REGIONAL PLANNING IN INDIA

REGIONAL PLANNING IN INDIA

MAHESH CHAND
VINAY KUMAR PURI

ALLIED PUBLISHERS PVT. LIMITED
NEW DELHI MUMBAI KOLKATA CHENNAI NAGPUR
AHMEDABAD BANGALORE HYDERABAD LUCKNOW

ALLIED PUBLISHERS PRIVATE LIMITED

1/13-14 Asaf Ali Road, **New Delhi**–110002
Ph.: 011-23239001 • E-mail: delhi.books@alliedpublishers.com

47/9 Prag Narain Road, Near Kalyan Bhawan, **Lucknow**–226001
Ph.: 0522-2209942 • E-mail: lko.books@alliedpublishers.com

17 Chittaranjan Avenue, **Kolkata**–700072
Ph.: 033-22129618 • E-mail: cal.books@alliedpublishers.com

15 J.N. Heredia Marg, Ballard Estate, **Mumbai**–400001
Ph.: 022-42126969 • E-mail: mumbai.books@alliedpublishers.com

60 Shiv Sunder Apartments (Ground Floor), Central Bazar Road,
Bajaj Nagar, **Nagpur**–440010
Ph.: 0712-2234210 • E-mail: ngp.books@alliedpublishers.com

F-1 Sun House (First Floor), C.G. Road, Navrangpura,
Ellisbridge P.O., **Ahmedabad**–380006
Ph.: 079-26465916 • E-mail: ahmbd.books@alliedpublishers.com

751 Anna Salai, **Chennai**–600002
Ph.: 044-28523938 • E-mail: chennai.books@alliedpublishers.com

5th Main Road, Gandhinagar, **Bangalore**–560009
Ph.: 080-22262081 • E-mail: bngl.books@alliedpublishers.com

3-2-844/6 & 7 Kachiguda Station Road, **Hyderabad**–500027
Ph.: 040-24619079 • E-mail: hyd.books@alliedpublishers.com

Website: www.alliedpublishers.com

First published, 1983

Reprinted 1985, 1988, 1990, 1991, 1993, 1995, 1997,
1999, 2000, 2001, 2003, 2004, 2005, 2006.
2008, 2009, 2010, 2011 , 2012 , 2013

ISBN 81-7023-058-6

Published by Sunil Sachdev and printed by Ravi Sachdev at Allied Publishers Pvt. Ltd., Printing Division, A-104 Mayapuri Phase II, New Delhi - 110064

Dedicated to the loving memory of

Mrs. CHANDRAMANI AGRAWAL

and

Miss SAVITA PURI

Preface

The large-scale interest generated in Regional Economics and Regional Planning in recent times (more specifically since the fifties) is a direct consequence of the acceptance of the need for planning in practically all countries of the world and the recognition that spatial elements can play an important role in guiding and shaping the planning process. It is through regional planning alone that a judicious pattern of location of industrial and all other economic activities can be ensured, growth process in lagging regions generated through the establishment of growth poles, growth centres, or growth points, the process of over-urbanization of large urban centres checked (and, in fact, countered by developing a series of small and medium towns and new urban centres), and the whole economy linked up in a hierarchy of human settlements in an integrated way. Neglect of regional planning, on the other hand, leads to a number of serious problems as has happened in our own case—widespread disparities among different regions, unchecked growth of large urban centres (especially million plus cities) with rapidly increasing pressure on urban infrastructure and amenities, failure to generate growth impulses in the rural hinterland, setting up of industries and other economic activities without paying any heed to the locational factors and the linkage processes, and the like. In fact (as we intend to show in this book), neglect of regional factors has made the planning process highly unrealistic and artificial and has reduced it to an exercise in sectoral allocation of investment and target-setting—nothing more, nothing less.

The plan of this book is as follows.

Chapter 1 starts with a discussion on the concept of 'region'. We note that there is no unanimity in the definition of a region and depending on whether we adopt the criterion of homogeneity, nodality, or administrative convenience, we can have different types of regions. Even in these categories we can have numerous possibilities. For example, we might seek homogeneity in physical geography, economic structure, or socio-cultural factors. Then, we might seek homogeneity in two or more features of a particular factor. For example, while considering the factor 'homogeneity in economic structure' we might take into account per capita income, productivity of land, industrial output, etc. Depending on how we choose to combine these features of a particular factor will depend our scheme of regionalization. For purposes of planning, we might seek to define 'planning regions' which take all possible criteria such as homogeneity, nodality and administrative convenience into account. We have tried to explain all such possibilities of defining (or more accurately, delineating) a region and follow up this explanation by different schemes of regionalization of India submitted by scholars from time to time based on various criteria, factors, and features discussed earlier in the chapter.

Chapter 2 is concerned with the definition, scope, and content of Regional Economics and Regional Planning. The last section of this chapter seeks to establish that *regional* planning is not necessarily opposed to *national* planning as is sometimes tried to be made out in certain quarters and that there are ample possibilities of 'integration between the two in an overall and comprehensive framework of regional planning'.

Chapter 3 presents an overview of the planning process in India. In addition to presenting a critical appraisal of the financial, agricultural, industrial, employment, and other strategies and the different policy measures adopted by the government, this chapter aims at highlighting the fact that *neglect of spatial and regional factors* is the basic flaw of the planning strategy in this country. We point out that the task of plan formulation is highly centralized in India and the lower levels of the planning process (States, districts, and blocks) enter only at the implementation level.

Chapter 4 is basically designed to present a brief summary of the various theories, methods, and techniques used in regional planning literature, but is not confined to such an exercise alone. We have also tried to illustrate the application of some of these techniques in the Indian context from various studies conducted by scholars from time to time. This exercise, we hope, will help clarify the utility and the applicability of different techniques of regional planning on the one hand, and present the regional problems of our country in a better perspective, on the other. Of particular importance is the last section of the chapter on "Modified Growth Foci Approach : The Contribution of R.P. Misra". We believe that a true integration between regional planning and national planning (of which we had talked in the concluding section of Chapter 2) can be accomplished only by adopting the growth foci approach advccated by Prof. Mishra which presents a brilliant synthesis of the growth pole theory with some other important theories concerned with the planning of space. This belief leads us to discuss this theory again and again in the context of different problems facing our country.

Chapter 5 discusses the problem of regional imbalances and inequalities in India. The major difficulty we had to encounter here (and practically in all other chapters) was the non-availability of requisite data. Data in this country are available at the State level only, and in some cases go down to the district level. Consequently, we had to limit our discussion to inter-State disparities. Have such disparities reduced over time? This is a difficult question to answer and our study does not present any conclusive evidence in this regard. The answer will ultimately depend upon what indicators of development are chosen and the methods of combining them. To illustrate this point we have discussed the studies of Hemlata Rao, S.K. Rao, B.N. Ganguli and Devendra Gupta, V. Nath, and Asok Mitra. We have also considered inequalities in per capita income and disparities in the agricultural sector, industrial sector, transport and communications, etc., to highlight the fact that substantial inter-State disparities continue to exist even after three decades of planning.

Chapter 6 on the 'Process of Urbanization in India' starts with the definition of urban areas. This is followed by a detailed account of the urbanization process with special emphasis on the growth of million plus urban agglomerations. After this comes a discussion on migration (with special emphasis on rural-to-urban migration), and problems of urban areas. The last sections of the chapter are devoted to a discussion on the relationship between urbanization and economic development, and urban planning in a comprehensive framework of regional planning. It is in the latter section that we advocate the establishment of a linked pattern of human settlements modelled after the growth foci approach of Prof. R.P. Misra.

Chapter 7 on 'Regional Planning in Agriculture' starts with a discussion on the Community Development programme—the first comprehensive programme of rural development. This is followed by a discussion of the New Agricultural Strategy. We have shown that the green revolution was basically confined to wheat areas where both quantitative changes (in terms of quantum and yield of output) and qualitative changes (in terms of a change in the attitudes of farmers) were in evidence. But this strategy has accentuated regional imbalances on the one hand, and disparities in inter-personal income on the other. After this comes a discussion on programmes of rural employment and development of the rural poor. The last section is devoted to 'integrated approach to rural development'.

Chapter 8 deals with 'Backward Area Development' and opens up with a discussion on the methods and criteria adopted by different committees for the identification of backward areas. This is followed by an account of the incentives for development given by different State governments. Measures for the development and industrialization of backward areas are then discussed. The last sections of the chapter are devoted to the strategy of integrated area development which again advocate the integration of rural with urban areas through the strategy of hierarchical pattern of human settlements on the lines of Prof. R.P. Mishra's approach. We have strongly advocated the formation of an Authority for Backward Area Development in which experts from backward areas are given adequate representation.

Chapter 9 on 'Resource Transfer from Centre to States' is closely linked up with Chapter 8 and discusses in detail how the scheme of transfer of resources has favoured the relatively developed States more vis-a-vis the backward States.

The best examples of inter-State regional planning in this country are the Damodar Valley Corporation and the Dandakaranya Project. In both cases, genuine regions cutting across the State boundaries have been adopted for purposes of planned development. We have accordingly devoted a separate chapter (Chapter 10) to a discussion of these projects.

Chapter 11 is devoted to 'Planning for Tribal Development'. After noting the State-wise distribution of the tribal population, we proceed to a discussion of the economic life of the tribals, patterns of agriculture in the tribal areas, and sources of authority in the tribal areas. This is followed by a review of the tribal development programmes under the various plans and their critical appraisal. The last section is devoted to a discussion of integrated development of the tribal areas.

Chapter 12 on 'Directions of Regional Policy' starts by considering in detail the multi-level planning structure as it has evolved over the years. We have discussed in detail the organization of levels below the State and have paid special attention to the organization of the panchayati raj institutions in different States because it was essentially these institutions through which popular participation of the people in the planning process was sought to be obtained. We have noted how a small class of the rural rich gained complete control over the panchayati raj institutions and utilized them for their own benefit. The general masses remained outside these institutions and consequently felt isolated and neglected. We have discussed the proposals of the Dantwala Working Group on Block Level Planning and the Ashok Mehta's Committee on Panchayati Raj Institutions in detail and have noted how the proposals of the latter committee could have resulted in a genuine regional planning approach to development but were unfortunately rejected by the National Development Council. The last two sections of the chapter are devoted to a discussion of social and environmental issues in regional planning. There is not much that can be said on these subjects because they have not emerged as yet as important issues in planning in this country. Yet it is expected that in all future economic planning in this country (and in all underdeveloped countries) these issues will increasingly assume greater importance.

Our attempt has been to review the developments in the regional planning field in this country and present a comprehensive book on the subject for the benefit of students (particularly post-graduate students), research scholars and teachers engaged in studying or teaching regional planning in different Universities of the country. Since the manuscript was submitted to the UGC in September 1979, its period of study also ends at 1979. Some data for later years and some other information available till 1982 have also been incorporated here and there. But the structure of the analysis does not go beyond 1979. We are in constant touch, however, with post 1979 developments and hope to build them in greater detail in subsequent editions of the book.

MAHESH CHAND
VINAY KUMAR PURI

Acknowledgements

Prepared under the "Preparation of University Level Books by Indian Authors" scheme of the University Grants Commission, this book would not have been possible without the active and financial assistance of the UGC and the NBT. The authors are grateful to them. The authors also wish to thank: the University of Delhi for providing three years' study leave to V.K. Puri; the numerous scholars whose articles and books have benefited the present work and whose number is so large as to defy attempts at individual acknowledgement; and to Vijay Batra for typing the manuscript with patience and efficiency.

Contents

Chapter 1

Region and Regionalization

THE CONCEPT OF REGION

It is very difficult to define a region because the concept has been used by different people to mean different things. The concept is generally linked with 'space' and has spatial dimensions, though it is sometimes also used as something 'subjective' (a 'mental construct') or 'spaceless'. The followers of the subjective approach treat region only as an 'idea' by accepting the nation as a one-point economy, and arbitrarily dividing it into as many regions as the need be, independent of considerations of space. This concept is favoured by many economists engaged in the formulation of regional growth theory. However, for most geographers and public in general, region is an objective reality linked with space and defined in terms of (and through) space. The major problem that has to be faced in such an analysis is the ambiguity that surrounds the term 'region'. Thus, sometimes part of a district (sometimes even a village) is called a region, sometimes a district is taken to be a region, sometimes a State and sometimes a group of States (or parts of them) is regarded as a region. In international trade and in discussions relating to international economic relations it is not infrequent to find a combination of nations as constituting a region. However, if one states clearly the object of one's enquiry the confusion can be considerably reduced, for depending on the purpose of one's enquiry the definition (or more accurately, the delimitation) of region will vary. As far as the methods of delimiting a region are concerned they can be grouped under three categories: homogeneity, nodality, and programming. "The first stresses *homogeneity* with reference to some one or combination of physical, economic, social or other characteristics; the second emphasizes the so-called *nodality* or *polarization*, usually around some central urban place; and the third is *programming* or *policy-oriented* concerned mainly with administrative coherence or identity between the area being studied and available political institutions for effectuating policy decisions."[1] However, as noted by Meyer, the three categories are not mutually exclusive. Thus, "a so-called programme or policy region is essentially homogeneous in being entirely under the jurisdiction of some one or a few specific government or administrative agencies". Similarly, "a nodal region is homogeneous in that it combines areas dependent in some trade or functional sense on a specific centre".[2]

This similarity should not be stretched too far since basically the idea of homogeneity emphasizes *uniformity* while the idea of nodality underlines *interdependence*. The one gives a *formal region* and the other a *functional region*. A formal region is a geographical area which is homogeneous in terms of selected geographic criteria (as similar topography or cilmate), or selected economic criteria (such as similar per capita income levels, similar production structures, similar consumption patterns, uniform unemployment situation, etc.), or social and/or political criteria (e.g., party allegiance). When physical homogeneity is stressed, i.e. when uniformity in topography or climate is taken into account in actual delineation of regions, we get the oft-discussed *natural regions* or *physical-geographic* (*or physiographic*) *regions*. When we stress economic homogeneity, i.e. when we emphasize uniformity or similarity in per capita income levels, production structure, consumption pattern, etc., we get *economic regions*. When homogeneity in some social factor(s) is stressed, we get what are generally called *socio-cultural regions*. Against all such classifications, the *functional region* emphasizes interdependence (or linkage). It is composed of heterogeneous units such as cities, towns, and villages which are nevertheless functionally interrelated. Obviously, the functional region is a nodal region since it emphasizes intra-regional spatial differentiation. Population and economic activities are seen as concentrated in or round some specific foci of activities (e.g., large urban centres). The functional interrelationships are usually revealed in *flows* of people, factors, services, commodities, or communications.

PLANNING REGIONS

When one comes to defining regions for planning purposes, administrative convenience assumes paramount importance. This is so because in actual implementation of development plans, the existing administrative boundaries cannot be easily ignored. In fact, it is generally these boundaries that have to be accepted as demarcating the different regions. Political realities and availability of data for specific administrative units only make this practically essential.[3] However, in the enthusiasm of practical (administrative) considerations, one must not forget the importance of the factors of homogeneity and nodality, for the neglect of these factors can introduce distortions in the whole planning process. For example, if functional linkages are ignored in defining planning regions we might face a situation where a region so defined includes "nodes which have greater interdependence with nodes outside the region".[4] Similarly, for ensuring proper implementation of development plans, the region should have a fairly homogeneous economic structure, some topographical homogeneity, and some socio-cultural homogeneity. Therefore, in actual delineation of regions for planning purposes, it becomes necessary to strike a balance between the considerations of homogeneity, nodality, and administrative convenience.

Keeping these arguments in view, Keeble defined a planning region to be an area that is large enough to enable substantial changes in the distribution of population and employment to take place within its boundaries, yet which is samll enough for its planning problems to be viewed as a whole. Klaassen believes that a planning region "must be large enough to take investment decisions of an economic size, must be able to supply its own industry with the necessary labour, should have a homogeneous economic structure, contain at least one growth point and have a common approach to and awareness of its problems".[5] According to another definition, a planning region should have the following characters: "(a) it should be large enough to contain a range of resources, conditions and attributes so as to serve a desired degree of economic viability and at the same time not too large to make the comprehensive approach too general, (b) its resource position is such that a satisfactory level of product combination for consumption and for exchange would be feasible, (c) the internal homogeneity of resources structure should logically link up the anticipated future so as to make future relevant to the present, (d) the region should be internally cohesive area . . ., and lastly (e) that planning region is essentially operational in character, therefore, a high degree of flexibility and elasticity should be maintained in the process of regional delineation."[6]

Perhaps the best definition of a planning region emphasizing the factors of homogeneity, nodality, and administrative convenience in a right perspective is the one given by P.D. Malgavkar and B.M. Ghiara which we quote below:

> Geographically, it should be a contiguous unit though it could be sub-divided into plain, hilly track, coastal belt, lake area etc.
>
> The people of the region should have social and cultural cohesiveness.
>
> The region should be a separate unit for data collection and analysis.
>
> The region should have an economic existence which can be assessed

from statistical records.

It should be small enough to ensure local people's participation in its development.

It should be under one administrative agency.

It should not be too small; its geographical size should be big enough to exploit resources and avoid duplication (by way of partially used capacity in neighbouring region). This is as much relevant for new investments in capital for production as for technical training, medical facilities, colleges, etc. It should be big enough to permit the major part of labour requirements in any employing centre to be met from within the region.

It should have fairly homogeneous economic structure, i.e., the variation in local proportions of employment and output in agriculture, industry and services should be within a narrow range. To this we may also add a minimum topographical homogeneity which ensures absence of seasonal or permanent breaks in road links.

It should have one or more growth points.

There should be common appreciation of local problems and common aspirations and approaches to their solution; it should permit and encourage competition but not rivalry or apathy between one area and the other.[7]

The discussion on the concept of region brings out clearly the difficulty in defining the concept. In addition to the fact that we can have three basic types of regions—homogeneous, nodal, and programming—within each of these categories, we can have a number of regions in the actual process of delineation depending on the *factors of classification* that are employed. Thus, as already pointed out, in the category of homogeneous regions we can have natural regions (or physiographic regions), economic regions, and socio-cultural regions, depending on whether we are seeking physical homogeneity, economic homogeneity, or socio-cultural homogeneity, respectively. In these categories we can again delineate regions in a number of ways depending upon what (and how many) factors of classification are adopted. Thus, in delineating economic regions we might take into account homogeneity in per capita income levels or homogeneity in production structure or homogeneity in consumption pattern or homogeneity in some other economic variable. Then we might try to consider two or more economic variables at the same time. Thus, we might have a single-factor region or a multi-factor region, and, as already noted, even they can be delineated in a number of ways depending on what factors are considered.

Coming down to nodal regions, they can also be delineated in a number of ways depending upon the factor(s) of classification adopted. The polarization flows, their rate and their orientation (which need to be studied while defining nodal regions) can be shown in a number of ways such as "the distribution area of retail and household goods and the relative traffic of such goods over different parts of the trade area; freight and passenger movements, such as intra-regional commodity flows, commuting patterns and migration flows; telephone communication densities and newspaper circulation areas; financial ties; domiciliary origin of students at educational institutions; the area supplied by centrally located social services and leisure facilities; labour catchment areas and journey to work patterns".[8] Depending upon what factor of the above list is adopted, we will get a different nodal region. Again, two or more factors can be considered together to define numerous other nodal regions. Then, there is another problem. As pointed out by Peter Hall, "there are a number of possible sets of nodal regions depending on the level of activity one is specifying".[9] We shall explain this point with the help of the example given by Hall. Let us consider the delineation of nodal regions on the basis of the shopping pattern. If regions are defined in terms of shopping for convenience goods such as food, we shall get a very large number of small regions for 'almost every small place will supply food needs'; but if we consider, say, furniture, the number of regions will get reduced and their size will increase for generally 'people are willing to go further for this type of shopping'. Thus, even if the same activity (shopping in this case) is considered, different sets of nodal regions will result according to the different 'levels' of the activity that are taken into account in the actual delineation of regions.

DELINEATION OF FORMAL REGIONS

As already noted, in the delineation of formal regions we seek to find out similarities, homogeneity, and uniformity in localities on the basis of a specific criterion (or a set of criteria). The localities possessing homogeneity are classified as constituting one region.[10] We have also emphasized that the criterion (or criteria) may relate to the physical geography, economic structure, or socio-cultural factors. The economic criterion that is most often used is 'per capita income level' and this is combined with some other criteria to introduce more sophistication and realism into the analysis. The simplest case will, of course, be that in which we consider per capita income only. For purposes of illustration, let us suppose that a and b are two localities with per capita incomes Y_a and Y_b respectively. The simplest procedure would be to classify a and b in the same region if $Y_a = Y_b$. Alternatively, we may include a and b in the same region if $Y_a - Y_b$ is small. Thus, we can prescribe certain definite limits for this purpose so that if $Y_a - Y_b$ is less than the limits, a and b are included in the same region, and if $Y_a - Y_b$ is greater than the prescribed limit (or level), *a* and *b* fall in different regions. Another method is to test whether the difference between Y_a and Y_b is significant with the help of statistical methods of testing of significance.

Problems arise when we try to delineate regions by taking into account more than one feature (especially if they are incc mmensurable such as per capita income, literacy, industrialization, etc.). The issue of assigning weights to the different features has also to be faced. The methods that can be adopted in such a case are basically three: (i) the fixed index method, (ii) the variable index method, and (iii) the cluster method. Under the fixed index method, a number of characteristics (indices) common to regions are chosen; e.g. per capita income, unemployment, rate of industrialization. An arbitrary weight is given to each index and a single weighted mean is obtained for each region. Then contiguous regions, with similar indices, are grouped together in order to minimize the variance within each group. Under the variable index method, variable weights are assigned to highlight different *levels* of activities in different regions. The weight given to each activity, in each region, is different and in accordance with the *value* or the *volume* regionally produced. For example, if region *A* is a wheat region and region *B* is a coal region, the weight of wheat index will be the largest in the former and the weight of coal index will be the largest in the latter. This method is good when the criteria can be compared with each other. However, in those cases where comparability is not possible (e.g., in the case when one feature is *literacy* and the other is *steel production*), it becomes necessary to employ the cluster method. The cluster method is used to detect the homogeneous character of the structures of different regional units. For this purpose, a study of the income and trade flows can be made. Such a study is resorted to while delineating functional regions (or polarized regions) also, but whereas in the former case we consider income and trade flows for the purpose of comparison only, in the latter we study the *linkage processes.*[11]

For tracing the clusters, we can take the help of mapping techniques wherein interrelated variables are mapped by superposing techniques. The regional divisions identified by Spate and Learmonth were obtained by superimposition of many individuals' multivariate studies on different parts of India and Pakistan, and the study on 'Resource Development Regions' couducted by V. Nath for the Planning Commission was based on multivariate superposition of natural and physical resources in India.[12] However, "when the variables are too many, particularly when they are not having strong interrelations, the mapping by superposing techniques is not much help in the identification of composite formal configuration, since the combinations of different classes of all variables that include one or more areal units become numerous. Again, it is possible to identify the differential levels between areas only through the ranks of areas in individual variables, but the composite ranking of areas with reference to all variables that are superimposed together to identify a composite formal configuration is very difficult."[13] Because of these reasons, it is essential to employ certain quantitative techniques also in addition to mapping techniques. In the application of such techniques, there are several possibilities. In those cases where many interdependent variables are involved two possibilities arise: (i) variables are interdependent having a particular order in them, with or without any causal relation among them, or (ii) all variables are simultaneously interdependent without the existence of any order among them. Examples of the first kind with two variables can be seen in the study pertaining to 'An Atlas of Resources of Mysore State' conducted under the supervision of A.T.A. Learmonth (1960). Pairs of such ordered variables are: "(i) the normal rainfall together with the temporal variability (coefficient of variation) as an inverse measure of reliability of the normal rainfall, or (ii) the exponential rate of population growth together with the deviation of actual to exponential population curves as an inverse measure of stability of the rate of population growth, or (iii) the mean morbidity rate of a disease together with the variability as a measure of the epidemic or endemic nature of the disease, etc."[14]

In the case of simultaneously interdependent variables of equal importance (where the identity of individual variables is not important), Pal advocated the use of a composite index of development.[15] In the case of simultaneously interdependent variables of varying importance, integration of all variables of development can be done either by the subjective or by the objective methods with or without weighting for the differential importance of constituent variables. In the subjective method, the "geographers usually apply the technique of superimposition of varieties of both commensurable and non-commensurable information obtained through field experiences, opinion surveys, and on the basis of available quantitative and non-quantitative data. This mode differentiating areas is not according to any strict quantitative formulation and as such the ranking of each area in comparison with all others, that may be needed in evolving the norms for decision-making, is not possible even though the areas could be differentiated qualitatively."[16] An attempt on these lines was made by Schwartzberg (1962) to delineate the different areas of India for grades of development and sought to give credibility to his analysis by carrying out opinion surveys from selected Indian economists and geographers.

An unweighted aggregation study to obtain a composite development index for ranking Indian districts was used by Asok Mitra using the 1961 census data. (Mitra's method is discussed in detail in Chapter 5.) When one comes to weighted aggregates, the weights can be either subjective or objective. Subjective weighting was used by Schwartzberg (in the way pointed out above) to determine the development ranks of 18 old Indian States.

Objective weighting method was used by the National Council of Applied Economic Research in estimating the per capita income of districts (1963) using 'price-weighted aggregation of economic activities of production and services'.

In a situation when we are to handle a group of heterogeneous variables that could be considered as to influence or be influenced by several characteristics or sub-characteristics, the technique employed for delineation of regions is known as the *principal component analysis.* This method was first employed by M.J. Hagood in 1943 to delineate regions of relatively greater homogeneity. In Indian conditions, M.N. Pal popularized the use of this technique after Hagood. The question that is sought to be answered relates to the assigning of weights to selected economic (development) indicators since, as we have tried to illustrate so far, this is the basic question in formulating any composite index of development. The guiding principle in the principal component analysis for determining individual or group indicator weights is the inter-correlation among them, high weights being assigned to those showing high inter-correlation and vice-versa. "The logic for applying this principle seems to rest on the view that the development process is propelled by the joint action of a number of inter-related variables and that, therefore, stronger the relationship between a set of indicators, the more important they are to development. Implicit in this logic is the notion of balanced growth and perhaps even more significantly, the insistence that only balanced growth is indicative of development."[17]

IDENTIFICATION OF FUNCTIONAL REGIONS

Delineation of formal regions on the basis of homogeneity considerations carried out in terms of either simple or composite characteristics (discussed above) is undoubtedly a useful method in regional planning and is necessary in those cases where regional differentials are important in planning policies. However, it is, in itself, incomplete because in it considerations of spatial interdependence are lost sight of. Therefore, "the next step is to identify what can be called the functional spatial configurations wherein the interdependence between diverse formal areas or localities is ascertained for one or more selected phenomena of spatial flows. Such interdependencies are usually so patterned as to form functionally organized units in the spatial configuration, with varying centripetal intensities of spatial flows in each such unit called functional regions. Major centres of different functional regions in the spatial configuration can again be linked axially (not centripetally) on the basis of macro-economic functional ties."[18] The techniques usually employed in actual delineation of functional regions are (i) the flow analysis and (ii) the gravitational analysis.

The *flow analysis* is based on an *empirical study* of flow data which may refer to different forms of spatial flows such as: intra-regional (i.e. within the region) commodity flows; commuting patterns and migration flows (to study movements of people); distribution area of retail and household goods and their relative traffic over different parts of the trade area; freight and passenger movement; telephone communication densities; newspaper circulation area; financial intra-regional ties; area served by centrally located social services and leisure facilities; journey work patterns; etc. Each flow will show a decreasing intensity as it becomes more distant from the main centre, and an increasing intensity as it approaches another centre. The boundary of area of influence (of the area being considered) will be where the flow intensity, reaches the minimum. To highlight the spatial flows, it is usual to construct flow maps since they are in a better position to illustrate actual lines or routes of flows while a tabular presentation 'does not say anything about the depth along different routes of flows'. However, the basic flaw in flow mappings is that they do not give the full story on account of *information gaps* in flow data (which are present in practically all countries but are present in a very serious form in underdeveloped countries). Therefore, it becomes necessary to undertake what is known as the *gravitational analysis.*

Gravitational Analysis: Under this analysis we study the theoretical forces of attraction between centres instead of actual flows as under the flow analysis. The importance of this technique is clear from the fact that it is an important instrument to study the *potential flows* between centres.

Stated in simple terms, the gravity principle merely states that the interaction between two geographical points or areas is directly related to their 'masses' and inversely related to the 'distance' between them. Both the terms 'mass' and 'distance' are, however, difficult to define and many controversies have arisen on this account. For example, 'mass' may be regarded as population or as employment or as income or as retail turnover or as economic activity of one type or the other (however measured); the distance may refer to road distance, airline distance, time distance, money distance, etc. Once mass and distance are defined (depending on the purpose of the study or the value judgement of the researcher), the gravitational force between two centres i and j is expressed as

$$G_{ij}=K\left[\frac{M_i M_j}{d_{ij}^2}\right] \qquad \text{(i)}$$

where G_{ij} represents the gravitational force between centres i and j, M_i and M_j represent the masses of the centres i and j, d_{ij} is the distance between them, and K is a constant.

Various levels of sophistication can be introduced in this model. A generalized version would be

$$G_{ij}=K\left[\frac{M_i^{\alpha}M_j^{\beta}}{d_{ij}^{\gamma}}\right] \tag{ii}$$

where α, β, and γ are exponential parameters. This is equivalent to (i) when $\alpha=\beta=1$ and $\gamma=2$.

Sometimes, the estimate of total interaction of a centre with all centres is obtained. This is called *potential at the centre*. This potential at centre *i* caused by a mass at centre *j* is defined as

$$P_{i,j}=K\left[\frac{M_j}{d_{ij}^2}\right]. \qquad \text{[following (i)]}$$

Then, the total potential at centre *i*, P_i, is given by

$$P_i=\sum_{j=1}P_{i,j}=\sum_{j=1}K\left[\frac{M_j}{d_{ij}^2}\right].$$

The method is to calculate the potential for the centres in a study area and plot contour lines of equal potential on a map. From such lines functional regions can be identified.

One of the earliest and a classic application of gravity models was done by W.J. Reilly[19] in his study of retail trade. Reilly's Law of Retail Gravitation is a particular form of the general gravitation law and states that "the force *F* of attraction, or scale of spending in a village with purchasing power *m*, is proportional to the number of retailers *N* in a town *V*, and inversely proportional to a certain power of the distance *d* separating the town *V* from the village, i.e. $F=k(N/d^{\alpha})m$".[20] The boundary of attraction between two towns 1 and 2 is, therefore, given by the formula:

$$\frac{N_1}{N_2}=\left[\frac{d_1}{d_2}\right]^{\alpha}.$$

In Reilly's formulation α was taken as 2.

Subsequently, the gravity model was developed by a psysicist,

J.Q. Stewart, in his study "Empirical Mathematical Rules Concerning the Distribution and Equilibrium of Population", and by a mathematician, G.K. Zipf, in his book *Human Behaviour and the Principle of Least Effort* (1949).

The most important criticism of the gravity model relates to the empirical problems such as how to measure the masses M_i and M_j, distance d_{ij}, and how to estimate the parameters α, β, and γ. Though these problems are very difficult, most of them are not unsurmountable. Thus, for studies estimating the influence over space of population centres, population can be used to measure the mass and this can sometimes be weighted by income. In considering the attraction of a retail centre the volume of retail sales can be taken into account. The number of shops can also be considered. The problems become difficult when different phenomena have to be considered together for, then, the problem of assigning weights arises. Whatever statistical methods are employed in deciding the weights, it is to be admitted that value judgements are likely to play an important role. It is therefore, better, to explicitly recognize their importance in such analyses. Similar problems arise when attempt is made to define 'distance'. The definition is likely to be determined by the problem studied. Stouffer used the term 'distance' in the sense of 'number of intervening opportunities' in his model of intervening opportunities developed in 1940 and this use has become quite popular in recent times.

After the definitions of the masses and the distance have been settled, the problem of the determination of exponents arises, i.e., what should be the values of α, β, and γ. Stewart argued that the value of the exponent of distance d_{ij} should be 1 or 2. Reilly used $\gamma=2$ in his study. But there is no inherent justification in assuming this value. Similarly, what should be the values of α and β. Generally α and β are taken to be unity giving the value of G_{ij} as given in equation (i), but again there is no justification in assuming this value. In some cases the agglomeration economies may be so important that the value taken should be either less than unity or greater than unity. The influence of external economies will necessitate the use of exponents greater than one and the influence of external diseconomies will necessitate the use of exponents less than one.

The concept of distance that is normally used is a static one. However, since different socio-economic groups have different mobilities and the process of development is generally expected to improve the economic condition of the people, mobility is likely to change over time and this must lead to a change in the concept of distance. However, determination of such a dynamic and flexible concept of distance is not an easy task. The utility of the gravity model is further reduced by the nature of predictions that it leads to. The gravity models "like most predictive models . . . forecast on the basis of past behaviour. In cases where new regions or new centres of agglomeration are being opened up and developed, they are of little value. Thus, in retail shopping studies, gravity concepts may be useful for assessing the effect of population growth on existing shopping centres but are unproductive for estimating sales at a new shopping centre, the growth of which requires customers to break away from past patterns of behaviour."[21]

DELINEATION OF REGIONS IN INDIA

Physiographic Regions

The first attempt to classify natural regions or physiographic regions was made by L. Dudley Stamp who, in 1922, presented his scheme of 3 major natural regions and 22 sub-regions of India. Stamp's scheme was based on the homogeneity of physiography, structure, and climate. Another attempt was that of J.N.L. Baker who, in 1928, presented a scheme of natural regions (based on the work of Wood) which showed a very close agreement to Stamp's scheme. Following the empirical lines of Stamp and Baker, Spate presented a detailed scheme of physiographic regions for India in 1954 (which was slightly modified later on). In the third edition of his bok published in 1967, Spate divided the whole country into 3 macro regions which were further divided into 34 regions of the first order (excluding islands), 74 of the second order, and about 225 sub-divisions of these. The three macro regions are (i) the mountain rim, (ii) the Indo-Gangetic plains, and (iii) the Peninsula.[22]

To present a picture of physiographic divisions of India, let us now consider the scheme presented by S.P. Chatterjee in detail. The scheme given below was published in the *Gazetteer of India*, Vol. I.[23]

Chatterjee divides the country into seven major physiographic divisions on the basis of topography: (1) Northern Mountains which include the Himalayas and the mountain ranges in the north-east, (2) Great Plains, (3) Central Highlands, (4) Peninsular Plateaus, (5) East Coast, (6) West Coast, and (7) Bordering Seas and Islands. The further divisions and sub-divisions of these major regions are as follows.

The Himalayas extend almost uninterruptedly for a distance of 2500 km and cover 500,000 km^2. This mountain range can be divided into Western Himalayas and Eastern Himalays. Between these two is the Himalayan country of Nepal. The Western Himalayas are further subdivided into the following four regions: (a) the North Kashmir Himalaya, (b) the South Kashmir Himalaya, (c) the Punjab Himalaya, and (d) the Kumaon Himalaya from west to east. The broadest part of the Himalayas lies in Kashmir. It is 700 km from west to east and 500 km from north to south, covering

350,000 km^2 of mountainous tract. The great Himalaya Range serves as the dividing line between the North Kashmir and South Kashmir Himalayas. The most densely populated part of the Kashmir Himalaya is the Valley of Kashmir. The valley is enclosed by a ring of mountains—Pir Punjab in the south and a branch of the Great Himalaya in the north. Srinagar, the capital city of the State of Jammu & Kashmir, is in the heart of the Kashmir Valley, 1893 m above sea level. The portion of the Himalayas lying in Himachal Pradesh and Punjab is known as the Punjab Himalaya. It covers 45,000 km^2 and in this part of the Himalaya the four important rivers of Chenab, Ravi, Sutlej, and Beas have their sources or upper reaches. The Kumaon region of the Himalaya forms an administrative part of Uttar Pradesh. It is from the Kumaon Himalaya that the rivers of Ganga and Yamuna emanate. This mountain tract covers approximately 30,000 km^2. The famous hill stations of Mussocrie, Naini Tal, Almora, and Ranikhet are to be found here and also the important religious places of Hardwar, Rishikesh, Kedarnath, and Badrinath.

The Eastern Himalaya can be divided into the following four regions: (a) the Sikkim Himalaya, (b) the Darjeeling Himalaya, (c) the Bhutan Himalaya, and (d) the Assam Himalaya. The Sikkim Himalaya "is an anticlinal valley" and includes a vast river basin. The Darjeeling Himalaya consists principally of two north-south ranges. Along the Darjeeling range are found the famous tea gardens for which this area is widely known. The Bhutan Himalaya covers approximately 22,500 km^2 of deep valleys and high ranges. The Assam Himalaya is the easternmost stretch of the Himalayas lying in the NEFA area of Assam. This stretch covers almost 67,500 km^2. The north-eastern mountains may be further sub-divided into the three physiographic provinces of Purvachal, the Meghalaya Plateau, and the Assam Valley. The Purvachal includes the "lofty ranges" which border India in the north-east, hills and plains in Manipur, Tripura, and adjoining districts of Assam. The Purvachal can be further sub-divided into six sub-provinces: Purva NEFA, Nagaland, the Manipur Hills, the North Cachar Hills, the Mizo Hills, and the Tripura Hills. The Meghalaya contains Cherrapunji (the area recording the highest rainfall in the world), the Khasi and Jaintia hills, the Garo hills, and the Mikir hills. The Assam Valley can be divided physiographically into two parts—Upper Assam and Lower Assam, "each about 75 km wide, with low relief, easy accessibility and extreme fertility of the land".

Great Plains

The Great Plains can be divided into three divisions—Western Plains, Northern Plains, and Eastern Plains. As would be clear from Fig. 1, this extends from the arid and semi-arid plains of Rajasthan on the west of the Ganga delta on the east. The total area of these plains is approximately 652,000 km², of which one-third lies in the arid Western Rajasthan, one-third in Uttar Pradesh, and the remaining one-third is approximately equally distributed among the States of Punjab, Bihar, and West Bengal.

The Western arid plains of Rajasthan cover 175,000 km² with a well-defined boundary on the east marked by the Aravalli range. This area is often referred to as a desert because it is a region of moving sands and deficient rainfall. The eastern part is less sandy, more humid, and is clothed with steppe vegetation. The Punjab plains are flat and the general elevation varies between 200 and 240 (except the Hoshiarpur plains). To the south of Punjab lies the State of Haryana. Approximately 55% of the Great Plains is occupied by the Ganga plains which lie in Uttar Pradesh, Bihar, and West Bengal. The region between the two rivers of Ganga and Yamuna in Uttar Pradesh is known as the Ganga-Yamuna Doab which is a highly densely populated area. It is generally divided into Upper, Middle, and Lower sections on the basis of rainfall, elevation, and character of older flood plains. The Upper Doab extends from Hardwar on the north to Aligarh on the south and is irrigated by the Eastern Yamuna and Upper Ganga Canals. Rainfall is much heavier than in the Middle and Lower Doabs. The Lower Doab is a flat area and ends at Allahabad where the Yamuna merges into the Ganga. East of the Ganga-Yamuna Doab is a vast stretch of alluvial plains, from the foot of the Himalayas to the Ganga. These are known as the Rohilkhand plains and lie entirely in Uttar Pradesh covering an area of approximately 35,000 km². The other plains in this State are the Avadh plains which end in Uttar Pradesh itself. The next stretch of the Great Plains lies in Bihar, covering approximately 88,000 km². The plains here can be divided into the North Bihar Plains and the South Bihar Plains. The North Bihar plains is a land of the rivers Ganga, Ghaghara, Gandak, and Kosi accompanied by a number of mountain streams passing through these plains. "The combined work of these streams has resulted in a 2,000 m deep trough at the foot of the Nepal Himalaya being filled up with alluvial deposits. One of the most extensive alluvial plains of the world, 54,400 km². in North Bihar, was thus formed." The portion of the Great Plains coming under North Bengal has an area of 23,003 km² and extends from the foot of the Eastern Himalaya to the northern limit of the Bengal basin. "This region has evolved from an extensive sheet of waste materials brought down from the Eastern Himalaya by a number of powerful streams like the Tista, Jaldhaka and Torsa", and its eastern part is drained by the rivers joining the Brahmaputra while the western part is drained by the tributaries of the Ganga. The Bengal basin embraces most of the alluvial plains of West Bengal and Bangladesh, and the Ganga delta occupies the major portion of this basin.

Central Highlands

The Central Highlands can be divided into North Central Highlands and South Central Highlands. As would be clear from Fig. 1, the Central Highlands separate the Great Plains of North India from the plateaus and coastal plains of the Deccan. "It forms a compact block of mountains, hills and plateaus, interspersed with valleys and basins, covering about one sixth of the total area of India." The physiographic division of the Central Highlands includes about one-half of Madhya Pradesh, one-third of Rajasthan, and a small portion of Uttar Pradesh.

The North Central Highlands can be divided into (a) the Aravalli Range, (b) Eastern Rajasthan Upland, (c) Madhya Bharat Pathar, and (d) Bundelkhand Upland. The South Central Highland can be divided into (a) Malabar Plateau, (b) Vindhya Scraplands, (c) Vindhya Range, and (d) Narmada Valley.

The Aravalli range extends from Delhi south-west to near Ahmedabad for a distance of about 800 km. To the east of the Aravalli range lies the East Rajasthan Upland that ranges in height from 250 to 500 m. The Chambal river enters the State of Rajasthan near the northern end of the Gandhi Sagar and flows for 360 km in Rajasthan. The Madhya Bharat Pathar area has a rocky surface and dense forests to the east of the Chambal. The other part of the northern part of the Central Highlands is that part of Bundelkhand which lies between the Yamuna and the northern arcuate scrap of the Vindhyan plateau. As already noted, the southern part of the Central Highlands comprises the Malwa plateau, the Vindhya scraplands, the Vindhya range, and the Narmada Valley. The Vindhya range "is really an escarpment which varies in character and height, depending on the structure and lithology of the underlying rocks. For the first 100 km from its western terminus, Gomanpur peak (554 m) in the Dhar district of Madhya Pradesh, the Vindhya range runs in curve, its convex side facing the Narmada valley and following a 300 m contour line. . . . [It is] heavily forested and sparsely populated. For the next 160 km a more open type of country prevails and the escarpment, still built of basalt, becomes more prominent. : . . Near Hoshangabad the rock type changes; the Vindhya mountain comes down very close to the Narmada river and presents a terraced slope built of hard sand stones alternating with shales." To the north of the Vindhya range lies the Malwa plateau in Madhya Pradesh with a general northward slope, good drainage, and black soil. The strong sandstones of the Kaimur, Rewa, and Bhander are the principal makers of the Vindhyan scraplands and also form the surface of the three constituent plateaus descending in steps from west to east. To the extreme south of the Central Highlands lies the Narmada Valley.

Peninsular Plateaus

As would be clear from Fig. 1, the Peninsular plateaus constitute the largest physiographic division of India facing the Bay of Bengal in the east and the Arabian Sea in the west. "Its maximum length from Pachmarhi on the north to Cape Comorin on the South is 1,600 km and the maximum width from the Sahyadri on the west to the Rajmahal hills on the east is 1,400 km." The Peninsular plateaus consist of five distinctive physiographic subdivisions: (i) Western hills, (ii) North Deccan plateau, (iii) South Deccan plateau, (iv) Eastern plateaus, and (v) Eastern hills. The Western hills cover all the three sections of the Sahyadri (Western Ghats), the North Deccan plateau comprises Satpura Range, and the Maharashtra plateau and the South Deccan plateau can be divided into Telengana plateau and Karnataka plateau. The Eastern plateaus consist of (a) Baghelkhand plateau, (b) Chotanagpur plateau, (c) Mahanadi basin, and (d) Dandakaranya.

The shape of the Peninsular plateaus is that of an inverted triangle. All important rivers of the Deccan emanate from the Sahyadri (or Western Ghats). These rivers are Godavari, Krishna, Tungabhadra, and Cauvery. All these rivers flow into the Bay of Bengal. The south portion of the Southern Ghats (South Sahyadri) is sparsely populated on account of its inaccessibility though jungles, which are now being cleared, and plantation crops—rubber, coffee, and tea have been introduced. The next sub-division of the North Deccan plateau comprises the Satpura Range and the Maharashtra plateau, as already noted. "Nearly the whole of the Maharashtra plateau is formed of plateau basalt, which on weathering has given rise to rolling plains with intervening shallow valleys." The west-flowing Tapti forms the northern boundary of this region. Farther south is the Godavari. It enters the Maharashtra plateau at Nasik and flows for 650 km eastwards to the farthest end of this region. Receiving other rivers on its way it enters the Telengana plateau and divides it into two sections. The northern section is very hilly and forested and contains few inhabitants. The southern section is dotted with low hills and shallow depressions. "One such depression, surrounded by low hills, 130 metres high, provided the site for the twin city of Hyderabad—Secunderabad, capital of Andhra Pradesh." On the basis of altitude the Karnataka plateau is also divided into two sections—northern section and the Mysore plateau. The Krishna and the Tungabhadra flow through the northern section. The Mysore plateau "is the loftiest and most well-defined plateau of South India. . . . This plateau abuts against the Sahyadri on the west and is bounded on the east by the Eastern Ghats.

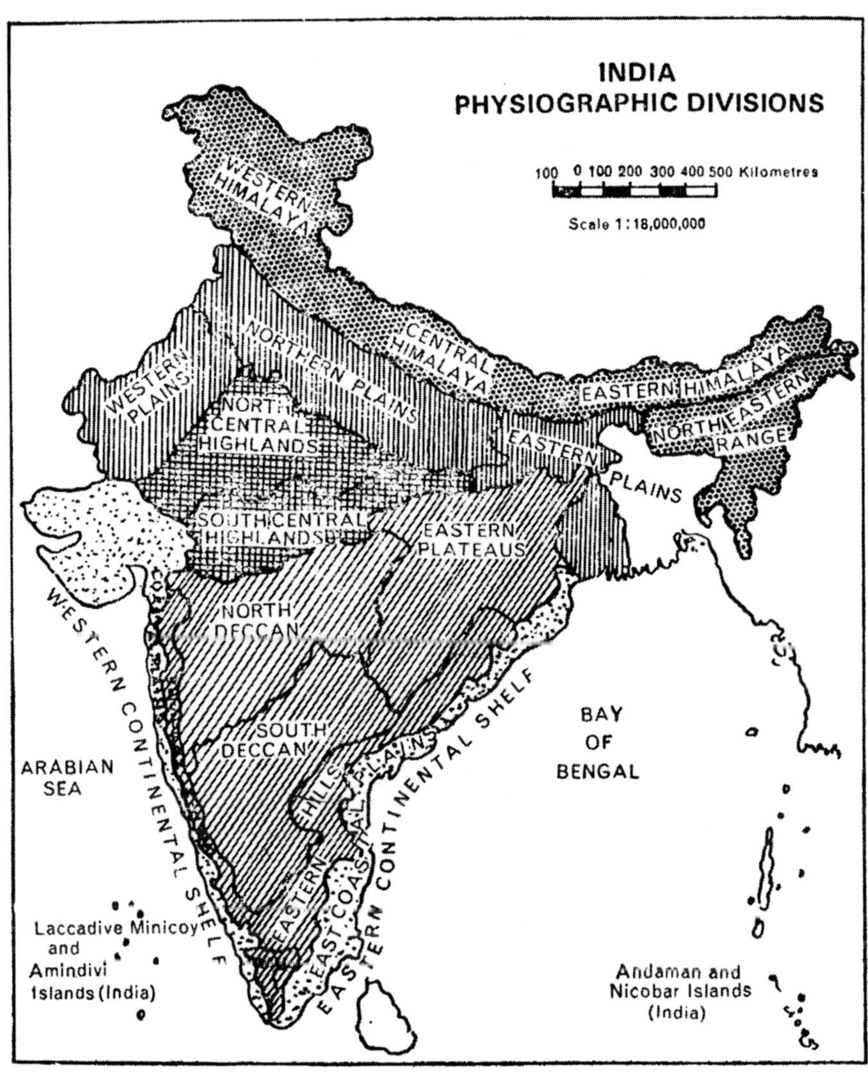
INDIA
PHYSIOGRAPHIC DIVISIONS
100 0 100 200 300 400 500 Kilometres
Scale 1:18,000,000
WESTERN HIMALAYA
CENTRAL HIMALAYA
EASTERN HIMALAYA
NORTH EASTERN RANGE
WESTERN PLAINS
NORTHERN PLAINS
EASTERN PLAINS
NORTH CENTRAL HIGHLANDS
SOUTH CENTRAL HIGHLANDS
EASTERN PLATEAUS
NORTH DECCAN
SOUTH DECCAN
EASTERN HILLS
EAST COASTAL PLAINS
WESTERN CONTINENTAL SHELF
EASTERN CONTINENTAL SHELF
ARABIAN SEA
BAY OF BENGAL
Laccadive Minicoy and Amindivi Islands (India)
Andaman and Nicobar Islands (India)

Figure 1

Along its southern boundary rises the Nilgiri. Physiographically the Mysore plateau may be divided into two sections, Malnad and Maidan. The Malnad portion is the billy area bordering the Sahyadri, and has an average width of 35 km and a mean elevation of 1000 m. It is dissected into steep hills and deep valleys and covered with dense forests. The Maidan is an area of rolling plains with low granitic hills." The most important river is the Cauvery.

Coming down to the Eastern plateaus, the Ranchi plateau is the largest and most typical part of Chotanagpur. Rounded hills of massive granite and slightly elevated terraces of older flood plains mark the topography of the Ranchi plateau. The Damodar river rises in the hills of Chotanagpur and drains areas in the Ranchi, Hazaribagh, Dhanbad, and Santhal Parganas districts of Bihar and the Bankura and Burdwan districts of West Bengal. Its length is 336 miles. The Damodar Valley formed by this river comprises the Upper Valley (including parts of Bihar) and the Lower Valley (including parts of West Bengal). This valley is the field of an inter-State planning effort in which the State governments of Bihar and West Bengal and the Central government have taken part.[24]

The central part of the Mahanadi basin is known as the Chhattisgarh basin. To its south lies Dandakaranya, a field of another inter-State planning effort. It comprises the districts of Bastar, Kalahandi and Koraput. The Bastar district forms part of Madhya Pradesh (in size it is even bigger than the State of Kerala) and Kalahandi and Koraput are in Orissa.[25] The true mountain character of the Eastern Ghats is exhibited between the Godavari and the Mahanadi. In the Deccan these Ghats do not constitute a continuous range. Down south, they turn to the west to meet the Western Ghats at the Nilgiri Hills.

East and West Coasts

The coastal plains of India are washed by the Bay of Bengal on the east and the Arabian Sea on the west, the Indian Ocean touching the southern toe. The western coast strip extends from the Gulf of Cambay in the north to Cape Comorin in the south, and from the Western Ghats in the east to the sea on the west. It is made up of mud brought down by the short rapid rivers from the Western Ghats. At the northern end are two peninsuas—Kutch and Kathiawar, and one vast extensive plain—Gujarat. "Farther south lies the coastal plains proper which have been subdivided into three areas, the Konkan coast, Karnataka coast and Kerala coast, their limits conforming to the state boundaries." The height of the Western Ghats ranges from 815 to 1220 m.

The East Coast has a number of deltas such as the Mahanadi delta, the

Godavari delta, the Krishna delta, and the Cauvery delta. The eastern coast strip stretches from the delta of the Ganga to Cape Comorin and lies between the Eastern Ghats and the Bay of Bengal. The coastal plains in Orissa are called the Utkal Plains and include the Mahanadi delta with Cuttack at its head. From the southern limit of the Utkal plains stretch the Andhra plains and the rivers of Godavari and Krishna flowing through this region form deltas in their lower reaches. The east of the East Coast comprises the Tamilnad plains, 675 km in length and with an average width of 100 km. The Cauvery delta is its most important physiographic unit. In Madras and Andhra Pradesh the East Coast is called the Payan Ghat, which extends from Cape Comorin northwards to the united deltas of the Krishna and the Godavari for 1100 km with an average width of 100 to 130 km.

Islands

India has a number of islands within its territory in both the Bay of Bengal and the Arabian Sea. The islands in the Arabian Sea are: (i) Amindivi Islands (consisting of six main islands of Amini, Keltan, Chetlat, Kadmat, Bitra, and Peremul Par); (ii) Laccadive Islands (consisting of five major islands of Androth, Kalpeni, Kavaratti, Pitti, and Suheli Par); and (iii) Minicoy Island. Far away from the mainland are more than 500 islands in the Bay of Bengal. They are the remotest region of the country and include Andaman and Nicobar Islands. The Andaman islands are divided into three main islands—North, Middle, and South. Separated from these islands by the Duncan passage is the Little Andaman. The North Andaman Island is 80 km long and has a maximum width of 20 km. The Middle Andaman is much wider and less indented. It is 70 km long and 30 km wide. The South Andaman consists of parallel ridges and valleys. Port Blair, the famous port and capital, lies in the South Andaman. Off these main islands lie numerous smaller islands. Below the Andamans are Nicobar islands consisting of 19 islands, 12 of which are inhabited. The Great Nicobar is the largest, occupying 862 km^2. The Car Nicobar is the northernmost island, 229 km from Port Blair. The extreme length of the sea space occupied by these islands is 261 km, and the extreme width 58 km.

ECONOMIC REGIONALIZATION OF INDIA

Though the knowledge of the natural regions is essential for understanding the basic geography of the country, it is of not much use as far as economic planning is concerned. It is static and merely describes the existing situation, while for purposes of planning it is necessary to study the natural resources of regions in detail,[26] and also to find out areas of potential development and to trace interlinkages among them (and within them) in such a fashion as to promote maximum development of resources. Depending upon the physio-geographical and economic features and the socio-cultural factors that we choose to emphasize and depending upon the method of combining them, we can have different types of homogeneous regions. As an illustration, we have discussed below some schemes of homogeneous regions for India presented by different scholars from time to time. This is followed by a discussion on polarized regions wherein we have highlighted the results of the studies conducted by Brain J.L. Berry, L.S. Bhat and R.G. Gidadhubly, and S.R. Hashim. After this comes a discussion on planning regions. Schemes taken up in this section include the schemes of Sen Gupta and Chandrasekhara. The concluding part of the chapter discusses whether the schemes given above have any practical utility in the overall context of the existing political realities where States are the only distinct political and economic entities and have to be treated as planning regions on administrative grounds, irrespective of considerations of theory.

The Scheme Proposed by V. Nath[27]

Guided by the twin objectives of (i) providing of framework for understanding the variety of physical conditions and resource development potentials in different parts of the country to those concerned with planning at the Centre and in the States, so that these differences are given due consideration in the planning of programmes, and adjustments in programme content and pattern are made to meet these, wherever necessary, and (ii) furnishing to those concerned with planning at the State level, a scheme of division of their States into internally homogeneous units, each of which can be used as a unit for planning of most of the programmes included in State plans, V. Nath prepared a scheme of Resource Development Regions and Divisions of ndia for the Planning Commission in 1964. His scheme is based on considerations of homogeneity in:

(i) physical factors—topography, soils, geologic formations and climate, and

(ii) agricultural land use and the cropping pattern.[28]

Though the regions cut across the State boundaries, Nath kept each resource division within the boundaries of a particular State (or Union territory) so that no administrative problems arise. On administrative considerations again, "districts have not been divided and the entire area of a district forms part of one or the other resource development division".

After collecting data on physical conditions (topography, soils, geologic formations, and rainfall), cropping pattern and development of irrigation, and mineral resources for each district, Nath divided the country into resource development regions. These were further sub-divided into sub-regions and divisions on physical and/or administrative considerations. Then after examining (i) the scheme of division of India into natural regions, sub-regions, and divisions used in the census of 1951, (ii) the scheme given by O.H.K. Spate, and (iii) the tentative scheme of regions for resource planning evolved by the Indian Statistical Institute, Nath divided the country into the following 15 resource development regions: (1) Western Himalayan Region, (2) Eastern Himalayan Region, (3) Lower Gangetic Plain Region, (4) Middle Gangetic Plain Region, (5) Upper Gangetic Plain Region, (6) Trans-Gangetic Plain Region, (7) Eastern Plateaus and Hills Region, (8) Central Plateaus and Hills Region, (9) Western Plateaus and Hills Region, (10) Southern Plateaus and Hills Region, (11) East Coast Plain and Hills Region, (12) West Coast Plain and Ghats Region, (13) Gujarat Plain and Hills Region, (14) the Western Dry Region, and (15) the Islands. These regions are divided into 61 resource development divisions.

The Western Himalayan Region has been divided into four Divisions—Himalayan Uttar Pradesh Division (having 5 districts), Himalayan Punjab Division (having 2 districts), Himachal Pradesh Division (6 districts) and Jammu & Kashmir Division (9 districts). The Eastern Himalayan Region contains the Himalayan sub-region (consisting of NEFA with 5 districts and one district of Himalayan West Bengal), the Assam and Associated Hills sub-region (consisting of Assam Hills, Nagaland, Manipur, and Tripura), and the Plains sub-region (consisting of Brahmaputra and Surma Valleys and West Bengal Doars). The Lower Gangetic Plain Region consists of 12 districts of West Bengal Plain; the Middle Gangetic Plain Region consists of North Bihar Plain (6 districts), South Bihar Plain (5 districts), and Eastern U.P. Plain (12 districts). Upper Gangetic Plain Region consists of Central U.P. Plain (12 districts), North Western U.P. Plain (9 districts), and South Western U.P. Plain (9 districts). The Trans-Gangetic Plain Region consists of Delhi, Punjab Plain (16 districts), and Western Rajasthan Plain (one district). The Eastern Plateaus and Hills Region consists of Chotanagpur Plateau (6 districts), West Bengal Plateau (one district), Orissa Inland (9 districts), Madhya Pradesh (8 districts), and Maharashtra (2 districts). The Central Plateaus and Hills Region consists of Bundelkhand (4 districts of Uttar Pradesh), Madhya Pradesh (7 districts of Northern Plain and Plateaus, 10 districts of Central Plateaus and Hills and 7 districts of Vindhyan Hills and Plateaus), East Rajasthan Plain and Hills (11 districts), and South Rajasthan Plateau and Hills (4 districts). The Western Plateaus and Hills Region consists of 20 districts of Maharashtra, 11 districts of Madhya Pradesh, and one district of Rajasthan Malwa Plateau. The Southern Plateaus and Hills Region consists of the Telengana, Rayalaseema, and Chittoor regions of Andhra Pradesh, Madras Inland (4 disiricts), Mysore Plateau (6 districts) and Mysore-Karnataka Plateau (8 districts). The East Coast Plain and Hills Region consists of Orissa Coastal (4 districts), Coastal Andhra (7 districts), Madras East Coast (6 districts), and Pondicherry. The West Coast Plain and Ghats Region comprises Madras West Coast (one district), Madras-Nilgiris (one district), Kerala (9 districts), Mysore Coastal (2 districts), Mysore Hills (3 districts), Maharashtra Konkan (4 districts), and Goa (one district). The Gujarat Plain and Hills Region comprises Gujarat Plain and Hills (9 districts), Saurashtra Plain (5 districts), Gujarat Hills (one district), and Gujarat Dry (2 districts). The Western Dry Region consists of the Rajasthan Division having 9 districts. The last Region, viz., the Islands, consists of all islands—its two divisions corresponding to islands in the Bay of Bengal and islands in the Arabian Sea.

The Scheme of Bhat and Rao[29]

On the basis of a study of the "distributional patterns of resources with the help of qualitative maps of distribution of important natural resources followed by a study of agricultural land-use structure on the basis of Districtwise data", Bhat and Rao identified eleven major regions and 51 sub-regions. In this scheme, "the guiding principle is that major regions should have minimum disparities within and distinctiveness from their neighbours in respect of regional character and resources for development. While the regional development *norm* is common for the major region as a whole, sub-regions are identified depending upon the concentration of resources, problems for development and administrative convenience".[30]

The major eleven regions given in the scheme are: (i) West Coast Region, (ii) Western Ghats, (iii) Central Plateau, (iv) Eastern Ghats, (v) East Coast, (vi) North-Eastern Plateau, (vii) The Ganges Plain, (viii) Assam, (ix) Gujarat, (x) Rajasthan, and (xi) Kashmir and the northern hilly areas. Besides these major regions, 51 sub-regions were identified.

States can be grouped in different ways to form macro economic regions depending on the purposes for which the process of regionalization is being carried out. Thus, "if we adopt the principle that each macro-economic region should have power-metallurgical base as strong catalysts for attaining balanced regional development implying certain level of self-sufficiency", the macro economic regions can be defined as under, by grouping parts of different States:[31]

Macro Economic Region	Groups of States or parts of States comprising the regions
1. South India	Mysore, Kerala, Tamil Nadu, and Andhra and parts of Maharashtra, Madhya Pradesh, and Orissa
2. Western India	Most parts of Maharashtra and Gujarat
3. East Central India	Parts of Madhya Pradesh, Orissa, Maharashtra, and Andhra Pradesh
4. North-Eastern India	Bihar, West Bengal, major part of Orissa and Assam
5. The Middle Ganges Plain	Uttar Pradesh except the hill districts
6. North-Western India	Rajasthan, parts of Punjab and Haryana
7. Northern India	Including parts of Punjab, Haryana, Himachal Pradesh, and Jammu & Kashmir

Considering the fact that there is a lack of inter-regional data, Bhat suggests that it is better (as far as utility is concerned) to define macro economic regions comprising groups of States rather than their parts. These macro economic regions are five and include the States mentioned below:

Macro Economic Region	Groups of States
1. Southern	Mysore, Tamil Nadu, and Andhra Pradesh
2. Western	Maharashtra and Gujarat
3. Eastern	Bihar, Orissa, West Bengal, and Assam
4. North-Western	Punjab, Haryana, Rajasthan, and Jammu & Kashmir
5. North-Central	Uttar Pradesh and Madhya Pradesh

OTHER SCHEMES OF REGIONALIZATION

Different schemes of regionalization have been put forward by P. Sen Gupta and Galina Sdasyuk based on different factors of classification in the monograph already mentioned (see note 26). Thus, there is a discussion of population resource regions of India, agricultural regionalization of India, industrial regions of India, etc. The importance of defining population resource regions arises from the fact that *man* is the centre of whole development process and there is a spatial dimension of social development. It is therefore necessary that while planning for national development, "the population characteristics should be considered in terms of territorial units, like states, districts and so on".[32] This practice is also necessary to assess the latent capacity of the country in supporting population. To fulfil this objective it is necessary to divide the country into population resource regions according to the combined impact of the demographic structure of population (density and growth rate), resource potentiality, and levels of socio-economic development. This Sen Gupta has done by classifying India into 19 regions according to homogeneity in demographic structure, resource potentiality, and levels of socio-economic development. They are further grouped into three characteristic population resource regions—five as dynamic, five as prospective, and nine as problematic. The dynamic regions support 'advanced industrial areas and predominantly urban population', the prospective regions have immense resource potentials but face socio-economic obstacles to technological transformation, while the problem regions are those which show little promise of development in the near future. The five dynamic regions are: (i) the deltaic plain of the Ganga coinciding with West Bengal; (ii) the Deccan trap area embracing Gujarat State (excluding Kutch Peninsula) and Maharashtra (excluding Marathwada and Konkan coast); (iii) the Tamilnad region identified with Madras State; (iv) the Punjab Plain and the Ganga-Yamuna *doab* area; and (v) the South-Eastern Karnataka Plateau. The five prospective regions are: (i) North-Eastern Peninsular Plateau; (ii) Godavari Basin; (iii) Aravalli Hills and Malwa Plateau; (iv) Western and Southern Karnataka Plateau including Goa district; and (v) Brahmaputra Valley. The problem regions are: (i) the Middle Ganga Plain (Eastern Uttar Pradesh and North Bihar Plain); (ii) the Orissa Coast; (iii) the Kerala Coast; (iv) the Laccadive, Minicoy and Amindivi Islands; (v) the Konkan coast and the central part of Southern Peninsula stretching from Marathwada through north-eastern part of Karnataka Plateau to Rayalaseema area of Andhra; (vi) the Rajasthan desert including the Kutch Peninsula of Gujarat; (vii) the North-Western Himalayas; (viii) the Eastern Himalayas and Eastern Hills and Plateaus; and (ix) Andaman and Nicobar Islands.

This scheme is immensely useful for planning purposes because it specifically points out the regions that are lagging behind in the development race and need special attention and regions where development efforts can show maximum returns. Another scheme useful for planning purposes is the one based on energy and power resources because these resources will play a dominant role in determining the distribution of industrial activities (and many other economic activities) in the future economic development of the country. An energy resource regionalization scheme was put forward by K.L. Vij and C.K. Chandran of the Central Water and Power Commission of India. Their scheme cut across State boundaries and divided the country into eight macro regions which in their opinion "should develop in a comprehensive manner with their own regional power grid systems".[33]

FUNCTIONAL REGIONALIZATION : ANALYSIS OF THE SPATIAL LINKAGE PROCESSES

In this section we have chosen for discussion the schemes of functional regionalization proposed by Brian J.L. Berry and S.R. Hashim. We have also considered another useful study conducted by Gidadhubly and Bhat that could be of some help to us in understanding the spatial linkage processes in India. However, a note of caution should be struck at the very outset. All studies included here are based on commodity trade flows, but on account of non-availability of data, transportation by road is left out. In fact, it is precisely because of this factor of non availability of data that very few studies relating to spatial interaction and spatial linkage processes have been carried out in this country though their importance in exploring economic relationships (and, accordingly, in planning economic activities) is very much evident.

It was Edward L. Ullman's pioneering study on commodity flows in the U.S. economy that opened up wide vistas on the study of spatial interactions and regional economic structure.[34] A study with a similar intent and format was conducted by Brian J.L. Berry for Indian economy with the help of *Inland Trade Accounts* mainly for the year 1959-60.[35] The inland trade accounts provided quantity figures of the trade in 63 commodities moving by rail and inland steamer between the 36 trade blocks of India. Since the inland trade flows were reported by quantity in 63 separate from-to flow tables, there was a $63 \times 36 \times 36$ series in that year.

Berry's exhaustive and classic study on Indian commodity flows brings out clearly the spatial linkage processes in the Indian economy. The basic techniques used are map representation and cartographic analysis. A total of about 750 maps have been drawn to provide a vivid cartographic portrayal of the principal patterns of spatial interactions in India in 1959-60. Help is also taken of the multiple factor analysis. The following two themes emerge from an inspection of the maps of commodity flows:

(a) the division of the sub-continent into a set of regional economies oriented about major metropolitan centres; and

(b) the spatial distribution of major resource complexes and the economic activities located upon them.[36]

The predominance of the four metropolitan centres of Bombay, Calcutta, Delhi, and Madras would be clear from the fact that of the flows, 40% by value and 30% by quantity originated or terminated in these four metropolitan centres. Figures 2 and 3, taken from Berry's study (where they are Figs. 66 and 69 respectively), show clearly the four polarized regions of the Indian economy concentrated round the four metropolitan centres of Bombay, Calcutta, Delhi, and Madras. About 70% of the spatial pattern of linkages are taken into account. Figure 2 gives the functional regions based upon the total quantity moving into trade blocks, while Fig. 3 gives

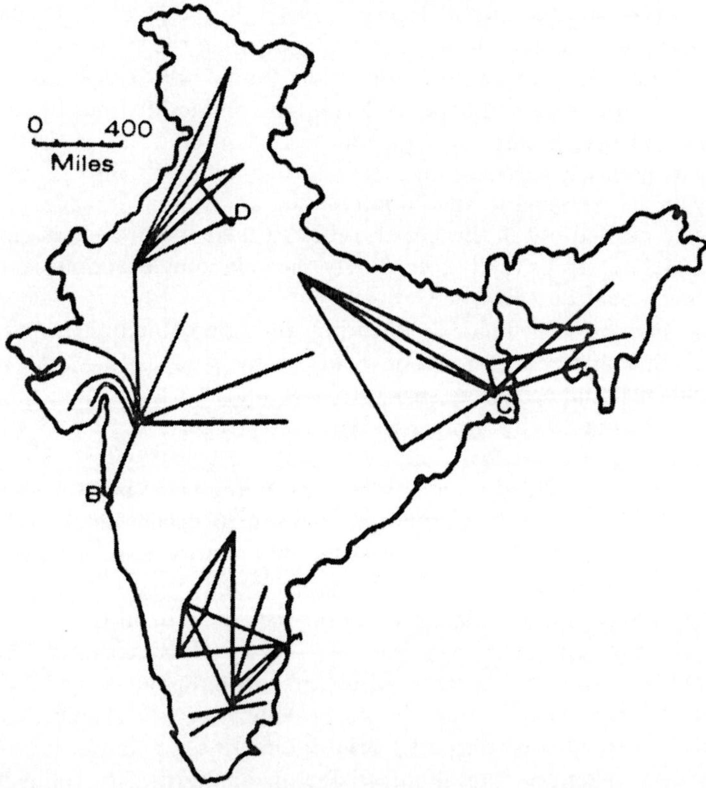

Figure 2: Functional regions based upon total quantity moving into trade blocks.
Source: Brian B.J.L. Berry, *Essays on Commodity Flows and the Spatial Structure of Indian Economy*, Department of Geography, Research Paper No. 111, University of Chicago, Chicago, 1966; Fig. 66, p. 156.

the functional regions based upon the total value moving into trade blocks. When we take into account the total quantity moving into trade blocks, four principal divisions of the economy are clearly evident. Each of these divisions is a polarized region with its own metropolitan centre. If the total value moving into trade blocks is considered, a similar regionalization emerges. But in this case the regions are larger, reflecting the ability of higher valued movements to move further. Also, the Delhi region is now embraced by that of Bombay.

If one considers Fig. 2, the economy seems to be consisting of four separate regional economies. These regional economies are held together in a national frame by inter-regional commodity flows of the following two kinds: "First, agricultural specialities move from one region to the metropolitan centres of others. Second, the specialized industrial products of the

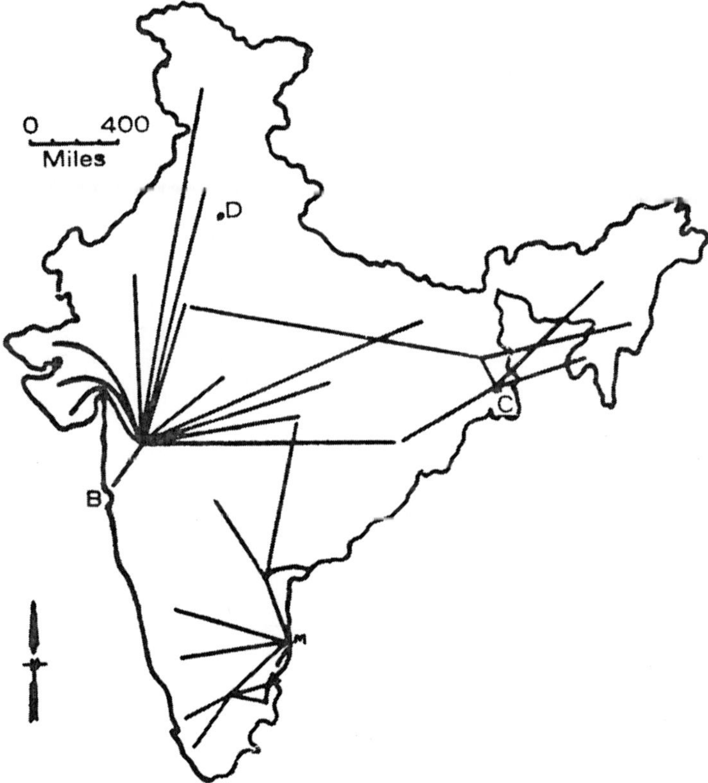

Figure 3: Functional regions based upon total value moving into trade blocks.
Source: **Brian B.J.L. Berry, op. cit.; Fig. 69, p. 160.**

metropoli are exchanged among themselves, creating a web of national interdependency."[37]

Study of S.R. Hashim[38]

Hashim's study is based on the *Inland (Rail and Riverborne) Trade Accounts* for the year 1965-66 and takes into account aggregate flows of 61 commodities. The major conclusions of Hashim are summarized below:

1. Assam, Manipur, Tripura, and Nagaland have high linkages with Calcutta.
2. Both in absolute and in relative terms, West Bengal and Bihar have strong mutual linkages. Orissa has strong links with both Bihar and West Bengal.
3. U.P.'s trade is more diversified and hence strong mutual links cannot be clearly discerned with any other single region. However, it has stronger relations with its eastern neighbours, viz. Bihar and West Bengal, than with its western neighbours, e.g. Punjab, Delhi, and Rajasthan.
4. Jammu & Kashmir depends more on Bombay for its exports and on U.P. for its imports.
5. Himachal Pradesh has stronger export relations with Bombay, and import relations with Punjab, Bihar, and Rajasthan.
6. Punjab, Himachal Pradesh, Delhi, and Rajasthan have strong mutual linkages, all of them depending mainly on Bombay for exports.
7. Madhya Pradesh has diversified trade relations but has stronger links with Gujarat and Maharashtra as compared with other States.
8. Goa and Mysore have very strong mutual linkages. Further, the four southern States, viz., Mysore, Andhra Pradesh, Kerala, and Madras, and all important parts in these States show quite strong inter-regional linkages.

With the help of these conclusions, Hashim suggests the following macro regions for the economy (important ports are mentioned separately):

1. Assam, Manipur, Tripura, and Nagaland
2. West Bengal, Bihar, Orissa, and Calcutta
3. Uttar Pradesh
4. Punjab (including Haryana), Himachal Pradesh, Delhi, Rajasthan, and Jammu & Kashmir

5. Gujarat (including Gujarat ports), Maharashtra (including other Maharashtra ports), and Bombay
6. Goa, Mysore and Mysore ports, Kerala and Kerala ports (including Cochin), Tamil Nadu and Madras port, Andhra Pradesh and Andhra ports.

The Study of Gidadhubly and Bhat[39]

The main objectives of the study are defined by the authors as follows: (i) analysing the spatial patterns and variations in the movement of selected commodities in India during the period 1955-56 to 1967-68; (ii) analysing the behaviour of inter-regional and intra-regional relationships among the different economic regions of India, and (iii) testing the emerging patterns and trends in space relations with certain hypotheses and concepts in the formation of economic regions and space relations. The data are obtained from the statistics of rail and riverborne trade of India (Government of India, 1955-56 to 1967-68) for the States and Union territories. The authors have selected the following five important industrial commodities for study: sugar, cotton textiles, cement, coal, and iron and steel. The major conclusions of the study are summarized below:

1. As a proportion of aggregate production the commodity flow has been generally on the increase.
2. The inter-regional flows were generally of a higher magnitude than the intra-regional flows.
3. The major flows were generally between regions with a relatively high level of development in respect of manufacturing activities. *A hierarchy of commodity flows as related to the regional hierarchy is to some extent evident.*
4. *Regions whose intra-regional flows were important revealed the complementarity in the formation of functional economic regions.* The patterns of intra-regional flows of sugar in the western region and of steel and coal in the eastern region reveal this aspect to a certain extent.
5. The patterns of linkages—intra-regional and inter-regional—not only reveal the relationship of flows to production structures in different regions but also the dynamic nature of those linkages with the changes in the spatial pattern of production and demand.

SCHEMES OF PLANNING REGIONS

Under this heading we propose to discuss the schemes submitted by P. Sen Gupta and C.S. the Town and Country Planning Organization.

Sen Gupta's Scheme[40]

Keeping natural regions of the country as a base and considerations of homogeneity, nodality, production specialization, energy resources utilization, etc., in view and accepting the importance of the State boundaries (on administrative and political grounds), P. Ser Gupta divides the country into seven major planning regions by grouping States approximately coinciding with the drainage-basins.[41] The regions are: (1) the North-Eastern Region, (2) the Eastern Region, (3) the North-Central Region, (4) the Central Region, (5) the North-Western Region, (6) the Western Region, and (7) the Southern Region. The North-Eastern Region conforms to Assam, Nagaland, North-East Frontier Agency, Manipur, and Tripura. The eastern Region comprises West Bengal, Bihar, and Orissa. The North-Central Region coincides with Uttar Pradesh, and the Central Region with Madhya Pradesh. The Western Region comprises Maharashtra, Gujarat, Daman, Diu, and Dadra, and Nagar Haveli. The North-Western Region embraces Rajasthan, Punjab, Haryana, Himachal Pradesh, and Jammu & Kashmir. The Southern Region comprises Andhra Pradesh, Mysore, Kerala, Goa, Pondicherry, Karaikal, Mahe, Yanam, Andaman and Nicobar Islands, Laccadive, Minicoy and Amindivi Islands.

Since it is only within a framework of a system of meso regions that resource-development of macro regions can take place, Sen Gupta proceeds to a delimitation of meso regions paying particular attention to the "core of economic growth—multipurpose projects, cities, industrial centres, etc., which radiate their production-impulses to their surrounding areas." The division of the macro-regions into meso regions is given in Table 2.

The Town and Country Planning Organization Scheme[42]

We shall note in Chapters 5, 6, and 8 the increasing regional disparities and imbalances in India despite the objective of balanced regional development included in all the Plan documents and the Industrial Policy Resolution of 1956. We shall also note that concentration of economic activity and processes of modernization and urbanization has continued unabated in the planning era in spite of the fact that large-scale public sector projects were set up in backward areas (especially of Bihar, Madhya Pradesh, and Orissa). One of the basic reasons accounting for this state of affairs was perhaps that no attempts were made to evolve an economic organization of activities around such projects to sustain and support them (for the purpose of ensuring adequate growth impulses to develop the whole area).[43]

Keeping these considerations in view, C.S. Chandrasekhara advocates the delineation of planning regions according to *minimum resource poten-*

TABLE 2: Macro and meso regions of India—Sen Gupta's classification

Macro Region*	Meso Region**
I. North-Eastern Region (Assam, Manipur, NEFA, Nagaland, and Tripura)	(i) Upper Brahmaputra Valley, (ii) Lower Brahmaputra Valley, (iii) Mineralized Plateau, (iv) Eastern and Northern Hills
II. Eastern Region (West Bengal, Bihar, and Orissa)	(i) Calcutta-Hooghly Region, (ii) Damodar Valley Area, (iii) Chotanagpur and Northern Orissa Plateau, (iv) Southern Hills and Plateaus of Orissa, (v) Lower Ganga Plain, Deltas and Coastal Plain, (vi) Darjeeling Hills and submontaine tracts (Duars)
III. North-Central Region (Uttar Pradesh)	(i) N. Himalayan Area, (ii) Western Ganga Plain, (iii) Eastern Ganga Plain
IV. Central Region (Madhya Pradesh)	(i) Eastern Madhya Pradesh, (ii) Western Madhya Pradesh, (iii) Bastar Area, (iv) Central Madhya Pradesh
V. North-Western Region (Rajasthan, Punjab, Haryana, Jammu & Kashmir, and Himachal Pradesh)	(i) Punjab Plain, (ii) The Union territory of Delhi, (iii) Western Rajasthan, (iv) Eastern Rajasthan, (v) Himalayan Hills including 'Dun' Area, (vi) Kashmir Valley and its surrounding Hills
VI. Western Region (Maharashtra, Gujarat, Dadra and Nagar Haveli, Daman and Diu)	(i) Bombay city and its Conurbation Area, (ii) Intervenings Area along the railway between Bombay and Nagpur, (iii) Coastal Part of Maharashtra, (iv) Western Maharashtra mainly Plateau Area, (v) Eastern Maharashtra, (vi) Central Maharashtra, (vii) Gujarat Plain, (viii) Saurashtra, (ix) Kutch
VII. Southern Region (Andhra Pradesh, Mysore, Tamil Nadu, Kerala, Pondicherry, Yanam, Goa, Andaman & Nicobar and Laccadive, Minicoy & Amindivi Islands)	(i) Coastal Plain of Andhra Pradesh, (ii) Telengana Area, (iii) Rayalseema Area, (iv) South-Central Industrial Area, (v) South-Eastern Coast, (vi) Anaimalai, Cardamom & Nilgiri Hills, (vii) Western Coast, (viii) Malnad and Western Ghat Area, (ix) Maidan Area, (x) Coral Islands

*Macro regions = 7
**Meso regions = 4 + 6 + 3 + 4 + 6 + 9 + 10 = 42

tials of different regions.[44] "Such a concept will lead to the areas rich in one type of resources being linked up with areas having complementary resources or even resource poor areas so that the benefits of activity in the former may flow into the latter." Planning regions delineated in this manner are to have within them three primary requirements for generating economic activities: (a) land, (b) raw materials for industrial development, and (c) power. "These three principal factors will enable each planning region to achieve a degree of self-sufficiency in food, an employment potential in the agricultural and non-agricultural sectors to meet the needs of the region's population and a power base which will serve the developmental needs of both agriculture and industry. Thus the region will have the basic elements to achieve a degree of economic viability."[45]

In the scheme submitted by the Town and Country Planning Organisation, the country is divided into thirteen macro-regions which are in turn divided into 35 meso regions. The macro regions are: South Peninsular, Central Peninsular, Western Peninsular, Central Deccan, Eastern Peninsular, Gujarat, Western Rajasthan, Aravalli Region, Jammu & Kashmir, and Ladakh, Trans-Indo-Gangetic Plains and Hills, Ganga Yamuna Plains, Lower Ganga Plains, and North-Eastern Region.[46] This scheme of planning regions cuts across State and district boundaries. However, Chandrasekhara feels that this "need not come into conflict with established boundaries of the state, as ***the state boundaries will continue to serve as administrative units for purposes of implementation of policies and programmes drawn up within a regional framework***".[47]

CONCLUSION : STATES AS REGIONS

India was reorganized on linguistic basis in 1956. The State of Bombay was divided into the States of Maharashtra and Gujarat in 1960, Nagaland was formed in 1962, and Punjab was divided into the States of Punjab and Haryana in 1966 on the same basis. At present, there are 22 States and nine Union territories. The States are: Andhra Pradesh, Assam, Bihar, Gujarat, Haryana, Himachal Pradesh, Jammu & Kashmir, Karnataka (formerly known as Mysore), Kerala, Madhya Pradesh, Maharashtra, Manipur, Meghalaya, Nagaland, Orissa, Punjab, Rajasthan, Sikkim, Tamil Nadu, Tripura, Uttar Pradesh, and West Bengal. The Union territories are: Andaman and Nicobar Islands, Arunachal Pradesh, Chandigarh, Dadra and Nagar Haveli, Delhi, Goa, Daman and Diu, Lakshadweep, Mizoram, and Pondicherry.

The formation of linguistic States has been a matter of great political importance after Independence. While on the one hand, it has promoted the economic consolidation of these areas, and has strengthened the intra-State production-economic links and integration of their economy (thus becoming a potent region-forming factor), on the other, it has led to a number of disputes and parochial claims for location of public sector plants and demands for Central assistance. The desire of the language groups to consolidate their economy coupled with the demand for the extension of benefits to less developed areas sometimes grows into a tendency towards economic autarky posing a threat to the economic progress of the country. Excessive emphasis on local, narrow interests often puts obstacles in the way of optimum utilization of national resources and rational allocation of industries.[48] A pertinent case in point is in regard to the utilization of water resources. Passions have flared up on the issue of distribution of water resources and invaluable time that could have been utilized in formulating and implementing schemes for expansion of irrigation facilities and generation of hydel-power (to help expand the industrial base) has been lost by States over senseless dog-fights. While, on the one hand, vast areas of land face acute shortage of irrigation facilities and are left dry, on the other, floods (which have become an annual occurrence) cause havoc and destruction over large areas. Both these problems could have been solved had States cared to mutually cooperate in programmes of inter-State planning to control and regulate the supply of water.

Perhaps the greatest difficulty, as far as considerations of regional planning are concerned, is that linguistic State do not correspond to economic regions of the country. The following comments of Sakharov are relevant in this context: "An economic-geographical analysis of the territorial structure of the Indian federation reveals numerous cases of bigger or smaller discrepancy between this structure and the country's actual regional economic distinctions. Several territories will be found whose inclusion in this or that State is doubtful, if we regard the States not merely administrative ethno-lingual units, but as economic regions." He further notes: "Some States, more or less homogeneous or integral economically and ethno-linguistically, constitute 'single region' formations. Others do not have this internal unity and homogeneity: there are States consisting of two or three large regions (at the same taxonomic level of major economic regionalization)."[49]

It would have been clear to the reader that most of the schemes of regionalization considered in this chapter divide the country into regions that are different from the linguistic States. Some authors such as V. Nath and P. Sen Gupta have sought to delineate regions by giving due importance to the existing State boundaries. For example, Nath's scheme keeps each resource division within the boundaries of a particular State and districts are not divided (the entire district forming the part of one resource division). However, this scheme was criticized by the Town and Country Planning Organization on the ground that it ran counter to the very concept of regional planning, which was meant to counteract the arbitrariness of administrative boundaries.[60]

This criticism would suggest that the requirements of theory and the requirements of practical planning are irreconcilable. We are faced with the task of evolving a satisfactory compromise formula. Once the States are able to cast away their narrow outlook and agree to participate and cooperate with each other in programmes of development, the gap between theory and practice could be bridged. For, then, the division of the national economy into macro, meso, and micro regions would assume specific significance. The States would then fall at the meso level which is the middle of the hierarchy. At the top of the hierarchy would be macro regions composed of a number of contiguous States with common problems of resource utilization. At the lowest level would be the micro regions. In this framework, States would serve as a link between local and national planning. Once this happens, the schemes of regionalization proposed by Rao and Bhat, Sen Gupta, Chandrasekhara, and others would become immensely useful in the actual task of regional planning.

NOTES

1. J.R. Meyer, "Regional Economics : A Survey", in L. Needleman (ed.), *Regional Analysis* (Penguin Modern Economics Readings, 1968), p. 23.
2. Ibid., p. 23.
3. For example, in India, States have been accepted as distinct political realities and data are normally available only at the State level. Therefore, it becomes essential to regard the States as representing different regions even if the homogeneity and/or nodality considerations deem it otherwise.
4. H.W. Richardson, *Elements of Regional Economics* (Penguin Modern Economics Texts, 1973), p. 109.
5. Quoted by John Glasson, *An Introduction to Regional Planning : Concepts, Theory and Practice* (London: Hutchinson & Co. Ltd., second impression 1975), p. 22-23.
6. C.R. Pathak and Amitabh Kundu, "Regionalization and Regional Planning—An Axiomatic Approach", *Indian Journal of Regional Science*, Vol. V, No. 2, 1973, p. 169.
7. P.D. Malgavkar and B.M. Ghiara, "Regional Development : Where and How?", in L.K. Sen (ed.), *Readings on Micro-Level Planning and Rural Growth Centres* (Hyderabad: National Institute of Community Development, 1972), p. 306.

   The economic viewpoint will try to incorporate growth and welfare aspects in the definition of region itself because no economic planning can ignore them. In this context, the region can be defined as "operationally the most convenient and economically the most gainful spatial, sectoral and/or temporal unit for resource-allocation, taking planning as merely a process, growth as the economic result and welfare as the ultimate goal". M.H. Gopal, "Region as a Developmental Concept", *The Indian Economic Journal*, Vol. XIX, No. 1, July-September 1971, p. 5.

8. Harry W. Richardson, *Regional Economics* (London: Weidenfeld and Nicolson, 1969), p. 228.
9. Peter Hall, *The Theory and Practice of Regional Planning* (London: Pemberton Publishing Co. Ltd., 1970), p. 16.
10. Of course, perfect homogeneity is not possible. What we aspire for is homogeneity 'within certain clearly defined limits'.
11. For a detailed and illuminating discussion on these and related issues, see J.R. Boudeville, *Problems of Regional Economic Planning* (Edinburgh: Edinburgh University Press, 1966, reprint 1974).
12. O.H.K. Spate and A.T.A. Learmonth, *India and Pakistan—A General and Regional Geography* (London: Mathuen & Co. Ltd., 1954), and V. Nath, *Resource Development Regions and Divisions of India* (New Delhi: Planning Commission, 1965).
13. M.N. Pal, "Regional Information, Regional Statistics and Regional Planning in India", in Antoni Kuklinski (ed.), *Regional Information and Regional Planning* (The Hague: Mouton and Co., 1974), UNRISD/Regional Planning/Vol. 6, p. 324.
14. Ibid., p. 324.
15. A composite index of development was developed by M.N. Pal in his sutdy "A Method of Regional Analysis of Economic Development with Special Reference to South India", *Journal of Regional Science*, 5, 1963 (pp. 41-58); reprinted in R.P. Misra, *Regional Planning* (University of Mysore, 1969). Also see: (i) M.N. Pal, "Quantitative Techniques for Regional Planning", *Indian Journal of Regional Science* Vol. III, No. 1, 1971, pp. 1-33; and (ii) M.N. Pal, *Regional Analysis for National Development : Techniques and Case Studies*, Doctoral dissertation (Delhi: University of Delhi, 1968).
16. M.N. Pal, "Regional Studies and Research for Consistent and Optimal Plan Formulation : The Need for a Right Kind of Orientation", *Indian Journal of Regional Science*, Vol. V, No. 1, 1973; p. 9.
17. Urmila Sandhu, "Identification of Backward Regions—A Brief Critical Review", *Margin*, Vol. 9, No. 2, January 1977, p. 55.

    A discussion on principal component analysis can be found in Harry H. Harman, *Modern Factor Analysis* (Chicago: The University of Chicago, 1967), especially Chapter 8. See also, M.N. Pal, *Regional Analysis for National Development : Techniques and Case Studies*, op. cit.
18. M.N. Pal, "Regional Information, Regional Statistics and Regional Planning in India", op. cit., p. 345. As noted by Boudeville, "The defining of polarized regions is most important for economic development. In new and growing countries, such as Latin America, the appearance, development, and integration of polarized regions is synonymous with the progress of industrialization and market economy. In older countries the identification of polarized regions stresses the location of the network of maximum economic interconnections and constitutes the best frame for the determination of efficient programming." Boudeville, op. cit., p. 38.
19. W.J. Reilly, *The Law of Retail Gravitation* (New York: 1931).
20. J.R. Boudeville, "A Survey of Recent Techniques for Regional Economic Analysis", in Walter Isard and John M. Cumberland (eds.), *Regional Economic Planning* (OECD), p. 384.
21. Harry W. Richardson, *Elements of Regional Economics*, op. cit., pp. 98-99 (footnote).
22. O.H.K. Spate and A.T.A. Learmonth, *India and Pakistan*, op. cit., p. 411 (Third edition, 1967).
23. Publications Division, Government of India, *The Gazetteer of India Vol. I*, August 1965 (reprinted in September 1973). All discussion on physiographic regions of India is taken from this source and all quoted matter is also from this source.

24. For details, see Chapter 10.
25. For details, see Chapter 10.
26. An attempt in this direction was made by Dr. (Miss) P. Sen Gupta, "Territorial Association of Natural Resources with Natural Regions", in P. Sen Gupta and Galina Sdasyuk, *Economic Regionalization of India : Problems and Approaches* (Census of India 1961: Monograph Series, Vol. I, No. 8). This article contains a detailed study of the natural resources of different natural regions of India and is supplemented by a series of immensely useful tables and maps.

    In fact, the entire monograph on *Economic Regionalization* . . . is indispensable for a study relating to economic regionalization of India and is recommended to all readers.
27. V. Nath, *Resource Development Regions and Divisions of India,* (New Delhi: Planning Commission, 1965).
28. Ibid., p. 2.
29. L.S. Bhat and V.L.S. Prakasa Rao, "A Regional Framework for Resource Development", *Bombay Geographical Magazine,* Vol. 10, No. 1, 1964. Also see, L.S. Bhat, *Regional Planning in India* (Calcutta: Statistical Publishing Society, 1972).
30. L.S. Bhat, *Regional Planning in India,* op. cit., p. 23.
31. Ibid., p. 28.
32. V.V. Pokshishevskiy, "Population geography : Problems of planned development of economic regions in developing countries", in *Economic and Socio-Cultural Dimensions of Regionalization* (Census of India, 1971; Centenary Monograph No. 7), p. 2.
33. Ibid., p. 18.
34. Edward L. Ullman, *American Commodity Flows* (Seattle: University of Washington Press, 1957).
35. Brian B.J.L. Berry and others, *Essays on Commodity Flows and the Spatial Structure of Indian Economy,* (Chicago: Department of Geography, Research Paper No. 111, University of Chicago, 1966).
36. Ibid., p. 187.
37. Ibid., p. 2.
38. S.R. Hashim, "Inter-Regional Linkages and Economic Regionalisation", *Indian Journal of Regional Science,* Vol. II, No. 1, 1970, pp. 11-20.
39. R.G. Gidadhubly and L.S. Bhat, "Economic regions and regional flows—a case study in the flow patterns and trends in selected commodities in India", in *Economic and Socio-Cultural Dimensions of Regionalization,* op. cit., pp. 175-215.
40. P. Sen Gupta, "Framework of Economic Regions", in *Economic Regionalization of India : Problems and Approaches,* op. cit., pp. 187-217.
41. "In developing country like India where resources are developed essentially in agricultural setting, the grouping of States having the common river-basins seems to be the most scientific approach to the delineation of planning regions." Ibid., p. 191.
42. For details of this scheme, refer to C.S. Chandrasekhara, "Balanced Regional Development and Planning Regions", in *Economic and Socio-Cultural Dimensions of Regionalization,* op. cit., pp. 59-74.
43. In this context, note the following comments of Chandrasekhara: "What is really necessary is the organisation of economic activities at all levels, primary, secondary and tertiary interacting with one another so as to produce an aggregate growth rate which will help to remove the deficiencies in the area. The growth rate that can be achieved in each area will depend upon the resource capability of that area; further a satisfactory organisation of economic activity requires a resource base wide enough and adequate to support the activity in each sector." Ibid., p. 62.
44. "If balanced regional development consistent with economic efficiency and equality

in economic opportunity is to be achieved, then it has to have as its primary basis, areas or regions which have the necessary minimum resources for supporting and sustaining development of a magnitude commensurate with the primary needs of that area or region." Ibid., p. 62.

45. Ibid., p. 62.
46. The reader is referred to Annexures I and II of Chandrasekhara's article for details of macro and meso regions. The annexures also give information on resources available in different regions. Ibid., pp. 65-73. Also see map on p. 74.
47. Ibid., p. 62. Emphasis added.
48. Sen Gupta and Sdasyuk, op. cit., p. 8.
49. Quoted in Ajit Kumar Singh, "States as Planning Regions", *Indian Journal of Regional Science*, Vol. IV, No. 1, 1972, p. 54.
50. B.K. Roy Burman, "Towards an Integrated Regional Frame", in *Economic and Socio-Cultural Dimensions of Regionalisation*, op. cit., p. 31. The criticism reveals that we cannot simultaneously meet the requirements of theory and practical feasibility.

    Sen Gupta has criticized Nath's scheme on another ground. According to her, "Nath's concept of resource-development regions, though first of its kind, is deficient in a sense that he has chosen only two out of four major categories of resources, such as, land, water, minerals and energy." Sen Gupta and Sdasyuk, op. cit., p. 34.

Chapter 2

Definition, Scope, and Content of Regional Economics and Regional Planning

Regional economics is a relatively new entrant to the field of economics, but within the past two or three decades it has come to acquire an invincible position. Literature on regional economics has grown at a tremendous pace, and academicians, planners, and administrators are showing increasing interest in this branch of knowledge. Considering the immediate relationship that it has with the process of planning and national development and its practical utility in deciding the locational pattern of industrial and other economic activity, one often wonders why interest in it developed so late. Perhaps the main reason for this is to be traced to the 'conservatism of the economics profession'. As noted by Harry W. Richardson, "The neoclassicists were steeped in marginalism, and marginal analysis was frequently not applicable to the space dimension. They liked smooth curves which were amenable to calculus, while distance functions and other spatial parameters tend to exhibit inconvenient discontinuities."[1] When they broke the shackles of 'static state', the economic analysis did make considerable advances, for now it became possible to incorporate the element of time. However, the locational and spatial aspects continued to be neglected on the pretext that they fell in the domain of geography. Neglect of these aspects was also born out of the conviction of many economists that given the conditions of perfect competition and perfect mobility of factors of production, factor prices in all regions would be equalized. Thus, according to them, there was no necessity for accepting the independent existence of 'regional economics' as such.

However, after the Second World War, there was a definite change in thinking. As regional data came to be collected and studied in a systematic way it became evident that convergence in economic growth was an ideal that could not be achieved and that it could not be explained in terms of non-existence of perfect competition alone. There are more causes that lie at the heart of the story, most of which are *spatial* in character. Also, several of the erstwhile colonies of the developed countries became independent and a strong urge to develop themselves as quickly as possible prompted them to plan their national economies. And, as Harvey S. Perloff pointed out, "planning does not take place on the head of a pin", it has to have spatial dimensions, these countries were forced to adopt spatial and regional planning as important constituents of national planning. And since regional planning has to be based on some economic considerations and some economic thinking, the importance of regional economics came to be recognized in a better way. We must, however, hasten to add that regional economics and regional planning continue to be in a backward state in most of the underdeveloped countries even now and most of the development that is taking place is in the developed countries. This is on account of the fact that there is a *knowledge gap* between the developed and the underdeveloped countries, i.e., we tend to teach and study things that were taught and studied in the developed countries a decade or even two decades earlier. This is very much true in economics, as all students of the subject will agree. On the basis of these considerations, we might expect a big boost-up to the study of regional economics in the underdeveloped countries in the decades to come.

THE TERMINOLOGY

Several interrelated yet distinct terms such as regional analysis, regional economics, regional science, regional economic analysis, regional planning, regional economic planning, regional policy, regional economic policy, etc., are in vogue in regional studies. There is a tendency to treat some of them interchangeably. Therefore, it is necessary to define them in such a way as to bring out the differences in them. Let us start by defining regional analysis and regional science. Both these terms are inter-disciplinary in character and include such diverse fields as economics, sociology, geography, demography, and history. It was to this inter-disciplinary character that Harvey S. Perloff was referring when he said:

> No fully satisfactory way of classifying regional studies was found not unexpectedly. Regional studies tend to deal with many features and often involve the use of several academic disciplines. Thus, no general system of classification can be expected to provide self-contained categories; there is inevitable spill-over. The subject classification employed in this report sets up categories whose cores, if not boundaries, are identifiable and whose titles are widely used, with popular and technical

meanings that are not too far apart. The topical categories employed are (i) Physical elements and natural resources; (ii) Population and human ecology; (iii) Regional Economic Development; (iv) Metropolitan studies and metropolitan planning; and (v) Regional history, literature, and socio-cultural elements. Two other categories were found necessary: (vi) Methods and techinques of regional analysis, and (vii) Comprehensive regional studies.[2]

A theorist would perhaps like to stress some difference between regional analysis and regional science by suggesting that the latter is a part of the former for it emphasizes a scientific approach to regional analysis: regional analysis would then assume a wider dimension than regional science. However, it is not useful to stress the difference too far, for both of them are generally referred to mean one and the same thing. Their canvas is so wide that it includes several disciplines and fields of study, and economists, geographers, ecologists, sociologists, town and city planners, regional scientists, etc. have all contributed to the progress of the subject. The leadership has been provided by that doyen of regional scientists, Prof. Walter Isard, who is regarded 'the father of Regional Science'. Walter Isard has been busy developing analytical tools for regional analysis since the 1940s and his magnum opus *Methods of Regional Analysis* (1960) is a 'classic' in regional science literature.

Regional economic analysis can be defined as a study of the *economic aspects* in regional analysis and the regional studies that adopt the *economic viewpoint* can be termed *regional economics*. Similarly, *regional economic planning* will constitute the *economic content* of regional planning and *regional economic policy* will constitute the *economic content* of regional policy.

DEFINITION OF REGIONAL ECONOMICS[3]

As in other branches of economics, the semantic problems in this field also are fairly complicated. Thus, according to Vinod Dubey, at least four approaches on the definition of regional economics can be shown to exist in the literature. The first approach is the one which we have noted above. It says that "regional studies that adopt the economic viewpoint may be considered as studies in regional economics". In this context the field of regional studies is defined on the lines of Harvey S. Perloff. The second approach is the opposite of the first one and "is based on the idea that a group of problems that form the subject matter of regional economics can be distinguished, and a listing of such problems could serve as a definition of the subject". This line is followed by Walter Isard who suggests a fairly exhaustive list of problems encountered in regional economics in the following passage:

> An analyst is perplexed with many problems when he looks at a region. One problem may be to identify specific industries which can individually or in groups operate efficiently and with profit in the region. Another related problem may be to improve the welfare of the people of the region, that is, to raise *per capita* incomes and perhaps achieve a more equitable distribution of income, the auxiliary problem of measurement of income and of the performance of a society is also present. Still another problem may be to avoid an industrial mix which is too sensitive to the ups and downs of national and world business, and which is composed too heavily of old, slow growing, or declining industries; this is the problem of diversification. Finally, a fourth problem which can be mentioned is to plan industrial development for a region, as part of a system of regions, in an internally consistent manner. . . . Another pressing problem . . . and which for many regions is the most critical, is the problem of how to put to best use a limited, if not a niggardly endowment of resources.[4]

Dubey criticizes this definition on the following grounds:

1. The definition is classificatory and not analytical.
2. It fails to bring out "the distinguishing character" of the problems studied and the unifying link (or links) of the subject.
3. It can never be complete since, with the passage of time, new problems will continue to get added. In time, the list would become very long and cumbersome.
4. "Regional economics is not the study of the economic problems of regions, as the 'list of problems' definition seems to imply. Rather, it is the study of all the problems of regions from the economic viewpoint."

The third approach to regional economics is the one that regards it as the 'economics of spatial separation'. Dubey regards this definition as incomplete for two reasons. First it does not describe the whole field of problems covered in regional economics. As noted by J.R. Meyer, this definition "would seem to be unduly confining since the policy problems considered by regional economists have been considerably wider in scope than the location problems emphasized by such a definition".[5] Secondly, the existence of spatial separation is a necessary but not a sufficient condition for the existence of regional economics. For example, "consider a situation in which resources and their production and consumption are evenly and uniformly distributed over a continuous plane. Assume that indivisibilities do not exist. In this situation there would be spatial separation, but it would have no modifying influence on economic activities. There would be no regional economics." Because of these two reasons, Dubey suggests that the definition of regional economics as the economics of spatial separation is to be rejected.

The fourth approach regards regional economics as the economics of *resource immobility*. Since "in actual regional analysis spatial separation as such hasn't been so much the policy concern as the fact that resources, particularly labour, are not completely mobile between regions", J.R. Meyer regards this approach as "a reasonably accurate, though still less than fully comprehensive, description of regional economics".[6] According to Dubey, the mere existence of resource immobility does not constitute regional economics unless and until the *type* of resource immobility is specified: e.g., (i) immobility of resources between two industries in the same location and (ii) immobility of a factor between two uses in the same plant, do not necessarily fall within the purview of regional economics. What is important is the fact that even if the type of resource immobility is defined, it is not sufficient to give rise to the regional economic problem. It becomes important only if resources are distributed unevenly over space. For example, if resources, products, and markets are evenly spread over space and indivisibilities are absent, the immobility of resources is not at all important and cannot give rise to regional economics.

After considering these alternative definitions, Dubey presents his own definition which we regard as the most satisfactory. Dubey's definition states: "Regional economics is . . . the study from the viewpoint of economics, of the differentiation and interrelationships of areas in a universe of unevenly distributed and imperfectly mobile resources, *with particular emphasis in application on the planning of the social overhead investments to mitigate the social problems created by these circumstances*." The italicized words, Dubey feels, are not really necessary for "there is nothing inherent in the subject matter of regional economics to make its orientation any more or any less problem solving than that of the rest of economic science".

Dubey's definition has two merits: (i) it is analytical rather than classificatory and (ii) the distinguishing characteristics of regional problems are brought out explicitly in the definition.

TASKS OF REGIONAL ECONOMICS

On pragmatic grounds, the tasks of regional economics can be summed up in the question posed by Edgar Hoover: *What is where, and why and so what?*[7] According to Hoover, "The first what refers to every type of economic activity: not only *production* establishments in the narrow sense of factories, farms, and mines, but also other kinds of businesses, households, and public and private institutions. *Where* refers to location in relation to other economic activity; it involves questions of proximity, concentration, dispersion and similarity or disparity of spatial patterns, and it can be discussed either in broad terms, such as among regions, or microgeographically in terms of zones, neighbourhoods, and sites, within the somewhat elastic limits of the economist's competence and daring."[8]

Thus, as would be clear from the statement of Hoover, the basic task of regional economics is to examine the *pattern of location of all economic activities* (in the initial stages of the development of this science, the study of the pattern of location of industries only was thought to be the task of regional economics). Under this general head, Hoover[9] would include the following activities:

(a) the locational behaviour of a business firm;
(b) choice of location as faced by a household, institution, or public facility;
(c) importance of transport and communications in determining locations;
(d) locational patterns of whole industries (or analogous groupings of residential or other non-business units);
(e) competition for space in determining locational patterns and analysis of the land-use pattern;
(f) "patterns of urbanization within a region: the spacing, sizes, and functions of cities, and particularly the relationship between size and function";
(g) consideration of the structure of functions of different regions with particular emphasis on the "internal economic ties or 'linkages' among activities and interests that give a region organic entity and make it a useful unit for description, analysis, administration, planning, and policy"; and
(h) study of 'population changes' in regions with particular emphasis on the topic of *migration;* causes of and constraints on regional growth; factors that contribute to regional growth and the policy measures that must be adopted to achieve it; and other related topics.

To this rather long list one must add the task of regional economics in *suggesting ways and means to reduce disparities between regions of the same country*. It becomes necessary to emphasize this because of the increasing concern at growing disparities in both the developed and underdeveloped countries, especially in the latter.

THE RATIONALE OF PLANNING

In a free market economy, the questions about 'what to produce', 'how to produce', 'how much to produce', and 'where to produce' are decided by the individuals themselves. The traditional economic analysis assumed that there was no need for interfering in the operations of the economic system since the guiding star—the profit motive—would itself ensure optimum utilization of resources provided the conditions of perfect competition for all goods obtained in the economy. In such a case the economy would be in a position of what is known in economics as Pareto optimum. In the state of Pareto optimum both production and consumption are economically efficient for it is not possible to make any person better-off without making some other person worse-off. Later on, the realization dawned upon the economists that real world was, at best, only an approximation to the ideal of a perfectly competitive economic system. In this framework, planning in the form of intervention was permitted but only "in order to remove, reduce or compensate for imperfections, and to re-allocate resources between individuals only when the distribution which results from the operations of the market is regarded as unjust".[10] It is this concept of planning that continues to be accepted in many developed countries of the West even today.

However, when one considers the case of the underdeveloped countries, the scope and area of planning widens considerably. In the underdeveloped countries, planning is not limited to only *intervention* but is regarded as the *necessary condition* for economic development. An underdeveloped country is generally faced with either non-availability of resources or inadequate resources or inefficient exploitation of resources. Indeed, it is because of either (or more) of these reasons that it remains underdeveloped. In all underdeveloped countries it has been observed that the private sector is not either capable to invest on a sufficient scale to initiate the process of development on its own accord or willing to do so. In most of the cases both the factors go together, i.e., the private sector is both not capable and not willing to invest in adequate quantities. Since the private entrepreneurs are guided by the profit motive, they prefer to invest in projects that yield quick returns to the neglect of projects with a long gestation period but essential from the socio-economic point of view (such as building of transport facilities, dams, and other infrastructure for development). On similar grounds, they are generally more interested in investing in quick-yielding (and high-yielding) luxury goods and consumer goods industries than in basic capital goods industries.[11]

Thus, either the basis for sound economic development is not laid in the underdeveloped countries or its base is too small. Economists have pointed out from time to time that the underdeveloped countries are caught in vicious circles of poverty[12] and, as a consequence, they remain underdeveloped. In the context of our discussion, the most important vicious circle is the one that encompasses the underdeveloped resources and the backward people. In the words of Meier and Baldwin, "The development of natural resources depends upon the character of human productive resources. The more economically backward are the people, the less developed will be the natural resources. Through illiteracy, lack of skills, deficient knowledge, and factor immobility, the resources will remain unutilized, underutilized, or misutilized. Underdeveloped resources are, therefore, both a consequence and cause of the backward population."[13] The magnitude of the task involved in breaking this and other vicious circles of poverty to initiate the process of development in the underdeveloped countries requires immense financial and physical resources. However, as already noted, it is basically because of the non-availability of resources for purposes of development that an underdeveloped country is compelled to remain as such.

This highlights the fact that whatever *technique* is adopted to break the vicious circles of poverty, *planning* of the distribution of resources and *planning* of the utilization of resources assume central importance. This is true irrespective of the fact whether one follows the logic of the ardent advocates of Balanced Growth: Ragnar Nurkse (who advocates simultaneous and balanced investment in a number of different industries, and agriculture) or Rosenstein Rodan (who presents three versions of the Balanced Growth theory—the first advocating balanced simultaneous investment in the production of light consumer goods; the second advocating balanced simultaneous investment in social overhead capital and light consumer goods industries; and the third advocating balanced simultaneous investment in social overhead capital, light consumer industries, and capital goods industries); or Hirschman's theory of unbalanced growth (which emphasizes deliberate imbalancing of the economy by investing in strategically selected industries having the maximum number of 'linkages' in the economy); or the theory of Critical Minimum Effort and Low Level Equilibrium Trap advocated by Nelson and Leibenstein (emphasizing the adoption of a development programme exceeding a certain 'critical minimum effort' and resulting in a rate of growth of per capita income in excess of the rate of growth of population).

Thus, the underdeveloped countries cannot escape planning if they want to develop themselves in a *reasonably short span of time*. It is necessary to emphasize the time factor, for, given a sufficiently long period of time, economic growth can be achieved even without planning (though even this is not certain). In addition to these economic factors, the new social and political consciousness that is emerging in the underdeveloped countries makes economic planning imperative. The governments of most of the underdeveloped countries are committed to the building of an egalitarian social order. Since the vast majority of their people are yet to attain a minimum level of subsistence, this commitment involves herculean efforts at [illegible] regulation and direction of all resources and all economic activities in desired directions of economic growth and welfare.

The need for planning, especially regional planning, also arises because of the widespread regional inequalities in the underdeveloped countries. It is the general experience that if things are left to market forces all economic and other activity (industrial, commercial, banking, science, art, literature, education, etc.) tends to get concentrated in a few regions. Once this happens, as a historical accident or otherwise, there is a tendency for regional disparities to widen.[14] In this era of increasing social and political consciousness it becomes necessary to counter these tendencies effectively and it can be done only with the help of a properly conceived regional planning strategy.

WHAT IS PLANNING?

But the question is: 'What is planning?' Though the term planning is generally understood to imply some sort of regimentation, regulation, and *guided direction* of economy and other activities of a country to develop the economy, it is necessary to define it precisely before we proceed further. According to the Planning Commission of India, "Planning involves the acceptance of a clearly defined system of objectives in terms of which to frame overall policies. It also involves the formation of a strategy for promoting the realisation of ends defined. Planning is essentially an attempt at working out a rational solution of problems, an attempt to coordinate means and ends; it is thus different from the traditional hit-and-miss methods by which reforms and reconstruction are often undertaken."[15] Perhaps the best definition is given by H.D. Dickinson, according to which, economic planning is "the making of major economic decisions—what and how much is to be produced and to whom it is to be allocated by the conscious decision of a determinate authority, on the basis of a comprehensive survey of the economic system as a whole".[16] This definition highlights three features of economic planning: (i) it involves making of major economic decisions, (ii) such decisions are to be made consciously (on the basis of some objectives that are generally taken as given), and (iii) the decisions are to be made by a certain determinate authority on the basis of a survey of the economy as a whole.

There are, however, at least two points that are not specifically included in the above definition—one relates to the 'notion of balance or consistency' and the other to the 'notion of optimization'. The notion of balance or consistency implies "taking proper account of the inter-connections and mutual repurcussions of the different elements of a composite system of action" and the notion of optimization implies "attaining the objectives at the least 'cost' in terms of time or effort or money".[17] If we neglect the notion of consistency, we might find ourselves in a situation where policies adopted to achieve a certain defined objective are mutually conflicting and contradictory. If we neglect the notion of optimization, we might be led to a situation where the objective is fulfilled after an unduly long effort in terms of time and money (while shorter methods existed but were not utilized).

CONSTITUENTS OF A PLAN

From the above discussion, it is possible to indicate the constituents of a plan:

(i) *Problem Identification:* Based upon the tasks which the planning process is expected to fulfill, the planners must identify the problems explicitly and, on that basis, specify a *set of objectives*.

(ii) After the objectives have been accepted, the planners should proceed to decide how they can be achieved. Since resources are scarce it becomes necessary to fix priorities. In general, the priorities are determined in such a way that the objectives can be realized in the *minimum possible time*. This is done by studying the alternative plan models and selecting the one that is expected to achieve the objectives in the minimum possible time or by devising a new model. The model selected should satisfy at least three criteria. "One criterion is *contingency*. There must be a clear relationship between the reality of the problem situation and the variables in the theoretical model. Another criterion is *consistency:* The postulated relationships within the model must not be contradictory. A third criterion is *completeness*. All key parameters that define the problem situation and in terms of which a solution can be operationally identified must be included."[18]

(iii) After the priorities have been determined, the least-cost method of carrying them out should be determined.

(iv) After this stage comes the actual process of implementation of the plan. For this purpose the phyical and financial aspects of the plan have to be integrated and the public administration geared to carry out the implementation.

(v) The last stage involves the provision for a continuous evaluation of the implementation programme. A continuous evaluation is necessary to determine whether the implementation of the plan is being carried out according to the strategy laid down.

REGIONAL PLANNING

As noted in the section on regional economics, interest in this field of study emanates from the fact that 'the element of space has become one of the key economic factors' and there is a growing concern among economists (and all other social scientists) to ensure *optimal utilization* of space and *optimal distribution pattern* of human activities. Regional planning is the instrument through which such optimality is sought to be brought about. In countries where the crucial questions regarding the size, the pattern, and the place of investment are determined by sectoral units under the overall supervision of national planning authorities, the role of regional planning is *passive* and is reduced to the following activities:

— to register the distribution of investment decisions made by the sectoral units;
— to analyse the impact of the decisions on the development of different regions in a given country;
— to indicate how the sectoral investment decisions can be integrated at the regional level and what advantages can be achieved by the integration.[19]

In such a framework, regional planning is only an 'instrument to improve the sectoral efficiency of the investment processes'. In those countries where the basic objectives of regional development are incorporated in the national plans, regional planning assumes a more positive and *active* role. Questions such as 'what is where and why—and so what' are decided with the help of regional economics and on the basis of this knowledge, regional planners seek to (i) improve the distribution pattern of human activity, and (ii) reduce the disparities between the rich and the poor regions of the country.[20]

Like planning at the national level, regional planning also has the objective of accelerating the processes of social advancement of the community through the techniques of economic (and social) planning though the sphere of influence of a regional plan is restricted to the given region or area of the country. Within the overall framework of a national plan, regional planning is designed to formulate measures to assist the growth of certain regions while restraining the growth of others (if that becomes necessary), assist the governments in examining the regional implications of undertaking infrastructural developments, and lay down detailed plans for economic activity in the different regions of the country. In the initial stages of its development in the 1930s, regional planning was generally understood to mean natural resource planning, and thus its role was confined to determining the ways and means of developing the natural resources of a region. Classsic examples of this belief were the TVA (Tennessee Valley Authority) and the regional planning studies of the Natural Resources Planning Board in the USA.

However, with the passage of time, the emphasis on natural resource planning reduced considerably as new dimensions of urban and metropolitan planning, environmental planning, human resource and community planning, planning for problem areas, etc., considerably enlarged the scope and content of regional planning. The emphasis on economic and social aspects in the writings of Ian Burton, James Henderson, Harvey Perloff, Edward Hearle, and others brought to the fore the problems of economic and social development, provision of education and social services, and equitable distribution of income and wealth. The inclusion of this spectrum of problems has made the concept of regional planning so comprehensive as to embrace all economic and social behaviour in a given region.[21]

METROPOLITAN AND URBAN PLANNING

In the developed countries, this element of regional planning is now receiving most of the attention of regional planners so much so that there is a distinct tendency in those countries to regard it as the whole of regional planning. In fact, John Friedmann assigns the entire field of regional planning in the USA to the planning of metropolitan complexes, as the definition of regional planning proposed by him proves. "Regional planning," according to him, "is the process of formulating and clarifying social objectives in the ordering of activities in supra-urban space."[22] This definition, says Friedmann, provides a 'link' with city planning which is concerned with the organization of intra-urban space. The two approaches meet and merge in the metropolitan region in whose context "the task of the regional planner will be to state the ordering of control centres within the area, to identify the functions to be performed by each centre, and to study the inter-regional effects of the expansion of metropolitan economies".[23]

Such a conception of regional planning arose out of the continuous and increasing concern of regional planners with the problems of urban and metropolitan areas. The increasing concentration of people in such areas on account of (i) natural increase of population and (ii) large-scale migration from rural areas and urban areas of a lower order has swelled their population leading to a complex of economic and social problems ranging from housing problem and traffic congestion to problems of personal and social disorganization.[24] The urban planner is faced with the task of preparing an urban land-use plan indicating the pattern of settlement of population and economic activities, determining the broad spatial characteristics of development and specifying the time-horizon development. Several issues have to be raised and solved before such a planning can be undertaken. Some of them are: (i) Should similar socio-economic groups be allowed to concentrate in residential areas? (ii) Should industry be allowed in residential areas? (iii) Should slums be cleared to enable private housing developments? (iv) Should every citizen have easy access to open space of a given standard? (v) Should land be kept vacant in the hope of major industrial development at a later stage?

When one comes to metropolitan area planning or metropolitan region planning, the canvas becomes considerably large, since in addition to the problems of the urban centre, problems of the core region and the peripheral regions have also to be tackled.[25] Depending upon the spatial perspective one has in view, the metropolitan planning can have a micro approach or a macro approach or a mega approach.[26] The micro approach regards the metropolitan region as an 'autonomous and individual phenomenon' while the macro approach considers such a region 'within the framework of a nationally integrated system of planning and decision-making'. The micro approach is concerned more with physical land-use problems than with economic and social considerations and planning is either very loosely associated or not at all associated with the national plans and policies. In the macro approach, however, economic and social considerations (and hence economic and social planning) play an important role and planning for the metropolitan region is an integral part of the national plan and policies. Information on the development of different sectors and other metropolitan and non-metropolitan regions influences the planning for a given metropolitan region which, in turn, influences the policies and planning of other regions. The mega approach goes beyond national boundaries and examines the problem from the scale of a continent or the whole world.

Many underdeveloped countries which have blindly followed the western path of development are also faced with the problems emanating from excessive concentration of population in large urban centres. As in the urban centres of metropolitan regions in the developed countries, physical, economic, social, and moral problems are plaguing large urban centres in the underdeveloped countries as well. However, there is an important difference that has to be noted. The difference lies in the nature of economic relationship between the urban centre of the metropolis and the periphery. In the developed countries the relationship is *two-way* where both the centre and the periphery move in a certain cohesion, and the positive growth in one also leads to a positive growth in the other. On the other hand, in the underdeveloped countries, the relationship is *one-way* so that the urban areas continue to assimilate the gains while the peripheral areas languish. Continuous migration of educated, skilled, and healthy people from peripheral areas to the centre accentuates this tendency. Increasing congestion in urban areas following this large-scale migration compels millions of people to live in slum areas and squatter settlements where conditions of living are, to say the least, inhuman.[27] The periphery also suffers because it is *denuded* of its best brains and best muscles.

The problems involved are indeed complex and any attack on them is to be oriented in two directions: (i) adoption of policies to mitigate the socio-economic evils of polarized development (mainly in the directions of providing social services, public utilities, housing facilities, etc. in over-congested large urban centres) and (ii) adoption of policies to plan out the construction of new industrial towns and urban centres in such a way that no problems arise in the future and the pressure of population on over-burdened large urban centres and metropolitan areas is relieved in a phased manner. While constructing new industrial towns (and making towns) it will be necessary to plan the social overheads, the infrastructure, and the environment keeping the long-term perspective in view and taking into account the *potential* population pressure and density, pattern of migration, etc. Because of the paucity of funds and resources, it might become necessary that in planning new towns, *standards* of services, utilities, and amenities are set radically different from those set in western countries.

Some observers of the Indian scene point out that these considerations were not kept in mind while planning new industrial towns in India and standards comparable with those in western countries were sought to be adopted. This led to much wasteful (and avoidable) expenditure. Ved Prakash[28] has pointed to the immense expenditure incurred in planning new towns in India. In seven towns studied by him it was found that the average capital costs per capita were as high as Rs.2856 (excluding non-residential buildings such as schools, hospitals, health centres, and other civic buildings) in 1963-64. The annual maintenance and operating costs were also found to be substantial. Ved Prakash also notes that after fifteen years (i.e., in 1978-79) such costs could be close to Rs.314 per capita which would be approximately 45% of the income. The reason for this is to be found in the fact that western standards had been followed in planning amenities and social services and instead of designing the new towns as *compact urban units*, most of them had a low density and were scattered. This resulted in high initial investment and recurring cost of maintenance.

Keeping the above considerations in view, it is necessary that while planning for new towns in the future, the emphasis should be on making them compact units and instead of individual open spaces, *community open spaces* should be the general rule. Because of the acute paucity of funds, the minimum standards should be curtailed considerably and care should be taken to ensure that whatever facilities are provided, they should cater to the needs of the maximum number of town dwellers. Thus, it would be immensely economical to go in for community water taps, community bathing facilities, community latrines, etc. instead of aiming to provide each such facility individually to every house. Unless this basic thing is accepted, the cost of establishing and maintaining new towns will be exorbitant and beyond the means of an underdeveloped country such as ours. Also, the net impact of such towns on the problems of urbanization will be marginal.

As far as the existing large urban centres are concerned, perhaps the biggest social problem is the slum areas and the accompanying human degradation. Here also, the scarcity of funds acts as the biggest constraint in improving the lot of slum dwellers. Therefore, it is wiser to aim for 'planned slums' where basic amenities are provided on a community basis and where people are either allowed to construct their own houses at minimal cost or skeletal houses are provided. Planning for the complete removal of slums is a luxury that India cannot afford.[29]

The underdeveloped countries that have just entered the stage of industrialization and where evils of polarized development have not yet appeared would do well to evolve their own patterns of development so that such problems do not arise at all, or, even if they arise, are kept within tolerable limits. There is nothing *sacred* about the pattern and strategy adopted by the western countries, and selection of alternative strategies of development can save the underdeveloped countries from the impending problems. The experience of many socialist countries in this regard should act as an eye-opener to the underdeveloped countries. The following observations of Antoni Kuklinski are relevant in this context:

> I am convinced, however, that it is wrong to accept the experience of the past as an unavoidable verdict for the future. In a worldwide perspective there is a growing dissatisfaction with the performance of

> the past and the different societies are looking for new models for the society of the future. Naturally, one could argue that new functional structures of the society will be accommodated by old regional patterns. But this accommodation is not a conflict-free process and, at least, in some cases the new functional structures must generate new regional patterns. If regional policy and regional planning is really an innovative activity, then a much more radical assumption should be accepted. The new regional pattern should accelerate the emergence of new social and functional structures.[30]

The interest in urban and metropolitan area planning has led to increasing interest in (and concern for) *environmental planning* in the developed countries. Rapid economic progress in the developed countries has polluted the environment and poses a threat to public health and natural ecological balance. The smoke rising from the chimneys of industrial units and emitted from the exhaust-pipes of moving vehicles on overcongested roads pollutes the air, and the industrial wastes that spread into the rivers and seas pollute the water. Thus, it is now being increasingly recognized that unless the environment is also planned, the full gains of development cannot be realized. This realization has extended the horizons of regional planning to include environmental planning as well. In the underdeveloped countries also, the necessity of planning the environment is being increasingly emphasized in seminars, symposia, and various discussion platforms, and public authorities and people are being educated on the evil consequences and hazards of ignoring the claims of environment planning. In actual planning processes, however, insufficient attention continues to be paid to this aspect of regional planning partly because of insufficiency of resources and partly because environmental problems in the underdeveloped countries have not, as yet, assumed dangerous proportions.[31]

REGIONAL PLANNING FOR RURAL DEVELOPMENT

In overpopulated countries such as India, having a predominantly rural base, the task of regional planning is much wider than merely planning for urban and metropolitan areas. There regional planning should aim at developing rural areas through the establishment of growth foci and through linking the different villages, service centres, growth centres, and growth poles in an integrated manner. The idea of growth poles and growth centres is quite basic to the theory of regional planning. As we shall have occasion to point out in Chapters 4, 7, and 8, the strategy of rural development implicit in this framework is one of 'selectivity' and specifying existing and potential linkages'.

It is generally found that villages in an area are linked with one another through a series of linkages which are mostly functional and are reflected by the frequency of trips people of a village make to other villages or towns. Generally there is a central village that provides some essential services to the cluster of villages around it—services that the villages around are not able to provide for themselves. The central villages, in turn, are linked to centres of a still higher order (maybe a town or a city) which provide higher order services. Such functional linkages can be traced to define a micro region with a certain focal point. This may be termed a *service centre.* Service centres are linked functionally with centres of a still higher order, and so on. Thus, we get a hierarchy of settlements.

The task of regional planning is to help us *define* this hierarchy and indicate what industries or activities should be located at different levels of the hierarchy so that an overall development of all villages and urban centres can be ensured in an integrated way at *minimum cost in terms of money, time, and effort*. We emphasize the cost aspect because development of rural areas can be accomplished even without following the above technique but such development is likely to be an unduly long and painful process involving a massive wastage of all resources, men, as well as material. Again, it is only by following the above method of integrated development of rural areas that the problems of poverty, unemployment, underemployment, and disguised unemployment can be solved effectively. Besides, proper encouragement of cottage and small industries (which is implicit in this method of development) will ensure the *cultivation* and *promotion* of entrepreneurship within rural areas themselves. Naturally, in this framework, specific attention will have to be concentrated on the building up of infrastructure, basically transport network and channels of communication. Unless these facilities are made available in ample measure, the locational utility of the growth foci will remain largely unutilized and the impact on the hinterland will be marginal.

This brief discussion shows that, in the Indian context, the basic task of regional planning is 'the deliberate promotion of growth centres as an instrument of rational rural planning'.[32]

REGIONAL DISPARITIES

The strategy of 'deliberate promotion of growth centres' can go a long way in reducing both inter-regional and intra-regional inequalities. Once the different levels in the hierarchy of human settlements are integrated and the different levels of growth foci (service centres, growth points, and growth centres) located in them according to the 'functional' (or 'linkage') approach, regional disparities should reduce appreciably. We must hasten to add that regional inequalities existed in all countries at all times and it will be ridiculous to expect that they can be altogether abolished. Complete equality among regions is not possible because resources and human skills are unevenly distributed over the different regions of a country and mobility of factors is imperfect. Thus, even in the USA, there is a vast underdeveloped area—Appalachia—characterized by rural poverty. There are seven other large areas spread in thirty States that have been earmarked for special development on account of their backward nature and "many smaller pockets of relative poverty and apparently arrested development exist in still other parts of the country".[33] In Canada, the Martime provinces; in Italy, the southern part; in Sweden, the far north; in the UK, large areas in Scotland, Wales, and south-west; in France, the west and the south-west areas; in Finland and Norway, the northern part; have all lagged considerably behind in the race of development and are designated 'problem areas'. The task of regional planning there is to ensure that the rate of development of the backward areas is considerably greater than the rate of development of other areas so that regional disparities can be narrowed down over time. The task of regional planning in the underdeveloped countries is far more complex. Because of the widespread poverty and below-subsistence level of existence of the vast majority of people in many backward regions in the underdeveloped countries, the task is twofold: (i) reduction of regional disparities, and (ii) ensuring at least a minimum level of subsistence to the majority of people inhabiting the backward areas and living below the level of subsistence.

One may perhaps point out, in the context of the underdeveloped countries, that greater equalization among regions will, on its own, ensure a minimum level of subsistence to the poor in the backward regions. It *might*, but there is no certainty that it *would*, because of the general backwardness of the economy. There is another related problem that must be tackled. Since planning in India is carried out at the State level it is generally the inter-State imbalances that are revealed by the data; therefore regional inequalities are not properly brought into focus. For example, we say that the four most advanced industrial States of India, viz. Maharashtra, Gujarat, Tamil Nadu, and West Bengal, are also the most developed States (excluding Punjab and Haryana). This should not mean that the whole of these States are well developed. In fact, considerable areas in all four of them fall under the category of *backward areas* or *problem areas*. To introduce all these considerations in the discussion, the objective of 'removal of regional inequalities' should be re-formulated in the Indian context as follows:

(i) reducing disparities among States; and
(ii) reducing inequalities among different areas of the same State in such a way that all the inhabitants are ensured a certain minimum level of subsistence.

When one suggests the rationale of regional planning in terms of removal (or reduction) of inequalities among regions, one is immediately encountered with that rather knotty (and somewhat mischievous) controversy of efficiency vs. equity: knotty because so much has been written on it and yet everything depends on 'what one thinks about it', and mischievous because the term 'vs.' suggests that these two are mutually contradictory and positively antagonistic to each other. Those who advocate (and believe in) the criterion of *efficiency* emphasize that efforts to increase regional balances will interfere with the desired rate of development. According to this belief, it is best to concentrate on highly developing regions since their chances of achieving a high level of development earlier are better. It is said that after they reach a high stage of development, the benefits of development will *trickle down* and the growth processes in the lagging regions will be automatically stimulated. A classic exposition of this belief is found in the following statement of Louis Lefeber:

> Barring some special and obvious cases, most industrial investments, if located in retarded areas, would have very low current yields, if any at all, and only questionable higher returns in the distant future. Similarly, many government sponsored rural programmes would be of the low-yield type. It might be argued that either approach to increase 'regional balance', i.e. low-yield type rural programmes or arbitrary location of industrial investment, is more in the nature of a transfer payment to improve income distribution than a contribution to economic development. In effect, it uses resources which otherwise would be available to increase national economic growth.[34]

This is the classical analysis in economic literature (with the difference that *individuals* are replaced by *regions*) and is supported by most of the economists. Yet, some important questions remain unanswered. For example, what is the *limit* to which the developed regions should be allowed to prosper (i.e., what is the time that should be allowed to lapse) before resources can be "channelled" to backward regions? Then, what would happen to the backward regions in the meantime? In the socially conscious world of today, will not the continuous rapid development (aided by substantial investments) of some regions promote discontent in regions lagging behind? Will not, as a consequence, the social and political stability of the nation as a whole be threatened? It will be ridiculous to advise the poor in the backward regions to wait, since progress will percolate to them in 'due course of time'.

Since the planning process in India has completed thirty years, it is necessary to pay specific attention to equity considerations. We shall be providing enough evidence in Chapter 5 to prove that the direction of *flow* of finance and investments has continued to be from depressed areas to progressive areas and governmental policies and policies of banks (despite nationalization) help this process. We strongly feel that the time has arrived to make some *hard* decisions. Regional planning should be given such an orientation that it helps locate growth centres and growth points in the lagging regions so that the need for the development of such regions can be looked after in a better way.

APPROACHES TO REGIONAL PLANNING

The approach to regional planning can be either 'total' or 'selective'. In the total regional planning approach an attempt is made to develop all regions of an economy, while in the selective approach the attention is concentrated on the development of some regions only. However, this differentiation between the 'total' and 'selective' approaches is possible only in the context of an economy where no national planning exists. In most of the underdeveloped countries, there is some sort of planning for all regions, at least in the overall framework of a national plan. Under these circumstances, it is better to define the total regional planning approach as the one which aims at *equal development rates* for all regions of the economy by providing equal investment in all of them. The selective regional planning approach will then be one that aims at *unequal development rates* for the different regions of the economy by providing unequal investments in them. When we talk of equal investment, we mean equal investment in relation to the size of the region (size can be determined in relation to either area or population or both). Thus, if region 1 is double the size of region 2, it receives investment twice as much compared with region 2. This is necessary, for otherwise equal investment will, in fact, imply unequal investments, as is fairly obvious. For example, if regions 1 and 2 receive the same investment, it clearly amounts to discrimination in favour of region 2.

As for the choice between the total regional planning approach and the selective regional planning approach, it is easy to see that the resources required by the former in terms of funds, physical resources, entrepreneurial and managerial skills, technical capabilities, etc., will be beyond the reach of an underdeveloped country. Therefore, an underdeveloped country has, of necessity, to rely on the selective approach in its regional planning strategy. Under such an approach it will devote more resources to the development of some regions and less resources to the development of others.

The advantages of the selective approach are many: (a) different kinds of regions for different purposes can be designated; (b) a loose delineation of regional boundaries can be adopted so that they can be changed whenever required (this introduces an element of flexibility in the planning process); (c) the regional effort can be dropped when the purpose has been largely accomplished; and (d) fewer planning personnel and organizational resources are required, and the available ones can be shifted from region to region as situations change.[35]

According to Perloff, the selection of a region for special attention will, in general, be guided by the following factors:

1. The possibility of developing an outstanding untapped resource, either of a limited type, such as a multi-purpose river basin development, or of a broad type involving a large spectrum of activities. . . .
2. The solution to a severe and nationally threatening problem, such as an extremely depressed area, a culturally backward area not in the national mainstream, or an area threatening to break away politically.
3. A combination of both significant potentials and tough problems, such as the planning of major metropolitan regions.[36]

Through the adoption of the selective approach, a country can concentrate more on the lagging regions and help them develop at a faster rate than other regions. As a consequence of this policy, employment opportunities will expand in the backward regions, per capita income will increase, and the incentive to migrate to prosperous regions will decline. This will also be to the advantage of the prosperous regions in the long run.

REGIONAL vs. NATIONAL PLANNING

There is a tendency in some quarters to think of *regional* as something opposed to *national*. The term 'regional' is often understood to imply a sectarian outlook and is consequently taken as a hurdle in the task of national integration. This belief is strengthened by the frequent clashes and conflicts between the regional and national authorities on the allocation of investment and other resources. Besides these practical problems, it is possible to think of situations where there are conflicts between national and regional goals on theoretical reasoning as well. Because the regions of an economy differ from one another in regard to their physical conditions and natural resources, level and stage of development, functional intra-regional and inter-regional interdependence, and human resources (both quantitatively and qualitatively), it becomes necessary to evolve different plans for different regions. Conflicts among regions can arise if their 'preference patterns' are different and if the economic policies devised by a region interfere with the development policies of the neighbouring regions. Inter-regional competition and a 'cut-throat policy' that might result can, in turn, interfere in the goals of optimization and economic development.

Charles L. Leven presents three reasons why optimization at the national level may be inconsistent with optimization at the regional level: "First, where there are multi-dimensional economic goals, the preference patterns of regions may be such that there will not be a consistent ordering of these goals at the national level. Second, even if maximum output were the only goal, each region's share in the relocation costs needed to achieve it may not be equal to their share in the resultant gains. Third, in either case, external economies or diseconomies in production extending across regional boundaries have not been taken into account."[37] The third type of inconsistency arises because it is generally not possible for a region to take into account the external economies or diseconomies of the investments undertaken in the region on production in other regions. The second type of inconsistency arises when the people of a region trained in various skills and provided with education migrate to other regions. (This has been happening in India on a fairly large scale, as we shall see in Chapter 6.) Thus, while the backward regions bear the *costs* of imparting education and skills they get a less than proportionate share of the *benefits* in relation to the costs. In such cases, it is necessary to follow Leven's advice that such activities should be financed on a multi-regional (frequently a national) basis.[38]

To focus the likely conflicts in national and regional planning in a clear perspective, let us think of a situation where a central government is faced with the task of deciding its allocation of investment between 'industries' and 'regions'. There are two alternatives open to it:

(i) first select the industry (on the basis of some national objective) and then decide about the region; or
(ii) first select the region (on the basis of some regional objective) and then decide about the industry.

Let us explain this by an example given by Richardson. There are two industries *A* and *B* and two regions *X* and *Y*. *X* is a prosperous region and *Y* is a backward region. Industry *A* is more efficient in region *X* while industry *B* is more efficient in region *Y*. Industry *A* is more efficient nationally.

If the planner adopts alternative (i), he will choose industry *A* and this will be an *efficient choice* for him. If he now decides on choosing region *Y* on equity considerations, the opportunity cost will be higher in comparison with the situation where industry *A* is set up in region *X* because it is assumed that industry *A* is more efficient in region *X*. If the planner chooses alternative (ii) and selects region *Y* for investment because of its backward nature, then, on the basis of efficiency, he must invest in industry *B* in that region for it is assumed that industry *B* is more efficient in region *Y*. Since on the national basis industry *A* is more efficient than industry *B*, adoption of efficiency considerations on a national basis will not justify the setting up of industry *B* and a clear case of conflict between regional and national goals arises.[39]

As pointed out by Richardson, "If efficient resource allocation resulted in an approximate regional balance in economic activity and growth rates, the conflicts that emerged would be negligible enough to be overlooked. But the nature of the growth process itself rules this out."[40] Regional growth is unbalanced on account of differences in resource endowments, etc.; therefore, conflicts are inevitable. Since a regional planner will be more concerned with the preference function of his own region, he may suggest policies which are not efficient on a national basis or which are positively harmful to other regions. Thus, if his region is a relatively backward one and if he notes the tendency of skilled and young people to migrate to prosperous regions, he might recommend stoppage of such out-migration. This may not be an efficient policy from the national point of view.

The Need for Integration

The above discussion would suggest the need for integrating regional planning with naticnal planning. Despite the inconsistencies that might arise between them, none can deny the necessity of ensuring that all regional plans get *fitted* into a coherent national development plan. It is wrong to regard that regional planning is opposed to national planning. On the contrary, it is part of "the new modern movement to manage the affairs of nations in a more constructive, considered and farsighted manner".[41] In large countries with diverse economic resources and distinct political States, it is not possible to formulate a plan at the nationl level which can take into account the specific detailed requirements of each region. The task of development can be tackled satisfactorily only by drawing up distinct regional plans for the several regions, and then integrating them into a national plan.

One line of integration can be to strike a compromise between the pursuit of national efficiency and the regional problems. Thus, we may seek to maximize some index of national welfare within certain regional constraints. For example, we might aim at maximizing the rate of growth of Gross National Product (a national objective) subject to the condition that the income of the poorest region does not fall relative to the national average (this would then be a regional constraint and would be termed a *minimum attainment constraint*). Let us suppose that there are only two regions (*A* and *B*) in an economy; Y_a and Y_b are the regional incomes (Y_a being lower); Y_p is the national income; and p_a and p_b are the growth rates of incomes. Then we would seek to maximize $Y_p = Y_a p_a + Y_b p_b$ subject to the constraint that $p_b \geqslant p$ (where p is the rate of growth of national income).

The difficulty in adopting this approach (i.e., the approach wherein regional considerations are accounted for in terms of constraints only) is that only broad regional objectives can be accommodated. It is possible that a severely depressed or backward region of an economy is compelled to adopt a number of different objectives simultaneously and to deploy an array of policy instruments to deal with them. Though most of these policies may be implementable at the national level, in some cases the task will fall on the regional policy-makers to administer the measures at the regional level. What about the potential conflict between the national and regional interests in these cases? The answer, according to Richardson, has to be a pragmatic one. Since there are likely to be several alternative policies that can be adopted to achieve a particular goal, "we should choose the method that interferes least with the most efficient allocation of resources. In this way conflicts between regional policies and national efficiency can be kept to a minimum".

In the actual planning process there is a vast scope for integrating regional and national planning. If intensive studies relating to resource availability in different regions of the country, potentialities of growth of different regions, and possibilities of developing growth centres and growth points in erstwhile backward regions are carried out before actually implementing the national plan, perhaps the tasks of integration will not appear as difficult as they are generally made out to be, *provided the required political will to coordinate planning efforts is available*.

NOTES

1. Harry W. Richardson, *Elements of Regional Economics* (Penguin Modern Economics Texts, 1973), p. 13.
2. Harvey S. Perloff in the introduction to the 'Resources of the Future Survey' entitled "Regional Studies at U.S. Universities : A Survey of Regionally Oriented Research and Graduate Education Activities"; quoted by J.R. Meyer in "Regional Economics : A Survey", reprinted in Needleman, *Regional Analysis* (Penguin Modern

Economics Readings, 1968), pp. 21-22.

3. Vinod Dubey, "The Definition of Regional Economics", in David L. Mckee, Robert D. Dean, and William H. Leahy (eds.), *Regional Economics : Theory and Practice* (New York: The Free Press, 1970). All quoted matter in this section is, unless otherwise stated, from this article.
4. Isard quoted by J.R. Meyer, op. cit., p. 22.
5. J.R. Meyer, op. cit., p. 26.
6. Ibid., pp. 26-27.
7. Edgar M. Hoover, *An Introduction to Regional Economics* (New York: Alfred A. Knopf, Inc., 1975), p. 3.
8. Ibid., p. 3.
9. Ibid., pp. 5-8.
10. Alan W. Evans, "Economics and Planning", in Jean Forbes (ed.), *Studies in Social Science and Planning* (Edinburgh: Scottish Academy Press, 1974), p. 82. Evans lists several reasons which might make planning (in the form of intervention) necessary. The ethical reasons that justify government's intervention might be that the government believes that the consumer is sometimes not the best judge of his welfare or it believes that the distribution of resources among the population is not equitable. On the economic side, the reasons for intervention might be the existence of external effects which lead to a divergence between private and social costs. Some such external effects (manifesting themselves in the form of external diseconomies) are: rising smoke from a factory chimney (which imposes costs on persons in the neighbourhood), noise, vibration, smell, air pollution, water pollution, etc. There are several ways of intervention that can be practised by the public authority (the most elementary and most widely used being the granting of subsidies and levying of taxes) and "which is chosen will depend upon the characteristics of the problem, the costs of administering each solution and also, of course, on what is regarded as an equitable solution". p. 89.
11. The lack of resources with the private sector strengthens this tendency.
12. A vicious circle of poverty is defined as "a circular constellation of forces tending to act and react upon one another in such a way as to keep a poor country in a state of poverty". See Ragnar Nurkse, *Problems of Capital Formation in Underdeveloped Countries* (Delhi: Oxford University Press, 1953; Indian reprint, 1973), p. 4. The whole process is summarized by Nurkse in the now-classic statement: "A country is poor because it is poor." p. 4.
13. Gerald M. Meier and R.E. Baldwin, *Economic Development : Theory, History, Policy* (Bombay: Asia Publishing House, 1960; reprint, 1970), pp. 316-317.
14. The processes that help this tendency are explained in Chapter 4. Also see Chapter 5.
15. Government of India, Planning Commission, *First Five Year Plan*, p. 7.
16. H.D. Dickinson quoted in D. Bright Singh, *Economics of Development* (Bombay: Asia Publishing House, 1966; reprint, 1971), p. 555.
17. Ashok Rudra, *Indian Plan Models* (New Delhi: Allied Publishers Private Limited, 1975), p. 1.
18. Michael F. Brewer, "An Alternative View of the Planning Process", in Maynard M. Hufschmidt, *Regional Planning : Challenge and Prospects* (New York: Frederick A. Praeger, 1969), p. 172.
19. Antoni Kuklinski, *Contributions to Regional Planning and Development* (Mysore: Development Studies No. 3, Institute of Development Studies, University of Mysore, 1971), p. 21.
20. Ibid., p. 22.
21. The social issues in the overall context of regional planning are discussed in Chapter 12.

22. John Friedmann, "Regional Planning as a Field of Study", in John Friedmann and W. Alonso (eds.), *Regional Development and Planning : A Reader* (Massachusetts: M.I.T. Press, 1964), p. 64.
23. Ibid., p. 66.
24. All these issues are discussed in the Indian context in Chapter 6.
25. The urban centre is the *centre* of the metropolitan region. The zone around this centre having a close association with the centre is known as the *core region* and the rest of the metropolitan region is termed *periphery*.
26. Antoni Kuklinski, *Contributions to Regional Planning and Development*, op. cit., p. 50.
27. For a discussion of these and related problems, the reader is referred to Chapter 6.
28. Ved Prakash, *New Towns in India* (Monograph No. 8 under the 'Programme in Comparative Studies on Southern Asia', Duke University, 1969).
29. See also Chapter 6.
30. Antoni Kuklinski, "Prospects of Regional Sociology", in Antoni Kuklinski (ed.), *Social Issues in Regional Policy and Regional Planning* (The Hague: Mouton & Co., 1977), p. 518.
31. Environmental planning is discussed in Chapter 12.
32. Preston Andrade and Prodipto Roy, *Pilot Projects for Integrated Area Development* (Delhi: Ministry of Agriculture, Government of India, 1969), Preface, p. 2. For a detailed discussion on how the 'deliberate' promotion of growth centres can become an instrument for 'rational' rural planning, the reader is referred to Chapter 4 (section on 'Growth Pole Policy and Regional Planning in India'), Chapter 7 (section on 'An Integrated Approach to Rural Development'), and Chapter 8 (section on 'Integrated Area Development').
33. Hoover, op. cit., p. 262.
34. Louis Lefeber, "Regional Allocation of Resources in India", in R.P. Misra (ed.), *Regional Planning : Concepts, Techniques, Policies and Case Studies* (Mysore: University of Mysore, (1969), pp. 380-381.
35. Harvey S. Perloff, "Regional Planning in Less Developed Countries", in Maynard M. Hufschmidt (ed.), *Regional Planning : Challenge and Prospects*, op. cit., pp. 327-328.
36. Ibid., pp. 328-329.
37. Charles L. Leven, "Establishing Goals for Regional Economic Development", in R.P. Misra (ed.) *Regional Planning*, op. cit., pp. 374-375.
38. Ibid., p. 375.
39. H.W. Richardson, *Regional Economics* (London: Weidenfeld and Nicolson, 1969), p. 367.
40. Ibid., p. 367.
41. F.B. Gillie, *Basic Thinking in Regional Planning* (The Hague: Mouton & Co., 1967), p. 10.

Chapter 3

Planning in India—An Overview

The planning process was initiated in India in April 1951 with the launching of the First Five Year Plan. So far five five year plans have been completed and the sixth one was initiated in 1978-79. The First Plan covered the period 1951-52 to 1955-56, the Second Plan 1956-57 to 1960-61, the Third Plan 1961-62 to 1965-66, the Fourth Plan 1969-70 to 1973-74, and the Fifth Plan 1974-75 to 1977-78. The three-year period intervening the Third and the Fourth Plans (i e., 1966-67, 1967-68, and 1968-69) was a period of 'plan holiday' when, though annual plans were prepared, there was no overall five-year framework. The plan holiday was forced on the economy by the Indo-Pak conflict in 1965 (and the subsequent suspension of foreign aid), devaluation of the rupee, and the two successive droughts in 1965-66 and 1966-67. The Fifth Plan, which had the terminal year 1978-79, was terminated one year earlier by the Janata government, and the Sixth Plan was initiated in 1978-79. However, before the Sixth Plan could get a real start, the government at the Centre changed. The Congress government proposes 1980-85 as the period for the new Sixth Plan.

The objectives and the tasks for the government were laid down by the Constitution itself when it said in the 'Directive Principles of State Policy':

> The State shall strive to promote the welfare of the people by securing and protecting, as effectively as it may, a social order in which justice, social, economic and political shall inform all the institutions of national life.

Further,

> The State shall, in particular, direct its policy towards securing:
>
> (a) that the citizens, men and women equally, have the right to an adequate means of livelihood;
>
> (b) that the ownership and control of the material resources of the community are so distributed as best to subserve the common good.

and

(c) that the operation of the economic system does not result in the concentration of wealth and means of production to the common detriment.

To fulfil this commitment, the Government of India constituted the Planning Commission in 1950 and entrusted it with the tasks of (a) assessing the country's material, capital, and human resources and to formulate plans for their most effective and balanced utilization; (b) determining priorities, defining stages through which the plan should be carried out, and proposing allocation of resources for the purpose; (c) specifying factors that retard economic development and determining the conditions which should be established to carry out the plans successfully; (d) determining the nature of the *machinery* that will be necessary to carry out the plan successfully; and (e) appraising from time to time the progress achieved by the plans and recommending adjustments of policies accordingly.

OBJECTIVES OF THE PLANS

The First Five Year Plan had two basic objectives: (i) correction of the disequilibrium in the economy caused by the war and the partition of the country, and (ii) initiation of a process of all round balanced development which would ensure a rising national income and a steady improvement in living standards over time. At the time of the formulation of the Second Plan, the objective of socialist pattern of society came to be adopted. This was meant to imply that "the basic criterion for determining the lines of advance must not be private profit but social gain, and that the pattern of development and the structure of socio-economic relations should be so planned that they result not only in appreciable increases in national income and employment but also in greater equality in incomes and wealth. Major decisions regarding production, distribution, consumption and investment—and in fact all significant socio-economic relationships—must be made by agencies informed by social purpose. The benefits of economic development must accrue more and more to the relatively less privileged classes of society, and there should be a progressive reduction of the concentration in incomes, wealth and economic power."[1] This statement has been the *guiding star* of all subsequent planning in the country. Each plan has reiterated its invincible faith in the concept of socialist pattern of society and modelled and remodelled the objectives and targets to accomplish it. We can broadly define the objectives of planning in India as under (following Pramit Chaudhury[2]):

(a) To secure an increase in national income;
(b) To secure an increase in the investment/income ratio;
(c) Reduction in income inequalities;
(d) Expansion of employment opportunities; and
(e) Adoption of measures to alleviate the three 'bottlenecks' regarded by the planners as being of critical importance, viz., agricultural production, the manufacturing capacity for producers' goods, and the balance of payments.

THE STRATEGY OF PLANNING

India is one of those few countries where the strategy of planning is based on specific growth models. The First Plan adopted a model based on the Harrod-Domar growth model to indicate the targets of income, consumption, and investment over time. The Domar equation can be represented as:

$$\Delta I \frac{1}{\alpha} = I\sigma$$

where I is the rate of investment in a given period, α the marginal propensity to save, and σ the potential social average productivity of investment.[3] In this model, I_0 (i.e. investment in the initial period) is taken as given and values to α and σ are assigned according to what seems feasible. In the First Plan, I_0 (the rate of investment in 1950-51) was taken as 5% of the national income; σ was taken as 0.33, and it was assumed that the value of α could not be raised above 0.20 in the plan period. On the basis of these assumptions, the likely rates of investment in subsequent years (and their impact on incomes) were worked out.

The initial attempt of P.C. Mahalanobis (whose models formed the basis of the Second and the Third Plans) was based on the Harrod-Domar formulation. In the course of a lecture delivered in 1952, he used the following mathematical model:

$$Y_t = Y_0(1+\alpha\beta-\rho)^t$$

where Y_t is the per capita net national income in year t, α is the rate of net investment, β is the addition to national product which is generated by a unit of net investment, and ρ is the rate of increase of population. On the basis of this model, Mahalanobis concluded that for achieving a reasonably high rate of growth, it would be sufficient if α was stepped up to 10-11% of the national income.

The really important model that formed the basis of the planning strategy in the Second Plan was presented by Mahalanobis in 1953. This model describes the growth path of the national economy in terms of the following curve[4]:

$$Y_t = Y_0 \left[1 + \alpha_0 \frac{\lambda_i\beta_i + \lambda_c\beta_c}{\lambda_i\beta_i} \{(1+\lambda_i\beta_i)^t - 1\} \right]$$

where Y_t is the gross domestic product in year t, α_0 is the rate of investment in the base year 0, λ_i is the share of investment going to investment goods industries, and λ_c is the share of investment going to consumer goods industries, β_i is the incremental output-capital ratio in investment goods, and β_c is the incremental output-capital ratio in consumer goods industries. Now if α_0 and β_i are constant and $\beta_c > \beta_i$ and $Y(\lambda'_i)$ and $Y(\lambda''_i)$ are curves corresponding to $\lambda_i = \lambda'_i$ and $\lambda_i = \lambda''_i$ and if $\lambda'_i > \lambda''_i$, then the curve $Y(\lambda'_i)$ will intersect the curve $Y(\lambda''_i)$ from below.[5] This has the following important significance for planning—*higher the allocation of investments to the investment goods industries, lower will be the rate of growth of income in the short run, but higher will it be in the long run.* Similar results hold for the curves representing the growth of consumption and this implies that *if one wants a high rate of growth of consumption in the long run, then the best policy is to give priority to the development of investment goods industries over consumer goods industries.*[6] This meant that the investment goods sector should get precedence over the consumer goods sector and the higher the proportion of investment goods output that was reserved for the investment goods industries, the sooner would the desired rate of investment be reached. And since the rate of investment was regarded as the king-pin of national development and growth,[7] it was found desirable to accept the strategy advocating more investment in investment goods sector (or the heavy and capital goods sector). Because of the ideological dominance of socialist thought, it was also deemed necessary to continuously increase the role of the public sector in the national economy. Thus, the strategy of industrialization as it finally emerged in the Second Plan had the following three basic elements:

(i) stepping up the rate of investment since the rate of development depends upon the rate of investment;

(ii) rapid expansion of the productive power of the economy by increasing appreciably the proportion of investment in heavy and capital goods sector; and

(iii) increasing the scope and importance of the public sector so that this sector comes to control 'the commanding heights' of Indian economy.[8]

These elements of the industrial strategy can be taken to be the *basic* elements of Indian planning strategy as it evolved in the Second Plan. The subsequent plans also accepted these elements as basic though the Third and the Fourth Plans did talk of giving more importance (compared with the Second Plan) to agriculture and allied activities. However, by 1970 a distinct change in the thinking of the planners was clearly discernible. As a result of the pioneering study by V.M. Dandekar and N. Rath on 'Poverty in India' in 1971 and the follow-up discussion in which several economists participated, the conviction grew strong that poverty and misery were widespread in India and there was urgent need to take account of this problem in plan exercises.[9] The revelation that more than 40% of the population was unable to achieve even the minimum necessary level of subsistence called for a drastic revision of plan priorities and programmes. Accordingly, for the first time in Indian planning history, the 'Approach Paper' to the Fifth Plan talked of a redistributive scheme aiming at bringing down the per capita consumption level of the richest 30% of the population so that the lowest 30% could be guaranteed a minimum level of subsistence. However, serious doubts were expressed about the proposed plan and it invited a scathing criticism from several quarters. Though the production process, with some changes, could be diverted to produce mass consumption goods, no definite strategy was enunciated to carry out the actual process of transfer of income to the poor. It was also not specified how the incidence of the cut proposed on the 30% upper strata of society was to be distributed among them. A considerable proportion of these people belonged to the lower strata of the middle class or even lower class and a cut in their income would spell misery to them.[10] Because of the difficulties involved in tackling these problems satisfactorily and of the lack of political will and courage to carry out the scheme, the Draft Fifth Plan abandoned the exercise. Though the importance of redistribution was stressed, the policy measures did not envisage any radical or bold redistributive scheme.

Another programme introduced in the Fifth Plan (keeping in view the objective of removal of poverty) was the Minimum Needs Programme. It was aimed 'to establish throughout the country a network of certain essential services on a coordinated and integrated basis' so that facilities such as elementary education, rural health, nutrition, drinking water, provision of housing sites, slum improvement, rural roads, and rural electrification could be provided in all the States (especially in those backward States which could not undertake these programmes on a sufficient scale on account of non-availability of resources). The content of the programme was as follows:

(i) the provision of facilities for elementary education for children up to the age of 14 at the nearest possible places to their houses;
(ii) ensuring in all areas a minimum uniform availability of public health facilities, which would include preventive medicine, family planning, nutrition and the detection of early morbidity and adequate arrangements for referring serious cases to an appropriate higher echelon;
(iii) supplying drinking water to villages suffering from chronic scarcity or having unsafe sources of water;
(iv) provision of all-weather roads to all villages having a population of 1500 persons or more; this minimum limit being conceived of as for a cluster of villages in the case of hilly, tribal and coastal areas;
(v) provision of developed home sites for landless labour in rural areas;
(vi) carrying out environmental improvement of slums;
(vii) ensuring the spread of electrification to cover approximately 30-40 percent of the rural population.[11]

The Approach Paper made a provision of Rs.3,300 crores for the programme which was scaled down to Rs.2,803 crores by the Draft Fifth Plan. The outlay for 1974-78 was Rs.2607 crores while the actual expenditure was only Rs.1038 crores. The Sixth Plan (1980-85) makes a provision of Rs.5807 crores for the programme. The objectives continue to be the same as for the Fifth Plan. More specifically, they can be classified as under:

(i) *Elementary Education:* (a) 100% enrolment in the age group 6-14 by 1990. It would be supplemented with non-formal education; (b) 100% coverage of adults in the age group 15-35 by 1990 through non-formal education.
(ii) *Rural Health:* (a) One Community Health Volunteer for a population of 1000 or a village by 1990;
(b) Establishment of one sub-centre for a population of 5000 in plains and 3000 in tribal and hilly areas by 2000 A.D.;
(c) One Primary Health Centre for 30,000 population in plains and 20,000 in tribal and hilly areas by 2000 A.D.;
(d) Establishment of one Community Health Centre for a popula-

tion of one lakh or one Community Development Block by 2000 A.D.

(iii) *Rural Water Supply:* Coverage of all the remaining problem villages by 1985 excepting in some difficult areas like hilly and desert regions.

(iv) *Rural Roads:* Linking up of all remaining villages with a population of 1500 and above and 50% of the total number of villages with a population of 1000-1500 by 1990.

(v) *Rural Electrification:* At least 60% of the villages in each State and Union Territory to be electrified by 1990.

(vi) *Housing Assistance to Rural Landless Labourers:* Provision of housing assistance to all landless labour households by 1990. Assistance to include house-sites, construction materials, drinking water well for a cluster of houses, and approach road.

(vii) *Environmental Improvement of Urban Slums:* 100% coverage of the urban slum population by 1990. Facilities to include water supply, sewerage, paving of streets, storm water drains, community latrines. Areas inhabited by scheduled castes, particularly scavengers would be given priority.

(viii) *Nutrition:* (a) The Special Nutrition Programme: 5 million children in 600 Integrated Child Development Service blocks and 5 lakh women to be covered by providing integrated services of feeding, health, welfare, etc.;

(b) The Mid-day Meals Programme: The existing level of beneficiaries i.e. about 17.4 million children, to be continued and the programme to be integrated with other essential services.

Of the total Rs.5807 crores proposed for this programme, expenditure under the above heads is to be distributed as under: Rs.1033 crores for elementary education, Rs.577 crores for rural health, Rs.2007 crores for rural water supply, Rs.1165 crores for rural roads, Rs.301 crores for rural electrification, Rs.354 crores for housing assistance to rural landless labourers, Rs.151 crores for environmental improvement of urban slums, and Rs.219 crores for nutrition.

DEVELOPMENT OUTLAYS AND PLAN EXPENDITURES

Table 1 gives the expenditure under different heads of development in the six plans. It shows that the successive plans have considerably increased in size (each plan being approximately double the size of the pervious one). Thus, the actual expenditure under the First Plan was Rs.1960 crores, which rose to Rs.4672 crores in the Second Plan, to Rs.8577 crores in the

Third Plan, and to Rs.15,779 crores in the Fourth Plan. The Fifth Plan kept the total outlay at Rs.39,303 crores which has been increased to Rs.97,500 crores in the Sixth Plan, representing an increase of more than 148% over the Fifth Plan.

While only 2.8% of total plan expenditure in the First Plan was devoted to industry, adoption of the heavy goods investment strategy (as advocated by Mahalanobis) remarkably increased the share of this sector to 20.1% in the Second Plan. The predominance of this sector has remained ever since. The sector that claimed maximum resources in the first four plans was 'Transport & Communications'. 'Village & Small Industries' could get only 2.1% of resources in the First Plan, 4.0% in the Second Plan, 2.8% in the Third Plan, 1.9% in the Three Annual Plans, 1.5% in the Fourth Plan, and 1.3% in the Fifth Plan. This is despite the fact that the plan documents glorified the role of this sector in providing employment and in ensuring a more even distribution of wealth and economic power.

Targets and Achievements of Plans

The First Plan aimed at increasing the national income at the rate of 2.1% and per capita income at the rate of 0.9% per annum. Against this, the actual achievements were 3.6% and 1.8%, respectively. Thus, the First Plan put up a good show. However, in all other plans the achievements were well below the targets. The Second Plan aimed at increasing the national income at the compound annual rate of 4.5% and per capita income at 3.3%. However, the annual growth rate was 4.1% in the former case and 2.1% in the latter. The Third Plan kept the target for increase in national income at 5.5% and for per capita income at 3.2% per annum. Against this, the national income rose by only 2.6% while the per capita income registered a nominal increase of 0.3% per annum. The Fourth Plan kept the target for increase in national income at 5.5% per annum while the actual achievement was merely 3.5%. The Draft Fifth Plan proposed a rate of growth of 5.5% per annum while the actual rate of growth was approximately 3.9%. The unsatisfactory performance of the economy is evident from the fact that the index number of per capita net national product which was 100.0 in 1950-51 (at 1970-71 prices) could increase only to 135.8 in 1970-71 (i.e., after two decades of planning) and to only 149.4 in 1980-81 (i.e., after three decades of planning).[13]

The above analysis shows that except in the First Plan, the (actual) annual rate of growth of national income has always been less than the target laid down. This has been the result of consistent failure to achieve targets in the different sectors of the economy. For example, the targetted rate of annual growth of output in the large-scale manufacturing sector was

TABLE 1: Plan outlays by heads of development: Centre, States and Union territories

(Rs. crores)

Head of development	First Plan (Actuals)	Second Plan (Actuals)	Third Plan (Actuals)	Annual Plans 1966-69 (Actuals)	Fourth Plan		Fifth Plan		Sixth Plan 1980-85 Outlay
					Outlay	Actuals	Outlay	Actuals	
1	2	3	4	5	6	7	8	9	10
1. Agriculture and Allied Sectors	290	549	1089	1107	2728	2320	4644	3413	12539
	(14.8)	(11.7)	(12.7)	(16.7)	(17.2)	(14.7)	(11.8)	(11.9)	(12.9)
2. Irrigation and Flood Control	434	430	665	471	1087	1354	3434	2716	12160
	(22.2)	(9.2)	(7.8)	(7.1)	(6.8)	(8.6)	(8.7)	(9.5)	(12.5)
3. Power	149	452	1252	1212	2448	2932	7016	5378	19265
	(7.6)	(9.7)	(14.6)	(18.3)	(15.4)	(18.6)	(17.9)	(18.8)	(19.8)
4. Village & Small Industries	42	187	241	126	293	243	510	375	1780
	(2.1)	(4.0)	(2.8)	(1.9)	(1.8)	(1.5)	(1.3)	(1.3)	(1.8)
5. Industry and Minerals	55	938	1726	1510	3338	2864	9691	6888	20507
	(2.8)	(20.1)	(20.1)	(22.8)	(21.0)	(18.2)	(24.7)	(24.0)	(21.0)
6. Transport & Communications	518	1261	2112	1222	3237	3080	6881	5087	15546
	(26.4)	(27.0)	(24.6)	(18.5)	(20.3)	(19.5)	(17.5)	(17.8)	(15.9)
7. Others	472	855	1492	977	2771	2986	7127	4796	15703
	(24.1)	(18.3)	(17.4)	(14.7)	(17.5)	(18.9)	(18.1)	(16.7)	(16.1)
Of which									
(a) Education and Scientific Research	149	273	660	354	963	905	1730	988	3388
	(7.6)	(5.8)	(7.7)	(5.3)	(6.1)	(5.7)	(4.4)	(3.4)	(3.5)
(b) Family Planning	—	—	25	70	315	278	498	384	1010
			(0.3)	(1.1)	(2.0)	(1.8)	(1.3)	(1.3)	(1.0)

(c) Health	98	216	226	140	433	335	682	525	1821.1
	(5.0)	(4.6)	(2.6)	(2.1)	(2.7)	(2.1)	(1.7)	(1.8)	(1.9)
Total	1960	4672	8577	6625	15902	15779	39303	28653	97500
	(100.0)	(100.0)	(100.0)	(100.0)	(100.0)	(100.0)	(100.0)	(100.0)	(100.0)

Notes: 1. Figures in parentheses indicate percentage of the total.

2. Figures of Fifth Plan outlay given in Col. 8 are those given in the *Revised Plan Document*, 1976.
3. Figures of actual expenditure under the Fifth Plan are the sum of expenditures incurred during years 1974-75, 1975-76, 1976-77, and 1977-78.
4. Sixth Plan outlay on 'Education and Scientific Research' has been obtained by summing up the figures for 'Education' and 'Science and technology'.

Sources: 1. Ministry of Information and Broadcasting, Government of India, *India A—Reference Annual, 1976*, Table 13.1, p. 172.

2. Government of India, *Economic Survey, 1980-81*, Table 2.4, p. 96 and Table 2.5, p. 97.
3. *The Economic Times*, 8 March 1981, p. 7.
4. Planning Commission, *Sixth Five Year Plan, 1980-85*, Annexure 4.3, pp. 57-58.

7% in the First Plan, 10.5% in the Second Plan, 10.75% in the Third Plan, and 8.10% in the Fourth Plan. Against this, the achievements were 6% in First Plan, 7.25% in the Second Plan, 8% in the Third Plan, and merely 3.9% in the Fourth Plan. The Draft Fifth Plan kept a target of 8.21%, but the actual rate of growth was likely to be in the range 5-6%. Many important industries faced substantial shortfalls (compared with the targets) as the sample data on some industries given in Table 2 demonstrate.

TABLE 2: **Plan targets and achievements for output of some selected industries in India**

% variation between Plan target and achievement for the last year of the five year plan (+ = excess; − = shortfall)

Industry	II Plan (1960-61 over 1955-56)	III Plan (1965-66 over 1960-61)	IV Plan (estimated 1973-74 over 1968-69)
(1)	(2)	(3)	(4)
Finished Steel	−45.5	−33.8	−32.8
Aluminium	−28.0	−32.5	−13.6
Machine Tools	+133.3	−2.0	0.0
Cement	−40.1	−16.9	−11.1
Cloth (mill-made)	−5.0	−17.0	−20.2
Fertilizers			
(a) Nitrogenous	−65.5	−71.0	−52.5
(b) Phosphatic	−56.5	−59.3	−61.1
Paper and Paper Board	−1.7	−20.3	−2.4
Sugar	+13.0	0.0	−8.5
Vanaspati	−16.2	−9.8	−8.0
Tractors	−100.0	−37.0	−20.0
Radio Receivers	−6.0	−24.3	−10.5
Iron Ore	−13.4	−27.1	−28.1

Source: C.D. Wadhva, "Performance Appraisal of Centralized Economic Planning in India : A Systems View", in C.D. Wadhva (ed.), *Some Problems of India's Economic Policy* (New Delhi: Tata-McGraw Hill Publishing Company Ltd.; Second Edition, 1977), Table 2, p. 149.

However, despite the shortfalls in the first three plans, the compound (annual) growth rate of industrial output was quite impressive. According to S.L. Shetty, it rose from 5.7% in the First Plan to 7.2% in the Second Plan, and further to 9.0% in the Third Plan. After this, the performance of the industrial sector deteriorated considerably. During the eleven-year period (1966-1976), the annual growth rate fell to about 4.1% including the 10.6% increase in 1976. If we leave out the year 1976, the annual growth rate falls to an even lower level of 3.7%.[14] Shetty notes that the share of the 'secondary sector' in net domestic product (at 1960-61 prices), which had continuously risen and reached the peak of 23.3% in 1965-66 and to 23.4% in 1966-67, failed to increase thereafter and stood at 22.8% in 1975-76 (the share of registered manufacturing, which was 6.3% in 1950-51, showed a continuous increase till 1965-66 when it touched the peak level of 10.4%, thereafter it tended to stagnate and stood at 10.4% even after a decade, i.e. in 1975-76), while the share of the tertiary sector continued to increase. Thus, the economy has had to face, 'the phenomenon of structural retrogression' since the mid-sixties.[15]

Let us now turn to the agricultural sector. The performance of the First Plan on this front was satisfactory. The target of additional production of foodgrains (7.6 million tonnes) was exceeded by 42%, the actual increase being 10.8 million tonnes. Agricultural production, as a whole, rose from 54 million tonnes in 1950-51 to 64.8 million tonnes in 1955-56 against the target of 61.6 million tonnes. The achievement was well above the target in the case of oilseeds and was marginally less than the target in the case of cotton. However, it was considerably below the target in the case of jute and sugarcane. The target for foodgrains production was kept at 75 million tonnes in the Second Plan while the achievement was 76 million tonnes. The achievement was greater than the target for oilseeds and sugarcane while it was less than the target for jute. The target of foodgrains production for the terminal year (1965-66) in the Third Plan was kept at 100 million tonnes, but the actual production was merely 72 million tonnes because of the fact that 1965-66 happened to be a drought year. The production in 1964-65 was 89 million tonnes. The performance of the Third Plan on the agricultural front can be considered quite unsatisfactory as the achievements were below targets for most of the crops. The Fourth Plan kept the target of 129 million tonnes for foodgrains production in 1973-74, while the actual production was merely 104.66 million tonnes. The achievements were below the targets in most of the commercial crops such as jute, sugarcane, cotton, oilseeds, etc. Taking agricultural production as a whole, the rate of growth was only 2.8% per annum in the Fourth Plan against the target of 5%. The Draft Fifth Plan kept the target of 140.0 million tonnes for foodgrains production (for the terminal year 1978-79). The target for sugarcane was kept at 17.0 million tonnes and for cotton at 80 lakh bales. The actual production of foodgrains in 1978-79 was 131.9 million tonnes and of sugarcane and cotton 15.73 million tonnes and 79.6 lakh bales respectively.

Because of a rapid increase in population the increases in foodgrains production were inadequate to meet the demand for foodgrains for a considerable period of planning and we had to resort to large-scale imports. Thus, the net imports of foodgrains, which were 1.39 million tonnes in 1956, rose to 3.49 million tonnes in 1961, to 7.45 million tonnes in 1965, to 10.34 million tonnes in 1966, and to 8.66 million tonnes in 1967. Naturally these large-scale imports of foodgrains put considerable pressure on the balance of payments which was already in a bad shape. As pointed out in the next section,[16] we did not have any export strategy for a considerable period of planning. This resulted in a situation where imports continually ran much ahead of exports. Right from the beginning of the First Plan to 1977-78 (except 1972-73 and 1976-77 when there were small surpluses of Rs.103.4 crores and Rs.68.9 crores respectively), the balance of trade has always been against India. For the most part of the planning period the net income from invisibles has been positive but too meagre to outweigh the deficit in balance of trade. Thus, balance of payments always remained adverse and the gap had to be filled through foreign aid. The extent of the problem would be clear from the fact that the deficit in balance of payments, which was only Rs.42.3 crores during the First Plan, rose to Rs.1724.6 crores during the Second Plan, to Rs.1951.2 crores during the Third Plan, and further to Rs.2015 crores during the Three Annual Plans. The Fourth Plan placed the target for exports at Rs.1900 crores in 1973-74 against Rs.1360 crores in 1968-69, implying a compound annual rate of growth of 7%. This target was overfulfilled because of a spectacular increase in export earnings in the last two years of the plan. Export earnings, which were Rs.1413.3 crores in 1969-70, rose to Rs.1970.8 crores in 1972-73 and further to Rs.2523.4 crores in 1973-74. The rate of growth was 28% in 1973-74 over 1972-73 and was 13.6% per annum taking the Fourth Plan period as a whole. But because of a sharp increase in the price of petroleum and petroleum products there was a sharp increase in import expenditure also. As a consequence, the Fourth Plan faced a deficit of Rs.1564 crores in balance of trade and Rs.2234.1 crores in balance of payments. In the Fifth Plan, exports were projected to grow at an annual rate of 8.5% in constant prices. The first three years experienced a buoyancy in exports when their rate of growth averaged 27%. However, the performance in 1977-78 was poor and the exports rose by only 4.5%. Against this, the imports rose by 19.6% and there was an overall trade deficit of Rs.693 crores in 1977-78.[17]

Before we conclude this section, let us briefly examine the targetted and the actual rates of savings and investment in the plans, for it is on the attainment of targets in this field that the success of an investment-oriented planning strategy (as the Indian strategy is) ultimately depends. The data for the planning period indicate a steady rise in the rate of saving and investment during the first three plans. In 1950-51, the rate of investment and the rate of saving were both estimated to be around 5.5% of national income. By the end of the Third Plan period, the rate of investment had risen to about 14% of national income while the ratio of domestic savings to national income rose to only about 10.5% in 1965-66. To make the economy self-reliant it was expressed in the Third Plan document that "net investment (at 1960-61 prices) as a proportion of national income would have to rise from about 11 percent at present to 14-15, 17-18 and 19-20 percent per annum by the end of the Third, Fourth and Fifth Plans. In other words, as compared to about Rs.10,500 crores postulated for the Third Plan, net investment over the Fourth and Fifth Plan periods should be of the order of Rs.17,000 crores and Rs.25,000 crores. Domestic savings would have to rise in corresponding measure from 8.5 percent at present to about 11.5, 15-16 and 18-19 percent of the national income at the end of the Third, Fourth and Fifth Plans."[18] The actual achievements were well below expectations. In the year 1963-64, the saving-income ratio was 10.0% while the investment-income ratio was 14.9%. During the period 1950-51 to 1970-71, the highest level of net investment recorded was 15.5% of national income in 1966-67 while the ratio of net savings to national income was 12.2% in that year.[19] The ratio of net investment to national income fell sharply after that year and was only 12.1% in 1967-68 (presumably because of industrial recession) and thereafter it could never touch the level of 1966-67. During the first four years of the Fourth Plan, the ratio of net savings to national income was 11.5%, 12.5%, 11.6%, and 12.5% respectively while the ratio of net investment to national income was 12.2%, 13.5%, 11.5%, and 12.2% respectively. Thus, the expectations expressed in the long-term perspective of the Third Plan were not fulfilled. Indeed for the most part of the planning period the supply of savings remained substantially less than the requirements for investment and we had to depend on foreign aid to fill the gap. Thus, the promises regarding self-reliance have remained largely unfulfilled.[20]

A CRITICAL EVALUATION OF THE PLANNING PROCESS

Absence of Financial Strategy

The planning process in India suffered from several deficiencies. The implementation of 'heavy investment goods' sector strategy required heavy resources, both domestic (monetary and real) and external (in the form of capital goods, machinery, industrial raw materials, and technical knowledge). On both the fronts, however, there was a surprising lack of concern and rational economic thinking and whatever planning was done was in the form of ad hoc measures. As regards raising the financial resources on the domestic front, it was necessary to lay down detailed policies and specify the wherewithals. This was not done. Both Mahalanobis and Pitamber Pant were essentially physical planners who believed that "provided the investments were technically feasible, savings ought to be forthcoming, somehow".[21] The obviously wrong assumption that 'what is physically possible is financially possible too' led to complacency on the financial front[22] and the neglect of financial strategy proved fatal. The plans continually increased in size (from Rs.1960 crores in the First Plan to Rs.4672 crores in the Second Plan, to Rs.8577 crores in the Third Plan, to Rs.15,779 crores in the Fourth Plan, and to Rs.28,653 crores in the Fifth Plan) and in the absence of a financial strategy the government was forced to depend more and more on deficit financing (which increased from Rs.333 crores in the First Plan to Rs.948 crores in the Second Plan, to Rs.1133 crores in the Third Plan, and to Rs.2000 crores in the Fourth Plan). The inflationary forces unleashed by such inflationary methods of financing have created various complications in the planning process.

Coming to the external methods of raising resources, we again find the absence of a strategy. All attempts or measures adopted were for a considerable period ad hoc in nature and were not interwoven into a well-thought-out strategy. The best method of raising external resources is by earning more through expansion of exports, therefore (as far as the necessity of raising external resources is concerned) the export strategy should have formed an integral part of the overall planning strategy. But this was not to be. In the first two plans, estimates were more in the nature of expected earnings rather than of firm targets and no definite programme of expanding exports earnings was adopted. Indeed, the Second Plan document took the position that only when industrialization had proceeded some way that increased production at home would be reflected in larger export earnings. The Third Plan did adopt some important export subsidization policies such as (i) exemptions from sales tax on final sales and refunds of indirect taxes, domestic and customs, on inputs; (ii) direct tax concessions; (iii) outright subsidies; (iv) rail freight concessions; and (v) import-entitlement schemes, in addition to certain other export incentives. However, even here, measures adopted were ad hoc and every thing was left vague, undecided, and uncertain 'to be considered from time to time in the light of the actual situation'.

It is difficult to say whether the attitude of indifference to exports was a result of the conviction that it would not be possible to increase exports or whether the model of Mahalanobis implicitly assumed a closed model. What is certain, however, is the fact that the export sector was a neglected field for a considerable period of planning. The planners paid more attention to the policy of restricting imports a ıd practically every import policy declared by the Government of India slashed imports, so much so that by the end of the Third Plan, it was felt that the policy of import restriction had reached its limits. It was only then that some serious thinking on the export front was done. Thus, for the most part of the planning period, we carried on without any export strategy and the huge balance of payments deficits had to be covered by foreign aid. Since foreign aid, in the ultimate analysis, depends upon the whims and prejudices of the donor countries it is always uncertain and cannot be planned in advance. Too much dependence on foreign aid, accordingly, introduces an element of uncertainty in the whole planning process. This has been the case in India.

Flaws in Industrial Strategy

While discussing the industrial strategy we had noted the primacy given to the rate of investment in the overall planning process. This emphasis on rate of investment as the growth-determining and growth-generating factor led to the belief that more investment was the panacea of all economic ills and consequently attention should be concentrated on increasing the rate of investment. This concealed from us the importance of many other factors in economic development such as improvement in skills, techniques, management, operational efficiency, and human capital in general. Neither was any attention paid to assess the adequacy and efficiency of the administrative machinery in the country which was to be entrusted with the task of implementing the ever increasing programmes of investment. Undue importance attached to the rate of investment part of planning also led to a neglect of certain fields which, though not contributing much to the rate of growth, would have helped make planning more broad-based and more purposeful and might have elicited the active cooperation and participation of masses which has been denied to us so far but which is essential if planning is to make a dent in poverty and economic backwardness.[23]

Emphasis on increasing the rate of investment in the industrial sector as a whole did not allow us to investigate the 'structure' of such investment. In his illuminating study, Shetty notes that the progsess of the industrial sector since the mid-sixties was characterized by a rapid growth of the consumer goods industries catering to the demands of the richer sections of the population, and a relatively slower rate of growth of basic and capital goods industries. The share of basic and capital goods industries in total net value added in the registered industrial sector at 1960-61 prices, which steadily increased from 31% during 1951-53 to the peak of 46.6% in 1965-67, declined to 44.0% in 1970-72 and remained at that level ever thereafter. Shetty notes that during the period 1965-66 to 1976-77 most of the industries belonging to the basic and capital goods sector (e.g., pig iron, steel ingots, finished steel, steel, castings and forgings, steel structurals, industrial machinery, machine tools and railway equipment, cement, etc.) registered rates of growth that were insignificant compared with the average of the previous five-year period. However, during the same period, disproportionately large increases were reported in the output of man-made fibres, beverages, perfumes and cosmetics, commercial, office and household equipment, watches and clocks, finer varieties of cloth etc.—signifying the emergence of an output structure that was increasingly getting elite-oriented. These tendencies in the industrial sector are a testimony to the increasing 'structural retrogression' in the Indian economy.[24]

The implementation of the industrial strategy required massive investment by the Central government in a number of industries. However, before undertaking actual investment, it is necessary to (i) determine the *type* of machines to be produced initially in the capital goods industries, (ii) define the time-phasing of different industries keeping the social considerations in view, (iii) determine the *capacity* of the existing skilled personnel and administration to actually carry out the plans, (iv) take into account the various managerial and organizational problems (both existing and potential), and (v) carry out detailed and in-depth studies at the micro level and link them to the macro-level plans to ensure that the whole programme is carried out in an efficient and integrated manner. However, these considerations were unfortunately ignored. This resulted in delays in the completion of major projects, lags causing inter-industry bottlenecks, bunching of capital goods projects, inefficient formulation and selection of actual projects, under-utilization of capacity in many industries, higher than estimated costs, and a number of other problems. On account of reasons such as these, the majority of the public sector projects took longer to complete than was originally estimated, benefits from them came in later than expected, and they cost the country more than what was estimated.[25] Major steel, heavy machinery, fertilizers, and chemical plants lagged behind schedules and, through forward and backward linkages, had an adverse effect on the development of several other industries.

The problems arose because the planners paid all their attention to the task of plan formulation and ignored its implementation aspects. Implementation was thought to be the business of the administrative machinery alone and it was forgotten that the successful implementation of plans required 'planning of implementation'. The lack of this planning not only created problems in the industrial sector, it also created problems in the successful execution of agricultural programmes and programmes related to the development of power, transport, communications, etc. Non-availability of data at the micro level and absence of planning machinery at the State and district levels further complicated the issue.[26]

Neglect of Employment Strategy

Provision of employment to all those seeking jobs has been explicitly recognized as an important objective of planning in many plan documents and is also implicit in the task the planners conferred upon themselves—establishment of a socialist pattern of society. Yet it is surprising to note the most casual way in which the problem has been faced. The planners assumed that production and employment were uniquely and directly related. Consequently, no attempt was made to formulate any employment strategy. However, the data reveal that the assumption of unique and direct relationship between production and employment was not justified. Thus, while over the period 1951 to 1969 factory production rose at an annual compound rate of 7%, employment rose at less than 3%.[27] The Draft Sixth Plan (prepared by the Janata Government) noted that though investment and output have growh at a high rate, the capital-intensive nature of the production-mix and the technology-mix has prevented employment from growing pari passu. Thus, between 1961 and 1976, although investment in modern factory sector increased by 139% and output by 161%, employment could increase only by 71%. As a consequence, employment per unit of gross output decreased by 34% and employment per unit capital declined by 28%.[28]

The extent of the unemployment problem would be clear from the fact that though 70 lakh jobs were created in the First Plan, 100 lakh jobs in the Second Plan, 145 lakh jobs in the Third Plan, and 185 lakh jobs in the Fourth Plan, the backlog of unemployment which was 53 lakhs at the end of the First Plan, rose to 71 lakhs at the end of the Second Plan and 96 lakhs at the end of the Third Plan. After 1966, the number of unemployed persons increased even faster. Shetty estimates that the number of unemployed persons had anywhere between trebled and quadrupled in the ten-year period from 1966 to 1976 (estimates of unemployed persons in 1976 vary from 280 to 380 lakhs).[29]

In addition to the unrealistic assumption about the relationship between production and employment, the neglect of employment strategy also arose from the nature of the planning models wherein attention was concentrated on scarce resources such as capital and foreign exchange, and labour (on account of its abundant availability) was not considered at all.[30]

In fairness to the planners it should be admitted that each plan provided for special schemes for provision of employment opportunities. The Third Plan introduced the Rural Works Programme which was carried forward to the Fourth Plan. The Fourth Plan introduced, in addition, a number of rural employment schemes such as CSRE, SFDA, MFAL, DPAP, etc. However, all these schemes were hurriedly drawn up, were ill-conceived and ad hoc, and consequently doomed to failure. Since no synchronization of these schemes was done with the plans, there was much wastage of resources and the implementing machinery did not undertake them seriously at all.[31]

Let us also note in passing the failure to evolve an integrated educational and employment strategy. The vast expansion of secondary and college education at a rate much faster than the requirements of the economy has created an imbalance in the system resulting in the problem of educated unemployed. Universities and colleges have tended to become places of 'refuge' where the student spends "as many years as possible in a socially acceptable environment and at public cost".[32] Education not related to the requirements of the economy has resulted in two destabilizing factors: (i) a vast army of educated unemployed has been created, the majority of them striving for white-collar jobs and despising manual work, and (ii) a situation has developed where "while on the one hand many trained persons go without jobs, on the other, right type of persons with specific (desired) skill and training are not available".[33] Though a number of vocational schools are being set up to deal with this problem, no attempt is being made to specify the requirements of specific skilled persons in different fields. Vocational training in such an atmosphere will only succeed in transferring the incidence of unemployment from one type of educated youth to another.[34]

Inequalities in Income and Wealth

There were extreme inequalities in income and wealth when planned progress was initiated in India. While the objective was to reduce these disparities it has been estimated that over the years they have actually increased. Price movements have been more against the poor as compared with the rich. Bardhan finds that the price of cereals paid by the poorest decile increased more sharply than that paid by the top-most decile (and 58.3% of the meagre budget of the poorest 10% people in rural India is spent on cereals). Thus, the index of the average price of cereals paid by the bottom 10% of rural population rose from 100 in 1954-55 to 186 in 1960-61 and further to 259 in 1964-65 while for the top 10% the increase was much smaller (from 100 in 1954-55 to 126 in 1960-61 and to 179 in 1964-65).[35] Another important, though less revealing, method to flash the increasing social injustice can be a study of the change in the general price structure. A cursory look at the index numbers of wholesale prices reveals that the price index for all commodities rose from 104 in 1962-63 (base 1960-61 = 100) to 131.9 in 1965-66 and to 181.5 in 1970-71. Against this, the index of foodgrain prices rose from 106.9 in 1962-63 to 144.7 in 1965-66 and to 204.1 in 1970-71. During the same period the index of prices of manufactured articles rose from 104.9 in 1962-63 to 120.7 in 1965-66 and to 158.3

in 1970-71. Thus, the prices of foodgrains increased more rapidly than the prices of manufactured articles and general price level.[36] Since the weightage to food articles is generally much higher in the consumption basket of the poor compared with the rich, the impact of inflation on the poorer sections had been much more severe.[37]

While on the one hand, rising prices made existence more and more difficult for the poorer sections of the population, on the other they helped to concentrate more and more income and wealth in the hands of a privileged section of the society. An estimate prepared by the Reserve Bank of India for the period 1953-54 to 1956-57 indicated that the top 5% accounted for 26% of urban income while the bottom 20% accounted for only 7% of urban income (the corresponding figures for the rural population were 17% and 9% respectively). A study conducted by NCAER for 1960 revealed that the top 5% of the population accounted for 31% of urban income, the bottom 20% accounting for only 4% of urban income. Similar tendencies existed in the rural sector; e.g., in 1961-62, the share of the lowest 30% of the rural households in total rural assets was a meagre 2.5% which further fell to 2.0% in 1971-72. Against this, the share of the top 30% of the rural households in total rural assets was 79.0% in 1961-62 which increased to 81.9% in 1971-72. The top 10% of rural households alone accounted for 51% of total rural assets in 1971-72. It should also not be forgotten that there are extreme inequalities in land ownership in the rural sector. The top 5% of households claim as much as 40% of the rural land, while the bottom 87% account for only 35% of land.[38]

Another pointer to substantial inequalities are the data on household consumer expenditure. In rural areas, the share of the bottom 30% was only 13.1% in 1958-59 which rose to 15.4% in 1972-73 but fell to 15.0% in 1977-78. Against this, the share of the top 30% stood at 52.6% in 1977-78. In urban areas, the share of the bottom 30% in household consumer expenditure was 13.2% in 1958-59, 13.8% in 1972-73, and 13.6% in 1977-78. Against this, the share of the top 30% was 55.1% in 1958-59, 54.3% in 1972-73, and 54.0% in 1977-78.[39]

It is important to note here that the per capita availability of cereals, pulses, and some other mass consumption goods tended to stagnate in the period after the Third Plan. This must have affected adversely the net availability of such commodities to the resourceless and poor people inhabiting both rural and urban areas. The per capita net availability per day of cereals which had shown a more or less consistent increase from 360.5 g in 1956 to 418.6 g in 1965 failed to increase thereafter and even showed a decline during some years. It stood at 391.2 g in 1977 and is estimated to be only 383.6 g in 1980. Similar trends were noticed for cereals and pulses considered together. Their combined net availability increased from 430.9 g in 1956 to 480.2 g in 1965 and declined thereafter. It stood at 434.7 g in 1977 and was expected to be only 413.7 g in 1980.[40]

The natural conclusion that emerges from these facts is that the benefits of growth have gone to a certain privileged section of the society. Indeed a parallel black money economy thriving on shortages (artificial, in many cases) concentrated tremendous economic power in the hands of this small section of the society. In 1972-73, black money was to the extent of Rs.9000-10,000 crores. Naturally, corruption and various anti-social activities got encouragement. The production pattern was also adjusted to the consumption needs of this privileged section of the society and the scarce resources that could have been utilized for increasing the welfare of the masses were wasted in the production of unnecessary luxury goods. Thus, while analysing the data for 1976-77, Shetty notes that "while output of goods catering to the requirements of the general masses registered either an absolute reduction or very moderate increase, that of patently elite-oriented products experienced astronomical increase". Thus, in the non-electrical machinery sector, the highest increases in production took place in room air-conditioners (108.4%), air-conditioning and refrigeration plants (39.0%), and domestic refrigerators. In the transport equipment sector, production of railway wagons declined by 1.6% and of railway locomotives by 8.9%, output of commercial vehicles rose by 5.9% and of bicycles by 14.9%; against this, production of cars shot up by 67.6%, scooters by 39.0%, and jeeps by 17.3%. Similar trends were observed in the case of other industries. For example, while the production of cotton yarn and cotton cloth increased by merely 1.8% and 3.4% in 1976-77, beer output rose by 66.2%, toothpaste by 55.7%, and infant milk food and biscuits by 23.0%.[41] This phenomenon is a natural outcome of the type of mixed economy we have in this country wherein the actual operation of the production process 'favours mostly those who own and control the means of production'. The control over the means of production and distribution and over the processes of income generation is exercised predominantly by the private sector. The government is forced to function through a variety of fiscal, monetary, and physical controls which bring a variety of administrative problems with them, encourage black money, red tapism, corruption, etc.[42]

We have already pointed towards the existence of mass poverty in India. A survey of the data reveals that it has shown no tendency to decline over the years. On the other hand, it might have actually increased. This is particularly so in States such as Uttar Pradesh, Bihar, Madhya Pradesh, Karnataka, West Bengal, Assam, and Kerala. Table 3 gives the percentage of population below the poverty line for different States in 1977-78.

Thus, the process of planning in India has generated growth 'but along with poverty, income inequality, and unemployment'. The growth-

TABLE 3: Percentage of population below the poverty line by States separately for rural and urban areas, 1977-78

State/U.T.	Rural	Urban	Combined
(1)	(2)	(3)	(4)
1. Andhra Pradesh	43.89	35.68	42.18
2. Assam	52.65	37.37	51.10
3. Bihar	58.91	46.07	57.49
4. Gujarat	43.20	29.02	39.04
5. Haryana	23.25	31.74	24.84
6. Himachal Pradesh	28.12	16.56	27.23
7. Jammu & Kashmir	32.75	39.33	34.06
8. Karnataka	49.88	43.97	48.34
9. Kerala	46.00	51.44	46.95
10. Madhya Pradesh	59.82	48.09	57.73
11. Maharashtra	55.85	31.62	47.71
12. Manipur	30.54	25.48	29.71
13. Meghalaya	53.87	18.16	48.03
14. Nagaland	N.A.	4.11	4.11
15. Orissa	68.97	42.19	66.40
16. Punjab	11.87	24.66	15.13
17. Rajasthan	33.75	33.80	33.76
18. Tamil Nadu	55.68	44.79	52.12
19. Tripura	64.28	26.34	59.73
20. Uttar Pradesh	50.23	49.24	50.09
21. West Bengal	58.94	34.71	52.54
22. All Union territories	34.32	17.96	21.69
All India (weighted)	50.82	38.19	48.13

Note: The above estimates are derived by using the all-India poverty line of Rs.65 per capita per month in 1977-78 prices corresponding to minimum daily calorie requirement of 2400 per person in rural areas and the poverty line of Rs.75 per month corresponding to daily calorie requirement of 2100 in urban areas.

Source: Planning Commission, *Sixth Five Year Plan 1980-85*, Annexure 1.12, p. 16.

focused strategy of investment planning naturally assumed (as is done so fashionably in economics with the help of beautiful abstract, theoretical, and mathematical constructs) that it is necessary to redistribute income in favour of upper income groups because this 'will increase the proportionate rate of saving and thereby accelerate economic growth' (one may note the contradiction between this assumption and the objective of 'socialist pattern of society'). Bagchi demonstrates that though such transfer of incomes in favour of the upper income groups did take place in India, it did not increase the rate of saving noticeably. "Thus India's experience explodes this particular myth about the beneficial effects of an increase in the inequality of distribution of incomes."[43]

Neglect of Spatial Factors

Not only planning has failed to tackle the problems of poverty, unemployment, inter-personal income inequalities, it has also failed to solve the problem of inter-regional and intra-regional inequalities and to divert the flow of migrants from rural to urban areas in an attempt to (i) reduce the pressure on metropolitan centres, and (ii) stop the process of *denudation* of rural areas and lower order urban centres of their best brains and best muscles. In fact, planning has only succeeded in accentuating these problems. We shall provide ample evidence in Chapters 5 and 8 to show that inter-regional and intra-regional inequalities have increased. And this has happened despite the stress on balanced regional development in the Third Plan and the introduction of a number of programmes aimed at the development of backward areas. We shall discuss the programmes initiated in the agricultural sector in Chapter 7 (e.g., community development, rural works programme, SFDA, MFAL and DPAP etc.), the programmes initiated for the rapid development of backward areas and reduction of regional disparities in Chapters 5 and 8 (e.g., use of industrial licensing policy to attract entrepreneurs to backward areas; location of public sector projects in such areas in those cases where techno-economic considerations do not absolutely rule out this possibility; development of infrastructure and social services particularly transport and communications in backward areas so as to reduce their comparative disadvantages; allocation of a large share of central fund and special assistance to backward areas, etc.), and the programmes initiated for tribal development in Chapter 11.

To reduce pressure on urban centres it was decided to launch programmes to (i) *shift away* industries from such areas and establish them in areas where new growth centres could emerge, and (ii) develop village and small industries spread all over the country so that dispersed industrial development could be encouraged (for this purpose industrial estates were to be located increasingly in small and medium sized towns). The approach towards regional development in India can be summarized, following V. Nath, as follows:[44]

1. The principal policy objective is balanced regional development. The phrase has not been explained adequately, though its principal operational connotation is reduction of regional disparities.
2. The scope for action for reducing regional disparities is limited because of limited resources. But as development proceeds and larger resources become available, the benefits of development will extend increasingly

to less developed regions.

3. The basic resource development and social service activities—in agricultural development, community development, irrigation, education, rural works, etc.—which are being undertaken under the plans throughout the country will benefit the less developed regions.
4. The disadvantage of the less developed regions, particularly for location of industries, is due to the lack of developed infrastructure facilities, such as power, transport, and water supply. This disadvantage will be removed progressively.
5. Location of large (basic, capital goods or producer goods) industries should be governed by techno-economic considerations, such as proximity to sources of raw materials. Since many of the public sector industrial projects are being located in backward regions because raw materials are located in them, these regions will benefit.
6. To the extent that industrial location is not determined by techno-economic considerations, however, balanced regional development should be aimed at. Concentration of industries in developed industrial areas and metropolitan cities should be avoided. As far as possible, new units in the public sector should be set up away from large cities and private entrepreneurs encouraged to invest in backward areas.
7. Regional patterns of development should be fostered in case of consumer goods and processing industries especially through the setting up of cottage and small-scale industries. Industrial estates should be located in small and medium towns.
8. Large projects should be thought of as nuclei of regional growth and related and complementary activities should be undertaken in the regions where they are located. It is noteworthy, however, that the activities mentioned include agriculture, education, training, and small- and medium-scale industries. Large-scale industries related to the projects through backward or forward linkages, or development of industrial complexes round the projects, are not mentioned.

In addition to these elements, mentioned by V. Nath, an element that has assumed considerable importance lately relates to the emphasis laid on an "integrated approach" to the special problems of backward areas, "calling for regional development measures to be coordinated with the organizational and institutional factors, on the one hand, and the needs of especially 'depressed' sections of the community, on the other".[45]

If such a wide spectrum of problems related to regional aspects of development were emphasized, why is it that planners are charged with ignoring regional planning? The answer to this question is to be found in the fact that whatever planning was done at the regional level was ad hoc in character since regional variables did not form part of the overall planning strategy. The models that have formed the basis of planning in India (e.g., Mahalanobis model) were sectoral in character and no regional variables were introduced. Therefore, regional aspects of planning never emerged in terms of an interwoven strategy of development. All discussions centred on the issues relating to the allocation of resources among different sectors (e.g., capital goods industries and consumer goods industries) and questions relating to allocation of resources (say, in industries) among different regions were not discussed. Whatever discussions on locations of industries are found did not directly emerge from the models themselves but were added simply as an appendage to justify the claim of planners that adequate attention was being paid to considerations of balanced regional development and regional planning.

A classic example of this statement is to be found in the policy regarding the setting up of large public sector projects in backward regions. The government has invested substantial amounts in public sector projects in the three backward States of Bihar, Orissa, and Madhya Pradesh (especially in steel plants). In fact, over the period 1951-74, per capita central industrial investment in these three States (combined) stood at Rs.158.8 while for all other States, it was a meagre Rs.42.8. The national average over the period was only Rs.68.6.[46] However, even this substantial investment has been unable to generate growth processes in these three backward States.[47] This is because of the fact that the policy pertaining to investment in public sector projects in these States did not form part of a regional planning strategy.

No in-depth studies were carried out to ascertain the effect of these investments on the rural hinterland and whether (i) a sufficient number of ancillary units would emerge and (ii) the ancillary units that might emerge would be able to spread the effects of development, i.e. whether the ancillary units would remain as a separate *pocket* (or *enclave*) of development or whether they could be linked up with the rural hinterland in such a way that growth impulses could be generated in the hinterland. Insufficient attention to these questions has severely restricted the ability of the public sector projects in backward regions to generate spread-effects and growth impulses. While in some cases the number of ancillary units was too small to have considerable effect on the rural economy, in some others, the type of ancillary-units set up were incapable of generating any growth impulses. In those cases where a considerable number of ancillary units did emerge, they remained in the form of 'uncoordinated enclaves' and created a number of problems.[48] In some cases, the public sector projects were not of the type that could ensure rapid diversification of the industrial base of the region (and hence rapid industrialization). Thus "In Orissa, public sector investment in the ferrous metals (iron and steel and ferrous alloys), related metal projects (castings and forgings, steel structurals and pipes and tubes, and fertilizers) clearly got reflected in the industrial base. However, the region has not diversified around this base, e.g. with an equipment group of industries or consumer goods manufactured primarily out of metal. The same situation holds for public sector investments in iron and steel, electrical equipment and fertilizers in Madhya Pradesh and to a lesser extent in Andhra Pradesh where the public sector projects are in ship-building and machine tools. In Bihar the situation is only slightly more complicated by the fact that public sector industries in the heavy machinery, railway equipment, fertilizers and petroleum sectors are supplemented by the well-known private sector industries in iron and steel, ferro alloys, related metal projects and transport equipment, but the lack of diversification around these major projects remains."[49]

The neglect of spatial factors in Indian planning strategy is also evidenced from the fact that the plans completely ignored the role of 'development poles' and 'growth centres' in the development process. Accordingly, no conscious efforts were made in the plans to evolve a *linked pattern of hierarchy of different settlements* (having central villages, services towns, growth points, growth centres, growth poles, etc.)[50] and therefore no spatially integrated socio-economic organization could emerge. What emerged was an immensely distorted and lopsided pattern of urbanization and economic development. Large metropolitan centres such as Bombay, Calcutta, Delhi, and Madras continued to attract industries and other economic activities. We shall show in Chapter 6 how all activities have tended to concentrate in these centres and how labour and capital have continued to flow from the backward areas and urban centres of lower order to these large urban centres.[51] The reader can understand the magnitude of the problems by observing that the Calcutta urban agglomeration alone had 64.11% of the urban population and 69.21% of the working urban population of West Bengal in 1971. Of the total workers in urban West Bengal engaged in different activities, the share of Calcutta urban agglomeration was 74.43% in manufacturing, processing, servicing and repairs; 72.5% in trade and commerce; 67.1% in transport and communications; and 68.4% in other services. Similar trends are revealed by the other large metropolitan centres as well.[52] This only shows that these centres have worked as great *suction pumps* swallowing the growth potentials of the vast rural hinterland, backward areas, and lower order urban centres. In the dazzle of economic growth models emphasizing the rate of investment as the growth-determining and growth-generating process, we forgot that the questions relating to *where* the investments should be made to maximize employment and 'to hasten and widen spatially the transforming process' were more important. It is only through the development of a hierarchical pattern of linked settlements that balanced regional development can be achieved; ad hoc measures such as the ones we have been practising are of no avail.[53]

While on the one hand the absence of a strategy of growth centres and development poles led to a lopsided pattern of urban development, on the other it led to the adoption of measures in the rural sector which did not form part of an integrated rural development strategy. The nearest that we came towards evolving such a strategy was the adoption of the Community Development programme. However, the absence of a regional planning framework led to a failure of the programme. Since no attempts were made to conceive of rural areas as part of a hierarchy of human settlements, functional linkages between rural and urban areas were not explored. As a consequence, growth impulses were not generated and rural areas remained backward and stagnant.[54]

The important features of the urban-rural dichotomy that have resulted from the planning process in India are summarized by Bijit Ghosh as follows:[55]

(1) Modernization has remained to be the privilege of urban and not rural population;
(2) "The inadequacies of resource utilization and imbalances in resource allocation have resulted in many backward regions, where the process of urbanization is grossly retarded—not to speak of rural development;"
(3) Traditional skills and crafts are dying out and sufficient attempts are not being made to preserve them. Materials used for traditional crafts (brass, wood, and stone) are being substituted by nylon and plastic;
(4) Inadequate measures to prevent waste are resulting in diseconomy. "In the case of land, it is resulting from misuse, abuse or disuse of land and from insufficient land reclamation;"
(5) Neglect of village and small industries in rural areas has forced these areas to remain dependent on agricultural activities. The importance of first- and second-degree manufacturing in transforming these areas has not been realised;
(6) The urban areas have attracted the dynamic, healthy, educated and enterprising youth of the rural areas and have thus taken away the very agents of change, dynamism and modernization; and
(7) The planners' attention is mostly confined to urban areas and development of rural areas is being neglected.

A significant development as far as regional planning is concerned was the formulation of master plans for the development of a number of important cities by the Town and Country Planning Organization of the Government of India and the State planning departments. Master plans have already been prepared for cities such as Delhi, Bombay, Bangalore, Kanpur, Lucknow, Ahmedabad, Patna, etc., and some more plans are under preparation. However, the approach adopted is the approach of city planners (for whom planning is basically *physical* in content concerned with questions of land-use pattern, place to be devoted to construction of residential buildings, office buildings, community parks, etc.), and no attempt is made to study the rural hinterland and the spatial interaction possibilities of the city in an overall framework of regional and national planning. City planning in India is also 'partial' and 'incomplete' in the sense that planning of environment has not been given due attention.[56]

The Centralized Nature of Planning

Neglect of spatial factors and genuine regional planning also stems from the nature of the plan formulation process which is a highly centralized one.[57] There are at least four important reasons why the dominant role of the Central government or of the Planning Commission seems justified at the stage of plan formulation:

1. The broad objectives of planning involve a perspective how the nation should develop in the future and this is a task that can be accomplished only by a central planning authority.
2. There are certain activities that cannot be delegated from the Centre to the States and thus their planning has to be done at the central level only. These include matters relating to foreign exchange, foreign aid, foreign collaboration, etc.
3. There are certain activities that require huge amounts of investment and some of them can be economically organized in very large plants only. It is necessary that the location of these activities is determined by a central planning authority so that there is no duplication and wastage.
4. Certain activities (such as railways) are immensely important from a national point of view and it is only proper that their planning is entrusted to a central authority.

However, on practically all other issues it is necessary that the States are given an important say while formulating the plans. Even on issues discussed above, it is extremely desirable that before adopting a particular strategy, States are taken into confidence. But, in the Indian planning set-up, the role of States has remained, over the years, unimportant and secondary. Most of the States do not possess any machinery for planning. Of course there is a department in the secretariat known as the planning department but it is like any other department. The staff consists of clerks, typists, stenographers, superintendents, assistant secretaries, deputy secretaries, and the secretary. Without any knowledge of economic and planning problems, the department functions as any other department of the State government. As noted by Gadgil, "The State plans are not made as the result of any wide consultation or effort at coordination. There is no specific definition of the objectives of state planning and no thinking out of a strategy appropriate to it. This follows from the fact that the State plans are prepared, basically, in the same manner as the annual state budget. The departmental proposals in the relation to each section, and sub-section are formulated in the departments, and put together by the heads of departments and forwarded to the secretariat. The plan is then prepared in the sense of being pieced together in the secretariat."[58]

Even these State plans (if they may be designated as such) "represent, in essence, the reactions of the State government and its officers to the known wishes and proposals of the Planning Commission. The standard Planning Commission schemes or similar departmental schemes, prepared in the States which have obtained the approval of the Planning Commission, are the basic materials from out of which the state and district plans are constituted."[59] Thus, the basic task in plan-formulation is done by the Planning Commission at the Centre and the State governments adjust their policies and programmes accordingly (with whatever little competence they have) in the 'piecing together' fashion described above.[60] The influence of the Centre on the States can be further highlighted if we consider the distribution of development outlays between these two levels of government. Since the Central government makes available more than 60% of the finances required to implement State plans, it obviously has a major say in deciding plan outlays of the States. In addition, all industrial and non-industrial projects sponsored by the Centre are totally financed by the Centre itself. Thus, the Central government has an important say in all State plans and programmes.

The agency through which the State governments voice their opinion is the National Development Council (NDC). The NDC was founded in 1952 and consists of the Prime Minister, the Chief Ministers of States, and the members of the Planning Commission. It was created with the purpose of securing the cooperation of States in planning. Its main functions are to review the working of the national plan from time to time, to consider important social and economic questions having a bearing on national development, and to recommend measures for the achievement of objectives and targets laid out in the national plan.

However, for several reasons, the role of the NDC has remained a subdued one: The Chief Ministers are generally not able to present a united front; the meetings of the NDC are conducted in a hurried way and are called for a very short period leaving no time for detailed discussions; and the NDC is not presented by the Planning Commission with alternative plans (this reduces the role of the NDC to merely making adjustments here and there in the proposed plan). On account of these reasons, over the years the NDC has become a forum to express the grievances (real or imaginary) of the Chief Ministers.[61]

In addition to the NDC, there are two agencies that are responsible for coordination between the national and the State plans. They are the Programme Advisors and the Programme Administration Division. The latter works under the Programme Advisors and its task is to maintain contacts with the State governments (to ensure that their programmes are in conformity with the overall plan outlays) and to advise the Planning Commission on issues relating to balanced regional development. The Programme Advisors work as a *link* between the Centre and the States and give necessary advice and guidance to the executive authorities at the State level and bring their difficulties and problems to the notice of the Central government and the Planning Commission. However, the Programme Advisors are generally hardpressed men since each one is in charge of several States. They are normally not in a position to pay adequate attention to the needs of individual States in their charge. What is more, they often work as representatives of the Centre. They present their own estimates of the needs of the States and what finally emerges as the State plan is the result of a compromise of the 'conservative' estimates of the Programme Advisor and the 'exaggerated' estimates of the State governments. Such a compromise is arrived at after considerable bargaining. Thus, the role of the States in the planning process is confined to 'bargaining for more financial resources and higher allocations'. Their role in the basic task of planning—that of plan formulation—continues to be negligible.

Role of District Planning

Since regional planning was not conceived as a framework for the planning experiment, the role of district planning was not appreciated by the Planning Commission. It was only after three plans had elapsed that a change in thinking took place and the need for adopting an area development approach was recognized. Accepting the importance of district planning in the overall planning process in general, and in the area development approach in particular, the Planning Commission prepared a set of guidelines for the formulation of district plans in 1969. The guidelines state, "it has become apparent that plan formulation undertaken exclusively at the state level cannot possibly take fully into account the variety of conditions existing in the different physio-geographical and economic regions of the state", and advocate the adoption of district planning on the following considerations:[62]

(a) the wide disparities which exist between the levels of development attained by different areas and community groups within a state and their full potential for development cannot be narrowed down unless the resources to be provided and the programmes to be taken up in each area or for each community are determined on the basis of a specific and local assessment of problems, resources and productive potentials;
(b) underutilization of the already available natural resources, infrastructural facilities and productive capacities in different areas cannot be properly assessed at the state level;
(c) the uniform application of development schemes formulated at the state level without regard to their suitability to local conditions, leads to inefficient utilization of physical and financial resources;
(d) meaningful assessment of on-going schemes cannot be undertaken except at the ground level and with the active participation of local officials and the beneficiaries of schemes;
(e) without a systematic study and planning of the local infrastructure, a firm and objective basis cannot be provided for the planning of the state superstructure nor can the time lags in its utilization reduced;
(f) proper phasing to ensure synchronization of the programme with other related programmes cannot be attempted without working out the details of programmes at the ground level;
(g) measures for the mobilization of local resources for development purposes cannot be planned realistically except in the specific context of the needs, aspirations and the economic condition of the people and the level of performance of local institutions; and
(h) integration of different levels of human settlements in a graded hierarchy requires the identification of growth centres. The deliberate steps required to be taken to identify the growth centres and to provide/locate the facilities and services required to meet the growing needs of the villages lying in their hinterlands cannot be taken except at the district level through the analysis of the emerging trends in economic activities and the pattern of facilities and services already available.

To undertake planning in these terms requires a certain amount of technical and statistical expertise at the formulation stage, and effective participation of people at the implementation stage. Both these requirements are woefully missing in our planning process. In addition, the absence of proper planning machinery at the State level and the complete non-existence of planning infrastructure at the district level, makes the task of preparing and implementing district plans still more difficult. An attempt in this direction was made by evolving a three-tier structure of panchayati raj institutions—village panchayat, panchayat samiti, and zila parishad. The zila parishad was to function at the district level. While the district collector continued to be the 'controller' of practically all governmental authority in the district, the institution of zila parishad considerably diluted the powers of the district collector in some States. Thus in Maharashtra and Gujarat, the district collector has been completely left out of the zila parishad. The administrative control here vests in the chief executive officer (or district development officer) who is responsible for coordinating all developmental programmes in the district. In U.P. and Bihar, the district collector can attend the meetings of the zila parishad and participate in discussions but has no right to vote. In Assam, Haryana, Orissa, Punjab, and Rajasthan, the district collector is associated with the zila parishad in an advisory capacity as a non-voting member.

Such an organization has created more problems than it has solved. Since the role of the district collector as a coordinator has not been precisely defined, the dichotomy between the administrative system and the political system has created severe problems. The local level government is political in character and it is natural that in the type of parliamentary democracy that we have, the local leaders should come to wield considerable power and influence. This gives them the necessary means to pressurize the district administrator for approving irregularities, doing illegal things (such as harassing a particular political group), indulging in corrupt practices, misallocating governmental benefits and funds, etc. Contrary to the expectations of the founders of the panchayati raj movement, the local leaders have not shown much interest in development programmes, programmes of education, family planning, and the like. On the other hand, on account of the structural dichotomy and on account of the lack of clear delineation of powers and duties, there are frequent delays at all stages of the planning process. In those cases where the administrator does not tow the lines dictated by local leaders, there are frequent struggles and interpersonal rivalries. Because of their local influence, the nature of their profession, and their contacts at the State political level, the local leaders are frequently at the winning end and the administrator gets transferred. While this dampens the spirit of other young enthusiastic administrators (who are thus compelled to tread the beaten track), it encourages the leaders of the local-level government to adopt more and more questionable means to accomplish their own selfish ends.

There is another serious problem that has not been referred to. Though the district collector has the district-level functionaries of all the departments such as health, education, cooperation, veterinary, engineering, etc., under him, these functionaries deal directly with their respective departments at the State level. Thus, there is 'dual supervision' and the possibility of frictions and disputes cannot be ignored.

What we are intending to drive at is that for district planning to be considered a serious proposition, it is necessary to provide for (i) *horizontal* coordination and integration between the district administrative system and the local political system; and (ii) *vertical* integration between the district level and the State level.[63]

Block Level Planning

When we consider planning at the block level, we are immediately confronted. with two important questions: (i) is block a proper unit of planning? and (ii) are district planning and block-level planning compatible? The Working Group on Block Level Planning appointed by the Government of India on 5 November 1977 under the chairmanship of M.L. Dantwala felt that the question of compatibility would not pose any problem because the district and block plans were visualized as part of the same exercise and the planning team charged with the responsibility of block level planning would be located at the district headquarters. As regards the first question, the Working Group felt that block is a relevant unit of planning because it is distinguished by a certain community of interests and is sufficiently small in terms of area and population to enable intimate contact and understanding between the planners, the authorities entrusted with the task of implementation, and the people. Because of these characteristics, it would help to:

(i) understand more clearly the felt needs of the people and factors inhibiting the uplift of the weaker sections;
(ii) ascertain area (block) specific physical and human resource potential;
(iii) identify constraints inhibiting socio-economic and technological growth; and
(iv) expand the area of people's participation in the preparation and implementation of plans.[64]

What are the activities that can be planned at the block level? This will depend upon the conditions prevailing in individual blocks. However, the Working Group felt that the following activities could be planned and executed at the block level without sacrificing planning efficiency:[65]

(i) Agriculture and allied activities
(ii) Minor irrigation
(iii) Soil conservation and water management
(iv) Animal Husbandry and Poultry
(v) Fisheries
(vi) Forestry
(vii) Processing of agricultural produce
(viii) Organizing input supply, credit and marketing
(ix) Cottage and Small Industries
(x) Local Infrastructure
(xi) Social Services
 (a) Drinking water supply
 (b) Health and nutrition
 (c) Education
 (d) Housing
 (e) Sanitation
 (f) Local transport
 (g) Welfare programmes
(xii) Training of local youth and upgrading of skills of local population.

The Working Group emphasized that the block plans prepared so as to cover the above activities should not only aim at the creation of productive assets but also generate maximum possible employment. Another important aim should be to provide basic minimum needs such as health care, drinking water, nutrition of children, education, housing sites, rural roads, and electricity.

What criteria will be adopted for the selection of blocks for purposes of block-level planning? While the ultimate task is to introduce such planning in all the 5004 blocks of the country, the sheer immensity of the task requires that the programme be introduced in stages. The selection of blocks every year will have to be based on some priorities. The priorities can be determined on the basis of unemployment and underemployment figures, low agricultural productivity, low consumption level and preponderance of people below the poverty line, preponderance of scheduled caste population, potentiality for development, etc. Since the basic task of block-level planning is the elimination of poverty and unemployment, the Working Group felt that *priority in selection should be given to blocks where backwardness is more pronounced.*

Location of Expertise

The formulation of district and block plans is a complex task. Before such plans can be actually prepared, it is necessary to carry out detailed studies of the resources available at the district and block levels and the possibilities of their quantitative and qualitative utilization, collect and analyse the data relating to various projects and schemes to identify their spatial and temporal linkages within an integrated framework, identify priorities and select a *catalytic programme*, study the availability and quality of economic infrastructure and social services, assess the availability of financial resources from the various sources, devise plans for fuller utilization of manpower resource after assessing the levels of unemployment and underemployment, etc. Obviously, the available planning machinery at the district and block levels is too inadequate for the task. The deficiencies of the planning machinery at the State and district levels are valid for blocks as well. In fact, the shortage of planning expertise at the block level is likely to act as a serious bottleneck in the formulation of block-level plans. The Working Group was quite realistic in suggesting that at the present stage of development, it would be much better to pool together the available planning skills at the district level instead of scattering this scarce resource in several blocks.[66] Such pooling of skills at the district level will, in addition to ensuring proper deployment of personnel resources, enable the planning team 'to take a broader perspective of resources potential and constraints, and ensure better coordination and integration of the block plans with the district plan'.

The Working Group proposed that the planning team at the district level should consist of a core group composed of (i) chief planning officer (next only to the collector in the district hierarchy), (ii) economist/statistician (for project formulation and evaluation), (iii) cartographer/geographer, (iv) agronomist, (v) engineer (irrigation/civil), (vi) industry officer (small and cottage industries), and (vii) credit planning officer. Other experts could be associated with this team keeping in view the requirements of the area or the programme. Such a planning machinery at the district level would prepare block plans as well in association with the block development officer, the panchayat samiti, voluntary agencies, and other concerned persons at the block level.

NOTES

1. Planning Commission, Government of India, *Second Five Year Plan*, 1956, p. 22.
2. Pramit Chaudhury (ed.), *Aspects of Indian Economic Development* (London: George Allen & Unwin Ltd., 1971), pp. 26-27.
3. This growth equation is similar to the growth equation given by Harrod. In fact, it can be easily converted to the form discussed in Chapter 4 (equation 5).
4. For a derivation of this curve the reader is referred to Ashok Rudra, *Indian Plan Models* (Delhi: Allied Publishers Private Ltd., 1975), pp. 96-97.
5. Ibid., p. 94; the graphs are given on page 95.
6. Ibid., p. 94.
7. This belief has got expressed in so many growth models and planning documents that its truth is almost taken for granted. The empirical studies (outlining high rate of investment in the developed countries and low rate of investment in the underdeveloped countries) only go to strengthen this belief.
8. C.T. Kurien, *Indian Economic Crisis* (Bombay: Asia Publishing House, 1969), pp. 92-93.
9. The Dandekar-Rath study (published in *Economic and Political Weekly*, January 1971) pointed out that 215.5 million people (166.4 million rural and 49.4 million urban) were below the poverty line in 1967-68. This meant that 40% of the population could not even procure the minimum level of subsistence even after seventeen years of planning, where the minimum level was defined as a meagre Rs.15 per capita per month for the rural population and Rs.22.2 per capita per month for the urban population (at 1960-61 prices). This disturbing revelation naturally aroused a lot of concern, discussion, and criticism of the planning process. Some other studies were also conducted to highlight the problem of poverty—the most important being the studies of P.K. Bardhan ("Green Revolution and Agricultural Labourers", *Economic and Political Weekly*, Vol. 5, Nos. 29-31, July 1970 and Vol. 5, No. 46, 14 November 1970), B.S. Minhas ("Rural Poverty, Land Redistribution and Development Strategy : Facts and Policy", *Indian Economic Review*, 1970), and P.D. Ojha ("A Configuration of Indian Poverty : Inequality and Levels of Living", *RBI Bulletin*, January 1970). All these studies pointed to the prevalence of large-scale poverty in India. P.K. Bardhan noted that 220.5 million rural people (constituting 53.0% of rural population) were below the poverty line where poverty line was defined to be monthly per capita consumption of Rs.15 at 1960-61 prices. Minhas took monthly per capita consumption of Rs.17 at 1960-61 prices as the poverty line and found that 154.0 million rural people (constituting 37.1% of rural population) were below the line in 1967-68. P.D. Ojha defined the poverty line at Rs.15-18 (at 1960-61 prices) per capita per month for rural population and Rs.8-11 per capita per month for urban population and found that 289.0 million rural population (constituting 70% of rural population) were below this minimum level of subsistence in 1967-68.
10. These and related issues were discussed at several forums. The *Economic and Political Weekly* alone brought out a series of brilliant articles on the subject, a sample of which is given below:

    (i) Phiroze B. Medhora, "Approach to the Fifth Plan : Issues and Pseudo Issues" (8 July 1972); (ii) K.N. Raj, "Approach to Fifth Plan" (Annual Number, February 1973); (iii) C.H. Hanumantha Rao, "Strategy for Removal of Poverty : Lopsidedness of Fifth Plan Approach" (Special Number, August 1973); (iv) T.N. Krishnan, "The Fifth Five-Year Plan Model : A Comment" (Special Number, August 1973); (v) Suresh D. Tendulkar, "Planning for Growth, Redistribution and Self-Reliance in the Fifth

Five-Year Plan" (12 January 1974, and 19 January 1974); (vi) Yoginder K. Alagh, "Planning Policy and the Fifth Plan" (Annual Number, February 1974); (vii) Suresh D. Tendulkar "Draft Fifth Plan and Removal of Poverty" (Annual Number, February 1974); (viii) Pranab K. Bardhan, "On 'Welfarism' vs. 'Radicalism' in Planning" (2 March 1974); and (ix) B. Nanjundaiya and K.C. Majumdar, "Planning for Growth, Redistribution and Self-Reliance : A Comment", and Suresh D. Tendulkar's "Reply" to the criticisms levied by Nanjundaiya and Majumdar (27 April 1974).

11. Planning Commission, Government of India, *Draft Fifth Five Year Plan*, Vol. I, p. 87.
12. Planning Commission, Government of India, *Draft Five Year Plan 1978-83*, (now defunct), p. 3.
13. Data on per capita net national product are taken from Government of India, *Economic Survey, 1980-81*, Table 1.1, p. 65.
14. S.L. Shetty, "Structural Retrogression in the Indian Economy since the Mid-Sixties", enlarged and updated reprint of the paper first published in *Economic and Political Weekly*, Annual Number, February 1978, p. 8.
15. Ibid., p. 14.
16. See under the section "A Critical Evaluation of the Planning Process".
17. Government of India, *Economic Survey, 1978-79*, pp. 45-46.
18. *The Third Five Year Plan*, p. 28.
19. K.N. Raj, "Growth and Stagnation in Indian Industrial Development", *Mainstream*, 21 February 1976, Table 5, p. 22.
20. K.N. Raj regards the imbalance between planned investment expenditure and savings as responsible for both slow rates of growth of output and savings, and price inflation. See K.N. Raj "Planning and Prices in India", *The Economic Times*, 15 March 1974 and 16 March 1974.
21. Jagdish N. Bhagwati and Padma Desai, *India : Planning for Industrialization* (London: Oxford University Press, 1970), p. 118.
22. "A study of the financing pattern of the Plans during the first three Plans and the three Annual Plans suggests that this is one area which is treated by the Planning Commission with utmost casualness." C.D. Wadhva "A Critique of the Fourth Five Year Plan", in C.D. Wadhva (ed.), *Some Problems of India's Economic Policy* (New Delhi: Tata McGraw-Hill Publishing Co. Ltd., 1973), p. 138. Also, "The argument presupposes that if, structurally, or physically, we can raise the proportion of investment in national income, the necessary *ex ante* savings can be found to make the program feasible without inflationary effects. While this is a tautology at one level, its implication that policy-makers can therefore raise as much savings as are necessary to support the planned investments is clearly untenable. There is no escape from having to investigate separately the problem of generating enough savings to support the projected investment, if inflation is to be avoided. Direct measures controlling the level and composition of consumption may be sometimes called for if the physical planning targets are to be implemented, a fact which was not fully emphasized by the physical planners." S. Chakravarti and J.N. Bhagwati, *Indian Economic Analysis : A Survey* (Bombay: Lalvani Publishing House, 1971), pp. 44-45.
23. For some comments on the inefficacy of the dependence on the rate of investment, see Edward S. Mason, "Comment on Planning in India", reprinted in Gerald M. Meier, *Leading Issues in Economic Development* (Oxford University Press, 1971), pp. 740-743; and Pradhan H. Prasad, "Production Relations : Achilles' Heel of Indian Planning", *Economic and Political Weekly*, 12 May 1973. According to Prasad, "Investment has remained the kingpin of the preferred models for development in our planning. . . . The principal urge towards planning in our country has

been the desire to achieve a high level of investment." This is reflected in the increasing size of the plans. Though there is nothing wrong in this emphasis, it overlooks much more essential things; e.g., it leads to a failure to assess the importance of the 'production relations' aspect of economic dynamics and this failure, according to Prasad, "is, by and large, responsible for so little achievement in development".

24. S.L. Shetty, op. cit., pp. 14-18.
25. V.G. Patel, *An Analysis of Plan Implementation in India* (Ahmedabad: Balgovind Prakashan, 1969), p. 46.
26. For a detailed discussion on the neglect of implementational aspects of planning, see V.G. Patel, ibid., especially Chapter IV on "The Capacity to Implement as a Constraint".
27. Ranjit Sau, "The New Economics", *Economic and Political Weekly*, Special Number, August 1972, p. 1571.

    It may interest the reader to note here that industrial employment in China increased at an annual average rate of 10% during 1950 and 1965 which was just one percentage point or two less than the growth of industrial output. This was mainly because of the fact that China took special pains to evolve and use labour-intensive techniques while we were engaged in fruitless discussion over the relative merits and demerits of capital-intensive and labour-intensive techniques. See Thomas E. Weisskopf, "China and India : A Comparative Survey of Performance in Economic Development", *Economic and Political Weekly*, Annual Number, February 1975.
28. *Draft Five Year Plan, 1978-83*, p. 82.
29. Shetty, op. cit., Table 26, p. 32.
30. Bhagwati and Chakravarty, op. cit., p. 33.
31. For a detailed discussion, see Chapter 7.
32. J.N. Kaul, "Development of Indian Higher Education", *Economic and Political Weekly*, Special Number, 1972, p. 1649.
33. D.G. Vashi, "Development Planning Models", *The Economic Times*, 21 December 1974.
34. For a complete discussion of this problem, see P.J. Foster, "The Vocational School Fallacy in Development Planning", reprinted in M. Blaug (ed.), *Economics of Education*, Vol. 1 (Penguin Books Series), pp. 396-423. A specific discussion of this point can be found on p. 411. Also see the article by J. Balogh and P.P. Streeten, "The Planning of Education in Poor Countries", in the same book, pp. 383-395. Balogh and Streeten suggest a rolling plan to solve the problem outlined above (p. 393).
35. P.K. Bardhan, "On the Incidence of Poverty in Rural India of Sixties", *Economic and Political Weekly*, Annual Number 1973, p. 245.
36. Planning Commission, *Basic Statistics Relating to the Indian Economy 1950-51 to 1970-71*, Table 7, p. 20. The data in this table (which give the wholesale price index for all years between 1960-61 and 1970-71) clearly show that during each year the foodgrains price index had remained higher than both the manufactured articles' price index and the general price index.
37. This is on top of the fact that an equal increase in price for the poor and the rich will have relatively much more serious implications for the former compared with the latter. One must also note that the existing public distribution system also discriminates against the rural poor. For a discussion of this point, see K.N. Raj, "Planning and Prices in India", *The Economic Times*, 15 and 16 March 1974. Raj points out, "In practice the spatial distribution of fair price shops is such that, except in a State such as Kerala, the population effectively covered is limited to those living in urban and semi-urban areas...". Also see G.R. Mishra, "Planning and Prices in India—A Comment on Prof. Raj's article", *The Economic Times*, 16 April 1974.

38. It may also be of interest to note that the real earnings of factory workers remained virtually constant over the whole planning period. Thus, the real earnings (base 1960=100) which were 99.2 in 1952 stood at 98.7 in 1965 and 100.2 in 1971. This was despite the fact that average productivity of factory workers had increased at the rate of 4% per annum since 1952. If this was the fate of the most organized and vocal section of workers, the fate of agricultural workers could be well imagined. See Weisskopf, op. cit., Table 4; and Ranjit Sau, "The New Economics", op. cit., p. 1571.
39. Planning Commission, *Sixth Five Year Plan, 1980-85*, Annexure 1.11, p. 16.
40. Government of India, *Economic Survey, 1980-81*, Table 1.11, p. 78.
41. Shetty, op. cit., p. 18. Shetty has given many other illustrations also.
42. "A critical dividing line between the fully socialist economies and underdeveloped mixed economies with apparently similar strategies of development is that the former can directly alter the distribution of incomes between different occupational groups or the distribution of means of production between different sectors so as to make them conform to the strategy of development, but the latter can try to do so only through a cumbersome apparatus of fiscal, monetary and physical controls supplemented by the market mechanism. The governments of the mixed economies are extremely inhibited about curtailing the right to private property fundamentally, and the alternative controlling mechanism it tries to set up comes ultimately to be governed by the more dominant forces in the economy, viz. the expenditure pattern of the private sector." A.K. Bagchi, "Long-Term Constraints of India's Industrial Growth 1951-1968", in E.A.G. Robinson and Michael Kidron (eds.), *Economic Development in South Asia* (London: Macmillan, 1970), p. 172.
43. Ibid., p. 174.
44. The summary follows V. Nath, "Regional Development in Indian Planning", *Economic and Political Weekly*, Annual Number, January 1970, pp. 255-256.
45. Shantilal Sarupria, "Approach to Regional Development in India", in Peter Meyer-Dohm (ed.), *Economic and Social Aspects of Indian Development* (Tubingen-Basel: Horst Erdmann Verlag, and Bombay: Shakuntala Publishing House, 1975), p. 75.
46. Computed from Shantilal Sarupria, Ibid., Table 3, p. 82.
47. Since these three States are very rich in natural resources, they were automatically qualified for a number of large-scale public sector investments on techno-economic grounds. And once the task was taken in hand, large-scale investment had to be directed to them on account of the "lumpiness" of investment in heavy industry sector. This would suggest that not all central investments in these three States were guided by regional considerations (such as balanced regional development). Therefore, it is not proper to regard all investment (in public sector) in the backward States as prompted by considerations of regional planning.
48. "In cases of new planned industrial townships like Bhilai, Durgapur and Rourkela, for instance, failure to cover their respective areas of influence has given rise to a number of problems. In Durgapur, where initially a steel plant was located, a number of ancillary and subsidiary industries have sprung up like uncoordinated enclaves each with its own township. Similarly, due to lack of forethought on the expansion needs of the main and allied industries, uncoordinated development has taken place. This in certain cases, has stifled the expansion programme of the main industry itself. Inefficient use of land, services, wasteful density and planning standards are other drawbacks in the planning of most of industrial townships." J.P. Sah and S.S. Dutta "Economic Development and Spatial Planning in India", *Ekistics*, 23 January 1967.
49. Yoginder Alagh, *Regional Aspects of Indian Industrialization* (Bombay: University of Bombay, Economic Series No. 21, 1972), p. 16

50. For a discussion and meaning of these terms, the reader is referred to Chapter 4, section "Modified Growth Foci Approach".
51. The industrial licensing policy helped this process instead of curbing it. See Chapter 5.
52. See Chapter 6 for details.
53. Also see Chapter 6 in this context.
54. For a detailed discussion, the reader is referred to Chapter 7.
55. Bijit Ghosh "Planning Process", in Lalit K. Sen (ed.), *Readings on Micro-Level Planning and Rural Growth Centres* (Hyderabad: National Institute of Community Development, 1972), p. 290.
56. "It is unfortunate to have to say that most of the physical plans for our cities and towns represent an outmoded Western approach, namely of pathological treatment of micro-environment. As such, these plans are merely occupied with internal problems of towns and cities, quite often severely confined to the formal city limits, heedless of the background of its region or hinterland. There hardly exists any framework for the coordination of such plans with each other and with economic development at the local, regional, State, or National level. Spatial planning activity is thus sporadic in nature, and devoid of any direction and perspective which, in fact, the economic development plans contain, but which physical planners have not yet begun to take serious note of." J.P. Sah, and S.S. Dutta, op. cit.
57. According to D.R. Gadgil, "Indian planning is highly centralized. Planning in the sense of attempting formulation of an integrated plan of development is undertaken only by the Planning Commission at the centre. Planning thought and information to the extent these are in evidence, exist only with the Planning Commission, and this body alone is concerned with planning techniques." D.R. Gadgil, *District Development Planning*, R.R. Kale Memorial Lecture, 1966, reprinted in abridged form in C.D. Wadhva (ed.), *Some Problems of India's Economic Policy* (New Delhi: Tata McGraw Hill Publishing Company Ltd., Second Edition, 1977), p. 202.
58. Ibid., p. 203.
59. Ibid., p. 203.
60. "Because of the *schematic matching* assistance, the States have almost always been compelled to accept not only particular schemes but even details such as patterns of staffing regarding the schemes suggested by the Central Ministries. Apart from the direct financial inducement, the power and prestige of the Planning Commission appears to be an important factor in the States' acceptance of the schemes suggested by the Centre. Hence it seems hardly surprising that 'genuine development properly related to the specific resource potential and felt requirements of each state' could not take place." Shantilal Sarupria, op. cit., p. 85.
61. Ajit Kumar Singh, "Planning at the State Level in India", *Commerce* Pamphlet 25, January 1970, p. 29.
62. Planning Commission, *Guidelines for the Formulation of District Plans*, 1969, pp. 1-2 (U.P. Government edition).
63. P.H. Vaishnav and K.V. Sundaram, "Integrating Development Administration at the Area Level", in Planning Commission, *Report of the Working Group on Block Level Planning*, 1978, Appendix III.

    Problems of vertical integration are best solved in the scheme submitted by Sudipto Mundle. Mundle suggests a change in the departmental structure of the State secretariat. Instead of the present system wherein departments in the secretariat correspond to sectors of government activity, it is suggested that ***each department should correspond to one district.*** This would involve a shift from an activity based line of demarcation of departments to an area-based line demarcation. See Sudipto Mundle *District Planning in India* (New Delhi: Indian Institute of Public Administration, 1977), p. 60.

64. *Reporting of the Working Group on Block Level Planning*, op. cit., p. 2.
65. Ibid., p. 3.
66. Ibid., p. 7. See also Anand Swarup, "Machinery for the Formulation of District and Block Plans", *Yojana*, Annual Number, Vol. XXII/1, 26 January 1978, pp. 43-44. Swarup states: "It is apparent that given the existing shortages of expert personnel and the cost of providing these, it would not be practical to think of setting up multi-disciplinary teams for data analysis, socio-economic appraisal, programme/project formulation or inter-sectoral and spatial integration at the block level. At this level, it would be possible only to assign to the block level machinery the responsibility of collecting data and preparing simple maps showing broad physio-geographic and socio-economic characteristics of the area, the coverage of infrastructure and the location of various economic and social services."

Chapter 4

Some Concepts, Methods, and Techniques Used in Regional Analysis

This chapter aims at providing a bird's-eye view of some of the important theories, methods, and techniques of regional planning. However, our object is not restricted to explaining the theories and the techniques only. We have tried to illustrate their application in the Indian context. Such illustrations provide important insights into the regional structure of our economy and also help us understand the role of regional planning techniques in the overall context of regional planning in our country. It is no doubt true that, compared with research in the field of regional science in the developed countries, very little work has been done in India. While interest in this discipline is developing at a very rapid pace in practically all the advanced countries (whether socialist or non-socialist) we have all along tended to treat it with scant respect. Undoubtedly some researchers are engaged in the task of developing and applying existing techniques in the Indian context, but their task has been rendered difficult due to acute shortage of reliable data at the district and block levels. That they have been able to achieve some significant results despite such limitations is indeed creditable. Therefore, while recognizing at the outset the total inadequacy of research in the field of regional planning and regional economics in India, we feel that due recognition should be given to the work that has already been done or is being done. Keeping such considerations in view, we have tried to illustrate the application of different techniques of regional planning from the works of researchers and have also given lists of important papers published, at various places in the chapter. Moreover, it is our belief that such illustrations will enable the reader to understand the application of regional planning techniques on the one hand, and provide him with a better perspective to understand some of the problems of regional planning in this country in a better way, on the other.

The framework of this chapter is as follows: We start with a discussion on the problem of regional growth and short-run changes and follow it up with a discussion of regional growth both as an exogenously induced process and as an endogenously induced process. Under the latter heading we discuss briefly, the sector theory, the stages theory, the Harrod-Domar Model, and the Neo-Classical Model of Growth. This is followed by a discussion of regional input-output analysis and its application in the Indian context. From here we proceed to discuss theories of industrial location and spatial development. We have discussed the theories of Weber, Walter Christaller, and August Losch in this context and have provided illustrations from India. Because of its close relationship with the central place theory, we have taken up rank-size rule immediately afterwards and its application in the Indian context. This is followed by a discussion on Perroux's growth pole theory and the contributions of Hirschman and Myrdal. The final section of the chapter is devoted to a discussion of the role of the growth pole theory in the context of regional planning in India. We have taken a special note of R.P. Misra's modification and enlargement of the *growth pole* strategy into a *growth foci* strategy and present it as the basic framework necessary for worthwhile regional planning in our country. Unless the country is divided into a hierarchy of human settlements and gaps in the linkage pattern noted, and unless specific attempts are made to implant growth points and growth centres at appropriate levels in the hierarchy, all talk of regional planning will remain useless and all efforts to introduce regional planning fruitless. But more of this later.

REGIONAL GROWTH

In economic theory when we talk of growth we mean increase of income —total income and/or per capita income. Therefore regional growth implies an increase in the total and/or per capita income of a region. Since the growth of income is always the result of the growth of the use of factors of production, regional growth should imply a better use of the factors of production, such as land, labour, capital, etc., of the region. In addition to these factors, a region can also grow due to an increase in the level of demand for its commodities from the other regions of the country. Thus, in regional analysis, growth of a region can result either from endogenous factors or from exogenous factors (or both). Consequently, there are some theories of regional growth that attempt to explain the growth of a region in terms of endogenous factors while some others attempt to explain it in terms of exogenous factors.

REGIONAL MULTIPLIERS : EXPLANATION OF SHORT-RUN CHANGES

Before we proceed to consider the theories of regional growth, it is necessary to explain how growth in one sector induces growth in another. This is done with the help of the multiplier concept. In mathematics, the word 'multiplier' refers to the quantity which multiplies another quantity to give a result. If in an economy we find that an initial employment of one more labourer results ultimately in an employment of four labourers, we may say that in the economy the multiplier action is 4. Similarly, if we spend or invest one more rupee and find that it leads ultimately to transactions worth four rupees, we may say that the multiplier action of investment on transactions (during a given period in time) is indicated by 4. In economics, the multiplier shows the effect of a change in a causal factor on another factor (usually national income or employment). The concept of employment multiplier was introduced in economic theory by Kahn which was defined by him as a coefficient relating an increment of primary employment (e.g., on public works) to the resulting increment of total employment, primary and secondary combined. Thus, if primary employment is increased by ΔE_P (where E_P is initial primary employment and Δ is the usual mathematical symbol used to denote *increment*) and this results in an increase of total employment by ΔE_T (where E_T is the initial total employment), then

$$k' = \frac{\Delta E_T}{\Delta E_P}$$

where k' is the employment multiplier.

The concept of investment multiplier was introduced by John Maynard Keynes. Investment multiplier is the coefficient relating an increment of investment to increment of income. Thus, if I is the initial investment, Y the initial total income, ΔI denotes an increase in investment and ΔY the increase in total income as a consequence of an increase in investment, then

$$k = \frac{\Delta Y}{\Delta I}$$

where k is the investment multiplier:

Coming to the regional level, we can think of two types of activity—basic and non-basic. Basic activities are those which produce goods (or services) for export, while non-basic activities produce goods (or services) for local use. Thus, while the former may be termed export activities, the latter can be termed local activities. Fluctuations in basic activities lead to fluctuations in local income which, in turn, induce fluctuations in various other activities and trades. This causes a multiplier effect. Thus, an increase in basic activity in a region increases the flow of income into that region. As a result, the demand for goods and services of non-basic activities increases leading to a spurt in such activities. On the other hand, a decrease in basic activity leads to a depression in the demand for non-basic activities. Thus, a fluctuation in basic activity has a multiplier effect on the regional economy.

This concept of multiplier corresponds to the economic base theory and is known as the *economic base multiplier*. The economic base multiplier is frequently calculated in terms of employment and is expressed as

$$k' = \frac{\text{increase in total employment in basic \& non-basic activities}}{\text{increase in employment in basic activities}}$$

$$= \frac{\Delta(TE)}{\Delta(E_B)}$$

where TE designates total employment and E_B employment in basic activities on the lines of Kahn's employment multiplier.

Thus, if in a region, employment in basic activities is increased by 10,000 and this results in increase in employment in non-basic activities by 20,000, we have

$$\Delta(E_B) = 10{,}000$$

and

$$\Delta(TE) = 20{,}000 + 10{,}000 = 30{,}000$$

and consequently

$$k' = \frac{30{,}000}{10{,}000} = 3.$$

The economic base multiplier does not take account of the effect of imports. But, since there is a system of regions in an economy where each region exports certain goods (or services) and, in turn, imports others, it becomes necessary to think of an inter-regional framework. A multiplier that takes account of such relationships is termed *inter-regional trade multiplier* and can be expressed in several ways. We discuss one form of this multiplier[1] to illustrate the concept.

Since in an open system (which we have to assume when we consider inter-regional trade) a region's exports and imports are to be taken into account, a region's income can be expressed as

$$Y = I+E+C-M \tag{1}$$

where Y is the region's income, I is the region's investment expenditure, C is the region's consumption expenditure, E denotes exports from the region, and M denotes imports into the region.

If ΔY denotes increment in income, ΔI increment in investment, etc., then, from equation (1)

$$\Delta Y = \Delta(I+E+C-M) = \Delta I+\Delta E+\Delta C-\Delta M \tag{2}$$

Let $M = M_c + M_i$

where M_c = consumer goods imports and M_i = investment goods imports.

Assuming that only consumer goods are imported, $M = M_c$, and dividing equation (2) by ΔY we get

$$1 = \frac{\Delta I+\Delta E}{\Delta Y} + \frac{\Delta C}{\Delta Y} \frac{\Delta M_c}{\Delta Y}$$

or

$$1 = \frac{\Delta I+\Delta E}{\Delta Y} + \frac{\Delta C}{\Delta Y}\left[1 - \frac{\Delta M_c}{\Delta C}\right] \tag{3}$$

Now $\Delta C/\Delta Y$ is the marginal propensity to consume and $\Delta M_c/\Delta C$ is the marginal rate of change of import of consumer goods with change in total consumption. Therefore,

$$\frac{\Delta C}{\Delta Y}\left[1-\frac{\Delta M_c}{\Delta C}\right]$$

is, in fact, the marginal propensity to consume local goods.

If $p = \Delta C/\Delta Y$ and $q = \Delta M_c/\Delta C$, we get from equation (3)

$$1 = \frac{\Delta I+\Delta E}{\Delta Y}+p(1-q) \tag{4}$$

In Keynesian analysis, we know that the multiplier k is given by

$$k = \frac{\Delta Y}{\Delta I} = \frac{1}{1 - \text{marginal propensity to consume}}$$

Since in equation (4), $p\,(1-q)$ is the marginal propensity to consume local goods, the multiplier k can be expressed as

$$k = \frac{1}{1-p(1-q)} \tag{5}$$

Equation (4) can be written as

$$\frac{\Delta Y}{\Delta I+\Delta E}=\frac{1}{1-p(1-q)}$$

From equation (5)

$$k = \frac{\Delta Y}{\Delta I+\Delta E} \tag{6}$$

k here is known as the *inter-regional trade multiplier* and its value is given by equation (6). It gives the change in regional income (ΔY) resulting from (and as a multiple of) a change in regional investment (i.e., ΔI) or regional exports (ΔE), or both.

REGIONAL GROWTH : THE EXPORT BASE MODEL

This model, initially developed by Douglass C. North, emphasizes the role of exogenous factors in regional growth. It points to the fact that regions are not 'closed areas' but are 'open' to the flows or trade. Therefore, the growth of a region depends upon the growth of the regional export base which, in turn, depends upon expansion in demand external to the region. As a consequence of export sales, income in the region increases leading to an expansion of residentiary activities, movement of factors of production, development of external economies, and further regional growth. A region will experience growth, if the demand for its exports increases. This can happen for several reasons: "(1) because per capita income in the exogenous sector is rising (historically, largely because of improving technology) and the income elasticity of demand for the exports is high; (2) because, even if its income elasticity of demand is low or negative, the increase in demand associated with a growing population is greater than the decrease due to a rising level of per capita income; (3) because of depletion or exhaustion in other areas producing the same item; (4) because improved transfer facilities have lowered total delivery costs, making marginal producers in other areas unable to compete; or (5) because technology has found new uses for the export."[2]

In addition to these factors, Stabler notes that a region can experience an increase in volume of activity if technological improvements are made in the production of export goods or if "the technology of the initial activity is such that linked activities are attracted to its location". Because of all such factors, the growth of exports is considered to be the basis of growth of the region in the export base model. Increased investment in residentiary activity is taken to be the consequence of expansion in income received from outside.

The export base theory is criticized on several grounds: First, the export base theory gives undue importance to the export sector and ignores the internal growth influences operative in the region. The growth of local activities can be of equal importance as the growth of the export base in pushing up the rate of growth of the region. Secondly, it is not necessary that the growth of the export base should invariably lead to the growth of the regional economy. If the additional income acquired through exports is frittered away on imported luxury goods, or the businessmen who acquire such income do not invest in the region itself, the regional economy may not experience any growth. Thirdly, it concentrates attention on only exports and does not consider the importance of autonomous variables, technical change, etc. Lastly, its highly aggregative nature conceals some important facts. Thus, the simple division into region and rest of the world hides the inter-regional relationships which are of basic importance in the process of regional growth. Because of similar factors, the theory fails also to realize that in inter-regional trade the level of exports of a region is determined by the import functions of other regions.

For these reasons, the export base theory is not of much importance. On the basis of the 1951 and 1961 census figures of population and occupational pattern, K.R.G. Nair has calculated the values of regional multipliers for each State of India in an attempt to examine whether the export base theory can be applied to Indian conditions.[3] Nair argues that "if the relative importance of the export base is to be the explanation for high per capita income, states with low regional multipliers (i.e. with relatively high export base) must have high per capita incomes". However, Nair's analysis gives the quite opposite conclusion. It is in the States with low per capita incomes such as Bihar and Orissa that the export base is large compared with the non-basic sector, while in States such as Gujarat and Maharashtra with high per capita incomes the export base is relatively less important than the non-basic sector in the regional economy. Thus, the regional employment multipliers for Bihar and Orissa are respectively 1.2 and 1.4 in 1951, and 1.3 and 1.4 in 1961. Against this, the regional employment multipliers for Gujarat and Maharashtra (States with a high per capita income) are respectively 3.2 and 3.7 in 1951, and 4.9 and 3.9 in 1961. To understand the nature of the relationship further, Nair has calculated the correlation coefficients between the regional multipliers and the per capita incomes of the state. The correlation has been found to be positive but had a low value of 0.40 for both the years, 1951 and 1961. From all these observations, Nair has concluded that the export base theory did not seem to be valid for India.

Growth as an Internal Process

The simplest theory of regional growth emphasizing the internal factors of growth is the *sector theory*. It begins with the Clark-Fisher hypothesis that a rise in per capita incomes in the regions would be accompanied by a decline in the proportion of resources employed in agriculture, and an increase in the proportion of resources employed in manufacturing (secondary) and later in service (tertiary) activities. As a result of this reallocation, division of labour and specialization will follow providing the main dynamic impetus for regional growth.

An extension of the sector theory is the *stage theory* which argues that the growth of a region is basically an internal evolutionary process involving different stages. In the first stage will be a self-sufficient subsistence economy depending wholly on agriculture (according to the localization of natural resources) with little investment or trade. In the second stage, improvements in transport induce a sort of regional specialization and development of trade. As a consequence, village industries based on simple production techniques are developed. In the third stage, increasing inter-regional trade introduces a diversification in regional production activities (such as introduction of dairying, fruit-growing, etc.). In the fourth stage, increasing population pressure on land and diminishing agricultural returns force the region to industrialize. Initially agricultural processing industries develop, and, over time secondary (and technically more advanced industries) are set up. In the final stage, tertiary industry producing for exports is developed. The region is now in a position to export capital, skills, technical knowledge, and specialized services to the less developed regions.

These development processes are accompanied by fundamental changes in the organizational structure of activities (especially industries), concentration in and expansion of large firms within industries, changes in locational and settlement patterns within regions, etc.

Let us now turn to two elementary models, both of which consider growth as an internal process and are popular in regional economic analysis. The first is the Harrod-Domar Model and the second is the Neo-Classical Model of Growth.

The Harrod-Domar Model

Harrod's model has two basic assumptions: (i) the saving of a community in period t is a constant proportion(s) of the income received during that period:

$$S_t = sY_t \tag{7}$$

and (ii) the desired investment during period t is a constant proportion (g) of the amount by which the income during period t exceeds that of the previous period ($t-1$):

$$I_t = g\,(Y_t - Y_{t-1}) \tag{8}$$

National income (Y_t) in period t is taken as the summation of consumption

(C_t) and investment (I_t) in that period:

$$Y_t = C_t + I_t \tag{9}$$

In the Keynesian system, ex post saving is equal to ex post investment, i.e., actual saving equals actual (or realized) investment. This is because of the fact that actual saving is income minus consumption while actual (or realized) investment is what is left over from income after consumption has taken place. Thus, they are, in fact, one and the same thing. Therefore, from equation (7), we can say that the realized investment in period $t = sY_t$. Equation (8) gives the desired investment for period t. For purposes of equilibrium, it is necessary that the realized investment is equal to the desired investment:

$$sY_t = g\,(Y_t - Y_{t-1}) \tag{10}$$

which yields

$$\frac{Y_t - Y_{t-1}}{Y_t} = \frac{s}{g} \tag{11}$$

as the equilibrium rate of growth of income. This rate is given the name 'warranted rate of growth of income' by Harrod. Since both s and g are constants, equation (11) requires that income must continue to increase at a constant rate, i.e. income must increase by a greater and greater amount if the system is to remain in equilibrium.

In addition to the warranted rate of growth, Harrod postulates a natural rate of growth. This is defined as the maximum possible rate of growth, given natural resources and a growing supply of labour and organization. It is not necessary that the actual rate of growth should coincide with the warranted rate of growth and the natural rate of growth or with either of them. If the natural rate of growth is denoted by n and the rate of growth of output by v then, for steady growth to take place, we must have

$$v = n = s/g.$$

What will happen if the actual rate of growth is different from the warranted rate of growth? To understand this, let us suppose that the actual rate of growth of income is less than the warranted rate. Then

$$Y_t - Y_{t-1} = \frac{s}{g} Y_t - c.$$

where c is a positive constant and indicates the amount by which $(Y_t - Y_{t-1})$ is less than $\frac{s}{g} Y_t$. Investment $I_t = g\,(Y_t - Y_{t-1})$, which would have been equal to sY_t [see equation (10)] is now equal to $g\{(s/g)Y_t - c\}$;

i.e., $$g\,(Y_t - Y_{t-1}) = sY_t - gc$$

or $$sY_t = g\,(Y_t - Y_{t-1}) + gc$$

Since the actual investment is sY_t (= realized saving), this expression shows that the investors have invested more than the desired investment by the amount gc. Consequently, they will find themselves in a position of over-investment and hence over-production. Therefore, they will be forced to cut down their investment. This will lead to a fall in income and c will increase leading to a further divergence between the actual and the warranted rates of growth. Thus, once the actual rate of growth differs from the warranted rate, forces are set into operation which further increase the divergences.

Harrod-Domar Model in a Regional Context[4]

Since regions are open economies it becomes necessary to introduce imports and exports. Then,

$$S + M = I + X \tag{12}$$

where M refers to imports and X to exports.[5]

If m is the constant propensity to import, we have

$$(s + m)\,Y = I + X$$

or $$\frac{I}{Y} = s + m - \frac{X}{Y}$$

Region i's exports (X_i) can be expressed in terms of the imports of other regions as

$$X_i = M_{i_1} + M_{i_2} + \ldots + M_{i_n} = \sum_{j=1}^{n} m_{ij} Y_j$$

where n is the total number of regions.

Thus the growth equation for region i can be written as

$$v_i = \frac{s_i + m_i - \sum_{j=1} m_{ij}.Y_j/Y_i}{g_i} \qquad (13)$$

[from equation (11), equilibrium rate of growth $v = s/g$].

There are two considerations that must be kept in view: (i) even if savings exceed investment, there can still be equilibrium between savings and investment if there is an export surplus equal to the gap; and (ii) the requirement for equilibrium with regard to labour is that excess labour should be eliminated by outmigration and if there is a deficiency in labour supply, it should be met by in-migration from other regions. Since both these conditions can be met more easily in a region than in a nation, equilibrium is easier to obtain in the region than in the nation. Yet, steady growth is an exception rather than a rule, for "attainment of equilibrium conditions in one region may alter the requirements of equilibrium in others, and this will have further repercussions on its own growth rate. . . . Whether or not there will be a tendency to steady growth depends on whether or not inter-regional flows of capital and labour are equilibrating, and these are not determined within the model."[6]

If, in this model, the equilibrium growth is higher in one region than in other regions, it will continue to increase at a higher rate.

This is so because if $v_i > v_j (j = 1,2, \ldots, n)$, then Y_j/Y_i becomes smaller. Thus, in equation (13),

$$\sum_{j=1} m_{ij} Y_j/Y_i$$

decreases and v_i rises further. Thus, "if regional growth rates initially differ, the divergence is likely to become wider in the absence of equilibrating factor flows".

Two other observations that can be made on the basis of equation (13) are : (1) Regions with a high propensity to save and/or a lower capital-output ratio will grow at a faster rate than other regions. This is so because a higher s_i will increase the numerator in the equation and a lower g will decrease the denominator. Both of them will have the effect of increasing v_i. (2) Regions with net import surpluses, i.e., those regions where

$$m_i = \frac{\sum_{j=1} m_{ij} Y_j}{Y_i} > 0$$

can grow faster than other regions.

THE NEO-CLASSICAL MODEL OF GROWTH[7]

The Neo-Classical Model of Growth has dominated general economic theory for a fairly long period. The most important contribution in this field came from R.W. Solow and T.W. Swan in 1956. The popularity of the neo-classical growth model in economic theory is basically because of its neat, precise predictions and the promise of adjustment in response to the Harrod problem of the divergence between the 'natural' and the 'warranted' growths. Though this model has been advocated as a model of regional growth as well, its highly restrictive assumptions make it practically useless for such analysis. As pointed out by Richardson, even if the assumptions of perfect competition and full employment can be made in aggregate economic analysis, they cannot be made at all in a regional context. "Space is incompatible with perfect competition, complete certainty, marginal adjustments in prices, outputs and locations, and the other background conditions of the neoclassical world. In other words, although a weak case for neo-classical models can be made in aggregate growth theory there is no case at all in regional analysis."[8]

The application of the neo-classical model to the problem of regional growth has been carried out chiefly by Borts and Stein. Let us consider the general production function for region i as

$$Y_i = f_i (K_i, L_i) \qquad (14)$$

where Y_i, K_i, L_i are income, capital, and labour of region i respectively. It is assumed in the theory that equation (14) is a linear homogeneous production function. In such a case, Euler's theorem yields

$$Y_i = L_i \frac{\partial Y_i}{\partial L_i} + K_i \frac{\partial Y_i}{\partial K_i} \tag{15}$$

which states that the total product is absolutely exhausted by capital and labour. Equation (15) can be written as

$$1 = \left[\frac{L_i}{Y_i} \cdot \frac{\partial Y_i}{\partial L_i}\right] + \left[\frac{K_i}{Y_i} \cdot \frac{\partial Y_i}{\partial K_i}\right] \tag{16}$$

If a_i denotes capital's share in regional output,

$$a_i = \frac{K_i}{Y_i} \cdot \frac{\partial Y_i}{\partial K_i}$$

and from equation (16) the share of labour

$$\frac{L_i}{Y_i} \cdot \frac{\partial Y_i}{\partial L_i} = 1 - a_i$$

Therefore if y_i, k_i, and l_i denote the rate of growth of output, capital, and labour, we can write

$$y_i = a_i\, k_i + (1-a_i)\, l_i$$

To take account of technical progress, which can also lead to increase in output, let us write the rate of growth of output as

$$y_i = a_i\, k_i + (1-a_i)\, l_i + t_i \tag{17}$$

where t_i denotes technical progress in region i.

The neo-classical model requires full capacity growth, and therefore a mechanism to equate investment with full employment savings. This mechanism is the rate of interest r. In the condition of an equilibrium, this rate of interest should be equal to the rate of profit which is assumed to be equal to the marginal product of capital MPK_i. The condition of steady growth requires that

$$MPK_i = a_i \frac{Y_i}{K_i} = r \tag{18}$$

If r is given, Y_i and K_i must grow at the same rate if a is to remain constant. Since the rate of growth of Y_i and K_i are designated by y_i and k_i, the condition for equilibrium can be written as $y_i = k_i$. Substituting y_i for k_i in equation (17), we get

$$y_i = \frac{t_i}{1 - a_i} + l_i \tag{19}$$

for the steady growth in the country as a whole $[t_i/(1-a_i)+l_i]$ must be the same for all i, i.e., equal in all the regions. If the rate of technical progress t_i and the rate of population growth l_i remain constant, y_i in equation (19) will vary according to variations in a_i. If a_i increases, the right hand side as a whole increases, i.e., y_i will also increase. If a_i decreases, y_i will decrease. This shows the importance of the capital-output ratio in the neo-classical model.

However, the main contribution of the neo-classical theory is its assurance of convergence in regional per capita incomes. But this result requires highly restrictive assumptions. Thus, we have to assume full employment, perfect competition, one homogeneous commodity, zero transportation costs, a fixed supply of labour and no technical progress, identical production functions in all regions of the form $Y = f(K, L)$ and subject to constant returns to scale. Under these restrictive assumptions, the marginal product of labour will equal the wage while the marginal product of capital will equal the return to capital. Also the marginal product of labour or the wage will be a direct function of capital-labour ratio and the return to capital will be an inverse function of capital-labour ratio. Now, since we have assumed that each region produces a homogeneous commodity with identical production functions, the region with the higher capital-labour ratio will have a higher real wage and a lower marginal product of capital. Similarly, the region with a higher capital-labour ratio will have a lower real wage and a higher marginal product of capital. This is not a position of equilibrium. For equilibrium, labour will flow from low- to high-wage regions and capital will flow from high- to low-wage regions (since regions with a lower real wage have a higher marginal product of capital). These flows continue until the factor returns are equalized in all regions and, thus, the process of regional growth will be accompanied by a *convergence in regional per capita incomes.*

THE INPUT-OUTPUT ANALYSIS

The Input-Output Analysis was evolved by Leontief as a method of determining inter-dependence among the various sectors of the economy. Leontief assumes that the economy consists of a number of interacting industries. Each industry produces a single good and uses only one process of production. To produce its good, that industry needs as inputs goods made by other industries and labour. Each industry must produce enough to supply the needs of other industries and to meet the external (exogenous or net) demand. The word 'inter-dependence' or 'interaction' is used to convey the idea that each industry employs the output of other industries as inputs while its output is used by other industries as an input. Leontief's analysis deals with only production and does not consider demand. Therefore, the demand theory plays no role in the input-output model.

To understand the basic elements of the model, let us suppose that there is an over-simplified economy consisting of only two industries—agriculture and manufacturing. Each industry requires some amount of a primary factor called labour and some amount of the output of the other (as well as of its own output) as input. Let us suppose that the data are as given in Table 1.

TABLE 1: Input-output data

Industries	Inputs to agriculture	Inputs to manufacturing	Final demand	Total output
(1)	(2)	(3)	(4)	(5)
Agriculture	25	175	50	250
Manufacturing	40	20	60	120
Labour Services	10	40	—	50

The total output in the agriculture industry is 250 units (say, million of tons) per year. Of this output, 175 units are used by the manufacturing industry to produce 120 units of output, while 25 units are used up in agriculture itself (as input). As is clear from col. 4 of Table 1, only 50 units are available for final consumption. Similarly, of the total output of 120 units of the manufacturing industry, 40 units are used in agriculture as inputs, 20 units are used by the manufacturing industry itself as inputs, and the remaining 60 units are available for final consumption. Col. 2 of Table 1 presents the input structure or the cost structure of agriculture. It shows that the 250 units of agricultural output are produced by using 25 units of agricultural goods, 40 units of manufactured goods, and 10 units of labour. This can be summarized in the form of a production function thus

$$250 = f(25, 40, 10).$$

Col. 3 of Table 1 presents the input structure of the manufacturing industry and the production function is given by

$$120 = f(175, 20, 40).$$

Keeping the two-industry model intact, Table 1 can be converted into Table 2 where X_1 is the total output of industry *A* and X_2 is the total output of industry *B*.

Of the total output of X_1 units of industry *A*, X_{11} units are used up by industry *A* itself as input while X_{12} units are used up by industry *B*. This leaves Y_1 units for final consumption. Thus, we have the equation

$$x_{11}+x_{12}+Y_1 = X_1.$$

Similarly, for industry *B*, we have the equation

$$x_{21}+x_{22}+Y_2 = X_2.$$

For labour, we have

$$x_{01}+x_{02} = X_0.$$

The Concept of Technical Coefficients

The units of output of industry *i* used as inputs for the production of 1 unit of output of industry *j* are known as technical coefficients (a_{ij}). Thus,

$$a_{ij} = \frac{x_{ij}}{X_j}.$$

For Table 2, the technical coefficients are a_{11}, a_{12}, a_{21}, a_{22}, a_{01}, and a_{02} and are given by x_{11}/X_1, x_{12}/X_2, x_{21}/X_1, x_{22}/X_2, x_{01}/X_1, and x_{02}/X_2, respectively.

TABLE 2: Total input-output of two industries

Industry	Inputs to industry *A*	Inputs to industry *B*	Final Demand	Total output
(1)	(2)	(3)	(4)	(5)
Industry *A*	x_{11}	x_{12}	Y_1	X_1
Industry *B*	x_{21}	x_{22}	Y_2	X_2
Labour Services	x_{01}	x_{02}	—	X_0

Thus, the equations given above for industry *A*, industry *B*, and labour can be converted to the form

$$a_{11}X_1+a_{12}X_2+Y_1 = X_1$$

$$a_{21}X_1+a_{22}X_2+Y_2 = X_2$$

and

$$a_{01}X_1+a_{02}X_2 = X_0$$

These equations can be expressed as

$$(1-a_{11})X_1-a_{12}X_2 = Y_1$$

$$-a_{21}X_1+(1-a_{22})X_2 = Y_2$$

and

$$a_{01}X_1+a_{02}X_2 = X_0$$

For the Leontief's system to be viable, it is necessary that the following conditions for the two-industry model are satisfied:

$$1-a_{11}>0,\ 1-a_{22}>0 \qquad \text{(i)}$$

and

$$(1-a_{11})(1-a_{22})-a_{12}a_{21}>0 \qquad \text{(ii)}$$

The system of inequalities (i) merely states that a_{11} and a_{22} should each be less than unity. A moment's reflection shows that a_{11} and a_{22} cannot be greater than unity, for that would imply that 1 unit of a commodity is being produced by using more than one unit of the same commodity as input—a possibility which shows that production is not viable. Inequality (ii) further assures that if the direct and the indirect inputs of a commodity, say coal, that go to produce 1 tonne of coal (the coal to make coal, the coal to make steel to make coal, the coal to make steel to make steel to make coal, etc.) are added up, the total will be less than 1 tonne.

Conditions (i) and (ii) are known as the *Hawkins-Simon conditions*.

The General Input-Output Table can be given as Table 3.

TABLE 3: **General input-output table**

Industry	Inputs to industry 1	Inputs to industry 2	...	Inputs to industry n	Final demand	Total output
Industry 1	x_{11}	x_{12}	...	x_{1n}	Y_1	X_1
Industry 2	x_{21}	x_{22}	...	x_{2n}	Y_2	X_2
Industry 3	x_{31}	x_{32}	...	x_{3n}	Y_3	X_3
.	.	.	.	.	.	.
.	.	.	.	.	.	.
.	.	.	.	.	.	.
Industry n	x_{n1}	x_{n2}	...	x_{nn}	Y_n	X_n

As before, the system of equations is

$$
\begin{array}{l}
x_{11} + x_{12} + \ldots + x_{1n} + Y_1 = X_1 \\
x_{21} + x_{22} + \ldots + x_{2n} + Y_2 = X_2 \\
\cdot \quad \cdot \quad \cdots \quad \cdot \quad \cdot \quad \cdot \\
\cdot \quad \cdot \quad \cdots \quad \cdot \quad \cdot \quad \cdot \\
x_{n1} + x_{n2} + \ldots + x_{nn} + Y_n = X_n
\end{array}
$$

This system of equations can be written as

$$\sum_{j=1}^{n} x_{ij} + Y_i = X_i \qquad (i = 1, 2, \ldots, n)$$

This shows that the total output of a given production sector is the sum of the flows to other production sectors plus the flow to final demand. In terms of technical coefficients, the system of equations can be expressed as

$$\left.\begin{array}{llll}(1 - a_{11}X_1) - a_{12}X_2 - a_{13}X_3 - & \ldots & - a_{1n}X_n = Y_1 \\ -a_{21}X_1 + (1 - a_{22})X_2 - a_{23}X_3 - & \ldots & - a_{2n}X_n = Y_2 \\ \cdot\ \cdot\ \cdot\ \cdot\ \cdot\ \cdot\ \cdot & \ldots & \cdot\ \cdot\ \cdot \\ -a_{i1}X_1 - a_{i2}X_2 - a_{i3}X_3 - & \ldots & - a_{in}X_n = Y_i \\ \cdot\ \cdot\ \cdot\ \cdot\ \cdot\ \cdot & \ldots & \cdot\ \cdot\ \cdot \\ -a_{n1}X_1 - a_{n2}X_2 - a_{n3}X_3 - & \ldots & + (1-a_{nn})X_n = Y_n \end{array}\right] \quad (20)$$

This system of equations can be solved with the help of the Cramer's rule. In matrix notation, the system of eq. (20) can be written as:

$$\begin{bmatrix} (1 - a_{11}) & -a_{12} & -a_{13} & \ldots & -a_{1n} \\ -a_{21} & (1 - a_{22}) & -a_{23} & \ldots & -a_{2n} \\ \cdot & \cdot & \cdot & \ldots & \cdot \\ \cdot & \cdot & \cdot & \ldots & \cdot \\ \cdot & \cdot & \cdot & \ldots & \cdot \\ -a_{i1} & -a_{i2} & -a_{i3} & \ldots & -a_{in} \\ \cdot & \cdot & \cdot & \ldots & \cdot \\ \cdot & \cdot & \cdot & \ldots & \cdot \\ \cdot & \cdot & \cdot & \ldots & \cdot \\ -a_{n1} & -a_{n2} & -a_{n3} & & (1-a_{nn}) \end{bmatrix} \begin{bmatrix} X_1 \\ X_2 \\ \cdot \\ \cdot \\ \cdot \\ X_i \\ \cdot \\ \cdot \\ \cdot \\ X_n \end{bmatrix} = \begin{bmatrix} Y_1 \\ Y_2 \\ \cdot \\ \cdot \\ \cdot \\ Y_i \\ \cdot \\ \cdot \\ \cdot \\ Y_n \end{bmatrix}$$

In summary form this is written as

$$(I - A)X = Y \quad (21)$$

If the inverse of $(I - A)$ exists, equation (21) can be written as

$$X = (I - A)^{-1} Y \quad (22)$$

Denoting the element of $(I - A)^{-1}$ by α_{ij}, we get

$$X_i = \sum_{j=1}^{n} \alpha_{ij} Y_j \qquad (i = 1, 2, \ldots, n) \quad (22a)$$

This gives the values of the total outputs. Thus, a knowledge of the final demands and the technical coefficients enables us to estimate the total required output of different industries.

Input-Output Analysis in Regional Framework

In the regional context, it becomes necessary to identify the regions. In this case, X_i becomes ${}_rX_i$, which represents the total output X, of industry i, in *region r*. If ${}_{rs}x_{ik}$ represents the flow from industry i in region r to industry k in region s, then the inter-regional model takes the form

$$ {}_rX_i - \sum_{s=1}^{m} \sum_{k=1}^{n} {}_{rs}x_{ik} = {}_rY_i \tag{23}$$

where $i = 1, 2, \ldots, n$, and $r, s = 1, 2, \ldots, m$ the number of regions.

Here ${}_rY_i$ represents the final demand for the products of industry i in region r.

The production coefficients are given as,

$$ \frac{{}_{rs}x_{ik}}{{}_rX_i} = {}_{rs}a_{ik} \tag{24}$$

This states that the inputs from industry i in region r to industry k in region s are some proportion of the total production (X) of good k in region s.

Equation (24) gives

$$ {}_{rs}x_{ik} = {}_rX_i \cdot {}_{rs}a_{ik} $$

Substituting this value in eq. (23), we get

$$ {}_rX_i - \sum_{s=1}^{m} \sum_{k=1}^{n} \left[{}_rX_i \cdot {}_{rs}a_{ik} \right] = {}_rY_i $$

This system of equations can be solved as equation (22) and the values of the total outputs obtained.

The regional input-output analysis is basically of the following three types: (1) local impact studies; (2) regional balance of payments studies; and (3) inter-regional flow studies. The regional impact analysis seeks to examine the impact of a new industry located in a given area on the *total* change in the level of economic activity. One method of studying the total impact is through the interrelations of an input-output matrix. The regional balance of payments studies based on input-output techniques try to *quantify* the relation of a region to the rest of the economy. The inter-regional flow studies seek to examine, in a quantifiable way, the structural relationships between regions.[9]

Limitations of Regional Input-Output Models

Despite the important interrelationships that the regional input-output studies can reveal, not much empirical research has been done in this direction. This is basically because of the fact that regional input-output studies require regional accounting data and also inter-regional and inter-industry flow estimates. Very limited data are available in these fields to make the use of such models feasible. In many underdeveloped countries such data are practically non-existent. Even where the regional input-output models have been used, they are open to serious criticism. As noted by Tiebout,[10] on account of operational necessity it has become necessary to use the national technical coefficients as regional technical coefficients. That is to say, "the production functions for various industries are assumed to be uniform throughout the whole country"—a very difficult assumption to accept especially in a country such as India. Then, the regional coefficients "not only specify the amount of needed inputs per unit of output, but they also specify the regional source. This source is assumed to be a constant proportion of total output, i.e., trading patterns are assumed to be stable."[11] As facts stand, it is unjustified to expect the trading patterns to exhibit stability.

In addition to these criticisms, the regional input-output models are subject to the customary criticisms levied against the national input-output analysis. Under the Leontief scheme, it becomes necessary to aggregate a large number of commodities into a relatively few outputs. For theoretical purposes there is nothing wrong in this practice, but in practical application it becomes necessary to lump together many separate activities into one sector. Also, as noted elsewhere in this section, the input-output model ignores the demand sector altogether. The usual economic assumptions of profit maximization, consumer utility maximization, optimal resource allocation, etc., do not find any place in the model. Everything is governed by "the dictates of productive necessity: each output requires its inputs and that is all there is to it."[12] The assumption of constant and linear production function solves all kinds of problems, e.g., it gets rid of factor substitution and economies of scale. But, in the process, numerous other problems are created. "Time is missing, yet the purchase of inputs by one industry to make goods to sell to other industries implies a period analysis. Assuming away substitution may simplify matters, but it leads to a sharp difference between input-output and most other conventional economic models. Moreover, the notion of a linear production function is not very meaningful in many non-industrial sectors such as agriculture, trade, service industries and the government sector. The model is starkly simple."[13]

Yet, all said and done, the regional input-output analysis is immensely useful in studying the *clusters* of industries and the linkage processes between them. It must be said to the credit of this model that in cases where it was used, it proved quite successful in unfolding the interactions and inter-relationships among industries and predicted reasonably well. Some of its assumptions are not all that serious as they seem to be. Thus, money values can be used as a measure of physical prices (to bring price considerations into account) and since, after all, the pace of technological change is slow, we can assume the input coefficient matrix of a given year to hold in the preceding and the succeeding years.[14]

Applications in Indian Context

The non-availability of sufficient regional data on inter-industry flows acts as a severe constraint on regional input-output studies. This constraint perhaps accounts for the limited work done in this field in India. However, in recent years, as the utility of the input-output model in understanding technological linkages, agglomeration economies, industrial clusters, etc., is being increasingly recognized, some studies (in spite of the data limitations) have been conducted. The first systematic attempt in this direction was carried out on the economy of Punjab by G.S. Bhalla using a 17-sector input-output table of Punjab for 1959.[15] A 20-sector input-output model of the industrial part of Gujarat was prepared by Yoginder Alagh and S.P. Kashap to examine the relationship between the industrial and the primary sectors of the regional economy and another model (which was a 24-sector model) was prepared for forecasting purposes.[16] An open, static three-region 18-sector model of the Indian economy was developed by Ranajit Dhar, Robert Venning, and Brian J.L. Berry.[17] The basis of this study was Ranajit Dhar's "Inter-regional Input-Output Analysis : A Study of the Interregional Intersectoral Relations of the Indian Economy, 1953-54." On the basis of the same data for 1953-54, Ranajit Dhar conducted another study, "Implications of Income Leakages in a Multi-Regional Frame.[18]" In this study, agriculture and allied activities, small-scale manufactures, and services emerged as local commodities whose growth "may be left entirely to the regional authorities". The eastern and the north-eastern regions had negligible income leakages in the iron and steel setor and accordingly ranked high in locational choice. In another study, Dhar [19] examined the nature of spatial clusters of the Indian economy and found that clusters in the various regions were not always uniform and were guided by the resource endowments, various types of demands, and such other factors. The sectors of agriculture and allied activities and other food processing industries were found to form regional clusters in four out of five cases and an inter-regional cluster only in one case. The sectors of cement and others (which constituted mainly construction activities), jointly formed regional clusters in all the cases, while the sectors of iron and steel and machinery formed inter-regional clusters.

The most comprehensive and immensely useful study (in both coverage and content) was carried out by Yoginder Alagh (and associates) to understand the regional pattern of Indian industrialization. This study throws significant light on inter-industry regional distribution, technological linkages, spatial clusters of industries, agglomeration tendencies, etc.[20] On account of these reasons, we intend discussing the results of this study in some detail. However, before we do so we must explain the theory of industrial location because Alagh's study also used concepts such as location quotient, agglomeration economies, etc., which belong to the field of industrial location. In addition to this, Alagh's study was basically meant to explain the locational pattern of Indian industries.

THEORIES OF INDUSTRIAL LOCATION AND SPATIAL DEVELOPMENT

The theory of industrial location attempts to explain why the industries are located where they are, why the locations are shifted, and what can be the best location for a particular industry keeping in view the resource endowments of different regions, transport network, existing demand, potential demand, etc. It is a field of study that interests both economists and geographers, because the location of industries is of particular importance in studying the internal structure of regions and, in many cases, guides the pattern of spatial development. The different approaches to the industrial location theory can be classified in either of the three following categories:

(a) those which emphasize cost factors
(b) those which emphasize demand
(c) those which are concerned with locational interdependence.

The first attempt in developing a theory of location emphasizing cost factors was made by a German scholar, Von Thunen, in regard to agricultural location. In his book *The Isolated State* (1826), Thunen considered the problem of location of various forms of agricultural production in relation to markets. For this purpose he imagined first an isolated state which had the following three characteristics: (1) A very large town was situated in the middle of a fertile plain which had neither canals nor navigable rivers, (2) At a considerable distance, the plain ended in an uncultivated wilderness; and (3) The town drew its produce from the plain, to which it supplied the manufactured products.

The question that Von Thunen asked was: "How will the agriculture of the plain be arranged in such circumstances"? The general answer of Thunen to this question was that cultivation would be arranged in a series of concentric circles round the town, according to the cost of transportation of the commodity and the ratio in which its value stood to its bulk and weight. A series of concentric rings would tend to grow up around the city and a specific pattern of land-use would dominate within each ring. In the ring closest to the city those items that could bear transportation least of all, or on which transportation charges would be out of proportion to the market price, would be produced. Green vegetables, horticulture, and dairy farming could be placed in this category. Other forms of cultivation would be arranged in concentric circles around the town in accordance with (i) the price of their products, and (ii) the cost of transportation.

The first comprehensive effort at developing a theory of location (and especially a theory of industrial location) was made by Alfred Weber in 1909 in his book *Theory of the Location of Industries.* Weber emphasized the cost factors. He assumed competitive pricing, i.e. a situation where individual firms were powerless to influence the price of their product which was the same everywhere. Therefore, to achieve the maximum profit, they had to minimize cost. It follows that a rational producer would choose a location where lowest costs were incurred. This is the reason why Weber's approach is known as *the least cost approach* to the theory of Industrial Location. On the basis of the costs of production, Weber arrives at three general regional factors of location, namely, the relative price range of deposits of materials, the costs of labour, and the costs of transportation. By assuming that the influence of material costs can be reduced to that of transportation costs (since costlier materials can be regarded as of more distant origin); only two regional factors, namely, transportation costs and labour costs remain. These can be termed as the primary causes of the regional distribution of industry (regional factors). To these causes could be added the secondary causes of a redistribution of industry; these are agglomerating and deglomerating factors and are themselves the effects of the primary regional factors.[21] Agglomeration refers to an advantage or cheapening of production due to the concentration of industry. Here the reference is mainly to external economies. The opposite tendency of deglomeration leads to a cheapening of production due to decentralisation. This is essentially caused by a rise in land value as a result of concentration.

Let us consider the influence of transportation costs, labour costs, and agglomeration and deglomeration separately. Weber divides all raw materials into two groups, namely, "ubiquities" and "localized materials". Ubiquities are those materials that are available everywhere, e.g. brick, sand, water, etc. Since they are available everywhere, they have very little influence on location. Localized materials are those materials that are available in certain specific regions only and therefore exert an important influence on location, e.g., iron, coal, etc.

Weber first shows the impact of transportation costs on location and then demonstrates how labour costs and agglomeration and deglomeration may change the situation. Assuming that transport costs are directly proportional to the distance covered and weight carried, Weber gives his famous locational triangle as shown below:

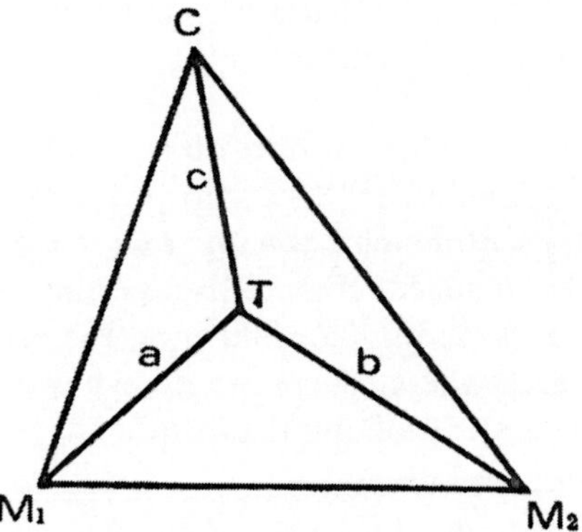

Figure 1: Weber's locational triangle.

M_1 and M_2 are two material sources and C the consumption centre. The entire weight of the material from M_1 has to traverse a distance '*a*' and the material from M_2 a distance '*b*' to reach the point of location *T*. The weight of the product has to move a distance '*c*' to reach the consumption point. Obviously, then, the weights represent the force with which the corners of the locational figures draw the location towards themselves.[22] To determine where the location will actually lie, Weber calculates the ratio between the weight of localized material and the weight of the product. This he designates as the *material index*. If the index is less than one, the location is oriented towards the consumption centre while if the index is greater than one, the location is material-oriented. If the two raw materials at M_1 and M_2 are $\frac{3}{4}$ tonne and $\frac{1}{2}$ tonne respectively, and they combine to produce a product of 1 tonne consumed at C, the optimum location will be nearer to C than to M_1 or M_2 and nearer to M_1 than to M_2.

What is the influence of labour costs and how can they vary the location determined by considering transportation costs alone? Obviously, "every change of location away from the point of minimum transportation costs to a favourable labour location means, in terms of transportation, a 'deviation' which lengthens the transportation routes and raises transportation costs above those prevailing under the most advantageous conditions. The changes of location can therefore take place only if the rise of cost per ton of product which it causes is compensated, or more than compensated, by savings of labour costs. A location can be moved from the point of minimum transportation costs to a more favourable lobour location only if *the savings in the cost of labour which this new place makes possible are larger than the additional costs of transportation which it involves*".[23] This is illustrated in Fig. 2.

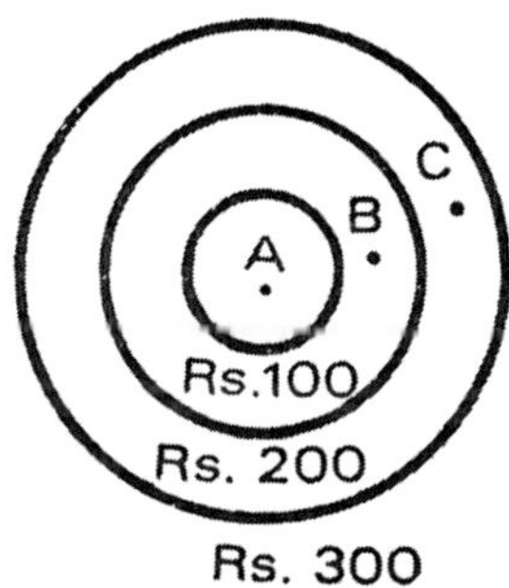

Figure 2: Influence of labour costs on location determination.

Point A is the minimum transport point and is surrounded by a series of *isodapanes*, lines of equal transport costs per tonne from A. In Fig. 2, isodapanes have been drawn at intervals of Rs.100. Let there be an alternative location where a saving of Rs.200 per tonne can be made in the cost of labour. Naturally, if this location is on the Rs.200 isodapane, the saving in labour costs will exactly balance the extra transportation costs. The Rs.200 isodapane will than be the *critical isodapane*. If the point of minimum labour cost lies outside of it (at point C) the location will stay at A, but if that point lies within it (at point B), the location will be shifted from point A to point B since, in the latter case, the saving in labour costs will exceed the extra transportation costs that will have to be incurred in shifting from the point of minimum transport cost A. The general conclusion that would emerge from this discussion is that "when labour costs are varied, an industry deviates from its transport location in proportion to the size of its labour coefficient" where the labour coefficient is the ratio of the labour cost per unit of product (at existing locations) to the 'locational weight' of that unit. The locational weight here would be equal to the sum of the required weight of localized raw materials plus product (excluding ubiquities). Other things remaining the same, a higher labour coefficient will imply greater labour cost savings in case the industry shifts to cheap labour area abandoning the minimum transport site.

The third factor considered by Weber is agglomeration. It is possible that because of concentration of industries at a specific point in space, the cheapening of production achieved compensates for the diversion of location away from either the point of least transportation cost or the point of least labour cost. The actual behaviour of industries will depend on the index of value added through manufacture. If we relate this index of value to the weight to be transported we get the 'coefficient of manufacture'. Whenever it is high, an industry has a tendency to agglomerate[24]

P. Sargant Florence introduced two new concepts in the theory of location, namely, "Location Factor" and "Coefficient of Localization." The coefficient of localization measures the degree of geographical concentration of a given industry. Judging the extent of the industrial activity by labour inputs, the formula for the coefficient of localization (C) can be written as follows:

$$C = \tfrac{1}{2} \sum_{j=1}^{N} | r_i - R_i |$$

where

$$r = \left[(a_i / \sum_{i=1}^{N} a_i) \right] \text{ for region } i.$$

a_i = labour in a given industry.

$$R_i = \left[A_i / \sum_{i=1}^{N} A_i \right] \text{ for region } i.$$

where

A_i = all industrial labour
N = total number of regions in the country.

The value of C varies from 0 to 1 and the relative magnitude of C characterizes the dispersal or localized nature of a given industry. The extent of industrial activity can, however, be measured by variables such as the value of output or the value of basic material input instead of the value of labour input.[25]

The location factor is an index of the degree of concentration of an industry in a given region and is given by the following formula:

$$P_i = d_i/D$$

where

$d_i = a_i/A_i$

$$D = \left[\sum_{i=1}^{N} a_i\right] \Big/ \left[\sum_{i=1}^{N} A_i\right]$$

a_i = labour input of a particular industry in region i.

A_i = all industrial labour (sometimes, all labour or total population) in region i.

If the location factor is unity, the industry is evenly distributed over the whole country because the proportion of the total industrial workers engaged in industry i in the region would be equal to the proportion of the total industrial workers engaged in the same industry in the country as a whole. If the location quotient is greater than one, the region has a higher share of the industry compared with the country as a whole and if it is less than one, the region has a lower share than the country as a whole. If A_i is the geographical area of region i, the formula becomes *absolute location factor*, say Q_i (P_i is the *relative location factor*).

M.N. Pal has suggested a method to consider both the absolute and the relative location factors together. As would have been clear from the above, the absolute location factor is proportional to the density of a given industrial labour per unit area and the relative location factor is proportional to the proportion of all industrial labour in the given industry. Since ranking of areas by density and proportion variables is likely to be different, there is a need for adopting a composite index wherein both the variables can be considered together. Pal has devised such a composite index. In his own words, "This combined index is characterised by its equal coefficient of correlation with both density and proportion variables. This coefficient of correlation is greater when the correlation between the variables is higher. By logarithmic or other suitable transformation of the variables, their correlation is often improved which is desirable for improving the combined index of the variables. Usually a logarithmically transformed density variable gives a distribution somewhat similar to that of the proportion variable; this results into an improved correlation between the variables".[26] If the density and proportion variables in their transformed form are denoted by Q and P and the combined index by I, the formula for I is given by Pal as

$$I_i = \frac{S(P)}{S(Q)E(P)+S(P)E(Q)}\,Q_i + \frac{S(Q)}{S(Q)E(P)+S(P)E(Q)}\,P_i \qquad (25)$$

where

$$E(Q) = \text{average value of } Q_i\text{'s} = \frac{1}{N}\sum_{i=1}^{N} Q_i$$

$$E(P) = \text{average value of } P_i\text{'s} = \frac{1}{N}\sum_{i=1}^{N} P_i$$

$$S(Q) = \text{standard deviation of } Q_i\text{'s} = \sqrt{\frac{1}{N}\sum_{i=1}^{N}[Q_i - E(Q)]^2}$$

$$S(P) = \text{standard deviation of } P_i\text{'s} = \sqrt{\frac{1}{N}\sum_{i=1}^{N}[P_i - E(P_i)]^2}$$

and the summation $\sum_{i=1}^{N}$ represents the summation over all N regions of the country.

The average value of I for the country is unity. The core areas of industrial activity will have a value of I considerably greater than unity. A mapping of I can show the areas of high concentration of the industrial activity.

Pal has used this method in his pioneering macro-regional study of southern India and for studying the concentration of industrial labour with reference to Indian districts as regions (or as areal units, as Pal prefers to call them).[27] For example, in the study of concentration of industrial labour, the density variable is taken to be the 'density of industrial labour per square mile' and the proportion variable is the 'number of industrial labour per thousand total labour'. Since the distributions of these variables were skewed a logarithmic transformation was carried out. The transformed variables Q and P are then given by

$$Q = \log_{10}(1+u) \text{ and } P = \log_{10}(1+v)$$

where *u* is the initial density variable and *v* the proportion variable.

The composite index was then computed, using equation (25), to be

$$I = 0.2077\,Q + 0.3771\,P.$$

The value of correlation coefficient of *I* with either *Q* or *P* was found to be as high as 0.909. The advantages of using such a composite index of *Q* and *P* for identifying concentration of industrial labour are explained by Pal as follows: "For example, in hilly and desert or dry areas where population density has been low, such as in the districts of Jaisalmer and Bikaner of Rajasthan, or in Kutch district of Gujarat, or in the districts of Lahul and Spiti, and Kinnaur in Himachal Pradesh, the proportion variable shows extremely high or very high levels of concentration, whereas the density variable shows extremely low or very low level of concentration of industrial labour. In other words, if judged by proportion variable alone, these districts are comparable with certain metropolitan districts like Calcutta, Bombay, Madras or Delhi in regard to the concentration of industrial labour, but that will be most unrealistic since it ignores the absolute level of areal concentration. Here the index *I* certainly gives an aggregate rank of the area which appears to be more realistic in relation to that of other areas."[28]

Consideration of Demand in the Theory of Location

The least cost approach ignores the fact that the demand can serve an important role in determining the location of industry. August Losch criticizes the main protagonist of this approach, Weber, for omitting the demand considerations in these terms: "Weber's solution for the problem of location proves to be incorrect as soon as not only cost but also sales possibilities are considered. His fundamental error consists in seeking the place of lowest cost. This is as absurd as to consider the point of largest sales as the proper location. Every such one-sided orientation is wrong. Only search for the place of greatest profit is right."[29] However, Losch's own theory is no less one-sided. He tried to incorporate demand by considering the size of the market and maintained that the best location would be that which would command the largest market area since this would bring in the highest sales revenue. But in making the theory into one of 'profit maximization', he tended to neglect supply almost to the extent that Weber had neglected demand.

Losch assumes an *isotropic plane*, that is a homogeneous land surface with an evenly distributed population of self-sufficient farm households each having the same tastes and similar technical capabilities; in short, a surface from which all irregularities and non-economic factors have been abstracted. He further assumes identical production, identical demand curves for each buyer of each product, and that transportation costs are proportional to distance. In such a situation, the shape and size of the market area will depend on the price of the product and the rate of transportation cost.

To take an illustration, let us consider the example given by Losch. Suppose there is a farmer who produces beer over and above his requirements. If *OP* is the price at the brewery, which is at *P*, those living there will buy *PQ* bottles of bear. Farther away the price is higher by the amount of the freight, and the demand consequently shrinks. When the freight costs are *PF*, the total price rises to *OF* and the demand shrinks to zero. Thus, *PF* will be the "extreme sales radius" for beer. By rotaing the triangle *PQF* on *PQ* as an axis we obtain the demand cone in Fig. 3b, whose volume gives the total sales of the brewery at point *P* and thus denotes the *market area* of the brewery.

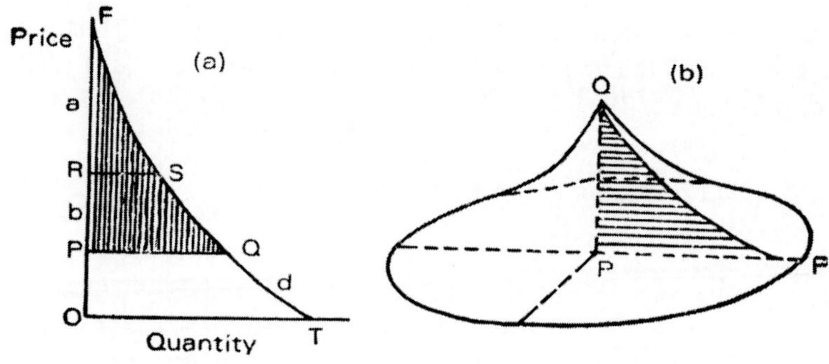

Figure 3a **Figure 3b**

Figure 3: Derivation of a Demand Cone (from A. Losch, *The Economics of Location*, Yale University Press, 1954).

It is possible that other farms may also produce surplus beer which they would like to sell in the market. As long as profits are made, new breweries will continue to be established, each brewery having a circular market area as in Fig. 4b. As the number of breweries increases the circular areas touch each other but even now the whole space is not covered. and some area remains unserved (Fig. 4c). The only possibility by which the total area can be covered is through overlapping circles (Fig. 4d). In the former case, firms will continue to be set up to serve the unserved market while in the latter, consumers in the shaded region will choose a centre that is nearest to them and leave others (we assume that the consumers are ratio-

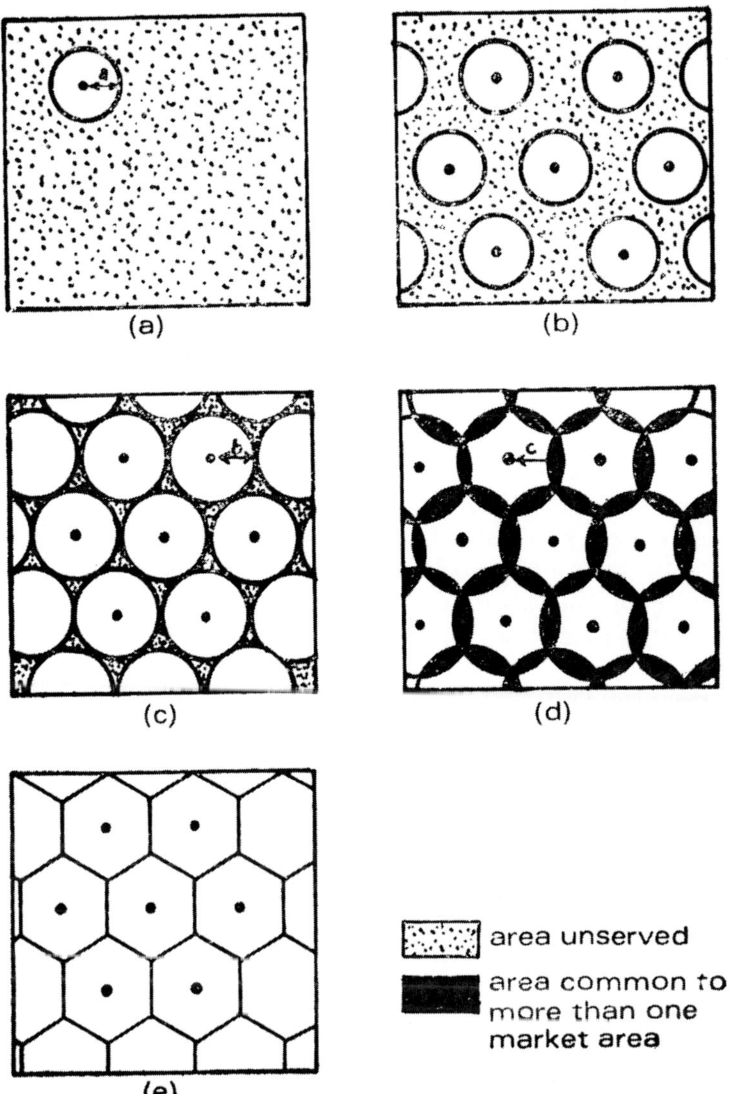

Figure 4: Areas unserved and areas common to more than one market area.

nal). Ultimately hexagons of the shape given in Fig. 4e are formed. The hexagonal form is the most efficient one since among all the possibilities of utilizing the corners, the hexagon retains most of the advantages of the circle.[30]

Each product will have a different network of market areas. When we consider different products each having its own network of market areas, we can see the emergence of an economic region or landscape. Since such a theory of spatial organization was first suggested by Walter Christaller while developing the theory of Central Places,[31] let us, at this juncture, turn to the central place theory before explaining the pattern of spatial organization.

The Theory of Central Places

From his study of *Central Places in Southern Germany* (1933), Christaller has discovered that there is some ordering principle governing the distribution of towns and cities, that is, settlements concerned with the provision of goods and services. Christaller proceeds to enunciate a 'general, purely deductive theory' claiming that his theory "could also be designated as the theory of location of urban trades and institutions" to be placed beside Von Thunen's theory of the location of agricultural production and the theory of location of industries developed by Alfred Weber.

A *central place* is defined as a settlement providing services for the population of its hinterland (known as complementary region), supplying it with central goods and services such as administrative, banking, and professional services, educational, leisure, and cultural facilities, as well as those of retail and wholesale trade.[32] Central places vary in importance. Depending upon the central functions performed by them and the population served, they can be classified as high order centres or low order centres. High order centres stock a wide array of goods and services and serve a large population; lower order centres stock a smaller range of goods and services and serve a smaller population.

Before we explain the emergence of central places let us explain three important concepts used in the theory: (i) Centrality, (ii) Threshold, and (iii) Range of a central good. The *centrality* of an urban centre is defined as the ratio between the services provided and the local needs of its inhabitants. However, no standard formulae are used to measure the centrality. Some of the measures adopted are: population size of the settlement, telephone calls weighted by telephone density, number of automobiles entering a city, business turnover of shops, number of central functions such as wholesale and retail stores, and professional services located in a settlement and *excess* of urban functions existing in a settlement *over* the normal. The *threshold* is the minimum sales volume needed to support a business. Below this level it will not be profitable to supply a good or a service. The *range of a central good* delineates the market area of a central good. It is the maximum distance that consumers are willing to travel (keeping in view the price of the good) to purchase the good. If we assume that travel is equally easy in all directions, the range of a central good will be a perfect circle round the central place.

The assumptions adopted by Christaller to explain his theory are: (i) the landscape is an even plain with an even distribution of natural resources and an even spread of population, producers, and consumers, and (ii) the movement in every direction is unimpeded and involves equal unit cost. Now let us assume a farmer selling his produce at point *A* in Fig. 4a. Other farmers are willing to travel distance '*a*' to purchase from this farmer. Since we have assumed that travel is equally easy in all directions, the market area for the farmer at *A* is given by the circle with radius '*a*'. In time more producers may develop their own separate market areas as shown in Fig. 4b. With the development of transportation and communications the market areas will expand and there will be an attempt to cover the maximum possible space. With circular market areas we can have a situation as in Fig. 4c or 4d. While in Fig. 4c there are several unserved areas (the shaded region in the figure), in Fig. 4d there is considerable overlapping. Neither of these instances gives a stable result. While in the former case the unserved areas will have to be split equally between neighbouring areas, in the latter consumers in the shaded region will tend to choose the nearest centre. Ultimately hexagonal market areas will emerge as given in Fig. 4e. It is only this hexagonal arrangement that ensures an efficient division of space between a number of central places.

Hierarchy of Central Places

Christaller's basic model is organized on the basis of what he calls the *marketing principle*. The hierarchy and nesting pattern in this case results in the maximum number of central places—a necessary condition if the supply of goods from the central places is to be as near as possible to the consumers (according to the requirement of movement minimization). Such a system is known as a $K=3$ network and is shown in Fig. 5. In this figure, the lowest order places (e.g., hamlets) are shown by filled circles; the next order places (e.g., villages) are shown by open circles; and the high order places (e.g., towns) are shown by double circles. Trade area boundaries of these three order settlements are indicated in the figure by solid lines, dashed lines, and double lines, respectively.

The *K*-value is the total number of settlements of a certain order served by a central place of the next higher order. As would be clear from Fig. 5, each hamlet is shared between three villages as shown by the arrows. Since a village has six hamlets at the corners of the hexagon surrounding it, each village serves $[(1/3)\times 6]=2$ hamlets. Adding to this the hamlet part of the functional structure of the village itself (which is obviously served by the village itself), each village serves the equivalent of 3 hamlets, i.e. $K=3$.

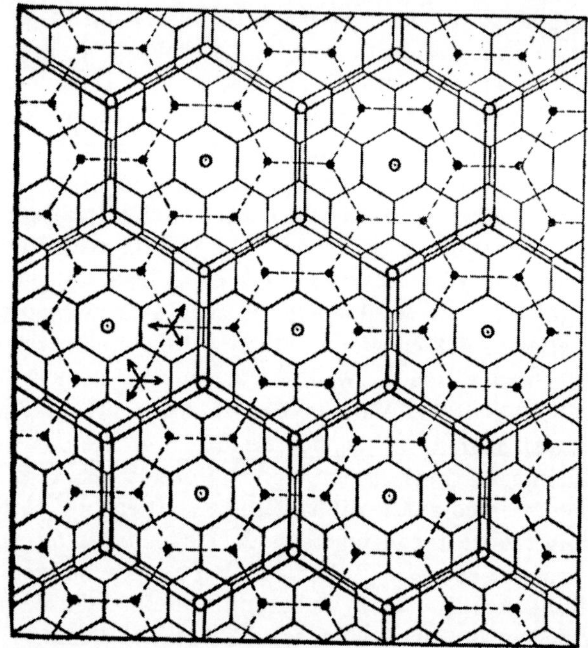

Figure 5: $K=3$ settlement pattern according to Christaller's marketing principle.

In a similar way it can be shown that a town serves three villages (and therefore nine hamlets). The central place of the next higher order (say, city) will serve 3 towns, i.e. 9 villages (3×3) or 27 hamlets (9×3). Thus, the number of centres at successively lower order levels in the hierarchy follows a geometric progression (i.e., 1, 3, 9, 27, etc.).

In addition to the principle of marketing Christaller proposes two other principles—the principle of transportation (or principle of traffic) and the principle of administration. The *principle of transportation* assumes importance in those cases where costs of transportation are significant. According to this principle, the distribution of central places is at an optimum when as many important places as possible lie on one traffic route between larger towns, the route being established in the cheapest possible manner. Thus, sub-centres lie along the routes between the main centres and we have an arrangement as given in Fig. 6. A hamlet is shared by two villages as represented by the arrows and since a village is surronded by six hamlets (each hamlet being situated midway between two corners of a hexagon and lying on the straight line connecting two villages), each village serves $(\frac{1}{2} \times 6) = 3$ hamlets. Adding to this, the hamlet part of the functional structure of the village itself, each village serves the equivalent of $(3+1)=4$ hamlets. Therefore $K=4$.

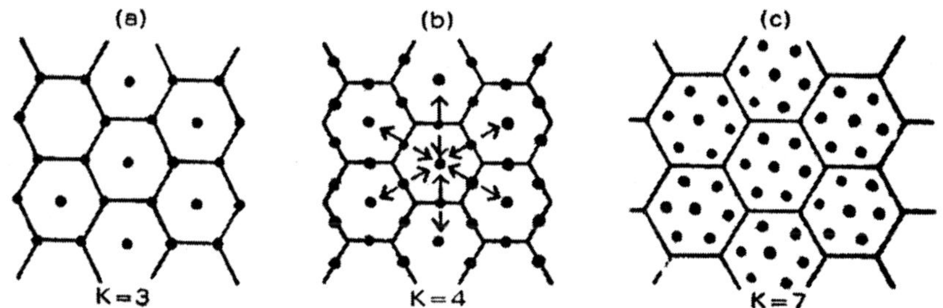

Figure 6: Christaller's model of hexagonal service areas.

The *administrative principle* is based upon the idea that each centre should have complete control of the six surrounding areas with no divided allegiance. Thus, in this case, sharing of the lower order centres between the higher order centres is not permitted. Therefore, $K=7$ (see Fig. 6c).

Refinements to Christaller : The Contribution of Losch

August Losch has put forward an elegant scheme to explain the structure of regions and spacing of settlements based upon Christaller's model of hexagonal service areas. He regards the K-value as being free to vary and, in his general case, Christaller's schemes of fixed K-values (3, 4, and 7) become only particular cases of a larger number of possible hexagonal systems. Thus, Losch has considerably elaborated and extended Christaller's scheme into a more complex model which is very close to the real world.

The market areas for different goods resemble nets of hexagons (as shown by Christaller). Let us lay them in such a way that all of them have at least one centre in common. Here a metropolis will arise, with all the advantages of a large local demand (see Fig. 7a).

By rotating the nets about this centre we can get six sectors with many and six with only a few production sites (see Fig. 7b). With this arrangement, according to Losch, (i) the greatest number of locations coincide, (ii) the maximum number of purchases can be made locally, (iii) the sum of the minimum distances between industrial locations is least, and (iv) not only shipments but also transport lines are reduced to the minimum.[33] Thus, six sectors can be identified with relatively many high order settlements (these can be described as 'city-rich' sectors) and six with relatively few high order settlements (these can be described as 'city-poor' sectors).

Walter Isard points out a serious deficiency in Losch's model: "It yields different sizes of concentrations of industrial activity and thus jobs at

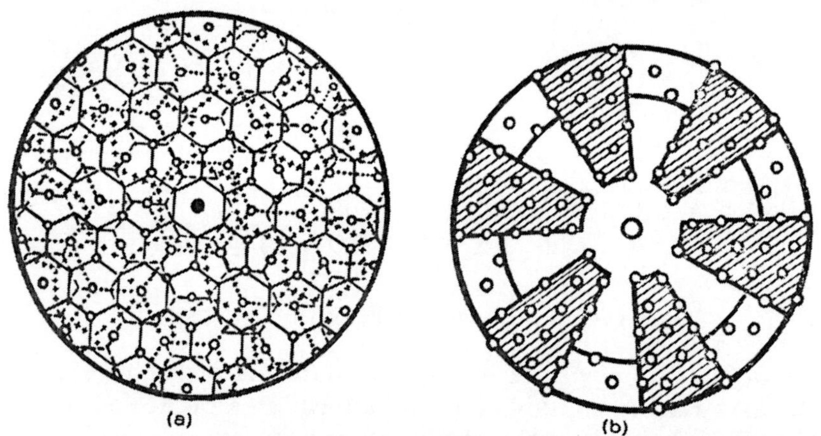

Figure 7: Losch's model of region and settlements (from August Losch, *The Economics of Location* (New Haven: Yale University Press, 1967), p. 125, figs. 28 and 29).

various production centres, and yet it postulates uniform distribution of consuming population."[34] To eliminate this inconsistency it would be necessary for the Losch diagram to exhibit "for each commodity greater concentrations of market areas and producers about the central city (the common production centre) in order to square with the central city's high level of industrial activity and large labouring population". To take account of this possibility, Isard gives a modified Losch system where a pattern of hexagons is presented in such a way that they decrease in size as one approaches the central city from any direction.[35]

Central Place Hierarchies : Illustration from Southern India

We have noted above how the central place theory tries to fit a hierarchy of linkages between localities on the basis of an assumption of regular hexagon market areas. Pal, however, feels that "this assumption seems to be inconsistent, more often for localities at the higher order of the hierarchy". He has accordingly evolved a procedure that establishes

> the hierarchical linkages among higher order localities (or central places) including metropolises, cities, towns and large villages, without the above mentioned regularity assumption, on the basis of following two consistent hypotheses:
>
> (i) people will try to move a route distance as minimum as possible for the satisfaction of their functional needs,

(ii) people of lower order central places will move to higher order central places only when the functional rank of higher central places is sufficiently higher as compared to that of lower order central places."[36]

A composite index *F* was constructed out of the *n* variables (say $y_1, y_2, \ldots, y_n$) measuring the extent of various central place functions.[37] This index was used by Pal to specify the spatial linkage pattern for southern India (having 797 towns and cities, all called central places) and the following nine variables were used to assess the concentration of functional activities: (i) number of factories and workshops, (ii) number of retail and wholesale shops, (iii) number of commercial and other offices, (iv) number of hotels and restaurants, (v) number of banks, (vi) number of schools, (vii) number of higher educational institutions, (viii) number of hospital beds, and (ix) urbanization 'index'.[38]

The following interesting facts have been revealed by the study:

1. Administrative set-up has wielded a more than proportionate share of influence in shaping the economic activities of the region (i.e. southern India). The metropolitan city of Bangalore and Mysore City act as strong centres:
2. A major functional region with Hyderabad as nucleus extends its influence over a wide region.
3. "The entire area in between the Deccan plateau and Bay of Bengal, stretching right from Nellore in the north down to the Kaveri delta in the south is dominated by the metropolitan centre of Madras."
4. A small but compact functional region with Madurai as nucleus has emerged in the southern end of Tamil Nadu (the functional hinterland extending over the districts of Madurai, Ramanathapuram, and Tirunelveli).
5. Coimbatore has emerged as an important centre with a strong industrial base and is extending its functional hinterland into Palghat, Nilgiris, and Madurai.
6. Functional activities to the west of the western ghats are organized around the four major cities of Trivandrum, Cochin, Kozhikode, and Mangalore. A small functional region with Dharwar as centre has extended its activities upto Belgaum.
7. On the east coast to the east of Vijayawada, "each of the third order centres, namely, Rajahmundry, Visakhapatnam, Kakinda and Vizianagram, exerts its influence independently over small adjoining areas around". The agro-industrial base of this strong agricultural region has not been able to create a 'well-integrated functional space' germinating

a strong nodal centre.

8. "The spatial integration force is still feebler in a major part of the Rayalaseema region where a good number of lower order centres remain scattered all over, almost in isolation." Functional force is not strong in the northern fringe area of the macro region. Even the strong metropolitan and industrial centre of Hyderabad has been unable to do much in this regard.[39]

Regional Pattern of Industrialization in India[40]

For the purpose of their study, Alagh (and associates) used disaggregated industry level data for 21 industry groups classified in the *Annual Survey of Industries* 1965. The search for industrial clusters was made from the 144-sector table of interindustry linkages made available by M.R. Saliya, of which 115 industrial sectors were utilized and classified into the following eleven blocks of interrelated industries: (1) Mechanical and Transport Equipment, (2) Electrical Equipment, (3) Metal Products, (4) Chemical-based, (5) Ferrous Metals, (6) Non-Ferrous Metals, (7) Non-Metallic Mineral-based, (8) Agro-based, (9) Textile-based, (10) Forest-based, and (11) Leather and Rubber. The objectives of the classification were (i) "to encompass the major technological interrelations from the input-output table within a group" and (ii) "to distinguish between resource based industry groups and those predominantly using the products of other industries as inputs". The industrial base of each region was defined, an industry being included in the industrial base of the region if its location quotient was equal to or greater than 0.75.

While estimating the industrial base of each region, industries were divided into two sets—resource-based and secondary industries, public sector being treated separately because of the autonomous nature of its investment and also because of its policy significance. Predominance of resource-based industries in the industrial base of a region would imply lack of regional industrial diversification and this category was "expected to account for a substantial part of the industrial base of the less developed States". The secondary industries were the industries using primarily the outputs of other industries as inputs and were expected to form part of the industrial base of more diversified States.

To highlight the spatial cluster of industries (as already illustrated above) the authors calculated location quotients and specialization coefficients in addition to the inputoutp-ut tables. The location quotient was defined as

$$l_{ik} = \frac{e_{ik}}{E_k} \Big/ \frac{E_i}{E}$$

where e_{ik} is the employment in industry i in region k ($i = 1, 2, \ldots, n$, $k = 1, 2, \ldots, m$), E_k the total industrial employment in region k ($E_k = \sum_{i=1}^{n} e_{ik}$), E_i is the employment in the industry i in all the regions ($E_i = \sum_{k=1}^{m} e_{ik}$), and E is the total employment in all regions. In case $l_{ik} > 1$, region k may be said to be specializing in industry i.

The other coefficient used was the specialization coefficient which was defined (for region k) as

$$S_k = \frac{\sum_{i=1}^{n} \frac{e_{ik}}{E_k} - \frac{E_i}{E} \; 100}{100}$$

If $S_k - 0$, region k has the same industrial mix as the national economy, and if $S_k = 1$, the region specializes in one industry only.[41]

Two types of industrial clusters were defined in the study: (i) empirical spatial clusters and (ii) technological clusters. "Empirical spatial clusters" would attempt to isolate the groups of industries 'which have in fact developed together in different regions of Indian economy'. Using techniques of clustering analysis, 102 industrial sectors of the Indian economy were estimated to fall into 18 such clusters of industries each of which displayed a tendency to cluster in space. "The equipment and engineering industries displayed a strong tendency to cluster in spatial units. In some cases equipment manufacturing and equipment using industries are found in spatial clusters. Agro-industries also emerge in spatial clusters." Technology clusters, on the other hand, isolated sets of industries which fell into relatively self-sufficient 'blocks of industries' where self-sufficiency was defined in terms of technological inter-linkages through input-purchase and output disposal. The technological structure of the Indian economy was shown to decompose into 12 blocks of relatively self-sufficient sets of industries.

Since the empirical spatial clusters of industries were found to be much smaller than the technological clusters of industries, it was concluded that *"in the regional context in India, full scale development of technologically interrelated industries has as yet not taken place, apart from in a few highly developed regions."*[42] Perhaps the most important conclusion from the point of view of future industrial development and spatial distribution of industries was that *"in the regional context in India, nascent complexes of interrelated industries have emerged"*. Such complexes "exist in almost every sector of the industrial economy, e.g. agro-based, or based around textiles, chemicals, mechanical equipment, electrical equipment, transport equipment, or metal products. Again in a few cases the equipment using industries are technologically clustered with equipment producing industries and are also spatially clustered with them."[43]

With the help of specialization coefficient and a study of industrial base of the regions of India in 1960 and 1965, it was found that Maharashtra was the most diversified industrial State of India in both 1960 and 1965 and Jammu & Kashmir was the least diversified. Uttar Pradesh and Madhya Pradesh had fairly diversified industrial structures in agro-based industries. Delhi and West Bengal had diversified engineering and chemical industries.[44]

Another important contribution of Alagh's study was the attempt to assess agglomeration tendencies in Indian industries. From Weber's theory of industrial location, we know the importance of such economies in understanding the location decision of industries (on account of the benefits that accrue from agglomeration economies). The methodology used in the study was 'preliminary' and the difficulties regarding the availability of data restricted the utility of the analysis.[45] Yet some broad trends of agglomeration are specifically brought out. Thus, according to Alagh, "In the mechanical and transport equipment blocks, the industries which reflect preliminary evidence of agglomeration economies . . . are railway locomotives, repair of motor vehicles, aircraft (industry as defined in ASI includes repairs), textiles machinery, sugar machinery, oil mill and rice dal, etc., machinery, power driven pumps, air compressors and air conditioning and industrial refrigeration plants, earth moving equipment, office machinery and tractors." Evidence of agglomeration economies was also found in some industries in the electrical equipment block, metal products block, chemicals block, textile based block, forest based block etc. In the agro-based block of industries, only sugar and milk and other miscellaneous food products exhibited these tendencies.[46]

THE RANK-SIZE RULE

We have shown how the central place theory explains the spacing of urban areas and their size. Actual experience has shown that the arrangement of urban areas follows a certain hierarchy. The *rank-size rule*, observed by Singer, Zipf, Auerbach, Lotka, and others, seeks to represent this hierarchy. Singer in his article "The 'Courbes des Populations' : A Parallel to Pareto's Law" (*Economic Journal*, Vol. XLVI, June 1936) tried to ascertain whether a relationship similar to Pareto's Law of Income Distribution existed between the number and size of towns. We know that Pareto's Law establishes a relationship between the 'number' and 'size' of incomes. On the basis of data from many countries Pareto constructed cumulative frequency distribution which indicated how many persons had incomes not below certain sums. Taking income x along the horizontal axis and number of persons with incomes of x or more on the vertical axis, Pareto found that the shape of the curves resembled that of a hyperbola whose equation is given by

$$y = \frac{B}{(x - b)^{\alpha}}$$

when $x \to b$, $y \to \infty$ and when $x \to \infty$, $y \to 0$. This shows that $x = b$ and $y = 0$ are two asymptotes of the curve. Thus, the curve is of the form as shown in Fig. 8.

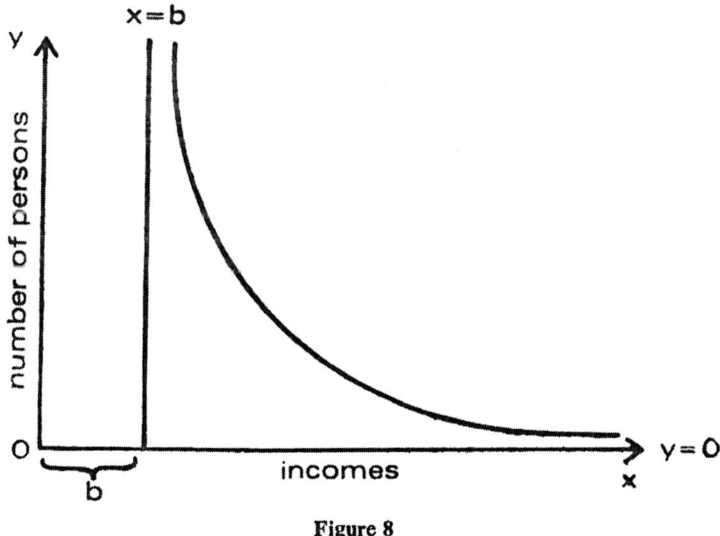

Figure 8

The form of the Pareto curve generally considered is obtained on putting $b = 0$, then

$$y = Bx^{-\alpha} \tag{26}$$

The logarithm transformation would be

$$\log y = \log B - \alpha \log x \tag{27}$$

which yields a straight line on logarithmic paper.

On these lines, the rank size rule is defined as

$$r = P_1 \cdot P_r^{-q} \tag{28}$$

where P_1 = Population of the largest/first-ranking settlement.
P_r = Population of the settlement of rank r.
q = Constant.

The logarithm transformation would be

$$\log r = \log P_1 - q \log P_r \tag{29}$$

which shows that *the plotting of ranks against size on double logarithmic paper yields a straight line with a slope of* $(-q)$.

Beckmann suggested in his article "City Hierarchies and the Distribution of City Size" (*Economic Development and Cultural Change*, 1958, pp. 243-248), that there was a strong correspondence between the central place hierarchy and the rank-size rule.[47] It can be shown that if r = order of place, P_r = population served by place of order r, C_r = population of place of rank r, K = proportion of population served located in the central place, n = number of places in order $(r - 1)$ served by places in order r, and S_1 = rural population served by place of lowest rank, then $P_r = S_1 n^{r-1}/(1-K)^r$ and $C_r = KS_1 n^{r-1}/(1-K)^r$.[48] The smallest central place has a population equal to $KS_1/(1-K)$ while each order place has a population equal to $[n/(1-K)] \times$[the population of the place of the next order]. If K is small relative to 1, then from $n/(1-K)$ we know that the product of the rank of a place and its population size will approximate to a constant. However, K may not be small especially in the heavily urbanized economy, and this fact leads to distortions in the rank-size rule.[49]

Application of the Rank-Size Rule to India

In her study "Urbanization and the Spatial Structure of Indian Economy",[50] Galina V. Sdasyuk considered the spatial structure of the Indian economy as reflected in its urban systems with the help of the rank-size rule. Such a study, according to her, "can provide an effective method for studying the distinctions in the structure of urban systems that are typical of the areas of various levels and types of development". Sdasyuk's data taken from the 1961 census show the primacy of two major metropolitan centres—Greater Calcutta and Greater Bombay. Figure 1 of the study covers the largest 50 cities of India. Though Greater Calcutta and Greater Bombay are at the top, "both of them are smaller than expected for the urban network of country as a whole". These two are followed by Delhi and Madras "which stand distinctly higher above other cities although they followed closely the rank size formula". Thus, four largest cities share the domination of the whole country. Other important conclusions, as far as spatial structure of regions is concerned, are summarized by Sdasyuk as follows:

1. The North East India comprising the three states of West Bengal, Orissa and Bihar reveal the strong domination of the primate city of Greater Calcutta. The city of Patna which is the second important city in that region is considerably smaller than the largest city of Calcutta.
2. The West-Indian urban system covering 50 major cities of Maharashtra, Gujarat and some districts of Madhya Pradesh and Rajasthan reveals the prominence of the city of Greater Bombay. The second largest city of that region *i.e.* Ahmedabad is "3 times as large as would be predicted from the size of the urban network of the Gujarat State, of which it is the capital, but of almost exactly the size that corresponds to distribution pattern of rank-size of West India".
3. The North-West India comprises Delhi, Punjab, Haryana, the western part of Uttar Pradesh and some areas of Rajasthan and Madhya Pradesh. The capital city of Delhi of this region "exceeds hypothetically primate city of the vast North-West territorial urban system". The next four major cities of the system—Agra, Jaipur, Amritsar and Gwalior "much inferior to Delhi in size, are located not too close to it (outside the capital's shadow) and belong to the four different states which constitute zone in question".
4. In the southern urban system, Madras is the leading city. But the

second largest city, is well above the size suggested by the Zipf rule. Thus, the spatial structure of the southern region corresponds to a "double-poles" pattern.[5]

THE GROWTH POLE THEORY

The concept of a growth pole was developed by the French regional economists, particularly Francois Perroux, in 1955. Perroux was basically concerned with the phenomenon of economic development and with the process of structural change that accompanied this phenomenon. In his theory of growth poles, he attempted to explain how modern process of economic growth deviated from the stationary conception of equilibrium growth. In doing this he based his argument heavily on Schumpeter's theories of the role of *innovations* and *large-scale* firms. In Schumpeter's analysis, development occurs as a result of discontinuous spurts in a dynamic world. Such 'discontinuous spurts' are caused by the innovative entrepreneur whose activities generally take place in large-scale firms. These large-scale firms are able to *dominate* their environment in the sense of exercising reversible and partially reversible influences on other economic units by reason of their dimension, negotiating strength, and by the nature of their operations.

The close relationships between scale of operations, dominance, and impulses to innovate become the most important features of Perroux's theory and lead to the concepts of *dynamic propulsive firm* and *leading propulsive industry*. The characteristics of a dynamic propulsive firm are that it is relatively large, has a high ability to innovate, belongs to a relatively fast growing sector, and the quantity and intensity of its interrelations with other sectors of the economy are important enough for the *induced* effects to be transmitted to them. The characteristics of a leading propulsive industry are also similar. Such an industry has (i) highly advanced level of technology and managerial expertise, (ii) high income elasticity of demand for its products, (iii) marked local multiplier effects, and (iv) strong inter-industry linkages with other sectors. Such linkages can be of two types—forward linkage and backward linkage. In the case of a backward linkage an industry encourages investment in the earlier stages of production by expanding its demand for inputs (which are the outputs of industries in the earlier stages of production). In the case of a forward linkage, an industry encourages investment in the subsequent stages of production either by transmitting innovation or effects of innovations forward. One possibility is that as a result of innovations, costs of production in the industry decline. This could lead to a fall in the price of its output. If this happens, the demand for this industry's output by those industries which use its output as input, will increase. In addition to this possibility, there are many other ways in which innovations or effects of innovations can be transmitted forward.

Thus, there are two cornerstones on which Perroux bases his theory: (1) Schumpeterian theory of development, and (2) theory of inter-industry linkages and industrial interdependence.[52] According to him, "*growth does not appear everywhere and all at once; it appears in points or development poles, with variable intensities; it spreads along diverse channels and with varying terminal effects to the whole of the economy.*[53] This concept of growth poles is closely related to Perroux's idea of an *economic space* as a field of forces consisting of centres (or poles or foci) "from which centrifugal forces emanate and to which centripetal forces are attracted. Each centre, being a centre of attraction and repulsion, has its proper field, which is set in the field of other centres."[54]

Perroux's conception of space was essentially an abstract one. It was Boudeville who gave it a *regional* character and a specific geographic content. Consequently it was with Boudeville that the growth pole theory received a specific geographical and regional importance. He defined a regional growth pole as a "set of expanding industries located in an urban area and including further development of economic activity throughout its zone of influence". The place where these 'expanding' or 'propulsive' or 'dominant' industries are located in the region becomes the pole of the region and agglomeration tendencies are promoted. Such tendencies arise because of *external economies* and result in polarization of economic activities around that pole. The external economies that become available in the area constituting the growth pole of a region are basically of the following three types:

1. *Economies internal to the firm* : These are the lower average costs of production resulting from an increased rate of output. These are the economies which any single firm by its own organization and effort can enjoy.
2. *Economies external to the firm but internal to the industry* : These are associated with localization of industry. On account of close locational proximity of linked firms, as industry expands at a particular location, cost per unit of output to a firm declines.
3. *Economies external to the industry but internal to the urban area* : These can be termed urbanization economies. They include development of urban labour markets, access to a larger market, and provision of a wider range of services.

In his theory of unbalanced growth, Albert O. Hirschman[55] emphasizes that because of these external economies there is a tendency among investors to concentrate in (and around) the growth poles. According to him, "what appears to happen is that *the external economies due to the poles, though real, are consistently overestimated by the economic operators*". Thus, a sort of 'dualism' in the economic progress of nations develops—a country is split up into developed and backward areas.

Trickling-Down and Polarization Effects

Despite the exaggerated space preferences of economic operators, notes Hirschman, development in geographical growth points will set in motion certain forces that act on the other regions of the country. Some of these forces will be favourable and others adverse. The favourable forces are referred to by Hirschman as the *trickling-down forces* while the adverse forces are named *polarization effects.* Through the trickling-down forces progress is 'trickled down' to the backward areas from the growth pole. Such forces work basically through (i) inter-regional trade and (ii) transfer of capital to backward regions. In addition, the growth pole might also attract labour from the backward areas and thus help in reducing the pressure of population (and consequently disguised unemployment) there. The polarization effects can discourage growth in the hinterland on account of the following factors:

1. The industries in such regions may find it difficult to compete with industry in the growth pole particularly as transportation facilities are improved.
2. Owing to better investment opportunities in the growth pole, the investors in the hinterland may invest their savings in the growth pole rather than in the hinterland.
3. Perhaps the worst polarization effect from the point of view of the hinterland is that it might be drained of the best part of its labour force. Instead of absorbing the disguised unemployed, the progress of the growth pole may denude the hinterland "of its key technicians and managers as well as of the more enterprising young men".

Hirschman's trickling-down and polarization effects are very much like Myrdal's spread effects and backwash effects, though Hirschman is more optimistic. Hirschman feels that in the long run external diseconomies will appear in the growth centre (industry will be congested and its expansion will be hampered by the insufficient size of the home market resulting from low income levels of the hinterland) and the existence of complementaries will ensure an extensive spread of development. On the other hand, Myrdal believes that this may not be the end result, for the existence of cumulative and circular causation may prevent this from happening.

Myrdal's Theory

To put Myrdal's view in a better perspective, let us see what he has to say on the subject. According to Myrdal, "If things were left to market forces unhampered by any policy interferences, industrial production, commerce, banking, insurance, shipping and indeed almost all those economic activities which in a developing economy tend to give a bigger than average return and, in addition, science, art, literature, education and higher culture generally—would cluster in certain localities and regions, leaving the rest of the country more or less in a backwater."[56] By whatever factors—natural, man made, or historical—growth gets started in a particular region and meets with initial success, all sorts of economic and non-economic activities start concentrating there. This happens because of ever-increasing internal and external economies—interpreted in the widest sense of the word to include, for instance, a working population trained in various crafts, easy communications, the feeling of growth and elbow room and the spirit of new enterprise".[57]

In Myrdal's analysis, the growth in progressive (or advancing) regions affects the growth in lagging (or depressed) regions through (i) spread effects, and (ii) backwash effects. The spread effects are the centrifugal forces of expansionary momentum emanating from the centres of economic expansion to other regions. Thus, the spread effects have a positive impact on the development of other regions. Because of growth in the progressive regions, on the one hand, demand for agricultural products and raw materials from other regions is increased, and on the other, advanced technology is made available to lagging regions which they did not formerly possess. On account of these two factors, growth in the other regions is promoted. In contrast to the spread effects, the backwash effects are those effects emanating from the centres of growth that discourage growth in other areas. Because of their rapid growth, in contrast to the stagnation of other regions, the centres of growth (or progressive regions) attract het immigration from other parts of the country. There is a net movement of population, capital, and goods in favour of the progressive regions while the backward regions are continually denuded. Since the migration from backward regions to progressive regions is generally selective in the sense that it is normally the young, the educated; and the healthy that migrate, the age structure in the lagging regions becomes lopsided. All these factors have an adverse effect on the growth of backward regions.

According to Myrdal, "In the marginal case the two kinds of effects will balance each other and a region will be stagnating. But this balance is not a stable equilibrium, for any change in the forces will start a cumulative movement upwards or downwards."[58] In whatever direction (upward or downward) the movement starts, it tends to be cumulative. This is so because, according to Myrdal, "In the normal case a change does not call forth countervailing changes but, instead, supporting changes, which move the system in the same direction as the first change but much further. Because of such circular causation a social process tends to become cumulative and often to gather speed at an accelerating rate."[59] If the initial starts are many and strong and if the spread effects work effectively, economic growth of all regions of the economy will be promoted. "The problem of inequality then becomes a problem of the different rates of progress between regions in the country." However, Myrdal notes that even in a rapidly developing country or in an advanced economy some regions are bound to lag far behind and even stagnate or decay. In the most advanced country of the world USA, the south remained till recently a stagnating region. This shows that the backwash effects are likely to dominate the spread effects for a number of years even in the advanced economies. The fate of the underdeveloped countries is still worse. As a rule, the spread effects in the underdeveloped countries are far weaker than the spread effects in the advanced countries because such effects are themselves "a function of the level of economic development actually attained". Therefore, under conditions of laissez-faire (i.e., under the conditions of a free market economy), the regional inequalities in the underdeveloped countries are expected not only to be larger than the inequalities in the developed countries but also possessing a tendency to increase at a faster rate.

Growth Pole Theory and Regional Planning

Because of the emphasis placed by the growth pole theory on various policy-oriented concepts such as propulsive firms, leading industries, polarization, agglomeration (resulting in various external economies), and the promise of the ensuing spread effects, it has acquired widespread popularity. It has come to occupy an important place in regional planning theory and most of the underdeveloped countries today regard it as the most promising hope for regenerating the economy of the backward regions. To develop such regions, one has to implant potential propulsive industries there and concentrate investments in the selected poles rather than spread them thinly over the whole region. It is true that this implies the promotion of a structural imbalance over the whole region, and the possibility that beyond the zone of influence of such poles the levels of income may actually stagnate has also to be admitted. Yet, the justification for this policy is that these areas are destined to stagnate in any event, and that concentration of 'expansionary momentum' at the poles will result in higher per capita income level in the region as a whole. Also, concentration of investments and public expenditure in a few selected points will enable more effective use of resources and there would be a better chance of generating enough external economies.

Viewed in the right perspective, the growth pole theory should be regarded as a conditional theory of regional growth that establishes conditions under which accelerated regional economic growth may occur. But, notes Hermansen, "The more intricate problem of establishing both necessary and sufficient conditions for regional economic growth seems, however, to remain unsolved."[60] To solve this issue and to make the whole concept operationally viable it is necessary to lay stress on the concept of polarized space that is defined in terms of interdependencies between economic units. Since this concept is closely related to the notion of hierarchy, it provides a link to the central place theory of Christaller. "A *polarized region* can then be defined as a heterogeneous continuous area localized in geographical space, whose different parts are interdependent through mutual complementary and interplay relations centred around a regional centre of gravity."[61] In this framework, growth pole theory and central place theory supplement each other. While the growth pole theory contributes to explaining the impact of propulsive industries and leading firms on regional economic development, it is not in itself a theory of location which explains where the functional poles are or where the most likely locations of the new poles may be. To explain this, it has to rely on the central place theory. On the other hand, the central place theory does not explain the growth phenomena. It is a static theory which only explains the existence of certain patterns of centres. It does not say how these patterns come into being and how they may undergo changes in future. To explain these dynamic phenomena, it needs the help of the growth pole theory.[62]

Modified Growth Foci Approach : The Contribution of R.P. Misra

R.P. Misra notes the following three important weaknesses in the conventional growth pole theory when it is applied to conditions prevailing in underdeveloped countries:

(i) The hypothesis has its roots in Western economic thought where its role has been defined in terms of *accelerating development through industrialization.* Undue emphasis on industrialization programmes introduces 'functional rigidity' in the growth pole theory;

(ii) In underdeveloped countries like India, the growth foci should not be concerned with industrial development alone. They have to perform two other basic functions: (a) they must function as service centres and meet the day-to-day needs of the area they serve (i.e., they must function as central places in the form postulated by Christaller); and (b) they must act as innovative and growth promoting centres. They must have processing and manufacturing activities of both basic and non-basic types and should be able to provide employment to the drop-outs of the agricultural system. Thus the role of growth foci is not limited to manufacturing of goods, *it includes the creation of conditions under which industrial development can occur*; and

(iii) In underdeveloped countries, the growth foci have to function as social interaction points also. *They have to act as the centres of diffusion of information.* Provision of extension services, educational services and meeting places is necessary to accomplish this task.[63]

Recognizing the importance of the growth pole theory in the process of regional planning and taking account of the above considerations, Misra extends the concept of growth pole to the concept of growth foci. This new concept of growth foci seeks to integrate the main elements of the central place theory, the growth pole theory, and the spatial diffusion theory.[64] The earlier version of the theory advocated the following four-tier hierarchy of growth foci.[65]

1. Service Centres at the local level
2. Growth Points at the sub-regional level
3. Growth Centres at the regional level
4. Growth Poles at the national level

The later formulation envisages a five-tier hierarchy with the central village at the local level, the service centres at the micro regional level, the growth points at the sub-regional level, the growth centres at the regional level, and the growth poles at the national level.[66] The central village, which will be the lowest level central place in the system, is designed to form the service and marketing nucleus for about 6,000 people living in about six villages. It will be a planned rural settlement offering marketing, recreational, and social services for the community. Each central village will have a standard primary school, a sub-post office, a cooperative, etc.

The service centres will serve a population of about 30,000 living in rural areas, apart from its own population of about 5,000. They will have grocery stores, general merchant shops, minor repair facilities, tailor shops, barbar shops, restaurants, primary and junior high schools, a sub-post office, cooperatives, a community centre, and other basic facilities. The service centre will also be the headquarters of an extension officer such as the village level worker, and other minor government functionaries. The service centres are aimed to serve as focal points for social intercourse from where developmental information will spread to the villages and hamlets. For any programme of integrated national development such service centres are vital, for in country where there is a serious lack of resources it is better to provide certain facilities such as cooperatives, schools, etc., at some determined centre rather than dissipate the resources in providing them in each and every village.

The next level in the hierarchy will be constituted by the *growth points*. Each growth point will serve about five service centres, serving about 150,000 people living in rural areas. The size of a growth point in terms of population will range from 10,000 to 25,000. The concept of a growth point here is similar to the concept of market towns. The growth points are so envisaged as to be 'the sub-regional innovative and propulsive urban centres'. They will be linked with sister growth points by state highways and with the service centres by district/local road networks. In terms of service specialization, the growth points will be predominantly agro-industrial. The economic activities at the growth points will be production, handling, and processing of agricultural and dairy products. Proper organization of such activites can help considerably in solving the problem of rural unemployment. The functions assigned to the growth points should be such as lead to 'social, economic and emotional integration of the respective sub-regions served by them'.

The next level in the hierarchy proposed by Misra will be constituted by *growth centres* which should be about 500 in number in the country as a whole. The population of each centre will vary from 50,000 to 500,000 depending upon the stage at which the regional economy is. The growth centres will serve a population of about 1,200,000 spread over a meso level region. In contrast with the growth points, the growth centres will have a preponderance of secondary activities and manufacturing as their chief function. Some of the characteristics of these centres noted by Misra can be summarized as follows:

1. They will have a preponderance of secondary activities especially manufacturing. Next in importance might be tertiary activities.

2. They will be determined according to the requirements of the industrial location theory and therefore the role of the industrial resources in the locational decisions will be quite substantial and so also will be that of regional development needs.
3. They will be the consumers of finished and semi-finished products produced at the growth points and of the agricultural products produced by the service centres and villages.
4. They will function as industrial hubs of the area they serve. The structure of their functions will be such that both internal and external economies will operate to their advantage.
5. They will have large collecting, storage, and processing facilities for agricultural products and will produce agricultural inputs such as fertilizers, pesticides, and machines.
6. Each centre will have a radio and/or television station, banking facilities, degree-level colleges or univesities, technical institutions and servicing facilities for everything in use in the rural or urban areas.
7. The most important characteristic of these centres, as far as urban planning is concerned, is that they will function as 'countermagnets' to large urban centres such as Bombay, Delhi, Calcutta, Madras, etc. By diverting the streams of migration away from large urban centres they shall relieve the increasing pressure of population on these centres.

At the apex of the hierarchy are the *growth poles*. The population of a growth pole will range from 500,000 to 2,500,000 (since towns larger than 2,500,000 are difficult to manage, Misra emphasizes the need for discouraging the expansion of existing towns, if they have attained or passed this limit). Each growth pole will serve a rural population of about 20 million and is designed to function as the 'heart' of one macro region of the country performing highly specialized secondary, tertiary, and quarternary activities, which other centres are not in a position to perform. The growth poles will also send out 'financial, technological, research and industrial impulses to all centres and points within the area of their command'. We have already noted while discussing the rank-size rule that Calcutta, Bombay, Delhi, and Madras function as 'hearts' of the macro regions of north-east India, western India, north-west India, and southern India respectively. Therefore, in Misra's scheme, metropolitan centres are destined to play the role of growth poles while intermediate towns such as Mysore, Jaipur, Bhopal, Meerut, etc., will play the role of growth centres. Market towns have to be planned as growth points.

Such an extension of the growth pole theory opens up immense possibilities for the application of this theory in promoting the processes of regional and national economic growth. By ensuring a linked pattern of hierarchy of human settlements it also successfully avoids the dangers of over-urbanization and of depressed areas coexisting with developed areas. The problem of providing an adequate institutional infrastructure in the rural areas is also properly looked after. Adoption of this strategy leads to what Misra calls 'decentralized concentration'.

Growth Foci : Illustration from India

In their book (see note 39) Misra, Rao, and Sundaram have illustrated the theory of growth foci by applying it to a tribal region (Bastar district of Madhya Pradesh), an agricultural region (Muzaffarnagar district of Uttar Pradesh), and an industrial region (comprising districts of Ranchi, Hazaribagh, Dhanbad, and Singhbhum of Bihar and Purulia, Bankura, and part of Burdwan in West Bengal). As far as the tribal region of Bastar district is concerned, it was divided into the following hierarchy: (i) Central villages (89), (ii) Service towns (30), (iii) Market towns (7), (iv) Growth points (3), and (v) Growth centres (2). Jagdalpur, Bailadila, Narayanpur, Geedam, and Barsus were designated as growth foci (the former two were excepted to become growth centres and the latter three growth points).[67] The industrial region comprising some districts of Bihar and West Bengal consisted of 47 towns (4 Class I, 2 Class II, 12 Class III, 13 Class IV, 13 Class V, and 3 Class VI). For the purpose of classification of urban centres, the following six major groups of functions are considered: "(1) law and general administration, (2) development administration, (3) presence of industries, (4) agricultural marketing, (5) modes of transportation, and (6) specialized services and skills".[68] Five categories of settlements were distinguished on the basis of the performance of the six functions considered above and the population size. The existing service centres, market centres, growth points, and growth centres were identified and potential centres indicated. For a discussion of the agricultural region of Muzaffarnagar, the reader is referred to Chaprer 11 (p. 293-335) of their book. For those interested in a more comprehensive analysis, V.L.S. Prakasa Rao's study (note 39) is highly recommended.

NOTES

1. Walter Isard, *Method of Regional Analysis* (Cambridge: M.I.T. Press, 1960), Chapter 6.
2. J.C. Stabler, "Exports and Evolution: The Process of Regional Change", in David L. McKee, Robert D. Dean, and William H. Leahy (eds.), *Regional Economics: Theory and Practice* (New York: The Free Press, 1970), p. 61.

3. K.R.G. Nair, "Inter-State Income Disparities in India," *Indian Journal of Regional Science*, Vol. 3, No. 2, 1971, pp. 53-54.
4. Discussion in this section is based on (i) H.W. Richardson, *Regional Economics* (London: Weidenfeld and Nicolson, 1969), Chapter 13 on 'Regional Growth'; (ii) H.W. Richardson, *Regional Growth Theory* (London: The Macmillan Press Pvt. Ltd., 1973); and (iii) H.W. Richardson, *Elements of Regional Economics*, Penguin Modern Economics Texts, 1973), Chapter 2 on 'Regional Growth :
5. Subscript t has been dropped for the sake of convenience.
6. H.W. Richardson, *Elements of Regional Economics*, op. cit., p. 49.
7. Discussion in this section is based on (i) H.W. Richardson, *Regional Growth Theory*, op. cit., (ii) H.W. Richardson, *Regional Economics*, op. cit. (Chapter 13), and (iii) H.W. Richardson, *Elements of Regional Economics*, op. cit. (Chapter 2).
8. H.W. Richardson, *Regional Growth Theory*, op. cit., p. 23.
9. C.M. Tiebout, "Regional and Interregional Input-Output Models: an Appraisal", in L. Needleman (ed.), *Regional Analysis* (Penguin Modern Economics, 1968), pp. 88-89.
10. Ibid., p. 90.
11. Ibid., p. 91.
12. Dorfman quoted in H.W. Richardson, *Input-Output and Regional Economics* (London: Weidenfeld and Nicolson, 1972), p. 8.
13. Ibid., p. 8.
14. Ibid., p. 9.
15. G.S. Bhalla, "Sectoral Income Multipliers in the Punjab and India", *Ninth Indian Econometric Conference*, Patna, 1969, published in *Anvesak* December 1971.
16. Yoginder Alagh and S.P. Kashyap, 'Structure of Gujarat's Industrial Economy: Some Experiments with Input-Output Approach", *Proceedings of First Gujarat's Economic Conference* (Ahmedabad, 1970) and "Problems and uses of Regional Input-Output Tables", *Third All India Input-Output Conference*, published in *Anvesak*, June 1971. The Indian Council of Social Science Research financed a project on "Economic Analysis of the Structure of Punjab and Haryana Economies—A Study in Regional Economic Development, 1969-70". The study was carried out by G.S. Bhalla. The results of this study have been published together with the results of the study conducted by Y.K. Alagh and S.P. Kashyap on Gujarat's economy in Y.K. Alagh, G.S. Bhalla, and S.P. Kashyap, *Structural Analysis of Gujarat, Punjab, and Haryana Economies* (New Delhi: Allied Publishers Private Limited, 1980).
17. Ranajit Dhar, Robert Venning and Brian J.L. Berry, "Interregional Intersectoral Relations of the Indian Economy", in Brian J.L. Berry (ed.), *Essays on Commodity Flows and the Spatial Structure of Indian Economy* (Chicago: Department of Geography, Research Paper No. 111, University of Chicago, 1966).
18. *Indian Journal of Regional Science*, Vol. IV, No. 1, 1972, pp. 59-68.
19. R. Dhar, "The Nature of Spatial Clusters of the Indian Economy", *Anvesak*, Vol. III, No. 1-2, June-December 1973, pp. 20-26.
20. Results of this study were published in (i) Y.K. Alagh, *Regional Aspects of Indian Industrialization* (Bombay: University of Bombay, Economics Series No. 21, 1972) and (ii) D.T. Lakdawala, Y.K. Alagh, and Atul Sharma, *Regional Variations in Industrial Development* (Ahmedabad: Sardar Patel Institute of Economic and Social Research, Monograph Series 2, 1974).

    Some other studies based on the input-output model are: (i) Jyoti D. Thakker, "A Note on the Level and Structure of Gujarat's Interregional Trade", *Anvesak*, June 1971; (ii) G.S. Bohra and S.S. Mehta, "An Input-Output Table of Rajasthan's Industrial Economy, 1964", *Anvesak*, December 1971; (iii) K.N. Prasad, "Input-Output Table for Bihar", *Seminar on Quantitative Economics* (Ahmedabad:

Sardar Patel Institute of Economic Research, 1971).

21. Alfred Weber, *Theory of the Location of Industries* (Chicago: The University of Chicago Press, 1929), Editor's Introduction, p. xxiii.
22. Ibid., p. 54.
23. Ibid., pp. 102-103. Italics in original.
24. Balkrishna, *Regional Planning in India*, (Bangalore: The Bangalore Printing & Publishing Co., Ltd., 1948), pp. 9-10.
25. Discussion here is based on M.N. Pal, "Quantitative Techniques for Regional Planning", *Indian Journal of Regional Science*, Vol. III, No. 1, 1971, pp. 1-33.
26. Ibid., pp. 4-5.
27. See, e.g., M.N. Pal, "A Method of Regional Analysis of Economic Development with Special Reference to South India", reprinted in R.P. Misra (eds.), *Regional Planning* (Mysore: University of Mysore, 1969), pp. 172-191; M.N. Pal, "Regional Analysis for National Development : Techniques and Case Studies" (Doctoral Dissertation, Delhi: University of Delhi, 1968); M.N. Pal, "Quantitative Techniques for Regional Planning", op. cit , pp. 1-33.
28. M.N. Pal, "Quantitative Techniques for Regional Planning", op. cit., pp. 6-7.
29. August Losch, *The Economics of Location* (New Haven: Yale University Press, 1954), pp. 28-29.
30. Ibid., footnote 8, p. 112; also see pp. 110-114.
31. Walter Christaller, *Central Places in Southern Germany* (Prentice-Hall, 1966). Originally published in German, 1933.
32. "The crystallization of mass about a nucleus is part of the elementary order of things. Centralistic principles are similarly basic to human community life. In this sense the town is a centre of a regional community and the mediator of that community's commerce; it functions, then, as the central place of the community." Brian J.L. Berry and Allen Pred, "Walter Christaller's Die Zentralen Orte in Suddeutschland—Abstract of Theoretical Parts", in Robert H.T. Smith, Edward J. Taaffe, and Leslie J. King (eds.), *Readings in Economic Geography—The Location of Economic Activity* (Chicago: Rand McNally and Co., 1968, Reprint 1972), p. 65.
33. Losch, op. cit., p. 124.
34. Walter Isard, *Location and Space Economy* (Cambridge: M.I.T. Press, 1956), p. 271.
35. Ibid., p. 271. Also see p. 272 for a diagrammatic representation of the modified Losch system as presented by Walter Isard.
36. M.N. Pal, "Regional Studies and Research for Consistent and Optimal Plan Formulation : The need for a right kind of Orientation", *Indian Journal of Regional Science*, Vol. V, No. 1, 1973, p. 16.
37. For methodology and related aspects, see (i) M.N. Pal and C. Subramaniam, "An Optimal Evaluation of Spatial Linkage in South India", *Indian Journal of Regional Science*, Vol. IX, No. 1, 1977; (ii) M.N. Pal, V.L.S. Prakasa Rao, and Tiwari, "A Technique of Ranking Central Places and Determining Linkages", paper presented at the 21st International Geographical Congress, Mysore, 1968; (iii) M.N. Pal, "Regional Information, Regional Statistics and Regional Planning in India", in Antoni Kuklinski (ed.), *Regional Information and Regional Planning*, UNRISD, 1974, Vol. 6, Mouton & Co.
38. M.N. Pal and C. Subramaniam, op. cit., p. 97.
39. Ibid., pp. 107-108.

    The application of the central place theory in a different context was made by

Vinod K. Gupta in his article "The System of Cities and Towns in Relation to Economic Development in India" (in NCAER, *Market Towns and Spatial Development*, 1972) to investigate the hierarchy (existing and expected) of cities and towns in India and also to find out the likely future patterns. The 'central place theory system' adopted here had six equations and eleven unknowns. Gupta finds that there is no substantial difference between the expected and the actual number of cities of various orders, except in the second order. Similarly, no substantial difference between the expected and the observed city size in various orders (except the seventh and second orders) was found.

Some other examples of the use of the central place theory are: (i) S. Folka, "Central Place System and Spatial Interaction in Nilgiris and Coorg", *Papers of the 21st International Geographical Congress*, India, 1968: (ii) R.C. Mayfield, "A Central Place Hierarchy in Northern India", in Garrison and Marble (eds.), *Quantitative Geography, Part I*, (Illinois, USA), 1967; (iii) K.V. Sundaram, "Settlement Pattern for an Irrigated Colony", paper contributed to the All-India Regional Planning Seminar, Mysore University, 1967. In their book *Regional Development Planning in India* (Delhi: Vikas Publishing House Pvt. Ltd., 1974), R.P. Misra, V.L.S. Prakasa Rao, and K.V. Sundaram have shown the applications of this theory in planning for (a) a tribal region (area of study being the Bastar district of Madhya Pradesh); (b) an agricultural region (area of study being the Muzaffarnagar district of Uttar Pradesh); and (c) an industrial region (constituted by some districts of Bihar and West Bengal). On account of its comprehensive nature and in-depth analysis perhaps the best study is that of V.L.S. Prakasa Rao on Muzaffarnagar district entitled *Development Strategy for an Agricultural Region—A Case Study of Muzaffarnagar District, U.P.* (Mysore: Institute of Development Studies, University of Mysore, 1976).

40. This section highlights the results of the exploratory work conducted by Yoginder K. Alagh (and his associates) in the field as revealed through (i) Yoginder K. Alagh, *Regional Aspects of Indian Industrialization*, op. cit., and (ii) D.T. Lakdawala, Yoginder K. Alagh, and Atul Sharma, *Regional Variations in Industrial Development*, op. cit.
41. Yoginder Alagh, et. al., *Regional Variations in Industrial Development*, op. cit., pp. 46-47.
42. Ibid., p. 41. Emphasis added.
43. Ibid., p. 43. Emphasis added.
44. Ibid., p. 75.
45. Ibid., pp. 88-90.
46. For details, see Yoginder Alagh, *Regional Aspects of Indian Industrialization*, op. cit., pp. 64-65.
47. As noted by B.J.L. Berry and W.L. Garrison, both suggest a situation where there are "many small cities, a lesser number of medium sized cities, but few large cities". But despite being stimulated by the consideration of a real area, southern Germany, Christaller's attempt was to build up a theoretical model while the rank-size rule is empirically derived from a large number of studies. Then, Christaller's urban hierarchy produces a tiered arrangement of urban sizes while the rank-size rule gives a continuous curve with a smooth progression from rank to rank. However, the discrepancy is not serious for the rank-size rule works best when a large area is being studied while tiered hierarchy is mostly found in a smaller area.
48. See Harry W. Richardson, *Elements of Regional Economics*, op. cit., pp. 92-93.
49. Ibid., p. 93.
50. Galina V. Sdasyuk, "Urbanization and the Spatial Structure of Indian Economy", *Economic and Socio-Cultural Dimensions of Regionalization*, Census of India 1971,

(Census Centenary Monograph No. 7), pp. 297-328.

51. The rank-size rule can be used to set a norm regarding the size of cities. The hierarchy thus obtained may be compared with the existing pattern, and the differences measured quantitatively. An exercise on these lines was carried out by S.K. Biswas in his article "Spatial and Demographic Behaviour among the Million Cities of India and other Leading Countries of the World" (*Indian Journal of Regional Science*, Vol IX, No. 2, 1977). The author examined fourteen countries (each with a population greater than 50 million in 1974) for the purpose. The average deviation of the million cities was calculated on the basis of difference between actual and expected size as per cent of (i) actual size, and of (ii) expected size, and (iii) by overall deviation (in percent) from the rank-size rule. India, Pakistan, USSR, Italy, Indonesia, and Nigeria are the six countries which showed maximum conformity to the rank-size rule.
52. Tormod Hermansen, "Development Poles and Development Centres in National and Regional Development", in Antoni Kuklinski (ed.), *Growth Poles and Growth Centres in Regional Planning* (UNRISD, Mouton & Co., 1972), p. 22.
53. F. Perroux, "Note on the Concept of 'Growth Poles'", in David L. Mckee, Robert D. Dean, and William H. Leahy (eds.), *Regional Economics : Theory and Practice*, op. cit., p. 94.
54. F. Perroux, "Economic Space Theory and Application", *Quarterly Journal of Economics*, (1950; Reprinted in Friedmann and Alonso, 1964).
55. Albert O. Hirschmann, *The Strategy of Economic Development* (especially 'Inter-regional and International Transmission of Economic Growth', pp. 183-201).
56. Gunnar Myrdal, *Economic Theory and Underdeveloped Regions* (London: Methuen & Co. Ltd., 1964), p. 26.
57. Ibid., p. 27.
58. Ibid., p. 32.
59. Ibid., p. 13. This is the famous theory of cumulative causation propounded by Myrdal.
60. Tormod Hermansen, *Spatial Organization and Economic Development* (Mysore: Institute of Development Studies, Mysore University, 1971, Development Studies Number 1), p. 73.
61. Boudeville as quoted in Hermansen, Ibid., p. 74.
62. Ibid., p. 74.
63. R.P. Misra, *Growth Poles and Growth Centres in Urban and Regional Planning in India* (Mysore: Institute of Development Studies, Mysore University, 1971, Development Studies Number 2).
64. Limitations of space do not allow us to discuss the spatial diffusion theory in detail. It was developed in the first part of the 1950s by T. Hagerstand. The main tenets of this theory are as under:

    (a) Diffusion of innovations takes place in a social system which can be conceived as localized in abstract space as well as in geographical space;
    (b) Mass media and personal contact provide the channels through which innovations are diffused;
    (c) There are barriers to the diffusion of innovations, one of them being the *friction of space;*
    (d) Communication fields of individuals and organizations vary and this variation is essentially *hierarchical;* and
    (e) Innovations *jump* from higher order settlements to the next level in the hierarchy

and hence if there are missing links in the hierarchy of settlements, the diffusion process is halted or slowed down.

See R.P. Misra, K.V. Sundaram, and V.L.S. Prakasa Rao, *Regional Development Planning in India*, op. cit., pp. 202-203.

The importance of spatial diffusion of innovations in any regional planning process can be easily realized. Unless such 'diffusion' takes place at an appropriate speed, development process cannot proceed smoothly. Once this theory is integrated with the central place theory, the close connection between a hierarchical ordering of individual communication fields and the hierarchy of centres within the central place system emerges clearly. Within the central place system, the centres can be ranked according to their respective strength in terms of innovations. Since, as noted above, innovations jump from higher order settlements to the next order settlements, the absence of a particular level in the hierarchy will slow down the transmission of the innovation considerably. Misra's scheme is designed to take account of all these eventualities. It defines a number of growth foci and attempts to integrate them functionally.

65. See, e.g., (i) R.P. Misra "Framework of a Modified Growth Pole Strategy for Urban and Regional Planning in India" in R.P. Misra, P.D. Mahadev, D.C. Jayashankar, *Urban Systems and Rural Development* (Part I) (Mysore: Institute of Development Studies, 1972); (ii) R.P. Misra, "Growth Pole Policy for Regional Development in India"; (iii) T.B. Lahiri, *Balanced Regional Development* (New Delhi: Oxford & IBH, 1972), p. 53; (iv) R.P. Misra, "*Growth Poles and Growth Centres in Urban and Regional Planning in India*", op. cit.
66. Misra, Sundaram, Prakaso Rao, op. cit., p. 206. Population figures at different levels of the hierarchy are taken from this study and not from the earlier ones.
67. Ibid., p. 279.
68. Ibid., p. 361.

Chapter 5

Regional Imbalances and Inequalities in India

Most of the countries of the world are faced with the problem of regional imbalances and regional inequalities. Even the most advanced nation of the world, viz. the USA, has not been able to solve this problem, and there are glaring regional disparities in the levels of development between northern and southern States. In most of the other developed countries as well regional inequalities and imbalances are present in substantial proportions. As far as the underdeveloped countries are concerned, the problem in many of them has assumed such a magnitude that their very political and economic stability is threatened. What differentiates the problem of the underdeveloped countries from that of the developed countries is the fact that whereas in the latter all inhabitants have an assured miniumm level of subsistence and the concern of lagging regions is just to 'catch up' with the leading regions, in the former the question before the lagging regions is a more basic one, i.e. how to provide a minimum level of subsistence to their teeming millions. Because of the complexities created by this economic necessity and their resentment over increasing disparities between them and the developed regions, the backward regions of the underdeveloped countries clamour for more resources and a discriminatory governmental policy in their favour. This is the reason why a strong 'desire' to ensure balanced regional development of the economy is incorporated as an important objective of planning in most of these countries. However, economic forces and compulsions often work to the opposite end as we shall soon point out (and illustrate from Indian experience) and the governmental policy in the name of economic growth, often adds fuel to the fire.

How is it that some regions of a country lag far behind others in economic development? The processes are to some extent natural and to some extent historical. Some regions of an economy are endowed with more natural resources and once the spiral of development starts, they attract more industries especially industries where raw material considerations play an important role in deciding the location. However, it has been observed that in many cases economic activity gets started at some particular place in the economy (because of political, social, or other considerations) and then economic and industrial activity tends to concentrate around that place. In many countries such historical forces have proved to be more important than the natural ones and have had a decisive impact on all future economic growth. For example, in India, the historical factors guided the development of the port towns of Bombay, Calcutta, and Madras (as shall be shown subsequently) and these three cities have, in turn, worked as nuclei for the development of Maharashtra, West Bengal, and Tamil Nadu respectively which are, at present, the most industrially advanced States of India. On the other hand, the areas having natural advantages in the form of mineral resources such as Bihar, Orissa, and Madhya Pradesh have lagged far behind.

Since we are concerned with regional imbalances and inequalities in India, we must examine how the historical processes forced a pattern of development which is not entirely in accordance with the pattern that would have emerged according to the natural processes of development. India is one of those countries which remained under foreign domination for a considerable period of time and, as could be expected, the development of the country was guided by the economic interests of the foreign power ruling the country. The interest of the ruling countries was to "use" the dependent countries or colonies both as a supplier of raw material to the home country's manufacturing industry and as a market for its products. Their attempt, therefore, was to hamper and suppress the growth of indigenous industries in colonies (as would be clear from the decline of handicrafts in India under British rule) and force them to become suppliers of important primary goods. The ruling powers paid special attention to the development of those regions of their colonies which could serve as suppliers of raw materials to the industry of the home country or which could supply other important basic primary goods to their economy. For this purpose they invested money on the development of railways in those specific regions and connected them with the ports, and sent skilled labour, enterprise, and capital to those regions while the rest of the economy was ignored. This resulted in the creation of 'pockets' or 'enclaves' of development in the dependent countries while the rest of the economy was continually impoverished. A dualistic economic structure was promoted, a high productivity sector producing for export coexisted with a low productivity sector producing for the domestic market. Such forcible creation of enclaves of development disregarded all natural potentialities of different regions of the dependent countries and, in some cases, proved to be positively harmful. In many dependent countries the enclaves of development never became part of their internal economic structure except in the purely geographical and physical sense. "Economically speaking, they were really an outpost of the economies of the more developed investing countries."[1] Since these enclaves had the advantage of an early start, they became centres of economic activity in due course of time.

In whatever way, natural or historical, development may get started in some particular regions, it tends to concentrate in and around these regions. There is a constant stream of inflow of labour, educated people, and entrepreneurs to these regions from the other regions of the economy. Labour migrates to these regions because of the expectations of better opportunities and more wages and since it is generally the dynamic, healthy, and young that migrate, the age-structure of the other regions (of the economy) gets lopsided in that there is an excessive burden of children and old people. This, however, is not the whole story. Because of increasing investment opportunities and expectation of higher profits, capital also tends to move to the rich regions. This outflow of capital accompanied by the generally poor and underdeveloped money and capital markets in the backward regions further depress economic activity in these regions. The banking system generally interested in assured income and profits and low risks also gives preference to the developed regions in granting loans and advances and even the deposits of the underdeveloped regions are transferred to the developed regions as advances.[2] Thus, the poor regions are continually denuded of their resources. A circular process of more investment and more income is initiated in the rich regions while an opposite circular process operates in the poor regions. According to Myrdal, both the processes are cumulative. Thus, while the rich regions have a tendency to grow richer, the poor regions are compelled to remain backward.[3] While the dictum "nothing succeeds like success" holds true for the developed regions, the dictum "nothing fails like failure" seems to be true for the poor regions.[4]

These processes are sustained and nurtured by the central government policies. Since the major objective before a government (especially the government of an underdeveloped country) is to maximize the rate of national development, it concentrates on those regions which are already well ahead of others because it is easier to develop them. It is maintained that once a sufficiently high level of economic development in these regions is attained, a transfer of 'benefits' in the form of developmental grants (and through supply of skilled labour, entrepreneurs, etc.) to backward regions will be carried out. According to the advocates of this view, emphasizing regional balances too early in the development process will mean *spill-over* of scarce resources in a number of regions leading to economic backwardness of all of them. However, concentration on developed regions will push up the rate of growth of not only these regions but of the whole economy. The logic here is somewhat (not entirely) similar to the one in the debate on economic growth versus social justice. The advocates of economic growth generally state that while growth can be redistributed poverty cannot be redistributed. Therefore, we must aim at economic growth first, redistribution can be considered afterwards. In fact, in economic theory it was for long maintained (and is even now maintained in many quarters) that the poor should be kept poor in the transitional process not only to ensure cheap labour supply to the capitalists but also to ensure maximum reinvestment which alone could push up the rate of growth of the economy. Later on, when the economy has progressed considerably, the state can undertake social welfare schemes and try to 'pull up' the *condemned* section of the community onto higher rungs of the ladder of economic prosperity. The choice, then, according to the propagators of this theory, is between 'a low level stagnation' and a 'high level equilibrium' approached through the process of creating and sustaining inequalities. In the context of our discussion, their view can be expressed in the form that choice is between 'low level stagnation of all regions' and 'overall national prosperity brought about by creating and sustaining regional imbalances' which, however, according to Williamson,[5] will diminish over time "allowing the more classical equilibrating effects to make themselves felt".

Williamson quotes Hirschman to substantiate his argument, who writes "Myrdal's analysis strikes me as excessively dismal. In the first place, he fails to recognize that the emergence of growing points and therefore of differences in development between regions . . . is inevitable and is a condition of further growth anywhere. Secondly, his preoccupation with the mechanism of cumulative causation hides from him the emergence of the strong forces making for a turning point once the movement toward North-South polarization within a country has proceeded for sometime."[6] For example, the rapid expansion of a few regions can (through labour immigration) help in solving the problem of disguised unemployment in the lagging regions thereby reducing the pressure on land in such regions; it can yield surplus for future investments in the lagging regions which, in turn, will raise the living standards of people residing in these regions, demand for products of the underdeveloped regions will increase, and so on. After some time, new growth centres will emerge in the lagging regions and gradually a balanced growth of national economy as a whole will be ensured.

It is because of these reasons that some economists advocate deliberate creation of regional imbalances for after some time these imbalances will themselves create external economies for the development of the lagging regions. The choice, according to them, is between regional balance at a low level or regional balance at a high level obtained after a long period of regional imbalances. Obviously the vote is normally cast in favour of adopting the latter course for it does, at least, ensure progress in the erstwhile stagnant regions (progress being defined in strictly economic and material sense and linked to the processes of industrialization and urbanization). Though regional disparities and imbalances will increase for some time (depending upon the resource endowment and institutional environment of the country being considered) they will *ultimately* decrease. Thus, "a statistic describing regional inequality will trace out an inverted 'U' over the national growth path".[7]

REGIONAL IMBALANCES IN INDIA

The historical growth processes described above explain the creation of regional imbalances in the early stages of development and modernization in India. The British rulers were interested in obtaining raw material to support their own industry in Britain and therefore concentrated specifically on those regions in India from where these raw materials could be procured. They initiated the construction of railways in 1853 and within 25 years the railways had a vast network of tracts but, as pointed out by S.R. Hashim, "the pattern of railway construction and the freight policy adopted at that time confirms that the railways looked more to the development of foreign trade of the country than to the growth of the internal trade and industry, and the effort was so deliberate in this direction that even the consideration of immediate profitability could not come in the way. The construction started from the main port towns of Bombay and Calcutta and spread towards the interior with the intentions of traversing the important agricultural tracts so as to facilitate the exports of agricultural produce."[8] Since the UK was interested in the import of raw cotton to nurture and develop its own cotton textile industry it made ample arrangements to ensure its supply from India and "Gujarat cotton tract, Khandesh and Berar cotton tracts and Karnatic cotton tracts were all connected with Bombay by 1870".[9] Thus, the sources of those raw materials as were required by the UK economy were linked to the ports from where these raw materials were shipped to Britain. Attention was not paid to connect the internal trading centres with each other. This practice of discrimination was also evident in the discriminatory freight policy of the railways which generally kept the rates of movement of raw materials comparatively low.

As is generally the case in the underdeveloped countries, the processes of industrialization and urbanization were closely linked with the development of port towns of Bombay and Calcutta in India. The development of transport (and especially railways) also played an important role in ensuring development of these towns. Though the development of transport was not done after taking into account the requirements of different regions, the growth centres of the regions, natural and comparative advantages of different locations, and the potentials of industrial development of different regions, it played a decisive role in guiding the pattern of development all over the country, the port towns and the various towns linked to them receiving most of the share of industrialization, urbanization, and modernization. This led to a neglect of a number of places and centres which could have been developed into centres of economic activity, and resulted in a lopsided development of the economy, distorting the evolutionary processes which could have emerged on the basis of natural advantages and potential growth possibilities. "The foreign trade oriented policy, thus, resulted in the industrial growth of a few centres near the port, and a general industrial deterioration of the interior. Corrective steps were taken, later, in the direction of abolishing the discriminatory practices of railways and providing protection to Indian industries against foreign competition. But, by this time the important port towns like Bombay, Calcutta and Madras, and their peripheral areas had already established themselves as industrial and commercial centres, and a complex of industrial and financial set-ups had already developed in these regions, which helped them in attracting more of new industries."[10]

The Period After Independence

Because of the glaring regional disparities and inequalities in India the planning process initiated in 1951 accepted the importance of regional balance and achievement of balanced regional development of the economy was incorporated as an important objective of planning in India. In July 1953, a Research Programmes Committee consisting of leading economists and other social scientists was set up by the Planning Commission. The Committee decided four broad categories of subjects on which research was to be concentrated. They were: (1) savings, investment, employment, and small-scale industries, (2) problems relating to regional development with special reference to problems of rapid urbanization, (3) land reforms, co-operation, and farm management, (4) social welfare problems and public administration.[11] A sum of Rs.50 lakhs was provided for the task. Thus, a small step in the right direction was taken in the First Plan itself.

The Second Plan expressed its concern over regional disparities and emphasized the necessity of balanced regional development in unequivocal terms: "In any comprehensive plan of development, it is axiomatic that the special needs of the less developed areas should receive due attention. The pattern of investment must be so devised as to lead to balanced regional development. The problem is particularly difficult in the early stages when the total resources available are very inadequate in relation to needs. But, more and more, as development proceeds and large resources become available for investment, the stress of developmental programmes should be on extending the benefits of investments to underdeveloped regions. Only thus can a diversified economy be built up."[12] The Second Plan adopted the following programmes for balanced development:

(1) priority was given to programmes of agriculture, community development, irrigation and local development works, etc. which spread over the entire area within the shortest possible time;
(2) facilities such as power, water supply, transport and communications, training institutions, etc. were provided in backward regions and in those regions that faced acute problem of unemployment;
(3) programmes for the expansion of village and small scale industries were adopted; and
(4) it was decided to keep the claims of underdeveloped regions in mind while deciding the location of new enterprises.[13]

The Third Plan devoted a separate chapter (Ch. IX) to 'Balanced Regional Development'. It was once again mphasized that "balanced development of different parts of the country, extension of the benefits of economic progress to the less developed regions and widespread diffusion of industry are among the major aims of planned development".[14] The Third Plan admitted that, on account of technological reasons, it might become necessary to localize production in large industrial sector. Therefore, it was necessary 'to provide for more dispersed advance in sectors like agriculture, small industries, power, communications and social services'. In certain consumer goods and processing industries regional dispersion was sought to be achieved. These include cotton textiles, sugar, light engineering industries such as bicycles, sewing machines, electric motors, radio receivers, re-rolling of steel and non-ferrous metals from billets and semis, moulded plastics and manufacture and further processing of bulk drugs from penultimate products. Some examples of such a regional distribution of industry are the setting up of textile units in Rajasthan, Orissa, Assam, and Punjab; sugar factories and distilleries in Andhra Pradesh, Madras, Mysore, and Maharashtra; steel rerolling mills in Assam, Madhya Pradesh, Kerala, and north Bihar, and tyre and tubes factory and electric lamps factory in Kerala.[15]

The approach in the Third Plan was to (i) help the States in reducing intra-State disparities (i.e., disparities among different regions of the same State) and (ii) initiate new programmes and extend programmes adopted in the previous plans to reduce inter-State inequalities (i.e., inequalities between different States). As far as the first issue is concerned, the programmes included related to (a) increasing agricultural production, (b) taking steps to ensure 'largest feasible' increase in income and employment, (c) developing social services (especially elementary education, water supply and sanitation and health services in rural areas), (d) developing communications and power, and (e) raising the standard of living for less developed areas of the State. All these programmes were "intended to be oriented towards greater production and employment and the welfare of weaker sections of the population." In assessing the needs and problems of different States and in proposing outlays, factors relating to backwardness (such as population, pressure on cultivated land, underdeveloped transport and communications facilities, etc.) and commitments arising out of the Second Plan and those arising from large projects were given due attention.

As far as the second issue is concerned, special attention was sought to be given to areas that were relatively backward in the past. Programmes to be implemented to achieve this purpose included (i) intensive development of agriculture, (ii) extension of irrigation, (iii) promotion of small and village industries, (iv) large-scale expansion of power, (v) development of roads and road transport, (vi) provision of universal education for the age-group 6-11 years, (vii) larger opportunities for secondary, technical, and vocational education, (viii) improvements in conditions of living and water supply, (ix) programmes for the welfare of scheduled castes, scheduled tribes and other backward classes, (x) programme of rural works to solve the problem of poverty and underemployment, and (xi) establishment of large industrial projects and river valley projects in the less developed regions of the country as long as this did not seriously conflict with the technological considerations.[16]

These policies were continued in the subsequent plans as well with some change of emphasis here and there. In addition to these programmes, the Fourth Plan introduced a number of other schemes for the benefit of the rural poor such as Small Farmers' Development Agency, Marginal Farmers' and Agricultural Labourers' Development Agency, Drought-Prone Areas Programme, Crash Scheme for Rural Employment, Pilot Intensive Rural Employment Project, etc. Since a large number of the rural poor live in relatively less developed regions, all these programmes were expected to benefit the less developed regions more in comparison with the developed regions. Some programmes such as Drought-Prone Areas Programme were meant specifically to help the backward areas.[17] Other specific programmes initiated in the Fourth Plan included identification of backward regions for purposes of granting concessions and financial assistance to industries established in such areas and weightage to backward States in the allocation of Central assistance. Besides, a number of State governments and financial institutions also announced special concessions to industries established in the backward areas so that entrepreneurs could be attracted to invest in such areas.

These policies and programmes were continued in the Fifth Plan period as well. Emphasis was laid on Area Development. Approaches adopted for this purpose included the resource-based or the problem-based development approach, the target-group approach, the incentive approach, and the comprehensive area approach. The various area development programmes undertaken during the Fifth Plan can be classified as follows:[18]

I	Resource/Problem-based Area Programmes:	The Drought-Prone Area Programme. The Command Area Development Programme. Hill Area Development
II	Target Group Programmes:	The SFDA Programmes, the Tribal Development Agency Projects
III	Area Specific Incentive Programmes:	Concessional Finance, Investment Subsidy and Transport Subsidy Schemes
IV	Comprehensive Area Development Programmes:	Sub-Plans for the Hills and Tribal Areas

Considering the period of planning as a whole, the policies adopted by the government can be classified into either of the following categories:

1. Policies aimed at industrialization of lagging regions;
2. Policies for development of irrigation, agriculture, and allied activities;
3. Policies aimed at providing infrastructural facilities such as transport, communications, banking, etc. in backward regions;
4. Transfer of resources from Centre to States in the form of plan assistance, non-plan assistance, and discretionary grants in such a way as to reduce regional disparities; and
5. Special programmes for the development of backward and less developed regions.

Under the first heading, the following measures were adopted: (a) location of public sector projects in backward regions, (b) use of industrial licensing policy to direct private investment to backward regions, and (c) encouragement to prospective entrepreneurs to set up industries in backward areas by granting them subsidies and concessional finance from nationalized banks and financial institutions. A number of public sector projects were set up in the backward States of Bihar, Madhya Pradesh, and Orissa. As a matter of fact, out of the total cumulative investment of Rs.11,451.2 crores in public sector projects as on 31.3.1977, as much as Rs.4648.3 crores were invested in these three States alone, which is more than 40% of the total investment in all States. However, the impact of such large public sector investment on the regional economies of Bihar, Madhya Pradesh, and Orissa has not been significant. The anticipated spread effects have not materialized and the economies of these States continue to be backward as usual.

We have discussed these issues in a detailed way in Chapter 8. A discussion on special programmes for development of backward areas can be found in the same chapter and in Chapter 7. Chapter 7 also includes a discussion on the programmes initiated for agricultural development. Discussion on transfer of resources from Centre to States (from the point of view of backward States) has been taken up in Chapter 9. In this chapter, therefore, we take up the study of only two policy measures in detail—industrial licensing policy of the government, and schemes of concessional finance initiated by the financial institutions. Since after the nationalization of banks in 1969, the avowed objective declared was to help economic development of the backward regions, we shall also examine briefly how far this objective has been actually fulfilled. But before we do this, let us turn to a discussion on the extent of regional imbalances and inequalities in India.

THE EXTENT OF REGIONAL IMBALANCES

After noting the intentions of the planners and the policy measures adopted by the government to reduce regional imbalances and inequalities, let us now try to analyse how far the intentions have been fulfilled and how far the measures adopted by the government have been successful. But before we try to do so, some comments are in order.

First, since States have been accepted as the planning units in India, we have data at the State level only which, in some cases, go down to the district level. Thus, we have inter-State data and, at the best, some inter-district data only. Consequently, we cannot study regional imbalances in the strict sense of the term but only inter-State imbalances and, to a very limited degree, intra-State imbalances. Second, most of the data available for different States are not comparable and, therefore, all results have to be accepted with reservations if not with some scepticism. At their best, the data can indicate 'broad trends' only. To give an example, data on per capita income are collected by States on the basis of prices ruling therein. Since (i) price levels are different in different States, (ii) commodities included in the compilation of price level by different States are different, and (iii) weights assigned to different commodities in the compilation of price levels are not the same in all States, per capita incomes of different States are not comparable. And yet differences in per capita incomes have for long been accepted as the best indicator of imbalances and inequalities. Third, to be able to make any worthwhile comments we must have comparable data for, at least, all districts in all States. In the absence of such data, we are likely to form a very wrong picture of the actul situation. Thus, a statement of the form that 'Maharashtra is the most developed State of India' should not lead the reader to expect that all districts of the State are well developed.[19] Indeed there are many districts which are well below the levels of development attained by many districts of much less developed States. Such intra-State differences are very important in any study on imbalances but are unfortunately concealed in inter-State data. Our problem is really very complex because we do not possess any reliable or comparable intra-State data in most of the States. And finally, what indicators should be used to highlight imbalances and inequalities? Should we use per capita income only? No, we cannot do so. We have already said that data on per capita income for different States are not strictly comparable. This indicator suffers from many other weaknesses also, some of which are mentioned below:

(a) A favourable population-resource relationship in a region (say, region *A*) compared with the population-resource relationship in another region (say, region *B*) may reveal that the per capita income in region *A* is greater than the per capita income in region *B*. Adoption of the per capita income indicator alone will lead us to conclude that region *A* is more developed than region *B*. However, it is possible that region *B* may be possessing a better infrastructure and other pre-conditions for development compared with region *A*;

(b) Generally the income data reveal the income *generated* in the region and not the income *accruing* to the region. Since the two can be materially different on account of inter-regional trade and commodity flows, the per capita income generated can be substantially different from the per capita income that actually accrues; and

(c) In an underdeveloped country like India, different States are likely to possess different levels of monetization. Some parts of the country might be still depending on barter exchange (i.e. exchange in kind). In such a situation, it would be unwise to consider the per capita income as a reliable index of development.

On account of all these considerations, per capita income alone cannot be considered to be a sufficient indicator of development. There are certain other indicators that cannot be lost sight of. For example, differences in industrial growth, disparities in agricultural growth, level of literacy in different States, percentage of urban population to total population in different States, percentage of workers in manufacturing industries to total workers, total road length, infant mortality rate, etc., can all be considered indicators for purposes of studying imbalances and inequalities in regional development. We can think of many more indicators. Which indicators should be chosen? This is a very difficult question to decide upon. The choice will inevitably have to depend upon (i) some value judgement about what is an important indicator and what is an unimportant indicator and (ii) availability of data. There may be indicators which according to our value judgement are important but for which comparable data for different units (States or districts, as the case may be) are not available. Then, there may be some indicators that do not seem very important but are included in the study because data for them are easily available. There is another difficult problem that has to be grappled with and it concerns with the assigning of weights to different indicators. For example, is the indicator of per capita income doubly important compared with literacy rate or trebly important? Questions such as this are very difficult to decide. An easy way out is to grant equal weights to all the indicators. But this approach is extremely unjustified. How can we regard per capita income, industrial growth, agricultural growth, percentage of urban population to total population, literacy rate, etc., as being of equal importance? The other way is to assign weights on the basis of *what one feels* about the importance of different indicators. However, recent developments in the field of statistical and mathematical analyses (particularly the development of principal component analysis) has reduced the amount of subjectivity considerably and we are now in a better position to choose weights more objectively.

STUDY OF PER CAPITA INCOME DATA

Table 1 gives estimates of per capita income for different States of India at current prices. Since data are at current prices, we cannot compare the figures for different years as prices have continued to rise over the years. Also because of the preceding discussion, it is not correct to derive any 'hard' conclusions from the data given in the table. Yet, it does reveal some broad basic trends which are indicated below:

TABLE 1: Per capita State net domestic product (at current prices)

(in rupees)

State	1960-61	1964-65	1967-68	1969-70	1975-76
1. Andhra Pradesh	314	438	522	544	897
2. Assam	349	441	509	586	848
3. Bihar	216	299	386	402	669
4. Gujarat	380	523	718	740	1236
5. Haryana	350	504	776	902	1514
6. Himachal Pradesh	—	—	576	724	1165
7. Jammu & Kashmir	287	341	416	503	825
8. Karnataka	292	420	538	571	1038
9. Kerala	278	393	567	643	1000
10. Madhya Pradesh	274	373	479	495	790
11. Maharashtra	419	526	663	736	1455
12. Manipur	—	—	420	542	904
13. Nagaland	—	—	282	328	949
14. Orissa	226	347	500	545	834
15. Punjab	385	575	867	1002	1688
16. Rajasthan	271	356	500	478	873
17. Tamil Nadu	344	434	529	591	997
18. Tripura	—	—	560	682	872
19. Uttar Pradesh	244	374	485	497	727
20. West Bengal	386	498	728	706	1100
All India	307	422	555	590	981
Mean	307	422	555	590	981
*S.D.	60.15	77.01	137.20	158.45	266.93
*C.V.	19.59	18.25	24.72	26.85	27.21
Range	203	276	585	674	1019

*Calculated from All-India Mean.

Sources: For the last column, *Report of the Seventh Finance Commission*, 1978, Annexure VII.3, p. 308. For all other columns, Om Prakash Mathur, "The Problem of Inter-Regional Disparities", *Indian Journal of Regional Science*, Vol. V, No. 1, 1973, Table I, p. 89.

(i) The States of Punjab, Maharashtra, and Haryana have continuously maintained a considerable lead over other States. In terms of per capita income, Maharashtra occupied the first place in 1960-61 but was pushed to the second place by Punjab in 1964-65. Since 1964-65, Punjab has occupied the first place with Maharashtra and Haryana vying with each other for the second place. The high level of per capita income in the States of Punjab and Haryana is due to the tremendous agricultural progress registered by these States especially after the advent of the green revolution while in the case of Maharashtra a large industrial base and impressive industrial progress accounts for the high level of per capita income.

(ii) Many States have continuously remained backward in terms of per capita income. The position of some big States such as Bihar, Orissa, Rajasthan, Uttar Pradesh, and Madhya Pradesh appears to be particularly bad. Bihar had the lowest per capita income during a number of years. In 1964-65, its per capita income was 70.8% of the national average and merely 52% of Punjab's per capita income. In 1969-70, its per capita income was 68% of the national average and 40% of Punjab's income. In 1974-75, its per capita income at Rs.669 was 68.2% of the national average (national per capita income was Rs.981 in that year) and 39.6% of Punjab's income. Some other examples can also be given to highlight the disparities. Thus, the per capita income of Orissa, Madhya Pradesh, Uttar Pradesh, and Rajasthan was merely 54.4%, 49.4%, 49.6%, and 47.7% respectively of Punjab's per capita income in 1969-70.

(iii) Data in the last three columns show that about 12 States out of the 20 have had per capita income below the national average. To highlight inter-State inequalities, we calculated the per capita incomes of different States as a percentage of per capita income of Punjab for 1964-65, 1969-70, and 1975-76. The results are presented below:

	1964-65	1969-70	1975-76
1. No. of States having per capita income less than 50% of Punjab's per capita income	1	4	5
2. No. of States having per capita income between 50% and 60% of Punjab's per capita income	3	10	8
3. No. of States having per capita income between 60% and 75% of Punjab's per capita income	10	2	4
4. No. of States having per capita income more than 75% of Punjab's per capita income	2	2	2
Total number of States considered	16	18	19

This shows that only two States had more than 75% of Punjab's per capita income. Another fact of considerable importance is that while only 4 States had less than 60% of per capita income of Punjab in 1964-65, their number rose to 14 in 1969-70 and stood at 13 in 1975-76. This observation reveals considerable increase in inter-State disparities as far as the indicator of per capita income is concerned.

(iv) We have calculated range, standard deviation, and coefficient of variation in the bottom half of Table 1 to highlight the fact of inter-State disparities in per capita income. The standard deviation of per capita income has risen consistently from 60.15 in 1960-61 to 77.01 in 1964-65, to 137.20 in 1967-68, to 158.45 in 1969-70, and to 266.93 in 1975-76. The true picture of disparities is, however, revealed by the coefficient of variation (since mean per capita income has also increased). The coefficient of variation shows a remarkable increase from 19.59 to 26.85 over the period 1960-61 to 1969-70 and further to 27.21 in 1975-76 highlighting a marked increase in disparities in per capita income.

DISPARITIES IN INDUSTRIAL GROWTH

As pointed out earlier in this chapter, the initial distribution of industries was determined by the historical processes of growth reflected in the development of transport facilities and the interests of the British rulers. In some cases such as jute these processes coincided with the potential natural processes. The jute industry got concentrated in Bengal and especially around Calcutta because of "the intimate agricultural connection of the industry, the long association of English investors with Calcutta and the good transport relations of the place for purposes of exportation".[20] Out of the 75 jute mills in 1919, as many as 71 were concentrated in Bengal while only three mills were located in Madras and one in the United Provinces. Out of the 100 jute mills in 1931, as many as 93 were located in Bengal. Though the first cotton mill was erected in Calcutta by the middle of the nineteenth century, the industry grew up in Bombay which also became its centre of concentration. The development of railways and the connection of Bombay with the cotton-growing tracts of Nagpur, Ahmedabad, and Sholapur, led to setting up of cotton mills in these cities and they spread rapidly. In 1919, out of the 246 cotton mills in British India, as many as 179 mills were in Bombay. By 1931, the cotton mill industry had gained a certain measure of dispersion; yet out of the 305 mills in that year, 208 were concentrated in Bombay. Similarly, in many other industries the growth of mills and firms has tended to concentrate at the original centres of establishment of these mills. Protective tariffs and the policy of discriminating protection did achieve a certain degree of dispersal but, on the whole, the original centres of location continued to gather firms around them.

Taking the period before independence as a whole, we can divide industries into three categories depending upon their tendency to concentrate at or disperse away from the original centres of location, following Balkrishna:

1. Industries which inspite of expansion in terms of an increase in the number of mills showed no significant dispersion. To this category belongs the iron and steel industry.
2. Industries which had a tendency to disperse and get located at places away from the original centres of location causing reduction in the importance of original centres. Under this category come the cotton textile industry, woollen industry, silk manufacture, soap, matches and cement.
3. Industries which showed dispersion but such dispersion did not lead to a reduction in the importance of original centres of concentration. This category includes the sugar industry, leather works, tanneries, chemical industry, paper and glass.

Points (1) and (3) above show that before independence there was a distinct tendency for industries to get located at a few centres. What is important from our point of view is the fact that even industries which showed a tendency to disperse away from the original centres of location tended to get concentrated at some other centres. Thus, the cotton industry merely changed its centre of concentration from Bombay to Ahmedabad. In the case of the soap industry, in 1919, the proportion of workers (as percentage of total workers engaged in soap industry) engaged in Bengal was 81.6 which fell to only 46.4 in 1937 because Bombay had emerged as a new centre. Together between them these two centres shared 86.3% of workers. In the case of the woollen industry, 78.8% of workers engaged in this industry were employed in the United Provinces and Punjab, but in 1937 this proportion went down to 59.7% because of the emergence of Bombay as a new centre. Taken together these three centres accounted for 80.0% of total workers employed. However, in the case of at least three industries—cement, matches, and silk—a remarkable degree of dispersion was achieved by 1937.

Taking the picture as a whole, we can say that at the time of independence, we inherited a lopsided pattern of industrial development with most of the industries concentrated at a few centres, and in some cases this concentration was not the result of natural advantages but was imposed by historical forces.

Let us examine the regional distribution of industries after independence. Table 2 gives an aggregative picture of the location of 28 large-scale manufacturing industries in India in 1950. Four indicators, viz. capital, employment, output, and value added, are considered in Table 2, and all of

TABLE 2: Distribution of 28 large-scale manufacturing industries in India in 1950

Region	Total productive capital (%)	Total No. of persons employed (%)	Gross ex-factory value of output (%)	Value added by manufacture (%)	Per capita value added by manufacture (Rs. per head)
1. Assam	0.56	0.39	0.62	0.35	1.095
2. W. Bengal	24.65	30.10	27.02	27.06	30.971
3. Bihar	10.49	6.79	8.01	10.78	7.610
4. Orissa	0.97	0.69	0.43	0.56	1.086
5. U.P.	9.64	9.85	10.36	9.04	4.058
6. Central Region	3.04	3.19	3.04	2.11	2.413
7. Northern Region	2.85	2.33	2.43	1.92	3.190
8. Rajasthan	1.25	0.99	0.65	0.43	0.757
9. Delhi	1.46	1.48	1.47	1.51	24.598
10. Western Region	34.60	32.93	33.39	36.89	28.677
11. Southern Region	10.49	11.28	12.58	9.35	3.991
Total	100.00	100.00	100.00	100.00	9.024
Total value (in lakhs of Rs.)	61,453	1,632,484 (in number)	102,802	28,392	—

Source: S.R. Hashim, op. cit., pp. 42-43. Compiled from Fifth Census of Indian Manufacturers, 1950.

Notes:

1. Factories with 20 or more workers are covered by the data.
2. Central region means—Madhya Pradesh, Madhya Bharat, Bhopal, and Vindhya Pradesh. Northern region means—Punjab, Himachal Pradesh, Pepsu, and Jammu & Kashmir. Western region means—Old Bombay State, Kutch & Saurashtra, Goa, Daman & Diu, Dadra & Nagar Haveli. Southern region means—Old Madras State, Old Mysore State, Travancore, Cochin, Coorg, and Pondicherry.
3. However, the following States were not covered by the census—Jammu & Kashmir, Madhya Bharat, Bhopal, Bilaspur, Manipur and Tripura, Saurashtra, Mysore, and Hyderabad.

   For calculating the per capita value added by manufacture (of 28 industries covered by the census) in each region, 1951 population has been used. The population of the areas/States not covered by the census has been excluded from the population of the respective regions, for this purpose.

them present more or less an identical picture and reveal the dominance of the western region and West Bengal in the regional distribution of industries. Thus, 34.60% of total productive capital was concentrated in the western region while 24.65% was concentrated in West Bengal, their combined share being as much as 59.25%. Taken together, the western region and West Bengal accounted for 63.03% of total persons employed, 60.41% of gross ex-factory value of output, and 63.95% of value added by manufacture. The table thus reveals the high level of concentration in the industrial sector in 1950. The rest of India (taken as total India minus West Bengal and western region) accounted for only 40.75% of productive capital, 36.97% of total persons employed, 39.59% of gross ex-factory value of output, and 36.05% of value added by manufacture for industries included in Hashim's table.

Table 3 reveals the extent of concentration in 1965, i.e. after 14-15 years of planned development. No decline of concentration is in evidence. The western region and West Bengal continued to dominate the scene. Thus, the three States of Maharashtra, West Bengal, and Gujarat with only 22.0% of total population accounted for 42.2% of total productive capital, 50.1% of total number of persons employed, and 53.1% of gross output. If another centre of development, viz. Tamil Nadu, is also included, the share of these four industrially advanced States in total productive capital rises to 50.3%. These four States together accounted for 58.8% of total number of persons employed and 61.6% of gross output while only 29.3% of the population lived in them. Against this, the combined share of the three industrially backward States of Bihar, UP, and Orissa having 31.1% of total population of the country (which is more than the combined population of the four most industrially advanced States) in total productive capital employed was merely 21.3% in total number of persons employed was 14.5%, and in gross output was a meagre 17.6%. This comparison explains the glaring inequalities in industrial development after fifteen years of planning.

The position regarding the factory sector in 1974-75 is summarized in Table 4. The table reveals that even after 25 years of planning there is no remarkable tendency of dispersion noticeable. In fact, the two States of Maharashtra and West Bengal alone account for more than one-third of total factory employment, output, and value added by manufacture. Their combined share in the total number of factories and aggregate fixed capital in 1974-75 was 26.0% and 25.0% respectively. If the four industrially advanced States of Maharashtra, West Bengal, Gujarat, and Tamil Nadu, are considered together, the true picture of regional concentration of industries is explicitly brought into prominence. Thus, in 1974-75, these four States together (having 29.81% of total population) accounted for 47.5% of total factories, 42.2% of total fixed capital, 53.1% of total employ-

TABLE 3: State-wise population, productive capital, employment, gross output of industries, 1965

	Maha-rashtra	West Bengal	Tamil Nadu	Gujarat	Bihar	Uttar Pradesh	Karnataka	Punjab & Haryana	Andhra Pradesh
(1)	(2)	(3)	(4)	(5)	(6)	(7)	(8)	(9)	(10)
Pop. (1968) million	47.7	42.6	38.2	25.2	55.1	86.9	28.0	23.4	41.6
% of total	9.1	8.1	7.3	4.8	10.5	16.7	5.3	4.5	7.9
Productive capital (employed by crores)	1048	1219	512	395	505	493	240	348	239
% of total	16.6	19.3	8.1	6.3	8.0	7.8	3.8	5.5	3.8
No. of persons employed (in '000)	775.3	866.9	345	338.6	209.2	295.5	163.5	136.2	215.4
% of total	19.6	21.9	8.7	8.6	5.3	7.5	4.1	3.5	5.5
Gross output Ex-factory value (Rs. crores)	1516	1376	545	518	439	463	229	249	253
% of total	23.6	21.4	8.5	8.1	6.8	7.2	3.6	3.9	3.9

(Contd.)

TABLE 3 (*Contd.*)

	Madhya Pradesh	Orissa	Kerala	Assam	Rajasthan	Jammu & Kashmir	Union Territories	Total
(1)	(11)	(12)	(13)	(14)	(15)	(16)	(17)	(18)
Pop. (1968) million	38.8	20.9	20.3	14.7	24.9	3.9	—	524.1
% of total	7.4	3.9	3.9	2.8	4.7	0.7	—	100.0
Productive capiial (employed by crores)	524	347	83	142	111	3.6	92	6300.4
% of total	8.3	5.5	1.3	2.3	1.8	0.1	1.7	100.0
No. of persons employed (in '000)	149.4	68.4	154.3	75.6	67.9	9.3	84	3953.2
% of total	3.9	1.7	3.9	1.9	1.7	0.2	2.1	100.0
Gross output Ex-factory value (Rs. crores)	228	141	130	114	80	4.9	135	64196
% of total	3.6	2.2	2.0	1.8	1.2	0.1	2.3	100

Source: A.J. Singh and M.V. George, "Regional Economic Development in India", *Balanced Regional Development* (Papers read at the Indian Economic Conference, 1969, Popular Prakashan, Bombay).

TABLE 4: **Principal data of factory sector, State-wise : 1974-75**

State	Factory		Fixed capital		Employment		Output		Value added	
	No.	% to total	Rs. crore	% to total	No.	% to total	Rs. crore	% to total	Rs. crore	% to total
1. Andhra Pradesh	5542	8.6	661	5.5	439943	7.3	1453	5.6	262	4.3
2. Assam	1945	3.0	129	1.1	106811	1.8	398	1.5	109	1.8
3. Bihar	2528	3.9	791	6.6	301744	5.0	1513	5.8	380	6.2
4. Gujarat	6860	10.7	1036	8.7	563860	9.3	2838	10.9	609	10.0
5. Haryana	1243	1.9	365	3.1	120259	2.0	658	2.1	132	2.2
6. Himachal Pradesh	151	0.2	35	0.3	22131	0.4	33	0.1	9	0.1
7. Jammu & Kashmir	230	0.4	12	0.1	16243	0.3	32	0.1	8	0.1
8. Karnataka	3978	6.2	526	4.4	292817	4.8	1034	4.0	275	4.5
9. Kerala	2583	4.0	451	3.8	243487	4.0	797	3.1	169	2.8
10 Madhya Pradesh	2562	4.0	682	5.7	254921	4.2	1124	4.3	287	4.7
11. Maharashtra	10835	16.9	1943	16.3	1165931	19.3	6569	25.2	1592	26.2
12. Orissa	914	1.4	419	3.5	98440	1.6	391	1.5	105	1.7
13. Punjab	3707	5.8	532	4.5	164093	2.7	842	3.2	136	2.2
14. Rajasthan	1399	2.2	423	3.5	122215	2.0	562	2.2	117	1.9
15. Tamil Nadu	6957	10.8	1012	8.5	603090	10.0	2586	9.9	577	9.5
16. Uttar Pradesh	4819	7.5	1475	12.4	507245	8.4	1778	6.8	395	6.5
17. West Bengal	5854	9.1	1036	8.7	877320	14.5	2880	11.0	786	12.9
18. Delhi	1648	2.6	198	1.7	104642	1.7	443	1.7	85	1.4
Total All-India	64215	—	11922	—	6052804	—	26099	—	6081	—

Source: The Economic Times, 6 April 1977; p. 6, Compiled from *Annual Survey of Industries, 1974-75.*

ment, 57.0% of total output, and 58.6% of total value added. Compared with the figures for 1965, these data show some reduction in the regional concentration of industries in the four industrially advanced States of Maharashtra, West Bengal, Tamil Nadu, and Gujarat; yet the reduction is too small to justify any tall claims of regional dispersal of industries. The mere fact that approximately half of total industries and approximately 60% of total value added and total output is found in these four States alone while the remaining 17 States and Union territories contribute only 40% of total output and total value added is a proof of substantial regional concentration of industries in the four industrially advanced States of Maharashtra, West Bengal, Tamil Nadu, and Gujarat.

Table 5 reveals disparities in per capita industrial consumption of electricity. In 1969-70 and 1976-77, per capita consumption was the highest in

TABLE 5: Per capita industrial consumption of electricity in States

(in Kwh)

State	1969-70	1976-77
(1)	(2)	(3)
1. Andhra Pradesh	27.3	40.0
2. Assam	10.8	16.6
3. Bihar	39.4	46.3
4. Gujarat	88.6	119.8
5. Haryana	46.3	78.2
6. Himachal Pradesh	—	12.9
7. Jammu & Kashmir	18.2	11.0
8. Karnataka	64.1	107.8
9. Kerala	57.3	68.1
10. Madhya Pradesh	36.9	61.1
11. Maharashtra	114.0	120.4
12. Nagaland	0.8	2.6
13. Orissa	57.6	71.2
14. Punjab	138.5	143.5
15. Rajasthan	21.6	42.2
16. Tamil Nadu	74.5	76.8
17. Uttar Pradesh	39.2	41.5
18. West Bengal	86.3	78.8
All India	57.5	68.4
Mean	57.5	68.4
S.D.	36.2	40.12
C.V.	62.9	58.65
Range	137.7	140.9

Sources: Col. 2 is from Om Prakash Mathur, op. cit., Table 6, p. 97.
Col. 3 is from *The Economic Times*, 3 August, 1978, p. 4.

Punjab followed by Maharashtra and Gujarat. The underdeveloped States of Bihar, Madhya Pradesh, and Rajasthan were way behind these States as far as industrial consumption of electricity is concerned. Range (which represents the difference between the highest and the lowest values) was as high as 137.7 Kwh in 1969-70 and 140.0 Kwh in 1976-77. Both standard deviation and coefficient of variation were also considerably high in these years.

OTHER INDICATORS OF DISPARITIES

In addition to disparities in per capita income and industrial growth, it is necessary to consider disparities in agricultural development, spread of educational facilities, development of banking facilities, transport and communications, etc. Disparities in agricultural development are revealed in cols. 2 to 5 of Table 6, where we have considered the following four indicators:

1. Per capita average foodgrain production
2. Consumption of fertilizers per hectare of cropped area
3. Per hectare yield of foodgrains
4. Percentage of gross irrigated area to gross cropped area

Column 2 shows that the highest per capita average foodgrain production was in Punjab (529 kg) and the lowest was in Kerala (57 kg). This gives a range as high as 472 kg. Coefficient of variation works out at 69. This column shows that per capita average foodgrain production was considerably higher than the national average of 173 kg in the agriculturally advanced States of Punjab and Haryana. Columns 3, 4, and 5 repeat the story of column 2. The agriculturally advanced State of Punjab is considerably above the national average in all these cases. Thus, against the national average of 20.1 kg fertilizer consumption per hectare of cropped area, consumption was as high as 61.6 kg in Punjab. Against the national average of 866 kg, yield of foodgrains per hectare was 1976 kg in Punjab. Similarly, while the nation as a whole had irrigation facilities in only 25.4% of gross cropped area, Punjab had irrigation facilities in 80.8% of gross cropped area. Coefficient of variation is 70.04 for col. 3, 44.9 for col. 4, and 72.6 for col. 5. These high values for coefficients of variation are indicative of large inter-State disparities in the agricultural sector.[21]

Table 6 also reveals widespread disparities in literacy and total road length per 100 km^2 of area. In both these cases, the first rank is occupied by Kerala. Column 10 states that the number of students in primary and secondary schools was 254.4 per thousand population in Kerala which is considerably above the second ranked State of Tamil Nadu where the number of students in primary and secondary schools was 186.7 per thousand population. Rajasthan was the most lowly placed State in this regard where the number of students was merely 85.5 per thousand population. Column 11 reveals that whereas the national average of total road length per 100 km^2 of area was 36 km only, in Kerala this road length was as high as 301 km which is more than eight times the national average. Kerala seems be an exception in this regard and is considerably above the other States. This would be clear from the fact that the second ranked State was that of Tamil Nadu having total road length of 71 km per 100 km^2 of area. At the bottom was the State of Jammu & Kashmir with only 6 km of road length. This gives a range of 295 km. The standard deviation for col. 11 works out as 66.63 and coefficient of variation 185.1. This shows that there are widespread inter-State disparities as fas as the indicator 'total road length per 100 km^2 of area' is concerned.

METHODS OF COMBINING INDICATORS

To obtain an overall view of inter-State disparities, it becomes necessary to combine indicators and form a composite index of development. In the analysis given above, we have considered various indicators of agricultural and industrial development and also indicators relating to per capita income, educational development, and infrastructure. Some States are more developed in agriculture and less developed in industry while others are more developed in industry and backward in agriculture. On a survey of data for different indicators of development given in Table 6 we find that as far as average foodgrain production per capita is concerned, Punjab ranked first followed by Haryana, Himachal Pradesh, and Madhya Pradesh in that order. The rank of the most developed industrial State (having first rank according to the indicator 'gross output in industry per capita'), viz. Maharashtra, was sixteenth out of the 21 States. The rank of Punjab according to 'gross output in industry per capita' was fourth. Similarly, Kerala which ranked seventeenth according to 'average foodgrain production per capita' and eighth according to 'gross output in industry per capita' ranked first according to the indicator concerning education (the only indicator employed for the purpose being 'the number of students in primary and secondary schools per thousand population') and the indicator concerning infrastructure (the only indicator employed for the purpose being 'total road length per 100 km^2 of area'). Because of such diversity in ranking according to different indicators of development, it becomes necessary to combine the indicators in some way so as to form an overall view of the regional disparities.

As noted by us elsewhere in this chapter, the choice of indicators depends on the value judgement of the researcher (i.e., what indicators are thought to be relevant or more important and are included in the study and what indicators are thought to be unimportant and are thus left out) and the availability of data on the various indicators. In general, care is taken that (i) each indicator selected is relevant, objective, and measurable and (ii) the indicators finally chosen are able to reflect the multi-dimensional character of development in a general way. Depending on what indicators are chosen and how they are combined will depend the results of our analysis. For example, if more indicators relating to agriculture are chosen the picture that will emerge will be entirely different from the picture that will emerge if more indicators relating to industrial development are considered. We shall illustrate this point later when we consider the data in Table 6. After the question of choosing indicators is settled comes the important problem of combining them. A simple method of combining them is just to add up the ranks that are assigned to different States on the basis of different indicators. The State having the minimum total rank score will then be the most developed State, the State having the second minimum total rank score will be the next developed State (second in order) and so on, the State having the maximum total rank score will be the least developed (or most backward). This method is the simplest and was employed by V. Nath and the former Registrar-General of India, Asok Mitra.

The next method is to assign weights to indicators before combining them. The technique that is now the most frequently used technique and has gained immense popularity in studies of regional imbalances and regional disparities is the 'Principal Component Analysis'. As noted in Chapter 4, in this technique the number of original indicators is reduced to a smaller number of indices, each of which is a linear combination of the original indicators. These indices are known as factors and the set of coefficients forming a linear combination of the original indicators are known as factor loadings (which are simply the maximum correlations between the factors and their constituent indicators). These factor loadings are, in fact, *weights* which reflect the relative importance of individual clusters or indicators of development. After the composite indicators of development are prepared for different sectors such as agriculture, industry, banking, infrastructure, education, etc., they can be combined once again following the technique described above to form a Composite Index of Development for the economy as a whole. The method of *principal component analysis* was applied in India for the first time by M.N. Pal to study regional imbalances and regional disparities in India.[22] Following the method formulated by Pal, Hemlata Rao also studied regional disparities in India taking the years

1956, 1961, and 1965. She also tried to assess whether or not disparities have tended to increase.

Let us now turn to a consideration of some of the important studies on the extent of regional disparities in India conducted by different scholars from time to time.

Asok Mitra's Study

Based on the 1961 census data, Asok Mitra, the then Registrar-General of India, conducted a pioneering study on 'Levels of Regional Development in India'.[23] Though, as noted above, Mitra's study was based on a simple method of 'assigning and adding up ranks' to highlight regional disparities, it was a *pioneering study* since it was the first study that used district-level data and which attempted to include a mammoth wealth of data. The indicators used by Mitra were divided by him into the following six blocks and information collected on them for each district of India:

Block I. (A) Geology, Topography, Rainfall, House Type, Language, and Scheduled Tribes and Castes. (B) Soils, Crops, and Yield of Rice.

Block II. Agricultural Infrastructure (including area under double crop percent of net area sown, gross area irrigated percent of gross area sown, Households cultivating 0-5 acres percent of all cultivating households, pure tenancy holdings percent of all cultivating households, hired attached workers percent of all workers at cultivation, cultivators and agricultural labourers per 100 acres of net area sown, cultivators and agricultural labourers percent of rural working population).

Block III. Participation Rates in traditional sector (including male participation rate, female participation rate, males working in agriculture percent of male working population, single and family workers in non-agricultural percent of total non-agricultural workers, workers in household industry percent of total working population).

Block IV. Potential of human resources (persons per square mile, females per 1,000 males, rural population per 1000 of total population, percentage increase of population in 1951-61, immigrants percent of total population, children 0-4 percent of women aged 15-44, crude literacy rate, scheduled tribe population percent of total population, scheduled caste population percent of total population).

Block V. Distributive trade, manufacturing and infrastructure (includes (1) workers in retail trade per 1000 of population, (2) workers in manufacturing per 1000 of total population, (3) census houses used as (a) business houses or offices, (b) as community centres, (c) as restaurants and eating houses, (d) as rest houses, (e) as school houses, and (f) as medical institutions per 1000 of all census houses, and (4) miles of surfaced roads per 1000 square miles of area).

Block VI. Organized industrial activity in the modern sector (includes establishments run on electricity percent of all industrial establishments, workers in registered factories percent of all workers, degree of congestion in housing, whether headquarters towns (1) generates own electricity, or (2) is connected to grid or (3) both or none, industrial specialization in organized sector—five industries graded according to declining ratio.

Block I was left out of computation as the data were 'largely descriptive and qualitative'. The technique employed by Mitra was as follows:

> For each column in blocks II to VI, except for those for housing congestion and industrial pattern, the districts were arranged in quartiles in order of their observed values. Each quartile was thereafter split as much as possible in two equal halves of values. In some cases the marks (1 to 8 or 1 to 4) were directly related to the ascending values of a cell on the assumption that a high value reflected credit on a district while a low value signified the reverse. In some others the eighths or fourths were inversely related to the value of a cell, a high eighth or fourth value being associated with a low actual value of the cell concerned. This too was a matter of simple rules; *e.g.* eighth values and actual values were inversely related in the column devoted to households cultivating 0·5 acres per 100 of cultivating households, but were directly related in the column devoted to gross area irrigated as percentage of gross area sown. It was decided to retain a positive grading of proportions of members of scheduled tribes and castes according to their strength—high eighths for high ratio and *vise versa*. . . . Greater Bombay, Calcutta and Madras Corporation, which have no rural areas, have been placed as a matter of course in the highest level of development.
>
> The next step was to pool the eighth values obtained for all the columns together by this process of ranking and obtain their total score for each district. All the districts, thereafter, were freshly arranged in quartiles in ascending order of their total scores. This rearrangement and the position of each district in terms of its total score formed the basis of the final ranking in the four levels of development. . . .[24]

Mitra's analysis shows that out of the total 327 districts in India, 79 were at the lowest level of development and 88 at the second lowest level of development. The number of districts at the fourth (or the highest level of development) was 84; 19.66% of the total population of the country lived in districts at the lowest level of development; and 30.72% of the total population lived in districts in the highest level of development. In the most advanced industrial State of India, viz. Maharashtra, 11 districts (out of a total of 26) were classified in the top level of development and 52.62% of population lived in them. Only 8 districts fell in the two lowest categories of development and 26.99% of population lived in them.

The position in some other developed States was as follows. In Gujarat, seven districts (out of a total of 17) were in the top level of development and 42.66% of population lived in them. Only 3 districts fell in the two lowest categories of development and a meagre 12.30% of population resided in them. In West Bengal, 8 districts (out of a total of 16) were placed in top level of development and 58.00% of population lived in them. Against this, 7 districts were placed in the two lowest levels of development and 37.86% of population resided in them. In Tamil Nadu, eight districts (out of a total of 13) were placed in top level of development and 61.41% of population lived in them. No district was placed in the lowest two levels of development. In the agriculturally advanced State of Punjab 13 districts (out of a total of 19) were placed in the top level of development and 78.33% of population resided in them. Against this, only 4 districts were placed in the two lowest levels of development and 14.10% of the population lived in them. Against this, the position of the relatively less developed States such as UP, MP, Rajasthan, Orissa, and Bihar shows a substantial concentration of population in districts placed in the lowest two levels of development. In UP, e.g., 59.28% of population (spread over 34 districts out of a total of 54 districts) lived in districts placed in the two lowest levels of development. The population in some other less developed States living in districts placed in two lowest levels of development was as under—77.90% in Bihar (spread over 12 districts out of 17), 85.48% in Kashmir (spread over 8 districts out of 9), 95.68% in Orissa (spread over 12 districts out of 13), and 55.22% in Rajasthan (spread over 16 districts out of 26).

V. Nath's Study

Utilising the conclusions of Asok Mitra's study and adopting a similar method of combining ranks (unweighted ranks are simply added up), V. Nath[25] attempted to highlight disparities between different regions of India. Nath considered data for 14 States and took the following indicators into account: (i) per capita income, (ii) proportion of urban population to total population, (iii) proportion of male workers in manufacturing industries to all male workers, (iv) proportion of population living in districts at the two higher levels of development (data for this indicator were obtained from Asok Mitra's study), and (v) Literacy rate for population in age groups of five years and above.

The method used by V. Nath was as follows. First of all, States were ranked according to the value of each indicator. Thus, Kerala having the highest literacy rate was given the first rank and Rajasthan having the lowest literacy rate was awareded the fourteenth rank as far as the indicator 'literacy rate (five years and above)' is concerned. Similarly, Maharashtra having the highest proportion of urban population to total population was awarded the first rank and Assam having the lowest proportion of urban population to total population was given the fourteenth rank as far as the indicator 'proportion of urban population to total population in 1961' is concerned. Ranks were awarded to different States in the case of other indicators in an identical manner. Ranks awarded to a particular State on the basis of the above five indicators were then added up to obtain the total rank score of that State. The States were then arranged in an ascending order of total rank score, the State having the lowest total rank score being the most developed State and the State having the highest rank score, being the least developed. In V. Nath's study, Maharashtra and Tamil Nadu had the lowest rank score of 14 and thus were considered as the most developed States. Gujarat with rank score 16 comes next. Then come West Bengal, Punjab, and Kerala. These six States were considered by Nath as the *relatively developed* States and the remaining eight States were considered as less developed.

Taking more recent data, we have adopted an analysis similar to V. Nath partly to illustrate the regional disparities with the help of recent data (V. Nath's data related to 1961) but more particularly to highlight the subjective element that inevitably enters any such study. It will amply demonstrate to the reader how the prejudices of a researcher (expressed in the choice of indicators) can vitally affect the results. The data are given in Table 6. We have considered eleven indicators, of which four relate to agriculture, four to industry, one to literacy, one to infrastructure, and one to per capita income. The four indicators relating to agriculture are: (i) average foodgrain production per capita, (ii) consumption of fertilizer per hectare of cropped area, (iii) yield per hectare of foodgrains, and (iv) percentage of gross irrigated area to gross cropped area. The four indicators relating to industry are: (i) average daily employment of factory workers per lakh population, (ii) gross output in industry per capita, (iii) value added in industry per capita, and (iv) industrial consumption of electricity per capita. The indicator relating to literacy is the 'number of students in primary and secondary schools per thousand population' and the indicator relating to infrastructure is 'total road length per 100 km^2 of area'. On the basis of Table 6, the following summary giving the order of development of States in different sectors can be prepared.

TABLE 6: Selected indicators of development for different States of India

State	Per capita average foodgrain production (kg)	Consumption of fertilizers per hectare of cropped area (kg)	Yield per hectare of foodgrains (kg)	Percentage of gross irrigated area to gross cropped area (P)	Average daily employment of factory workers per lakh population	Gross output in industry per capita (Rs) (P)
Reference Year	Average of 1970-71 to 1974-75	1976-77	Triennial average of 1973-74 to 1975-76	1974-75	1974	1975-76
(1)	(2)	(3)	(4)	(5)	(6)	(7)
1. Andhra Pradesh	166 (10)	30.3 (4)	942 (9)	33.3 (6)	846 (9)	3616 (9)
2. Assam	127 (14)	1.3 (17)	971 (8)	18.4 (11)	521 (13)	276.5 (11)
3. Bihar	139 (13)	14.5 (11)	852 (12)	28.1 (7)	566 (11)	324.9 (10)
4. Gujarat	114 (15)	20.0 (8)	760 (14)	17.5 (13)	1959 (3)	1014.2 (2)
5. Haryana	410 (2)	26.6 (5)	1037 (7)	53.6 (2)	1076 (7)	671.5 (5)
6. Himachal Pradesh	273 (3)	9.9 (13)	1276 (4)	16.5 (14)	434 (14)	139.5 (16)
7. Jammu & Kashmir	194 (8)	13.6 (12)	1260 (5)	39.6 (5)	282 (17)	78.2 (17)
8. Karnataka	210 (6)	19.0 (9)	928 (10)	13.6 (15)	1089 (6)	386.5 (7)
9. Kerala	57 (17)	23.1 (6)	1477 (2)	21.5 (8)	1223 (5)	373.8 (8)
10. Madhya Pradesh	234 (4)	6.4 (15)	636 (15)	8.3 (17)	571 (10)	272.8 (12)
11. Maharashtra	103 (16)	14.9 (10)	585 (16)	9.3 (16)	2168 (1)	1301.2 (1)
12. Orissa	197 (7)	8.5 (14)	796 (13)	17.9 (12)	342 (16)	215.2 (14)
13. Punjab	529 (1)	61.6 (1)	1976 (1)	80.8 (1)	974 (8)	688.4 (4)
14. Rajasthan	225 (5)	5.5 (16)	514 (17)	20.0 (9.5)	388 (15)	246.5 (13)
15. Tamil Nadu	150 (12)	36.3 (2)	1328 (3)	45.7 (3)	1252 (4)	652.5 (6)
16. Uttar Pradesh	185 (9)	31.7 (3)	903 (11)	40.3 (4)	528 (12)	212.2 (15)
17. West Bengal	152 (11)	20.4 (7)	1180 (6)	20.0 (9.5)	1995 (2)	705.1 (3)
INDIA	173	20.1	866	25.4	1032	499.5

State	Value added in industry per capita (Rs) (P)	Industrial consumption of electricity per capita (kWh) (P)	No. of students in primary and secondary schools per thousand population	Total road length per 100 km² of area	Per capita income at current prices (Rs) (P)	Total rank score
	1975-76	1976-77	1974-75	31/3/75	1975-76	
(1)	(8)	(9)	(10)	(11)	(12)	(13)
1. Andhra Pradesh	67.6 (11)	40.0 (14)	111.0 (15)	33 (11.5)	897 (10)	108.5
2. Assam	69.7 (9)	16.6 (15)	142.2 (11)	40 (8)	847 (12)	129
3. Bihar	81.8 (8)	46.3 (11)	97.0 (16)	69 (4)	669 (17)	120
4. Gujarat	192.9 (2)	119.8 (3)	170.5 (5)	23 (14)	1236 (4)	83
5. Haryana	137.0 (4)	78.2 (6)	149.5 (10)	33 (11.5)	1514 (2)	61.5
6. Himachal Pradesh	52.8 (14)	12.9 (16)	167.5 (6)	25 (13)	1165 (5)	118
7. Jammu & Kashmir	13.4 (17)	11.0 (17)	120.5 (13)	6 (17)	825 (14)	142
8. Karnataka	101.6 (7)	107.8 (4)	163.7 (8)	43 (6)	1038 (7)	85
9. Kerala	68.8 (10)	68.1 (9)	254.4 (1)	301 (1)	1000 (8)	75
10. Madhya Pradesh	60.2 (12)	61.1 (10)	115.6 (14)	20 (15)	790 (15)	139
11. Maharashtra	284.5 (1)	120.4 (2)	179.4 (4)	34 (10)	1455 (3)	80
12. Orissa	42.4 (16)	71.2 (8)	125.7 (12)	37 (9)	834 (13)	134
13. Punjab	115.2 (6)	143.5 (1)	179.6 (3)	44 (5)	1688 (1)	32
14. Rajasthan	54.9 (3)	42.2 (12)	85.5 (17)	13 (16)	873 (11)	144.5
15. Tamil Nadu	121.7 (5)	76.8 (7)	186.7 (2)	71 (2)	997 (9)	55

(*Contd.*)

TABLE 9 (*Contd.*)

(1)	(8)	(9)	(10)	(11)	(12)	(13)
16. Uttar Pradesh	43.8 (15)	41.5 (13)	165.0 (7)	42 (7)	727 (16)	112
17. West Bengal	174.8 (3)	78.8 (5)	151.0 (9)	64 (3)	1100 (6)	64.5
INDIA	106.8	68.4		36	918	

Notes: 1. Figures in parentheses indicate the ranks.

2. Out of 22 States, we have considered data for 17 States only. Data for the remaining States were not available for some of the indicators included in this table.

Sources: (i) *The Economic Times*, 3 August 1978; p. 4, Table A.

(ii) *Report of the Seventh Finance Commission*, 1978, Annexure VII. 3, p. 308.

Agricultural sector		Industrial sector	
State	Rank	State	Rank
Punjab	1	Maharashtra	1
Haryana	2	Gujarat	2
Tamil Nadu	3	West Bengal	3
Uttar Pradesh	4	Punjab	4
Andhra Pradesh	5	Tamil Nadu & Haryana	5
Jammu & Kashmir	6	Karnataka	6
Kerala	7	Kerala	7

Other indicators		Total development	
State	Rank	State	Rank
Punjab	1	Punjab	1
Kerala	2	Tamil Nadu	2
Tamil Nadu	3	Haryana	3
Maharashtra	4	West Bengal	4
West Bengal	5	Kerala	5
Karnataka	6	Maharashtra	6
Gujarat	7	Gujarat	7

As far as the agricultural sector is concerned, Punjab ranks first with Haryana, Tamil Nadu, Uttar Pradesh, and Andhra Pradesh occupying the next four places in that order. If attention is concentrated on the industrial sector alone, the six most industrially advanced States are Maharashtra, Gujarat, West Bengal, Punjab, Tamil Nadu, and Haryana.[26] Taking an overall view and considering the total rank score, the first seven States in order of development are: Punjab, Tamil Nadu, Haryana, West Bengal, Kerala, Maharashtra, and Gujarat. This would seem strange for generally Maharashtra is considered to be the most developed State while according to our analysis it is pushed to the sixth place. This is because of the reason that we have considered an equal number of indicators for agriculture and industry. Since industrialization is generally equated with economic progress, dynamism, modernization, and growth, it is argued that either indicators of industrial development should be given more weightage or more indicators of industrial development should be considered as compared with agricultural development. For example, if we consider only one indicator of agricultural development (relating to 'average foodgrain production per capita'), four indicators of industrial development (as given in cols. 6, 7, 8, and 9), and other indicators (as given in cols. 10, 11, and 12), we get an entirely different picture. The total rank score (in ascending order) and ranks are then as given below:

State	Total rank score	Rank	State	Total rank score	Rank
Punjab	29	1	Andhra Pradesh	89.5	10
Maharashtra	38	2	Bihar	90	11
West Bengal	42	3	Rajasthan & Madhya Pradesh	92	12
Tamil Nadu	47	4	Assam	93	13
Haryana	47.5	5	Uttar Pradesh	94	14
Gujarat	48	6	Orissa	95	15
Karnataka	51	7	Jammu & Kashmir	120	16
Kerala	59	8			
Himachal Pradesh	87	9			

These ranks also give the first place to Punjab. But the ordering of the other States is substantially changed. Thus, the most industrially advanced State of Maharashtra gets the second place. The other industrially advanced States of West Bengal, Tamil Nadu, and Gujarat get the third, the fourth, and the sixth rank respectively. This shows that any study of Nath's type is materially affected by the indicators that are included in it.[27]

The method of using unweighted ranks, as employed by Asok Mitra and V. Nath, is a very crude method. It is difficult to accept how 'per capita income' and 'proportion of workers in manufacturing industry' can be assigned equal weights In Asok Mitra's study as many as 30 variables are considered and they range widely from 'area under double crop percent of net sown area' to 'census houses used as restaurants and eating houses per 1000 of all census houses'. Assigning equal weights to all indicators implies giving equal importance to all such indicators which are very different in nature and content and which have varying levels of importance in any development process. Then, as noted by S.K. Rao, "while this method has simplicity, it ignores the magnitude of variation between any two regions with respect to any one variable. For example, *A* could be leading *B* in literacy by a large margin, but *B* might be leading *A* in mortality by a very small margin; if one sums up the ranks, both *A* and *B* might have the same rank score in such an instance. Thus rank-ordering gives no weight to the *magnitude of variation* between any pair of States."[28]

In his own attempt at studying regional disparities in India, S.K. Rao considers six variables, of which three relate to industry. The variables included in the study are: (a) crop output per head, (b) male workers in manufacturing other than household industry, (c) per capita consumption of industrial power, (d) per capita output from organized industry, (e) infant death rate, and (f) literacy rate. The method used by S.K. Rao is based on the multiple factor analysis. In this technique "new variables are formed which are linear combinations of the above six variables, such that they are themselves uncorrelated. Each one of the new variables represents an independent strand that make up the total variation." After calculating the factor loadings and employing the method used by Richard Stone (in his study relating to the building up of regional economic distances for the UK) with some modifications, S.K. Rao groups the States into three categories —the most developed, not so developed, and the least developed. The results of the study are presented for the early fifties and early sixties below:

Classification of States	In early fifties	In early sixties
(A) Most developed group	West Bengal, Maharashtra, Gujarat	West Bengal, Maharashtra
(B) Not so developed	Madras, Mysore, Punjab	Gujarat, Madras, Mysore, Punjab, Andhra Pradesh
(C) The least developed	Kerala, Andhra Pradesh, Rajasthan, Bihar, Assam, Orissa, Madhya Pradesh, Uttar Pradesh	Assam, Orissa, Madhya Pradesh, Uttar Pradesh, Rajasthan, Bihar, Kerala

Thus, Rao's study reveals that during the period between the early fifties and the early sixties there was no evidence of reduction in disparities. The position in the early sixties is practically the same in both the periods except that (a) Gujarat slipped from the group of most advanced States to the group of not so developed States; and (b) Andhra Pradesh moved up from the group of least developed States to the group of not so developed States. This suggests that "development during the first 15 years of planning in India seems to have led to no reduction in regional disparities; if at all, it seems to have been polarised in the two top groups of States. If one has to name the States which seem to remain depressed one may mention the following: Assam, Orissa, Madhya Pradesh, Uttar Pradesh, Rajasthan, Bihar and Kerala."[29]

Hemlata Rao's Study

Before we conclude this section, let us consider two other studies, both of which employ the technique of principal component analysis. One is Hemlata Rao's study[30] and the other is the study by B.N. Ganguli and Devendra B. Gupta.[31] While the former depends exclusively on the technique of principal component analysis (and is based on the methods evolved by M.N. Pal), the latter is more broadbased and employs a number of other techniques in addition to this technique. Ganguli and Devendra Gupta have constructed levels of living indices for 15 States of India by taking into account factors such as nutrition, housing, medical care, education, leisure, security, and environment. Compared with this study, Hemlata Rao's study is limited in scope. However, both of them try to estimate regional disparities in their own way and also attempt to answer whether regional disparities have reduced over time. Let us consider Hemlata Rao's study first.

Hemlata Rao selected 24 variables from the following four specific sectors —agriculture, industry, education, and banking. Five indicators selected related to agriculture, eight to industry, six to banking, and five to education. Indicators chosen from the agricultural sector were: (1) agricultural output per lakh of population, (2) agricultural output per worker, (3) gross area irrigated as percentage of gross area sown, (4) consumption of chemical fertilizers per 1000 hectares, and (5) mechanization index. Indicators from industrial sector were: (1) number of factories per lakh of population, (2) number of factories per 1000 km^2, (3) percentage of workers in the total population, (4) percentage of industrial employees, (5) factory workers per 1000 km^2, (6) factory employees per 1000 km^2, (7) high voltage industrial power consumption per factory, and (8) value added by manufactures per capita. Indicators included in the banking sector were: (1) number of bank offices per lakh of population, (2) deposits of banks per lakh of population, (3) credits of banks per lakh of population, (4) percentage of bank offices in the total number of bank offices in the country, (5) percentage of deposits in the total deposits, and (6) percentage of credits in the total deposits. Indicators selected from the education sector were: (1) literates as percentage of population, (2) scholars as percentage of population, (3) teachers as percentage of population, (4) school-going children as percentage of population, and (5) college-going children as percentage of population. Because of limitations of data, Hemlata Rao selected data for 1956, 1961, and 1965 only. A total number of 14 States were chosen for study.

Hemlata Rao's study of the agricultural sector reveals that there has been a slight rise in the level of agricultural development in the States but their relative position has not registered any noticeable change. Moreover, inter-State disparities in agriculture have increased since 1956 and the difference between levels of development in the agriculturally advanced and backward States is substantial. Glaring disparities were also found in the industrial sector where the industrially advanced States of West Bengal, Maharashtra, Gujarat, and Tamil Nadu were considerably above the backward States of Madhya Pradesh, Rajasthan, Assam, and Orissa. However, disparities over the years in the industrial sector have tended to go down. Substantial disparities existed in the banking and education sectors as well but over the years they also have shown a tendency to decrease.

To form an overall view of regional disparities, Hemlata Rao has combined the indices obtained from the agricultural, industrial, banking and educational sectors into a composite index of development. The composite index shows that West Bengal was the most developed State in all the three years—1956, 1961, and 1965. The second position was occupied by Maharashtra in all the three years. Tamil Nadu occupied the third position in 1956 and 1961, and Gujarat was fourth in both these years. In 1965, these two States interchanged their places. The agriculturally most advanced State of Punjab occupied the fifth position in all the three years. The value of composite index for the nation as a whole was 13.37 in 1956, 14.85 in 1961, and 15.96 in 1965. The index value for the States of Orissa, Rajasthan, Madhya Pradesh, Assam, and Bihar was below the national average in all the three years and consequently these States are classified by Hemlata Rao as 'less developed States'. Uttar Pradesh was just around the national average in all the three years.

Have regional disparities declined over the period? Yes, concludes Hemlata Rao. Her conclusion is based on the following three observations: (i) there has been a general decline in absolute differentials between the developed and the less developed States, (ii) the national average of composite index has registered an upward trend over time, and (iii) the coefficient of variation of the estimated values of composite index has declined from 19.70% in 1956 to 13.72% in 1965. While the absolute differential between the first and the last ranked State was 8.8 index points in 1956, it fell to 6.08 index points in 1965. Over the same period, the national average rose from 13.37 to 15.96 index points.

Ganguli and Gupta's Study

As already stated, B.N. Ganguli and Devendra B. Gupta have constructed Levels of Living Indices for 15 States of India. They have taken into account three periods of time—around 1955, around 1960, and around 1965. The following components of levels of living have been considered in the study—nutrition, housing, medical care, education, clothing, leisure, security, and environment. The first five represent what are called 'primary' components and the latter three represent 'secondary' components. Three sets of composite indices have been presented. The first covers the 'primary' components, the second covers the 'secondary' components, and the third is an overall index of the level of living (which is constructed by taking into account both the 'primary' and the 'secondary' components). As far as the primary aspects of levels of living are concerned, it was found that in all the three years considered (1955, 1960, and 1965) the States of Punjab, Tamil Nadu, Maharashtra, Kerala, and West Bengal showed the highest levels of living. Bihar, Orissa, Uttar Pradesh, Madhya Pradesh, and Andhra Pradesh showed the lowest levels. Punjab led as the 'highest' State with respect to the nutritional level, Kerala in respect of housing and education, and Tamil Nadu and West Bengal in respect of medical care. Examining whether inter-State disparities have reduced over the period 1955-65, Ganguli and Gupta find that in the matter of nutrition and medical care they had indeed reduced but in the field of education they had widened. As far as the overall primary aspects of living are concerned, it was found that the value of the 'critical minimum distance' had declined from 6.04 in 1955 to 5.61 in 1960 and further to 4.88 in 1965.

No definite pattern emerged for the secondary components. Yet, it was seen that West Bengal, Kerala, Tamil Nadu, and Punjab were the top States while Bihar, Orissa, Assam, Madhya Pradesh, and Uttar Pradesh occupied rather low positions. It was also observed that over the period 1955-65, disparities had decreased only in the field of 'leisure'. In other fields they had either increased or remained more or less at the same level. The value of the 'critical minimum distance' for the secondary components stood at 3.3 in 1955, at 4.62 in 1960, and at 3.81 in 1965.

By using the methods of principal component analysis and taxonomy, Ganguli and Gupta calculated a composite index of the levels of living by combining all primary and secondary indicators. It was found that in 1955, Tamil Nadu, West Bengal, Punjab, Maharashtra, and Kerala had the highest levels of living while Orissa, Bihar, Uttar Pradesh, Madhya Pradesh, and Assam were at lowest levels. The same grouping existed in 1960 and 1965 as well although while Karnataka and Jammu & Kashmir improved their position considerably, Rajasthan declined to the bottom group.[32]

A very important conclusion of the study related to reduction in disparities. It was found that the value of the critical minimum distance declined from 6.04 in 1955 to 5.61 in 1960 and further to 4.88 in 1965; which shows that *the disparities in the overall levels of living between the States declined during the period 1955-65.*

INDUSTRIAL LICENSING POLICY AND REGIONAL IMBALANCES

After considering the extent of regional inequalities and imbalances in India, let us now turn to enquire how the industrial licensing policy of the Government of India and the policies of the financial institutions and commercial banks actually helped in accentuating regional disparities though their purpose was exactly the opposite, i.e. reducing regional disparities.

First of all, let us consider the impact of industrial licensing policy. This policy was intended to regulate the private sector. For this purpose an Act of Parliament known as the 'Industries (Development and Regulation) Act, 1951' was enacted which came into force on 8 May 1952. The objectives that the Act sought to accomplish were: (i) the regulation of industrial investment and production according to Plan priorities and targets, (ii) protection of small entrepreneurs against competition from large industries, (iii) prevention of monopoly and concentration of ownership of industries, and (iv) balanced regional development with a view to reducing disparities in the levels of development of different regions of the economy. Since we are at present concerned with regional imbalances, let us consider how far the industrial licensing policy was able to fulfil the objective of balanced regional development. The obvious policy which was expected to be followed to achieve this objective was to grant more licences for establishment of industries in the lagging regions and controlling the establishment of more industries in the leading regions by denying licences to them.

In his study on 'Levels of Regional Development in India' (based on the 1961 census) A. Mitra divides all districts into four levels of development and provides evidence to the fact that districts at the top level of development received a large chunk of total industrial licences issued between 1953 and 1961. Out of a total number of 4971 industrial licences issued, districts in the top level of development cornered as many as 2293 licences, which comes to 46.13% of total licences issued. The three industrial cities of Bombay, Calcutta, and Madras got as many as 1778. This means that the share of these three cities in total licences issued in the period 1953 to 1961 was 35.77% (i.e. more than one-third). Districts at the first level of development got merely 84 licences, districts at the second level got 179 licences, and districts at the third level got 637 licences.[33] Mitra notes that during the period 1953 to 1961 "Districts in the first level of development did not find it possible to ask for more than 17 out of a total of 36 items under the Act (of 1951), and even out of these 17 items no more than one licence each was issued for such modern lines of manufacture as electrical equipment, transportation (including railway wagons), commercial, office and household furniture and leather products. . . . Of the more sophisticated lines of production districts in level II claimed the following additional items which were not claimed by any district in level I: machine tools (1 licence), drugs and pharmaceuticals (3), cement (6) and prime movers (2)."[34]

Most of the licences were claimed by districts in the third and fourth levels of development. Even here, districts in the third level of development claimed "no more than a handful of licences in agricultural machinery, miscellaneous mechanical and engineering industries, mathematical, surveying and drawing instruments, soaps, cosmetics and toilet goods, rubber goods, glues and gelatine and miscellaneous industries the total of all of which comes to only 12. . . ." On the other hand, the share of districts in the top level of development was 86.34% in licences issued to metallurgical industries, 89.58% in licences issued to electrical equipment industry, 93.15% in transportation (including railway wagons), 92.55% in industrial machinery, 80.19% in chemicals, 74.18% in vegetable oils and vanaspati, 89.28% in leather products, and 78.7% in glass, ceramic, and gypsum products. What is more significant from the point of view of regional concentration is the fact that in all these fields the share of the three industrialized cities of Bombay, Calcutta, and Madras has been substantial. Thus, the share of these three cities in licences issued to metallurgical industries was 32.25% and in licences issued to electrical equipment industry was 53.51%. In some other industries the share of these cities was as follows: 45.62% in transportation, 60.63% in industrial machinery, 33.33% in chemicals, 24% in vegetable oils and vanaspati, and 26.19% in textiles.[35]

The Industrial Licensing Policy Enquiry Commitee appointed in July 1967 under the chairmanship of Subimal Dutt revealed that the four industrially advanced States of Maharashtra, West Bengal, Gujarat, and Tamil Nadu benefited most from the operations of this policy. For example, in the decade 1956-1966 these four industrially advanced States accounted for 59.31% of the applications and 62.42% of the licences approved (the share of Maharashtra, West Bengal, Tamil Nadu, and Gujarat in total licences approved being 27.37%, 16.47%, 9.69%, and 8.89% respectively). On the other hand, the mineral-rich States of Bihar and Orissa got a meagre 5.16% and 1.18% of licences approved. The fate of Uttar Pradesh (biggest State population-wise) and Madhya Pradesh (biggest State area-wise) seems no different. The former got only 6.71% and the latter only 2.46% of licences approved. The more disturbing factor is the fact that not only the most industrialized States received a large proportion of licences issued, the highly industrialized areas within them cornered a very high proportion of licences. Thus, out of the total number of licences issued for Maharashtra, about 51% went to the three districts of Bombay suburban, Thana, and Poona alone while in West Bengal, 71% went to Calcutta, Howrah, and Hooghly and in Tamil Nadu about 59% went to Madras and Coimbatore.

Table 7 gives the State-wise break-up of licences issued under the Industries Act, 1951, from 1963 to 1967, 1972 and 1973, and 1976 to 1978. It reveals that during 1963 to 1967 Maharashtra received 25.89%, Tamil Nadu 11.49%, West Bengal 15.09%, and Gujarat 8.10% of licences issued. Thus, these four States together accounted for as much as 60.57% of the total licences issued. Though the Dutt Committee recommended a more even distribution of industrial licences between different regions, the subsequent data reveal that the old trends continued. Thus, in 1972 and 1973, Maharashtra got 27% of the licences issued and the share of West Bengal, Gujarat, and Tamil Nadu was 8.68%, 11.61% and 8.60% respectively. Thus, the combined share of these four States in the total licences issued was as high as 55.89%.

During the years 1976, 1977, and 1978, the share of Maharashtra, West Bengal, Gujarat, and Tamil Nadu in total licences issued was 25.78%, 7.79%, 12.32%, and 7.92% respectively (see cols. 6 and 7 of Table 7). Thus, these four States together accounted for as much as 53.86% of the licences issued. The backward States of Bihar, Assam, Madhya Pradesh, Rajasthan, and Orissa together received only 9.28% of the licences over the same period. The total number of letters of intent issued during 1976 to 1978 was 1520, of which Maharashtra, West Bengal, Gujarat, and Tamil Nadu received 353, 231, 110, and 85 respectively. Their combined share comes to 51.25%.[36]

After the Pande Working Committee[37] specified the backward areas of the country, it was expected that these areas would be granted more licences so that they would be able to develop their industries at a faster rate compared with other areas. This indeed did happen. The total number of licences issued to backward areas rose from 59 in 1970 to 103 in 1973 and to 216 in 1975. During the period 1976 to 1978, as many as 394 licences were issued to backward areas (which is 25.78% of the total licences issued during the period). However, the cause for concern is the fact that even in issuing licences to backward areas, it is the backward areas of the relatively more industrialized States of Maharashtra, West Bengal, Gujarat, and Tamil Nadu that have received favourable treatment. Thus, of the total 59 licences issued to backward areas in 1970, the backward areas of these four States together received as many as 39 licences. Of the 79 licences issued to backward areas in 1971 the backward areas of these four States together accounted for as many as 34 licences. Their share in 1972 was 43 licences

TABLE 7: State-wise break-up of licences issued under Industries (Development and Regulation) Act, 1951

State	Licences issued from 1963 to 1967		Licences issued in 1972 and 1973		Licences issued during 1976, 1977 and 1978	
	No.	% of total	No.	% of total	No.	% of to
(1)	(2)	(3)	(4)	(5)	(6)	(7)
Andhra Pradesh	117	4.07	59	5.07	95	6.22
Assam	17	0.59	16	1.37	9	0.59
Bihar	255	8.88	27	2.32	45	2.94
Gujarat	233	8.10	135	11.61	189	12.37
Karnataka	99	3.44	88	7.57	114	7.46
Kerala	66	2.29	22	1.89	48	3.14
Madhya Pradesh	78	2.71	22	1.89	34	2.22
Maharashtra	744	25.89	314	27.00	394	25.78
Orissa	34	1.18	4	0.34	11	0.72
Punjab & Haryana	179	6.23	96	8.25	120	7.85
Rajasthan	59	2.05	26	2.23	43	2.81
Tamil Nadu	330	11.49	100	8.60	121	7.92
Uttar Pradesh	175	6.08	110	9.46	122	7.99
West Bengal	434	15.09	101	8.68	119	7.79
Others	55	1.91	43	3.70	64	4.19
Total	2875	100.00	1163	100.00	1528	100.00

Sources: (1) For col. 2, A.I. Singh and M.V. George, op. cit. (see Table 3).
(2) For cols. 4 and 5, *Records and Statistics*, August 1974, Vol. 25, No. 4, p. 216.
(3) For col. 6, *Statistical Outline of India, 1980*, Tata Services Ltd., Bombay, Table 116, p. 119.

out of a total of 83 licences and 43 licences out of a total of 103 licences in 1973. In the first six months of 1974 the total number of licences issued to backward areas was 162 and the backward areas of the industrialized States of Maharashtra, West Bengal, Gujarat, and Tamil Nadu received 68 licences (which comes to approximately 42%).

The above analysis amply demonstrates that the industrial licensing policy has all along favoured the already developed States while the claims of the backward States were ignored. Even when recommendations were made to grant more licences to backward areas, the backward areas of the developed States received a preferential treatment. At times, licences for backward areas of the backward States were rejected on the plea that sufficient capacity had aready been licensed for the industry. Examples can also be found of instances where the choice of the projects licensed in backward areas was not appropriate. They did not possess sufficient spread effects and significant linkages within the regional economy so that no sizable impact was made on the local economy.

FINANCIAL INSTITUTIONS AND REGIONAL IMBALANCES

After examining the role of the industrial licensing policy in accentuating regional imbalances, let us consider how the financial institutions contributed to this state of affairs. The first institution to be set up was the Industrial Finance Corporation of India (IFC) which was established in 1948. A number of institutions were later set up to assist the private sector. Among them are the Industrial Credit and Investment Corporation of India (ICICI), the Industrial Development Bank of India (IDBI), State Financial Corporations (SFCs), the National Industrial Development Corporation (NIDC), the National Small Industries Corporation (NSIC), the State Industrial Development Corporations (SIDCs), the Refinance Corporation for Industry, and the Unit Trust of India (UTI). The ICICI was set up in 1955, the NIDC in 1954, the Refinance Corporation for Industry in 1958, and the IDBI in 1964. The IDBI was to act as the apex industrial finance institution and was to be a wholly owned subsidiary of the Reserve Bank of India. It provides direct financial assistance to industrial units and also coordinates the operations of other institutions providing term finance to industries. It can undertake research surveys, techno-economic surveys, provide technical and administrative services to industry, and help industries to fill up gaps in industrial structure. To enable it to play a more positive role in the field of industrial development, it was converted into an independent corporation in 1975 after it had worked as a subsidiary of the Reserve Bank of India for eleven years. To assist the growth of the small-scale and medium enterprises in their States, the State governments have formed State Financial Corporations. Each State has one such corporation. In all, there are 18 SFCs, one for each State plus one for the Union territory of Delhi. The Union territory of Chandigarh is served by Delhi, Goa, Daman & Diu by Maharashtra, Dadra & Nagar Haveli by Gujarat, Pondicherry by Tamil Nadu, and Manipur and Tripura by Assam. Most of the States also set up State Industrial Development Corporations around 1961 to promote industrial growth.

ASSISTANCE BY CENTRAL FINANCIAL INSTITUTIONS

Since 1970 the three central financial institutions (IDBI, IFCI, and ICICI) have been granting direct assistance on concessional terms to units located in backward areas. Since the IDBI is the apex development bank it provides a large range of facilities compared with the IFCI and ICICI. "The concessions in respect of direct loan assistance to units in backward areas include a lower interest rate of 8.5 percent, a reduced commitment charge of 0.5 percent, lower underwriting commission of 1.25 percent and 0.75 percent for shares and debentures, respectively, initial moratorium period up to 5 years, longer amortisation period of 15 to 20 years and participation in risk capital on a selective basis. IDBI also adopts a flexible attitude in respect of promoter's contribution to project cost, margin on security, rescheduling of debts etc., depending on merits of each case. In respect of refinance, IDBI charges a special rate of 5.5 percent with the primary lenders rate pegged at 9.0 percent."[38] In addition to these concessions, the IDBI provides concessional refinance assistance to the State Financial Corporations and Banks (at a special rate of interest of 6.5%). Along with the IFCI and ICICI, it also provides direct loan assistance up to Rs.2 crores and underwriting assistance up to Rs.1 crore on concessional terms to a new project as well as for expansion, diversification, renovation, and rehabilitation programmes of existing units.

It may interest the reader to note that the developed States accounted for 71% of the assistance granted by the IDBI as on 30 June 1977. The combined share of Maharashtra, Gujarat, and Tamil Nadu accounted for as much as 48% of the total assistance. The story of the performance of the IFCI is no different. The developed States accounted for about 63% of the total financial assistance sanctioned by this institution as on 30 June 1977. The two developed States of Maharashtra and Tamil Nadu together obtained 32% of the total sanctions and about half of the financial assistance sanctioned to all developed States. Table 8 gives data on the State-wise distribution of total and per capita assistance sanctioned by all financial institutions up to 1977. It shows that of the total financial assistance of Rs.5132.20 crores sanctioned by the financial institutions till 1977, the four advanced

TABLE 8: State-wise distribution of total and per capita assistance sanctioned by financial institutions (IDBI, IFCI, ICICI, ARDC, SFCs, IRCI) LIC and HUDCO up to 1977

(Rs. crores)

State	Total financial assistance sanctioned by financial institutions	Total financial assistance (including LIC and HUDCO)	
		Amount	Per capita (Rs.)
1. Andhra Pradesh	336.65	434.13	99.79
2. Assam	65.15	80.51	54.91
3. Bihar	243.98	318.91	56 91
4. Gujarat	617.52	845.73	316.79
5. Haryana	208.34	269.38	268.39
6. Himachal Pradesh	21.25	27.61	79.80
7. Jammu & Kashmir	30.15	38.00	82.30
8. Karnataka	369.58	478.82	163.43
9. Kerala	153.48	230.49	107.97
10. Madhya Pradesh	195.81	272.63	65.45
11. Maharashtra	1023.51	1288.25	255.54
12. Manipur	0.43	0.95	8.85
13. Meghalaya	7.47	13.65	134.88
14. Nagaland	1.64	2.40	46.51
15. Orissa	98.02	156.28	71.21
16. Punjab	165.98	228.20	168.40
17. Rajasthan	171.38	261.94	101.66
18. Sikkim	—	0.05	2.38
19. Tamil Nadu	588.73	775.61	188.26
20. Tripura	2.55	3.10	19.92
21. Uttar Pradesh	490.05	664.52	75.22
22. West Bengal	340.83	438.38	98.93
Total (All States)	5132.50	6829.34	126.12

Source: D.T. Lakdawala, "Plan Finances in a Federal Economy", *Yojana*, 16 May 1979; Table XII, p. 13.

industrial States of Maharashtra, Gujarat, Tamil Nadu, and West Bengal together accounted for approximately 50%. If the LIC and HUDCO are also included, the share of these four developed States together stands at approximately 49%. The last column on per capita financial assistance also reveals that the developed States have benefited more. Of the total 22 States, only 7 States had per capita financial assistance greater than the national average. Of these, only Jammu & Kashmir and Meghalaya were backward

States. The remaining five were developed States. The per capita financial assistance was the highest for Gujarat (about 2.5 times of the national average) followed by Maharashtra (about 2 times the national average).

The bias of the financial institutions in favour of the developed States and against the backward States can also be highlighted by observing the pattern of assistance to backward areas of the different States. Thus, the share of the backward areas of the developed States was 56% in the total amount sanctioned by the IDBI to units located in the backward areas. Similarly, about 55% of the total assistance to industrial units in the backward areas sanctioned by the IFCI went to the backward areas of the developed States. During 1971-72, a total financial assistance of Rs.71.7 crores was granted to the backward areas by the IDBI, IFC, and ICICI together. Of this, Rs.25.7 crores (i.e. 36%) was cornered by the four advanced industrial States of Maharashtra, Gujarat, Tamil Nadu, and West Bengal. Of the total assistance of Rs.48.2 crores granted by the above-mentioned institutions to the backward areas in 1972-73, the backward areas of these four advanced States received as much as 38%.[39]

Reasons for this state of affairs are not far to seek. Entrepreneurs in the advanced States are technically more qualified, skilled labour is easily available, infrastructural facilities (in the form of water, electricity, transport and communications, etc.) are present in ample degree, demand for the products of the firm is already existent or can be generated easily (compared with the backward States), and a better and conducive atmosphere for industrialization prevails. Entrepreneurs of the backward States contend that the decisions of the development banks are influenced by the entrepreneurs of the advanced States. The boards of directors of such institutions are filled by persons from advanced States and even the representatives of industrialists come either from Maharashtra or other industrially developed States. Against this, the financial institutions contend that the entrepreneurs of backward States do not have much sound industrial projects for help. 'Either the project is too small to be financed or the validity of the scheme is questionable'.

COMMERCIAL BANKS AND REGIONAL IMBALANCES

A review of the lending behaviour of the commercial banks reveals that they too behaved in a manner similar to that of the financial institutions. They also gave a large proportion of their advances to the developed industrial States. A more serious allegation levied against them is that they worked as 'channels' through which funds from the backward States kept flowing to the developed States. Thus, there was a paradox. Instead of the developed States contributing to the development of the backward States, it was the other way round in India.

A study of data on deposits mobilized and advances made by the commercial banks in 1956 and 1966 reveals that the four industrially advanced States of Maharashtra, West Bengal, Gujarat, and Tamil Nadu together accounted for 70.71% of advances in 1966 though they had contributed only 55% of deposits. In 1956, the combined share of Bombay, Madras, and West Bengal in total advances was 72% while they had contributed only 61% of deposits. When 14 major banks were nationalized in 1969 one of the important tasks assigned to them was to ensure a balanced development of the economy by granting more advances to the backward States. It has to be admitted that after nationalization, there was a rapid expansion of branches in backward States which rose from "2032 at the end of 1966 to 2879 by the end of 1969 and stood at 5262 as on last Friday of December 1972 and 5470 on last Friday of June 1973. Thus, as against 1,38,000 people being served by each bank branch at the end of 1966, only 58,000 were being served by each branch by the end of 1972 and 56,000 by the middle of 1973."[40] This expansion of branches had an immediate impact on deposit mobilization which increased rapidly from Rs.790.1 crores at the end of 1966 to Rs.1084.9 crores by the end of 1969 and, thereafter, to Rs.2143.8 crores by the end of 1972 and to Rs.2410.1 crores by the end of June 1970 in the backward States. The average annual rate of growth of deposit mobilization in these States increased from 12.4% in the three years before nationalization to 32.3% in the three years following nationalization.

As regards banking assistance, bank nationalization does not seem to have changed the position substantially. By the end of 1969, the developed States contributed 67.4% of total deposits but received 84.1% of total advances. By the end of 1972, these States contributed 64.1% of total deposits but received 82.6% of total advances. Thus, it seems that the trend before nationalization continued unabated even after nationalization. The assistance deposit ratio for the backward States ranged from 41.6% to 57.3% during the period 1966-73, exceeding 50% in only two years 1969 and 1970. On the other hand, the ratio ranges from 74.3% to 81.7% over a similar period for the developed States with 67.1% to 75.9 being the all-India average range.

Table 2 of Stuti Lall's study gives a comparion of incremental figures for deposits mobilized and assistance rendered by the nationalized banks in the backward States and the developed States during 1966-69 (taken as the pre-nationalization period) and 1969-72 (taken as the post-nationalization period). It shows that during 1966-69, the deposits increased in the backward States by as much as Rs.294.1 crores while advances increased by Rs.234.1 crores. This gives the assistance-deposit ratio as 0.79 which is not bad. However, in the three years after nationalization this ratio fell drastically to 0.42. Against this, the assistance-deposit ratio which was 0.95

for the developed States in 1966-69 fell to 0.75 in 1969-72

The evidence given above shows that funds have tended to flow from the backward States to the developed States. Thus, the former have contributed to the growth in the latter. As noted elsewhere in this chapter, this does happen in the initial stages of development in an underdeveloped country because of a number of factors. Thus, the backward regions do not have proper infrastructural facilities, they have unexplored national resources, they lack enough supply of entrepreneurs, and there is an apprehension of low (or even negative) returns on investment in them. The developed States, on the other hand, do not suffer as much from these handicaps and therefore artract more investment. It was expected that the nationalization of banks would bring about a marked transformation of this state of affairs but this has not happened. This is because of the following two basic causes (among others): (1) the pre-1969 era bankers still dominate the scene with their traditional outlook of 'playing safe'. They do not have that radical outlook and courage which are necessary to carry out the transformation, and (2) credit policies and norms are generally laid down on an all-India basis as if the entire economy were one homogeneous unit. The fact is that the economy is made of several economic regions with diverse conditions and it is necessary to consider the need of each region separately.

The *Economic Survey 1980-81* provides data on State-wise distribution of bank offices-aggregate deposits and total credit of public sector banks at two points of time—June 1969 and March 1980. With the help of these data one can highlight the performance of public sector banks in spreading banking facilities to the underdeveloped States and in helping the process of balanced regional development. A part of the table is reproduced as Table 9. We have converted the data into percentages to highlight the relevant information in a better perspective. The table shows that between the period June 1969 to March 1980 as many as 16129 new branches were opened of which 4862 were established in the backward States of Uttar Pradesh, Madhya Pradesh, Bihar, and Orissa. In June 1969, 42.66% of total branches were in the four advanced States of Maharashtra, Tamil Nadu, West Bengal, and Gujarat while in 1980 this percentage went down to 36.0. However, the matter for concern is the fact that out of 16129 new branches, as many as 5350 or 33.17% were opened in the above four industrially advanced States, the remaining 17 States and Union territories getting only 66.83% of the increase. The data also reveal the percentage distribution of deposits and credits for all States for the period ending June 1969 and March 1980. It shows that the four advanced industrial States accounted for 51.17% of total deposits and 64.06% of total credits in the period ending June 1969 showing that these States got a greater share

TABLE 9: State-wise distribution of bank offices—aggregate deposits and total credit of public sector banks (as percentage of total)

State/Union Territory	Number of offices at the end of				Deposits (in percentage)		Bank Credit (in percentage)		Credit-Deposit Ratio	
	June 1969		March 1980		June 1969	March 1980	June 1969	March 1980	1969	1980
	No.	Percentage to total	No.	Percentage to total						
(1)	(2)	(3)	(4)	(5)	(6)	(7)	(8)	(·)	(10)	(11)
1. Andhra Pradesh	444	6.66	1490	6.5	3.11	4.23	4.02	4.92	1.01	0,81
2. Assam	67	1.00	378	1.7	0.85	1.05	0.42	0.66	0.39	0.43
3. Bihar	269	4.03	1373	6.0	4.33	4.74	1.71	2.90	0.31	0.42
4. Gujarat	750	11.25	2113	9.3	10.30	8.24	6.42	6.62	0.49	0.56
5. Haryana	140	2.10	487	2.1	1.25	1.57	0.76	1.62	0.48	0.71
6. Himachal Pradesh	41	0.61	259	1.1	0.32	0.55	0.12	0.25	0.28	0.32
7. Jammu & Kashmir	17	0.25	151	0.7	0·46	0.51	0.03	0.27	0.05	0.36
8. Karnataka	510	7.65	1595	7.0	4.82	4.74	4.71	5.86	0.76	0.86
9. Kerala	331	4.96	976	4.3	3.00	3.27	2.54	3.02	0.66	0.64
10. Madhya Pradesh	332	4.96	1523	6.7	2.76	3.57	2.08	2.69	0.59	0.52
11. Maharashtra	946	14.18	2692	11.8	23.16	19.24	30.05	23.06	1.01	0.83
12. Manipur	2	0.03	32	0.1	0.03	0.05	0.005	0.02	0.14	0.36
13. Meghalaya	7	0.10	49	0.2	0.23	0.16	0.08	0.04	0.28	0.16
14. Nagaland	2	0.03	30	0.1	0.03	0.06	0.002	0.02	0.06	0.24
15. Orissa	96	1.44	576	2.5	0.76	1.20	0.48	0.90	0.50	0.52
16. Punjab	290	4.35	966	4.2	4.76	4.50	1.66	2.79	0.27	0.43
17. Rajasthan	311	4.66	985	4.3	1.89	2.14	1.26	2.08	0.52	0.67

(*Contd.*)

TABLE 9 (*Contd.*)

(1)	(2)	(3)	(4)	(5)	(6)	(7)	(8)	(9)	(10)	(11)
18. Tamil Nadu	721	10.81	1748	7.7	6.00	6.68	10.26	8.74	1.33	0.91
19. Tripura	5	0.07	45	0.2	0.10	0.10	0.005	0.06	0.04	0.45
20. Uttar Pradesh	639	9.58	2726	12.0	8.65	9.79	5.07	6.51	0.46	0.46
21. West Bengal	428	6.42	1642	7.2	11.71	11.88	17.33	10.36	1.15	0.60
Union Territories										
Delhi	207	3.10	623	2.7	9.23	9.74	8.07	13.84	0.68	0.98
Other union territories*	124	1.76	339	1.5	2.30	1.96	2.918	2.74	1.00	0.97
Total	6,669	100.00	22,798	100.00	100.00	100.00	100.00	100.00		

*Include Andaman & Nicobar Islands, Arunachal Pradesh, Dadra and Nagar Haveli, Lakshadweep and Mizoram for June 1969 and Sikkim also for March 1980.

Source: Computed from *Economic Survey, 1980-81*, Statement 4.7, p. 106.

of the credit than their percentage share in total deposits. In March 1980, the share of these States was 46.04% in total deposits and 48.78% in total credits.

The last two columns of the table have been computed from the table given in the *Economic Survey* and reveal that for a number of underdeveloped States (such as Assam, Bihar, Himachal Pradesh, Jammu & Kashmir, Madhya Pradesh, Manipur, Meghalaya, Nagaland, Orissa, Rajasthan, Tripura, and Uttar Pradesh) the credit-deposit ratio was less than the national credit-deposit ratio of 0.78 in June 1969. Against this, the credit-deposit ratio was greater than the national credit-deposit ratio in the case of the relatively more advanced States of Maharashtra, Tamil Nadu, and West Bengal. This shows a flow of funds from the less developed to the more developed States. At the end of March 1980 also, the situation remained virtually the same with the credit-deposit ratio being less than the national credit-deposit ratio of 0.69 for the underdeveloped States of Assam, Bihar, Himachal Pradesh, Jammu & Kashmir, Madhya Pradesh, Manipur, Meghalaya, Nagaland, Orissa, Rajasthan, Tripura, and Uttar Pradesh. The ratio was greater than the national credit-deposit ratio in the case of the relatively more advanced States of Maharashtra and Tamil Nadu. The only underdeveloped State having credit-deposit ratio greater than the national credit-deposit ratio, in both 1969 and 1978, was Andhra Pradesh. The combined credit-deposit ratio for the four industrially advanced States was higher than the national credit-deposit ratio in 1969 (being 0.97 against the national ratio of 0.78) and marginally higher in 1980 (being 0.73 against the national average ratio of 0.69).

The above analysis shows that, contrary to expectations, there has been a diversion of resources away from the underdeveloped States and towards the advanced States and bank nationalization has not been able to stall this process though some improvement in the situation is very much in evidence. This position needs a drastic improvement and a considerable diversion of resources to less developed States has to be carried out if regional imbalances and inequalities are to be narrowed down.

NOTES

1. Singer quoted in Benjamin Higgins, *Economic Development—Problems, Principles and Policies* (Indian Reprint, 1966), p. 369.
2. We shall show subsequently how financial institutions and banks in India promoted this process.
3. This is the famous theory of *cumulative causation* expounded by Gunnar Myrdal. It says: "In the normal case a change does not call forth countervailing changes but,

instead, supporting changes which move the system in the same direction as the first change but much further. Because of such circular causation a social process tends to become cumulative and often to gather speed at an accelerating rate." Gunnar Myrdal, *Economic Theory and Underdeveloped Regions* (London: Methuen & Co. Ltd., 1964), p. 13.

4. Ibid., p. 12.
5. J.G. Williamson, "Regional Inequality and the Process of National Development: A Description of the Patterns", in L. Needleman (ed.), *Regional Analysis* (Penguin Modern Economics Readings, 1968), p. 106.
6. Hirchman quoted by Williamson, Ibid., p. 106, footnote 8. It may be pointed out that the problem of regional imbalances is sometimes referred to as North-South problem because as noted by us earlier in this chapter the problem of regional imbalances in the USA basically resolves itself into the problem of North-South imbalances.
7. Ibid., p. 108.
8. S.R. Hashim, "Locational Flows and the Problem of Regional Development : Some Views Along with an Historical Review of Indian Situation", *Balanced Regional Development*, proceedings of Indian Economic Association, 1969 (Bombay: Popular Prakashan), pp. 46-47.
9. Ibid., p. 47.
10. Ibid., pp. 49-52.
11. Planning Commission, *Second Five Year Plan*, p. 246.
12. Ibid., p. 36.
13. Planning Commission, *Third Five Year Plan*, pp. 143-144.
14. Ibid., p. 142.
15. Ibid., p. 146.
16. Ibid., pp. 147-148.
17. For a discussion of these programmes, see Chapter 7.
18. Planning Commission, *Draft Five Year Plan 1978-83* (now defunct), p. 159.
19. In fact, 13 districts of Maharashtra covering 54% of the State's area and 42% of its population were classified by the Planning Commission as backward. Another developed State, West Bengal, had 13 of its 16 districts classified as backward and they covered 82% of the total area of the State and 68% of its population. See Chapter 8, Table 2.
20. R. Balakrishna *Regional Planning in India* (Bangalore: Bangalore Printing & Publishing Co. Ltd., 1948), pp. 29-30. We have utilized the analysis contained in this book to explain the regional distribution of industries in the pre-independence period.
21. For a detailed discussion on disparities in agriculture and other related topics, the reader is referred to Chapter 7 of this book.
22. Specific mention may be made of the following studies of M.N. Pal in this context: (i) 'A Method of Regional Analysis of Economic Development with special Reference to South India', *Journal of Regional Science*, 1963, Vol. 5, No. 1, reproduced in R.P. Misra (ed.), *Regional Planning*, 1969, pp. 172-191; (ii) 'Quantitative Delimitation of Regions', *Bombay Geographical Magazine*, 1961, 8-9, pp. 1-14; (iii) 'To Construct a Combined Concentration Index', *Raumforschung and Raumardung*, Koln, June 1963, 21, pp. 87-93; (iv) 'Regional Disparities in the Levels of Development in India', Paper contributed to the Fifth Econometric Conference of India, Delhi School of Economics, 1965; (v) 'Use of Principal Component in Regional Analysis', Paper contributed to the Symposium on Regional Planning, 21st International Geographical Congress, 1968; (vi) 'Regional Analysis for National Development : Techniques and Case Studies' (Doctoral Thesis, Delhi School of Economics, 1969); (vii) 'Quantitative Tech-

niques for Regional Planning', *Indian Journal of Regional Science*, 1971, Vol. 3, No. 1, pp. 1-33; (viii) 'Regional Information, Regional Statistics and Regional Planning in India', in Antoni Kuklinski (ed.), *Regional Information and Regional* Planning (UNRISD/Regional Planning/Vol. 6) (The Hague: Mouton & Co., 1974).

23. Asok Mitra, *Levels of Regional Development in India*, Government of India, 1965.
24. Asok Mitra, 'Levels of Regional Development in India', in Galina Sdasyuk and P. SenGupta, *Economic Regionalization in India : Problems and Approaches* (Census of India 1961: Monograph Series Vol. I, No. 8), p. 227.
25. V. Nath, 'Regional Development in Indian Planning', *Economic and Political Weekly* Annual Number, January 1970, pp. 242-260.
26. Throughout this text we have regarded Maharashtra, Gujarat, West Bengal, and Tamil Nadu as the most developed industrial States of India. This is in accordance with the normal pattern of industrial development in different States. However, in the table given here, the order of industrial development is slightly different with Punjab pushing down Tamil Nadu to the fifth place. This is on account of the rapid industrialization of Punjab in recent years. Thus, while in Punjab the gross output in industry per capita rose from Rs.584.7 in 1974-75 to Rs.688.4 in 1975-76, it could increase only from Rs.589 to Rs.652.5 over the same period in the case of Tamil Nadu. Similarly, if we consider value added in industry per capita we find that while it rose from Rs.94.5 in 1974-75 to Rs. 115.2 in 1975-76 in the case of Punjab, for Tamil Nadu it actually registered a fall from Rs.131.5 to Rs.121.7. We have carried out an exercise by taking data for 1974-75 also (in place of 1975-76 data) and found that Maharashtra was the most developed industrial State followed by Gujarat, West Bengal, Tamil Nadu, Punjab, and Haryana in that order. This is more in accordance with general belief.
27. Since industrialization is considered to be an index of development, it is better to adopt a procedure wherein more indicators of industrialization are included. It is frequently necessary to emphasize the various aspects of the industrialization process (keeping in view the various aspects of socio-economic policy) and each 'aspect' needs a separate indicator. On including more indicators of industrial development, S.K. Rao has this to say: "Our justification for this is that the pattern of regional growth in the long run will be predominantly influenced by where industry gets located; and in the absence of planned intervention, industry has the notorious habit of getting concentrated where it is. Further, industrial output by itself would not completely capture the dynamic aspects of manufacturing; one needs to consider its other dimensions—employment on the one hand and how modern it is in its technique on the other." S.K. Rao, "A note on Measuring Economic Distances between Regions in India", *Economic and Political Weekly*, 28 April 1973; p. 793. On these considerations, the alternative analysis discussed above (in which more industrial indicators are included as compared with agriculture) is perhaps more justified. Thus, the ranking according to which Punjab is the most developed State followed by Maharashtra, West Bengal, Tamil Nadu, Haryana, and Gujarat in that order, expresses the situation better.
28. S.K. Rao, "A Note on Measuring Economic Distances between Regions in India", *Economic and Political Weekly*, 28 April 1973, p. 796 (emphasis supplied).
29. Ibid., p. 799.
30. Hemlata Rao, "Identification of Backward Regions and the Trends in Regional Disparities in India", *Artha Vijnana*, June 1977, Vol. 19, No. 2, pp. 93-112.
31. B.N. Ganguli and Devendra B. Gupta, *Levels of Living in India—An Inter-State Profile* (New Delhi: S. Chand & Co. Ltd., 1976).

32. Ibid., See Table 4.8, p. 137.
33. In Mitra's analysis, districts at first level of development are districts at the lowest rung of the ladder of development, districts at second level of development are districts at the second rung of the ladder, districts at the third level of development means districts at the third rung of the ladder of development, and districts at the fourth level of development are districts at the fourth and the top rung of the ladder.
34. A. Mitra, *Levels of Regional Development in India*, op. cit., p. 287.
35. The percentages have been calculated from A. Mitra, Ibid., Statement VI. 1, pp. 287-88.
36. See *Statistical Outline of India, 1980*, Tata Services Ltd., Bombay, Table 116, p. 119.
37. See Chapter 8 for a discussion on Pande Working Committee's recommendations.
38. "IDBI and Backward Area Development", *The Economic Times*, 17 December 1975, p. 5.
39. K.S.V. Menon, op. cit. Recently the Parliamentary Committee on Public Undertakings has pulled up the IDBI for its "pronounced regional imbalance" in the assistance rendered. The Committee notes that out of the Rs.5391 crores assistance given by the Bank till 1980, the share of the two industrially advanced States of Maharashtra and Gujarat was as much as 32%. Of the total sanctions since IDBI's inception (till 1980) the western and southern regions accounted for 36% and 28% respectively while the share of the northern, central and eastern regions was around 12% each. The western region comprises the industrially advanced States of Maharashtra and Gujarat and the southern region has the developed State of Tamil Nadu and the emerging industrial state of Karnataka. In the eastern region, with the exception of West Bengal, all other nine States are industrially underdeveloped.

    An analysis of IDBI's assistance to backward areas indicates that the top 50 of 247 backward districts assisted by the IDBI accounted for the bulk of the assistance, their share ranging from 67% to 85%. State-wise, top three districts accounted for 60% to 70% of the assistance.
40. Stuti Lall, "Bank Nationalisation and Backward Areas—Regional Disparities Stay", *The Economic Times*, 29 July 1974, p. 5. Following B.D. Pande Committee, Stuti Lall has defined the following States as backward—Andhra Pradesh, Assam, Bihar, Himachal Pradesh, Jammu & Kashmir, Madhya Pradesh, Nagaland, Orissa, Rajasthan, Uttar Pradesh, and Meghalaya. .

Chater 6

The Process of Urbanization in India

DEFINITION OF AN URBAN AREA

"The concept of urban is almost universally understood to have reference to relatively large and relatively densely settled populations engaged primarily in non-agricultural economic pursuits. By contrast, the concept of rural ordinarily is understood to refer to relatively small and relatively sparsely settled populations, typically with large proportions engaged in agriculture."[1] This statement reflects the fact that two criteria—one quantitative and the other qualitative—distinguish the urban element from the rural element in a country's population. The quantitative criterion relates to population concentration and qualitative refers to the characteristics of the population. "The correlation between these two criteria varies with time, location, and the 'urban' features of the particular locality."[2] Thus, the broad consensus about the nature of the difference between urban and rural notwithstanding, in actual practice the designation of localities as urban or rural varies widely and is often dependent upon administrative, political, cultural, and historical as well as upon demographic and economic considerations. A United Nations Report[3] identified the following five main concepts among the definitions used for urban areas:

1. Administrative Area
2. Population Size
3. Local Government Areas
4. Urban Characteristics
5. Predominant Economic Activity

If classification of urban areas is done according to the quantitative criterion alone, we would consider the factor 'population size' only.

Such an approach is known as a *conglomeration approach*. A certain minimum size of population is prescribed and all areas having population greater than this size are termed *urban areas*. Naturally, all areas having population less than the prescribed minimum would then constitute rural areas. Adoption of the conglomeration approach alone simplifies matters considerably but can lead to misleading conclusions. For, it is frequent to find areas where population is greater than the minimum prescribed limit but no urban characteristics are present. Such areas can, at best, be termed 'overgrown villages' but not urban areas. If the conglomeration approach alone is adopted, a number of places which are classified as 'rural' in a particular census will enter the category of 'urban' in the next census merely because their population has increased and has crossed the minimum prescribed limit. To take account of these possibilities it is generally necessary to consider whether the area in question has acquired some urban characteristics or whether there has been a change in the predominant economic activity. For example, if we find that while previously more than 60% of the people were engaged in agriculture while now merely 20% are engaged in it, a distinct change in predominant economic activity has taken place (in the sense that the majority of the people have shifted to non-agricultural occupations). Similarly, the area might have acquired some distinct urban characteristics. For example, new educational institutions, courts of law, police stations, hospitals, etc., might have been built up or public services such as sewerage, piped water supply, electric lighting, etc., provided. If neither any change has occurred in the predominant economic activity nor any urban characteristics have been introduced, it would be a misnomer to call the area 'urban' even though its population is now larger than the minimum prescribed limit. In the Indian censuses, e.g., the minimum prescribed population size for a settlement to be designated as urban is 5000.[4] Then, according to the conglomeration approach, all settlements having more than 5000 inhabitants should be classified as urban. However, a significant number of settlements fulfilling this requirement have to be included under rural areas because they do not possess urban characteristics. In the 1951 census, the number of such settlements was 2136 and their total population was 15.52 million. In the 1961 census, their number rose to 4197 and total population to 34.63 million. In the 1971 census, the number of such settlements stood at 6332 and their total population was 55.05 million.

Just as it is possible to think of areas which have population greater than the minimum prescribed limit but are to be classified as 'rural', similarly it is possible to think of areas which have to be classified as 'urban' even though their population is less than the minimum limits. All municipalities, cantonments, notified areas, etc., have to be regarded as urban even if their population falls below the minimum limit. If this is not done, serious administrative problems would arise. In the 1951 census, 611 settlements each with a population of less than 5000 had to be included in urban areas in India on these considerations. Their total population was 2.03 million. In the 1961 census, such settlements were 268 in number and their total population was 8.87 lakhs. In the 1971 census, their number stood at 303, total population being 9.17 lakhs.

Let us now consider the definition of towns as adopted in India to see in what way qualitative criteria were sought to be incorporated. The Census of India 1901 defined a town so as to include (i) municipal corporation, municipal area, all civil lines not included in municipal limits and cantonment, and (ii) every other continuous collection of houses permanently inhabited by not less than 5000 persons, which the Provincial Superintendent might decide to treat as a town for census purposes. This definition continued to be adopted with some modifications right up to the 1951 census. The 1961 census tried to be more specific and defined a town so as to include (a) all places with a municipality, corporation, town committee, notified area committee or cantonment board and (b) all other places which satisfied the following criteria: (i) density of not less than 1000 per sq. mile (i.e. 400 per km)^2; (ii) a minimum population of 5000; (iii) at least 75% of the male working population being non-agricultural.

This definition was adopted in the 1971 census as well. In all the censuses some discretionary powers were given to the Census Superintendents to include such places in urban areas that possessed pronounced 'urban characteristics and amenities' and to exclude undeserving cases. The definition of urban characteristics and amenities, though vague, "yet meant to cover newly-founded industrial areas, large housing settlements, or places of tourist importance which have been recently served with all civic amenities".[5]

TOWN GROUPS AND URBAN AGGLOMERATION

The census of 1951 introduced the concept of town groups. A town group was defined as "a group of towns which adjoined one another so closely as to form a single inhabited urban locality". This was done to distinguish a group of towns from an isolated town so that areas of conglomerate growth can be marked off for purposes of better planning and development. This practice was continued in the census of 1961 as well with the difference that while in the census of 1951, the distinction between town group and town "was limited only to town groups with an aggregate population of 100,000 and over" the census of 1961 extended the concept of town group to all urban classes and did not limit it to class I urban areas (i.e., areas with population of 100,000 and above) alone.

The census of 1971 introduced two new concepts: (i) Urban Agglomeration and (ii) Standard Urban Areas. Urban Agglomeration would be constituted in the following situations:

(a) a city with a continuous out-growth (the part of outgrowth being outside statutory limits but falling within the boundaries of the adjoining village or villages);
(b) one town with a similar out-growth or two or more adjoining towns with their outgrowths as in (a); and
(c) a city and one or more adjoining towns with their outgrowths all of which form a continuous spread.[6]

In this connection, the census had this to say: "In several areas, fairly large railway colonies, university campuses, port areas and military camps have come up around a core city or statutory town. Though these are outside the statutory limits of a corporation, municipality or cantonment, they fall within the revenue boundary of the place by which the town itself is known. It may not be altogether realistic to treat such areas lying outside the statutory limits of a town as rural units; at the same time each such area by itself may not come up as the minimum population limit to be treated as an independent urban unit. Such areas deserve to be reckoned along with the main town and the continuous spread including such urban out-growths would deserve to be treated as an integrated urban area which is being called 'Urban agglomeration' (in the Census of 1971)."[7]

The "Standard Urban Area" was defined as the projected growth area of a city or town as it would be after 20 years (i.e., in 1991), taking into account not only the towns and villages which will get merged into it but also the intervening areas which are potentially urban. The SUA was thus defined to be an area which extends beyond the main city or town and contains all likely developments over the next 20 years up to 1991.[8]

TRENDS OF URBAN GROWTH AND URBANIZATION IN INDIA

Before we discuss the trends of urbanization in India, let us distinguish between 'urban growth' and 'urbanization'. Technically speaking, 'urban growth' denotes the net population increase of towns and cities while 'urbanization' refers to the *proportionate* increase of the urban population in relation to the total population in a given country.[9] It is obvious that urban growth and urbanization are not identical. For example, it is possible that on

TABLE 1: **Increase in urban and rural population in India**

(population in millions)

Year	Urban population	Rural population	Total population	Percent increase in		
				Urban population	Rural population	Total population
1901	25.85	212.48	238.33			
1911	25.94	226.06	252.00	+ 0.35	+ 6.39	+ 5.73
1921	28.09	223.15	251.24	+ 8.27	− 1.29	− 0.31
1931	33.46	245.41	278.87	+19.12	+ 9.98	+11.00
1941	44.15	274.39	318.54	+31.97	+11.81	+14.22
1951	62.44	298.51	360.95	+41.42	+ 8.79	+13.31
1961	78.93	360.14	439.07	+26.41	+20.65	+21.64
1971	109.09	438.86	547.95	+38.22	+21.85	+24.80

Source: Computed from Census of India 1971 *General Population Tables* Series I, Part II-A (i); Statement 5, p. 45 and Statement 11, p. 50.

account of natural increase, urban population registers a substantial increase. If, however, the rate of growth of urban population is the same as that of rural population so that the actual percentage of urban population remains stable, urban growth has occurred but not urbanization. If, on the other hand, urban population increases at a faster rate than rural population so that the percentage of urban population in the total population of the country increases continuously, it is a clear indication that urbanization is taking place. Table 1 shows that the percentage increase in urban population in India has been considerably greater than the percentage increase in rural population for all decades since 1901.

The average rate of increase in urban population for the seven decades works out at 22.8% per decade from Table 1 while the average rate of increase in rural population is 10.9% and in total population is 12.2%. On account of this factor, the percentage of urban population to total population has increased consistently from 10.84 in 1901 and 10.29 in 1911 to 13.86 in 1941, 17.97 in 1961, and 19.97 in 1971 as Table 2 clearly demonstrates.

It is important to note some important facts about the urbanization process revealed from Table 2 before proceeding further. From 1911 to 1951 there was a continuous increase in the number of towns. However, during the decade 1951-61, the number of towns registered a marked decline from 3059 to 2699. This was the result of adopting a stricter definition of towns in the 1961 census. Some places which were classified as towns in 1951 were declassified in 1961. On account of this, the percentage increase of urban population was 26.41 which was consi-

TABLE 2: Growth of urban population in India : 1901-1971

Census year	Number of towns	Total urban population (in millions)	Urban population as a percentage of total population	Increase in each decade (million)	Percent increase (decade)
1901	1917	25.85	10.84	—	—
1911	1909	25.94	10.29	0.09	+ 0.35
1921	2047	28.09	11.18	2.15	+ 8.27
1931	2219	33.46	11.99	5.37	+19.12
1941	2424	44.15	13.86	10.69	+31.97
1951	3059	62.44	17.29	18.29	+41.42
1961	2699	78.93	17.97	16.50	+26.41
1971	3119	109.09	19.91	30.16	+38.22

Sources: (i) Table 1.
(ii) Census of India 1971 *General Population Tables* Series I, Part II-A (i): Statement 3, p. 43.

derably less than the previous decade. If definitional changes are eliminated, the growth rate in the decade 1951-61 will be found to be higher than 26.41. Ashish Bose[10] has estimated that if the 1951 census definition is accepted by hypothetically including in the 1961 urban population the 1961 population of places which were urban in 1951 but eliminated in 1961 on account of stricter definition, the increase in urban population in the decade comes out to be 32.4% and not 26.41% as shown in Table 2. If, on the other hand, adjustment is undertaken by adopting the 1961 census definition to the 1951 census, the percent increase in the decade 1951-61 works out to be 30.7.[11] Thus, in whatever way adjustments are carried out, the percentage increase comes out to be higher than that given in Table 2. However, no adjustment for 1971 data *vis-a-vis* 1961 data is required for they are fairly comparable. One methodological issue did arise and it was in applying the test that at least 75% of male working population should be engaged in non-agricultural activities. Though both the censuses had accepted this test, a problem arose because of a difference in the definition of worker adopted by them. The 1971 census report noted that in the 1961 Census, the definition of worker was on a liberal side and, as a consequence, inflated the participation rates. However, it has been shown by Pethe[12] that though the 1961 definition of the worker did inflate participation rates for all population and females in some categories of economic activity, it did not effect the pattern of male participation rates and the participation rates in broad divisions of agriculture and non-agriculture. Therefore, the figures of 1961 and 1971 are fairly comparable and no adjustment needs to be made.

There are two important facts about the urbanization process in India which need to be noted: (1) in terms of the percentage of the total population, the level of urbanization is low, and (2) in terms of absolute numbers, the level of urbanization is rather high. Thus, in 1951, the percentage of urban population to total population was only 17.29. In 1961, this percentage was 17.97 and in 1971 it was 19.91. This was less than the average for Asia, Africa, and Latin America. On the other hand, the total urban population of India was 78.93 million in 1961 which rose to 109.09 million in 1971. In terms of total urban population, India is well ahead of most of the developing countries and many developed countries such as Japan, UK, Federal Republic of Germany, etc. In fact, "next to USSR, USA and perhaps China, India has the largest urban population in the world".[13] Again, in accordance with the pattern of population concentration in urban areas in developed countries, India also has the majority of its urban population concentrated in large urban centres. In 1971, India had 151 cities, each having a population greater than one lakh and 49% of total urban population was concentrated in them. In this respect (i.e , in respect of the share of large cities in total urban population) India is on par with such developed countries as the USA, the UK, Germany, and Japan. As we shall see later on, it is precisely on this account that large cities in India are plagued by a number of complex social and economic problems. The low level of economic development of the economy and the consequent unavailability of resources further reduce our capacity to successfully meet the challenges thrown up by the rapid process of urbanization.

PATTERN OF GROWTH OF TOWNS BY SIZE-CLASSES

It is customary in Indian censuses to classify towns into the following six classes according to population size:

Class I Population of 100,000 and above
Class II Population of 50,000 to 99,999
Class III Population of 20,000 to 49,999
Class IV Population of 10,000 to 19,999
Class V Population of 5,000 to 9,999
Class VI Population of less than 5,000

In consonance with the experience of the developed countries, population in India has tended to concentrate in Class I towns.[14] Again, as in the developed countries, in India also the maximum concentration of urban population is found in the largest urban centres within cities, especially in cities with population more than ten lakhs each (hereafter referred to as 'million plus cities'). Table 3 exhibits the pattern of concentration of population as between different classes and Table 4 shows the tendency of urban population to concentrate in million plus cities.

Table 3 shows that there has been a significant rise in the number of Class I, Class II, and Class III towns. The most spectacular rise is in the case of Class I towns whose number went up from 25 in 1901 to 76 in 1951, to 107 in 1961, and to 151 in 1971. Therefore, over the period of 70 years (i.e., from 1901 to 1971) the number of Class I towns rose by 504%. During the same period, the number of Class II towns rose by 398%, Class III towns by 354%, Class IV towns by 131%, and Class V towns by 6.36%. Against this, Class VI towns registered a decline of 42%. The number of towns in the first three classes therefore registered an increase of more than 300% over the period 1901-1971, Class I towns being much ahead of the other two. As far as percentage of population in each class to total urban population is concerned, the data can be divided into three categories—under the first category come Class I towns which have shown a considerable increase in the share of urban population (from 22.02% in 1901 to 48.93% in 1971); under the second category come Class II and Class III towns whose combined share increased by a small percentage from 28.35 in 1901 to 31.77 in 1971; and under the third category come Class IV, Class V, and Class V towns whose combined share has actually declined (from 49.63% in 1901 to 19.3% in 1971). The situtation is depicted in the graph (drawn on the basis of Table 3).

Table 3 and the graph show emphatically the increasing role of Class I towns in the urbanization process in India. In fact, the population of Class I towns registered an increase of 68.8%, 48%, and 52% in the decades 1941-51, 1951-61, and 1961-71 respectively. The population of Class II and Class III towns (combined) increased at the rate of 36%, 35%, and 37% respectively during the same period. The combined population of Class IV, Class V, and Class VI towns increased by 22.45% during 1941-51 and by 13.6% during 1961-71. During 1951-61, it had registered a decline of 7.2%.

STATE-WISE PATTERN OF GROWTH

Let us now analyse the State-wise pattern of growth of towns since 1951. The data are presented in Table 4 which throw light on, at least, three aspects: (i) The total urban population in different States, (ii) percentage of

TABLE 3: Change in the number of different size-class towns in India and the percentage of population in each class to total urban population, 1901-1971

Year	Urban classes												Total number of towns
	Class I		Class II		Class III		Class IV		Class V		Class VI		
	No. of towns	% of urban population	No. of towns	% of urban population	No. of towns	% of urban population	No. of towns	% of urban population	No. of towns	% of urban population	No. of towns	% of urban population	
1901	25	22.02	44	11.40	144	16.95	427	22.62	771	20.63	503	6.38	1917
1911	26	23.63	38	9.53	158	18.85	388	20.75	750	20.18	546	7.06	1909
1921	29	24.45	49	11.23	172	18.20	395	19.21	773	19.39	626	7.52	2047
1931	31	24.41	59	12.42	218	19.76	479	19.62	849	18.01	580	5.78	2219
1941	49	31.84	88	12.97	273	18.25	554	17.47	979	15.90	478	3.57	2424
1951	76	38.00	111	12.21	374	17.80	675	15.02	1195	13.63	628	3.34	3059
1961	107	44.50	139	12.07	518	19.95	820	14.32	847	8.03	268	1.13	2699
1971	151	48.93	219	13.49	654	18.28	987	12.80	820	5.68	290	0.82	3119
% increase in the No. of towns over the period 1901-1971	504		398		354		131		6.36		—42		

Source: Census of India 1971, *General Population Tables*, Series I, Part II-A (i), Statement 1, p. 182 and Statement 3, p. 183.

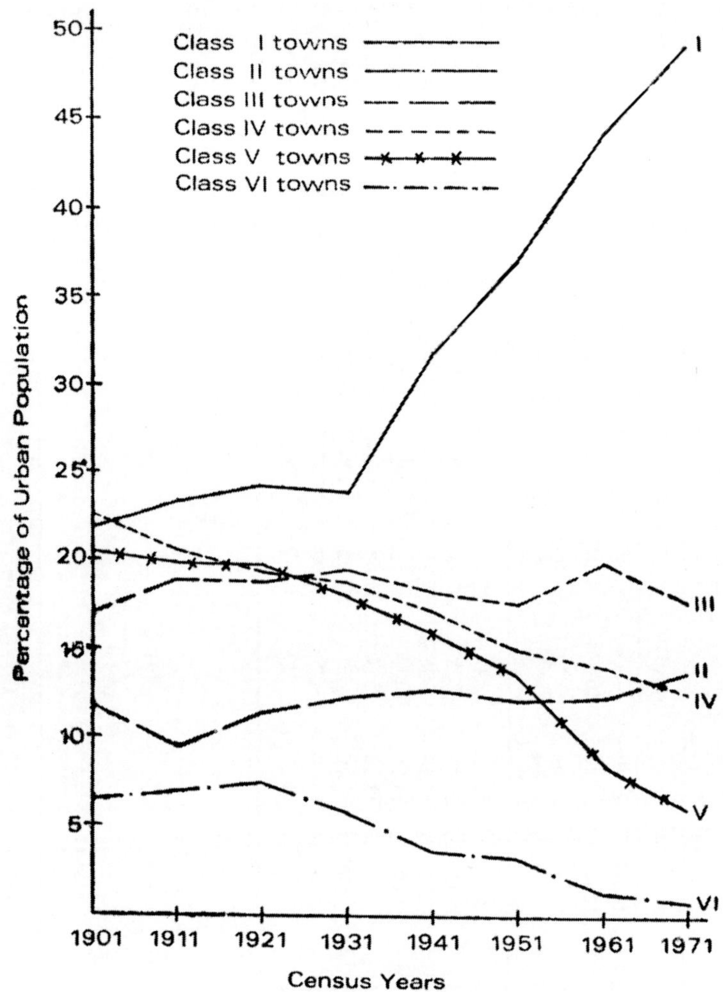

urban population in different States to total population of those States, and (iii) percentage increase (or decrease) of urban population in different States in the decades 1951-61 and 1961-71. Let us consider these aspects one by one.

(i) The data on total urban population in States show that the largest urban population was in the State of Maharashtra in all the three censuses. U.P. occupied the second place in the 1951 and 1961 censuses and Tamil Nadu was third. However, in 1971 Tamil Nadu pushed U.P. to the third place. The States of Assam, Manipur, Nagaland, Tripura, Meghalaya, and Orissa had a very small urban population.

(ii) The picture shows an important change when percentage of popula-

TABLE 4: Urban population in different States of India : 1951-71

(in millions)

State	1951		1961		1971		% increase or decrease in 1951-61	% increase or decrease in 1961-71
	Population	% of total population	Population	% of total population	Population	% of total population		
1	2(a)	2(b)	3(a)	3(b)	4(a)	4(b)	5	6
1. Andhra Pradesh	5,42	17.42	6.27	17.44	8.40	19.31	15.68	33.92
2. Assam	0.41	4.64	0.79	7.69	1.33	8.87	121.95	66.80
3. Bihar	2.63	6.78	3.91	8.42	5.63	10.00	48.67	43.95
4. Gujarat	4.43	27.24	5.32	25.77	7.50	28.08	20.09	41.00
5. Haryana	—	—	1.31	17.26	1.77	17.66	—	35.48
6. Himachal Pradesh	—	—	1.78	—	2.42	6.99	—	35.68
7. Jammu & Kashmir	0.46	14.11	0.59	16.66	0.86	18.59	28.26	44.65
8. Kerala	1.83	13.51	2.55	15.11	3.47	16.24	39.34	35.72
9. Madhya Pradesh	3.13	12.01	4.63	14.29	6.79	16.29	47.92	46.63
10. Maharashtra	9.20	28.75	11.16	28.22	15.71	31.17	21.30	40.75
11. Manipur	—	—	0.07	—	0.14	13.19	—	108.95
12. Meghalaya	—	—	0.12	—	0.15	14.55	—	25.27
13. Mysore	4.45	22.94	5.27	22.33	7.12	24.31	18.43	35.23
14. Nagaland	—	—	0.02	5.40	0.05	9.95	—	168.28
15. Orissa	0.59	4.03	1.11	6.32	1.84	8.41	88.14	66.30
16. Punjab	3.07	19.03	2.57	20.13	3.22	23.73	33.22	25.27
17. Rajasthan	2.96	18.53	3.28	16.28	4.54	17.63	10.81	38.47

(Contd.)

TABLE 4 (*Contd.*)

I	2(a)	2(b)	3(a)	3(b)	4(a)	4(b)	5	6
18. Tamil Nadu	7.33	24.34	8.99	26.69	12.46	30.26	22.65	38.64
19. Tripura	—	—	0.10	—	0.16	10.43	—	57.64
20. Uttar Pradesh	8.63	13.65	9.48	12.85	12.39	14.02	9.85	30.68
21. West Bengal	6.28	23.88	8.54	24.45	10.97	24.75	35.99	28.41
Union territories	1.61	—	2.82	—	—	—	75.16	—
All India	62.44	17.29	78.93	17.97	109.09	19.91	26.43	38.22

Sources: (i) Ashish Bose, *Studies in India's Urbanization 1901-1971*, op. cit., p. 59 and p. 69.
(ii) Census of India 1971, *General Population Tables*, op. cit., Statement 5, pp.184-188 and Statement 13, p. 51.
(iii) Central Statistical Organization, *Basic Statistics Relating to the Indian Economy 1950-51 to 1970-71*, Table 70, p. 118.

tion in urban areas to total population of the States is considered. The first position continues to be held by Maharashtra. Gujarat occupied the second place in 1951 but was pushed to the third place in 1961 by Tamil Nadu. In 1971 also, Tamil Nadu continued to hold the second place while Gujarat was a close third. After these States came the State of West Bengal which had 23.88% of its population living in urban areas in 1951. In 1961 this rose to 24.45% and in 1971 to 24.75%. Uttar Pradesh which had the third largest urban population in the country in 1971 showed merely 14.02% of its population living in urban areas in that year. Thus, on the criterion of the percentage of total population living in urban areas, it finishes a poor fourteenth out of the 21 States. Since it is on the basis of the percentage of population living in urban areas that urbanization can be determined, the States of Maharashtra, Tamil Nadu, Gujarat, and West Bengal can be regarded as the most urbanized States of India (in that order). The States of Assam, Bihar, and Orissa have continued to lag far behind in the urbanization process. Thus, only 7.69% of total population in Assam lived in urban areas in 1961. This proportion registered a small increase to 8.87 in 1971. The percentage of population living in urban areas was 6.32 in 1961 and 8.41 in 1971 in Orissa. For Bihar, these percentages were 8.42 in 1961 and 10.00 in 1971.

As is clear from column 3(b), the percentage of population living in urban areas was 17.97 in 1961 for India as a whole. In nine States (out of 15 in 1961), viz. Andhra Pradesh, Assam, Bihar, Jammu & Kashmir, Kerala, Madhya Pradesh, Orissa, Rajasthan and Uttar Pradesh, the percentage of population living in urban areas was less than the national average. In 1971, the average for India as a whole was 19.91 and fifteen States (out of 21) were below this average. These States were Andhra Pradesh, Assam, Bihar, Haryana, Himachal Pradesh, Jammu & Kashmir, Kerala, Madhya Pradesh, Manipur, Meghalaya, Nagaland, Orissa, Rajasthan, Tripura, and Uttar Pradesh. The six States which were relatively more urbanized in both instances were Maharashtra, Tamil Nadu, Gujarat, West Bengal, Mysore, and Punjab (in that order).

(iii) Another important indicator giving the trend of urbanization is the percentage increase (or decrease) in urban population. As would be clear from col. 5, the percentage increase in urban population during the decade 1951-61 for India as a whole was 26.43 (the reader should note that data given in col. 5 are unadjusted data in the sense that changes due to the adoption of a new definition of town are not accounted for). Six States out of fifteen in 1961 experienced a percentage increase less than this level. In the case of remaining nine States that experienced a percentage increase in urban population in 1951-61 greater than the national average there were great variations. The highest increase was recorded in Assam.

The percentage increase in this State was as high as 121.95. Incidentally, it may be pointed out that Uttar Pradesh registered the lowest percentage increase in the decade 1951-1961 which was a meagre 9.85. In the decade 1961-1971 the percentage increase in urban population in India as a whole was 38.22. Of the 21 States, as many as nine States, viz., Andhra Pradesh, Haryana, Himachal Pradesh, Kerala, Meghalaya, Mysore, Punjab, Uttar Pradesh, and West Bengal had a percentage increase less than the national average. Two States registered percentage increase approximately equal to the national average. These States were Rajasthan and Tamil Nadu.

Table 5 presents percent distribution of urban population in different size classes of towns in 1961 and 1971. It brings out the importance of large urban centres in the urbanization process. It shows that 44.50% of urban population was concentrated in Class I towns in 1961 and this rose to 48.93% in 1971. In 1961, Jammu & Kashmir and Maharashtra had more than 60% of their urban population concentrated in Class I towns. In 1971, Manipur and Tripura were added to this list. The number of States having population living in Class I cities in the range of 40-60% of total urban population was four in 1961 (viz., Andhra Pradesh, Gujarat, Uttar Pradesh and West Bengal) and nine in 1971 (viz., Andhra Pradesh, Gujarat, Kerala, Madhya Pradesh, Mysore, Rajasthan, Tamil Nadu, Uttar Pradesh, and West Bengal). Thus, in 1971, 13 out of 21 States had more than 40% of their urban population concentrated in Class I cities. The proportion of urban population living in Class I cities was 39.90% in Punjab in 1971 which is very close to the lower limit of 40%.

CONCENTRATION IN MILLION PLUS URBAN AGGLOMERATIONS

As explained elsewhere in this chapter, the 1971 census introduced the term 'urban agglomeration' (hereinafter referred to as UA) which includes the suburban outgrowths of a particular town with that town itself. This concept enables us to compare more effectively the sprawl of different urban centres, especially the spread of large cities into their adjoining areas. In the 1971 census, 339 UAs were recognized of which 87 UAs belonged to Class I (each having population greater than one lakh), 57 UAs belonged to Class II (each having population in the range 50,000 to 99,999), 86 UAs belonged to Class III (each having population in the range 20,000 to 49,999) 56 UAs belonged to Class IV (each having population in the range 10,000 to 19,999), 51 UAs belonged to Class V (each having population in the range 5000 to 9999) and 2 UAs belonged to Class VI (each having population less than 5000).

The UAs having population greater than one million each were Calcutta, Greater Bombay, Delhi, Madras, Hyderabad, Ahmedabad, Bangalore,

TABLE 5: Percent distribution of urban population in different size-class of towns in 1961 and 1971

State	Year	Size-class of towns						Total
		I	II	III	IV	V	VI	
(1)	(2)	(3)	(4)	(5)	(6)	(7)	(8)	(9)
INDIA	1961	44.50	12.07	19.95	14.32	8.03	1.13	100.0
	1971	48.93	13.49	18.28	12.80	5.68	0.82	100.0
Andhra Pradesh	1961	40.55	9.73	24.23	16.23	8.99	0.27	100.0
	1971	45.41	14.47	21.49	13.89	4.40	0.34	100.0
Assam	1961	12.66	7.35	36.56	17.83	20.42	5.18	100.0
	1971	11.00	23.74	24.32	25.92	13.04	1.98	100.0
Bihar	1961	33.15	12.63	25.60	18.68	9.17	0.77	100.0
	1971	32.32	13.51	28.80	18.67	6.48	0.22	100.0
Gujarat	1961	42.42	10.55	24.20	13.48	8.66	0.69	100.0
	1971	45.10	15.66	17.72	14.04	7.20	0.28	100.0
Haryana	1961	8.07	36.22	28.39	15.68	8.24	3.40	100.0
	1971	12.82	39.75	26.06	12.54	7.84	0.99	100.0
Himachal Pradesh	1961	—	—	23.89	25.81	25.49	24.81	100.0
	1971	—	22.89	8.81	27.18	17.51	23.61	100.0
Jammu & Kashmir	1961	65.39	—	3.55	9.99	6.70	14.37	100.0
	1971	66.79	—	9.52	5.33	12.67	5.69	100.0
Kerala	1961	26.95	14.81	34.68	18.49	4.95	0.42	100.0
	1971	42.32	13.38	31.77	10.11	2.15	0.27	100.0
Madhya Pradesh	1961	31.55	10.62	24.61	16.97	14.82	1.42	100.0
	1971	41.06	12.48	20.38	14.72	10.67	0.69	100.0
Maharashtra	1961	60.49	9.17	13.00	11.17	5.65	0.52	100.0
	1971	64.75	11.07	11.71	8.78	3.39	0.30	100.0

(Contd.)

TABLE 5 (*Contd.*)

(1)	(2)	(3)	(4)	(5)	(6)	(7)	(8)	(9)
Manipur	1961	—	100.0	—	—	—	—	100.0
	1971	70.93	—	—	—	22.18	6.89	100.0
Meghalaya	1961	—	61.66	—	18.24	20.10	—	100.0
	1971	—	59.56	—	31.16	6.07	3.21	100.0
Mysore	1961	36.77	12.79	18.16	20.82	8.99	2.47	100.0
	1971	45.39	10.17	17.32	20.60	5.30	1.22	100.0
Nagaland	1961	—	—	—	—	100.0	—	100.0
	1971	—	—	41.92	58.08	—	—	100.0
Orissa	1961	13.18	20.55	20.27	28.00	17.13	0.87	100.0
	1971	30.03	7.97	31.72	17.13	12.69	0.46	100.0
Punjab	1961	37.71	8.14	28.86	12.06	10.38	2.85	100.0
	1971	39.90	15.68	21.74	14.40	6.99	1.29	100.0
Rajasthan	1961	37.83	7.35	20.34	21.56	11.87	1.05	100.0
	1971	40.94	10.74	20.03	20.62	7.30	0.37	100.0
Tamil Nadu	1961	37.76	14.15	20.85	18.07	7.95	1.22	100.0
	1971	43.80	13.78	20.86	13.51	5.76	2.29	100.0
Tripura	1961	—	53.28	—	12.85	33.87	—	100.0
	1971	61.75	—	—	32.49	5.76	—	100.0
Uttar Pradesh	1961	50.45	13.23	17.80	11.79	6.32	0.41	100.0
	1971	53.03	11.57	17.87	11.55	5.67	0.31	100.0
West Bengal	1961	55.48	14.93	17.00	7.45	4.52	0.62	100.0
	1971	54.91	19.38	13.84	7.52	4.02	0.33	100.0

Source: Computed from Census of India 1971, *General Population Tables*, op. cit., Statement 5, pp. 185–188.

Kanpur, and Poona. Table 6 highlights the concentration of urban population in these million plus UAs. Calcutta UA is the largest in India having a population of more than 70 lakhs followed by Greater Bombay, Delhi, Madras, Hyderabad, Ahmedabad, Bangalore, Kanpur, and Poona in that order. In 1961, there were seven UAs having more than a million inhabitants and in 1971 their number rose to nine with the addition of Kanpur UA and Poona UA. In the 1971 census, all the nine UAs except Poona had more than one million persons, each living within municipal corporation limits. Thus, there were eight million plus cities and nine million plus UAs.

Table 6 reveals the growth of population in the million plus UAs over the decade 1961-71 and the increasing pressure of population on these metropolitan centres. Columns 5 and 6 show that the percent increase of population in almost all of them is considerable. Delhi shows a most consistent and rapid increase. If this rate of increase continues, its population will double itself in less than two decades. Greater Bombay shows more than 40% increase in population in the decade 1961-1971. At this rate, its population will double itself in the next 20-25 years. Similar trends are revealed by some other UAs as well. The increase in population of Calcutta UA seems to be on the lower side compared with some other UAs but it should be remembered that it already contains 64.11% of the urban population of West Bengal. The other UAs are far behind Calcutta in this respect. The second position is occupied by Greater Bombay which contains 38% of Maharashtra's urban population. The two million plus UAs of Maharashtra, viz., Greater Bombay and Poona, together contain 45.22% of the urban population of Maharashtra. The share of Madras, Hyderabad, Ahmedabad and Bangalore in the total urban population of their respective States is between one-fifth to one-fourth. The Kanpur UA contains only 10.29% of the urban population of Uttar Pradesh. In fact, it is the only million plus UA in Table 6 where population density per km^2 in 1971 was less than the population density in the total urban area of the State.[15]

The total population of the nine UAs given in Table 6 was 193.13 lakhs in 1961 which constituted 24.5% of total urban population in that year. This proportion fell marginally to 22.7 in the 1971 census. This would reveal the fact that out of 339 UAs in India in 1971, *more than one-fifth of the urban population was concentrated in merely nine UAs.*

It would be illuminating to consider the interaction between the process of industrialization and urbanization while discussing concentration of urban population in million plus cities and UAs. A study of the data shows that industrial activity has tended to get concentrated in the million plus UAs. Thus, in 1971, out of a total urban working population of 3,303,228 in West Bengal as much as 2,286,147 (or 69.21%) was concen-

TABLE 6: Concentration of urban population in million plus urban agglomerations

UA	Population (in lakhs)		Population living within the limits of municipal corporation (in lakhs)		Percentage variation in the population of UA in the decade		Percentage share of UA in the total urban population of the State		Population density in 1971 (per km²)	
	1961	1971	1961	1971	1951-61	1961-71	1961	1971	in UA	in total urban area of the State
Calcutta	57.37	70.31	29.27	31.49	25.01	22.57	67.17	64.11	12362	5628
Greater Bombay	41.52	59.71	41.52	59.71	39.95	43.80	37.18	38.00	9901	2555
Delhi	20.62	36.47	20.62	32.88	64.17	54.57	—	—	8172	—
Madras	19.45	31.70	17.29	24.69	26.08	63.02	21.63	25.43	5972	2115
Hyderabad	12.49	17.96	11.18	16.07	10.77	43.83	19.90	21.38	6018	2360
Ahmedabad	12.06	17.42	11.50	15.92	37.46	44.40	22.68	23.23	—	1625
Bangalore	12.00	16.54	11.41	15.40	54.04	37.82	22.78	23.22	9466	2272
Kanpur	9.71	12.75	8.81	11.54	37.66	31.32	10.24	10.29	4265	4356
Poona	7.91	11.35	6.06	8.56	30.66	43.53	7.08	7.22	3498	2555

Source: Census of India 1971, *General Population Tables*, op, cit., Statement 5, p. 45 and Table A-IV, pp. 239-250.

trated in Calcutta UA alone. Of the people engaged in manufacturing, processing, servicing, and repairs in urban West Bengal in 1971, as many as 76.43% were working in Calcutta UA alone. Again, Calcutta UA employed 72.5%, 67.1%, and 68.4% of the working population of urban West Bengal in 1971 engaged in trade and commerce, transport, and communications, and other services respectively.[16] The second largest UA of India, viz., Greater Bombay, had 14% of urban Maharashtra's area in 1971, and 27.08% of total manufacturing, processing and servicing establishments, 40.70% of trade or business establishments, 24.97% of total educational establishments, 39% of public health establishments, and 34.88% of other establishments. Its share in all establishments (taken together) stood at 35.34% in 1971. Of the total 1,132,336 persons employed in 14,346 registered manufacturing, processing, and servicing establishments in the whole of Maharashtra in 1971, as many as 542,093 (i.e., 47.87%) were employed in Greater Bombay alone. In the same year, 41.06% of workers engaged in construction activity in urban Maharashtra were concentrated in Greater Bombay. This proportion was 50% in trade and commerce and 49.5% percent in transport, storage and communications.[17] The third important sea-port town of India after Calcutta and Bombay is Madras. In the pre-independence period these three urban centres were centres of trade and handled the imprt-export trade of India. Thus, they were the 'Gateways of India'. The growth of trade, commerce, and industrial activities that followed (and got concentrated) in these towns accounted for a substantial increase in the population of these towns which, in turn, was a consequence of large-scale in-migration into these cities. The continuing sprawl of Madras would be clear from the fact that in 1971 the Madras UA had 58 constituents of which as many as 41 were introduced in the 1971 census. An idea of the concentration of industrial activities in this UA would be clear from the fact that with 9% of the area af urban Tamil Nadu in 1971, it accounted for 9.33% of total manufacturing units and 16.76% of trade or business establishments. Its share in all establishments was 13.25%. Of all the workers engaged in manufacturing, processing, servicing and repairs in urban Tamil Nadu in 1971, 24% were concentrated in Madras UA. The share of Madras UA in some other activities was: 32% in construction, 25% in trade and commerce, and 41% in transport, storage and communications.[18]

These processes are natural, for, according to Galina Sdasyuk, "Industrialization greatly intensifies the formation of industrial-territorial complexes in the old regions which are most advanced industrially and which gravitate towards major port and industrial centres."[19] Sdasyuk gives the example of the Bombay-Ahmedabad industrial belt, 'the country's chief cotton-growing and cotton textile manufacturing area', which has seen an 'accelerated development of texile machine-building, the production of dyes, detergents, bleaching powder and other products connected with traditional specialisation' and growth of new branches of heavy industry such as the machine-tool making, the chemical industry, the oil processing and petro-chemical industry. The processes of metropolitan expansion and industrial growth have also led to the creation and rapid growth of a number of satellite industrial towns. Thus, all along the Bombay-Poona industrial belt a number of satellite towns have cropped up and towns such as Thana, Ulhasnagar, Ambarnath, Bhiwandi, Pimpri, etc., have registered phenomenal growth of population. Similarly, industrial satellite towns have sprung around the capital city of India, Delhi, and are continuously expanding. These satellites are Narela, Ghaziabad, Modinagar, Faridabad, Ballabhgarh, Gurgaon, and Bahadurgarh.

In fact, the three major port-and-industrial cities (Calcutta, Bombay, and Madras) and the capital city (Delhi) have a 'focal role' in the territorial structure of the economy. They are the centres of regional urban systems and are the 'region-forming nuclei of the most mature economic regions'. During the short period of ten years (1961 to 1971) considerable changes have occurred in the maps of India's urban population potentials. According to Sdasyuk, the limits of closed areas gravitating towards the four major metropolitan centres have got considerably extended and "the zones of the main metropolitan centres are stretching out towards each other and are tending to merge". Sdasyuk notes in this context the increasingly important role being played by the 'Bombay-Calcutta corridor' in the industrial development of the nation and the consequent growth of new industrial towns in this corridor. The development of towns such as Nasik, Melegaon, Dhulia, Akola, Amaravati between Bombay and Nagpur belt of the corridor and Jamshedpur, Raipur, Bhilai, Rourkela, etc., in the stretch between Nagpur and Calcutta is a testimony to the interdependent nature of urbanization and industrialization process. To further emphasize this point, one may note the role of the four large steel plants set up in the public sector (and located at Bhilai, Durgapur, Rourkela, and Bokaro) in the urbanization process. The establishment of Bhilai steel plant has helped in making Durg an important urban agglomeration. Thus, the population of Durg-Bhilainagar urban agglomeration which was merely 20,249 in 1951 (i.e., before the establishment of Bhilai steel plant) rose to 133,230 in 1961 and further to 245,124 in 1971 registering an increase of 557.96% over the decade 1951-61 and 83.99% over the decade 1961-71. The setting up of the steel plant was accompanied by the development of mining industry in the area and a fuel and power base was set up at Korba. Thus, "the emerging urban system of Durg-Bhilainagar-Raipur-Bilaspur-Korba furnishes the pivot for a new economic region that is taking shape"[20] in the

State of Madhya Pradesh. Similarly, the Rourkela steel plant set up in the Sundargarh district of Orissa in the Second Plan, built up a township around it and soon the Rourkela urban agglomeration started its sprawl. From its area of 95.31 km^2 in 1961 it increased its area to 121.73 km^2 in 1971 and within this period its population registered an increase of 91.06% The Bokaro Steel City urban agglomeration (constituted of Bokaro Steel City and Chas) also increased its population very rapidly. The Bokaro Steel City urban agglomeration which had a population of only 5873 in 1951 and was declassified as a town in 1961 emerged as a Class I UA in 1971 with a population of 1.07 lakhs. Because of the Durgapur steel plant established in Burdwan (West Bengal), the Durgapur urban agglomeration has emerged as an important centre on the industrial map of the country. In a single decade 1961-1971, its area rose from 73.69 km^2 to 154.20 km^2 and its population from 41,696 to 206,638 registering an increase of 396%.

MIGRATION AND URBANIZATION

The factors responsible for rapid urban growth are: (i) the natural increase of population as a result of excess of births over deaths, and (ii) migration from rural areas to urban areas. In large urban centres (especially metropolitan centres) additional factor of migration from lower order urban centres is also operative. People living in urban areas of a lower order are attracted to urban areas of a higher order because of better prospects of employment, scope for enlarging their incomes, and the opportunities such areas offer for leading a more sophisticated and a modern social life. In many western countries, on account of the industrial revolution and the consequent economic growth, there was a big flow of migrants from rural areas to urban areas in the nineteenth century. The technological changes and the era of specialization was bound to concentrate in certain specific areas and it was these areas which attracted substantial migrants from other places. Because of the closer integration of economic activities that such concentration of population in specific areas made possible, efficiency of the socio-economic organization was enhanced. This further increased the drift of people towards these areas and their population increased further.[21]

Thus, in the nineteenth-century Europe, the process of urban growth was a consequence of the growth in manufacturing industry and the economic development propelled by such industrial growth. People were attracted to areas of industrial growth and soon the process of large-scale migration from rural areas to such urban areas was unleashed. The question that is frequently asked is—can the rapid expansion of urban population in countries of Asia be regarded as being caused by similar forces that were in evidence in the nineteenth-century Europe? In other words, are the migrants from rural areas being 'pulled in' by urban centres, i.e., are the urban areas acting as magnets to attract rural population as was the case in the West in the nineteenth century? This brings us to the popular controversy between the 'pull' and the 'push' factors. Protagonists of the 'pull theory' believe that urban centres attract people from non-urban areas by promising them (or so the migrants believe) better employment opportunities, better income, and, in general, a better life. In addition to these factors the protagonists of the pull theory believe that some other pull factors operate in the developing countries of Asia. These can be summarized as follows:

(i) the tendency of the public authorities to concentrate greater investments in both industry and social overheads in urban areas;
(ii) availability of social services such as medical care, environmental sanitation, educational facilities, housing, recreation, etc., in urban areas and their total absence or inadequate availability in rural areas;[22] and
(iii) some people, especially those belonging to the younger generation, migrate from rural to urban areas in search of greater psychological satisfaction in urban environment which offers rapid changes, innovations, fashions and thrills. In a way, the young migrants may also be rebelling against the restraints and authoritarian character of traditional family life of rural areas.

The protagonists of the 'push theory' believe that in countries of Asia, it is not the pull of the urban centres but the 'push' of the rural areas that swells the population of urban areas. Because of the widespread poverty in rural areas and the pressure of population on land, economic pressure forces out people from rural areas who move into urban areas in search of employment and livelihood. Some of the important push factors that seem to be operative in India are: (i) rapid increase in population growth, (ii) high pressure on available land, (iii) low productivity of land, (iv) low per capita income and the disparity between urban and rural levels of income, and (v) prevalence of widespread unemployment and underemployment in rural areas. Such 'push' factors are found to exist in most of the over-populated countries of Asia and are used by the protagonists of the push theory to explain the large-scale exodus of people from rural areas to urban areas.

Before we can proceed further, we must point out that though rural push seems to be the most valid (or, at least, the most popular) explanation of rapid urban growth in most of the underdeveloped countries of Asia, it alone cannot be relied upon to explain the causes behind rural-urban migration. We must answer, at least, the following two questions before a judgement can be passed: (i) Do the migrants to urban areas from the rural areas constitute a substantial proportion of the potential migrants? and (ii) Are the migrants economically worse off than those who remain in the villages? These questions, posed by Sovani,[23] are of basic importance. For, (i) if only a small proportion of the potential migrants (all of them being more or less equally poor) actually migrate while the remaining ones continue to hang on in villages, the motivations of actual migrants behind their decision to migrate cannot be summed up easily in the form of push factors, and (ii) if evidence suggests that it is not really the poor and the desperate that migrate but those who are relatively well off, then such migration cannot be attributed to the push factors but must be accounted for by the pull factors. Sovani has collected some evidence to show that only a small proportion of potential migrants actually migrate and it is the relatively well off that have a greater tendency to migrate thus questioning the validity of the push theory. He admits, however, that his study based as it is on a very small sample can only be 'suggestive' and should not be considered as 'conclusive'. In fact, both push and pull factors play an effective role in the process of migration. Therefore, it is safe to summarize the situtation thus: "Although the push factors of falling incomes and underemployment in agriculture in most of the less developed countries are now very strong, they do not, in the absence of strong pull factors, suffice to cause the large shifts in manpower between occupations."[24]

ANALYSIS OF MIGRATION DATA IN INDIA

Migration is a vague concept and different definitions and concepts of migration are used in different parts of the world. Thus, data on migration are frequently not comparable across countries. Generally a person who crosses an 'administrative boundary' is considered to be a migrant. However, in India, up to 1961, the census data were derived through the particulars on birth place alone. In the censuses prior to 1961, a person was considered a migrant if he was born outside the *State* in which he was enumerated. This naturally gave a very low mobility of population. Thus, in 1901, only 3.3% of persons were enumerated in States other than the State of birth. This proportion has remained more or less constant throughout. It was thus maintained by many scholars that population mobility in India was extremely low and various explanations were provided to explain this phenomenon. For example it was maintained that an average villager in India 'clings on' to his native place irrespective of his economic condition in his village and the opportunities available in other places. Indian population is traditionally immobile and therefore unresponsive to economic changes and better opportunities, and so on. A little reflection will show the shallowness of this thesis. As already noted, such an opinion is based upon the migration data that include only those persons who were born outside the State of enumeration, therefore considerable actual migration was not revealed at all. In the 1961 census, data were collected for the first time with reference to the exact place of enumeration. If we regard all persons who are born outside *the place of enumeration* (even if they are born in another district of the same State) as migrants, as should indeed be the case, the percentage of migrants to total population in 1961 rises to 30.8 (from 3.31 which is the percent of persons enumerated in a State different from the one in which they were born to total population). This is considerable by any standards and shows that about one-third of the total population came under the category of migrants in 1961. Similarly, in the 1971 census, 160.1 million persons were reported to be born outside the place of their enumeration and since the total population was 548.16 million, the percentage of migrants to total population was 29.21 which is again considerable by any standards (see Table 7).

Table 7 presents data on migration during the decades 1951-1961 and 1961-1971. Migrants are divided into four classes according to the types of movement which are (i) rural to rural (known as Rural Turnover), (ii) rural to urban (known as Rural Push), (iii) urban to rural (known as Push back, Reverse or Return migration), and (iv) urban to urban (known as Urban Turnover).

Table 7 reveals some important facts about the migration streams which can be stated as follows:

(1) Out of the four migration streams, rural to rural migration is the most important. Thus, in 1961, 73.2% of total migrants belonged to this category and in 1971 their percentage was 70.6. This is not unexpected in an underdeveloped country where more than 70% of the population depends on agriculture.

(2) Migration in the case of females is much higher compared with males according to both the 1961 and the 1971 census. Thus, out of a total migrant population of 135.3 million according to the 1961 census, 93.5 million (i.e., 69.1%) were females. According to the 1971 census, the total migrant population was 160.1 million out of which 112.2 million (i.e., 70%) were females. This high migration in females is the result of the fact that after marriage the girl goes to her husband's place to live with him. It would interest the reader to know that marriage migration and associa-

TABLE 7: **Volume of migrant population by types of movement**

(in millions)

Type of movement	1961 census			1971 census		
	Males	Females	Total	Males	Females	Total
Rural to rural	23.5	75.6	99.1	25.3	87.7	113.0
	(56.2)	(80.8)	(73.2)	(52.8)	(78.2)	(70.6)
Rural to urban	10.6	9.0	19.6	12.4	11.3	23.7
	(25.4)	(9.6)	(14.5)	(25.9)	(10.1)	(14.8)
Urban to rural	1.19	2.9	4.8	2.9	5.0	7.9
	(4.5)	(3.1)	(3.6)	(6.0)	(4.4)	(4.9)
Urban to urban	5.4	5.4	10.8	6.8	7.2	14.0
	(12.9)	(5.8)	(8.0)	(14.2)	(6.4)	(8.8)
Unclassified	0.4	0.6	1.0	0.5	1.0	1.5
	(1.0)	(0.7)	(0.7)	(1.1)	(0.9)	(0.9)
Total	41.8	93.5	135.3	47.9	112.2	160.1
	(100)	(100)	(100)	(100)	(100)	(100)

Note: Data in parentheses are percentages to the total.
Source: G.K. Mehrotra, Census of India 1971, Monograph No. 1 on *Birth-Place Migration in India*, Statement 2.0, p. 32.

tional migration (i.e., accompanying migrant husbands) of females from rural to rural areas alone accounted for 56% of total migration in 1961 and 55% of total migration in 1971 (since according to Table 7, out of 135.3 million migrants in 1961, 75.6 million were female rural to rural migrants and in 1971, out of 160.1 million total migrants, 87.7 million were rural to rural female migrants).

(3) As far as rural to urban migration is concerned, male migration is more than female migration. Thus, in 1961, 25.4% male migration was from rural areas to urban areas while in 1971 it was 25.9%. However, female migration was only 9.6% in 1961 and 10.1% in 1971. This is explained by the fact that it is generally the male section of the population that is 'pushed out' from rural areas in search of employment and better opportunities and this phenomenon is found in most of the developing countries. However, a note of caution needs to be struck here. While in percentage terms the share of male migration from rural to urban areas is definitely much more than female migration, Table 7 reveals that in absolute numbers the difference is not much. Thus, against 10.6 million males who migrated from rural to urban areas in 1961, the number of females who migrated from rural to urban areas was 9.0 million. In 1971, against 12.4 million males, 11.3 million females migrated from rural to urban areas.

(4) After rural to rural and rural to urban migration, comes urban to urban migration. The data show that according to the 1961 census, the magnitude of this form of migration was 10.8 million which went up to 14.0 million in 1971, registering an increase from 8% to 8.8%. Thus, intra-urban migration is showing an increase over time, a phenomenon which is accounted for by the strong pull force of large urban centres especially metropolitan centres which attract persons from urban areas of lower order.

(5) As far as magnitude is concerned, the least important is urban to rural migration or push back migration. It was 4.8 million in 1961 and 7.9 million according to the 1971 census. In percentage terms, its share was 3.6 in 1961 and 4.9 in 1971. This implies that the share of urban to rural migration is gradually increasing. Perhaps this is because of the fact that increasing unemployment and underemployment in urban areas and deteriorating living conditions in metropolitan centres (especially the mushroom growth of slums in such areas) are forcing back people from urban to rural areas.

It is frequent to classify migration into (i) short-distance migration, (ii) medium-distance migration, and (iii) long-distance migration. Short-distance migration is generally taken to be intra-district migration (i.e., within the district), medium-distance migration is inter-district but intra-State migration, while long-distance migration is inter-State (i.e. from one State to another) migration. In both 1961 and 1971, approximately two-thirds of the migrants were short-distance migrants and a little more than one-fifth were medium distance migrants. Long-distance migration has continued to contribute merely 10 to 11% of total migrants. However, as far as the volume of long-distance migration is concerned, it increased from 14.6 million in 1961 to 18.5 million in 1971.

Since we are interested in the rural to urban migration in particular, it may be noted that in 1961 out of the total male migrants from rural to urban areas, 35% were short-distance, 34% medium-distance, and 31% long-distance migrants. In 1971, these percentages were 37, 34, and 29 respectively. This gives the significant conclusion that a little less than a third of rural to urban migrants have continued to be long-distance migrants showing thereby that as far as male rural to urban migration is concerned, *long-distance migration claims approximately the same importance as short-distance and medium-distance migration.* It is also important to note that whereas in intra-district and inter-district migration among males, rural to rural migration is most important, *in inter-State migration rural to urban migration becomes most important.*[25] This is because of the fact that large urban centres especially metropolitan centres such as Bombay, Calcutta, Delhi, and Madras attract people from far-flung rural areas. For example, the metropolitan centres of Bombay and Calcutta have attracted continuous migration streams from the rural areas of Uttar Pradesh and Bihar.

Since the States of Maharashtra, Gujarat, Tamil Nadu, and West Bengal are most advanced industrial States of India, we should expect the rural to urban migration to be more important in these States. This indeed is the case. Mehrotra's analysis (Statement 4, page 38) shows that as far as male migrants are concerned, the highest percentage of rural to urban migrants was found in Maharashtra, followed by Gujarat and West Bengal in that order in 1971. Thus, 35% of total male migrants in Maharashtra, 32% in Gujarat, and 29% in West Bengal were rural to urban migrants. Among the underdeveloped States, Bihar was at the top having 20% of male migrants as rural to urban migrants (which was, in fact, very close to West Bengal and higher than Tamil Nadu). As far as our general observations above are concerned, the pattern seemed more consistent in 1961 when each of the four developed States had 30% or more migrants as rural to urban migrants and the other States were far behind. This pattern is not observed in the case of female migrants. This is also to be expected, for in Indian conditions, as noted earlier, the push or pull factors are not very much in operation as far as female migrants are concerned.

Some other conclusions of Mehrotra's[26] study regarding the State-wise pattern of migrants are summarized below:

(i) Uttar Pradesh, being the most populous State of the country, has contributed maximum to the total intra-district and inter-district migration in rural sector. Bihar and Maharashtra are the next largest contributors.

(ii) The highest contribution to all-India intra-district migration in the urban sector comes from Tamil Nadu though according to urban population it has a second rank. Maharashtra (the State having the largest urban population) stands second with regard to intra-district migration and first in respect of inter-district migration in the urban sector.

(iii) In Maharashtra and West Bengal, where heavy industrialization has taken place, the inter-State in-migration to urban areas has been quite heavy compared with other States. Maharashtra contributes about one-fourth of the total inter-State in-migration. West Bengal has maintained its second rank even though it has attracted fewer migrants in 1971 compared with 1961. Delhi ranks third and has shown an upward swing in its inter-State in-migration in 1971 over 1961.

(iv) In rural areas, the largest share (12%) of inter-State in-migration is recorded by Madhya Pradesh, followed by Punjab group, West Bengal, and Uttar Pradesh in both 1961 and 1971.

PROBLEMS OF URBAN AREAS

When we talk of problems of urban areas we undoubtedly have large urban centres in mind. Even among the large urban centres it is the metropolitan areas that suffer from these problems in their worst form. In most of the discussion that follows, the reader must bear this in mind.

Broadly speaking the problems of urban areas can be classified under the following categories—economic, physical, social, governmental, and administrative.[27] Because of their immediate appeal, physical problems have received most of the attention. Under this category come land-use pattern, housing problem, and problems of water supply, sewerage, drainage, air and water pollution, congestion, transport, etc. Because these problems have an immediate impact on the city dwellers they naturally receive most of the attention of all cities and planners. We shall discuss some of them in detail to highlight their seriousness in India, after having discussed the other problems mentioned above.

THE ECONOMIC PROBLEMS

Under this head, the most important problem is that of finding resources for provision and maintenance of urban infrastructure. Most of the developing countries have acute scarcity of resources and their natural desire is to invest in programmes of economic development. Thus, they are faced with a problem of choice. Huge investments are needed for providing urban infrastructure including public utilities and housing while resources are extremely limited. In their anxiety to promote economic growth, the underdeveloped countries have been tempted to devote more attention to productive projects (projects productive in the short run, for in the long run investment on urban infrastructure must also be considered productive) neglecting or paying insufficient attention to problems of urbanization which get accentuated to alarming proportions with the passage of time. This is the natural outcome of ignoring the investment claims of urban infrastructure in an atmosphere where urbanization always keeps on running ahead of economic development and productivity. However, even with the best of intentions, it is not possible to spend a sufficient amount for financing urban overhead capital. The sheer paucity of resources makes this impossible. It is a tremendous strain on the scarce capital resources of a poor country to provide even tolerable housing facilities, electric supply, water supply, sewerage and drainage facilities, sanitary units, schools, hospitals, transport and communications facilities, etc., on an ever increasing scale for a continuously increasing urban population.

Some underdeveloped countries are trying to overcome this problem by reducing the rate of urbanization, by inducing people in urban areas to go to villages and by decentralizing new industrial development. However, such efforts are often not successful because the large urban centres have become centres of cultural, political, commercial, industrial activity and this process was in many cases initiated long back. With the passage of time this process has gained such a strength and momentum that it is not likely to slow down. For example in India, the sea-coast cities of Bombay and Calcutta (and to a lesser degree Madras) served as colonial trading ports in British India and they gradually developed into centres of commercial and industrial activity. Now, as already shown, they have developed into large metropolises and continuous streams of in-migration have continued to increase the population pressure on these centres. On account of this pressure a serious problem of urban unemployment has arisen. A number of autochthones fail to get employment on account of competition from migrants and since this section of unemployed urbanites is far more vocal and volatile compared with the rural unemployed or underemployed, the fear of political and social eruptions and instability are greater in metropolitan areas.

Urbanization also creates some other economic problems. For example, it encourages the production and consumption of non-essential goods leading to a diversion of scarce economic resources away from the production of essential goods. Because of 'demonstration effect' of the consumption patterns in the developed countries and better 'communication' in urban areas compared with rural areas, the consumption of semi-luxuries and luxuries is promoted at the cost of necessary goods and services.

THE SOCIAL PROBLEMS

The social problems thrown up by urbanization are complex and many. In addition to the social instability that results from unemployment in urban areas (as noted above) urbanization tends to break down traditional behaviour and produces many problems of *personal disorganization*.'[8] It precipitates problems such as 'juvenile delinquency, crime, prostitution, alcoholism, drug addiction, suicide, mental diseases, social unrest, and political instability'. The migrants usually come alone to cities where they find it difficult to adjust to the new atmosphere while their own family life is disrupted on account of such migration; stresses and strains of the fast city life promote a gloomy outlook and frustration in life and encourages alcoholism, drug addiction and suicides; inequalities in income and wealth breed crime, social unrest and political instability; and low sex ratio (frequently because of the fact that most of the migrants are generally males who leave behind their families in villages) promotes the practice of prostitution. In his study of the social effects of urbanization on industrial workers conducted at Worli in Bombay, Prabhu notes[29] that the compulsion to live in cities away from their families is the cause of their social and personal disorganization. 'Pathological manifestations of impulses' are frequent and abnormal sex practices have grown sufficiently common. Because of acute housing shortage and their inability to pay rent (or build their own houses) a large proportion of the migrants are condemned to living in slums. The nauseating and filthy atmosphere prevailing in such areas is a real health hazard. In his study quoted above, Prabhu notes that there is terrible congestion in the quarters and chawls at Worli (his area of study) with ten to fifteen people packed in a small room of 10'×10'. Latrines are just cesspools and bathrooms are pools of filth and dirt. Out of 523 respondents in Prabhu's study, as much as 61% stated that stay in the city had an adverse effect and caused illness every now and then.

Similar observations are scattered all over in various case studies related to the process of urbanization in cities and metropolitan centres. To take just one more example, we consider the study *Urbanization Trends in Agra* by D.S. Chauhan.[30] Chauhan's study notes the personal and social disorganization which persons living in urban areas have to suffer and the resulting dwarfing and disintegration of human-personality. His study of 2599 persons reported frustration (of one kind or another) in 2231 persons. Boredom was found to have increased in 88.6% cases, isolation in 69.7% cases, nervous strain in 86.4%, and emotional depression in 45.2% cases. The urban atmosphere was felt to be more polluted by 95.13% persons. The most common frustrations and tensions in order of importance were: "unwholesome environment, blighted hopes, boredom, nervous strain, emotional depression, strenuousness of work and fear in daily life".

The Governmental and Administrative Problems

On account of the existence of a number of urban bodies and problems relating to distribution of functions, allocation of resources for tax purposes, etc., serious governmental and administrative difficulties arise quite frequently in urban areas. For example, in Delhi, there is a New Delhi Municipal Corporation, Municipal Corporation of Delhi, Cantonment Board, Metropolitan Council, etc., with no clear demarcation and separation of functions. Not surprisingly, there are conflicts and controversies and it is sometimes not possible to *fix* responsibility for lapses in providing civic amenities or in solving other urban problems. Admittedly, the administrative and governmental problems are, as yet, confined to a few metropolitan centres only but with the progress of urbanization as more and more cities attain the metropolitan status, these problems are expected to increase.

Physical Problems

On account of limitations of space, we propose to discuss only two problems (which are, nevertheless, basic problems) under this heading. They are: (i) problems relating to civic amenities and (ii) problem of housing and slums.

Problems Relating to Civic Amenities. It is a known fact that a large number of urban areas in India are plagued with inefficient and insufficient civic amenities. Public facilities and utilities are frequently very inadequate. The Town and Country Planning Organization noted in 1962 that "out of 13 medium-sized towns (the Class II towns with a population range of 50,000 to 99,999) only 4 had piped water supply and 3 had sewerage system. Out of 10 major towns (the Class I cities with population of 100 thousand and more each) 6 had no sewerage. In all of the urban areas of the country, only 38 percent of the dwellers had water taps and only 16 percent had sewerage system for their uses.[31] Because of continued pouring in of a large number of migrants, the problems of large cities and especially million plus cities have assumed alarming proportions. The mushroom growth of slums in these cities has led to a sharp deterioration of sanitation, water supply position, and transport facilities. Undoubtedly some of these problems are present in the developed countries as well but what separates the problems of the underdeveloped countries from the developed countries is the lack of financial and other resources in them to provide even a minimum amount of civic amenities to their citizens.

Less than 1% of urban areas in India have filtered water supply. Of these few towns, a very small number can boast of a 24-hour water supply, and only a minority of them have a system of distribution of water on taps.[32] The per capita availability of water continues to be pathetically low in metropolitan cities. For example, the daily per capita water supply is only 12 gallons in Bangalore, 19 in Madras, 27 in the Calcutta Metropolitan District, 34 in Bombay, and 45 in Delhi.[33] Since these are only averages, there must be areas of severe shortage of this basic amenity in all these million plus cities. Though the governments (both Centre and State) provide financial assistance in the form of loans and grants to municipal corporations to carry out various water supply schemes yet (i) the assistance is totally inadequate and (ii) the general attitude of many municipal corporations and municipalities is one of apathy and lethargy, if not that of sheer neglect.

The same story is found in the case of sewage disposal systems. It has been estimated officially that only about 38% of the urban population has a sewerage system. Since this is only an average, the actual position in many parts of cities and metropolitan areas must be deplorable. In many cities, the old sewer systems have not been improved, modernized, or replaced. The treatment and disposal of sewage is carried out by crude and outdated methods. For example, the three metropolitan cities of Calcutta, Bombay, and Madras continue to discharge a major part of sewage into the sea. Similarly in Delhi, more than half of the total inflow of sewage goes into the river Jamuna leading to its pollution. The drainage facilities are also inadequate to cope with the increased strains on the system. The open drains often serve as depositors for road sweepings and also human wastes. In rainy season water overflows and spreads into streets presenting a dingy view, promoting unhygienic conditions and causing outbreak of numerous infectious diseases.

These problems relating to water supply, sewage, and other facilities have been noted by all city surveys, especially those relating to metropolitan centres. The conditions are particularly bad in slum areas. As an example, we point out the results of a survey conducted in the city of Surat by the Centre for Regional Development Studies, Surat, in mid-1973.[34] This survey noted that as many as 91% of the households dwelling in slums depend on public water stand posts. On an average, about 150 families use one tap. Heavy rush for water creates tension and often results in quarrels. On latrine facility, the survey notes that only 6% households of the slums have private lavatory facility either of their own or in common with others. One-third of the population of the slums uses public latrines. Approximately, 150 to 200 persons use one lavatory. Consequently, people have to stand in queue, sometimes, for more than half an hour to avail of lavatory facilities. Moreover, most of these latrines are in extremely dilapidated condition. Because of these factors, many slum dwellers are forced to defecate in the open or anywhere near their *basti*. Their excreta causes odour, uncleanliness and hence flies, mosquitoes and diseases such as dysentry and cholera.

Most of the surveys of metropolitan cities confirm that such hostile environment to human life is not the legacy of slums in Surat alone, it is the general condition prevailing in the majority of slums scattered all over the major cities of the country.

The Problem of Urban Housing and Slums: One of the most serious problems generated by the rapid urbanization process in the developing countries is the acute shortage of housing facilities and the related problems of explosive growth of slums. An overall picture of housing shortage in urban India is presented in Table 8.

TABLE 8: **Estimated housing demand, supply and shortage in urban India owing to population growth, 1951 to 1971**

(in million)

Year	Urban India		
	Demand	Supply	Shortage
1951	12.500	10.305	2.195
1956	14.160	11.764	2.396
1961	15.780	14.063	1.717
1966	18.640	16.021	2.619
1971	21.640	18.413	3.227

Note: Demand estimated year-wise on the basis of one dwelling unit for five persons. Population figures obtained from census reports. Supply of housing stock obtained for 1951, 1961, and 1971 from census reports. The 1956 and 1966 figures were estimated on the basis of the census data.

Source: Gopal Bhargava and P.N. Dougre, "Housing for the Urban Poor", *The Economic Times*, 14 July 1977. This table has been taken by Bhargava and Dougre from Bakshi D. Sinha's study on "Housing Growth in India".

Table 8 shows that the supply of housing has continuously remained less than the demand. The shortage was 21.95 lakhs in 1951, 17.17 lakhs in 1961, and 32.27 lakhs in 1971. The spectacular increase in shortage over the decade 1961-1971 was on account of 37.14% increase in demand while supply increased only by 30.93%.

The Study of 1971 Census Data. In the 1971 census, 1,985,761 persons belonging to 565,180 households were counted as houseless.[35] The number of houseless persons in urban areas was 465,863 belonging to 177,252 households. Out of the 465,863 houseless persons in 1971 found in urban India as much as 106,260 were found in Maharashtra alone. Then came West Bengal with 64,876, Rajasthan with 48,340, Gujarat with 42,429 and Andhra Pradesh with 39,981. In percentage terms, share of these States was: Maharashtra 22.81%, West Bengal 13.93%, Rajasthan 10.38%, Gujarat 9.11%, and Andhra Pradesh 8.58%. It would seem strange that the most developed State of India, viz. Maharashtra, should also possess the largest number of houseless people (incidentally, it may also be pointed out that Maharashtra possesses the highest number of houseless rural people as well). Out of the first four States having maximum number of urban houseless population as many as three States, viz. Maharashtra, West Bengal, and Gujarat, are among the four most developed States of India. Their combined share in urban houseless population is as much as 45.85%. If the fourth industrially developed State, viz. Tamil Nadu, is also added, the share of the four most developed States in urban houseless population comes out to more than 50%.

This may seem paradoxical but an answer can be found in the observations already made on migration. It is quite possible that a considerable number of people might have come to the urban areas of these States from the rural areas of these States themselves and from the rural and urban areas of other States in search of employment and have not been able to find any accommodation. These houseless people, or pavement dwellers as they are usually called, sleep on side-walks in the porches and corridors of public buildings, in public parks, or suburban railway stations.

Table 9 presents data on urban housing problem in States according to the 1971 census. The following facts are revealed by it:

(1) Approximately half of urban households have only one room and as much as 40% of urban population lives in them. The situation is worst in Maharashtra where 63.36% of urban households have only one room and 58.03% of urban population lives in them. In West Bengal as much as 62.84% urban households have only one room and 50.66% of urban population is condemned to living in such houses. In fact, as far as the percentage of households with one room to total number of households and the percentage of population living in them is concerned, only five States, viz. Maharashtra, West Bengal, Gujarat, Tamil Nadu, and Andhra Pradesh, exceeded the national average and out of these States, the first four are the most developed States of the country. Thus, 54.37% urban households in Tamil Nadu had only one room and 48.16% of urban population lived in them. In Gujarat, 52.16% of urban households had only one room and 47.03% of urban population lived in them.

(2) Column 8 reveals that on the average more than 4.7 persons live in one-room households in urban India. The States that exceed the national average are Maharashtra, Gujarat, Tamil Nadu, Kerala, and Karnataka. In Maharashtra, Gujarat, and Kerala approximately 5 persons are squeezed into such one-room households and the situation in respect of Tamil Nadu and Karnataka looks only a shade better. This brings into prominence the *congestion* in single-room households in urban areas and the consequent loss of privacy and unhealthy atmosphere for growth and living in such areas, a situation to which approximately 40% of people living in urban areas in India are condemned.

(3) Columns 6 and 7 present data on urban households having two rooms and the percentage of people living in them. They show that 26.93% urban households had two rooms and 28.08% of urban population (excluding houseless population) lived in them. These data combined with the data in cols. 4 and 5 bring out a distressing picture. They show that 77.03% of urban households had either one or two rooms and 69.79% of urban population lived in them. This implies that only 22.97% of urban households had more than two rooms and only 30.21% of urban population lived in them.

TABLE 9: Statewise data on urban housing problem, 1971

State	Houseless population in urban areas		Percentage of households with one room to total number of households in urban areas	Percentage of number of members living in households with one room to number of members in all households in urban areas	Percentage of households with two rooms to total number of households in urban areas	Percentage of number of members living in households with two rooms to number of members in all households in urban areas	No. of persons living in one room households in urban areas / Total number of one room households in urban areas	Total number of rooms in all households in urban areas / Total number of households in urban areas
	No. of Households	Persons						
(1)	(2)	(3)	(4)	(5)	(6)	(7)	(8)	(9)
INDIA	177,252	465,863	50.10	41.71	26.93	28.08	4.57	1.98
Andhra Pradesh	12,119	39,981	52.84	45.49	26.76	28.14	4.51	1.87
Assam	1.122	2,542	48.93	36.77	29.89	31.87	4.16	1.91
Bihar	3,161	8,951	40.57	28.63	29.24	28.88	4.07	2.30
Gujarat	13,498	42,429	52.16	47.03	29.39	30.60	5.03	1.84
Haryana	1,042	4,456	40.69	31.30	32.48	33.39	4.30	2.15
Himachal Pradesh	252	756	46.46	32.76	31.45	34.33	2.76	1.97
Jammu & Kashmir	165	413	23.33	16.29	25.93	23.39	4.38	3.10
Kerala	2,665	6,372	18.10	13.96	27.29	26.11	5.04	3.18
Karnataka	13,173	28,926	41.29	34.05	30.82	31.36	4.71	2.18
Madhya Pradesh	11,579	31,462	41.14	31.56	31.94	37.94	4.08	2.16
Maharashtra	49,387	106,260	63.36	58.03	21.92	23.19	5.00	1.62
Orissa	2,421	6,490	40.47	30.73	31.92	32.13	3.63	2.19

(Contd.)

TABLE 9 (*Contd.*)

(1)	(2)	(3)	(4)	(5)	(6)	(7)	(8)	(9)
Punjab	1,643	7,488	41.08	32.43	30.73	31.54	4.37	2.19
Rajasthan	2,516	48,340	38.59	29.13	27.60	27.46	4.19	2.40
Tamil Nadu	8,478	28,724	54.37	48.16	25.90	27.65	4.61	1.83
Uttar Pradesh	5,389	13,680	45.36	35.67	28.85	29.69	4.41	2.11
West Bengal	35,370	64,876	62.84	50.66	22.20	25.20	4.50	1.66

Sources: (i) Cols. 4 to 9 computed from Census of India 1971, Series I—India, Part IV-B, *Housing Tables*, Table H-III.
(ii) For Cols. 2 and 3, Census of India 1971, Series I—India, Part II-A (i), *General Population Tables*, Table A-I (Appendix III).

In all the four most developed States of India, viz. Maharashtra, Gujarat, West Bengal, and Tamil Nadu, only 15-20% of urban households had more than two rooms and less than 25% of the population lived in them.

(4) Column 9 presents data on average number of rooms per household in urban areas. It shows that in a number of States the average is approximately 2 rooms only (which is also the average for urban India as a whole).

Table 10 presents data on housing problem in metropolitan cities. The most precarious position is seen in Greater Bombay where the number of houseless persons is 59,169, Calcutta being second with 48,802 houseless persons. In Bombay, as much as 77.40% households had only one room and 75.07% population lived in them. On average, 5.26 persons were squeezed in one-room households (which is incidentally the highest in all metropolitan cities—see col. 8). On an average, a household in Bombay had only 1.36 rooms (which is the lowest among all metropolitan cities—see col. 9). In Calcutta, 67.64% of urban households had only one room and 54.68% of urban population lived in them. These percentages were 57.35 and 49.14 for Delhi and 53.59 and 48.81 for Madras respectively. The situation seems comparatively better in the metropolitan cities of Hyderabad and Bangalore. Thus, in Hyderabad 42.75% of urban households had one room and 33.42% of urban population lived in them. In Bangalore, 45.07% of urban households had a single room and 38.51 of urban population lived in them. However, if one considers the number of persons per one-room households, the situation seems best in Kanpur and worst in Greater Bombay (see col. 8).

Because of the acute housing shortage (as evident from the above analysis), a considerable proportion of urban dwellers in metropolitan cities are forced to live in slum areas. A UNO report defines slums as "a building, group of buildings, or area characterized by overcrowding, deterioration, unsanitary conditions, absence of facilities or amenities which, because of these conditions or any of them, endanger the health, safety or morals of its inhabitants or the community".[36] There are two related issues as far as slum dwellers are concerned: (i) there is an acute housing shortage in metropolitan cities, hence they are not in a position to find any other accommodation; and (ii) the majority of them are so poor that even if some good or tolerable accommodation is available (or can be provided for them by government agencies), they are not in a position to pay the rent (or instalments, if the dwellings are sold to them). Therefore, even where the government has tried to provide alternative accommodation to slum dwellers, they have not been able to avail of the opportunity and such accommodation is generally taken over by somewhat better-placed individuals (compared with the slum dwellers). As a result the population of the slums has continued to increase and the slums have spread over vast areas of the

TABLE 10: Data on housing problems in metropolitan centres, 1971

Urban area	Houseless population		% of households with one room to total No. of households	% of No. of members living in households with one room to No. of members in all households	% of households with two room to total No. of households	% of No. of members living in households with two rooms to No. of members in all households	No. of persons living in one room households / total No. of one room households	Total No. of rooms in all households / Total No. of households
	No. of households	Persons						
Calcutta M. Corp.	28,202	48,802	67.64	54.68	17.25	20.10	4.46	1.62
Greater Bombay	31,133	59,169	77.40	75.07	14.22	14.84	5.26	1.36
Delhi (urban)	11,181	15,728	57.35	49.14	25.42	28.43	4.46	1.73
Madras	1,634	7,049	53.59	48.81	24.43	25.48	5.23	1.91
Hyderabad	1,669	4,722	42.75	33.42	29.63	29.98	4.57	2.14
Ahmedabad	2,832	6,095	57.35	53.16	27.90	29.01	5.08	1.71
Bangalore	4,745	8,057	45.07	38.51	28.80	29.39	4.77	2.12
Kanpur	1,119	1,997	59.72	50.13	27.02	30.01	4.15	1.67
Poona (urban)	2,239	5,240	63.26	57.74	22.57	24.69	4.82	1.64

Source: Census of India, 1971, Part IV-B, *Housing Tables*.

metropolitan cities. It has been reported that in Calcutta, there are about 3000 slums spread over one-twelfth of the city's area and one-fifth of city's population lives in them. If together with these official slums, tenements and houses which are not listed but are in all respects part of the slums are also counted, it will be observed that over one-fourth of Calcutta's population lives in slums.[37] In Bombay, about one-sixth of the population lives in slums. The dwellings are constructed with the help of discarded racks, flattened sheets of metal cans, and with almost any material that comes to hand. The Economic Survey of Bombay City conducted more than twenty years ago found that out of 13,369 families for which data were obtained, as many as 10,504 (i.e., 78.6%) lived in chawls and another 5.5% in hutments.[38] In their revealing study on the housing problem in Ahmedabad, Mahesh Bhatt and V.K. Chawda have noted that the total number of slum dwellers in Ahmedabad is 7,89,004 which is 49.6% of that city's total population.[39] This means that 'out of every ten citizens, five live in slums'. The eastern side of the city inhabited by the working class is full of such slums and 5 lakh people are cramped in an area of 2 sq. miles 'side by side with shopping centres and many public buildings'. On the other hand, the western side of the city is inhabited by employers. Here only 2.5 lakh people live in an area of 11 to 13 sq. miles. In the words of Bhatt and Chawda, "the western side looks like a garden suburb, the eastern side a terribly overcrowded, structurally decayed ghetto".[40]

Bhatt and Chawda have divided the slum dwellers into two categories—those living in hutments and those living in chawls. Altogether there are 80,000 hutments housing 28.65% of the population (i.e., more than one-fourth of the total population of the city). These hutments are the worst type of slums and are "*kacha* mud and bamboo structures using scrap tin sheets and old gunny bags". There are 59,456 chawls housing one-fifth of the city's population. The floor space available to an individual in these chawls is a mere 22 sq. feet which "is much less than what a convict in a jail should have, namely 40 sq. feet, according to jail manual".[41]

To provide financial support to State governments, housing boards and other local bodies for implementing housing and other urban development projects, the Housing and Urban Development Corporation (HUDCO) was established in the Fourth Plan. This Corporation started functioning in 1970 with an authorised capital of Rs.10 crores against which it received Rs.6 crores from the Central government. It raised resources through other means as well. HUDCO has provided loans for the construction of tenements at very low rates of interest. The prospective buyers are required to make a first down payment equal to 20% of the cost of the tenement. The balance is to be paid in instalments. People belonging to low-income group (i.e., those drawing between Rs.350 and Rs.600 per month) are required to repay the loan in 15 years at 7½% rate of interest. Persons belonging to the economically weaker sections (i.e., those earning less than Rs.350 per month) are required to repay the loan in 20 years at 6½% rate of interest. Bhattacharya[42] has estimated that an economically weak household which might occupy 20 sq. metres of built-up accommodation) will have to pay Rs.3600 as initial payment and Rs.133.00 as monthly instalment under this scheme. If we assume that the rent paying capacity is 10% of income, then a person earning Rs.350 per month can, at the most, pay Rs.35 per month as rent. Obviously it is not possible for him to pay Rs.133 per month as instalment which would constitute 38% of income. In circumstances where expenditure on food alone of this group of people lies between 70% and 75% of total income, it is not possible to pay 38% of income as instalment. The point to be remembered is that we are considering only the people at the top level of the bracket earning less then Rs.350 per month. The position of others can be well imagined. Obviously under the circumstances that exist, the poor continue to dwell in slums where rents are Rs.30 to Rs.35 per month (in those cases where slum dwellers live in rented accommodation) and the 'cheap houses' constructed for them go to the lower middle classes.

There seem to be only two alternatives—first, the low income group can be heavily subsidized and the cost obtained from the upper strata of the society; second admitting the fact that decent houses cannot be provided to the poor we must plan for colonies similar to shanty towns where the settlers will be given small plots of land on which they construct houses suiting their pockets or they can be given 'rudimentary skeletal houses' which they can complete themselves. The difference between such settlements and the unplanned slums which are mushrooming all over the large urban areas is that they shall be planned in such a way that minimum civic amenities can be provided. More specifically, it is the environment which shall be improved by providing sewerage, surface drainage, public latrines, garbage clearance arrangements, pathways, etc. Proper provision of water will also be made. Though the first alternative seems to be more attractive, it is full of difficulties. It is only a small proportion of the upper starta of society that is in a real position to provide resources whereas the majority of other people are already facing acute financial problems. But this does not mean that this alternative should not be adopted at all. In fact, where a number of people are condemned to living in inhuman and unhygienic conditions, a small number of people have no right to a luxurious living. The argument here is the same as is given by the underdeveloped countries in international forums when they demand more aid from the developed countries. If the poor do not live or continue to live in appalling conditions, the volcano of unrest will erupt and then neither the rich nor their riches will survive.

However, coming to more sober economic arguments, it must be pointed out that whatever resources can be squeezed from the rich will always be entirely inadequate to solve the problems of millions of slum and shanty town dwellers. Thus, though the first alternative should also be explored, it is the second alternative alone that can solve the problem. Adopting this alternative thousands of houses can be provided by the government in urban areas at a very low cost. This is perhaps the only solution to the housing problem in large urban centres in India and other developing countries. Slums will, no doubt, remain but they will be 'controlled' or 'planned' slums as against the unplanned slums that exist at present.

URBANIZATION AND ECONOMIC DEVELOPMENT

The origin of city goes back to ancient times. In old civilizations it played an important role as a political and administrative centre.[43] In the medieval period also there were a number of cities performing predominantly political, economic, and social functions. Then, why is it that there is a tendency to link up urbanization with the advent of industrial revolution? Why do we regard industrial revolution as the initiator of the process of urbanization? Answers to these questions are to be found in the new sense of dynamism imparted by the industrial revolution in the European society and the change it introduced in the traditional and orthodox ways of life. The industrial centres became vibrant centres for almost all the manufacturing, servicing, and other activities. They became focal points for economic development and attracted large-scale migration. A large stream of people flowed into these areas in search of employment and better opportunities. Improved transport and communication facilities encouraged such widespread and substantial migration. The industrial centres soon emerged as large urban centres and the population of many of them swelled rapidly and touched the million mark. Between 1800 and 1850 the large city population of Europe and America increased by 184% and in the next fifty years by 220%. Against this, the large city population in agriculture-oriented Asia could increase by only 25% between 1800 and 1850, and by 60% between 1850 and 1900. Thus, the processes of industrialization, economic development, and urbanization moved together in cohesion and were closely related to each other.

Lampard[44] distinguishes three phases of city development—(i) the pre-industrial phase, (ii) industrial phase, and (iii) the metropolitan phase. The pre-industrial phase was present in Europe roughly up to the nineteenth century and was a "loose-knit system of food economies with some inter-regional commerce but no marked territorial division of labour". The industrial city was a product of the industrial revolution in the nineteenth century and was characterized by "marked territorial division of labour, and centripetal development generated by steam power and belt and pulley technology". The key motive force behind industrial activities in this period was specialization among men and machines "which gradually transformed the techno-organization base of society and with it, the spatial order of economic activities". Thus, urbanization minimized a great obstacle to human production—the phenomenon known as 'the friction of space'. The gradual concentration of numerous other activities such as banking, insurance, brokerage, fire services, police protection, etc., in urban areas further accelerated the pace of economic development in these areas. The workers in different industries got acquainted with different types of technical and mechanical jobs and slowly transformed themselves into a skilled working force. Because of better educational facilities available in urban areas and because of the general atmosphere around, the children of the working class got trained in carrying out various industrial activities and this process continued, feeding on itself. Thus, a constant stream of the required type of industrial workers emerged in such centres. The inhabitants of such centres inculcated new outlook on life, experienced a new variety of complex human relations, received better educational facilities, and developed into a progressive force seeking economic and social progress. This became an asset for future economic development. Because of the generally high level of per capita income in them, the urban centres also provided a strong and ready-made market for a number of industrial products and thus provided the necessary impetus to industrial growth. Since industry is inevitably attracted by market, it tended to concentrate in the urban areas. Population of such areas grew further on account of natural growth and more migration, the latter growing because of the progress registered by urban centres. Supply of labour in these centres increased, markets expanded and as a consequence there was a further expansion of industries. Cities helped in removing excess manpower from rural areas and in providing it with better jobs and opportunities; they helped in stimulating the demand for agricultural products; and through the provision of capital and new organizational techniques to rural enterprise, they also contributed to the modernisation of agriculture.[45]

After the industrial phase in European countries, the metropolitan phase arrived. This is essentially the creation of the twentieth-century technology. The development of new modes of transport and communications (e.g., the automobile and the telephone) no longer required the concentration of people in small congested areas. People started 'spreading out'. They could stay in the periphery of the large urban centres while continuing to work in the centre itself. As population pressures in the centre grew and housing conditions started deteriorating fast, the great sprawl of urban centres into the surrounding areas was encouraged. Gradually economic activities expanded in the suburbs and adjoining areas of the old urban centre and a closely linked-up metropolitan areas developed around the old urban centre. Such a metropolitan community represents at once "a gigantic population agglomeration which combines centralization with decentralization, and specialization and differentiation of functions with integration and interdependence relationships . . . (and) may be thought of as both an effect and a cause of rapid and great economic development".[46] Interactions and inter-connections between different nearby towns and cities grew as the borders of the metropolitan sprawl spread and thus complex 'systems' of cities and settlements were produced. Such systems of cities and urban areas are sought to be explained by scholars with the help of rank-size rule and some complex geometrical constructs as hexagonal arrangements, etc. We have already examined some of these techniques in Chapter 4.

THE INDIAN CONTEXT

Hauser notes that during the first half of this century the increase in the large-city population was more rapid in Asia compared with Europe or North America. In fact, it was mainly the increase in the urban population of the Asian countries that has kept the rate of urban growth high during the twentieth century. We have already shown how, in our own case, the urban population has continued to increase rapidly ever since the turn of this century and how population has continued to concentrate in large urban centres. Is it because of the process of economic development that such concentration of population in urban areas is taking place? As discussed earlier, it is very difficult to give any conclusive answer. We are not sure whether it was the 'urban pull' or the 'rural push' that led to this process. However, our study on trends of urbanization and patterns of migration in India gives an indication that probably rural push has been more important than urban pull in pushing up the rate of urban growth. It is alleged by many observers that in such a case it is not economic development that fosters urban growth but the very opposite, i.e., it is because of underdevelopment of these economies that rural poor are pushed to swell the population of urban areas. So, it is maintained, as far as the Asian countries are concerned that there is a positive relation between economic backwardness and urbanization rather than between economic development and urbanization.

Such a criticism misses the basic point. Though none can deny that the processes of urbanization in Asia are essentially different from that obtained in the nineteenth-century Europe since the dominant role of the push factor is very important, yet the economic difference in the levels of development of urban and rural areas do play an important role. Since urban areas have more industries and since they are, on the whole, much more developed economically compared with the rural areas, the rural poor are tempted to come to such areas. Thus, it is not a question of developed and underdeveloped countries, it is a question of difference in the levels of development of different regions (or areas) in a country. A relatively more developed area attracts people from other parts of the country. The population of the developed area increases as more and more people come from near and far places and the process of urbanization gathers momentum. This is what is happening in India and most other Asian countries. Economic development of some areas is leading to the process of urbanization.

However, the reverse does not seem to be true. As noted above, in the European countries of the nineteenth century, the processes of urbanization and economic development supported each other. Economic development initiated the process of urbanization which, in turn, created many external economies to aid economic growth. These external economies were in the nature of skilled labour, availability of market, scientific and technological advances, and the economies of 'urban atmosphere' (e.g., availability of complementary commercial and industrial activities, socially conducive atmosphere for development, etc.). However, in the case of India and many other developing economies of Asia, it does not appear that urbanization is helping economic development. A litte development in urban areas attracts a large number of migrants from rural areas and the population of urban areas increases in a greater proportion to the level of economic development. Slums swell, pressure on urban infrastructure intensifies, and misery increases. This is the form of over-urbanization prevalent in India. The urban infrastructure which is already very weak tatters and crumbles under the pressure of increasing population and the state of urban services (which includes provision of basic amenities, public utilities, transport and communication, etc.) further deteriorates. It becomes necessary to choose between investment on urban amenities to provide tolerable living conditions for a great mass of population, on the one hand, and a faster economic growth on the other, by channelling resources towards capital formation.[47] Urbanization, instead of acting like a 'catalyst' is actually acting like a 'retarder' in the process of economic development. It is forcing the diversion of many valuable resources that can be utilized for economic progress into creation of urban services and amenities, investments which are not productive in the short run. As already noted above, urbanization helped the process of economic development in the nineteenth-century Europe by providing external economies and the necessary infrastructure for development. As emphasized by Sachin Chaudhuri, "It is industry-based urban development that exhibits these features, not urbanization of whatever sort. Where urban growth is a direct adjunct of industrial development, as in the case of new steel towns, the question of choice does not arise. In other cases, it does ".[48]

Though strong and passionate claims are made to the contrary, it is in villages and small towns that solutions will have to be found. It is only by investing more in agriculture and rural industry and by developing a number of small towns that the problems can be solved. All indicators suggest that as Indian economy develops, disparities between rural and urban areas will grow. This will promote and increase the exodus of rural people from their native places in the direction of urban areas. Many demographers note this 'dislocation' with a certain amount of admiration for it helps the process of urbanization and, as a consequence, modernization. But the thinking that such 'dislocation' will be able to solve the problem of poverty in a country where 70% of the population lives in villages and where urban areas are already hard pressed with acute problems is, to say the least, totally misconceived and basically wrong. The western models do not fit the Indian situation and it is not necessary for us to follow the western path. The thinking prevalent in this country that whatever the West did was right and we should also pass through the same path that West followed (as if it is a ritual that must be performed) to achieve the goal of economic development has already done ample harm to the country.[49]

NEED FOR URBAN PLANNING IN A FRAMEWORK OF COMPREHENSIVE REGIONAL PLANNING

We have already noted the declining importance of small towns as far as urban growth is concerned and the tendency of the population to concentrate in Class I cities and especially in great million plus cities. We have also noted that mainly as a consequence of this rapid population growth in them, the large cities are confronted with a number of problems as that of housing and slums, traffic congestion, water supply shortage, sewage, sanitation, personal and social disorganization, etc. To view this process as essential on the basis of the historical experience of western countries and adopt an attitude of complacency will inflict irreparable damage to the whole national fibre. As noted by a UNESCO report, there are at least two new factors which make it unnecessary for the countries of Asia to repeat the mistakes of the nineteenth-century West: "One is the fact that present technology offers a wider range of possibilities for the region wide distribution of population and for community structure than was possible in the nineteenth century. The other is the increasing role of government and public responsibility in the planning and development process".[50]

There is no unanimity of opinion regarding the type of urbanization policy that should be followed in India. Persons who believe that urbanization acts as a catalyst for economic development and large urban centres are the 'carriers' of economic growth, favour uninhibited growth of such centres. Their major concern is with improving the conditions of living in such cities through a better provision of basic urban amenities and ample housing facilities so that the problems of slum dwellers can be tackled satisfactorily. Against this, the protagonists of rural-oriented approach point to the cancerous growth of large urban areas and the dwarfing of individual personality in urban areas. On the economic front, they feel that an underdeveloped country can ill-afford the costs necessary to maintain and continuously expand urban infrastructure and basic amenities in large cities. According to them, it would be much better to provide jobs and amenities in rural areas so that migration is reduced and the progress of increasing income disparities between town and country halted and, if possible, reversed.

Both these approaches have an element of truth in them and it is necessary to strike a compromise. Such a compromise has been found by urban planners in the plea for accelerating the development of small and medium sized towns. Development of such towns offers the possibility of reducing the urban pressure on large urban centres on the one hand, and relieving surplus labour from agriculture and providing it with gainful employment on the other. It is maintained that the infrastructure cost in small and medium towns will be substantially less than in large cities, therefore an economy in the use of scarce resources of the country can be effected. Also, the possibility of spreading modernization and a progressive attitude to life will increase because the small towns will be larger in number and will be located in close proximity to villages, possibly one such town catering to the needs of 40 to 50 villages. Perhaps the greatest advantage of such a strategy of urbanization will be that regional disparities and regional imbalances will be reduced over time.

At the instance of the Department of Works, Housing and Urban Development of the Government of India, NCAER organized a seminar on "Market Towns and Spatial Development" in mid-April 1971. In the Background Paper prepared by the NCAER it was pointed out that even after taking an optimistic view of family planning measures, the urban population would exceed 300 million by the end of this century which would be approximately three times the level of urban population according to the 1971 census (assuming 2.5% rate of growth of population and urban population as 30-40% of total population). In the 1961 census there were 567,338 villages in India against 2699 cities and towns. In the 1971 census there were 575,936 inhabited villages against 3119 towns. The total number of towns having population less than 20,000 was 1935 in 1961 and 2097 in 1971. Designating all such towns as small towns or market towns, we find that in 1961, on average, there was only one market town for 293 villages and in 1971 there was one such town for 275 villages. Taking the Background Paper's estimate of the need of one market town for 40-45 villages, it would be evident that the present number of towns is entirely inadequate.[51]

An intense debate has been carried out since long on the comparative virtues of large and small towns. Supporters of the large-town strategy emphasize that since the underdeveloped countries have a scarcity of entrepreneurial and other resources, their concentration in one, or at most two or three large cities has considerable advantages in the initial stages of development. Moreover, development of new towns is an expensive affair in terms of both financial and administrative resources. "A fairly large 'minimum mass' is needed for the town to operate as an efficient largely self-contained unit. In the process, considerable underutilized capacity has to be created".[52] It is also pointed out that managerial and professional staff are generally unwilling to move from major cities to such small towns and considerable incentives in the form of higher wages and/or perks have to be offered to induce them to work in small towns.

These considerations are no doubt important but they do not distract from the importance of small and medium sized towns. In a country of India's size providing a fairly large 'minimum mass' should not pose any problem. The only relevant point in the above observations relates to the problem of providing resources for the development of small towns. However, keeping in view the fact that maintenance and expansion of urban amenities in large towns is becoming more and more unmanageable and expensive with the passage of time, perhaps the time has arrived when the strategy of small and medium towns has to be effectively included in the urbanization policy. We have reached a stage in our development process where it is imperative to spread out industrial growth to the countryside and ensure a proper integration of the major industrial centres with the neighbouring industrial zones and rural industries. A network of small and medium towns can accomplish this task reasonably well. Such towns can function as processing and marketing centres for neighbouring villages, and can also work as markets for the products of rural industries.[53] A small town working as a central place for 40 to 50 villages can serve to convert them 'into a spatially-integrated social and economic organization'. It can serve as a place where agricultural processing can be conducted, social and health services which villages cannot afford can be provided, younger generation trained in the art of handling various machines and more educational, cultural, and employment opportunities for the villagers can be made available. These towns can also provide many other services such as repair facilities for agricultural machinery, veterinary services, supply of farm inputs and farm credit, etc. The most significant advantage is that such towns serve in broadening the outlook of villagers, bring them into close contact, make them politically more conscious, and economically and socially more active. They help, so to say, the task of 'transformation of underdeveloped countries' without which economic development is either not achieved at all or even if achieved, is distributed inequitably and injudiciously. An ardent advocate of the policy of establishing small towns, E.A.J. Johnson (in a paper presented to the NCAER seminar) argues that "by a gradual transfer of young workers to new occupations, a steady improvement in the average capital equipment of workers in both agriculture and industry, and a progressive improvement in the bundle of goods and services that consumers can afford as their family incomes rise", the small towns can prove to be 'germinating places for genuine economic progress'.[51]

Along with the task of developing small and medium towns, it will be necessary to tackle the problems faced by large urban centres (especially metropolitan centres). The policy to be adopted for this purpose will have to take into consideration both the present requirements of urban areas and the long-term needs. It is necessary to have a long-term perspective in view constantly because it is estimated that in about 25 years, the urban population will be about 30-40% of the total population against 20% now. The National Committee on Environment Planning and Coordination (NCEPC) has estimated that increase in urban population would be between 175 and 270 million (even the lower limit is greater than the Census Commissioner's estimate of additional 169 million) by 2001.[56] If the present trends continue, approximately half of this increase will take place in metropolitan cities. These considerations call for phased research on transport problems, housing materials and designs, problems of civic amenities and pollution, sewage, sanitation, water shortage, etc., at a national level.

Thus, we have emphasized the need for adopting an urbanization policy at two different levels: (i) at the city level, and (ii) at the regional and national level. At the city level, we have advocated the adpotion of a policy that can mitigate the misery of the urban poor (especially slum dwellers) as early as possible and can also ensure that problems of urban amenities and the like do not arise in the future. At the regional and national level, we have advocated the adoption of a policy aimed at developing a sufficiently large number of small and medium towns so that the flow of migrants can be diverted to these smaller urban centres. Morever, since we are advocating the development of a large number of such towns in close proximity of villages, not much incentive will be left to the villagers to migrate at all. What we are suggesting here is the bringing of urbanization itself to the villages. The best strategy is to conceive the development of small towns in the overall framework of an urban hierarchy with village at the first level, central village at the second level, market towns at the third level, and the establishment of various growth foci exactly in a manner already described in Chapter 4. It is only through such planning of human settlements that a judicious distribution of population, resources and development all over the country can be accomplished. It is a gigantic task but a task that is worth undertaking and perhaps even essential. However, the adoption of such an urbanization policy will require a basic change in the thinking, attitudes and motivations of planners and the government. It will become necessary to give greater weight to this policy in development plans and strategies than economic considerations which, by adopting a short-run microscopic view, often approve a locational strategy recommending concentration in a few large urban centres.[56]

NOTES

1. Philip M. Hauser and Judah Matras, "Areal units for urban analysis", in Philip M. Hauser (ed.), *Handbook for Social Research in Urban Areas* (Belgium, UNESCO, 1965), p. 26.
2. United Nations, *Urbanisation : development policies and planning* (UNO: New York, 1968), p. 9.
3. C. Chandrasekaran and K.C. Zachariah, "Concepts used in defining Urban Population and data available on its Characteristics in Countries of Southern Asia", in UNESCO, *Urban Rural Differences in Southern Asia* (Delhi 1964), pp. 52-53.
4. It may be noted that the minimum population sizes prescribed in different countries differ significantly from one another. In Denmark, places with 250 or more people are classified as urban and in Greenland urban status is granted to places with 300 or more people. Against this, in the USA a settlement must have at least 2500 inhabitants, in India 5000 inhabitants and in Korea 40,000 to be classified as urban. It would thus be clear that making international comparisons is a very risky affair unless proper adjustments are made.
5. Ashish Bose, *Studies in India's Urbanisation 1901-71* (New Delhi: Tata-McGraw Hill Publishing Co. Ltd., 1973).
6. Census of India, 1971 *General Population Tables* Series I, Part II-A (i), p. 3.
7. Ibid., p. 3.
8. For a critical evaluation of the town group concept and application of the SUA concept to the 1971 census (including methodology) the reader is referred to K.V. Sundaram, *Urban and Regional Planning in India* (New Delhi: Vikas Publishing House Pvt. Ltd., 1977), Chapter II, especially pp. 52-67. Sundaram was one of the chief architects in evolving the concept of SUA and in specifying the methodology to be adopted in the actual delimitation of such areas.

9. In fact, things are not as simple as that. Urbanization has been defined differently by different scholars and definitions of urbanization range from "terse definition determining urbanization as a mere growth of the share of urban population in the world, or in a particular country or region, to an overall definition according to which urbanization is a world-historic process involving increasing concentration and intensification of human interaction and the integration of the forms of Man's activity which are becoming evermore varied". Thus, urbanization is understood as (i) growth of towns and an increase in the proportion of the urban population, (ii) growth of importance of towns and cities in the life of a country or a region conditioned by social and economic progress, (iii) a complex social process accompanied by the emergence of a specific way of life, which turns the cities into the prevalent form of organization of social activity in our century and the centuries to come, and (iv) a process leading to a spatial concentration of activity in relatively few areas and centres where labour efficiency is the highest. In this context, see I.V. Kantsebovskaya's article on "Some Definitions of Urbanization in Geographic literature and the Relevant Ideas", in S. Manzoor Alam and V.V. Pokshishevsky (eds.), *Urbanisation in Developing Countries* (Hyderabad: Osmania University, 1976).

   Commenting on the definition of urbanization as the *increase* in the proportion of the urban population, Kantsebovskaya notes that this definition is inadequate because (i) it cannot distinguish between areas that have 'fundamentally different levels of economic development and population concentrations' but practically the same proportion of urban population, (ii) it can lead to false notions of the real state of affairs. Thus, accepting this indicator we might perhaps say that Hawaii might be as urban as England or Wales, or that Kuwait could be as urban as Scotland, Australia and the United States, 'which evidently contradicts the generally accepted idea of the urbanisation levels of these countries and regions', and (iii) since it does not include the distribution of towns by size, countries 'with a large number of small urban settlements can fall into the category of highly urbanized countries, and countries with an intensive growth of metropolitan cities and a simultaneous increase in rural population can be ranked among countries with a low urbanisation level'. On account of reasons such as these, Kantsebovskaya suggests that the proportion of urban *dwellers does not reveal such an important aspect of urbanization as the growing role of large cities in the life of society.* To highlight the role of large cities, Kantsebovskaya proposes a set of indices.

   In the discussion on urbanization in the present chapter, we have adopted the traditional definition of urbanization as increase in the proportion of urban population since this definition gives a fairly good account of urbanization trends in India. However, keeping Kantsebovskaya's arguments in view, we have discussed in detail the role of large cities in the urbanization process in India with particular emphasis on the growth of the metropolitan centres of Calcutta, Bombay, Delhi, and Madras.

10. Ashish Bose, op. cit., pp. 37-38.
11. Approximately 35% according to Pethe. See Vasant P. Pethe, "On Assessing trends in Urbanization between 1961 and 1971", *Artha Vijnana*, March 1977, Vol. XIX, No. 1, p. 36.
12. Ibid.
13. Galina V. Sdasyuk, "Urbanization and the Spatial Structure of Indian Economy" in *Economic and Socio-Cultural demensions of Regionalization* (Census of India 1971: Census Centenary Monograph No. 7), p. 298.
14. According to Indian census convention, all such towns (having more than 100,000 inhabitants each) are known as cities.

15. So far only one report of the 1981 census entitled 'Census of India, 1981 Series I, India, Paper No. 1 of 1981—Provisional Population Tables' is available. It does not present statistics on urban growth or rural-urban distribution of population. The only relevant information from our point of view relates to the population of million plus urban agglomerations. According to the report, the number of such UAs has risen from 9 in 1971 to 12 in 1981. The new entrants are Nagpur, Lucknow, and Jaipur. The growth of population in the decade 1971-81 in million plus urban agglomerations is given below:

UA	Population (in lakhs) 1971	Population (in lakhs) 1981	Percentage variation in the population of the UA in 1971-81
1. Calcutta	70.31	91.66	30.4
2. Greater Bombay	59.71	82.03	37.4
3. Delhi	36.47	52.28	43.3
4. Madras	31.70	42.77	35.0
5. Bangalore	16.54	29.14	76.2
6. Hyderabad	17.96	25.66	42.9
7. Ahmedabad	17.42	25.15	44.4
8. Kanpur	12.75	16.85	32.2
9. Poona	11.35	16.85	48.5
10. Nagpur	9.30	12.98	39.6
11. Lucknow	8.14	10.07	23.7
12. Jaipur	6.37	10.05	57.8

This table shows that the most spectacular rise has been in the population of Bangalore UA which registered an increase of 76.2% in the decade 1971-81 and thus rose to the fifth position pushing down Hyderabad and Ahmedabad. The population of the four largest urban agglomerations—Calcutta, Bombay, Delhi, and Madras—registered an increase of 30.4%, 37.4%, 43.3%, and 35% respectively in the decade 1971-81. Taken together, their population rose from 198.19 lakhs in 1971 to 268.74 lakhs in 1981 registering an increase of 36%. If we consider this table along with Table 6 we find that over two decades 1961 to 1981, the population of most of the million plus urban agglomerations has doubled (in the case of Delhi and Bangalore it increased by two and a half times). This staggering increase in the population of million plus UAs has brought with it numerous problems as we shall see later on in this chapter.

16. Census of India 1971, Series 22 (on West Bengal), Part II-B(i), Table B-I Part A and B-II, pp. 44-45 and pp. 164-165.
17. Census of India 1971, Series 11, Maharashtra, Part II-B(i) *General Economic Tables*, Table B-II; and Census of India 1971, Series II, Maharashtra, Part III-B *Establishment Tables*, Table E-I.
18. Census of India 1971, Series 19 (on Tamil Nadu), Part II-B (i), *General Economic Tables* Table B-I, Part A, pp. 552-555.
19. Galina V. Sdasyuk, "India's Urban Growth and Problems of Regional Planning",

in Manzoor Alam and V.V. Pokshishevsky (ed.), *Urbanization in Developing Countries*, op. cit., pp. 245-246.
20. Ibid., pp. 248-249.
21. In this context, the reader is referred to Eric E. Lampard, "The History of Cities in the Economically Advanced Areas", *Economic Development and Cultural Change*, Vol. III, No. 2, January 1955. For instance, see the statement, "*Specialization of functions makes inevitably for specialization of areas: it promotes a territorial division of labour between town and country and differentiates town from town.* . . . From a socio-ecological standpoint *city growth is simply the concentration of differentiated but functionally integrated specialisms in rational locales.*" (italics in original), p. 92.
22. "The individual in question may migrate because of an existing need, or a hope to improve possibilities of meeting the future needs (in education and health, for example) of himself or his family. . . . The need can be temporary but result in permanent migration. Thus, villagers who do not have the means to travel to and from urban hospitals or clinics go and camp outside, and their stay in the city often becomes a permanent one." United Nations, *Urbanization : development policies and planning*, op. cit., p. 92.
23. N.V. Sovani, *Urbanization and Urban India* (Bombay : Asia Publishing House, 1966), pp. 69-70.
24. ILO Report, *Why Labour Leaves the Land? A Comparative Study of the Movement of Labour out of Agriculture*, quoted by Sovani, ibid., p. 9.
25. G.K. Mehrotra, *Birth Place Migration in India*, Census of India 1971, Series-I India, Special Monograph No. 1, p. 35, (Statement 3.0).
26. Ibid., pp. 20-23.
27. Philip M. Hauser, "Comprehensive Urban Studies", in Philip M. Hauser (ed.), *Handbook for Social Research in Urban Areas*, op. cit., p. 99.
28. "The individual who cannot accept the values or does not follow the behaviour norms of the social group of which he is a member is said to be characterized by personal disorganization. The unemployed individual, the delinquent, the homeless man, the prostitute are examples of individuals characterized by personal disorganization." Judah Matras, "Social and Personal Disorganization", in Philip M. Hauser (ed.), ibid., p. 180.
29. P.N. Prabhu, "A Study on the Social Effects of Urbanization", in *The Social Implications of Industrialization and Urbanization* (UNESCO, Research Centre on the Social Implications of Industrialization in Southern Asia, Calcutta, 1956), p. 102.
30. D.S. Chauhan, *Trends of Urbanization in Agra* (Delhi: Allied Publishers Pvt. Ltd., 1966); Chapter 7.
31. Quoted by Lidia I. Bonifatieva in "Problems of Urban Planning in India", *Economic and Socio-Cultural Dimensions of Regionalization*, Census of India 1971, Census Centenary Monograph No. 7, p. 344.
32. M.S. Gore, "Social Development and a Strategy for Urbanization", *Economic and Political Weekly*, 25 January 1975, p. 113.
33. A Draft Paper of TCPO (January 1975) quoted by K.C. Sivaramakrishnan, *Indian Urban Scene* (Indian Institute of Advanced Study, Simla, 1978), p. 6.
34. As given in Ghanshyam Shah, "Anatomy of a Slum", *The Economic Times*, 16 February 1975.
35. According to the definition adopted in the 1971 census, houseless persons are those who have no fixed place of residence and no regular house to live in. A house is defined as a building or part of a building having a separate main entrance from the road, common courtyard, staircase, etc., used or recognized as a separate unit. The

test of a 'room' was that it should have four walls with a door-way and a roof overhead. It should be wide and long enough for a person to sleep in, i.e. it should have a length of not less than 2 metres and a breadth of at least 1½ metres and be 2 metres in height. It would interest the reader to note that people living in *jhuggi-jhonpari* were not treated as 'houseless' since their *jhuggi-jhonpari* generally satisfied the definition of a house specified above.

36. Quoted in Mahest Bhatt and V.K. Chawda, "Housing the Poor in Ahmedabad", *Economic and Political Weekly*, 8 May 1976, p. 736.
37. Sunil K. Munsi, *Calcutta Metropolitan Explosion* (New Delhi: People's Publishing House, 1975), p. 114.
38. D.T. Lakdawala et al., *Work, Wages and Well-Being in an Indian Metropolis—Economic Survey of Bombay City* (Bombay: Bombay University Press, 1963), p. 715.
39. Mahest Bhatt and V.K. Chawda, op. cit., Table A, p. 707.
40. Ibid., p. 706.
41. Ibid., p. 710.
42. Arabendu Bhattacharya, "Housing Urban Poor". *The Economic Times*, 29 November 1974, p. 5.
43. At the time of the Buddha, there were at least six important cities in north India—Sraavasti, Campaa, Raaj agrha, Saaketa (later known as Ayodhya), Kausambi, and Kaasi. In the time of Mauryas, Patliputra developed into an important political centre. In the south, Vijayanagara was larger and more populous than Rome and contained 100,000 houses "from which we may infer that its population was at least half a million, and probably more". A.L. Basham, *The Wonder That was India* (London: Sidywick & Jackson, 1967), pp. 200-201.
44. Eric E. Lampard, "The History of Cities in the Economically Advanced Areas", in *Economic Development and Cultural Change*, Vol. III, No. 2, January 1955.
45. Kingsley Davis and Hilda Hertz Golden, "Urbanization and the Development of Pre-industrial Areas", *Economic Development and Cultural Change*, Vol. III, No. 1, October 1954, pp. 23-24.
46. Philip M. Hauser, "World and Asian Urbanization in Relation to Economic Development and Social Change", in Philip M. Hauser (ed.), *Urbanization in Asia and the Far East* (Calcutta: UNESCO Research Centre on the Social Implications of Indusrialization in Southern Asia, 1957), p. 71.
47. Sachin Chaudhuri, "Centralization and the Alternative forms of Decentralization: A Key Issue", in Roy Turner (ed.), *India's Urban Future* (Bombay Oxford University Press, 1962), p. 219.
48. Ibid., pp. 219-220.
49. "Despite an enormous turnover of research in urban geography, we have failed to evolve a theory of urban growth or even test the validity of the western theories of urban growth. Most of the researches in urban geography make us feel that the Indian cities are carbon copies of the western cities and, therefore, the theories of growth for the latter are applicable to our cities as well.... This intellectual following of the western scholars has prevented the development of our own theoretical formulation of the processes of growth of Indian cities." A. Manzoor Alam, "Metropolitan Planning—A Trend Report", in *A Survey of Research in Geography* (A project sponsored by the Indian Council of Social Science Research) (Bombay: Popular Prakashan, 1972), pp. 104-105.
50. Chapter XI, "Urbanization and Policies for Town and Country Planning" prepared by the Bureau of Social Affairs of the United Nations in Philip M. Hauser (ed.), *Urbanization in Asia and the Far East*, op. cit., p. 265.

51. "Considering villages located at 3-mile intervals, and taking a 12-mile radius as the maximum area that can be effectively transport-linked to one town, in the sense of being accessible to a villager within a day's to and from travel with such transport facilities as would normally be available to him, a market town would seem to be necessary for each group of 40-45 villages. On this basis some 12,500 to 14,000 market towns would be needed for the country." National Council of Applied Economic Research, *Market Towns and Spatial Development*, (New Delhi, 1972), p. 37. The paper admits that this is a very rough and crude estimate. But even if we regard half the number indicated here as the required number of market towns (i.e., 6000 to 7000 towns), the present number of 2097 is very inadequate.
52. World Bank, Sector Working Paper on *Urbanization*, June 1972.
53. NCAER, op. cit., pp. 36-37.
54. Ibid., pp. 73-74.
55. Quoted in *The Economic Times* editorial "Urban Growth and Slums", 6 August 1976.
56. See, e.g., Gerald M. Desmond, "The Impact of National and Regional Development Policies on Urbanization", in Leo Jakobson and Ved Prakash (eds.), *Urbanization and National Development* (California: Sage Publications, 1971), esp. pp. 75-78.

Chapter 7

Regional Planning in Agriculture: The Task of Rural Development

Agriculture forms the backbone of Indian economy and more than 70% of the population of the country depends on this sector for its livelihood. Even after 20 years of planning and giving utmost importance to programmes of industrialization (especially in the Second Five Year Plan based on Mahalanobis model), approximately 69% of the working population was engaged in agriculture in 1971 and this sector contributed more than 40% of the national income. Thus, we can say that agricultural development is the sine qua non of economic development and without it all talk of economic progress is meaningless and futile. And when we talk of agricultural development we imply the development of the whole rural sector in an integrated way and not merely increases in agricultural production and productivity. Programmes in this direction were initiated in some places of the country in the pre-independence period though planning on a national scale was initiated in the post-independence period—and more specifically in April 1951 when the First Five Year Plan was launched.

Notable experiments in the pre-independence period included the Martaindem Project initiated in 1921, the Rural Development Scheme initiated in 1932 in Baroda State, the experiments conducted by F.L. Brayne in Gurgaon during 1920-28, by R.N. Tagore in Sriniketan, and by Mahātma Gandhi in 1920 at Sevagram and then in 1938 at Wardha. In 1935-36, the Government of India initiated a rural development programme with a grant of Rs.1 crore for rural reconstruction through an integrated development of village industries, agricultural improvement, village communications, rural sanitation, etc. An attempt on these lines was made by the U.P. government as well when in 1937 it created a separate rural development department to carry out the programmes of rural reconstruction throughout the State

Most of the above-mentioned projects were comprehensive in nature and had the aim of developing agriculture, industries, credit facilities, production, marketing and supply, transport and communications, public services, etc. They were action-cum-research projects aimed at evolving (i) suitable programmes and institutional and administrative patterns for a balanced physical, social, and economic development of rural communities, (ii) a spirit of cooperation among the people, the government, and the voluntary agencies (engaged in the task of rural development) in the actual execution of these programmes, and (iii) methods of balancing modern scientific and technological advances and techniques of production with the socio-cultural traditions of the people.

However, all such attempts at comprehensive development initiated in the pre-independence period were restricted in scope because they were the results of the endeavours of some particular individuals, were confined to some specific areas only, and lacked coordination, adequate support, and sufficient financial assistance from a central authority. A real beginning in these directions was made only in the post-independence period when on 2 October 1952 the programme of Community Development was launched. It is to this programme that we now turn our attention.

THE PROGRAMME OF COMMUNITY DEVELOPMENT

According to a UNO report on community development, "the term Community Development has come to cannote . . . the process by which the efforts of the people themselves are united with those of governmental authorities to improve the economic, social and cultural conditions of communities, to integrate these communities into the life of the nation, and to enable them to contribute fully to national progress." Thus, the community development is a comprehensive programme of development of communities wherein the government and people cooperate with each other to improve the general level, condition, and environment of living of the people. The principal responsibility for improving the living conditions rests with the people themselves while the government is assigned the role of guiding and assisting them by supplying technical advice and the wherewithals of development including the supply of seeds, fertilisers, pesticides, insecticides, agricultural machinery, irrigation facilities, etc. In general, a community development programme should include the following measures:

(a) to educate, guide and assist the people for good citizenship by developing, amongst other things, their talent potentialities, encouraging their initiative and civic consciousness, and evoking the desire for self-help and community action;
(b) to secure by total mobilisation of available resources, the participa-

tion on an essentially self-help basis, of the people whom the programme is designed to benefit;

(c) to bring to the people of the community the benefits of modern scientific and technical knowledge in a form they can use to meet their own needs; and

(d) to use democratic methods designed to ensure that progress is directed towards goals valued by the community and is of a character which contributes to the preservation of self-respect and the advancement of human dignity and freedom.[1]

The basic input of all community development programmes is 'Man' and all efforts are geared towards using this input in the best possible way to bring about an integrated development of the community life. It is a project 'of the people, by the people and for the people' wherein the role of the government and administrative authorities is to help the people to help themselves.

Obviously in such a comprehensive programme of rural upliftment which community development was expected to be, the role of education is most important. Following the United States pattern, it is usual to term such adult education as 'extension education' though in an underdeveloped country like India its task is more varied and complex. For, in such countries it is bound to include programmes for learning to read and write and other social welfare training, programmes aimed at motivating the farmers and sharpening their decision-making skills, and programmes for supplying the farmers with necessary information especially regarding changes in attitudinal behaviour of the farmers in other community development projects. The task of extension education is to effect changes in the following four broad areas:

1. *Changes in what people know*—their knowledge of themselves, of their society and of their physical environment.
2. *Changes in what people can do*—their skills, mental and physical.
3. *Changes in what people think and feel*—their attitude toward themselves, toward their society and toward their physical environment.
4. *Changes in what people actually do*—their actions related to factors determining their own welfare.[2]

The community development programme was initiated on a 'pilot project basis in 55 community project areas all over India on 2 October 1952. Initially a community development block covered an area of about 1300 km² with about 300 villages and a population of about 200,000. The budget provision was of Rs.65 lakhs for three years. Later on, the pattern was revised and under the revised scheme a CD block was expected to cover approximately 100 villages. As can be calculated from cols. 6, 7, and 8 of Table 1, a CD block now covers about 110 villages and a population of about 92,000. Keeping the importance of extension education in view, national extension service blocks (NES blocks) were introduced in 1953. All new areas chosen for development were to function as NES blocks for three years with a budget provision of Rs.45 lakhs per block. After this period they were to be converted into blocks of intensive development type for three years. Each such block was to consist of a population of about 66,000 and the budget provision was Rs.15 lakhs for three years. At the end of the intensive development phase, these blocks were to be developed according to the NES pattern and were to be known as post-intensive blocks. The basic desire underlying these organizational patterns was to *transform* the traditional rural life by injecting forces of dynamism in the erstwhile stagnant rural economy. Community development was conceived as the "method" and extension education as the "agency" through which such transformation could be accomplished. The programme, as approved by the Government of India, included the following fields of action:

I. Agriculture and Allied Fields:
(i) reclamation of available virgin and waste land, (ii) provision of (a) irrigation facilities, (b) seeds and manure, (c) improved agricultural implements, (d) new agricultural technology, (e) veterinary aid, (f) credit and marketing facilities, (g) breeding centres for animal husbandry, (h) plantation of forests.

II. Communications:
(i) provision of roads, (ii) encouragement of mechanical and transport services, (iii) development of animal transport.

III. Education:
provision of (a) compulsory and free education at elementary stage, (b) high and middle school, (c) social education and library services.

IV. Health:
provisions of (a) sanitation and public health measures, (b) medical aid, (c) ante-natal care of expectant mothers, (d) midwifery services.

V. Training of agriculturists, artisans, supervisors, managerial personnel, health workers, extension assistants and executive officers for projects.

TABLE 1: State-wise position of CD blocks, village panchayats, panchayat samitis and zila parishads

State/Union territory	Village panchayats as in 1971-72	Panchayat Samitis as in 1971-72	Zila parishads as in 1971-72	Data relating to Community Development blocks			
				No. as on 31 March 1969	No. as on 1 April 1976	Population covered (lakhs) as on 1 April 1976	Villages covered ('00) as on 1 April 1976
	(2)	(3)	(4)	(5)	(6)	(7)	(8)
1. Andhra Pradesh	15906	324	21	445	324	380	296
2. Assam	2602	121	19	160	130	142	234
3. Bihar	10844	209	5	575	587	527	782
4. Gujarat	13067	182	17	224	218	218	189
5. Haryana	4590	82	7	82	87	94	71
6. Himachal Pradesh	1695	29	8	69	69	33	190
7. Jammu & Kashmir	1496	—	—	70	73	38	68
8. Karnataka	8307	175	—	268	175	240	298
9. Kerala	960	—	—	143	144	194	16
10. Madhya Pradesh	12815	390	—	416	457	368	771
11. Maharashtra	22356	296	25	425	343	383	389
12. Manipur	224	—	—	14	14	9.3	20
13. Meghalaya	—	—	—	—	24	9.4	50
14. Nagaland	—	—	—	21	21	4.9	10
15. Orissa	3826	314	—	307	314	208	517
16. Punjab	9645	116	11	116	117	115	130
17. Rajasthan	7351	232	26	232	232	226	359

(Contd.)

TABLE 1 (*Contd.*)

(1)	(2)	(3)	(4)	(5)	(6)	(7)	(8)
18. Tripura	449	—	—	15	17	15	52
19. Uttar Pradesh	72846	657	51	899	875	773	1,249
20. Tamil Nadu	12651	384	23	375	374	330	171
21. West Bengal	19662	325	15	341	335	358	416
22. Sikkim	N.A.	N.A.	N.A.	N.A.	N.A.	N.A.	N.A.
Union Territories:							
23. Andaman & Nicobar Islands	39	—	—	5	5	1.2	22
24. Arunachal Pradesh	623	44	5	41	43	4.5	30
25. Chandigarh	18	1	1	½	1	0.2	0.3
26. Dadra & Nager Haveli	10	—	—	2	2	0.7	1
27. Delhi	195	—	—	5	5	4.2	3
28. Goa, Daman & Diu	173	—	—	11	12	8.0	4
29. Lakshadweep	—	—	—	—	4	0.3	0.2
30. Mizoram	—	—	—	—	20	2.3	—
31. Pondicherry	—	—	—	—	4	4.5	4
Total—All India	221720	3871	233	5265½	5026	4,697	6,325

Sources: (1) Government of India, Planning Commission, *Draft Fifth Five Year Plan*, Vol. 2 (New Delhi, 1974), Annexure X and Annexure XI, pp. 103 & 104.

(2) Govt. of India, *India—A Reference Annual 1977-78* (New Delhi, Ministry of Information and Broadcasting, 1978), Table 15.1, p. 237.

VI. Employment:
encouragement of cottage and small-scale industries, and other services such as trade, auxiliary, and welfare services.

VII. Improving the housing conditions of people covered by the project.

VIII. Social welfare:
(i) provision of (a) community entertainment based on local talent and culture, (b) audio-visual aid for recreation and instruction, (ii) organization of (a) local and other sports activities, (b) melas, and (c) cooperatives.

By the end of the First Plan, community projects and NES programme had been taken up in about 140,000 villages situated in 988 development blocks and was serving a population of 77.5 million persons. The total expenditure on these programmes was Rs.4602 lakhs, of which Rs.3229 lakhs was on community projects/blocks and the remaining Rs.943 lakhs was on NES blocks. At the end of the plan there were 43 extension training centres where approximately 5000 workers were trained annually. It was resolved by the National Development Council in 1955 that during the Second Plan, "the entire country should be served by the NES and that not less than 40% of the National Extension blocks should be converted into Community Development blocks". Target was of covering 3800 additional development blocks under the NES programme and of these, 1200 were to be converted into CD blocks. The plan provided a sum of Rs.200 cores for implementing the programme, of which approximately Rs.12 crores were to be spent on education and Rs.55 crores on agriculture (animal husbandry and agricultural extension, irrigation and reclamation). During this plan it was decided to give foremost attention to programmes of increasing agricultural production and providing employment opportunities especially in the non-agricultural rural sector. At the beginning of the plan, work had been taken up in 950 development blocks of which about 370 were under the community projects scheme and about 580 under NES scheme. By the end of the plan, the community development programme was serving over 3100 development blocks comprising 370,000 villages.

The following three aspects of the programme were emphasized by the plan: "In the first place, national extension and community projects are intended to be areas of intensive effort in which development agencies of the government work together as a team in programmes which are planned and coordinated in advance. . . . In the second place, the essence of the approach is that villagers come together for bringing about social change, are assisted in building up a new life for themselves and participate with increasing awareness and responsibility in the planning and implementation of projects which are material to their well-being. . . . Thirdly, the movement should bring within its scope all rural families, especially those who are 'under-privileged', and enable them to take their place in the cooperative movement and other spheres in their own right."[3]

To undertake a review of the community development programme and to examine questions relating to the execution of the programme (including coordination and people's participation in the programme) a Study Team was appointed under the chairmanship of Balwantrai Mehta in 1957 by the Committee on Plan Projects. The Study Team made some important recommendations that changed the pattern of the CD programme. So far it was divided into three phases—(a) NES stage, (b) Intensive Development stage, and (c) Post-intensive Development stage. The Study Team gave a unified conception to the programme. It advocated a single scheme of community development in each block which was to pass through two stages. Accordingly, in April 1958 it was decided to replace the three phases by two stages of five years each. The budget provision for a block in stage I was Rs.12 lakhs and for a block in stage II was Rs.4 lakhs. In 1959, one pre-extension phase was prescribed for a block before it entered stage I. As far as the implementation/execution part of the programme is concerned each CD block "was to have a minimum administrative set-up consisting of the block development officer, extension officers for agriculture, animal husbandry and cooperation, two social education organisers, an overseer with public health bias, 10 village level workers, each serving a group of about 10 villages, and some ancillary staff". Block was conceived to be a unit of development and the 'Block Plan' was seen to be a vital part of the planning effort. A block plan was intended to include all social and economic activities undertaken within the block which call for (a) planning initiated locally at the block and village levels, and (b) coordination with the plans of various departments which are implemented within the block. At the end of the Third Plan, the number of depelopment blocks included under the programme had risen to 5245, the number of villages brought under the programme to 565,000, and the population covered to 404 millions.

The Study Team also gave a concrete shape to the idea of democratic decentralization to which Nehru gave the name of 'Panchayati Raj'. As already mentioned, the programme of community development depended for its success on the active participation of the people themselves. However, such a participation cannot be expected unless local democratic and representative institutions are evolved. The failure to evolve such institutions was, according to the Study Team, responsible for the poor response and poor participation of the people in the CD programme. According to the Study Team, "So long as we do not discover or create a representative and democratic institution which will supply the local interest, supervision and care necessary to ensure that expenditure of money upon local objects conforms with the needs and wishes of the locality, invest it with adequate power and assign to it appropriate finances, we will never be able to evoke local interest and excite local initiative in the field of development." Accordingly, it proposed the establishment of an elected self-governing institution at the block level. This institution was to be a statutory body called the panchayat samiti. It was to be constituted by indirect elections from the village panchayats. The panchayats within the block area could be grouped into different units and each unit was to elect one member to the panchayat samiti. The functions of the samiti included the development of agriculture and allied activities, supply of drinking water, sanitation and public health, construction and maintenance of roads, management of primary schools, etc. It was also to act as the agent of the State government in executing any special schemes for development. To enable the panchayat samiti to carry out its duties, sufficient resources were to be transferred to it. Its sources of income were to include a share in some tax revenue and grants from the State government.

The Study Team had proposed a three-tier structure of panchayati raj, with the village panchayat at the lowest level, the panchayat samiti at the intermediate level (functioning at the block level), and the zila parishad at the top level (functioning at the district level). The proposal was accepted and this three-tiered structure of rural local government has been gradually instituted. The village panchayat is constituted by direct election on the basis of adult franchise. The zilla parishad at the district level is composed of the presidents of the panchayat samitis, members of the State legislatures and of Parliament who represent the district, and the district officers. The district collector is the chairman of the zilla parishad.

In order to ensure that the three-tier structure functions in an 'organic way' in the task of rural development. The Third Plan proposed that: (1) village panchayats should receive 'greatest stress' and should function with the general consent and goodwill of the community, (2) technical officers at the district level should assist and advise extension officers and panchayats in formulating schemes of development, (3) village level workers, extension workers and the block development officer, should work as a team, (4) mutually interlinked and integrated village and block plans should be evolved to ensure 'intensive and continuous development' and the panchayat samitis should take proper steps in this direction, (5) the technical departments at the State level should extend full cooperation to help the elected representatives under panchayati raj in discharging their duties efficiently, and (6) the collector has an important part to play in the whole process and should play the dual role of maintaining *coordination* among different agencies at work (viz., zilla parishad, extension officers at the block level, and panchayat samitis) on the one hand, and ensure a continuing flow of technical advice and guidance from departments at the State level to panchayat samitis and other institutions of the lower order, on the other.[4]

At the beginning of the Fourth Plan in 1969, all villages were covered by blocks and there were 5265 of them, including 492 tribal development blocks. Of these, 999 were in stage I (less than five years) and 2585 in stage II (more than five years). The rest had completed ten years of existence and had passed both the stages. Village panchayats existed in all States and most Union territories while panchayat samitis (at the block level) and zilla parishads at the district level were yet to be constituted in some States as would be clear from Table 1. The panchayati raj institutions exist in all States and Union territories in some form or the other except the States of Meghalaya and Nagaland and the Union territories of Lakshadweep, Mizoram, and Pondicherry. In Nagaland, area, range and tribal councils and in Dadra and Nagar Haveli gram panchayats and a varishtha panchayat are in existence. In Assam, the panchayati raj bodies ceased to exist from 7-5-1973 to 13-5-1974 due to repeal of the old Act of 1959 and enforcement of the new Panchayati Raj Act of 1972. The new Act provides for two tiers—gaon panchayats and mohkuma parishads. The number of the CD blocks came down to 5026 in 1976 from 5265½ in 1969 on account of reorganization in many States. The population covered by these blocks was 46.97 crores as on 1 April 1976 and the number of villages covered was 632,500. According to '*India—A Reference Annual, 1977 and 1978*', the number of panchayat samitis has now risen to 4015 (from 233 in 1971-72).

Expenditure on the Programme

Table 2 gives the expenditure in different plans in absolute figures and in percentages.

Of the Rs.290 crores spent on agriculture and allied sectors in the First Plan, only Rs.45.98 crores which is 15.8% of the expenditure on agriculture and merely 2.3% of the total plan expenditure) were spent on the community development programme. Expenditure on the CD programme amounted to a mere Rs.187.12 crores in the Second Plan and Rs.292.00 crores in the Third Plan. Thus, over the first fifteen years of planning, the actual expenditure on the CD programme was Rs.525.10 crores out of a total expenditure of Rs.1928 crores on agriculture and allied sectors. This shows that the CD programme accounted for 27.23% of expenditure on agriculture and allied sectors. Since the total plan expenditure under the

TABLE 2: Expenditure on agriculture and allied sectors in different plans

(Rs. crores)

Plan	Total plan expenditure	Expenditure on agriculture and allied sectors	(3) as percentage of (2)
(1)	(2)	(3)	(4)
First Plan	1960	290	14.80
Second Plan	4672	549	11.75
Third Plan	8577	1089	12.70
Three Annual Plans	6625	1107	16.70
Fourth Plan	15779	2320	14.70
Fifth Plan			
(i) Outlay	39303	4644	11.80
(ii) Actual	28653	3413	11.91
Sixth Plan Outlay	97500	12539	12.86

Notes: (a) Data on expenditure up to the Fourth Plan relate to 'actual expenditure under the plan'.
(b) Since the Fifth Plan was terminated one year before schedule, figures for actual expenditure under the Fifth Plan were obtained by adding up the figures for 1974-75, 1975-76, 1976-77, and 1977-78.

Sources: (i) Government of India, *Statistical Pocket Book 1975*, Table 126, pp. 185-92.
(ii) Government of India, *Economic Survey, 1980-81*, Table 2.4, p. 96.
(iii) *The Economic Times*, 8 March 1981, p. 7.

first fifteen years of planning was Rs.15,209 crores, the expenditure on the CD programme works out to be merely 3.45% of the total expenditure. The inadequacy of resources would be revealed by the following statements as well:

1. Since by the end of the Third Plan, there were 5245 development blocks all over the country and actual expenditure on CD programme was Rs.292.00 crores, expenditure per block works out to be merely Rs.5.57 lakhs. Of this, as much as 33% was spent on administration, leaving only a very small amount for the actual programme.
2. Since total expenditure on CD programme worked out at Rs.525.10 crores by the end of the Third Plan, the annual outlay over the fourteen-year period of the CD programme (which was initiated in 1952) comes out to be Rs.37.57 crores. If the strength of rural population depending on agriculture is roughly taken to be appro-

ximately 37.50 crores, the per capita outlay per year works to a meagre Rs.1.00 only.

3. The contribution of the people over the 14-year period was only Rs.151.52 crores which comes to only 49 paise per capita per year.[5]

From 1967-68 to 1973-74, the expenditure on the CD programme amounted to Rs.172.38 crores. The expenditure in 1973-74, the last year of the Fifth Plan, was Rs.34.83 crores. Of the Rs.4644 crores kept for agriculture and allied sectors in the Fifth Plan, only Rs.127.45 crores was proposed to be spent on the CD programme.

Village Level Functionaries

The three important aspects of rural administration are revenue, development, and panchayat administration. The functionaries corresponding to them are the revenue accountant, the village level worker (VLW), and the panchayat secretary. There are considerable differences in the revenue and panchayati raj set-ups in different States and the nomenclature of the funtionaries also varies. In Gujarat, Kerala, Maharashtra, Karnataka, and some other States, there are full-time panchayat secretaries whereas in Punjab and Tamil Nadu they are part-time employees. In Gujarat the same functionary looks after both revenue and panchayat duties whereas in many States the functions are clearly bifurcated. Depending on the size of the villages, the jurisdiction of the functionaries also varies. For example, the revenue accountant has about 3 villages under him in Gujarat, 20 in Assam, 8 to 10 in Himachal Pradesh, and 2 in Uttar Pradesh. The gram panchayat secretary has normally 5-7 panchayats under his charge in Punjab whereas in U.P. his jurisdiction is limited to only one or two villages. The VLW (generally known as Gram Sevak) has normally 10 villages to look after. The VLW was initially supposed to be a multi-purpose worker. He was trained for about two years in various programmes of rural development such as agriculture and rural engineering, crop husbandry, horticulture and plant protection, animal husbandry and veterinary science, cooperation, panchayat and panchayati raj, extension and social education, planning, community development programme and administration, public health and family planning, and rural industries. In most of the States, 80% of the work of the VLWs was to be devoted to programmes of agricultural development. The minimum qualification for the VLW was, in most cases, matric and salary less than Rs.150 p.m. There were some exceptions to this rule. For example, in Assam the scale of pay was Rs.110–200 p.m. plus allowances; in West Bengal it was Rs.125–200 p.m.; and in Orissa Rs.100.00 plus allowances (totalling Rs.170 p.m.). The initial basic pay in most cases was about Rs.100 p.m. (in Andhra Pradesh and Mysore it was even less, being Rs.80).[6] Thus, with limited educational qualifications and average abilities, poor salary, and few avenues of promotion, the VLW was expected to work as an "originator" of community development concept, train villagers in this programme by ascertaining their needs, awakening their interest in change, and spread the message of the CD programme through friendly conversations and group discussions. Obviously, this was hoping for too much. Only a highly qualified and well-paid person with a missionary zeal can do the job effectively.

Evaluation of the Programme

Jawaharlal Nehru regarded community development and panchayati raj as a 'tremendous adventure' that would change the face of rural India. The community development programme had drawn its inspiration from various experiments conducted in different pockets of the country in the pre-independence period. Thus, Mahatma Gandhi had conducted a successful experiment at Wardha and Rabindranath Tagore had carried out a programme of rural reconstruction at Sriniketan. In south, Spencer Hatch of the YMCA had launched a similar programme at Martaindem (south of Travancore). In Baroda, V.T. Krishnamachari was engaged in implementing the Baroda Rural Development Programme.

After independence, experience of two projects—the Etawah project and the Nilokheri project—was available to the planners. The Etawah project was initiated in 1948 under the expert guidance of an American (Albert Mayor) while the Nilokheri project was initiated by S.K. Dey in the township set up by the government about 100 miles north of Delhi to rehabilitate the displaced persons pouring in from West Pakistan. All these experiments were confined to specific areas, yet they provided the basic rationale of adopting a community approach to the programmes of development. Accordingly, the programme of community development was launched on an ambitious scale in 1952 under the supervision of the Deputy Chairman of the Planning Commission, V.T. Krishnamachari, who had considerable experience in the field.

However, the mere magnitude of the task demanded utmost cooperation and assistance from the people and one-pointed devotion from the administration both of which were not available to the extent that was necessary to make the programme a success. Most of the observers of the Indian scene agree that the programme of community development and panchayati raj has failed to fulfil its role. The programme, according to them, was sustained more by *hope* than by *achievement*. The philosophic and romantic view of village life implicit in the very conception of community development and panchayati raj could not be given a practical shape because the *man* is intrinsically not as good and cooperative as the programme expected him to be. There are a number of other reasons, some of which are mentioned below.

The programme was implemented on a very large scale without having amply trained personnel with a missionary zeal and right aptitude. Then, as already noted, the VLW was poorly paid and in the absence of proper avenues for promotion he had no incentive to carry out the programme in right earnest. A person just coming out of school and engaged as a VLW cannot be expected to fully understand or appreciate the problems of villagers and cannot command much respect especially on account of the fact that with improved communications and mass education there are a number of people in the villages themselves who are better equipped to do the job. The reliance on the VLW as a "messenger of new ideas of change and improvement" is, therefore, no longer valid. Also, since the VLW has no powers to exercise, he does not command any respect (or importance) in the eyes of the villagers who are used to respect persons who have power and authority. This is the reason why the VLW has no firm footing in the rural scene.

By its very nature, the community development programme had to be officially sponsored. It was a programme formulated by the higher official machinery and people's participation was sought to be obtained through the VLW. Though much has been said about CD being a programme by the people, the programme was essentially *thrust* from outside and was not *inspired* by the people themselves. It was to correct this state of affairs that the institution of panchayati raj was established. But as many studies have noted, this institution itself became an obstacle to people's participation. This was on account of many administrative, economic, psychological, social, and political obstacles and problems. The 50th orientation course held at the National Institute of Community Development noted that the very structure of the panchayats was defective because "due to adult franchise and factions which often became stronger with elections, not always the best persons stood for elections, nor the best persons were elected".[7] Conflicting claims to leadership breed rivalries, tensions, and struggles and the faction that dominates the panchayat is busy exploring ways and means to perpetuate its hold over the village. Programmes of community development and people's participation in developmental activities are neglected and people, in general, get disillusioned and try to dissociate themselves from all development programmes, whatever their initial enthusiasm.

On the economic front, the village panchayats find it difficult to carry out the programmes because most of them are existing 'in a hand-to-mouth' condition. They are vested with powers to raise their own resources but generally they are not willing to exercise them either on account of the fact that people are too poor or because they do not want to incur the displeasure of the villagers. On the psychological side, the enthusiasm of the elected representatives is marred by numerous rules of procedure, laws and rules, limitations of finance and resources. Sometimes the elected representatives of the panchayats have high hopes of doing something useful for the people but such a plethora of rules combined with the fact that their planning has to conform to a cut and dried plan already set as a goal by the government acts as a brake and promotes gradually an attitude of negligence and apathy in them

On the social side, the traditional caste system has imposed a *stratification* of functions which works considerably against the very concept of community participation and development. For example, the work of sanitation will never be done by persons belonging to a higher caste while persons belonging to lower castes will not be allowed to participate in programmes of education, health and other decision-making processes. Individuals belonging to higher castes will not cooperate in programmes aimed at improving the condition of the village sweepers, cobblers, and persons belonging to other lower castes. Similarly, a person belonging to a lower caste will never be accepted as a sarpanch, however 'enlightened' or educated he may be. Thus, "caste and the social stratification on one side and the will to participate in developmental activities on the other hand, are opposing forces".[8]

According to John M. Mellor and associates,[9] there were numerous defects in the administrative structure as well. Thus, (i) there was a tendency for the administrative structure to become a line organization from the block development officer to the assistant to the VLW further isolating the higher order of competence in the block from farmers, (ii) adequate technical advice was not made available to the blocks in time because there was no clear tie with agricultural experiment stations, (iii) blocks were not well coordinated and were not linked at district and local levels, (iv) since promotions were gained by impressing distant administrators much of the time was wasted in writing reports and too little time was devoted to actual programmes of development,[10] and (v) because of frequent transfers, the block personnel did not get sufficient time to understand the local problems and consequently took little interest in the community development programme of that area. On account of such factors the administrative machinery could not (or did not) explore the directions of cooperation in full earnest and no sound programmes for eliciting participation of the people were taken in hand. The different levels of administration did not work as a team and their efforts lacked the sense of purpose and direction.

It was expected by the planners that after a ten-year initial period of their development, the community development blocks would become 'self-reliant' and no external assistance in the form of financial resources would be necessary. This expectation was not realized and the programme continued to remain dependent on the government for initiative and funds. As noted by the Draft Fourth Plan, where administrative and financial support was forthcoming, the community development and panchayati raj programme made significant contributions "in the formulation and implementation of local development plans" but where such support was lacking "activities languished and the staff remained almost supernumerary".[11] The programme failed to generate resources basically because it failed to elicit popular response, cooperation, and participation of the people for whom it was intended.

Perhaps the most important criticism of the CD programme is that it totally ignored considerations of regional planning. Blocks were defined at the top and the headquarters were either selected for administrative convenience or under local pressure. No micro-level studies were conducted to define the blocks and the headquarters were frequently not the central place of the area. No attempt was made to define the functional linkages, hence villages were not integrated functionally in an organic manner. Since urban areas were specifically excluded from the ambit of the programme, no attempt was made to link up the villages with the urban areas. Thus towns, which could regenerate the rural areas by acting as focal points of development, were entirely left out of the picture.[12]

As reiterated at various places in this chapter, the most important objective of the community development programme was to elicit popular participation and involvement of the people. The institutions through which this could come about were basically two—panchayati raj (already described) and cooperatives. While the former was necessary to implement the will of the people, the latter was necessary to directly organize the rural people (and harness their energies) in the task of rural development. The cooperative form of organization was found desirable in a number of fields such as agricultural credit, marketing, and processing, all aspects of production in rural areas, organizing artisans and labourers, and in ensuring supply of essential consumer goods at reasonable prices. Since the agricultural credit societies accounted for the greater part of development in the field of cooperation ever since the movement got underway in 1904, they were taken as the *starting point* for the cooperative experiment in the planning era. The target was to expand the coverage of the movement substantially and bring large areas under cooperative farming.

The Second Plan advocated that to evolve better methods of management and organization, pilot projects in cooperative farming should be undertaken 'in each district and later in each national extension and community project area'. These centres were to be developed later on into 'practical training centres for cooperation, agricultural and other extension workers'. Groups of persons were to be encouraged to form cooperative farming societies, which were to be provided assistance on the following lines: (i) credit from the government or cooperative agencies and preference in financial assistance from the government for agricultural programmes, (ii) preference in the supply of improved seeds, fertilizers, and materials for local construction, (iii) preference in the grant of leases of land reclaimed by the government, culturable waste lands, lands whose management is assumed by the government, and lands under the management of village panchayats, (iv) provision that after a cooperative farming society is formed and so long as it continues and is managed in accordance with the conditions prescribed under the law, no new rights adverse to the interests of its members will accrue, (v) technical assistance of personnel in farm operations, marketing, preparation of production programmes, etc., (vi) technical or financial assistance in developing non-agricultural employment for members of the cooperative farming society and others associated with them, as in cottage industries, dairying and horticulture, etc., and (vii) subsidy for managerial expenses for a limited period whenever desirable.[13]

The cooperative movement (along with community development and panchayati raj) was acclaimed as the *means* of transforming the rural society in all plan documents and high hopes were pinned on it. For example, the Draft Fifth Plan has this to say in this regard: "Cooperation represents institutionalisation of the principle and impulse of mutual aid. It has the merit of combining freedom and opportunity for the small man with the benefit of large-scale management and organization. Cooperation is, therefore, eminently suited to bring about the desired socio-economic changes in the context of the existing conditions in the country. *There is no other instrument as potentially powerful and full of social purpose as the cooperative movement.*"[14]

The cooperative movement also faced a fate similar to community development and panchayati raj. Popular participation in the movement did not come about and the attitude of the administrators was one of apathy and indifference. Just as in the case of the community development programme, a sufficient number of willing and efficient people were not available to carry out the programme. The cooperative societies benefited mostly the affluent section of the rural population like the CD programme and panchayati raj institutions. This was not unexpected in an atmosphere where too little was done to change the institutional structure and the feudal organization of the villages wherein all power—political, economic, and social—was concentrated in the hands of a few people.

Undoubtedly, the CD programme, cooperative movement, and panchayati raj institutions were implemented precisely to bring about a change in the institutional structure and feudal organization of the villages but they failed because (i) they were implemented over a very wide area more or less simultaneously, (ii) the illiterate villagers did not possess adequate mental maturity to implement these programmes, (iii) the actual implementation of these programmes benefited mostly the rural rich and consequently the much desired popular support and participation of the majority of the rural poor did not come about, (iv) multiplicity of agencies created confusion in the minds of the rural people and corrupt practices adopted by the administrative agencies at many places compelled them to stay away from the programmes, (v) the elected members of the panchayats were usually representatives of factional and vested interests and often a substantial number of ill-suited candidates were selected, and (vi) at many places the bureaucratic machinery has connived with the affluent section of the rural population in cornering the benefits of development while the majority of the rural people remained practically unaffected by the programme of development. Often loans to the small and marginal farmers are ruled out on the pretext that they do not have the repaying capacity. Another technique employed to deny them credit facilities is the insistence on the security of mortgage of land. The Fourth National Convention of the All-India Panchayati Raj held in 1964 made the following pertinent observation on the panchayati raj movement, which summarizes the problems very ably:

> The progress of the movement of democratic decentralisation is painfully slow and there has been a lack of promptitude in the implementation of plans. Lukewarm interest shown by the people, casteism and communalism, poor leadership, unwillingness of panchayats to impose taxes, lack of self-reliance and increasing dependence on State governments, bickerings and factionalism, corruption and manipulation of accounts, continuation of the old district board attitude, emphasis on desk work at the cost of real field work, bureaucratic approach and lack of guidance from superior authorities, and the habit of the *panches* to ignore people are some of the causes explaining the unsatisfactory state of affairs.[15]

HYVP—THE NEW AGRICULTURAL STRATEGY

A team of experts sponsored by the Ford Foundation was invited by the Government of India in the latter half of the Second Plan to suggest ways and means to increase agricultural production and productivity. This necessity arose out of the need for increasing the agricultural production in the face of continuing stagnation of production on the one hand, and rapidly increasing demand on the other. The Team submitted its report, entitled *India's Food Crisis and Steps to Meet it*, in April 1959. The report suggested 'intensive' efforts for increasing the agricultural production and productivity in *selected regions* of the country with stress on modern inputs, especially fertilizers, credit, marketing facilities, etc. On the basis of the recommendations of this Team, the government introduced an intensive development programme in seven districts selected from as many States in 1960 and this programme was named Intensive Area Development Programme (popularly known as IADP). The programme was basically a plan to increase agricultural production and productivity and did not possess the comprehensive character of the community development programme. Therefore, from 1960 onwards, there was a distinct change in the rural development strategy. From a *multi-dimensional* community development programme embracing varied aspects of rural life the emphasis shifted to a *uni-dimensional* development programme oriented towards increasing the agricultural production and productivity.

A district selected under the IADP was required to fulfil the following conditions:

1. The district should as far as possible have assured water supply.
2. It should have minimum hazards such as susceptibility to floods, drainage problems, acute soil conservation problems, etc.
3. It should as far as possible have well-developed village institutions like cooperatives and panchayats.
4. It should have maximum potentialities for increasing agricultural production within a comparatively short time.[16]

The seven districts selected under the programme were: West Godavari in Andhra Pradesh, Shahabad in Bihar, Raipur in Madhya Pradesh, Thanjavur in Tamil Nadu, Ludhiana in Punjab, Aligarh in Uttar Pradesh, and Pali in Rajasthan. The first four were selected for rice, the next two for wheat, and the last one for millets. This programme was later extended to the remaining States also by selecting one district from each State. In October 1965, the net was further widened and 114 districts (out of 325) were selected for intensive development and the programme labelled as Intensive

Agricultural Areas Programme (IAAP).

New high-yielding varieties of foodgrains were successfully used in Mexico and elsewhere and considerable increases in production and productivity recorded. This brought a Nobel Peace Prize to the discoverer of these varieties (Dr. Norman Borlaug) and new hope and enthusiasm in the developing countries which saw a hope of breaking the age-long stagnation in the agricultural sector through the introduction of these varieties. The Government of India evolved a New Agricultural Strategy in the form of a Package Programme woven around the new high-yielding varieties. This strategy was implemented for the first time in kharif season of 1966 and was termed High-Yielding Varieties Programme (popularly known as HYVP). Initially the total area covered under this programme was 1.89 million hectares. "Within a year of their introduction, it was conclusively demonstrated that the yields from the new varieties, at the farm level, exceeded 25 to 100 percent compared to the yield from traditional varieties."[17]

Following the adoption of this programme significant increases in foodgrain output were recorded. The foodgrain output which was 72.35 million tonnes in 1965-66 and 74.23 million tonnes in 1966-67 shot up to 95.08 million tonnes in 1967-68 which was 28% higher compared with 1966-67, the previous year. Rightfully there was a tone of optimism and victory in the planning circles. But soon the critics struck. They pointed out that the years 1965-66 and 1966-67 were years of drought and it was a folly to measure gains keeping these years in mind. Instead production in 1964-65 (which remains an ideal year for future comparison) should be taken into consideration for purposes of comparison. The production in that year was 89.00 million tonnes and thus less than the foodgrain output in 1967-68 by only 6.05 million tonnes. Thus, though there was an increase, its extent was not of the magnitude to justify the label 'revolution' since revolution implied 'a complete change', a 'great reversal of conditions' and a 'fundamental reconstruction' which was not in evidence. The second argument put forth by the critics was that spectacular results were achieved only in the case of wheat and therefore even if there was a revolution, it was only a wheat revolution and not a green revolution, as Table 3 amply demonstrates.

Wheat production increased from 12.99 million tonnes in 1964-65 to 16.54 million tonnes in 1967-68 and to 18.64 million tonnes in 1968-69 Except, for a year or two this increasing trend has been maintained more or less consistently. In fact, as is clear from Table 3, there is a 115% increase in wheat production over the period 1964-65 to 1971-72 which by all means is 'spectacular' or 'revolutionary' as one likes to put it. The production of rice, jowar, and maize has remained virtually constant taking the period 1964-65 to 1979-80 as a whole. Bajra production has shown an erratic movement,

TABLE 3: Foodgrain production

(million tonnes)

Crop	1960-61	1964-65	1967-68	1968-69	1969-70	1970-71	1971-72	1972-73
Rice	34.60	39.03	37.61	39.76	40.43	42.23	43.07	39.25
Wheat	11.00	12.99	16.54	18.65	20.09	23.83	26.41	24.73
Jowar	9.90	9.75	10.05	9.80	9.72	8.10	7.72	6.97
Bajra	3.29	4.45	5.18	3.80	5.33	8.03	5.32	3.93
Maize	4.12	4.66	6.27	5.70	5.67	7.49	5.10	6.39
Others	19.42	18.12	19.40	16.30	18.26	18.74	17.55	15.76
Total	82.33	89.00	95.05	94.01	99.50	108.42	105.17	97.03

Crop	1973-74	1974-75	1975-76	1976-77	1977-78	1978-79	1979-80
Rice	44.05	39.58	48.74	41.92	52.67	53.77	42.19
Wheat	21.78	24.10	28.85	29.01	31.75	35.51	31.56
Jowar	9.10	10.41	9.50	10.52	12.06	11.44	11.32
Bajra	7.52	3.27	5.74	5.85	4.73	5.57	4.03
Maize	5.80	5.56	7.26	6.36	5.97	6.20	5.58
Others	16.42	16.91	20.94	17.51	19.11	19.41	14.17
Total	104.67	99.83	121.03	111.17	126.41	131.90	108.85

Sources: Government of India, *Economic Survey 1975-76*, Table 1.5, p. 63; and *Economic Survey 1980-81*, Table 1.5, p. 69.

Notes: 1. Since HYVP was confined to only five crops—rice, wheat, jowar, bajra, and maize—separate data for only these five crops have been given in the table.

2. Since the years 1965-66 and 1966-67 were years of drought, they have been included in the table.

a year of very good crop is followed by a year of a very bad performance. It shot up rapidly from 3.80 millon tonnes in 1968-69 to 8.03 million tonnes in 1970-71 but fell back to 3.93 million tonnes in 1972-73. This analysis shows that the revolution has remained confined to wheat only. Therefore, we should talk of 'wheat revolution' only and not of 'green revolution' since the latter term should signify spectacular increases in other crops as well.

To find out the truth about the green revolution the methodology that is generally adopted consists in comparing the recent increases in annual foodgrain output "with the long-run trend of growth established in the period 1949-50 to 1964-65, that is the period before the advent of the high-yielding varieties. If output increases turn out to be substantially higher than what would be expected on the basis of the past trend, one could conclude that the green revolution has had an impact on foodgrain output. The expectation is that since the green revolution represents a sharp break from the past, it will have raised the long-run trend rate of growth of foodgrain output considerably over the rate of 3.05 percent per annum established during the period 1949-50 and 1964-65".[18]

Sen has plotted the indices of foodgrain production and productivity separately (in natural logarithm) against time and has fitted two trend lines—one for the period 1949-50 to 1964-65 and the other for the period 1949-50 to 1970-71. Obviously, if the latter is well above the former it is an indication of a 'spectacular achievement'. But no such conclusion emerges since "comparison of the two trend lines shows that there has been some improvement in the rate of growth of foodgrains production—but an improvement that can be termed as best nominal". The long-run trend growth rate increased from 3.05 to only 3.26 per annum when the period 1967-68 to 1970-71 is also taken into account (years 1965-66 and 1966-67 being drought years were left out). Similarly, the long-run trend rate of growth in yield rose from 1.63 in 1949-50 to 1964-65 to 1.99 in 1949-50 to 1970-71. According to Sen, these small improvements are not significant enough to merit the term revolution.[19] It would be interesting to note that if the last three years of the Fourth Plan (i.e. 1971-72, 1972-73, and 1973-74) are also taken in account, the rate of foodgrain output over the entire period 1949-50 to 1973-74 works out to only 2.7% per annum. Similarly, the rate of growth of foodgrain yield over the period 1949-50 to 1973-74 works out to merely 1.3% per annum. These rates are lower than the rates of growth attained during 1949-50 to 1964-65, the pre-HYV period.[20]

Only wheat stands out as an exception whose performance has continued to remain consistently good. In this context it may be of interest to note that the percentage of wheat in total foodgrains rose from 13.4 in 1960-61 and 14.6 in 1964-65 to 22 in 1970-71 and further to 29 in 1979-80 forcing rice to tumble down from 42% in 1960-61 and 44% in 1964-65 to 39% in 1970-71 and to 38.7% in 1979-80, and other foodgrains (including jowar, bajra, maize and all other foodgrains) from 44.6% in 1960-61 and 41.5% in 1964-65 to 39% in 1970-71 and 32.2% in 1979-80 (computed from Table 3). Thus, wheat has been the mainstay of the green revolution and, as noted by Wolf Ladejinsky, it is a "mighty significant mainstay". To quote him: "Wheat yields have doubled in many districts of Punjab, Haryana and Western U.P. Even in the bad year 1972-73 the total wheat output was 26 or 28 million tonnes, depending on how one looks at estimates, compared with an output of 12 million tonnes on the eve of the new package of practices, and more a function of increased yields rather than expanded acreage. More specifically, the growth of wheat production at a compound rate of nearly 14 percent per year since 1964-65 (the year of peak production immediately preceding the launching of the High Yielding Varieties Programme) through 1970-71 is an outstanding achievement. Even more impressive, the per acre yield has increased over the same period at a compound rate of 7.5 percent per year."[21] Thus, whereas the index of foodgrain production in India, with triennium ending 1961-62 as the base, increased from 89.6 in 1965-66 to 117.1 in 1967-68 and to 133.9 in 1970-71 and stood at 125.6 in 1974-75 that of wheat increased from 93.4 in 1965-66 to 148.7 in 1967-68 and to 214.2 in 1970-71 and stood at 217.8 in 1974-75. Also, while the yield per hectare of all foodgrains, which was 710 kg in 1960-61, could increase only to 872 kg in 1970-71 and to 878 kg in 1979-80, that of wheat rose from 851 kg in 1960-61 to 1307 kg in 1970-71 and further to 1437 kg in 1979-80.[22]

On this plus side must also be considered the fact, according to A.S. Kahlon, that dramatic change had taken place in "(a) the status of agriculture as a money-making activity, and (b) the willingness of Indian agriculturist to accept technical change in the pursuit of profit."[23] According to him, this is, in itself, a revolutionary breakthrough. In his article quoted above, Wolf Ladejinsky also noted similar trends in these unmistakable term: "Where the ingredients for the new technology are available, no farmer denies their effectiveness. The desire for better farming methods and a better standard of living is growing not only among the relatively small number of the affluent using the new technology, but also among countless farmers still from the outside looking in." This factor, as noted by him, cannot be underestimated as an opening to future progress. The objective evidence of these micro-level or 'qualitative' changes (according to what one chooses to call them) is provided by the change in the short- and long-term investment decisions of the farmer, i.e., by changes in the consumption of current inputs such as fertilizers and efforts aimed at land development through construction of tubewells and installation of irrigation pumpsets.[24]

From a mere 1.89 million hectares in 1966-67, the area under HYVP increased to 15.38 million hectares in 1970-71 and to 26.00 million hectares in 1973-74. This further increased to 41.10 million hectares in 1978-79. The consumption of fertilizers which was only 0.294 million tonnes in 1960-61 rose to 1.10 million tonnes in 1966-67, to 2.26 million tonnes in 1970-71, and further to 2.84 million tonnes in 1973-74. Because of a rapid rise in the prices of fertilizers the consumption in 1974-75 suffered a slight setback and was 2.58 million tonnes, but again resumed its upward trend from the very next year. The consumption stood at 5.12 million tonnes in 1978-79. By the end of the Third Plan there were only 80,000 tubewells. In 1969-70 the number of private tubewells installed had risen to 371,000 which further increased to 483,000 in 1970-71 and to 719,000 in 1973-74. The total number of agricultural pumpsets energized in 1969-70 was 1354 thousand units which further increased to 1900 thousand units in 1970-71 and to more than 2400 thousand units in 1973-74. The number of tractors in use which was merely 21 thousand units in 1956 and 31 thousand units in 1960-61 went up to 108 thousand units in 1969-70. The use of improved seeds in the IADP districts grew at about 40% per annum in the 1960s.[25] In the words of Khusro, "no one could see such remarkable figures of annual percentage increases in inputs and yet surmise that a structural change had not occurred".[26]

THE REGIONAL DIMENSION

This brief review shows that there are at least two positive achievements of the new agricultural strategy that must be acknowledged: (i) it has helped in the expansion of wheat production and productivity substantially ushering the nation into an era of wheat revolution, and (ii) it has induced revolutionary changes in the outlook and attitudes of farmers. These two factors—one quantitative and the other qualitative—have together introduced an element of dynamism in the erstwhile stagnant rural economy. But one must not forget that it is precisely these two factors that have created an imbalance in the rural economy—a fact that has to be viewed with concern. Some experts[27] have ventured to prove that the HYVP does not accentuate regional imbalances but, as N. Krishnaji has rightly pointed out,[28] much depends on how one defines regions. For, if States are taken as regions the impact of the new technology in increasing imbalances would not be revealed since it is only small areas within States that have benefited from it. Aggregation of data for the State as a whole is likely to conceal imbalances. It is only in two States, Punjab and Haryana, where this danger is not present since in both these States the use of high-yielding varieties of seeds has been quite widespread.

Table 4 gives inter-State data of the State-wise growth rates of crop

TABLE 4: State-wise growth rate of crop production, 1962-65 to 1971-74

(% per annum

State	Growth rate	State	Growth rate
1. Punjab	8.35	11. Karnataka	2.68
2. Haryana	6.66	12. Assam	1.88
3. Kerala	4.94	13. Gujarat	1.75
4. Tripura	4.34	14. Bihar	1.67
5. Rajasthan	3.80	15. Madhya Pradesh	1.29
6. Manipur	3.73	16. Andhra Pradesh	1.19
7. Himachal Pradesh	3.68	17. Jammu & Kashmir	0.69
8. Uttar Pradesh	3.28	18. Orissa	−0.19
9. West Bengal	3.14	19. Nagaland	−2.33
10. Tamil Nadu	3.12	20. Maharashtra	−2.44

Source: Economic Times, 10 May 1976, p. 5.

production during 1961-62 to 1973-74. While Punjab shows the rate of growth of 8.35% per annum, Haryana shows the rate of growth of 6.66% per annum. It would be interesting to note that U.P. show a growth rate of 3.28% per annum only despite the fact that western U.P. is one of the major regions of green revolution in India. The reason is not difficult to seek. Stagnation of eastern and central U.P. camouflages the progress of western U.P.

Obviously, these trends should show up in per capita availability as well. In 1971-72 the per capita availability of foodgrains was 1357 per day in Punjab and 1053 per day in Haryana against the national average of only 462 per day.[29] Thus, per capita availability was about twice in Punjab and more than twice in Haryana as compared with the national average. As would be clear from Table 5, the per capita output in Punjab and Haryana registered remarkable increases. Thus, over the period 1964-65 to 1970-71, the increase in per capita output of these States (combined) was 57.0% which was much higher than progress registered by other States. From their combined per capita output of 336.8 kg in 1964-65, they increased their combined per capita output to 528.54 kg in 1970-71. The combined share of these States in the total output of food grains rose from 7.5% in 1964-65 to 11.12% in 1970-71 and further to 15.5% in 1979-80. In 1970-71, the per capita output of foodgrains was 565 kg in Punjab which was approximately three times the national per capita output. The per capita output in Haryana in that year was 479.1 kg which was about two and a half times the national per capita output. The position of these States vis-a-vis other States would be clear from the fact- hat the per capita output in Madhya Pradesh (which

TABLE 5: State-wise estimates of foodgrains output, percentage share in total output and per capita output (Total output in million tonnes)

	Output of total foodgrains			Percentage to all-India			Per capita output in kg[2]			Percent change in per capita output		
	1964-65	1970-71	1979-80	1964-65	1970-71	1979-80	1964-65	1970-71	1978-79	1964-65 to 1970-71	1964-65 to 1978-79	1970-71 to 1978-79
Andhra Pradesh	7.42	7.41	9.35	8.3	6.8	8.6	197.9	175.1	196.6	−11.5	−0.7	12.3
Bihar	7.51	7.88	7.01	8.4	7.3	6.4	153.9	149.3	139.9	−3.0	−9.1	−6.3
Gujarat	2.86	4.41	4.01	3.2	4.1	3.6	129.3	153.2	130.5	18.5	0.9	−14.8
Haryana	—	4.75	5.03	—	4.4	4.6	—	479.1	482.4	—	—	0.7
Kerala	1.16	1.32	1.30	1.3	1.2	1.2	64.6	63.7	52.6	−1.4	−18.6	−17.4
Madhya Pradesh	10.28	10.92	7.17	11.5	10.1	6.6	296.9	267.7	211.4	−9.8	−28.8	−21.0
Maharashtra	6.79	5.59	10.36	7.6	5.2	9.5	161.4	119.6	176.0	−25.9	9.0	47.2
Mysore	4.83	5.96	7.08	5.4	5.5	6.5	194.1	210.8	216.9	8.6	11.7	2.9
Orissa	4.92	5.10	3.85	5.5	4.7	3.5	264.9	227.5	199.6	−14.1	−24.6	−12.3
Punjab	6.71[1]	7.31	11.89	7.5[1]	6.7	10.9	336.8	565.0	733.5	57.0[3]	85.9	29.8
Rajasthan	5.27	8.84	5.21	5.9	8.1	4.8	244.6	266.9	223.5	9.1	−8.6	−16.3
Tamil Nadu	5.72	6.97	8.36	6.4	6.4	7.7	163.6	169.1	169.6	3.4	3.7	0.3
Uttar Pradesh	15.29	19.59	16.15	17.1	18.1	14.8	198.8	213.1	204.4	7.2	2.8	−1.4
West Bengal	6.26	7.49	6.87	7.0	6.9	6.3	167.1	176.0	152.6	5.3	−8.7	−13.3
Others	4.38	4.88	5.21	4.9	4.5	4.9						
All India	89.40	108.42	108.85	100.0	100.0	100.0	192.6	197.0	194.2	2.3	0.8	−1.4

1. Includes output in Haryana also.
2. Per capita output for 1970-71 has been estimated by considering the average output for the triennium ending 1971-72 and dividing it by the mid-year population of 1970 as given in the *Report on Currency and Finance, 1971-72*. Similarly, per capita output for 1978-79 has been estimated by considering the average output of the years 1977-78, 1978-79, and 1979-80 and dividing it by the mid-year population of 1978.
3. For calculating the percent change in per capita output over the period 1964-65 to 1970-71, combined output and population for Punjab and Haryana has been considered because the data for the year 1964-65 consider Punjab and Haryana together (under Punjab). Similar considerations have been observed while calculating the percent change in per capita output over the period 1964-65 to 1978-79.

Sources: (i) C.H. Hanumantha Rao, *Technological Change and Distribution of Gains in Indian Agriculture* (Delhi: Macmillan Co. of India Ltd., 1975) Table 8.5, p. 100, for estimates of output in 1964-65. (ii) Government of India, *Economic Survey, 1980-81*, Table 1.9, pp. 73-76. (iii) Reserve Bank of India, *Report on Currency and Finance 1971-72*, Statement 2, pp. 58-59 for estimates of mid-year population of 1964, 1970, and 1978.

ranked third in 1970-71) was merely 267.7 kg and in Rajasthan (which ranked fourth in 1970-71) was merely 266.9 kg. Thus, the per capita output of foodgrains in Punjab was more than twice the per capita output in the third ranked State. The per capita output in Punjab in 1978-79 was 733.5 kg which was more than three and a half times the national per capita output and more than three times the per capita output of Rajasthan, the third ranked State.

Another measure to highlight inter-regional disparities in agricultural growth can be agricultural productivity per worker which can be defined as land productivity divided by the number of agricultural workers per hectare of the net sown area. It has been shown by Narottam Shah that per agricultural worker average net domestic product of agricultural sector at current prices was Rs.3195 for Punjab (average for the period 1967-68 to 1969-70) against the average of Rs.1213 for all States in the same period. The lowest agricultural productivity per worker was recorded in Nagaland where it was a meagre Rs.409. Thus, the regional differential (the ratio between the lowest and the highest) was as high as 1 : 8. Table 6 summarizes the position in this regard wherein data for 18 States are given. It shows that even in the third ranked State of Kerala, agricultural productivity per worker was only 65% of the productivity in Punjab. In fact, agricultural productivity per worker was less than 50% in as many as 13 States compared with agricultural productivity per worker in Punjab.

The question that naturally arises at this juncture is: 'Why is Punjab the heartland of green revolution?' A number of factors have combined to make Punjab 'ideally suited' to benefit from the new technology. Some of these factors are:[30]

1. The ownership of land in Punjab is mostly vested in those who actually cultivate the land. Thus, the area under owner-occupiers increased from 51.4% in 1947 to 66.4% in 1957 and further to 80.89% in 1969-70. The introduction of farm machinery on a large scale and availability of repair services, etc., in medium sized towns has encouraged more and more rich landowners to cultivate the land themselves. Since they were in a position to invest substantial sums on land, agricultural production and productivity rose rapidly.

2. The average size of holding in Punjab is larger than in the rest of the country. Thus, more than half of the holdings are bigger than 4 hectares and about 10% are bigger than 12 hectares. Besides, Punjab is the only State where the entire farming area has been consolidated.

3. Availability of irrigation has been much greater in Punjab than in any other State of India. Thus, by the early seventies, 70% of the net sown area of the State was irrigated, compared with about 20% irrigated area for the country as a whole.[31] Since the new high-yielding varieties could be

TABLE 6: **Relative levels of agricultural productivity per agricultural worker : average for 1967-68 to 1969-70**

Rank (1)	State (2)	Per agricultural worker average net domestic product of agricultural sector at current prices (in Rs.) (3)	% agricultural productivity in other States compared with that of Punjab (4)
1.	Punjab	3195	100
2.	Haryana	2922	91.46
3.	Kerala	2072	64.85
4.	West Bengal	1819	56.93
5.	Assam	1707	53.43
6.	Gujarat	1457	45.60
7.	Orissa	1400	43.82
8.	Jammu & Kashmir	1393	43.60
9.	Mysore	1321	41.35
10.	Uttar Pradesh	1236	38.69
	All States	1213	37.97
11.	Himachal Pradesh	1134	35.49
12.	Rajasthan	1129	35.34
13.	Andhra Pradesh	993	31.08
14.	Tamil Nadu	955	29.89
15.	Maharashtra	949	29.70
16.	Madhya Pradesh	856	26.79
17.	Bihar	755	23.63
18.	Nagaland	409	12.80

Sources: Columns 1 to 3 are taken from Narottam Shah, "Indian Agriculture since Independence", in Vadilal Dagli (ed.), *A Regional Profile of Indian Agriculture* (Bombay: Vora & Co. Publishing Pvt. Ltd., 1974), p. 24; col. 4 is calculated from col. 3 to highlight regional disparities in agricultural development by comparing the position of other States *vis-a-vis* Punjab, the most advanced State in agriculture.

used in irrigated areas only, Punjab derived the greatest advantage from the introduction of these varieties.

4. Punjab paid special attention to the provision of infrastructure. A network of roads has been laid and every field is accessible by road.

5. There was a remarkable spurt in the use of inputs such as improved and high-yielding varieties of seeds, fertilizers, insecticides, and pesticides and farm machinery. In 1969-70, "of the total gross cropped area of 5.5 million hectares, plant protection measures covered an area of 2.9 million hectares or 53 percent, against the national average of 21 percent". The fertilizer use in Punjab was 58.7 kg per hectare in 1972-73 against the national average of only 16.5 kg per hectare.[32]

6. Punjab was blessed to have easy and substantial availability of electricity because of the Bhakra Dam, Nangal Dam, and other electricity generating plants. "In terms of annual per capita electricity consumption for irrigation, Punjab with 10.86 kwh stood third to Tamil Nadu and Haryana."[33] The ample availability of electric power has made extensive use of pumping sets, threshers, chaff-cutters, etc., possible.

7. Credit facilities are available to farmers on a more 'generous' and 'less obstructive' basis and even small farmers have been able to benefit from them. This is because of the strong cooperative movement in this State.

8. The Punjab Agricultural University set up in 1962 at Ludhiana has established a sound reputation for agricultural research in the fields of plant breeding, agronomy, agricultural engineering and plant protection. It evolved a number of high-yielding varieties of seeds of wheat—PV 18, Kalyan Sona 227, and S 308—from the material originally received from Mexico. In addition to this, the University has established a directorate of extension which maintains links with districts through its farm advisory services. Fairs are organized by the university at Ludhiana in September and March every year to demonstrate the improved implements to the farmers. A workshop for agricultural officers is set up twice a year at which the extension staff of the State department is briefed on the latest research findings. Training camps are held for the farmers at the district and block levels and short courses on agriculture and allied activities are also arranged.

9. Punjab has the most hard-working and intelligent farming population in the country which has a 'rare' and 'aggressive' courage to better its living conditions. Other dynamic factors of the farming population of Punjab, according to Biplab Das Gupta, are (i) high propensity of the population to migrate in search of more income and profits and their tendency to remit substantial amounts of money to their family members in the villages to purchase land and machinery; (ii) "the long tradition of Punjabi village folk of work in the army, which again creates the opportunity for saving and remitting it back to the village for buying machinery"; (iii) the regular contact of the persons living abroad and/or in the army with their village folk back at home widens the horizons of outlook of the latter and makes them aspire for a better life; and (iv) the technological awareness promoted by these and other factors (such as working in transport trade in other States) "is also an important factor both in the adoption of farm machinery and in the growth of their servicing industries".

The other seats of the green revolution, viz. Haryana and western Uttar Pradesh, also had many of these advantages and their success can also be explained in terms of "the high share of owner-occupier holdings, the development of credit and irrigation facilities, and the presence of an enterprising group of rich farmers with a background in the army or outside the state with a high propensity to save and invest in productive farm assets".[34] Thus, in Haryana 43% of the net sown area had irrigation facilities (against the national average of 20%), per hectare consumption of fertilizers was 19.0 kg in 1972-73 against the national of average of 16.5, and plant protection measures covered 36% of the area against the national average of 21.0%. Because of the large size of holdings and availability of irrigation facilities, mechanization has shown rapid progress.

The coverage under HYVP was 1.89 million hectares in 1966-67 which rose to 22.09 million hectares in 1972-73 and to 38.38 million hectares in 1979-80. Even then, the HYV area was only 23.7% of the total cropped area in 1979-80. Naturally, the benefits of the new technology remained concentrated in this area only. What is more, as already pointed out, the green revolution remained limited to wheat which means, in other words, that the benefits of the green revolution were actually concentrated in the 15.03 million hectares of the area under wheat where HYVs were practised in 1979-80. Thus, out of the total area of 38.38 million hectars under HYVP in 1979-80, at the most, only 15.03 million hectares can be taken to have benefited from the new technology. Even within this area, the benefits could accrue to only those regions that had assured water supply because the success of the new technology depended on proper irrigation facilities. Consequently, the so-called structural change induced by the new technology, as mentioned by A.S. Kahlon, A.M. Khusro, and others (discussed above), also remained confined to some specific areas only. Again, within the regions adopting the new strategy the major part of the gains have gone to the privileged section of farmers who were in a position to 'afford' the new strategy which was a package programme involving the use of high-yielding seeds in combination with other inputs such as irrigation, fertilizers, pesticides, insecticides, and improved implements.

The new technology calls for substantial investments that are generally beyond the means of the majority of this country's small and marginal farmers. Some observers have ventured to prove that the new technology is size-neutral. Even if one accepts this view, it has to be emphasized that the new technology is not resource-neutral. Size-neutrality does not imply resource-neutrality. It is basically on account of the non-availability of resources that in many HYV areas small and marginal farmers have failed to implement the new technology while large and medium farmers accepted it on a large scale. Thus, disparities in the regions adopting the HYVP have increased.

In a sample study to examine the trend in the spread of the HYVP for wheat and paddy for the period 1971-72 to 1974-75 and to assess the adequacy and timely availability of various inputs, the programme Evaluation Organisation of the Planning Commission found that in many areas included in the study, small and marginal farmers could not adopt the new strategy.[35] In both the districts (Ludhiana and Amritsar) included in the study in Punjab, there were some initial problems for small and marginal farmers and therefore their participation in the HYVP was low. However, this phase existed for a very short period and by 1969-70 virtually all farmers were participants. In the Khalilabad block of the Basti district in 1969-70, the majority of marginal farmers (in the 0-1 hectare group) were non-participants but later on practically all of them adopted the new varieties. In the Basti blocks and Muzaffarnagar also, a number of small and marginal farmers remained non-participants for a considerable time. In Sitapur, the non-participants were concentrated in the 0-1 hectare group. The report notes, "Amongst those blocks and districts where participation was not complete by 1974-75, non-participants were completely concentrated in the 0-1 hectare group. In Gaya blocks there was a large proportion of cultivators and non-participants in this group. In the case of Obra block (Gaya) this was significant as the proportion of non-participants with 0-1 hectare was high (63%)".[36] In Hissar, even by 1974-75 few were participating with holdings below 4 hectares. In the Sonepat block, participation amongst the smallest size group was quite high by 1969-70 but in the next five years most persons in the 0-1 hectare group left the programme while the numbers in the 8-20 hectare group increased, 'again indicating a positive association with holding sizes'.

As far as the paddy areas are concerned, the report notes that the smaller the size of holding, the greater are the constraints in adopting the HYVs in early years. Participation of small and marginal farmers has continued to be low. According to the report, "The significance of low participation in paddy blocks is underlined by the façt that first, in 15 of the 27 blocks in 1974-75 cultivators in the 0-1 hectare group comprised more than 50 percent of the total cultivator population and range upto 83 percent. Secondly, out of all non-participants in each of the 27 blocks, 60 to 100 percent were in the 0-1 hectare group in 18 blocks in 1974-75. In the selected blocks as a whole, 51 percent of cultivators were in the 0-1 hectare group and almost two-thirds were non-participants. A further 20 percent were non-paticipants in 1-2 hectare group, thus giving a total of 85 percent of non-participants in the lowest two size-groups."[37]

These results are not unexpected. Since the small and marginal farmers do not have sufficient resources, they are generally not in a position to participate in the HYVP. Thus, while the HYVP has increased disparities among regions, it has also increased disparities within regions adopting the new strategy. The new technology accordingly has to face two criticisms. First, it has aided the emergence of two rural Indias: one that is irrigated, progressive and prospering, and the other that is dry, stagnant, and poor and inhabited by millions of small and marginal farmers. It may interest the reader to note that in June 1971 the average assets per cultivator household in Punjab were Rs.62,789 and in Haryana Rs.41,825. The third and the fourth States of Himachal Pradesh and Gujarat with average assets per cultivator at Rs.24,107 and Rs.18,502 respectively were far behind. The all-India average was at Rs.14,627 only. The contribution of the new strategy in increasing disparities is evident from the fact that while the average assets of the cultivator household in composite Punjab (Punjab and Haryana) at Rs.15,053 in December 1961 were 2.25 times the all-India average of Rs.6,696, the average assets of the cultivator household in Punjab and Haryana in June 1971 were respectively 4.29 times and 2.86 times the all-India average.[38]

The second criticism against the new technology is that within the regions adopting it, participation among the medium and large farmers has been much greater compared with the participation among the small and marginal farmers. Therefore, a greatar share of the benefits derived from the HYVP have been pocketed by a small section of the privileged farmers. It has been pointed out that under traditional agriculture the small farmer was not much at a disadvantage since productivity per acre was more on small farms. The adoption of the new capital-intensive technology has shifted the advantage of productivity per acre in favour of the big farmers. As opposed to the small farmers, capital is more easily available to the large farmers and they can make a more judicious use of it on account of favourable farm size. Investment in agricultural machinery can be cited as an illustration. Besides, the large farmers have a greater risk-bearing capacity and thus are in a better position to exploit new opportunities. Ranjit Sau[39] has estimated that the adoption of new strategy in traditional irrigated areas increases the total expenses by more than three times per acre of wheat produced. Thus, it seems that the small farmers are at a distinct disadvantage compared with the large farmers in the adoption of the new strategy. This disadvantage is, in turn, reflected in the distribution of benefits from the new technology in the regions that adopted it.

The study of the distribution of benefits can, of course, be conducted at the micro-level only and a number of empirical studies carried out for different regions confirm the assertion that the class of large farmers has benefited the most from the green revolution while the small and marginal farmers and agricultural labourers have lagged far behind. Let us illustrate from the studies of different micro regions to support this contention and consider first of all the study of five IADP districts carried out by Francine R. Frankel.[40] The districts included in the study are Ludhiana (the seat of the green revolution) in Punjab, West Godavari in Andhra Pradesh,

Thanjavur in Tamil Nadu, Palghat in Kerala, and Burdwan in West Bengal. From her study of Ludhiana, Frankel finds that "it appears that most classes of cultivators have made some gains as a result of the green revolution Nevertheless, the benefits have been heavily weighted in favour of the larger farmer (the cultivator with 25 to 30 acres or more). . . . Although 15 to 25 acre farmers have also experienced absolute increases in output and income the gap between the large and medium farmers has undoubtedly widened. Small farmers, those with 10 to 15 acres have so far made only marginal gains, and ultimately they may even find their farm operations over-capitalized and uneconomic. Some farmers with less than 10 acres have experienced an absolute deterioration in their economic position with the increasing difficulty of finding leased land on reasonable terms" (p. 39).

Frankel's study of West Godavari also indicates that the medium holders and large landowners have benefited more from the new strategy. "Over the last few years alone, large farmers estimate that they have doubled their net income" but such gains were not in evidence in the case of small farmers. In Thanjavur the adoption of ADT 27 benefited the largest landowners (those with 30 acres and above) the most in terms of both absolute and relative gains. While the larger farmers increased their income by at least three times, the small farmers report little improvement in real income or standard of living. In Palghat, only 23% of holdings are of the size 10 acres or more and the gains of the new technology have generally accrued to this small minority of farmers. In the case of Burdwan, Frankel notes that "it is only when one comes to the upper one-fourth or one-third of rural families, and these in the irrigated areas of the district that any signs of tangible improvement appear" (p. 173). Though some farmers owning between 3 and 6 acres reported improvement, it was generally in holdings of more than 6 acres that the gains were found. (It may interest the reader to note that more than 50% of the holdings were less than 5 acres in size and thus this large group of landowners was not benefited by green revolution.) The greatest gains have been pocketed by farmers in the large size category, i.e. those with holdings between 12 and 20 acres.

On the basis of the Farm Management Surveys, P.K. Bardhan and G.R. Saini[41] have studied disparities in farm business income. Bardhan has studied four districts—Ferozepore (in Punjab), Muzaffarnagar (in western Uttar Pradesh), Hooghly (in West Bengal), and Ahmadnagar (in Maharashtra). G.R. Saini has studied two districts—Ferozepore and Muzaffarnagar. Bardhan notes that as a consequence of the new technology, farm business income (at currrent prices) has registered remarkable increases in all the four districts but the matter for concern is that inequalities have also increased. Bardhan's analysis reveals that of the four districts studied concentration ratio of farm business income has registered increase in three districts. In Ferozepore it increased from 0.45688 in 1956-57 to 0.47605 in 1969-70, in Hooghly it increased from 0.55188 in 1956-57 to 0.59766 in 1970-71, and in Ahmadnagar from 0.53198 to 0.63847 during the same period. Only in the case of Muzaffarnagar the concentration ratio of farm business income fell from 0.44857 in 1956-57 to 0.38673 in 1968-69. Thus, Bardhan's analysis reveals that except in the case of Muzaffarnagar, inequalities in the other three districts have increased.

To explain the results obtained from Muzaffarnagar, Bardhan sets up the hypothesis that the base year might be an 'abnormal year'. To take account of this possibility, Saini in his study takes averages of two years—1955-56 and 1956-57. His study shows that the Lorenz ratio/specific concentration coefficient for land fell from 0.3421 in 1955-57 to 0.3365 in 1967-69 for Ferozepore and from 0.3878 to 0.3617 in Muzaffarnagar during the same period. On the other hand, the Lorenz ratio for farm business income recorded an increase in both the districts from 0.2901 to 0.3767 in Ferozepore and from 0.3495 to 0.3512 in Muzaffarnagar during the period 1955-57 to 1967-69. Thus, inequalities in farm income have increased in both the districts and this despite the fact that in both these districts distribution of land had become slightly more equal as would be clear from the above. Thus, Saini concludes that the fate of the small farmers in Muzaffarnagar has not been different from that of their counterparts in the Ferozepore district though increase in inequality has been markedly less in this case. Saini points out that this may be due to the presence (and relatively more important position) of sugarcane in the cropping pattern of that region.

Coming to the fate of the agricultural labourers, Frankel finds that the green revolution has benefited the agricultural workers in Ludhiana and West Godavari while the lot of the workers in the other three districts has not improved and might have even deteriorated in some cases. In Ludhiana, the landless labourers now find work all the year round and their wages have doubled.[42] Similar is the case in West Godavari. In Thanjavur, on the other hand, wage rates have remained frozen at the same level for the past several years. In Palghat also the fate of the majority of the landless labourers has been the same. In fact, in the face of rising prices their standard of living might have actually deteriorated. In Burdwan, permanent labourers are divided into two categories—*mahinders* and *nagare*, and both the categories report either no improvement or deterioration in their economic condition. As far as casual labour is concerned, "there has been little change in wage rates over the last few years" (p. 176).

In his pioneering study "Green Revolution and Agricultural Labourers"[43] Pranab Bardhan reaches the conclusion that, on the whole, green revolution has not led to any improvement in the condition of agricultural labourers. His study of the data in *Agricultural Wages in India* for Punjab and Haryana reveals that the average real wage has slightly declined. The Farm Management Surveys for Ferozepore and Muzaffarnagar also reveal similar trends. In Muzaffarnagar out of the eight villages studied, decline in the average *real* wage rate was in evidence in seven villages, Gagore being the exception. Despite the progress registered under the green revolution, the average *real* wage rate remained nearly constant in western U.P. Kerala emerges as an exception in Bardhan's study which shows a 'considerable rise in the real wage rate'. In his later study[44] Bardhan find more or less the same trends to continue.

On the basis of the NSS data for three years—1956-57, 1964-65, and 1970-71—Deepak Lal[45] seeks to disprove Bardhan's thesis. He finds that the real wages of agricultural labourers increased in all States except one or two over the period 1956-57 to 1970-71. The best performance seems to be of Uttar Pradesh where, according to him, the index of real wage rates rose from 100 in 1956-57 to 110 in 1964-65 and to 175 in 1970-71. Rohini Nayyar[46] criticises the use of the NSS data by Deepak Lal which is available for the years 1956-57, 1964-65, and 1970-71 only, thus entirely missing the yearly variations in the wage rates of the agricultural workers. On the basis of a more reliable data source, she successfully refutes Deepak Lal's thesis that the wages of agricultural labourers have increased in Uttar Pradesh. Bringing up her analysis to 1973-74 she finds that in western Uttar Pradesh the real wages show no tendency to rise. In fact, after 1970-71 they declined steadily (from Rs.1.62 per day in 1970-71 to Rs.1.47 in 1972-73 and further to Rs.1.31 in 1973-74). For U.P. as a whole, the real wage rate was Rs.0.95 in 1957-58, which happened to be the rate in 1973-74 as well.

These observations gleaned from various micro studies bring out the fact that the small and marginal farmers (and in some cases the agricultural labourers) have benefited from the green revolution to a very limited extent and the major part of the benefits has gone to the large farmers. If one remembers the fact that approximately 70.7% of the cultivator-households had less than 5 acres of land in 1971[47] (and can be termed small and marginal farmers), it will be evident that the majority of the rural population failed to benefit from the new technology. It has also to be pointed out that a major part of the benefits of the green revolution were obtained by cultivators whose size of holding was more than 10 acres. Since this section of the cultivators accounted for only 13.1% of the total cultivator-households, the benefits of new technology got concentrated in the hands of this small section of rural population only.

Obviously the difficulties of the small and marginal farmers could have been mitigated to a large extent had the cooperative credit institutions directed their resources to help them. Timely financial assistance could have helped the small and marginal farmers in purchasing the HYV seeds, fertilizers, and other inputs. However, this was not to be. The large farmers have continued to obtain the major chunk of the cooperative credit. In 1974-75, only 28% of the small- and medium-term loans were advanced to farmers with holdings up to 2 hectares. The long-term credit provided by the land development banks to this category of farmers was 32%. Thus, approximately 70% of the farmers could manage to get even less than 30% of the credit from the cooperatives. Similarly, a major part of the term loans from both the public sector and the private sector banks went to the large farmers. Thus, in 1973-74, 62.29% of the term loans from public sector banks and 77.29% of such loans from the private sector banks went to farmers having an average size of holding of more than 10 acres.[48]

The report of the Programme Evaluation Organisation (mentioned above) also noted similar trends. In all wheat areas included under the study (except Ludhiana and Muzaffarnagar) the small and marginal farmers faced problems in obtaining institutional credit. "The farmers in the districts of Hissar, Rohtak and Basti had frequently to resort to private money-lenders (and big landlords who were displacing the moneylenders, in recent years, as a source of credit for tenants and share croppers etc.), with rates of interest varying from 18 to 40 per cent. In some of the districts viz. Amritsar, Gaya and Basti, a number of cooperative societies were defunct, on account of accumulation of heavy overdues."[49]

Similar problems existed in paddy areas. The report notes that in Basti, the small farmers were preempted from institutional credit in many instances by the large farmers who dominated these sources. In Shahabad, the small cultivators suffered from lack of credit which reduced the fertilizer dosage. In Burdwan, neglect of the small and marginal farmers by the cooperatives compelled them to continue their dependence on private moneylenders. In Midnapur, Cuttack, West Godavari, and all other areas as well, the large cultivators continued to receive a major part of the advances while the claims of the more needy persons were neglected.[50] The report notes that the cooperatives failed to serve the needs of the small farmers because of the increasing number of defaulters in this class of farmers. This was one of the reasons why a large portion of the advances granted by the cooperative societies went to the large farmers. The cooperatives functioned keeping the general norms of banking and financing in view (viz., creditworthiness, etc.) and thus failed to fulfil the role of a 'development agency'.

As pointed out by C.H. Hanumantha Rao,[51] the new technology was evolved in the developed countries where the prices of fertilizers were declining, capital was abundant, labour was scarce, and land per worker was rising. Obviously, "the accent on the increase in crop yields rather than in cropping intensity suited the factor endowments" of these countries. But, did this accent suit our own factor endowments? In a brilliant article, Arthur Gaiskell[52] warns the developing countries of ignoring their own realities and relying on 'short cuts' by backing the larger farmers to increase food output expecting the benefits to 'seep down to the masses' in the long run. Of course, this policy has many attractive features for it can help achieve the desired growth in output without having to bother about the questions of distribution.

Since it seems that the new agricultural strategy has come to stay as an important plank of overall agricultural strategy, it is necessary to devise supplementary programmes to ensure that the 'distribution aspect' is properly looked after. For example, there is a need for (i) introducing "varietal improvements which may not raise yield per cropped acre but reduce the crop duration significantly" since they can "enable a significant increase in output and employment by facilitating multiple cropping"; (ii) providing 'institutional machinery' to meet the requirements of small farmers, marginal farmers and landless labourers; and (iii) expanding irrigation facilities to as much area as possible and as early as possible. Only 20% of the cropped area has irrigation facilities at present and it is estimated that it is possible to expand irrigated areas by at least 150% at a reasonable cost. In fact, if only this could be achieved agricultural production would register a remarkable increase on the one head, and the rural poor would also share the benefits of progress more equitably on the other.

PROGRAMMES OF RURAL EMPLOYMENT AND DEVELOPMENT OF THE RURAL POOR

As noted in the preceding pages and as pointed out by most of the observers of the Indian rural scene, the programmes of rural development, especially the HYVP benefited mostly the large farmers. The majority of the small and marginal farmers and agricultural labourers did not experience improvement in their economic welfare. Keeping these facts in view and sharing the widespread concern of the public at increasing poverty of the rural poor during the planning period, the Government of India introduced a number of special programmes for the rural poor in the Fourth Plan. The important programmes introduced were: Small Farmers' Development Agency (SFDA), Marginal Farmers' and Agricultural Labourers' Development Agency (MFAL), Drought-Prone Areas Programme (DPAP), Crash Scheme for Rural Employment (CSRE), and Pilot Intensive Rural Employment Project (PIREP). These programmes were meant to cover the small and marginal farmers, agricultural labourers, farmers in chronically drought-prone areas, and rural artisans, etc.

Under the SFDA programme, the Fourth Plan provided for 46 pilot projects throughout the country with a view to covering 50,000 potentially viable farmers with holding between 2.5 and 7.5 acres. Some of the important schemes included under the SFDA were: state help for irrigation purposes, land levelling, soil conservation, better agricultural implements, provision of services on hire, warehousing and marketing facilities, and schemes for the development of related occupations such as dairy development, poultry breeding, piggery development, etc. It was also planned to provide help to the rural artisans under this scheme. The SFDA does not extend credit to the small farmers directly but functions as an agent for stimulating the flow of credit from the existing agencies such as cooperative banks, land development banks, commercial banks, etc. These institutions have been asked to forward to the SFDA the names of the small farmers who have been sanctioned loans. After these names are forwarded, the SFDA office sends to the concerned credit institutions a subsidy equivalent to 25% of the loans sanctioned to the small farmers. This subsidy is distributed by the credit giving institution to the farmers who had been earlier given loans.

A separate agency—MFAL—was created to serve the needs of the marginal farmers (i.e., non-viable small farmers) and agricultural labourers. Farmers with land holdings below the limit prescribed for the small farmers were designated as *marginal farmers*. Under the category of agricultural labour, those rural households that derived more than 50% of their income from agriculture were to be included. However, those identified persons who have a steady off-farm income of Rs.200 or more per month for the family will not be included under any programme of the agency. The rationale for its creation was the same as for the SFDA though in its programme content much more effort was to be made to the provision of supplementary occupations and other employment opportunities. The Draft Fourth Plan had this to say on their scope and modus operandi: "These projects would, as far as possible, be market-based (e.g., centred around towns or other areas of demand) so that there is scope for development of employment-oriented activities, such as poultry and dairy farming. Stress will be laid on using the funds for development of various marketing and processing facilities with a view to giving organised support, preferably through cooperatives to the activities of sub-marginal cultivation and agricultural labourers".[53] A total of 41 projects in different districts all over the country were adopted under the MFAL in the Fourth Plan.

Most of the agencies under the SFDA/MFAL were formed in 1970-71, though the real work of implementation could be taken up only in 1971-72. An outlay of Rs.115 crores was originally earmarked for the SFDA/MFAL programmes for the Fourth Plan in the Draft Paper of that plan. Subsequently, this was revised downwards to Rs.103 crores and Rs.12 crores were diverted for six special projects taken up in predominantly tribal areas. It was expected that Rs.1.5 crores would be granted to each SFDA and Rs.1.0 crore to each MFAL project. As far as the organizational set-up is concerned, the existing developmental machinery and the existing institutional framework were sought to be utilized though a small nucleus staff was to function at the agency headquarters. Therefore, each agency has a small membership consisting mainly of the concerned district officers and representatives of the institutional agencies. The collector or the deputy commissioner acts as the chairman.

The Fifth Plan abolished the distinction between the SFDA and the MFAL and merged them into a single programme. The coverage of this composite programme was extended to 160 projects. A provision of Rs.200 crores was made in the Central plan for the implementation of the programme. This was expected to be supplemented by 'suitable outlays in the State Plans for extension of infrastructural support'. The basic approach in the new projects was to implement crop husbandry programmes such as intensive agriculture, multiple cropping, application of the HYV of seeds, fertilizers, minor irrigation, etc. for the identified participants with special emphasis on dry farming practices and better management techniques. The selection of the new projects had been completed and some of the projects were taken up in 1974-75 while a number of them were taken up in 1975-76. The normal life of a project is five years, with a financial outlay of Rs.1.50 crores. Each project is to be confined to one revenue district and is expected to cover 50,000 beneficiaries. The proportion of the small and marginal farmers in the beneficiaries is to be kept in proportion to their total numerical strength in the project area. Those porjects which had completed the first phase on 31-3-1976 have been allowed to continue for another three years and can cover another 30,000 beneficiaries within a maximum outlay of Rs.1.00 crore for the extended period.

Progress under the Programmes[54]

As in other fields, the official evaluation of the performance of the SFDAs and MFALs has generally run in terms of the quantum of loans disbursed, the number of tubewells/dugwells constructed, the number of pumpsets installed, the quantity of inputs supplied, etc. Up to the end of June 1974, 27.7 lakh small farmers were identified in the 46 SFDA projects and of these 15.4 lakhs were brought into the cooperative fold. A sum of Rs.28.9 crores was released to the agencies (since their inception) up to June 1974 of which actual utilization was Rs.28.0 crores. Under the 41 MFAL projects,

12.9 lakh persons were identified of which 5 lakhs were brought into the cooperative fold till the end of June 1974. The finances released since their inception amounted to Rs.19.6 crores of which Rs.17.2 crores were actually utilized. The total number of tubewells/dugwells constructed till June 1974 under the 87 SFDA and MFAL projects together was 122,252, the number of pumpsets installed was 37,228, the number of milch cattle units set up was 82,035, the number of poultry units set up was 8715, the total number of rural artisans trained was 9150, and the number of labourers employed under rural works was 262,181. The participants identified under the 87 projects received term loans aggregating Rs.70.67 crores. In addition, short-term production loans of Rs.29.64 crores were disbursed by the cooperative and commercial banks during July 1973 to June 1974.

Up to June 1975, 46 new SFDA projects were registered in different States and a sum of Rs.365 lakhs was released to them. Thus, the total number of SFDA/MFAL projects rose to 133 by June 1975 which further increased to 168 by March 1978. The *Report on Currency and Finance* for the year 1979-80 summarizes the progress as shown in Table 7.

Table 7 reveals that by the end of January 1980 the total number of projects under the SFDA and MFAL had risen to 168, the number of participants identified to 165.58 lakhs (of which 71.28 lakhs were brought under the cooperative fold), and the finance released (since inception) to the agencies to Rs.209.53 crores. The number of beneficiaries under minor irrigation had risen to 8.57 lakhs. The total number of milch cattle units, poultry units, and other animal husbandry units had risen to 8.41 lakhs till January 1980 from 7.59 lakhs till March 1979 and 1.95 lakhs till June 1975. The programmes relating to animal husbandry have been geared to benefit the small and marginal farmers and agricultural labourers, "Under the calf-rearing programme subsidy is provided at the rate of 50% of the feeding cost for small/marginal farmers and 66% for agricultural labourers. Programmes for poultry, piggery and sheep rearing envisage subsidy at the rate of 25% for small farmers and 32% for marginal farmers and agricultural labourers." Some other facilities extended by the SFDA include: (i) encouraging small farmers to sink wells and install pumpsets either individually or on a group basis by subsidizing capital cost by 25%, (ii) writing off the entire cost in case of failure to strike water, (iii) where there is scope for a community well, the small farmers coming in the command area of the well have been subsidized to the extent of 50% of the capital cost; other capital cost on land, such as levelling, is subsidized to the extent of 25%, (iv) provision of custom service on a priority basis by the Agro-Industries Corporation to small farmers at a subsidized rate of 25%, and (v) provision of assistance to cooperative institutions in the form of (a) risk fund, (b) grant for supervisory staff, and (c) finance to improve the share capital

TABLE 7: **Progress under SFDA and MFAL projects (combined)**

Item	Progress up to		
	June 1975	March 1979	January 1980
1. No. of project areas	133	168	168
2. No. of participants identified (in lakhs)	47.56	163.23	165.58
3. No. enrolled as members of cooperatives (in lakhs)	24.05	70.32	71.28
4. Finance released (since inception) to the agencies (Rs. in crores)	65.23	198.39	209.53
5. Funds utilized (Rs. in crores)	61.85	196.33	215.72
6. Physical results			
(i) No. of beneficiaries under minor irrigation (in lakhs)	2.41	7.96	8.57
(ii) Milch cattle (in lakhs)	1.21	5.12	
(iii) Poultry (in lakhs)	0.16	0.19	8.41*
(iv) Other animal husbandry (in lakhs)	0.58	2.20	
(v) Improved agriculture (in lakhs)		55.35	59.68

*Sum of items 6 (ii), (iii) and (iv).

Source: Reserve Bank of India, *Report on Currency and Finance, 1979-80*, Vol, I, Table III.11, p. 30.

position.[55]

The results of physical performance are indeed impressive. But the basic thing is to find out who the actual beneficiaries of the schemes are. A study conducted by the Division of Rural Surveys of the RBI for the year 1972-73 and relating to 13 SFDAs pointed out that it was the relatively better-off section of the farmers that got the benefits of the operation of these agencies. Thus, the study reported that in all but three agencies studied the tenant-cultivators had been altogether kept out. The two basic reasons for excluding them were: (i) the fear of strong opposition from the landlords and landowners; and (ii) "the majority of tenants were oral lessees where tenancy arrangements were concealed".[56] What is more important is the fact that even the three agencies which did not completely ignore the tenant small farmers could include only those with recorded cultivation rights and left out the oral lessees and share-croppers. Undoubtedly in doing so the agencies were trying to be "practical", but in the process they left out lage numbers of small farmers who were tenants and who deserved every incentive.

There is evidence to prove that a large number of farmers who are taking advantage of the schemes are by no means small farmers. This tendency has been noted by the RBI report mentioned above. It states that "in almost all the agencies, the land owned/cultivated by the farmers in a village other than that in which they resided was not generally taken into account". Thus, a large landlord of a particular village could pass off as a small or even as a marginal farmer in a neighbouring village. Examining the working of the SFDA in the Ambala district of Haryana, H. Laxminarayan[57] notes that a number of large farmers took advantage of the schemes by claiming themselves as small farmers. For the purpose of analysis, Laxminarayan took a sample of 75 households from amongst the small farmers who had received tubewell loans. But, out of these, as many as 50 households had to be dropped because a large number of them were cultivating more than 7.5 acres. Then, "many other households had to be dropped because, though they own less than 7.5 acres they have larger cultivation holdings as they have taken considerable land on lease". The Ambala SFDA has also a programme of giving subsidies to the small farmers for dairy development programme. But this loan is given to only those farmers who are members of the milk producing cooperatives. Also, "out of nearly 60 'small' farmers who have taken loans for buying of buffaloes, only 20 own and cultivate holdings below 7.5 acres. The remaining 40 cultivate larger holding as they have taken land on lease."

A study of the MFAL programme in rural Delhi was conducted during 1975-76 by S.M. Pandey and J.S. Sodhi.[58] Their study notes that though the scheme was meant to cover farmers with holdings less than 2.50 acres, many 'marginal' farmers were actually found to possess cultivated holdings of more than 2.50 acres. According to the report, such mistakes occur basically because no attempt is made to collect fresh and uptodate land records. Thus, a large number of tenant-farmers could not be enrolled as potential beneficiaries in the category of marginal farmers though they had a strong case for inclusion in the programme. Whereas, on the one hand, such valid and desirable cases were excluded from the programme, on the other, a number of farmers belonging to the upper category posed themselves as marginal farmers and cornered the benefits.

There is another aspect of the problem that is revealed by a study conducted by Mahendra D. Desai on the working of the SFDA programme in the Surat district.[59] The thirteen talukas of the Surat district are classified into 'advanced', 'average', and 'backward' according to the level of agricultural development attained by them. The proportion of small and marginal farmers as on 31 August 1973 together in the three groups of talukas was: advanced 24.6%, average 27.9%, and backward 47.5%. Desai's study indicates that during the period June 1971 to March 1972, only 26.62% of the financial expenditure was incurred in the backward talukas while 39.88% was incurred in the advanced talukas and 33.50% in the average talukas. The share of the backward talukas was satisfactory in the case of marketing and storage and rural artisans. In all other fields, the share of the backward talukas was much less than desirable. This is especially true for expenditure on agriculture where only 16.37% went to the backward talukas and 51.25% went to the advanced talukas. This experience of the working of the SFDA in the Surat district suggests that "the strategy devised by the Agency for small and marginal farmers in the district is such that such farmers in the relatively backward areas would not be able to benefit much in the short run, whereas such farmers in the relatively better-off areas would benefit substantially from the programme in the short run".

Since detailed evaluation studies of all the SFDA/MFAL agencies are not available, it is not possible to generalize from these observations. Yet given the present organizational set-up and the responsibility conferred on the existing institutions to carry out the programme, nothing much different is expected in the case of other projects. As noted in the context of cooperation and community development, the richer sections of the rural society have gained ascendancy in all matters of rural policy and practically control the reins of rural economy. In such circumstances it is not unexpected to find that all programmes operated through the existing institutional set-up are geared to help the rural rich. Programmes such as the SFDA, MFAL, etc., have no chance of success unless a radical change is brought about in the existing rural institutions and the attitude of hostility towards the small, resourceless man is radically altered.

In addition to all these considerations, one must also not forget that the *imposition* of all schemes on the same existing institutions and staff has overburdened them and has thus created an attitude of apathy and indifference in them. The study of the MFALDA in rural Delhi, referred to above, points to this tendency. Almost all the agency officials contacted in the study opined that they were overburdened with work and found it difficult to effectively implement the various programmes. Thus, the project officer, MFAL, was also in charge of the IADP and the Multiple Cropping Programme. The manager of the cooperative society, the BDO, the extension staff, all viewed the MFAL as additional burden without any incentive. Probably all of them feel that the MFAL work is not their responsibility. Also, as noted in the report, "the reported absence of any financial or non-financial incentives to extension staff at block and village levels might have induced them to accept gratifications from beneficiaries as was alleged by some of them". These factors considerably eroded the credibility of these agencies.

Drought-Prone Areas Programme

The object of this programme is to create permanent works which will mitigate the effects of drought when it occurs and at the same time provide employment to the rural households. Initially the scheme was concerned with rural works and employment generation. Subsequently, its scope was enlarged since it was thought that a mere rural works programme would not help towards solving the problems of these areas and in mitigating drought conditions. The programme was oriented on an *area approach* and was given the name of Drought-Prone Areas Programme at the time of the Mid-term Appraisal of the Fourth Plan. In January 1973 it was decided that funds under the programme would not be restricted to the four fields of minor and medium irrigation, afforestation and soil conservation, road and drinking water supply, but would also be available for cattle development, animal husbandry, dairying, etc., "which are highly relevant to the land and water resources situation in most of the drought prone areas".

During the Fourth Plan, an outlay of about Rs.112 crores was sanctioned for the implementation of the plans. Of this, nearly 54% was allocated for irrigation works, 24% for road construction, approximately 17% for soil conservation and afforestation, and the residual for drinking water and miscellaneous works.

The Draft Fifth Plan explained the necessity of the Drought-Prone Areas Programme on, at least, three counts: (i) the drought-prone areas account for a considerable proportion of the area and population of the country (19% of the total area and 12% of the total population), (ii) the drought-prone areas are a major factor contributing to regional imbalances in the country for their overall productivity continues to be very low, and (iii) these areas remain a "continuing source of strain" on the financial resources of the nation. Keeping these considerations in view, the Draft Fifth Plan aimed at the restoration of ecological balance and stable growth in the drought-prone areas through optimal utilization of land, water, and human resources. Some of the important elements of this strategy were:

(i) Development and management of irrigation resources;
(ii) Soil and moisture conservation and afforestation;
(iii) Restructuring of cropping pattern and pasture development;
(iv) Changes in agronomic practice;

(v) Livestock development; and

(vi) Development of small and marginal farmers and agricultural labour.[60]

The DPAP lays considerable emphasis on the 'total approach to development' and long-term strategy of development and is therefore a truly comprehensive plan. It emphasizes a *total* and *interlinked* development effort simultaneously on a number of fronts so that the achievements are more enduring and permanent. Thus, the DPAP ensures a continuity in planning efforts. This is in contrast to the schemes of the CSRE type (discussed later on in this chapter) where it is not known what will be the fate of those persons who are provided employment under them once these programmes are withdrawn after the completion period. The unit for the purpose of the project formulation under the DPAP is the district. Even when the area under the DPAP is only a portion of the district, the resource endowment situation for the entire district is to be assessed so that proper integration of the plan with the general plan can be done. Since the strategy of integrated agricultural development in drought prone areas concerns not one department but at least five departments, viz., agriculture, irrigation, animal husbandry, forestry, and cooperation, there is a danger that the DPAP 'may flounder on the rock of departmentalism'. Consequently, the Fifth Plan suggested that a coordinating corporate body should be formed with the responsibility of designing, coordinating, and catalysing a programme of integrated development in each drought-prone district. Such a body would have the requisite financial and operational flexibility and would be able to utilize effectively the facilities and the manpower of various development departments operating in the district. It would be so patterned that it is able to directly undertake some activities, particularly land development.

Appraisal of DPAP. The programme is in operation in 557 blocks spread over 74 districts in 13 States. The State-wise distribution of districts covered is as follows: Andhra Pradesh (7); Bihar (4); Gujarat (10); Haryana (3); Jammu & Kashmir (2); Karnataka (10); Madhya Pradesh (6); Maharashtra (6); Orissa (2); Rajasthan (13); Tamil Nadu (2); Uttar Pradesh (6); and West Bengal (3). The programme covers 6 crore people and 5.65 lakh km^2 area. The expenditure under the programme was Rs.92 crores in the Fourth Plan which resulted in the generation of employment of the order of 1500 lakh mandays, provided about 1.54 lakh hectares with irrigation, covered about 46 lakh hectares under soil conservation measures and afforestation. Nine thousand kilometres of roads were also constructed.

Since its inception up to March 1980 a total expenditure of Rs.426 crores was incurred on this programme. Under this programme up to December 1979, 13.30 lakh hectares of land was treated with soil and moisture conservation measures, irrigation potential of 2.72 lakh hectares created, afforestation and pasture development taken up on 4.77 lakh hectares, and 72,000 milch animals distributed to individual beneficiaries.[61]

A number of deficiencies in the DPAP have been pointed out. As noted in the case of the SFDA and MFAL, it has been observed that in the DPAP also the benefits have not accrued to the section of the population whose needs are the greatest. Thus, in the case of some projects, small and marginal farmers and agricultural labourers have not benefited from the programme. Then, in some project areas there were delays in the implementation due to the non-availability of personnel and their frequent transfers. Though the DPAP was expected to be a comprehensive programme wherein all programmes operating in the district would be coordinated and complementarity with the State plan would be ensured, this has not happened in practice. In the absence of such coordination, 'pooling of investible funds and plan of action has not been done' resulting in duplication of efforts, waste of time and resources, and confusion among the programme execution authorities. The lack of expertise in plan formulation, absence of knowledge about the potential areas of development, and sectoral push and pulls are some of the other factors that have created problems.

Programmes for Rural Employment

No precise estimates of rural unemployment are available in India. This is because of the fact that the labour supply available for productive activity is of an 'extremely heterogeneous character' and a significant proportion of the rural labour is self-employed of which a considerable number works as unpaid family labour in household enterprises. Accordingly, the estimates of rural unemployment considerably differ from one another. Then, there is the problem of estimating the number of the underemployed people because their problems are no less acute than the unemployed people. However, all estimates are agreed on the point that there is a considerable number of unemployed and underemployed people in India and their number is constantly on the increase. The Committee on Unemployment (Bhagwati Committee), 1973, used the 19th round NSS to estimate rural unemployment in India. Its estimate for rural unemployment in India for 1969 stood at 9.12 million man-years including 7.82 million as totally uemployed (a man-year was taken as 273 man-days). According to Raj Krishna, the number of totally unemployed persons plus underemployed available for additional work was 29.29 million in India in 1971. Of this, 26.22 million (i.e. 89.4%) were found in rural areas alone. The number of totally unemployed people was 9.25 million of which 8.26 million (89.3%) were found in rural areas alone.[62]

With a view to providing employment to this large mass of unemploped people, the Government of India has introduced various rural employment schemes from time to time. A start was made in the Third Plan when a Rural Works Programme (RWP) was initiated. This programme was expected to provide work for an average of, say, 100 days in a year for about 2.5 million persons, and if possible. more. It was expected to involve an outlay of Rs.150 crores over the plan period and was envisaged to cover the following five categories of works:

(i) Works projects included in the plans of states and local bodies which involve the use of unskilled and semi-skilled labour;
(ii) Works undertaken by the community or by the beneficiaries in accordance with the obligations laid down by law;
(iii) Development works towards which local people contribute labour while some measure of assistance is given by Government;
(iv) Schemes to enable village communities to build up remunerative assets; and
(v) Supplementary works programmes to be organised in areas in which there is high incidence of unemployment.[63]

A scheme of pilot projects for works programmes was initiated as the first step and 32 pilot projects were taken up in hand. These projects included schemes for irrigation, afforestation, soil conservation, drainage, land reclamation, and improvement of communications. In the programme of construction of roads, preference was to be given to roads which connected villages with market centres. However, on account of its ad hoc nature, the programme of rural works failed to make any impact on rural unemployment. Therefore, in April 1971, a new scheme for providing employment was introduced under the name of Crash Scheme for Rural Employment (popularly known as CSRE). The programme was introduced in almost all districts with an annual outlay of Rs.50 crores initially for a three-year period (i.e., up to March 1974). The scheme had a two-fold purpose: (i) generating employment for 1,000 persons on average per year in every district, and (ii) production of assets of a durable nature in consonance with the local development plans.

The scheme envisages that if a year is taken as consisting of 10 working months and a month as consisting of 25 working days, on average 2.50

lakh man-days of employment will be created in every district. The second objective is meant to ensure that all-round development of the district is assisted through the execution of the projects which are basically labour-intensive. The works undertaken under the scheme were to be such as would be completed within two working seasons. To avoid the undertaking of schemes which in their size were too small to be really worthwhile, and which would only create problem of adequate supervision, it was laid down that the minimum size of a project should be such that it could employ at least 50 persons continuously for a period of 15 weeks. This was in modification of an earlier guideline which had laid down that the minimum size of a project should be such as involving an outlay of Rs.5000. The change was obviously meant to link up the programmes with the creation of rural employment.

In the directives given, it was stated that the selected rural work should be located in those areas of each district (i) where other special programmes (such as the SFDA, MFAL, DPAP etc.) were not in operation, (ii) where the percentage of landless labour and incidence of unemployment was quite high, and (iii) which were relatively less developed.

A special rural employment programme was launched by Maharashtra in May 1971. This was known as the "Employment Guarantee Scheme". The objective of the scheme was to provide gainful and productive employment to all such rural people who were able and willing to work in manual and unskilled jobs through employment on rural works programme. The scheme guaranteed jobs to all those who demanded and got themselves registered at the place of registration or at the work site within 15 days. Up to 15 June 1972, 254 works—roads, percolation tanks, soil conservation, etc.—were sanctioned in 16 districts of the State. The programme faced some rough weather in the initial period and out of 244 works (for which information was collected), Dantwala reports, 81 works were sanctioned but not started while 97 were started but discontinued. About half the persons who had registered were either covered under the scarcity programme or offered employment under the scheme. Only about one-tenth of the people who were offered jobs accepted them—the remaining nine-tenths did not even accept the job. Half of the workers who joined the work discontinued it, 80% on their own accord. This lack of response was accounted for by the low level of wages (generally less than Rs.2.00 per day), distance from the place of residence, and unsuitability of the type of work.[64]

In the year 1973-74, 14.80 lakh persons registered themselves under EGS. However, the scheme made a real start only in 1974-75. In six years, from 1974-75 to 1979-80, expenditure under the programme rose from Rs.14 crore to over Rs.71 crore. The average labour attendance under the programme grew from 3.31 lakhs in 1975-76 to 6.60 lakhs in 1979-80 and man-days of employment provided increased from 11 crores to 22 crores in the same period. In 1974-75, 3000 works came under the EGS. In 1979-80 their number had gone up to 11,000.[65]

The success of the EGS in providing employment has prompted many to advocate it as a model for special rural public works programmes for other States in the country. The Karnataka government sanctioned an Employment Affirmation Scheme (EAS) in November 1978. The scope of the scheme is restricted to 100 days of employment guarantee during the slack agricultural season every year in rural areas (against the EGS which guarantees employment to all the rural people round the year). The scheme was launched in 45 talukas, to begin with, on 1 March 1979. The wage rate under the EAS was Rs.4 per day up to May 1980 and Rs.5 per day afterwards.[66]

In view of the new employment generating programmes such as the SFDA, MFAL, etc., the CSRE was virtually dropped and a Pilot Intensive Rural Employment Project (PIREP) was initiated in 15 blocks of the major States for an initial period of three years in October 1975. This project was an *action-cum-study* project implemented with a view to knowing fully the problems involved in coping with the problem of unemployment and thus enabling the government to draw useful plans for the future. The PIREP was selected after taking into account all existing programmes that were being implemented in the block under different schemes. After considering the total employment provided (or likely to be provided) by all such schemes, the PIREP planned to make available employment for the remaining number of unutilized mandays in projects such as construction of drinking water wells, school buildings, houses, etc. The scheme was expected to impart new skills to the workers, help them in finding regular employment in the secondary and tertiary sectors, and help in integrating the rural works programme with other development programmes.

During the first year of the implementation of the scheme, i.e. from October 1972 to October 1973, Rs.155 lakhs were released of which Rs.118.31 lakhs were spent. The corresponding figures for the next year were Rs.240.85 lakhs and Rs.214.44 lakhs respectively. A number of schemes were taken up in the 15 States that undertook the implementation of the programme. These included construction of roads, minor irrigation, programmes of soil conservation and afforestation, drinking water schemes, construction of school buildings, etc. The maximum expenditure was on construction of roads (the expenditure on this programme being 54.3% in 1972-73 and 61.7% in 1973-74) followed by minor irrigation works (expenditure being 19.5% in 1972-73 and 17.2% in 1973-74). During the first year, 33.70 lakh man-days of employment were generated and during the second year 49.29 lakh man-days of employment was generated.

A Food-for-Work Programme (FWP) was introduced in 1976-77 to tackle the problem of rural unemployment through a programme of infrastructural development and creation of community assets in rural areas to provide additional employment opportunities to the rural unemployed/underemployed with wages wholly or partly paid in foodgrains.[67] In 1977-78, 2.04 lakh tonnes of wheat were allocated to the States under the FWP, but only 1.27 lakh tonnes were actually utilized. The programme really took off in 1978-79 when 12 lakh tonnes were utilized. In that year, the FWP provided 2864 lakh man-days of employment—the equivalent of a year's employment for one million people.[68] During 1979-80, approximately 25 lakh tonnes of foodgrains were distributed under this programme and a total additional employment to the tune of nearly 100 crore man-days was generated.

The Food-for-Work Programme has now been redesignated as the National Rural Employment Programme (NREP) and an outlay of Rs.340 crores provided for it in 1980-81 to generate employment of an order of 850-900 million man-days.

AN INTEGRATED APPROACH TO RURAL DEVELOPMENT

We have discussed in this chapter some of the schemes and plans adopted for developing the rural areas during the planning period. Most of these plans have had only a marginal success because of their ad hoc character and because they were conceived in isolation. On account of these factors, they remained poorly formulated and haphazardly implemented. The grand exception to this general rule was of course the community development programme which was very comprehensive in nature and had the object of transforming the whole rural life. It included various programmes of minor irrigation, soil conservation, distribution of agricultural inputs, promotion of animal husbandry, dairying, cottage and small industries, programmes for the construction of roads, school buildings, etc., and programmes for ensuring adequate supply of drinking water to rural people, and development of cooperatives. We have already noted the various shortcomings and defects of this programme. It was a *comprehensive* but not an *integrated* plan of development. It tried to do everything whereas in an integrated plan the basic emphasis is not on *doing everything* but doing whatever is to be done in a most *effective* manner so that maximum linkages in the production process can be exploited to the maximum advantage. An integrated plan has to take into accout the following factors: (i) what are the projects that are *interlinked* to each other in the area of planning under consideration and what are the activities that are 'basic' and/or 'catalystic'?,[69] and (ii) where should the selected projects be located in the given physical space? These questions can be answered only in the overall context of a regional plan; sectoral planning alone can be of no avail. Since the CD plan was implemented in the framework of sectoral plans only wherein these questions were not even raised, let alone tackled satisfactorily, it cannot be regarded an integrated plan.

Once we talk of tracing interlinked projects and finding *appropriate* location for them, we necessarily emphasize the idea of *selectivity*. On this count, we have the support of all location theorists. Thus, Weber, Christaller, Losch and other location theorists are agreed on the basic fact that each and every settlement cannot have each and every function and that there is a hierarchy of settlements based on the number of functions of different orders and specialization and also on the basis of the area served by a settlement. It is, therefore, necessary to find out the functions that are central to each settlement and the means through which these functions are linked to functions in other settlements. Such a study should be based on both the *existing* and the *potential* linkages and should be followed by a selective location of appropriate functions in different settlements.

The concept of rural growth centre is latent in the statement made above that integrated development is possible 'only in the overall context of a regional plan'. Let us see how. We all know that a single village constitutes an inefficient unit of planning because of the sheer smallness of size. Considered in isolation it cannot make available the necessary social services or the basic facilities required to ensure a tolerable level of existence to its inhabitants. This is borne out by the fact that villages are generally linked up with one another through a series of linkages which are mostly functional and are reflected by the frequency of trips people of a certain village make to other villages or towns. Because of the difficulty in transportation and communication in rural India, such linkages do not generally extend beyond a radius of 10 to 15 km. Within that radius one can discern a common centre around which villages tend to cluster. This common centre is the *central village* which provides certain services to the cluster of villages around it—services that the villages are not able to provide for themselves. Generally, such central villages are, in turn, linked with larger centres called towns or cities which provide higher order services. Such functional linkages can be traced to define a sub-region (or micro region) which will also have a certain focal point. Such a focal point can be called a *service centre* which is of an higher order than the central village and in addition to the services provided by the central village provides a set of more complex services. The service centres (or growth centres) are, in turn, linked to centres of a higher order, and so on. In this way, depending on the functional linkages and the services provided by each centre, a complete hierarchy of human settlements can be defined.

All this is merely to repeat what we have said in Chapter 4 in the sections on central places, growth centres, and growth poles. Yet it has become necessary to repeat it here since, according to regional scientists, planning which takes these functional linkages into account can serve the needs of an area better than such comprehensive programmes as community development which spread scarce resources of an underdeveloped economy thinly over the entire country and, consequently, achieve nothing. The community development programme failed because it was not conceived in functional terms. The blocks were defined keeping administrative considerations in view and economic factors were not considered at all. Block boundaries were arbitrary and block headquarters were frequently not the functional centres of their respective areas. Also, as noted elsewhere in this chapter, since urban areas were specifically excluded from the programme, rural areas were deprived of the growth impulses that towns and cities could generate.

The idea of growth centres is basic to the theory of integrated rural development. Accordingly, the first task of a strategy aiming at integrated rural development should be to specify *the existing and potential linkages*, and with the help of such linkages to *select* areas for investment and development. The development of these areas makes them nuclei of the future economic growth and acts as a powerful stimulant to the development of surrounding areas. Since the market for agricultural products is limited and the bulk of the rural labour are employed in agriculture where they face problems of unemployment and underemployment, it is necessary that adequate attention is paid to the creation of industries at the growth centres. Such industries could be agro-industries, repair workshops, cottage industries, and small-scale industries. They can produce agricultural implements or simply process agricultural raw meterials. As a consequence of these industries it will become possible to tackle the problems of unemployment and underemployment, promote development in the surrounding areas (via the multiplier and accelerator effects), and help in 'cultivating' entrepreneurship within rural areas themselves.

Another programme that will need specific attention in the strategy of integrated rural development is the development of infrastructure. Infrastructure here means transport network and channels of communication. Unless these facilities are provided in an ample measure, the locational utility of the growth centre will remain largely unrealized. Creation of communication channels, especially between the growth centre and the hinterland, is important so that quick diffusion of knowledge of agricultural innovation is ensured. In the absence of such knowledge, the process of 'interdependent growth' of the centre and the surrounding areas will be hampered and full potentialities of the growth centre will not be realized. The Indian farmer is generally charged with traditionalism and apathy to modernization. But it has been observed that he has responded favourably to changes if he is convinced that they aim at his betterment.

INTEGRATED RURAL DEVELOPMENT PROGRAMME (IRDP)—APPROACH OF THE SIXTH PLAN

The Janata government embarked on the integrated rural development programme in 1977, which was to be confined in the initial phase to 2000 out of the 5004 development blocks in the country. The programme was intended to generate gainful employment for all able-bodied persons in rural areas within a period of about ten years by introducing such schemes as would help (1) development of production potential of each area, and utilization and upgrading of the human skills available, and (2) to take up measures of livestock and poultry development, fishery, forestry, and village and cottage industries in order to raise the standard of living of the weaker sections of population, such as landless labourers, artisans, sharecroppers, and marginal and small farmers. The coverage under this programme was 2600 blocks as on 31-3-1980. Till that date 5.3 million families were identified for assistance of which 2 million families have been already given assistance in some form or other.

The IRDP has now been extended to cover all the 5004 blocks in the country. During the Sixth Plan period (1980 to 1985), it aims at assisting on a priority basis, the poorest 3000 families selected per block from "the bottom deciles of the rural population below the poverty line". The main elements of the programme during the Sixth Plan period are proposed to be as under:[70]

1. A five-year development profile will be drawn up for each district, dis-aggregated into blocks, based on practical (achievable) possibilities of development in agriculture and allied sectors. This will form the 'framework of action' for the relevant schemes of development in these sectors.

2. A specific operational programme will be drawn up by the extension agency to provide farm guidance on a systematic basis to the small and marginal farmer families.

3. A special programme of assistance to the poorest of the rural households will be drawn up to raise the specific households, so identified, above the poverty line.

4. A blueprint for exploiting the available potential in the secondary and tertiary sectors, which also spells out linkages for training and marketing, will be prepared for each block and families from among the target group

identified for assistance based on such a blueprint.

5. The IRDP has been conceived essentially as an anti-poverty programme. This objective is proposed to be achieved by enabling the poorest families to acquire productive assets, technology and skills as would make their economic activities viable. These families will also need support from social services such as health, education, and housing. It will be necessary to link to the extent possible the prospective beneficiaries under the IRDP to these social services, particularly programmes such as applied nutrition, compulsory education, adult education, family welfare, children's and women's welfare activities, etc.

As the reader must have noticed, the type of integration that the Sixth Plan seeks to accomplish is not the type of integration we envisage. In fact, the scope and content of the IRDP gives an impression that, at best, it is a modified community development programme oriented towards the objective of providing employment to the unemployed and underemployed people in rural areas. As noted by M.L. Dantwala, "merely packing together of existing sectoral or departmental plans does not automatically make an integrated plan. A plan becomes integrated only when backward and forward linkages are thoroughly analysed and *interlinked* projects in the area of planning are clearly specified."[71] Such an exercise will reveal the *basic* or the *catalystic* activities that need to be developed in the area. Armed with this knowledge, the planner has then to decide where the selected activities have to be precisely located in the area. Such an exercise is highly technical and has to be carried out separately for each district of the country. This requires a competent multidisciplinary planning team at the district level, which unfortunately wo do not have at present. Till such an organization is evolved at the district level and conferred with the task of formulating plans, we cannot have a genuine integrated planning.

NOTES

1. S.N. Bhattacharyya, *Community Development : An analysis of the Programme in India* (Calcutta: Academic Publishers, 1970), p. 3.
2. J. Paul Leagans, "Extension Education for Community Development", *Extension Education in Community Development* (New Delhi: Ministry of Food and Agriculture, Government of India, 1961), p. 5.
3. Planning Commission, Government of India, *Second Five Year Plan*, p. 235.
4. Planning Commission, Government of India, *Third Five Year Plan*, pp. 339-340.
5. National Institute of Community Development, *Report of Syndicate No. 3 on Impact of Community Development on Agricultural Production* (50th Orientation Course, 22-6-1967 to 22-7-1967).
6. National Institute of Community Development, *Report of Syndicate No. 2 on Village*

Level Functionaries (50th Orientation Course, 22-6-1967 to 22-7-1967), Appendix IV.

7. National Institute of Community Development, *Report of Syndicate No. 1 on People's Participation—Panchayati Raj & Community Development* (50th Orientation Course, 22-6-1967 to 22-7-1967).
8. Ibid.
9. John W. Mellor, Thomas F. Weaver, Uma J. Lele and Sheldon R. Simon, *Developing Rural India : Plan and Practice* (Bombay: Lalvani Publishing House, 1972), pp. 37-38.
10. "In an output-oriented scheme again the reporting about work, the proforma, statements and returns that are to be filled very often assume an unduly large proportion of the total work effort. In the absence of more dependable yardsticks of judging work performance, expenditure comes in handy as a basis for measurement of execution of various works programmes. The basic limitations involved in yardsticks of this type are often forgotten with the result that undue emphasis may get placed on *how much* was spent rather how well the amount was spent." J.G. Kunte, "Community Development and Development Administration : Some Reflections", *Community Development and Panchayati Raj Digest*, Vol. 6, July 1974, No. 1, p. 43.
11. Planning Commission, Government of India, *Fourth Five Year Plan*, p. 228.
12. L.K. Sen, *Readings on Micro-Level Planning and Rural Growth Centres* (Hyderabad: National Institute of Community Development, 1972), pp. 31-32.
13. *Second Five Year Plan*, op. cit., pp. 228-229.
14. Planning Commission, Government of India, *Draft Fifth Five Year Plan*, Vol. II, p. 78, emphasis added.
15. Quoted by John Mellor *et al.*, *Developing Rural India*, op. cit., p. 78.
16. Caprihan, *Fight Against Hunger in Developing Countries* (Delhi: J.K. Jain Brothers, 1975), p. 1.
17. V.S. Vyas, "Green Revolution—A Promise and the Problems", *Industrial India*, Annual Number, 1969, p. 35.
18. Bandhudas Sen, *The Green Revolution in India—A Perspective* (New Delhi: Wiley Eastern Private Limited, 1974), pp. 11-12.
19. A similar study was conducted by T.N. Srinivasan earlier and two trend lines—one for the period 1949-50 to 1964-65 and the other for the period 1949-50 to 1969-70—were fitted and practically similar results were obtained. See T.N. Srinivasan, "The Green Revolution or the Wheat Revolution?" in *Comparative Experience of Agricultural Development in Developing Countries*, Indian Society of Agricultural Economics, Bombay, October, 1972.
20. See the review of the Report of the National Commission of Agriculture in *The Economic Times*, 10 & 11 May 1976.
21. Wolf Ladejinsky, "How Green is India's Green Revolution?" *Economic and Political Weekly* (hereinafter *EPW*), 29 December 1973, p. A-134.
22. Government of India, *Economic Survey, 1980-81*, Table 1.7, p. 71.
23. Quoted in Amritananda Das, "Understanding the Green Revolution", in *Green Revolution—The Unfinished Task*, Centre for the Study of Social Change, Calcutta, p. 121.
24. Preface to *Comparative Experience of Agricultural Development in Developing Countries*, op. cit., by M.L. Dantwala, p. 40.
25. Data are from (i) M.L. Dantwala, op. cit., p. 41; (ii) *Report on Currency and Finance, 1973-74*, RBI; (iii) *Economic Survey 1978-79*; and (iv) A.M. Khusro, "Structural Change in Indian Agriculture", *Agriculture and Economic Development—Structural Readjustment in Asian Perspective*, The Japan Economic Research Centre, May 1972, Tables III & IV, p. 3.
26. Khusro, ibid., p. 316.

27. For example, see V.S. Vyas, "New Agricultural Strategy and Regional Variations in Foodgrains Production", in *Green Revolution—The Unfinished Task*, op. cit., pp. 65-77. Vyas considers State-level data only.
28. N. Krishnaji, "Inter-Regional Disparities in Per Capita Production and Productivity of Foodgrains", *EPW*, Special Number, August 1975, p. 1377. N. Krishnaji's article is an excellent attempt in disaggregating and studying data up to the district level.
29. V. Ramachandran, op. cit. Availability here has been taken as 85% of production.
30. The discussion that follows is mostly based on (i) Biplab DasGupta, "India's Green Revolution", *EPW*, Annual Number, 1977, pp. 241-260 and (ii) Vadilal Dagli (ed.), *A Regional Profile of Indian Agriculture*, op. cit. pp. 25-26 and p. 180 ff.
31. Biplab DasGupta, ibid., p. 259, Note 10.
32. *Basic Statistics Relating to the Indian Economy, Vol. II: States*, Commerce Research Bureau, October 1974, Table 6.3.
33. Biplab DasGupta, op. cit., p. 259, Note 13.
34. Ibid., p. 253.
35. Programme Evaluation Organization, *The High Yielding Varieties Programme in India, 1970-75*, (Government of India: Planning Commission). Under this study 16 blocks in 8 districts from 4 States were selected for wheat and 27 blocks in 14 districts from 10 States were selected for paddy. The districts selected for wheat were Amritsar and Ludhiana in Punjab, Muzaffarnagar, Basti, and Sitapur in U.P., Gaya in Bihar, and Rohtak and Hissar in Haryana. The districts included for paddy were Thanjavur and Coimbatore in Tamil Nadu, Shimoga in Karnataka, West Godavari and Nizamabad in Andhra Pradesh, Basti in U.P., Amritsar in Punjab, Shahabad in Bihar, Burdwan and Midnapur in West Bengal, Cuttack in Orissa, Palghat in Kerala, and Thana in Maharashtra.
36. Ibid., p. 3.
37. Ibid., p. 32.
38. S.L. Shetty, "Structural Retrogression in the Indian Economy since the Mid-Sixties", (Bombay: *Economic and Political Weekly*, 1978), pp. 25-26.
39. R.K. Sau, *Indian Economic Growth : Constraints and Prospects* (Calcutta: Orient Longmans, 1973), p. 89.
40. Francine R. Frankel, *India's Green Revolution—Economic Gains and Political Costs* (Bombay: Oxford University Press, 1971). The important point to be remembered here is that the definitions of large, medium, and small land owners are not uniform for the five districts and vary considerably in the study, depending upon the circumstances prevailing in the districts.
41. Pranab K. Bardhan, "Inequality of Farm Incomes—A Study of Four Districts", *EPW*, Annual Number, 1974, pp. 301-307; G.R. Saini, "Green Revolution and the Distribution of Farm Incomes", *EPW*, 27 March 1976, p. A-17-A-22. Also see G.R. Saini, "Green Revolution and Disparities in Farm Incomes—A Comment", *EPW*, 13 November 1976.
42. Similar results have been arrived at by Partap C. Aggarwal in his book *The Green Revolution and Rural Labour—A Study in Ludhiana.* In this study three villages have been selected for detailed analysis. Aggarwal notes that on account of the increase in crop intensity, demand for labour has increased. This has resulted in scarcity of labour and hence wage rates have increased. They have more than doubled and the earnings of labour households have increased nearly fourfold.
43. Pranab Bardhan, "Green Revolution and Agricultural Labourers", *EPW*, Vol. 5, Nos. 29-31, July 1970; reprinted in C.D. Wadhva (ed.), *Some Problems of India's Economic Policy* (New Delhi: Tata-McGraw Hill Pub. Co. Ltd. 1973), pp. 346-361.

The estimates of poverty given in this study have made it extremely popular along with the study of Dandekar & Rath, Minhas and Ojha.

44. Pranab Bardhan, "Variations in Agricultural Wages", *EPW*, 26 May 1973, pp. 947-950.
45. Deepak Lal, "Agricultural Growth, Real Wages, and the Rural Poor in India", *EPW*, 26 June 1976, pp. A-47-A-60.
46. Rohini Nayyar, "Wages of Agricultural Labourers in Uttar Pradesh—A Note", *EPW*, 6 November 1976, pp. 1771-1772. Rohini Nayyar used data from the *Quarterly Bulletin of Statistics* of the Directorate of Economics and Statistics, Government of Uttar Pradesh.
47. Reserve Bank Staff Occasional Papers, Vol. 2, No. 1, June 1977, Table 2, p. 38.
48. A.C. Minocha, "Some Aspects of Income Distribution in India", *Indian Economic Journal*, Vol. 25, No. 2, October-December, 1977, pp. 6-7.
49. PEO, op. cit., p. (xiii). Also see pp. 22-24.
50. Ibid., pp. 56-59.
51. C.H. Hanumantha Rao, "Factor Endowments, Technology and Farm Employment", *EPW*, 26 September 1976, Review of Agriculture.
52. Arthur Gaitskell, "Some of the Puzzles facing Development Strategy in the Seventies and their Influence on the Choice of Institutional Machinery in the Agricultural Sector", *Agricultural and Economic Development—Structural Readjustment in Asian Perspective*, op. cit., pp. 275-302.
53. Planning Commission, Government of India, *Fourth Five Year Plan*, op. cit., p. 152.
54. Data in this section have been taken from various issues of *Report on Currency and Finance* especially those of 1973-74, 1974-75, 1975-76, and 1976-77.
55. R.N. Tripathy, "Distribution of Benefits of Technological Advancement in Agriculture", *Community Development and Panchayati Raj Digest*, Vol. 5, January 1974, No. 3, pp. 129-130.
56. *EPW*, 24 January 1976, p. 86.
57. H. Laxminarayan, "Small Farmers Development Programme", *EPW*, 28 April 1973, p. 806.
58. Published in *The Economic Times*, 11 & 12 May 1977.
59. Mahendra D. Desai, "Small Farmers' Development Agency : Experience in Surat District", *EPW*, 3 August 1974, pp. 1245-1255.
60. Planning Commission, Government of India, *Fifth Five Year Plan*, Vol. II, p. 91.
61. Planning Commission, Government of India, *Sixth Five Year Plan, 1980-85*, p. 168.
62. Raj Krishna "Unemployment in India", *EPW*, Vol. VIII, No. 9, 3 March 1973, p. 477, (Table 2).

The *Draft Five Year Plan, 1978-83*, (prepared by the Janata government) estimated that in 1971 chronic unemployment was 3.6 million of which 1.73 million was in rural areas. The number of chronically unemployed people in rural areas had risen to 1.83 million in 1973 and was expected to have crossed the mark of 2.00 million in 1978. If weekly unemployed people are also added to this, the number of unemployed people in rural areas rises to 7.04 million in 1971, 7.46 million in 1973, and 8.15 million in 1978. Even this is an understatement because "millions of workers do not get regular work even for a whole week". Therefore the Draft suggested the counting of unemployed *days* rather than unemployed *persons*. If this method is adopted, person day unemployment is found to be 130.0 million days per week in 1973 which is equivalent to 18.6 million persons being unemployed on a typical day. Of these 18.6 million persons, 15.1 million persons were in rural areas. Assuming the person-day unemployment rate in 1978 to be at least as much as in 1973, unemployment in March 1978 is found to be 20.6 million person-years of which 16.5 million were in rural areas. See Planning Commission, *Draft Five Year Plan, 1978-83* (now defunct), Chapter 4.

63. Planning Commission, Government of India, *Third Five Year Plan*, op cit., pp. 163-164.

64. M.L. Dantwala, "Approaches to Growth and Employment", *EPW*, 16 December 1972, p. 2462. The wages paid to labourers working in the Works Programme are kept below the normal wage level to ensure that the Programme does not alter the existing pattern of employment.

65. Amrita Abraham, "Maharashtra's Employment Guarantee Scheme", *EPW*, 9 August 1980, p. 1339.

66. D.M. Nanjundappa, "Karnataka Job Scheme", *The Economic Times*, 15 & 16 April 1981.

67. Government of India, *Economic Survey, 1979-80*, p. 11.

68. Kaushik Basu, "Food for Work Programmes: Beyond Roads that Get Washed Away", *EPW*, 3-10 January 1981, p. 37.

69. This has been referred to as *sectoral-cum-temporal integration* elsewhere in this book. See Chapter 8, Section "Integrated Area Development".

70. Planning Commission, *Sixth Five Year Plan, 1980-85*, pp. 170-172.

71. M.L. Dantwala, "Block Level Planning Revisited", *EPW*, 26 July 1980, p. 1281.

Chapter 8

Development of Backward Areas

IDENTIFICATION OF BACKWARD AREAS

It is frequent to regard areas with relatively low per capita income as backward. But, as noted by us elsewhere in the book[1] per capita income alone is not a reliable measure. Various other measures have also to be considered in addition. For the purpose of identificatian of backward areas such measures can be (i) the percentage of the scheduled caste and scheduled tribe population in the total population of the area, (ii) the ratio of population to the cultivated land, (iii) the percentage of the working force engaged in agriculture, (iv) the ratio of urban to rural population, (v) availability of transport, communications, and other services, (vi) availability of water, electricity, and other facilities, (vii) level of literacy, etc. During the first decade of planning no attempt was made to specify the backward areas and pockets of underdevelopment taking into account these various indicators. Perhaps the Committee on the Dispersal of Industries, set up by the Small Scale Industries Board in 1960, was the first to identify the backward areas for purposes of rural industrialization. The criteria for backwardness suggested by this Committee were as follows:

(1) Poverty of the people as indicated by
   (a) Low per capita income; and
   (b) Low per capita consumption.

(2) High density of population in relation to development of productive resources and employment opportunities as indicated by the following factors:
   (a) High ratio of population to cultivable land (50% below the national average of per capita land holding should be considered as backward);

(b) Low percentage of population engaged in output (50% or more below the national average should be considered as backward);
(c) Absence or under-exploitation of other natural resources, viz., minerals, forests and animals;
(d) Low percentage of population engaged in secondary and tertiary activities (25% below the national average should be considered as backward);
(e) Low ratio of urban to rural population (districts where the ratio was less than 50% of the national average might be considered as backward);
(f) Low percentage of factory employment (50% below the national average might be considered as backward).

3. Poverty of communications as indicated by small lengths of railways and metalled roads per square mile (districts where the railway and road mileage fall below 50% of the national average might be considered as backward).
4. High incidence of unemployment or gross underemployment.
5. Consumption of electric power.[2]

At the time of formulating the Fourth Plan (1966-1971) the Planning Commission appointed a Study Group to suggest the criteria for identifying the backward areas. The Group suggested 5 different indicators as given below:

(1) Total population and density of population;
(2) Number of workers engaged in agriculture including agricultural labourers as pecentage of total workers;
(3) Cultivable area per agricultural worker;
(4) Net area sown per agricultural worker;
(5) Percentage of gross irrigated area to net sown area;
(6) Percentage of area sown more than once to net sown area;
(7) Per capita (rural population) gross value of agricultural output;
(8) Establishments (manufacturing and repair) using electricity:
    (a) Total
    (b) Household
    (c) Non-household
(9) Number of workers per lakh of population employed in registered factories;
(10) Mileage of surfaced roads:

(a) Per 100 sq. miles
(b) Per lakh of population
(11) Number of commercial vehicles registered in a district;
(12) Percentage of literate population:
(a) Men
(b) Women
(13) Percentage of school going children:
(a) Boys
(b) Girls in age groups of (i) 6-11 years, and (ii) 11-14 years
(14) Number of seats per million population for technical training:
(a) Craftsmen
(b) Diploma level
(15) Hospital beds per lakh of population.[3]

Commenting on the inadequacy of these indicators, Pathak notes that "the suggested indicators do not appear to have been selected very precisely. For instance, in what way and at what stage is the density of population related with the degree of backwardness? In what way is the cultivable area per agricultural worker or net area sown per agricultural worker related with the degree of backwardness? How are the absolute numbers of manufacturing and repair establishments relevant? Similarly, information about the number of seats for technical training in a region is not meaningful. If the idea is to have some information about the level of skill, the more relevant figures would be those of number of technically trained persons per 1000 of population."[4]

The National Development Council (NDC) in its meeting held on 13 September 1968 decided that two working groups should be set up for studying the question of regional imbalances. In pursuance of this decision, two Working Groups were set up by the Planning Commission—one for recommending the criteria for the identification of backward areas and the other for recommending the fiscal and financial incentives for starting industries in the backward areas. The committee for specifying the criteria for identification of backward areas was set up under the chairmanship of B.D. Pande (and is popularly known as the Pande Committee) and the committee for recommending the fiscal and financial incentives in the backward areas was set up under the chairmanship of N.N. Wanchoo (and is popularly known as the Wanchoo Committee).

The terms of reference of the Pande Committee were: "To recommend the objective criteria to be followed in identification of backward regions which would qualify for special treatment by way of incentives for industries to be set up in such regions. Among other things, the broad techno-economic factors which are relevant to the establishment of industries on a regional basis should be taken into account, so that the grant of special concessions does not lead to irrational growth in industrial development."[5] For the lack of data, the committee restricted its attention to the State and district levels and did not go beyond the district level. Thus, it is possible that, "backward pockets" in the developed districts were ignored by the committee. The committee restricted itself to the *identification of backward districts in industrially backward States only*. The identification of backward districts in industrially advanced States was not considered at all on the plea that the advanced States had the necessary industries and resources that could be diverted towards the backward areas.

The criteria for the identification of industrially backward States and Union territories adopted by the Pande Committee were as follows:

(1) Total per capita income.
(2) Per capita income from industry and mining.
(3) Number of workers in registered factories.
(4) Per capita annual consumption of electricity.
(5) Length of surfaced roads in relation to:
    (a) the population, and
    (b) the area of the State.
(6) Railway mileage in relation to:
    (a) the population, and
    (b) the area of the State.

On the basis of these criteria, the following ten States were classified as industrially backward: Andhra Pradesh, Assam, Bihar, Himachal Pradesh, Jammu & Kashmir, Madhya Pradesh, Nagaland, Orissa, Rajasthan, and Uttar Pradesh. All Union territories except Chandigarh, Delhi, and Pondicherry were also classified as industrially backward.

The committee suggested the following criteria for identifying the backward districts in the backward States:

(1) Districts outside a radius of about 50 miles from large cities or large industrial prjoects.
(2) Poverty of the people as indicated by low per capita income starting from the lowest to 25% below the State average.
(3) High density of population in relation to utilization of productive resources and employment opportunities as indicated by:
    (a) Low percentage of population engaged in secondary and tertiary activities (25% below the State average may be considered as backward).

(b) Low percentage of factory employment (25% below the State average may be considered as backward).
(c) Non- and/or underutilization of economic and natural resources like minerals, forests etc.

(4) Adequate availability of electric power or likelihood of its availability within the next one or two years.
(5) Availability of transport and communication facilities or likelihood of their availability within the next one or two years, and
(6) Adequate availability of water or likelihood of its availability within the next one or two years.

On the basis of these criteria, the committee identified 238 districts all over India comprising 60% of the country's area and an equal proportion of its population as industrially backward. Since a large number of districts were declared backward the Pande Committee suggested that, initially at least, States should identify one or two districts with a potential for development so that efforts of development were 'concentrated' and were not dissipated. Such a policy of concentrating on selected areas in the backward regions is justified on the grounds that the total resources available to the economy are limited and the distribution of limited resources in all areas leads to a *dissipation* of resources, time, and energy. Thus, instead of spreading the available resources thinly over all the backward areas, efforts should be concentrated on some selected areas in the backward regions which have development potential. To study such potential it is necessary to conduct techno-economic surveys of different areas in the backward regions and a study of the inter-industry linkages has to be carried out. It is necessary to locate the areas which have water, electricity, transport and communications, raw materials, entrepreneurial ability, etc., and concentrate on those districts (or selected pockets of those selected districts) which have these facilities in adequate measure. These areas can serve as the growth centres for the future development of the backward regions.

INCENTIVES FOR DEVELOPMENT

Wanchoo Committee Report

The terms of reference of the Wanchoo Committee were:

(a) To consider the nature of concessions to be given for encouraging the development of industries in backward regions and in particular to examine procedural, financial and fiscal incentives;

(b) To consider the role of State governments and financial institutions in the development of industries in backward regions; and also

(c) To examine the type of dis-incentives that should be introduced to avoid concentration in metropolitan or highly industrialised areas.[6]

The fiscal incentives recommended by the committee for attracting the entrepreneurs to set up industries in the backward areas were the following:

(a) Grant of higher development rebate to industries located in backward areas.

(b) Grant of exemption from income-tax, including corporate tax, for 5 years after providing for the development rebate.

(c) Exemption from the payment of import duties on plant and machinery, components, etc., imported by units set up in backward areas.

(d) Exemption from excise duties for a period of 5 years.

(e) Exemption from sales tax, both on raw materials and finished products, to units set up in specified backward areas for a period of 5 years, from the date of their going into production.

(f) Transport subsidy. We feel that there is a case for giving transport subsidy for reasons of special remoteness of certain areas, for taking out the finished products for a period of 5 years. Upto 400 miles the distance should be considered as normal and beyond that the transportation cost for finished products should be subsidized for such backward areas as may be selected in the States of Assam, Nagaland, Manipur, Tripura, NEFA and Andamans. The transport subsidy should be equivalent to 50% of the cost of transportation in case of the backward areas specified in J & K State.[7]

In addition to these incentives, the committee advocated that "in order to create the desired situation and to provide the lever in favour of backward areas, it is necessary to offer certain special incentives, to the entrepreneurs in the backward areas, *inter alia*, in the matter of fixed assets, i.e. supply of developed plots, built-up accommodation, machinery and equipment etc."[8] For example, in regard to making available developed plots to entrepreneurs in the backward areas, the committee recommended that the developed plots should be given to entrepreneurs on a down payment of 10% of the value of the land and no further payment should be asked from them during the first five years. The balance should be recovered in easy instalments spread over a period of nine years, after the expiry of the first five years. In those cases where the entrepreneur is provided built-up accommodation in industrial estates or industrial areas, a subsidy to the extent of 50% of the cost of construction was recommended, the balance 50% to be collected in easy instalments over a fairly long time-period, say 20 years. In case the entrepreneur wishes to construct the shed himself, his cost of construction should be subsidized to the extent of 25%. In regard to supplying machinery and equipment on hire-purchase basis, it was recommended that the rate of interest should be merely 3%, earnest money required to be deposited should be 10% (instead of 20%), and no surcharge should be levied.

Against the recommendation of the Pande Committee to restrict concessions to the backward States only, the NDC in its meeting held in September 1969 decided that such concessions should be made available to *selected backward areas in all the States and Union territories*. The criteria for the selection of the industrially backward districts in the States and Union territories were to be decided by the Planning Commission in consultation with the financial institutions and the State governments, in the light of the two sets of criteria recommended by the Pande Committee. The following set of criteria was evolved by the Planning Commission for the purpose of identification of the industrially backward districts to qualify for concessional finance:

(1) Per capita foodgrains/commercial crops production depending on whether the district is predominantly a producer of foodgrains/cash crops. (For inter-district comparisons, conversion rates between foodgrains and commercial crops may be determined by the State government on a pre-determined basis where necessary.)
(2) Ratio of agricultural workers to population.
(3) Per capita industrial output (gross).
(4) Number of factory employees per lakh of population or alternatively number of persons engaged in the secondary and tertiary activities per lakh of population.
(5) Length of surfaced roads in relation to population or railway mileage in relation to population.

On the basis of these criteria, 241 districts (later raised to 247) all over the country were classified as industrially backward. The list is given in Table 2. The list of industrially backward districts selected to qualify for concessional finance from the financial institutions (as on 3 January 1976) is given in Annexure I to this chapter. As far as the scheme for capital subsidy is concerned, it was decided that instead of giving incentives such as higher development rebate, exemption from income tax, corporate tax, import and excise duties as recommended by the Wanchoo Committee, only one incentive in the form of an outright subsidy amounting to one-tenth of the fixed capital investment for projects in the backward areas be given. The only condition was that total fixed capital investment should not exceed Rs.50 lakhs. Subsequently, for units coming up after 1 March 1973, the subsidy was increased to 15% of the total fixed capital investment provided the total investment did not exceed Rs.1 crore. The lists of districts/areas qualifying for the subsidy are given in Annexures II and III to this chapter.

According to a recent decision of the industry ministry, all industrial units, other than those run departmentally, which made investments in land, building, plant, and machinery on or after March 1973, and located in areas identified as backward by the Central government, will be eligible to claim 15% of the amount invested as outright grant subject to a maximum of Rs.15 lakh per unit. Out of the 247 districts declared backward by the Planning Commission, 103 districts have been selected to qualify for Central investment subsidy. These have been selected on the pattern of six districts or areas each for industrially backward States and three each in the case of other States.

Following the recommendation of the Wanchoo Committee regarding transport subsidy, the Central government provides 50% reimbursement to industrial units in the hill areas on transportation charges incurred on raw material and finished goods to and from selected railheads.

A scheme of providing income tax concession to new industrial projects (including hotels) located in the backward areas and employing ten or more workers was introduced in April 1974. The scheme provides a deduction of 20% of profits for computation of taxable income and applies to any industrial undertaking which fulfils the following conditions:

(i) It has begun or begins to manufacture or produce articles after the 31st of December, 1970 in any backward area.

(ii) It has not been formed by the splitting up, or the reconstruction of a business already in existence in any backward area: Provided that this condition shall not apply in respect of any industrial undertaking which is formed as a result of the re-establishment, reconstruction or revival by the assessees of the business of any such industrial undertaking as is referred to in section 338 of the I.T. Act, 1961 in the circumstances and within the period specified in that section."[9]

In addition, small-scale units including ancillaries are eligible to procure machinery on hire-purchase basis from the National Small Industries Corporation Limited. The NSIC has liberalized the terms and conditions for the supply of machinery on hire-purchase basis to industries located in the backward areas which qualify for investment subsidy. According to these terms, with effect from October 1975 the earnest money payable by technocrats and entrepreneurs from the declared backward areas is 10% against 15% in other cases. The rate of interest is 11% in their case as against 13½% in other cases. This concessional rate is available to units having a total investment in plant and machinery up to Rs.2 lakhs, a rebate of 2% is allowed for prompt payment.[10]

Measures Adopted by State Governments

A number of State governments have adopted various measures to attract industries to the backward areas. We give a brief account below:

Andhra Pradesh: (i) Efforts are being made to develop backward areas such as Telengana, Rayalaseema and Coastal Andhra through the formulation of regional plans and area development plans; (ii) the State Financial Corporation provides loans on a concessional rate of 7%; (iii) power is supplied at concessional rate to power-oriented industries varying from Rs.525 to Rs.600 per KVA; (iv) concessions on sales tax are provided.

Assam: Concessions and assistance granted include: (i) concession on sales tax and provision of financial assistance; (ii) provision of technical guidance; (iii) provision of developed land with power, water and other facilities for establishing small scale industries; (iv) training of local youths in industries as apprentices; (v) contribution to the extent of 50% by the State government towards the cost of preparation of feasibility reports.

Bihar: Special programmes have been prepared for the development of the backward areas of Chotanagpur, Santhal Parganas, and North Bihar; (ii) supply of water required by the industrial units on no-profit-no-loss basis; (iii) concession on sales tax; (iv) provision of loans at concessional rate of 6½% with amortization period of 10-12 years; (v) subsidy of 10% on investment in addition to the Central subsidy for industrial housing.

Gujarat: (i) Provision of loans at concessional rate of 7%; (ii) exemption from the payment of water charges for a period of five years; (iii) concessions on sales tax; (iv) the Gujarat State Industrial Corporation charges a meagre 5% rate of interest on purchase of machinery compared with normal 20%; (v) sheds in industrial estates in the backward areas are allotted on a payment of 12½% compared with 25% everywhere else. The balance of 12½% is recovered by instalments in two years and the remaining 75% in monthly instalments spread over a period of ten years.

Haryana: (i) New units in the identified backward areas are exempted from payment of electricity duty; (ii) loans are provided at a concessional rate of 6%; (iii) sales tax is treated as interest-free loan for seven years in the case of backward regions which can be repaid in ten half-yearly instalments; (iv) during the Fourth Plan, Rs.42 crores were spent on special schemes (belonging to agriculture, soil conservation, animal husbandry, dairy development, minor irrigation, rural industry, etc.) for the development of backward areas. This scheme was continued in the Fifth Plan as well; (v) contribution to the extent of 50% by the State government towards the cost of preparation of feasibility reports in the case of selected industrial projects; (vi) allotment of land on no-profit-no-loss basis and on easy instalments for construction of subsidized industrial houses and residential colonies for workers.

Himachal Pradesh: (i) Provision of loans at the concessional rate of interest of 7%; (ii) provision of industrial plots on lease of 95 years; (iii) contribution to the extent of 75% by the State government towards the cost of preparation of feasibility reports.

Jammu & Kashmir: (i) Exemption of new units from the payment of electricity duty; (ii) preparation of feasibility studies and their free supply to entrepreneurs provided the cost of the study is less than Rs.10,000; (iii) exemption of new industries from payment of sales tax for the first five years; (iv) interest-free loans are advanced for the acquisition of generating sets: 25% of the amount is treated as subsidy and the remaining 75% is recovered in yearly/half-yearly instalments over a period of 7 years.

Karnataka: (i) Exemption from sales tax in respect of capital goods purchased within the State; (ii) exemption from payment of electricity duty; (iii) the concessional refinance given by the IDBI to the State Financial Corporation for new units in the backward areas is supplemented by a further subsidy of interest by 1% by the State government; (iv) district plans for all districts are being prepared wherein the problems of the backward areas will be accorded special attention by giving weightage to the backward areas in the allocation of plan outlays.

Kerala: (i) Supply of water to industrial units on no-profit-no-loss basis; (ii) rebate in electricity duty; (iii) acquisition of land and its development for industrial purposes (developed industrial plots are made available to the industrialists either on full payment or on lease or on easy hire-purchase instalment basis); (iv) preparation of project reports on medium- and small-scale industries and making them available to the entrepreneurs free of cost.

Madhya Pradesh: (i) Supply of water to industrial units on no-profit-no-loss basis; (ii) sales tax concessions in the form of either subsidy or 15 years' interest-free loan (subsidy is available to new units with an investment of less than Rs.50 lakhs at the rate of 50% of the sales tax paid in the developed areas, and 75% to 100% of the annual payment in the backward districts. The interest-free loan is applicable to units with investment in the range of Rs.50 lakhs-Rs.5 crores); (iii) preparation and supply of feasibility reports; (iv) development of industrial plots and providing them at a lease of 99 years; (v) relatively more allocation of plan funds to the backward areas compared with developed areas (recommended ratio being 60 : 40).

Maharashtra: (i) Rebate on eletricity tariff; (ii) exemption from the payment of octroi duty on raw materials, capital equipment and building materials imported within the limits of local authorities; (iii) cash refund of sales tax paid by the industry on raw materials purchased by it and on finished products; (iv) guarantee of loans raised by the new industries; (v) contribution to the extent of 75% by the State government towards the cost of preparation of feasibility studies; (vi) reservation for industries in the government purchase programmes; (vii) supply of building material for the construction of sheds on loan to entrepreneurs; (viii) financial assistance to the industries for providing housing to workers; (ix) provision of loans at concessional rate (of 5% for industries located in Konkan, Vidarbha, and Marathwada and 5½% for industries in respect of other parts of the State except Greater Bombay-Thana for loans exceeding Rs.25,000 but not exceeding Rs.50,000); (x) provision of industrial plots to entrepreneurs in the backward areas (it was decided that no rent would be charged for the first two years, 50% of the economic rent would be charged for the next two years, while full economic rent would be charged from the sixth year).

Manipur: (i) Provision of land at 50% of market rate to entrepreneurs; (ii) 50% concession in water charges for units in the backward areas; (iii) allocation of about one-third of the total plan outlay to more backward areas and preparation of integrated area programmes.

Meghalaya: (i) Preparation of special projects for the accelerated development of the backward areas; (ii) contribution to the extent of 75% by the State government towards the cost of preparation of feasibility studies of projects.

Nagaland: Keeping in view the backwardness of the district of Tuensang, special safeguards were provided for taking care of the needs of this district for a period of ten years (from the date the State was constituted). These safeguards are likely to be continued even after ten years.

Orissa: (i) Provision of guarantee on loans sanctioned to entrepreneurs in the backward areas; (ii) provision of loans at one-third of market rate; (iii) exemption from payment of octroi duty on machinery brought for setting up new industries, expansion and renovation of the existing ones (raw materials are also exempt from payment of octroi duty for a period of five years in the case of new industries); (iv) provision of developed sites having power, water supply, and raw materials, etc., to entrepreneurs in the backward areas; (v) refund of sales tax on raw materials purchased by entrepreneurs during the initial 5-year period of starting of their units; (vi) provision of land and electricity at concessional rates (e.g., land is allotted at 50% of the market rate); (vii) availability of water to industrial units at no-profit-no-loss basis; (viii) contribution to the extent of 50% by the State government towards the cost of preparation of feasibility studies of projects.

Punjab: (i) Exemption of new units totally from the payment of electricity duty for a period of five years; (ii) provision of land on concessional rate (the allottee has to pay 10% of the cost on allotment and the remaining amount is to be paid in six instalments after an initial grace period of two years); (iii) underwriting share capital up to 20% to 25% of the paid-up capital of the new ventures; (iv) contribution to the extent of 50% by the State government towards the cost of preparation of feasibility studies of projects; (v) purchase and sales tax including inter-State sales tax are refunded for a period of five years to new and expanding units; (vi) for a period of 10 years, additional price preference of 2½% over the existing rate of 15% for small-scale industries is allowed in government purchases.

Rajasthan: (i) Provision of land at concessional rate to entrepreneurs in the backward areas (the allottee has to pay 10% of the cost on allotment and the balance is to be paid in four years after an initial grace period of three years); (ii) exemption of new units from payment of electricity duty; (iii) concessions on sales tax; (iv) provision of special assistance for the development of backward areas and preparation of special integrated (drought) area schemes for their development.

Tamil Nadu: (i) Water royalty concessions for industries set up in the backward areas; (ii) concessional power tariff for new industries; (iii) provision of land at concessional rates (e.g., the allottee is required to pay 10% of the cost on allotment and the balance is to be paid in six annual instalments after an initial grace period of two years); (iv) preparation of feasibility reports on industrial projects and their cost-free supply to entrepreneurs; (v) sanction of interest-free sales tax loans to major and medium industries in the backward areas.

Tripura: Provision of credit facilities to small-scale units set up in the backward areas. Loans are made available under State Aid to Industries Rules, liberalized credit schemes of the State Bank of India and the Assam State Financial Corporation. For Rural Industries Projects area, the interest on loan and mode of payments have been liberalized as follows: (i) Loan is repayable in 10 equal instalments; (ii) first instalment of the principal amount is to be paid on completion of five years from the date of disbursing; and (iii) the rate of interest has been reduced to 2½% for cooperative societies and 3% for new units.

Uttar Pradesh: (i) Provision of land at concessional rate and on a lease of 90 years; (ii) exemption of new units from the payment of electricity duty; (iii) provision of loans on concessional terms by the U.P. Financial Corporation to small- and medium-sized projects in the backward areas [concessions include (a) low rate of interest of 7-7½% with a rebate of 1% to 1½% for timely repayment, (b) longer grace period extending up to 4 years, (c) long repayment period extending up to 15 years, (d) reduced margin ranging from 15 to 35%]; (iv) increasing allocation of plan funds to the development of the backward areas and on provision of infrastructural facilities such as roads, irrigation, transport and communication; (v) setting up of special regional corporations/boards for the development of the backward areas such as the Poorvanchal Vikas Nigam, the Bundhelkhand Vikas Nigam, and the Parvatiya Vikas Nigam.

West Bengal: (i) Water royalty concessions up to 50% for a period of three years to new industries set up in backward areas; (ii) provision of loans at a concessional rate of 6% to small-scale units; (iii) provision of

1% interest subsidy by the State government on loans given by the West Bengal Financial Corporation to units having capital investment not exceeding Rs.20 lakhs; (iv) provision of a subsidy of 10% of the investment in addition to the Central subsidy for industrial housing; (v) setting up of special boards and corporations for the development of the backward areas such as the North Bengal Development Board, the Sunderbans Development Board, the Jhargram Development Board, and the Darjeeling Hill Areas Development Advisory Committee.

In addition to all these incentives provided by the State Governments for the development of backward areas, a number of States gave numerous other incentives in both financial and physical terms and also provided technical assistance either through the programme of industrial estates or rural industries projects. Programmes of assistance were also adopted by many administrations in Union territories.

OTHER MEASURES TO PROMOTE INDUSTRIALIZATION

In addition to the above measures adopted by the Central and the State governments to encourage the potential entrepreneurs to set up industries in the backward areas, a number of other programmes were initiated to promote industrialization of such areas, the most important being:

1. Use of the Industrial Licensing Policy to encourage setting up of industries in backward areas.
2. Location of large public sector projects in the backward areas.
3. Setting up of rural industries projects.
4. Establishment of industrial estates.

We have already discussed the industrial licensing policy in Chapter 5 and have pointed out how the actual implementation of the policy went against the desired objective of promoting industrialization of the backward areas. Let us now discuss other measures briefly.

Location of Large Public Sector Projects

Several public sector projects were located in the backward areas in the belief that their location in such areas would unleash a *propulsive mechanism* in them and cause economic development of the hinterland. Such projects included steel plants, fertilizer plants, heavy electrical plants, etc. Though economic and technical considerations cannot be ignored while deciding the location of these projects, the Third Plan felt that "the disadvantages which particular areas may have for the location of the larger projects are not always basic or irremediable, for at times they may reflect only the lack of basic facilities and services."[11]

Table 1 shows that a considerable proportion of the public sector investment has gone into the backward States of Bihar, Madhya Pradesh, and Orissa. The total share of these three States in the cumulative investment in public sector units till 31.3.1977 amounted to Rs.4648.3 crores which is 40.6% of the total investment in all States. The individual share of these States was: 22% for Bihar, 13% for Madhya Pradesh, and 5.6% for

TABLE 1: Value of property (gross block) invested by Central government in public sector undertakings in different States

(Rs. crores)

State	Cumulative investment as on 31-3-1977	Per capita (Rs.)
1. Andhra Pradesh	390.7	90
2. Assam	312.9	214
3. Bihar	2509.1	445
4. Gujarat	523.4	196
5. Haryana	142.7	142
6. Himachal Pradesh	11.8	34
7. Jammu & Kashmir	5.7	12
8. Karnataka	268.2	92
9. Kerala	274.1	128
10. Madhya Pradesh	1492.7	358
11. Maharashtra	630.3	125
12. Manipur	—	—
13. Meghalaya	—	—
14. Nagaland	—	—
15. Orissa	646.5	295
16. Punjab	197.8	146
17. Rajasthan	227.1	88
18. Sikkim	—	—
19. Tamil Nadu	466.9	113
20. Tripura	—	—
21. Uttar Pradesh	376.2	43
22. West Bengal	768.3	173
Unallocated and others (including Union territories)	2206.8	—
Total	11451.2	209

Source: D.T. Lakdawala, "Plan Finances in a Federal Economy", *Yojana*, 16 May 1979, Table IX, p. 13.

Orissa. There were only four States recording a per capita investment greater than the national average. These were Bihar, Madhya Pradesh, Orissa, and Assam. In fact, the per capita investment in the case of Bihar was more than two times the national per capita investment as Table 1 clearly shows.

Even such large-scale public sector investment has failed to create any remarkable impact on the backward economies of Bihar, Madhya Pradesh, and Orissa. In many cases the industries set up in these States had linkages outside. For example, the lead industry in Bhilai "was closely linked with the distant economy of Bombay. Small scale and ancillary industries based on the lead industry developed in far-off regions completely bypassing the next village economy".[12] In many cases the inputs had to be imported from outside the State where these projects were located. Also, because of the non-availability or inadequate availability of skilled labour in the backward areas, the employment-generating effects of these projects did not benefit the inhabitants of the area. This is on top of the fact that being capital-intensive, the employment potential of large-scale projects is already very limited. A study of 80 units located in the backward regions shows that in as many as 65 units a capital of more than Rs.50,000.00 was required to employ one person.[13] The same study reveals that the public sector projects were highly capital-intensive and had a very low employment-generating capacity. Thus, in Bihar, it required an investment of Rs.107,243 to employ one person. In Orissa and Madhya Pradesh, it required Rs.79,773 and Rs.71,141 respectively to employ a single person.

Rural Industries Projects

In 1962, a Rural Industries Planning Committee was set up with the object of providing non-farm employment to workers in rural areas and stimulating the process of industrialization of these areas. There were four criteria according to which the rural industries projects were located:

(i) where agricultural conditions were favourable and considerable agricultural effort was being organized but at the same time there was heavy pressure of population;
(ii) where agriculture was undertaken mainly under unirrigated conditions and there was considerable need for additional employment;
(iii) where there was considerable underemployment because of unfavourable natural conditions and lack of development of potential resources, and
(iv) tribal and other backward areas.[14]

It was purposely decided to select eight projects so that two projects belonged to each location category. Under the first category came the projects initiated in Nawadah (Bihar) and Sangamner (Maharashtra); under the second and third categories, projects were started at Kozhikode (Kerala), Anantapur (Andhra Pradesh), Churu (Rajasthan), and Mahasu (Himachal Pradesh); and under the fourth category, projects were started at Panchmahals (Gujarat) and Tarikhet (Uttar Pradesh). The rural industries projects scheme was a Centrally sponsored scheme covering 45 areas, each covering 3 to 5 development blocks with a population of 300-500 thousand, for intensive development of small industries in rural areas. Later on, 4 more areas, near large-scale projects of Durgapur, Bhilai, Bhadravati, and Ranchi, were added in 1965. Expressing satisfaction over the performance of the rural industries projects, the Fifth Plan envisaged the initiation of 57 new projects and the extension of the coverage of the existing projects to the whole district excluding towns with population of more than 15,000.[15]

Assistance to entrepreneurs under this scheme is given in the form of loans, grants, technical assistance, and assistance for hire-purchase of machinery, etc. Though no specific criteria have been laid down for the selection of industries for extending the loan facilities, one can discern the following norms in the selection procedure adopted: " (1) to ensure the stability of certain existing industries like blacksmithy, carpentry, etc., (2) to help the industries in the industrial estates like manufacture of polythene bags and stainless steel utensils, (3) to help the industries utilising local raw materials like manufacture of paper bags, varnishes, (4) to help the traditional artisans by providing technical and financial assistance, and (5) to start industries which have a bearing on the maintenance of the present industries and future development".[16]

Several deficiencies in the actual operation of the rural industries project have been noted. The Programme Evaluation Organization of the Planning Commission noted in its report (published in December 1968) that in as many as 6 projects (at Mahasu, Kozhikode, Nawadah, Panchmahals, Sangamner, and Tarikhet) out of the original 8 projects there was no integration of the project with the district and block plans. This happened even in those cases (e.g., in Tarikhet) where the views of the officials associated with the formulation and implementation of the district and block plans were taken into account while preparing the programmes for setting up of rural industries. Again, in six out of eight rural industries projects, marketing facilities were not provided by the project authorities and the projects faced difficulties of water supply and electricity. It has also been revealed that there had been some deviations in the implementation of the programmes to the extent that some part of the assistance was provided to relatively larger ones among the small-scale units and also in towns which were excluded from the purview of the scheme. On the other hand, the rural artisans did not receive adequate assistance, particularly in respect of technical advice, credit, training, and marketing.

Industrial Estates Programme

The industrial estates programme was initiated in 1955 when, following the recommendations of the Small-Scale Industries Board, a total number of twelve estates were sanctioned. The construction, organization, and management of ten estates was entrusted to the State governments while the development of two estates (one situated in Naini at Allahabad and the other in Okhla at Delhi) was the responsibility of the National Small Scale Industries Corporation. The ten estates entrusted to the respective State governments were situated at Rajkot in Gujarat, Guindy and Virudhunagar in Tamil Nadu, Kanpur and Agra in Uttar Pradesh and Palghat, Trivandrum, Kottayam, Quilon, and Trichur in Kerala. The State governments were sanctioned a loan of Rs.57.89 lakhs and a grant of Rs.0.495 lakhs each for the purpose.

The principal objectives of the programme, varying to some degree with time and place, have been:

(i) to encourage the growth of small scale industries;
(ii) to shift small scale industries from congested areas to estate premises with a view to increasing their productivity;
(iii) to achieve de-centralised industrial development in small towns and large villages; and
(iv) to encourage the growth of ancillary industries in the townships, surrounding major industrial undertakings, both in public and private sectors.[17]

Under the industrial estates programme, the government provides factory accommodation to small industries at suitable sites with facilities of water, electricity, steam, transport, banks, post offices, canteens, watch and ward, first aid, etc. The sheds constructed for the purpose are rented out to potential entrepreneurs who are also provided with expert advice and opportunities for institutional credit. An industrial estate brings a number of units together and thereby facilities the establishment of common service centres, introduction of modern techniques, collective purchase of raw materials and sale of finished goods, joint publicity, etc., thus giving the small firms in the estate an opportunity to avail of the numerous external economies. The representatives of advisory and information services, research services, financing services, training centres, etc., are also attracted to the area because of a cluster of industrial firms situated. Another external economy that can emerge is in the form of inter-trading between the small firms themselves. The member-enterprises can avail of the goods and services of each other thereby becoming complementary and inter-dependent on each other.

Initially conceived as a measure to promote small-scale industries, the industrial estates programme was seen as an important means to ensure the industrial spread of industries and development of the backward areas in the Third Plan. Under the new arrangement, the task of the industrial estate programme was threefold: (i) to promote the rapid development of small-scale industries, (ii) to help the industrialization of the backward areas, and (iii) to stimulate industrial development in rural areas. During the Third Plan, the schemes of industrial estates were classified into three categories:

(i) *Uurban Estates:* i.e. those in cities and large towns, or in the vicinity thereof.
(ii) *Semi-Urban Estates:* i.e. those in semi-urban areas comprising small towns located at a reasonable distance from large cities and having population of 5000 to 50,000.
(iii) *Rural Estates and Worksheds:* i.e. those in villages with a population of less than 5000 and situated at a sufficient distance from large cities and towns.[18]

While initially all industrial estates were established in urban areas, their percentage in these areas came down to 63.5 by the end of 1963 and to 46.5 by end 1969 on account of the new role assigned to the programme in developing rural and backward areas. The Third Plan emphasized that rural industrial estates should be located in those villages where power, water supply, transport, and other facilities were either available or could be provided and where sufficient number of artisans and craftsmen were available to make use of modern techniques, better tools and relatively modern facilities—in short, in those villages where the *potentialities* of industrialization existed. The total cost of each rural estate was estimated to be between Rs.2 and Rs.3 lakhs.

Expansion of the Programme

During the Second Plan, the total expenditure on village and small-scale industries amounted to Rs.180 crores of which Rs.11.6 crores was spent on industrial estates. The corresponding expenditures during the Third Plan, the three Annual Plans, the Fourth Plan and the Fifth Plan were Rs.240.5 crores and Rs.22.2 crores, Rs.132.6 crores and Rs.7.6 crores, Rs.251.1 crores and Rs.15.7 crores, and Rs.387.8 crores and Rs.17.6 crores respectively. The total expenditure on village and small-scale industries from the Second to the Fifth Plan thus amounts to Rs.1192.0 crores of which Rs.74.7 crores (i.e. 6.3%) were spent on industrial estates.[19]

By the end of 1970, 535 industrial estates were sponsored out of which 397 were completed and 340 were functioning. Among the functioning estates, 154 were located in urban areas, 110 in semi-urban areas, and 76 in rural areas. While in 1961 the number of estates was 83 and the number of sheds completed in all estates was 2692, in 1970 the number of estates had risen to 397 and the number of sheds completed to 10,133. Of these, 8827 sheds were allotted. Of these 8827 sheds, 7999 were occupied but merely 6316 were working. The proportion of sheds working to the total number of sheds completed comes to only 62.3%. Over the decade 1961-70, the employment provided by the industrial estates rose from 14,695 to 104,862, while the value of half-yearly production increased from Rs.6.50 crores to Rs.76.66 crores. The latest figures available for the industrial estates are till 1975. According to them, there were about 700 industrial estates in India by the end of 31 March 1975 housing 12,830 small units. These units were producing goods worth Rs.500 crores and providing employment to 1.86 lakh people.

The maximum number of estates were in Maharashtra which was also much ahead of other States in terms of number of sheds completed, number of sheds working, total employment, and value of half-yearly production. Thus, at the end of 1970, 1564 sheds were completed in Maharashtra of which 1207 was working. The total employment provided was 20,940 and the total half-yearly production was Rs.19.50 crores. The second position was occupied by Uttar Pradesh where the total number of sheds completed was merely 824, of which 584 were working. The total employment provided was 10,108 while the total half-yearly production was only Rs.4.44 crores (which is merely 33% of the production in Maharashtra).[30]

Critical Appraisal of the Programme

The industrial estates programme has not been able to fulfil its role in the development of the backward areas. The estates turned out to be highly capital-intensive and have provided very meagre employment opportunities. Thus, "in the sample of factories studied by Dhar and Lydall, about half employed 10 workers each, only a sixth more than 40 workers. The same study showed that the capital employed per person in the sample estate was 2½ to 3½ times as large as in Delhi light engineering industries. Considering the scarcity value of capital in India, the conclusion seems inescapable that the factories in these estates have generally not been planned in conformity with the relevant economic criteria."[21] Also, the very limited surge of the industrial estates in the countryside seriously limits their role as an agency of industrial spread. It has been observed that the industrial estates in or near about metropolitan centres such as Delhi, Bombay, Calcutta, Madras, etc., had proved successful while those in the backward areas had not. The reasons are not far to seek and can be summarized as follows:

1. The industrial estates in the backward areas were set up without undertaking adequate techno-economic surveys. This resulted in the selection of unsuitable places within these areas.

2. There was a considerable time-lag between sanctioning, construction, and allotment of sheds. The main reasons for the time-lag between the sanctioning and the construction of the sheds are procedural delays in acquiring land, time taken in the preparation of lay-out, designs, and estimates, delay in financial sanctions, difficulties in procuring building material such as cement, steel, etc. The time-lag between the construction of estates and the allotment of sheds is because of non-availability of essential facilities such as power, water, drainage, and sewage facilities, non finalization of terms and conditions of giving sheds on rent, calling of applications for the allotment of sheds after the completion of estates, delays in getting the schemes approved from the State directorate of industries, the lack of demand from entrepreneurs, etc.

3. The cost of land development and construction has been on the higher side leading, in turn, to high rentals.

4. Entrepreneurs are generally not willing to go to the backward areas because of high initial costs in such areas, the lack of supporting facilities and services, difficulties in obtaining skilled labour, etc.

5. The firms in industrial estates set up in the backward areas suffer from a number of disabilities leading to under-utilization of the installed capacity. Some of these problems are: shortage of skilled labour, lack of finance (particularly for working capital), inadequate supply of power even during day time, improper balancing of equipment, etc.

6. Various agencies connected with the provision of infrastructure, State departments and financial institutions have failed to work in a coordinated manner. Instead, there are ample examples of political and official bickerings, red-tapism, and corruption. These factors combined to dampen the spirit of the potential entrepreneurs. There are also examples of some units which were forced to close down after a hesitant start.[22]

Development of Backward Areas: Other Policy Measures

In addition to the programmes aimed at industrialization of the backward areas (discussed above) a number of other programmes were initiated in different plans to promote the development of such areas. These included programmes aimed at intensive development of agriculture, extension of irrigation, development of roads and road transport, provision of universal education, improvements in conditions of living, and water supply. Special schemes were initiated for the development of problem areas. Thus, in 1953-54, a programme of permanent improvements in scarcity areas was taken in hand in several States at a total cost of Rs.40 crores. This included medium and minor irrigation schemes, land reclamation, contour bunding schemes, and some other measures. Additional programmes were undertaken in 1957. The governments of Uttar Pradesh, Punjab, Orissa, Madhya Pradesh, and Assam made specific provisions for the development of the backward areas. Schemes for the development of mineral resources such as lignite deposits in Arcot, iron ore in Orissa, bauxite and lead and zinc deposits in Rajasthan were all expected to benefit the backward areas also. With a view to providing employment to the unemployed people in rural areas, the Third Plan introduced the Rural Works Programme.

The Fourth Plan proposed that a multi-directional Area Development approach should be adopted in order to accelerate the pace of development of the backward areas. Since each backward area presented its own set of problems, it was suggested that no uniform programme should be imposed from the national level. Instead, specific strategies based on cause of backwardness (of the particular region under consideration) should guide the location policy of industries and other activities in the region. For this purpose, the backward areas were grouped broadly into two categories:

(a) areas with unfavourable physio-geographic conditions, terrian, climate and regions inhabited by people with typical cultural characteristics. These included hill areas, drought-prone areas and tribal areas;

(b) economically backward areas marked by adverse land-man ratios, lack of infrastructure or inadequate development resource potentials.[23]

For areas falling in the first category, the Fourth Plan initiated a series of measures which are summarized below.

(a) Central projects in 54 drought-prone areas with an outlay of Rs.2 crores per project for four years.[24]

(b) Central projects for the integrated development of tribal areas in six districts taken up in 1971-72.[25]

(c) "In recognition of the higher costs and poor returns from investments in hill areas, it was decided that special allocations of Central assistance should be made to the hilly States, and the pattern of Central assistance to the hill areas in other States should also be liberalised in order to encourage them to make substantial allocation of funds from their plan resources. The pattern provided for 50 percent grant component in the Central assistance accruing on account of expenditure incurred in these areas as compared to a 30 percent grant component available in other areas. For a few backward and strategically important areas on tne Himalayan border, a more liberalised pattern involving 90 percent grant and 10 percent loan was introduced during the Fourth Plan. In addition, a Hill Areas Cell was set up in the Planning Commission for providing assistance to the States in the preparation of integrated plans for their hill areas." [6]

As far as the economically backward areas in the second category are concerned, it was accepted that their problems did not lend themselves to aneasy soultion on account of the following factors: "Firstly, it presented conceptual and methodological problems in the identification of such areas. There were difficulties both in the selection as well as assignment of suitable weights to the indicators of development. Secondly, meaningful programmes for such areas could be evolved only out of location-specific strategies based upon a careful assessment of potentials and priorities arising out of the resource endowment, infrastructure, settlement pattern and marketing opportunities in various identified areas. For the kind of detailed work involved in the development of the appropriate strategies and programmes, neither the requisite data nor adequate personnel with the required skills were available at local levels. Thirdly, private entrepreneurs as well as financing institutions and banks were unwilling to invest in these areas in the absence of either the requisite infrastructure or the proper identification of development prospects."[27] Keeping these problems in view, the Fourth Plan initiated a number of measures, the most important being the identification of the backward areas and the granting of considerable financial and other concessions, subsidies, incentives, etc., for setting up industries in such areas. We have already considered these policy measures in detail.

In addition to these measures, task forces/committees were set up to undertake development of regions such as Western Ghats, Dandakaranya, and Bundelkhand which required the participation of more than one State government. Certain financial and promotional institutions also introduced a number of measures to develop the backward areas. Surveys were conducted under a Committee of Direction constituted with representatives from the RBI, IDBI, ICICI, IFCI, ARC, and the Government of India to specify projects for investment in different backward areas of the country. The Rural Electrification Corporation, set up in 1969, approved, out of a total of 499 schemes, 214 schemes for the backward and underdeveloped areas up to the end of August 1973.

The strategy for the development of the backward areas in the Fifth Plan recognized that the problem of backwardness was a long-term problem and though financial incentives were important, many other incentives and developmental programmes were needed to develop backward areas (in the form of strengthening and coordinated functioning of financial, promotional, and consultancy institutions, restructuring of the field organization to suit the functional requirements of the identified development programmes, evolution of locally-oriented integrated strategies, etc.). Emphasizing that the development of backward areas was basically the responsibility of the State governments, the Plan gave an important role to the Central government which was to participate in the programme of development by making special allocations for hilly and tribal areas and by "(i) providing technical support in respect of planning as well as programme development; (ii) channelising institutional resources on a priority basis; (iii) continuing and further extending the liberal pattern of Central assistance; and (iv) providing special incentives for the flow of private investment to identified backward areas".[28] The programmes for drought-prone areas, tribal areas, and hill areas were reinforced and programmes for the rural poor (especially programmes for the small and marginal farmers) given due importance. The total outlay on these programmes was Rs.1490 crores in the Fifth Plan period, of which Rs.645 crores was in the Central Plan.

As noted earlier, one of the important schemes introduced for the development of the backward areas is the Central investment subsidy scheme. Since the inception of this scheme in 1970, an amount of Rs.10.71 crores was disbursed till 30 March 1976. Of this, the share of the developed States was as much as 59%. Of the developed States, more than one-fifth (22 percent) of the amount has been cornered by Maharashtra alone. Among the backward States, Andhra Pradesh alone received 13% of the amount disbursed.[29] During the past three years (1978-79, 1979-80 and 1980-81) a total sum of Rs.58.1 crores was paid to projects in the backward areas under this scheme.

We have also noted earlier that the term lending institutions also operate a scheme of concessional finance and refinance for industrial projects in specified districts/areas. The total amount of concessional finance (inclusive of refinance) sanctioned by the IDBI, IFCI and ICICI for units in the specified backward districts amounted to Rs.273.99 crores in 1976-77. The share of assistance (concessional and non-concessional) sanctioned to units in the backward areas was 45% in 1976-77. However, as noted in the Draft Five Year Plan, 1978-83 (now defunct),[30] the entire amount indicated above cannot be considered to be a grant for the development of the backward areas. Since the interest differential in favour of the backward districts is around 1.5 to 3.0% the grant component assuming a 15 year repayment period and a five-year grace period, would amount to about Rs.32 crores in 1976-77.

As we shall see in Chapter 9, the distribution of plan and non-plan assistance from the Centre to the States takes into account the factor of backwardness. The distribution of plan assistance is done according to the Gadgil formula (slightly modified in the meeting of the NDC held on 31-8-1980). Whereas previously 10% of assistance was given to those States whose per capita income was below the national average, under the modified version, the share of these States has been raised to 20%. The backward north-eastern States and Jammu & Kashmlr are outside the formula and aid is given to them more liberally. As far as the distribution of non-plan assistance is concerned, practically all the Finance Commissions appointed so far have tried to take account of the special needs of backward areas in their own ways. These issues are discussed in detail in Chapter 9.

With the aim of removing unemployment, the disparities between the rural and urba nareas, and the increasing incidence of industrial sickness, District Industries Centres (DICs) were set up by the Janata government. The present government has decided to continue this scheme with minor changes. Under the existing arrangements, the Central government finances each of the DICs to the extent of 50% of the total annual expenditure in no case exceeding Rs.2.5 lakhs per annum, while the remaining 50% is borne by the State governments. There are a total of 392 DICs in the country with only eight districts remaining to have such centres.

A Critical Review of Government's Policy for the Development of Backward Areas

The casual and indifferent attitude of the government towards the problems of the backward areas is evident from the very fact that it was only after two decades of planning that an attempt was made to demarcate and identify the backward areas and a package of incentives to develop such areas were seriously considered (through the appointment of the Pande Committee and the Wanchoo Committee, respectively, in 1968). Though much had been said on the necessity of developing the backward areas in the Third Plan, the approach was evolved basically within the framework of overall planning wherein it was assumed that the overall economic growth would automatically lead to the development of the backward areas and the regional imbalances that might get accentuated on account of the operation of the planning process could be rectified with the help of such instruments as industrial licensing, provision of education and training facilities, provision of infrastructure facilities, etc.

It is worth while noting that some important recommendations of the Wanchoo Committee were not implemented while the basic recommendations of the Pande Committee were set aside. Thus, the Pande Committee had suggested that efforts of development should be concentrated only on the backward districts of industrially backward States on account of limitations of resources. However, probably because of political pressures, the Planning Commission was led to specify backward districts in all States. This led to a discrimination against the backward States and distribution of limited resources thinly over wide areas in both the developed and the backward States. Also, as already noted, the Planning Commission modified the criteria adopted by the Pande Committee. The modified criteria suffered from anumber of serious drawbacks. Thus, the weightage given to various criteria was not specified. Hence, it is not possible to judge whether justice was done to the backward States. However, the presence of the criterion "length of surfaced roads in relation to population or railway mileage in relation to population" and the insistence of the Planning Commission that the districts selected should possess a minimum level of infrastructure facilities points to a built-in bias in favour of the developed States.

The adoption of the new set of criteria by the Planning Commission has led to a paradoxical situation wherein some of the most backward States have lesser percentage of their districts declared as backward compared with some of the most developed States. Also, the proportion of the population covered by the backward districts in some of the most backward States is less than those covered by the backward districts of the most developed States. Thus, "West Bengal, the state which ranked first according to the composite index of development of Pande Working Group has the highest percentage of districts declared as backward barring Jammu & Kashmir, the north-eastern States and the Union territories. All but three of its 16 districts have been declared backward. On the other hand, its neighbour, Bihar, whose rank in the industrial development is only 10 according to the Pande panel index, has the lowest percentage of districts eligible for the package of incentives. Kerala, the least developed among the developed States, has the lowest percentage of backward districts among developed States, except Haryana and Punjab."[31] Similarly, "the percentage of population in the backward districts of West Bengal to the total population in the State was the highest among all States barring Madhya Pradesh, Jammu & Kashmir and the north-eastern States. Tamil Nadu ranking second in the matter of industrial development and Karnataka ranking seventh had larger proportion of their population eligible for incentives under the package than States like Orissa, Himachal Pradesh, Rajasthan, Bihar, Assam and Andhra Pradesh."[32] (See Table 2.)

Since the Planning Commission insisted on the availability of a minimum level of infrastructure in the districts that could be given incentives, the incentives went more to the backward districts of the developed States compared with the backward districts of the backward States. Because of their comparatively better economic position, the developed States are in a position to invest more on provision of infrastructure in their backward districts compared with the backward States. This investment, in turn, leads to a situation where backward districts of the developed States fulfil the minimum infrastructure requirement as required by the Planning Commission, and hence they are given incentives in preference to the backward districts of the backward States.

There is another important weakness of the Planning Commission's criteria noted by K.K. George. According to him, while only the districts with indices well below the State averages in respect of the specified criteria were to be selected as backward it was not clear as to what exactly was the distance from the State average denoted by the expression "well below". If it is uniform in all States, it would imply a situation wherein some of the districts in highly developed States get classified as backward though they are relatively more developed than some of the districts in the backward States which get classified as developed. Also, since the distance of the backward district is measured from the State averages of the indicators and not the national average, the not-so-backward districts of the developed States were classified as backward and made themselves eligible for incentives and concessions.

We have already presented a critical analysis of the programmes relating to industrialization of the backward areas and the arguments need not be repeated. For a critical appraisal of the policy of resource transfers from the Centre to the States, the reader is referred to Chapter 9, and for a critical review of the industrial licensing policy and policy of financial institutions, the relevant sections of Chapter 5 may be consulted.

NATIONAL COMMITTEE ON DEVELOPMENT OF BACKWARD AREAS (NCDBA)

To examine afresh the backward area development approach, the Planning Commission set up the National Committee on Development of Backward Areas in November 1978. Evaluating the existing policy for industrial dispersal, the Committe notes that the Central investment subsidy and the scheme for concessional finance have benefited a small number of districts,

TABLE 2: **Industrially backward districts: State-wise summary**

State/Union territory	Backward districts		
	Number	As per cent of	
		Total area of the State	Total population of the State
Developed (A)			
West Bengal	13	82	68
Tamil Nadu	8	64	60
Gujarat	10	67	49
Maharashtra	13	54	42
Punjab	4	39	35
Haryana	4	50	39
Karnataka	11	67	63
Kerala	5	42	50
Total (A)		53	52
Backward (B)			
Andhra Pradesh	14	72	59
Bihar	9	47	55
Rajasthan	16	62	54
Madhya Pradesh	36	87	83
Assam	7	78	76
Uttar Pradesh	37	68	62
Orissa	8	61	48
Jammu & Kashmir	10	100	100
Nagaland	3	100	100
Himachal Pradesh	7	88	73
Manipur	5	100	100
Meghalaya	2	100	100
Tripura	3	100	100
Goa, Daman & Diu	3	100	100
Pondicherry	4	100	100
Andaman & Nicobar Islands	1	100	100
Arunachal Pradesh	5	100	100
Dadra & Nagar Haveli	1	100	100
Lakshadweep	1	100	100
Mizoram	1	100	100
Total (B)		69	61
All India	241*	71	58

*The number of districts declared backward has since risen to 247.

Source: Ministry of Industrial Development, *Guidelines for Industries 1974-75*, June 1974.

mostly in close proximity to relatively developed industrial centres; that with a few exceptions the industrial estate programme has not helped relocate industries away from developed areas; that licensing policy is only a negative instrument and cannot, by itself, promote industrial development in backward areas. Having regard to this experience as also the natural tendency of industry to congregate at certain locations, the committe has recommended a policy of encouraging location of industry in suitable growth centres with due weightage for such centres in industrially backward States. For example, it has advocated the creation of 100 growth centres during the Sixth Plan of which 30 are to be in industrially developed States and 70 in the backward States. Of the 70 centres proposed for the backward States, 10 are to be allocated to the hill States of Jammu & Kashmir and Himachal Pradesh, the north-eastern States (excluding Assam) and the Union territories. The balance is to be distributed within each category, the share of each State being proportional to the area and population assigning equal weights to both.

The 100 industrial growth centres would be set up where the population is 50,000 or more and in such backward areas where sufficient infrastructure is "already in position" with a view to minimizing the cost of infrastructure. The criteria also include that such identified areas should have less than 10,000 workers in non-household manufacturing industries and that such centres should not be 'near' the existing centres where employment in non-household manufacturing exceeds 10,000 persons. The committee has recommended the setting up of Industrial Development Authorities (IDA) in each of these 100 growth centres.

In addition to these, the committee has recommended a package of incentives. These include extension of the income tax concession to the units set up in areas outside the area of influence of the "existing industrial centres", modification of the Central subsidy to cover such units, dispensing with the concept of "selectivity" in the existing subsidy and concessional finance scheme and linking the State subsidy schemes with the locational approach in the Central subsidy and concessional finance schemes.[33]

INTEGRATED AREA DEVELOPMENT

The concept of integrated area development is being discussed at present in various seminars and forums all over the country and is being presented as a panacea for all major planning problems in general, and for the development of backward regions in particular. However, the concept of *integrated development* is not altogether clear. For example, it is difficult to decide *what* type of integration should be sought and *what* ways should be adopted to accomplish it. In general, four aspects of integration can be differentiated.[34]

The first aspect concerns itself what is known as *sectoral-cum-temporal integration*. Since all elements of development strategy are not equally important, it becomes necessary to fix priorities and find out what activities have to be developed, when they should be developed, and what should be the pace and intensity of their development keeping in view the underlying linkages among various activities. This can be designated *sectoral-cum-temporal integration*.

The second aspect of integration is *spatial integration*. Just as there are linkages among various activities, there are also linkages among various places that constitute an area. By locating activities at certain places we can divert the patterns of flows of people and goods as between different areas. Spatial integration is concerned with this aspect of integration. In our planning policy we should aim at such spatially integrated plans that ensure a balanced development of all regions of the country. Normally the attempt should be to ensure that each area is able to develop all its potentialities to the fullest possible extent and no area develops at the cost of others.

The third aspect of integration concerns itself with the development of individuals and groups of people. It is a frequent experience of practically all countries that fruits of development tend to get concentrated in a few hands while a considerable majority of people continues to lead a miserably poor life. The problem is more acute in the developing countries such as India where a substantial proportion of the population is below the poverty line (which, itself, is generally defined at a low subsistence level). It is the task of the integrated development to ensure that the benefits of development are conferred more on such poorer sections of society so that interpersonal disparities of income can be considerably brought down.

The fourth and final aspect of integration involves 'the integration of conflicting goals of economic, social and environmental development'. Obviously in a country plagued by widespread poverty and economic backwardness, the considerations of economic growth are likely to govern all other considerations on account of the necessity to provide the basic needs of food, clothing, and shelter to all and sundry. However, the social considerations and the considerations regarding environmental improvement cannot be altogether ignored if some basic quality of human life is to be preserved. By adopting an integrated approach to problems of economic development, all such considerations can be given due importance in the planning process.

The planning process can be considered satisfactory only when it pays due regard to all the aspects of integration discussed above. Our own planning efforts have failed to achieve the desired results in the socio-economic field precisely because they did not take into account the need for integrated planning. The second and fourth aspects of integration were, more or less, entirely ignored. Attention was concentrated on the first aspect, and to some extent, on the third aspect. However, as far as the former is concerned success was very limited because sectoral-cum-temporal integration was not entirely conceived in the manner we have described above. As far as the latter is concerned, nothing seems to have been achieved so far (for proof of this statement, the reader is referred to Chapter 3, Section on "Inequalities in Income and Wealth"). For most of the planning period, we have tended to adopt a tentative, ad hoc and piecemeal approach with the result that national planning has more or less bypassed large rural and backward areas. It is in this overall context that one must view the widespread interest generated in recent years in India, for adopting an integrated area development approach and the role given to Integrated Rural Development in the Draft Sixth Plan. However, before any attempts are made in this direction, it is necessary to clarify certain issues. Let us see what these issues are.

Unit of Planning

The first issue that confronts us is—What should be the unit of planning? Normally a village is taken as the unit of planning in the belief that it can serve as an *effective* and a *viable* unit for development purposes. However, as emphasized by V.K.R.V. Rao,[35] the village is not a homogeneous unit nor is it necessarily a viable unit. Some of the important questions raised by Rao are: ". . . is the census village a viable unit? Does it contain the area and population base necessary for integrated development? Can we bring about either full employment or distributive justice and elimination of poverty or provision of a minimum of developmental and welfare schemes or popular participation or even maximization of output or productive application of science and technology by treating the village identified as the unit for development?" The answers to most of these questions are in the negative. The majority of villages in India in 1971 (352,023 out of 567,338, i.e. 55.34%) had a population of less than 500 each and out of these more than 50% had a population of less than 200 each. How, asks Rao, can these small villages having between 40 and 100 families be treated as *viable economic units* for development purposes? In the absence of viability, the vast amounts spent on their development are likely to go waste. Therefore, it is necessary to determine the minimum size of rural settlements that is necessary to implement the various programmes of development. According to Rao, "The problem is not only to determine the size of such a minimum unit but also to devise ways and means for bringing suh minimum units into existence by grouping clusters of villages with necessary social, economic and resource links into new viable villages and establishing the necessary transport facilities between the villages composing any given cluster so that each cluster of villages constituting a new village can function as one integrated unit." This basioally is a domain of regional economics and regional planning for the decision on what clusters should be formed, how the villages should be integrated, and in what manner transport linkages should be provided, are all decided by regional economics with the various methods and techniques at its disposal.

Once such clusters of villages are demarcated, it becomes necessary to identify the *dynamic clusters* among them and locate the growth foci within them. Such growth foci have to be interlinked with one another in such a form that a hierarchy is established with service centres at the local level, growth points at the sub-regional level, growth centres at the regional level, and growth poles at the national level.[36] Attention, in this general framework, has to be concentrated on those clusters that have the largest development potential. Such a selective approach is necessary because of the paucity of resources. Spreading the limited resources over large areas thinly implies a wastage of resources as amply demonstrated by the community development programme in India.[37] The selective approach emphasizes the development of areas having the greatest potential of development and their linking up with the hinterland in such a way that maximum spread effects are generated.[38]

The preliminary steps in a growth strategy for the development of the backward areas would therefore include: (i) formation of clusters of Villages, (ii) selection of dynamic clusters, and (iii) locating growth centres within them. For these purposes it will be necessary to carry out detailed industrial potential surveys of the backward districts and "preparation of a series of project profiles based on feasible products identified in the district surveys".

Development of Entrepreneurship

After these preliminary steps are completed comes the task of *planting* entrepreneurs in areas specified in the above manner (through industrial potential surveys and project feasibility reports). While at the formulation level of the development strategy *selection of areas for development purposes* is the basic task, at the implementation level *planting of entrepreneurs* is the basic task. The task is basic because the role of the entrepreneurs in the process of economic development is very important. In fact, J.A. Schumpeter assigns a central role to entrepreneurs in his theory of economic development. Since development occurs by discontinuous spurts in a dynamic world, Schumpeter argues that there is a high degree of risk and uncertainty involved in the industrial development process. Accordingly, "a specially motivated and talented type of individual— the entrepreneur—is therefore necessary in this environment both to see potentially profitable opportunities and to exploit them".[39] Since the backward areas have an acute paucity of this 'specially motivated and talented individual' it becomes necessary to plan for (i) importing entrepreneurs from relatively more developed areas and (ii) *creating* entrepreneurs from within the backward areas themselves. The former is generally sought to be accomplished by providing subsidies, concessions, and incentives in the backward areas and the latter is achieved by provision of technical and other training to prospective entrepreneurs and creation of an atmosphere (having the necessary socio-economic infrastructure) conducive to industrial activity. Also, it is expected that the entrepreneurs who come to these areas from the developed areas will, through demonstration effect, encourage young, trained, and skilled people of the backward areas to take risks and set up industries themselves.

The setting up of a large project in a backward area provides opportunities to a number of ancillary units to come up as suppliers of various parts and components. The establishment of industrial estates also leads to a rapid growth of small enterprises. But, for the success of either of these programmes, it is necessary that (i) there is an adequate provision of pre-requisites in the form of water, power, transport, and technical knowledge; (ii) there is a ready market for the products of these industries and payments to the entrepreneurs on account of the purchase of their products are made early (it is frequently observed that small-scale industrialists are generally short of funds and cannot (a) afford to stock their products for long and (b) wait for payments to be made to them for long); and (iii) the aspirations of the people are so aroused that they participate enthusiastically in exapanding industrial and economic activity.[40]

The technique advocated for developing entrepreneurship in the backward areas is known as the *intensive campaign technique*. The basic purposes of this technique are: (i) making the potential entrepreneurs aware of the opportunities and potentialities of industrial development (in these areas), and (ii) making the potential entrepreneurs aware of the incentives and concessions to which they are entitled (in these areas). For carrying out an intensive campaign, it is usual, first of all, to specify the area that is selected and is to be covered. The second step involves (i) surveying the potentialities and investigating the possibilities of development of industries in the area and (ii) preparing a pamphlet incorporating (a) the findings of the survey and (b) the incentives announced by the different levels of the government to entrepreneurs setting up industries in the area. The final step involves circulating the pamphlets among the potential entrepreneurs and utilizing other media (such as lectures, demonstrations, exhibitions, etc.) in making the results known to the general public.

As far as developing entrepreneurship in the backward areas is concerned, the most important role is played by the special inducements and incentives offered to potential entrepreneurs in these areas by the Central and the State governments and the local bodies. In addition to tax incentives in the form of tax rebate, tax holiday, depreciation allowances, lower income-tax rate, exemption from excise duty, sales tax and octroi duty, it is necessary to plan out a number of other concessions and facilities to attract the entrepreneurs from other regions and to develop entrepreneurship within these regions because the advantages of setting up industries in the developed areas are so overwhelming that unless substantial efforts are made (in the form of special concessions and assistance), the backward areas will fail to attract industries. The special concessions required include provision of construction grants (because construction costs are high in the backward areas and there is the non-availability of skilled labour to carry out the job), grants to offset the transportation disadvantages, grants to pay for the import of skilled labour from relatively more developed areas, and housing grants for the construction of housing colonies by medium and large units set up in the backward areas. Infrastructure, in the form of land, power, transportation facilities, constructed sheds, shopping centres, telephone exchange, dispensary, schools, canteens, etc., will also have to be provided. As noted elsewhere in this chapter, the programme of industrial estates was initiated precisely to provide such an infrastructure. It is necessary to regenerate and revitalize the programme. If instead of locating the industrial estates at random (i.e., without any consideration of growth foci, growth potentials, and inter-industry linkages) as had been done in the past, they are located in *selected* growth foci areas having maximum linkages, the programme can achieve astounding successes.

In areas selected for intensive development, entrepreneurial training programmes should be organized and technical assistance guaranteed. For this purpose, technical consultancy service centres should be set up. One such centre was set up in Kerala (Cochin). The function of such a consultancy centre would be "assisting entrepreneurs in selection of project ideas, preparation of feasibility studies, provision of technical and administrative assistance in promotion and management of industries, undertaking techno-economic appraisal of projects on behalf of the local financial institutions, conducting market research and surveys for specific projects and acting generally as industrial, management and financial consultants".[41]

The Lead Industry Strategy for Development of Backward Areas

In the first IFCI Lecture delivered under the auspices of the Faculty of Management Studies, University of Delhi, A.V. Srinivasan[42] advocated the adoption of a *lead industry* strategy for the development of backward areas. An industry is termed leading if it generates significant growth impulses and has high ability to innovate. According to Srinivasan, "The lead industries should be patterned after lead banks and asked to support and contribute to the development of backward areas. Each such industry (chosen from both private and public sectors) be identified with a district *which has potential for development* and made responsible for promoting, developing, and assisting industries in that district. Then, the lead industry will conduct techno-economic surveys and sociological studies and match the development objectives of the state with its economic efforts. This would result in an investment plan for the district, participated by the lead industry, financial institutions, development agencies, and State administration."[43] Since big business houses in the private sector and successful large corporations in the public sector are multiproduct-multiplant-multicity, have numerous backward and forward linkages, possess ample (and sophisticated) managerial talent, are experienced in high technology, have research and development facilities and have capital and market approach, Srinivasan advocates that big business houses and successful large corporations in the public sector should be considered *lead* industries.

Where should such lead industries be located? Srinivasan advocates that they should be located in *developable* regions since only then can they exert a powerful pull effect on the *underdeveloped* regions of the hinterland. The characteristics to be considered while identifying such developable districts would be: "(i) dispersal of population; (ii) percentage of population in relation to poverty line; (iii) extent of agricultural productivity; (iv) literacy level; (v) indications on the existence of social infrastructure facilities; (vi) level of investment per individual; (vii) potential for developing a market growth centre; (vii) possibility of industrialization". Very high, medium, and very low intensity of these characteristics delineates districts as developed, developable, and underdeveloped respectively. Justifying his stand for the concentration of projects in developable districts alone with the help of the growth centre theory (which, as noted in chapter 4, maintains that the most efficient way to generate development in lagging regions is to concentrate projects in a relatively few places with growth potential), Srinivasan advocates that the lead industry should be located in *one* or *two* developable districts of each State. Table 3 gives a list of the developable districts according to Srinivasan and identifies two lead firms—one in the public sector and the other in the private sector.

The tasks conferred on the lead firms are: "The lead firm should be assigned the task of total industrial development of the district with the state providing the necessary support. This task must comprise techno-economic survey, sociological studies, resource investigation, identifying growth centre, product choice, research for decentralised production, iden-

TABLE 3: Lead firms and developable districts

State	Developable districts	Lead firms
(1)	(2)	(3)
Himachal Pradesh	Simla, Bilaspur, Mandi, Sirman	Oil & Natural Gas Commission, Mafatlal Group
Jammu & Kashmir	Jammu, Anantnag, Baramula	Hindustan Machine Tools Ltd., Mahindra and Mahindra Group
Orissa	Puri, Ganjam, Balasore, Mayurbhanj, Bolangir, Dhenkanal, Keonjhar	National Mineral Development Corporation Ltd., Birla Group
Uttar Pradesh	Kanpur, Gorakhpur, Ghazipur, Agra, Faizabad, Bareilly, Basti, Allahabad, Moradabad, Aligarh, Bulandshahar, Muzaffarnagar, Pratapgarh, Rampur, Saharanpur, Sultanpur, Barabanki, Etah, Farukhabad, Mathura, Mainpur, Etawah, Sitapur	Indian Drugs & Pharmaceuticals Ltd., J.K. Group
Assam	Cachar, Goalpura, Sibsagar	Oil India Limited, McNeil Magor Group
Madhya Pradesh	Raipur, Bilaspur, Sehore, Sagar, Balaghat, Satna, Dhar, Shajapur, Rajgarh, Tikemgarh, Narsimhapur, Raigarh, Mandsaur, Jhabua, Khargone, Vidisha, Morena, Dewas Chindwara	Bharat Almuinium Company Limited, Walchand Group
Rajasthan	Jhunjhunun, Ajmer, Sikar, Kota, Banswara, Durgapur, Udaipur, Sawai Madhopur, Bhilwara, Jhalawar, Chittorgarh, Tonk, Sirohi, Bundi	Hindustan Copper Limited, Bangur Group
Bihar	Darbhanga, Dhanbad, Monghyr, Champaran, Saharsa, Bhagalpur, Gaya, Purnea	Heavy Engineering Corporation Ltd., Indian Tobacco Company Ltd.

(*Contd.*)

TABLE 3 (*Contd.*)

(1)	(2)	(3)
Andhra Pradesh	Guntur, Visakhapatnam, Srikakulam, Chittoor, Karimnagar, Warangal, Nalgonda, Medak, Nizamabad	Bharat Heavy Electricals Ltd., ICI (India) Private Ltd.
Kerala	Ernakulam, Trichur, Kozhikode, Quilon, Malappuram	Fertilizers and Chemicals (Travancore) Ltd., Tata Group
Karnataka	Belgaum, Kolar, Dharwar, Mysore, Tumkur, Hassan, Bidar, Shimoga, Chitradurga	Bokaro Steel Ltd., Kirloskar Group
Haryana	Ambala, Karnal, Jind	Indian Oil Corporation Ltd., Sri Ram Group
Punjab	Amritsar,Gurdaspur, Patiala, Hoshiarpur, Ropar, Kapurthala	Fertilizer Corporation of India Ltd., Thapar Group
Maharashtra	Poona, Jalgaon, Nagpur, Sangli, Nasik, Ratnagiri, Satara, Bhandara, Buldhana, Ahmednagar, Akola, Sholapur, Osmanabad	Hindustan Petroleum Corporation Ltd., Khatau Group
Gujarat	Gandhinagar, Vadodara, Valsad, Mahansana, Surat, Pandimahal, Junagadh, Sabarkantha, Rajkot	Indian Petrochemicals Corporation Ltd., Kasturbhai Lalbhai Group
Tamil Nadu	Chingleput, South Arcot, Salem, Madurai, North Arcot, Coimbatore	Madras Fertilizers Limited, Larsen & Toubro
West Bengal	Nadia, Burdwan, Malda, Murshidabad, Midnapore, Cooch Behar	Hindustan Steel Ltd., Associated Cement Companies

Source: A.V. Srinivasan, *Lead Industry Strategy for Developing Backward Areas* (Delhi University: Faculty of Management Studies, 1978), Appendix C.

tifying process units and entrepreneurs, and arranging finance. Besides, the lead firm should make available industrial facilities and material, provide technological supports, and act as a singular institution to channelise development efforts and process demands of various state institutions which extend development support, finance etc. Its responsibility includes starting of an industry based on decentralised production, thereby developing entrepreneurial skill and setting the pace for progress in the assigned developable district. This in turn will provide diffusion of management into other areas."[44]

In his comments on Srinivasan's thesis, D.T. Lakdawala has raised a number of objections. The basic defect of the thesis is that it assigns a *pivotal* and *predominant* role to multiproduct-multiplant firms of big houses. How, Lakdawala argues, can the big houses now, all of a sudden, assume the role which they have failed to assume in the past thirty years? How can they be expected to assume the social responsibility of playing a pivotal role in the development of industries in underdeveloped areas when in the past they have functioned as "self-sufficient (and self-dependent) enclaves" and their relationship with other industries and areas has been an exploitative one? Lakdawala also notes that the strategy of *selectivity* advocated by the thesis is irrational and injudicious in a socio-economic farmework wherein more than 40% of the population lives below the poverty line. Another important drawback of the thesis is its emphasis on *industry* to the neglect of agriculture. Following western economic thinking it is fashionable to talk of the location of *propulsive* and *leading* industries in backward areas of the underdeveloped countries. In labour surplus agricultural economies such as India, where more than 70% of the population is dependent on agriculture, it is far better to concentrate on the development of agriculture. It is *agriculture* and not one or two *industries* that can serve as the vehicle of development. Lakdawala also notes that the cost of carrying out the new strategy advocated by Srinivasan would be much higher compared with an agriculture-oriented strategy.

Authority for Backward Area Development

The discussion above shows that the concept of lead industry cannot be too much relied upon in the task of backward area development. Yet, in some backward areas of the economy (especially in some backward areas of the developed States) it does have some chances of success. In other backward areas, it is much better to follow the strategy of development of growth foci advocated by R.P. Misra.[45] Keeping in view the observations of D.T. Lakdawala discussed above, it would be desirable to define inter-industrial linkages (in the overall framework of growth foci) in such a way that forward linkages are established between rural and urban economies through appropriate infrastructural and institutional network. Here, by 'forward' link is meant the linkage that connects the rural features of the district economy with the industrial economy of the neighbouring regions by establishing consumer goods and ancillary or auxiliary industries. By 'backward' linkage is meant the connection of the industrial features of the district or region with agrarian and rural economy by establishing agro-industries, etc., so that there is a coordinated development of the entire region in a phased manner. Such an approach will ensure both the development of industry and the development of agriculture in the backward regions. Since development of industry will be based on the industrial potential surveys of the regions, demand for regional resources (regional agricultural produce, regional labour, regional minerals, etc.) will increase giving a spurt to agricultural activity on the one hand and initiating a process of transfer of labour from primary to secondary activity on the other. While the former will have the effect of making agriculture more efficient and diversified, the latter will have the effect of reducing the pressure of population on agriculture.

Because of the complexity of the task of backward area development and its specialized nature, it is not likely that the Centre and the State governments can carry out the job effectively. Study of the *linkage patterns* in the spatial organization of economic activity, conducting industrial surveys, carrying out entrepreneurial development programmes, initiating specific programmes for the development of infrastructure (power, transport, communications, factory accommodation, etc.), and linking up the processes of agricultural development with industrial development are tasks too complex to be treated by the existing politico-administrative set-up. This is the reason why the Seminar on "Backward Area Development: Strategies and Policies" organized by the Management Development Institute, New Delhi (from 23 to 25 April 1976 at Bangalore) suggested the setting up of a separate authority for the development of backward areas. Such an authority can be termed the Authority for Backward Area Development (ABAD). The seminar recommended that such an authority should be a central organization at the national level and should be headed by a high level board of ministers and secretaries to the Government of India (viz., Minister for Industries, Minister for Finance, Deputy Chairman of the Planning Commission, Minister for Company Law, Development Commissioner, Small Scale Industries, etc.). The authority should decide where the industries are to be located in the backward areas and how the licensing capacity is to be sanctioned. It should also ensure that an adequate share of subsidies and incentives go to the development of the most backward areas which hold a promise of development and that the most backward States get their due share. For this purpose the authority will have to devise 'suitable promotional and development measures'. The seminar recommended that the proposed authority should have the following objectives:

1. A rapid development of backward areas.
2. Preparation of project reports of propulsive industries based on local resources leading to rapid development of backward areas.
3. Dissemination of information to investors of the facilities and incentives available for promotion of their projects in backward areas.
4. To provide technical assistance for development of backward areas.
5. To actively develop, promote and sponsor programmes of industrial development of backward areas.
6. To administer as an agent of the Government of India schemes on incentives, subsidies and facilities for development of backward areas.
7. To raise additional resources from the market for promotion of industrial development of backward areas.[46]

A careful review of the plan for the establishment of the ABAD reveals, at least, two flaws in the approach: (i) the authority proposed is to be a *central organization* where no provision is made to incorporate the representatives of the local bodies of the backward areas (and representatives of the backward States) and (ii) the basic approach is to help *industrialize* the backward areas with all emphasis being given to development of industries through schemes of incentives, subsidies, technical assistance, etc. As far as the former issue is concerned, we believe that unless the most backward States and the most backward areas of these States are given representation on the ABAD, neither the voice of the backward States (and areas) will be heard nor their requirements for development appreciated. In the absence of this, it will not be possible to carry out detailed, relevant, and in-depth studies of inter-industry and rural-urban linkage processes in the development strategy because such processes are likely to be different in different backward areas. If we do not have such *regional* studies, schemes for the development of backward areas cannot be planned in a right perspective nor can a desirable scheme of resource-transfer worked out.

As far as the second issue is concerned, we feel that the ABAD should not unduly restrict its field to industrial development alone. It is possible that the committee that formulated the above objectives for the seminar had such linkage-processes in mind as we have described above (e.g., establishment of consumer goods and auxiliary industries on the one hand and agro-industries on the other so that the agrarian economy can be developed in an integrated manner) but a study of the report does not reveal it.

We believe that the role of the ABAD in promoting development of agricultural activities in particular, and rural areas in general, should be explicitly acknowledged and incorporated as one of the basic objectives of the ABAD. Since linkage processes and rural environment were not paid sufficient attention in the past, many large industrial complexes set up in the backward areas did not materially influence the hinterland as we have already noted in the case of steel cities. It is not appreciated by the planners that far more important than the size and sophistication of an industrial complex is the spread effect which its establishment sets in motion. On account of all these factors, it is also necessary that the proposed ABAD should lay ample emphasis on the 'social diffusion process' and this calls for (i) adequate representation to the backward States and the backward areas of these States on the ABAD and (ii) emphasis on rural-urban linkage and rural development in the ABAD's programme.

NOTES

1. See Chapter 5.
2. Mahesh T. Pathak, "Development of Backward Areas : Problems and Prospects", *Artha Vikas*, Vol. X, Nos. 1-2, January-July 1973, p. 41.
3. Ibid.
4. Ibid.
5. Planning Commission, Government of India, *Identification of Backward Areas,* 1969.
6. Government of India, Development Commissioner (Small Scale Industries), *Fiscal and Financial Incentives for Starting Industries*, 1969, pp. 2-3.
7. Ibid., pp. 16-17.
8. Ibid., p. 14.
9. R.N. Lakhotia, "Tax Incentives for Backward Areas", *The Economic Times*, 17 December 1974, p. 5.
10. *The Economic Times*, 6 April 1981.
11. Planning Commission, Government of India, *The Third Five Year Plan*, p. 145.
12. Vibhooti Goyal, "Area Development Strategy: Diffusion of Growth Forces", *The Economic Times*, 9 December 1975, p. 5.
13. M.N.V. Nair, V. Srinivasan and S.P. Kumar, "Need for New Policy Perspectives on Regional Development", in *Backward Area Development: Strategies and Policies* (New Delhi: Management Development Institute, 1977), p. 157.
14. Programme Evaluation Organisation, Planning Commission, *Report on Evaluation of Rural Industries Projects*, December 1968, p. 2.
15. Planning Commission, Gorvernment of India, *Draft Fifth Five Year Plan*, Vol. II, p. 163.
16. Programme Evaluation Organisation, op. cit., p. 34.
17. Development Commissioner, Small Scale Industries, *Study of Industrial Estates*, 1966, p. 5.
18. Development Commissioner, Small Scale Industries, *Study of Industrial Estates*, 1967, p. 10.

19. S.V. Char, "Role of Industrial Estates", *The Economic Times*, 16 May 1981.
20. Data are from N. Somsekhara, *Efficiency of Industrial Estates in India with particular reference to Mysore* (Delhi: Vikas Publishing House Pvt. Ltd., 1975), Table 2.1, p. 11 and Table 2.2, p. 12. At present there are 60 well-knit estates in Maharashtra with at least one in each district of the State. A total of 3048 factories are operating in that State giving employment to 136,282 persons. *The Economic Times*, 16 May 1981, p. II (Supplement).
21. NCAER, *Market Towns and Spatial Development* (New Delhi, 1971), p. 44.
22. Thus, the observation of rural industrial estates of Baruipur and Shaktigarh in West Bengal leads Kalyani Bandyopadhyaya to conclude that the industrial estates suffer from non-availability of skilled labour, high rent, shortage of electricity, delay in decision-making, lack of good and efficient administration at the local level, lack of the spirit of mutual cooperation and understanding between the entrepreneurs and estate authorities as well as among the different government departments. See Kalyani Bandyopadhyaya. *Industrialisation through Industrial Estates: A Pattern of Economic Decentralisation* (Calcutta: Bookland, 1969), pp. 229-235.
23. *Draft Fifth Five Year Plan*, Vol. II, op. cit., p. 282.
24. See Chapter 7 for details.
25. See Chapter 11, Section 'Integrated Development of Tribal Areas', for details.
26. *Draft Fifth Five Year Plan*, Vol. II, op. cit., p. 283.
27. Ibid., p. 283.
28. Ibid., p. 284.
29. K.S.V. Menon, "Backward Areas Development", *The Economic Times*, 27 May 1979, p. 5.
30. Planning Commission, Government of India, *Draft Five Year Plan, 1978-83* (now defunct), p. 111.
31. K.K. George, "Development of Backward Regions: Strategy Distorted", *The Economic Times*, 1 & 2 October 1976.
32. Ibid.
33. *The Economic Times*, 19 February 1981 and 7 June 1981. Also see, Planning Commission, Government of India, *Sixth Five Year Plan, 1980-85*, pp. 87-88.
34. K.V. Sundaram, R.P. Misra and P.S. Tiwari, "Micro Level Planning and Development Processes" Vol. II (University of Mysore, 1976), Cyclostyled Report, pp. 43-45.
35. V.K.R.V. Rao, "An Integrated Approach to Rural Development", *Yojana*, 15-28 February 1977, pp. 11-12.
36. For a discussion on these issues, see Chapter 4.
37. For a discussion on community development programme, see Chapter 7.
38. Compare with the following statement:

    "The very scarcity of resources forces a need for priorities. A few districts do possess more locational strong points for rapid industrial development than others. Maximum results of the massive concessions or grants could be generated in a short time if adequate resources and efforts are concentrated on selected areas rather than spreading thin the limited resources over all districts at the same time leading to partial and inadequate incentives thereby hurting all areas equally including those with better potential. It is essential to identify 'New growth districts' on which attention may be focused since they have potential for immediate development. As basic infrastructure is developed, sufficient industrial activity takes place, these will become self-sustaining. The efforts then can be concentrated on the next ranking new districts." Anil C. Shah and V.G. Patel, "An Integrated Strategy for Backward Districts' Industrial Development", *Artha Vikas*, Vol. IX, op. cit., pp. 204-205.

39. Gerald M. Meier and Robert E. Baldwin, *Economic Development: Theory, History, Policy* (Bombay: Asia Publishing House, 1970), p. 89.
40. The National Small Industries Corporation Ltd., *How to Motivate Entrepreneurship in Backward Areas,* Okhla, New Delhi), 1966, p. 2.
40. N.D. Joshi, "Review of the Policy for the Development of Backward Regions in India", *Artha Vikas,* Vol. IX, op. cit., p. 16.
42. A.V. Srinivasan, *Lead Industry Strategy for Developing Backward Areas,* First IFCI Lecture delivered under the auspices of Faculty of Management Studies, University of Delhi on 30 March 1978; published by the Faculty of Management Studies.
43. Ibid., p. 15.
44 Ibid., p. 18.
45. For a discussion of Misra's thesis, see Chapter 4.
46. Management Development Institute, *Backward Area Development,* op. cit., p. 284.

ANNEXURE I

List of industrially backward districts selected to qualify for concessional finance from the financial institutions (as on 3 January 1976):

Andhra Pradesh	: Anantapur, Chittoor, Cuddapah, Karimnagar, Khammam, Kurnool, Mahbubnagar, Medak, Nalgonda, Nellore, Nizamabad, Ongole, Srikakulum, Warangal.
Assam	: Cachar, Goalpara, Kamrup, Mikir Hills, North Cachar Hill, Nowgong, new Lakhimpur district.
Bihar	: Bhagalpur, Champaran*, Darbhanga*, Muzaffarpur*, Palamau, Purnea, Saharsa, Santhal Parganas, Saran*, and new districts of Nalanda, Aurangabad, Nawadah, Gaya, Bhojpur, Begusarai and Monghyr.
Gujarat	: Amreli, Banaskantha, Bhavnagar, Broach, Junagadh, Kutch, Mehsana, Panchmahal, Sabarkantha, Surendernagar
Haryana	: Bhiwani, Hissar**, Jind, Mohindergarh.
Himachal Pradesh	: Chamba, Kangra*, Kinnaur, Kulu, Lahaul and Spiti, Solan, Sirmur.
Jammu & Kashmir	: Anantnag, Baramula, Doda, Jammu, Kathua, Ladakh, Pooch, Rajori, Srinagar, Udhampur.
Kerala	: Alleppey, Cannanore, Malapuram, Trichur, Trivandrum.
Karnataka	: Belgaum, Bidar, Bijapur, Dharwar, Gulbarga, Hassan, Mysore, North Kanara, Raichur, South Kanara, Tumkur.
Madhya Pradesh	: Balaghat, Bastar, Betul, Bilaspur, Bhind, Chhatarpur, Chindwara, Damoh, Datia, Dhar, Dewas, Guna, Hoshangabad, Jhabua, Khargone, Mandla, Mandsaur, Morena, Narsimhapur, Rajgarh, Raisen, Ratlam, Rewa, Sagar, Seoni, Shajapur, Shivpuri, Sidhi, Surguja, Tikamgarh, Vidisha and new Sehore district.
Maharashtra	: Aurangabad, Bhandara, Bhir, Buldhana, Chanda, Colaba, Dhulia, Jalgaon, Nanded, Osmanabad, Parbhani, Ratnagiri, Yeotmal.
Manipur	: All the 5 districts.
Meghalaya	: Garo Hills and United Khasi & Jaintia* Hills.
Nagaland	: Kohima, Mokokechung, Tuensang.
Orissa	: Balasore, Bolangir, Dhenkanal, Kalahandi, Keonjhar, Koraput, Mayurbhanj, Phulbani.
Punjab	: Bhatinda*, Gurdaspur, Hoshiarpur, Ferozpur, Sangrur.
Rajasthan	: Alwar, Banswara, Barmer, Bhilwara, Churu, Dungarpur, Jaisalmer, Jalore, Jhunjhunu, Jhalawar, Jodhpur, Nagaur, Sikar, Sirohi, Tonk, Udaipur.

Sikkim	: All the 4 districts of Gangtok, Mangan, Gyalshing and Namchi.
Tamil Nadu	: Dharmapuri, Kanyakumari, Madurai, North Arcot, Ramanathapuram, South Arcot, Thanjavur, Tiruchirapalli, and new Pudukkottai district.
Tripura	: All the 3 districts.
Uttar Pradesh	: Almora, Azamgarh, Badaun, Bahraich, Ballia, Banda, Barabanki, Basti, Bulandshahr, Chamoli, Deoria, Etah, Etawah, Faizabad, Farrukhabad, Fatehpur, Garhwal, Ghazipur, Gonda, Hamirpur, Herdoi, Jalaun, Jaunpur, Jhansi, Mainpuri, Mathura, Moradabad, Pilibhit, Pithoragarh, Pratapgarh, Rai Bareli, Shahjahanpur, Sitapur, Sultanpur, Tehri Garhwal, Unnao, Rampur, Uttar Kashi.
West Bengal	: Bankura, Birbhum, Burdwan, Cooch-Behar, Darjeeling, Hooghly, Jalpaiguri, Malda, Midnapur, Murshidabad, Nadia, Purulia, West Dinajpur.
Andaman & Nicobar Islands	: Entire Area.
Arunachal Pradesh	: Entire Area.
Dadra & Nagar Haveli	: Entire Area.
Goa, Daman & Diu	: Entire Area.
Lakshadweep	: Entire Area.
Mizoram	: Entire Area.
Pondicherry	: Entire Area.

*District as it existed prior to its recent reorganization.

**District as reorganized recently.

Source: K.V. Sundaram and R.P. Misra, *Micro Level Planning and Development Processes*, Vol. I (Cyclostyled Report by Institute of Development Studies, Mysore University, August 1976); Annexure VII.

ANNEXURE II

List of industrially backward districts/areas selected to qualify for the Central scheme of investment subsidy (as on 10 July 1972).

Andhra Pradesh	: Two areas—
	One 'area' from Rayalaseema region comprising
	13 blocks, viz., Chittoor*, Bangarupalem*, Pulicherla*, Pattur*, Chandaragiri and Kalahasthi* (from Chittoor district) and Kodur, Rajampet, Sidhout, Cuddapah, Kamalapuram, Proddatur and Pulivendla (from Cuddapah district).
	The other 'area' from Telengana region comprising
	14 blocks, viz. Mahbubnagar*, Jadcherla*, Shadnagar*, Kalwakurthy and Amangal (from Mahboobnagar district) and Nalgonda, Mungadi, Nakrakal, Suryapet, Kodad*, Kuzuranagar*, Mirgalaguda*, Peddavora* and Devarakonda* (from Nalgonda district).
Assam	: Goalpara and Mikir Hills districts.
Bihar	: Bhagalpur and Darbhanga** districts.
Gujarat	: Panchmahals districts.
Haryana	: Reorganized Mohindergarh district (comprising Rewari* and Mohindergarh Sub-divisions).
Himachal Pradesh	: Kangra** district.
Jammu & Kashmir	: Jammu and Srinagar districts.
Karnataka	: Raichur district.
Kerala	: Alleppey district.
Madhya Pradesh	: Two areas—
	One 'area' from eastern region comprising
	12 blocks, viz., Korba, Baloda, Shampa, Kota, Masturi and Bilha, (Bilaspur) blocks (from Bilaspur district), Bhatapara, Simga, Tilda, Dharsiwa (Raipur), Abhanpur, and Rajim blocks (from Raipur district);
	The other 'area' from western region comprising
	10 blocks, viz., Dewas and Tonk Khurad blocks (from Dewas district), Gulana, Shujalpur and Shajapur blocks (from Shajapur district), Panchor (Sarangpur), Biaora blocks (from Rajgarh district) and Chachaura. Raghogarh and Guna blocks (from Guna district).
Maharashtra	: Ratnagiri district.

Manipur	: All the 5 districts.
Meghalaya	: Garo Hills and United Khasi & Jaintia** Hills districts.
Nagaland	: Kohima & Mekokchung districts.
Orissa	: Kalahandi and Mayurbhanj districts.
Punjab	: Hoshiarpur district.
Rajasthan	: Alwar and Jodhpur districts.
Tamil Nadu	: One 'Area' comprising 11 Taluks (including Sub-taluks) viz., Ramanathapuram, Mudukulathur, Sivaganga, Parmakudi, Thiruvadani and Thirupathur Taluks (from Ramanathapuram district), Melur* Taluk (from Madurai district), Pudukkottai, Thirumayam, Alangudi and Kalathur Taluks (from Pudukkottai district).
Tripura	: All the 3 districts.
Uttar Pradesh	: Ballia and Jhansi districts.
West Bengal	: Purulia district.
	Union territories
Andaman & Nicobar Islands	: Entire territory.
Arunachal Pradesh	: Entire territory.
Dadra & Nagar Haveli	: Entire territory.
Goa, Daman & Diu	: Entire territory excluding the area within the municipal limits of territory's capital.
Lakshadweep	: Entire territory.
Mizoram	: Entire territory.
Pondicherry	: Entire territory excluding the within the area municipal limits of territory's capital.

*Represents Taluks/Blocks/Tehsils/Sub-divisions selected after 10-7-1972.

**Represents Districts as they existed prior to their recent reorganization.

Source: K.V. Sundaram and R.P. Misra, *Micro Level Planning and Development Processes*, Vol. I (Cyclostyled Report by Institute of Development Studies, Mysore University, August 1976), Annexure VIII.

ANNEXURE III

List of additional industrially backward districts/areas selected (after 10-7-1972) to qualify for the Central scheme of investment subsidy (as on 3 January 1976).

Andhra Pradesh	: *Srikakulam district and 3 'areas'* *One area from Rayalseema region comprising* 9 blocks, viz., Tadpatri*, Singanamala*, Gooty*, Kudair (from Anantapur district) and Dhone*, Kurnool*, Banganapalli, Nandyal and Giddalur (from Kurnool district). *Two areas 'from' Telengana region* One area comprising 14 blocks, viz., Khammam*, Thirumalaipalam*, Kallur, Yellandu, Kothagudam, Aswaropeta, Burgampad and Bhadrachalam (from Khammam district) and Mahbubabad*, Narsampet*, Hanamkonda*, Ghanapur, Jangaon and Mulug (from Warangal district). *The other 'area' comprising 15 blocks, viz.* Zaheerabad, Patancheruvu, Narasapur, Medak and Siddipet (from Medak district), Yedapalli, Nizamabad, Kamareddy and Damokonda, (from Nizamabad district) and Sircilla, Karimnagar*, Sultanabad*, Peddapalli*, Manthani and Huzurabad* (from Karimnagar district).
Assam	: Kamrup, Newgong, Cachar and new Lakhimpur district.
Bihar	: Champaran**, Palaman, Saharsa and Santhal Parganas.
Gujarat	: Broach and Surendranagar.
Haryana	: Bhiwani district (comprising Bhiwani and Dadri* sub-divisions) and one area comprising 8 blocks, viz., Hissar Block No. 1 and Barwala Block (of Hissar Tehsil), Hansi Block No. 1 (from Hansi Tehsil), Bahuna block (from Fatehabad Tehsil), Tohana Block/Tehsil (from Tohana Tehsil)—from the district of Hissar—Jind Block and Julana Block (from Jind Tehsil), Uchana Block (Narwana Tehsil)—from the district of Jind.
Himachal Pradesh	: Chamba, Kulu, Sirmur and Solan (additional proposal for one district awaited).
Jammu & Kashmir	: Anantnag, Doda, Baramulla and Poonch.
Karnataka	: Mysore and Dharwar.
Kerala	: Cannanore and Malapuram.
Madhya Pradesh	: 4 areas— *One 'area' from north region* Comprising 9 blocks, viz., Shivpuri & Kerara (from Shivpuri

	district), Datia & Seondha (from Datia district), Bhind, Mehgaon and Gohad (from Bhind district) and Morena and Jaura (from Morena district). *Second 'area' from central region* Comprising 11 blocks, viz., Bina-Itawa, Khuri Banda (Binaika), Rahatgarh, Sagar, Shahgarh (Amarmau) (from Sagar district), Tikamgarh and Baldeogarh (from Tikamgarh district), Vidisha and Gyaraspur (from Vidisha district) and Chhatarpur (from Chhatarpur district). *Third 'area' from western region (II)* Comprising 12 blocks, viz., Potlawad & Meghnagar (from Jhabua district), Badnawar Dhar and Nalcha (from Dhar district), Mahesh and Barwaha (from Khargone district), Ratlam and Jaura (from Ratlam district), Mandsaur, Malhargarh and Neemuch (from Mandsaur district). *Fourth 'area' from north eastern region* Comprising 11 blocks viz., Rewa and Raipur (Garh) (from Rewa district), Majhauli, Sidhi, Doosar and Waidhan (from Sidhi district), Sonhat, Baikunthpur, Manendargarh, Surajpur and Ambikapur (from Sarguja district).
Manipur Meghalaya	: All the districts already covered.
Maharashtra	: Aurangabad and Chandrapur.
Nagaland	: Tuensang.
Orissa	: Bolangir, Dhenkanal, Keonjhar and Koraput.
Punjab	: Sangrur and Bhatinda**.
Rajasthan	: Bhilwara, Churu, Nagaur, Udaipur.
Uttar Pradesh	: Almora, Basti, Faizabad, and Rae Bareilly.
Sikkim	: All the four districts of Gangtok, Mangan, Gyalshing and Namchi.
Tamil Nadu	: Two tracts. One comprising Taluks of: 1. Dharmapuri 2. Hosur 3. Krishnagiri 4. Uthangarai 5. Harur } From Dharmapuri district. 6. Tirupattur 7. Vaniyambadi 8. Vellore 9. Walajapet } From North Arcot district. and the other tract comprising Taluks of: 1. Aruppukottai 2. Sattur 3. Srivilliputtur } From West Ramanathapuram of Ramanathapuram district.

(*Contd.*)

ANNEXURE III (*Contd.*)

	4. Tirumangalam 5. Usilampatti 6. Nilakothai 7. Dindigul and 8. Vedasandur	From Madurai district.
Tripura	: All the districts already covered.	
West Bengal	: Midnapur and Nadia.	

*Represents Taluks/Blocks/Sub-divisions selected prior to 10-7-1972.

**Represents districts as they existed prior to their recent reorganization

Source: K.V. Sundaram and R.P. Misra, *Micro Level Planning and Development Processes*, Vol. I, (Cyclostyled Report by Institute of Development Studies, Mysore University, August 1976), Annexure IX.

Chapter 9

Transfer of Resources from Centre to States

India is a federation of States. As in other federations, here also governmental functions are divided between two sets of authorities—the Central or federal government on the one hand and the governments of States on the other. Though a strict division of functions is not possible in any federal set-up, the general convention is to assign tasks of national importance to the Central government and tasks of local or regional importance to the State governments. In India, e.g., subjects such as foreign affairs, defence, communications, and currency are Central subjects while education, public health, maintenance of law and order are State subjects.

Problems of federal finance arise on account of the division of functions. The first problem, in this context, is to decide as to what sources of finance should be assigned to each of these authorities. It has been generally observed that the needs and resources of each government are not balanced. There is either a surplus or a deficit. The second problem, thus, is to ensure a balance between needs and resources by transferring resources from the government which has a surplus to the government which has a deficit. For example if the Centre has a surplus and the States have deficits, it is necessary to provide for the transfer of resources from the former to the latter. If the States have a surplus and the Centre has a deficit, a mechanism should be there to ensure transfer from the States to the Centre. The latter is only a hypothetical case in modern federations because, with the increase in its powers and resources, the revenues of the federal government have registered phenomenal increases while the State governments generally incur deficits. Since it is necessary to have those taxes under the control of the Central government which are likely to affect the economic life and activities of the country as a whole, excise duties, customs duties, income tax, corporation tax, etc., are generally levied by the Central government. Since most of these taxes are rapidly expanding ones the revenues of the Central government increase at a more rapid speed compared with those of the State governments.[1] This introduces an imbalance between the revenues and expenditures of these two levels of government. Accordingly, in practically all federal set-ups there is a provision for the division of tax revenues between the Centre and the States. In India, the two most important taxes from this point of view are the income tax and the Union excise duties. The share of the States in both these taxes has shown a consistent increase.[2]

Before the question of division of tax-revenues arises, it is necessary to determine the basis of division and the amount that should de divided. The Indian Constitution recognized that due to changing needs and circumstances it might become necessary to change the criteria and the amount of division between the two levels of government (Centre and State) from time to time. Hence it did not lay down any hard and fast rules in this regard. Instead, it provided for the appointment of a Finance Commission at the expiry of every fifth year or earlier, if necessary, to investigate these questions. The Commission is appointed under article 280 of the Constitution and is entrusted with the task of recommending:

(i) the distribution between the Union and the States of the net proceeds of taxes which are to be or may be divided between them and the allocation between the States of the respective shares of such proceeds;
(ii) the principles which should govern the grants-in-aid of the revenues of the States out of the Consolidated Fund of India; and
(iii) any other matter referred to the Commission by the President in the interests of sound finance.

In addition to the devolution of resources from the Centre to the States on the basis of the recommendations of the Finance Commission thus constituted, there are two other sources of transfer: (i) assistance for plan purposes from the Planning Commission, and (ii) discretionary grants from the Centre to the States. As we shall show subsequently,[3] these sources of transfer have together contributed a significant proportion of total transfers. In fact, taking the total period up to the end of the Fifth Plan, these sources together contributed approximately 60% of the total transfers (computed from Table 4).

TRANSFERS THROUGH THE FINANCE COMMISSIONS

Let us start by considering the transfers through the Finance Commissions. Before we do this, let us see what the Constitution has to say on the subject of financial transfers from the Centre to the States. Articles 268, 269, 270, 272, 275, and 282, deal with this subject. Under Article 268, stamp and excise duties on medicinal and toilet preparations "shall be levied by the Government of India but shall be collected (a) in the case where such duties are leviable within any Union territory, by the Government of India, and (b) in other cases, by the States within which such duties are leviable". Thus, as far as Article 268 duties are concerned, their proceeds can be collected directly by the States and retained by them.

Article 269 lists seven types of duties and taxes: "estate duty in respect of property other than agricultural land", "taxes on railway fares and freights", and "taxes on the sale or purchase of goods other than newspapers, where such sale or purchase takes place in the course of inter-State trade or commerce". The entire net proceeds of Article 269 taxes, though levied by the Union, are to be assigned and distributed among the States "in accordance with such principles of distribution as may be formulated by Parliament by law".

As for tax on income other than agricultural income, Article 270 provides that it too "shall be levied and collected by the Government of India" but only a *prescribed percentage* of it shall be assigned to the divisible pool for distribution among the States. Article 272 is concerned with Union excise duties which are to be levied and collected by the Union government and can be retained by it unless Parliament by law provides for its distribution among the States. However, once Parliament does so, a *prescribed proportion* of the net proceeds is to be distributed.

Thus, while under Article 269 the entire proceeds of the taxes and duties, though levied by the Union, are assigned and distributed among the States, and while under Article 270 (pertaining to income-tax) a prescribed amount is to be assigned to the States' pool, there is no such compulsion under Article 272 relating to Union excise duties. But once Parliament, by law, lays it down that they have to be shared, then a prescribed amount has to be assigned to the States' pool.

Article 275 of the Constitution relates to "grants-in-aid of revenues" to be given to the States "in need of assistance". Different sums can be fixed for different States, so that the weaker States can be given specific assistance to meet the necessary expenditure in the proper discharge of their duties to the people. Article 282 provides for grants by the Union to the States for any public purpose. Article 275 grants-in-aid are fixed on the advice of the Finance Commission while Article 282 grants can be fixed by the Union government at its own discretion.

The Finance Commissions have concerned themselves with allocating the net proceeds from income-tax, Union excise duties, additional duties of excise, estate duty in respect of property other than agricultural land, grants-in-aid in lieu of jute export duty (issue that concerned the first two Commissions only), taxes on railway fares and freights (levied for the first time in 1957) and grants-in-aid to fill in the budgetary gaps of the States. In addition, some Finance Commissions gave grants for the upgradation of standards of administration. The Sixth and the Seventh Finance Commissions were also asked to undertake a general review of the States' indebtedness to the Centre and examine the policy and arrangements in regard to the financing of relief expenditure.

Let us consider the recommendations of the different Financing Commissions in detail.

The First Finance Commission was appointed in 1952 with K.C. Neogy as chairman. While making its recommendations, the Commission kept the following three basic considerations in view: "Firstly, the additional transfer of resources from the Centre must be such as the Centre could bear without undue strain on its resources, taking into account its responsibility for such vital matters as the defence of the country and the stability of its economy. Secondly, the principles for the distribution of revenues between the States and the determination of grants-in-aid must be uniformly applied to all the States. Lastly, *the scheme of distribution should attempt to lessen the inequalities between States.*"[4] The Commission recommended that 55% of the net proceeds of income-tax should be made available to the States and its distribution should be governed by (a) a general measure of needs, furnished by population and (b) the collections of income-tax from each State. Keeping these considerations in view, the Neogy Commission recommended that 80% of the States' share of the divisible pool of income-tax should be distributed among the States on the basis of their relative populations and 20% on the basis of the relative collections of income-tax in different States. As regards excise duties, the Commission considered that three Union excise duties (tobacco, vegetable products, and matches) were suitable for distribution among the States. It recommended that 40% of the net proceeds of these duties should be allocated to the States and distributed in proportion to their population. In lieu of jute export duty, the Commission recommended the following annual grants-in-aid to four States: Rs.150 lakhs to West Bengal, Rs.75 lakhs each to Assam and Bihar, and Rs.15 lakhs to Orissa. As far as distribution of grants under Article 275 is concerned, the Commission formulated a number of principles for regulating grants-in-aid to the States: (1) budgetary needs, (2) tax effort, (3) economy in expenditure, (4) standards of social services, (5) special obligations, and (6) broad purposes of importance. However, in actual transfer of resources under this heading, the Commission considered mainly the budgetary needs of the States.[5] Because of the national importance of the primary education programme, the Commission also recommended special purpose grants to eight States for improving primary education ranging from Rs.1.5 crores in

1953-54 to Rs.3.0 crores in 1956-57.

The Second Finance Commission was appointed in May 1956 with K. Santhanam as chairman. It submitted its report in September 1957. It recommended that the share of the States in income-tax should be increased to 60% from 55% and the distribution of the share of different States should basically be done according to their population. It decided that 90% of allocation should be done according to population and the remaining 10% on the basis of collection (of income-tax revenue). The number of excise duties to be shared was increased from three to eight and the States' share in these duties was reduced from 40% (as under the First Finance Commission) to 25%. The five new excise duties that were included in the divisible pool were those to be levied on sugar, tea, coffee, paper, and vegetable non-essential oils. The criteria for distribution among the States was 90% population and 10% for adjustments. As regards estate duty, the Second Finance Commission recommended:

1. that out of the net proceeds of the duty in any financial year, a sum equal to one percent be retained by the Union as proceeds attributable to Union territories;
2. the balance be apportioned between immovable property and other property in the ratio of the gross value of all such properties brought into assessment in that year;
3. the sum thus apportioned to immovable property be distributed among the States in proportion to the gross value of the immovable property located in each State;
4. the sum apportioned to property other than immovable property be distributed among the States in proportion to their population.

The Second Commission also dealt with the division of additional duties of excise for the first time. These are those duties which are levied by the Central government in lieu of sales tax by the States. The net proceeds of these duties are to be divided between the States in such a way that no State gets less than what it was deriving from sales tax on the relevant items in 1956-57.[6] Thus, the States were *guaranteed* a payment equal to their sales tax revenue on these items in 1956-57. The basis for distributing the amount that remained after paying the guaranteed amounts was not made clear. The National Development Council had considered consumption as the relevant basis. Consequently, after having allotted 1% of the net proceeds to the Union territories and 1½% to Jammu & Kashmir and after having set apart the guaranteed amounts for individual States, the Second

Finance Commission distributed the remaining amount by using consumption figures corrected by population factor. It was decided to continue the scheme of grants-in-aid in lieu of jute export duty to the four States of West Bengal, Assam, Bihar, and Orissa till 1959-60. In the case of grants-in-aid, the Commission took into account the requirements of States for development purposes and the special needs of border States (viz., Punjab, Assam, West Bengal, and Jammu & Kashmir).[7]

The Third Finance Commission was appointed in December 1960 under the chairmanship of A.K. Chanda and it submitted its report in December 1961. It recommended an increase of States' share in income-tax from 60% (proposed by the Second Finance Commission) to 66⅔% and this was to be distributed among the States by giving a weightage of 80% to population and 20% to collection (thus restoring the formula adopted by the First Finance Commission). As regards Union excise duties, the number of excisable items in the divisible pool was increased from 8 to 35 by including all commodities on which duties exceeding Rs.50 lakhs were collected in 1960-61 excluding the duty on motor spirit. The Commission did not explicitly state the criteria for determining the distribution of excise duties. However, it seems that population was taken as the major criterion though some account was also taken of relative financial weakness, disparity in development, etc.[8] The share of the States in the excise duties was reduced from 25% to 20% on account of the fact that the net had been widened from 8 commodities (as under the Second Commission) to 35 commodities.

The Commission did not recommend any change in the principles governing the distribution of estate duty and the principles adopted by the Second Commission were to continue with the change that population according to the 1961 census was to be considered. As far as additional duties of excise are concerned, the Third Commission kept the share of the Union territories at 1% of the net proceeds but increased the share of Jammu & Kashmir to 1½% from 1¼%. The pattern of distribution of the balance amount remained the same as under the Second Commission. After having set apart the guaranteed amounts for individual States, the Third Finance Commission estimated the percentage increases in sales tax revenue in each State since 1957-58 and modified these figures with the population factor. As far as grants-in-aid are concerned, the Commission recommended the total aid so as to cover together with tax devolution, the non-plan revenue gap plus 75% of the plan revenue gap of the States. The Commission also recommended the distribution of Rs.36 crores in four years (from 1962-63 to 1965-66) among ten States as a special purpose grant for improvement of communications. In this context the Commission had this to say: "We had not intended to make any special purpose grant, but, in the course of our visits to the States and the discussions we had with their Cabinets, we became convinced that impetus should be given to the development of communications more extensively. There is the pressing need to open up backward areas, to break down barriers of isolation and stagnation, to develop social services and social sense, to mobilise economic resources, and above all to bring about a feeling of oneness in the minds of the people of these regions with the rest of the community."[9]

The Fourth Finance Commission was appointed in May 1964 under the chairmanship of P.V. Rajamannar and it submitted its report in August 1965. As far as distribution of income-tax revenue is concerned, the Commission recommended that after deducting 2.5% of the proceeds as the share of the Union territories, 75% of the divisible pool should be allocated to the States. Rejecting the plea of many States that factors such as area, backwardness, financial weakness, and proportion of scheduled castes and scheduled tribes in total population of the States should be given weightage while allocating proceeds from income-tax, the Commission justified the continuation of population and collection as the only bases for the determination of the States' share in income-tax, proceeds on the ground that frequent changes in the scheme were not desirable. In the distribution of income-tax proceeds among the States, the recommendations of the First and the Third Commissions were to be followed (implying a weightage of 80% to population and 20% to collection). The Commission made no change in the scheme adopted earlier for the distribution of estate duty except that the share of the Union territories was increased from 1% to 2%.

In the distribution of excise duties while population was recognized as the major factor for determining the share of the States, *relative economic and social backwardness* of the States was also taken into account. Rejecting the criterion of financial weakness as adopted by the Third Finance Commission on grounds that "a State may be economically backward and yet it may have fairly comfortable position on revenue account", the Fourth Finance Commission considered the economic and social backwardness indicated by the following factors in the distribution of Union excise duties:

(i) *Per capita* gross value of agricultural production;
(ii) *Per capita* value added by manufacture;
(iii) Percentage of workers (as defined in the Census) to the total population;
(iv) Percentage of enrolment in Classes I to V to the population in age group 6-11;
(v) Population per hospital bed;
(vi) Percentage of rural population to total population; and
(vii) Percentage of the population of Scheduled Castes and Tribes to total population."[10]

The factor of relative economic backwardness (determined in accordance with the above indicators) was given a weight equivalent to 20%. The other factor, namely population, was accorded a weight of 80%. As regards estate duty, the Commission favoured the continuance of the existing principles with the only change that the share of the Union territories was raised from 1% to 2% of the net proceeds. As far as additional excise duties are concerned, the share attributable to the Union territories, Nagaland, and Jammu & Kashmir was kept at 1%, 0.05%, and 1.50% respectively. From he balance, the guaranteed amounts were to be paid. The share of the rates in the excess amount was to be determined by "proportion of sales tax revenue realized in each State to the total sales tax collections in all the States taken together".[11] While determining grants-in-aid, the Fourth Commission also (like the earlier Commissions) gave maximum importance to the need to cover up the budgetary deficits. On account of this approach, the backward States of Bihar and Uttar Pradesh could not qualify for any grants. Other States that did not receive grants were Maharashtra, Punjab, and West Bengal.

The Fifth Finance Commission was appointed under the chairmanship of Mahavir Tyagi in February 1968 and it submitted its final report on 31 July 1969. As regards the devolution of income-tax the Commission recommended that the allocation of this tax according to collection (or contribution) should be reduced from 20% to 10% and of population should be increased from 80% to 90%. This was justified on the ground that three-fourths of income-tax collections were made from four advanced industrial States only and if a larger share of income-tax revenues is given to States according to the factor of collection, these four advanced States would corner a major share of the resources transferred to the States. Reduction of the importance of collection factor from 20% to 10% would imply a greater recognition of the needs of less developed States.

In regard to the distribution of excise duties also, the Commission paid special attention to the factor of backwardness. It stated that the distribution of excise duties "should be based mainly on population alongwith some criteria to take into account lower potential for raising resources and relative backwardness in economic and social development. We feel that as a broad measure of needs of different States, due regard should be had to criteria like populatian and suitable indicators of backwardness, rather than the relative financial weakness or budgetary deficits of the States At the same time, since the States having less per capita income have lower potential for raising resources and are therefore placed at a disadvantage as compared to the States with higher per capita income, we consider it reasonable that some portion of the States' share should be distributed to States with per capita income less than the average of all States."[12] Having regard to these considerations, the share of the States in Union excise duties was determined on the following basis:

(1) 80 percent on the basis of population of respective States.
(2) Out of the remaining 20 percent
 (a) 2/3rd should be distributed among States whose per capita income is below the average per capita income of all States in proportion to the shortfall of the State's per capita income from all States' average, multiplied by the population of the State. For this purpose, Nagaland, for which the requisite per capita income statistics are not available, should be equated with Assam.
 (b) 1/3rd should be distributed according to the integrated index of backwardness on the basis of the following six criteria, *viz.*,
  (i) Scheduled tribes population;
  (ii) Number of factory workers per lakh population;
  (iii) Net irrigated area per cultivator;
  (iv) Length of railways and surfaced roads per 100 square kilometres;
  (v) Shortfall in number of school going children as compared to those of school going age;
  (vi) Number of hospital beds per 1,000 population.[13]

The pattern of distribution of estate duty was to remain as under the earlier Finance Commissions except that the share of the Union territories was increased to 3%. As regards additional duties of excise in lieu of sales tax, the Fifth Finance Commission was required to examine the desirability or otherwise of maintaining the existing arrangements and the scope for extending such arrangements to other items in addition to the normal task of specifying the principles of distribution. As far as the distribution of additional duties of excise is concernded, the Commission increased the share of the Union territories and Nagaland to 2.05% and 0.09% respectively but reduced the share of Jammu & Kashmir to 0.83% (these percentages were fixed on the basis of population figures while the earlier Commissions had fixed them on an ad hoc basis). After setting apart the amounts thus calculated, guaranteed amounts (like the earlier Commissions) were to be paid. Regarding the distribution of the excess amount (which represents the excess over the guaranteed amount) the Commission recommended that it should be divided by assigning equal weights to population and sales tax collection. As far as the question of the desirability of the scheme and its extension is concerned, the Commission maintained that the rationale of the scheme and the advantages which it was expected to bring would continue to hold good. However, in view of the opposition from the States, it suggested that it would not be desirable to continue the scheme unless the Government of India, in consultation with the State goverments could arrive at a general agreement for its continuance with suitable modifications. In view of this suggestion, the Commission did not make recommendations in regard to the extension of the existing arrangements to other items or commodities.

As far as the distribution of grants-in-aid is concerned, the Commission did not recommended any grants to the States of Bihar, Gujarat, Haryana, Madhya Pradesh, Maharashtra, Punjab, and Uttar Pradesh because they were expected to have surpluses Another State, Karnataka, was also expected to have a small surplus but since the average amount of devolution of taxes during the five-year period for this State was expected to be less than what it had received under the Fourth Finance Commission, a small amount in the form of grants was made available to it. Karnataka and other nine States (Andhra Pradesh, Assam, Jammu & Kashmir, Kerala, Nagaland, Orissa, Rajasthan, Tamil Nadu, and West Bengal) were given a total sum of Rs.710.7 crores as grants-in-aid.

The Sixth Finance Commission was constituted on 21 June 1972 with K. Brahmananda Reddy as chairman. Its recommendations covered the period of the Fifth Five Year Plan. In addition to its constitutional function of recommending distribution of Central taxes such as income-tax, excise duties, and estate duty and distribution of grants-in-aid to the States, the Commission was required to make recommendations on two other issues which were presented to Finance Commission for the first time. These issues were:

(a) assesment of the non-plan capital gap of States on a uniform and comparable basis for the five years ending 1978-79; and
(b) review of the policy and arrangements in regard to the financing of relief expenditure by the States affected by natural calamities.

As far as distribution of net proceeds of income-tax is concerned, the Sixth Finance Commission recommended:

1. Out of the total net proceeds of income taxes, 1.79% should be given to the Union territories.
2. Of the balance, 80% should be divided between the States.
3. The share of different States in the total divisible pool thus determined should be on the following basis—90% on the basis of population and

the remaining 10% on the basis of collection. Thus, the basis of distribution was kept the same as in the Fifth Commission.

In respect of estate duty, the principles of distribution were kept the same as under the earlier Finance Commissions but the share of the Union territories was reduced from 3% to 2.5%. This was justified on the ground that the area under Union territories had declined as some Union territories had been conferred Statehood. In determining the share of individual States, population according to the 1971 census was to be considered. As far as Union excise duties are concerned, the weightage of population factor which was 80% under Fifth Finance Commission was reduced to 75%. This meant an increase in the weightage of the backwardness factor from 20% under the Fifth Commission to 25% under the Sixth Commission. To determine the backwardness of a State, only one factor, viz. per capita income, was taken into account. The actual distribution of the 25% portion was to be done in relation to the 'distance' of a State's per capita income from that of the State with the highest per capita income multiplied by the population of the State concerned according to the 1971 census.[14] This marked a distinct change in emphasis vis-a-vis the approach adopted by the Fifth Commission. While the latter had considered a number of other factors in addition to per capita income to measure backwardness, the Sixth Finance Commission considered per capita income as the sole criterion. There was another, and perhaps a more important, difference in the approach. While under the award of the Fifth Finance Commission, States having per capita income above per capita national average were not granted any share as per State income component of backwardness factor, the Sixth Commission granted a share in Union excise duties to all States except Punjab (which had the highest per capita income) under the criterion of 'backwardness'. This change benefited the relatively advanced States (except Punjab) whose share in Union excise duties registered an increase. As can be seen from Table 2, the share of the relatively advanced States such as Maharashtra, Gujarat, Tamil Nadu, West Bengal, and Haryana in the Union excise duties rose as a result of the recommendations of the Sixth Commission (compared with the transfers under the Fifth Commission). On the other hand, the share of the States with low per capita income (such as Uttar Pradesh, Bihar, Rajasthan, Kerala, Orissa, and Madhya Pradesh) declined.

As far as additional duties of excise in lieu of sales tax are concerned, the Sixth Finance Commission made a remarkable departure from the practice adopted by the earlier Commissions. As we have already noted, all the earlier Commissions distributed a certain amount as guaranteed amount (which was determined in such a way that no State got less than that it was deriving from sales tax on the relevant items in 1956-57). The Sixth Commission dropped this procedure on the plea that, in any case, each State was sure to get more than the guaranteed amount because the estimated yield from these duties for the five years was Rs.1037 crores against the guaranteed amount of Rs.162 crores for the same period. For determining the share of the States, the Commission adopted a new set of criteria—70% was to be distributed according to population 20% on the basis of State domestic product, and the remaining 10% on the basis of production of these commodities. This marked an attempt by the Sixth Commission to take into account the backwardness of States while determining their share in additional duties of excise.

The Sixth Commission increased the grants-in-aid to States substantially from Rs.710.7 crores under the Fifth Commission to Rs.2509.6 crores (see Table 1). This increase is partly on account of grants recommended by the Sixth Commission to the States of Himachal Pradesh, Jammu & Kashmir, Manipur, Meghalaya, Nagaland, and Tripura. These are the States which have practically no resource base of their own and whose requirements have consequently to be met almost completely through Central transfers. The substantial increase in grants-in-aid is also on account of the fact that the Commission made special financial provisions for 'upgradation of standards of administration'. Under this heading, grants were released for the following activities: (1) general administration, (2) administration of justice, (3) jails, (4) police, (5) primary education, (6) medical and public health, and (7) welfare of scheduled castes and scheduled tribes and other backward classes. A total amount of Rs.815.84 crores was released for the purpose.[15]

Table 1 gives the total amount of resources transferred from the Centre to the States according to the recommendations of the first six Finance Commissions. It shows that while the gross revenue receipts of the Central government rose from Rs.2921.4 crores during the period of the First Finance Commission to Rs.48,502.4 crores during the period of the Sixth Finance Commission (registering an increase of about 17 times), the resources transferred through the Finance Commission rose from Rs.421.3 crores to Rs.10,760.2 crores during the same period (registering an increase of about 25 times). On account of this, the percentage of transferred resources to gross revenue receipts of the Central government registered an increase from 14.4 during the period of the First Finance Commission to 22.1 during the period of the Sixth Finance Commission. The grant component in total resources transferred increased from 11.9% under the First Finance Commission to 23.3% under the Sixth Finance Commission.

Table 2 gives the percentage share of the different States in income-tax and Union excise duties as recommended by the Second, Third, Fourth, Fifth, and Sixth Finance Commissions. It can be seen from Table 2 that the combined share of the four advanced industrial States of Maharashtra,

TABLE 1: Resources transferred from the Centre to the States through Finance Commissions

(Rs. in crores)

	Gross revenue receipts of the Central Govt.	Resources transferred through Finance Commissions					Percentage of transferred resources to (2)	(4) as percentage of (3)
		Share of taxes	Grants	Total	(3) as percentage of (5)	(4) as percentage of (5)		
(1)	(2)	(3)	(4)	(5)	(6)	(7)	(8)	(9)
First Finance Commission (1952-57)	2921.4	371.3	50.0	421.3	88.1	11.9	14.4	13.5
Second Finance Commission (1957-62)	5270.9	822.4	197.2	1019.6	80.6	19.4	19.3	23.97
Third Finance Commission (1962-66)	8737.3	1067.5	250.4	1317.9	81.0	19.0	15.1	23.69
Fourth Finance Commission (1966-69)	9151.1	1328.0	421.8	1749.9	75.9	24.1	19.1	31.76
Fifth Finance Commission 1969-74)	24655.7	4643.0	710.7	5353.8	86.7	13.3	21.7	15.37
Sixte Finance Commission (1974-79)	48502.4	8250.6	2509.6	10760.2	76.7	23.3	22.1	30.41

Source: H.L. Bhatia, *Centre-State Financial Relations in India*, Study sponsored by the Birla Institute of Scientific Research (New Delhi: Abhinav Publications, 1979), Table 4.7, p. 127.

TABLE 2: Percentage share of States in income-tax and Union excise duties as recommended by Finance Commissions

	Second Commission		Third Commission		Fourth Commission		Fifth Commission		Sixth Commission	
	Income-tax	Excise duties	Income-tax	Excise duties	Income-tax	Excise duties	Income-tax	Excise duties	Income-tax	Excise duties
States' share in divisible Pool	60.00	25.00	66.67	20.00	75.00	20.00	75.00	20.00	80.00	20.00
States:										
Andhra Pradesh	8.12	9.38	7.71	82.3	7.37	7.77	8.01	7.15	7.76	8.16
Assam	2.44	3.46	2.44	4.73	2.44	3.32	2.67	2.51	2.54	2.71
Bihar	9.94	10.57	9.33	11.56	9.04	10.03	9.99	13.81	9.61	11.47
Gujarat	*	*	4.78	6.45	5.29	4.80	5.13	4.17	5.55	4.57
Haryana	**	**	**	**	**	**	1.73	1.49	1.77	1.53
Jammu & Kashmir	1.13	1.75	0.70	2.02	0.73	2.26	0.79	1.12	0.81	0.90
Kerala	3.64	3.84	3.55	5.46	3.59	4.16	3.83	4.28	3.92	3.86
Madhya Pradesh	6.72	7.46	6.41	8.46	6.47	7.40	7.09	8.48	7.30	8.15
Maharashtra	15.97	12.17	13.41	5.73	14.28	8.23	11.34	7.93	11.05	8.58
Nagaland	—	—	—	—	0.07	2.21	0.08	0.08	0.09	0.11
Orissa	3.73	4.46	3.44	7.07	3.40	4.82	3.75	4.72	3.73	4.06
Punjab	4.24	4.59	4.49	6.71	4.36	4.86	2.55	2.17	2.75	1.87
Rajasthan	4.09	4.71	3.97	5.93	3.97	5.06	4.34	5.28	4.50	5.00
Tamil Nadu	8.40	7.56	8.13	6.08	8.34	7.18	8.18	6.50	7.94	7.43
Uttar Pradesh	16.36	15.94	14.42	10.68	14.60	14.98	16.01	18.82	15.23	17.03
West Bengal	10.08	7.59	12.09	5.07	10.91	7.51	9.11	6.84	8.89	7.79
Total	100.00	100.00	100.00	100.00	100.00	100.00	100.00	100.00	100.00***	100.00****

*Included under Maharashtra.

**Included under Punjab.

***Includes the share of Himachal Pradesh, Manipur, Meghalaya, and Tripura as well which was 0.60%, 0.18%, 0.18% and 0.27%, respectively.

****Includes the share of Himachal Pradesh, Manipur, and Tripura which was 0.63%, 0.21%, 0.19%, and 0.30% respectively.

Source: Reports of the Finance Commissions.

Gujarat, Tamil Nadu, and West Bengal in income-tax revenue has continuously remained more than one-third of the total transfers (being 34.45% 38.51%, 38.42%, 33.76%, and 33.43%, under the awards of the Second, Third, Fourth, Fifth, and Sixth Finance Commissions respectively). However, the combined share of these four States in Union excise duties was lower (being 27.32%, 23.33%, 27.72%, 25.44%, and 28.37% under the awards of the Second, Third, Fourth, Fifth, and Sixth Finance Commissions respectively). This was because of the fact that all Commissions tried to take into account the factor of backwardness in some way or the other while determining the allocation of Union excise duties. Change in the definition of backwardness in the Sixth Commission from that adopted in the Fifth Commission increased the share of these four advanced industrial States from 25.44% under the Fifth Commission to 28.37% under the Sixth Commission.

RECOMMENDATIONS OF THE SEVENTH FINANCE COMMISSION

The Seventh Finance Commission was appointed in June 1977 and it submitted its report on 28 October 1978. S.M. Shelat was the chairman of the Commission and Raj Krishna, C.H. Hanumantha Rao, and H.N. Ray were its members. In addition to the sharing of the net proceeds of divisible income-tax, Union excise duties, distribution of additional excise duties in lieu of States' sales tax, estate duty on property other than agricultural land, payment of grants in lieu of the repealed tax on railway passenger fares and on account of wealth tax on agricultural property, and payment of grants-in-aid under article 275(1) of the Constitution, the Commission was asked to

(a) assess the non-plan capital gap of the States on a uniform and comparable basis for the five years ending 1983-84 and in the light of such an assessment to review the States' debt position and suggest appropriate measures; and
(b) review the policy and arrangements in regard to the financing of relief expenditure by the States affected by natural calamities and suggest appropriate modifications.

As far as distribution of proceeds from income-tax is concerned, the Seventh Commission increased the share of the States from 80% to 85% and the share of the Union territories from 1.79% to 2.19%. The determination of the share of different States in the divisible pool was done according to the basis used in the Fifth and the Sixth Finance Commissions—90% on the basis of population and 10% on the basis of collection. The recommendations of the Commission in the field of Union excise duties are very important. It recommended that the entire collections of revenue from the Union excise duties on electricity, levied from 1 March 1978, be transferred to the States. As far as other excise duties are concerned, the Commission increased the share of the States considerably to 40% of the net proceeds, against 20% adopted by most of the previous Commissions. As far as distribution of Union excise duties among the States is concerned, the Commission determined the percentage share of each State by assigning a weight of 25% each to the following factors:

(i) Population according to 1971 census;
(ii) Inverse of per capita State domestic product multiplied by projected population of the State as on 1 March 1976;
(iii) Percentage of the poor in each State measured by a method evolved by the Commission; and
(iv) A formula of revenue equalization worked out by the Commission.

As far as distribution of the net proceeds of additional excise duties on sugar, textiles, and tobacco is concerned, the Seventh Finance Commission made a departure from the Sixth Commission which (as we have already noted) recommended distribution according to the following criteria—70% on the basis of population, 20% on the basis of State domestic product, and 10% on the basis of production of the commodities. The Seventh Commission determined the shares attributable to Union territories and each State on the following basis:

(a) In the case of sugar, average despatches to the Union territories and each State during the three years ending 1976-77; and
(b) In the case of textiles and tobacco, population according to the 1971 census and the average per capita State domestic product.

As regards estate duty, the Commission recommended its distribution among the States in proportion to the gross value of the immovable property as also property other than immovable property taken together located in each State except in regard to property located abroad. Sikkim also will be entitled to a share in the net proceeds of this duty if and when the duty becomes leviable in that State. As far as grants in lieu of railway passenger fares are concerned, the Commission determined the percentage share of each State on the basis of the non-suburban passenger earnings of the railways allocated State-wise with reference to the originating stations in each State, instead of the State-wise route kilometre as used by earlier Commissions (see note 7).

The Commission estimated that five States, namely, Gujarat, Haryana, Karnataka, Maharashtra, and Punjab, were expected to have surplus on non-plan revenue account during the period 1979-84, even without tax devolution from the Centre. After taking into account the tax devolution, the Commission felt that only eight States were expected to have a non-plan revenue gap and consequently recommended payment of grants-in-aid to these States only amounting to a total of Rs.1173.12 crores (see Table 3). For upgrading the standards in non-developmental sectors and services in the States which are backward in general administration, the Commission recommended separate grants-in-aid amounting to Rs.436.79 crores to all States except the five States of Gujarat, Haryana, Karnataka, Maharashtra, and Punjab.

The percentage shares of different States in income-tax, excise duties, and additional excise duties are given in Table 3 which also gives details about the grants-in-aid recommended by the Seventh Commission:

TABLE 3: **Percentage shares of States in devolution of Central taxes and duties and also grants-in-aid recommended by the Seventh Commission**

State	Percentage share of				Grants under Art 275 (Rs. crore)	
	Income-tax	Excise duties	Additional excise duties			
	*	*	Sugar	Textiles & tobacco	Gap	Upgradation
(1)	(2)	(3)	(4)	(5)	(6)	(7)
Andhra Pradesh	8.023	7.698	5.245	8.018	—	19.60
Assam	2.522	2.793	2.408	2.297	—	21.71
Bihar	9.540	13.025	5.933	7.219	—	63.02
Gujarat	5.959	4.103	8.742	6.013	—	—
Haryana	1.819	1.177	2.666	2.789	—	—
Himachal Pradesh	0.595	0.521	0.860	0.734	207.07	7.74
Jammu & Kashmir	0.818	0.839	0.831	0.744	199.56	18.28
Karnataka	5.442	4.877	4.901	6.081	—	—
Kerala	3.950	4.036	3.783	4.019	—	4.18
Madhya Pradesh	7.356	8.727	6.019	6.419	—	63.58
Maharashtra	10.953	8.633	17.082	13.506	—	—

(*Contd.*)

TABLE 3 (*Contd.*)

(1)	(2)	(3)	(4)	(5)	(6)	(7)
Manipur	0.188	0.218	0.143	0.185	146.32	9.95
Meghalaya	0.178	0.200	0.029	0.171	92.61	4.86
Nagaland	0.085	0.097	0.115	0.084	218.35	4.33
Orissa	3.739	4.682	2.178	3.456	136.92	32.26
Punjab	2.714	1.226	6.220	4.268	—	—
Rajasthan	4.364	4.813	4.729	4.365	—	19.29
Sikkim	—	—	0.057	0.034	35.72	0.65
Tamil Nadu	8.050	7.641	6.449	7.707	—	27.20
Tripura	0.258	0.373	0.172	0.256	136.57	3.61
Uttar Pradesh	15.429	18.293	13.184	12.544	—	112.02
West Bengal	8.018	8.028	8.254	0.091	—	24.51
Total	100.000	100.000	100.000	100.000	1173.12	436.79

Note: *Excluding Sikkim.
Source: Report of the Seventh Finance Commission, 1978, pp. 121-127.

Two other recommendations of the Seventh Finance Commission merit attention. One relates to financing of relief expenditures by the States affected by natural calamities and the other to debt relief. Financing of re lief expenditure concerns with the provision of margin for relief expenditure in the expenditure forecasts of each State. When a calamity—flood, cyclone, earthquake, drought, etc.—occurs necessitating expenditure on relief measures the States have this margin to draw upon immediately. Debt relief concerns with the filling up of non-plan capital gap of the States, after taking into account the States' debt position. As far as financing of relief expenditure is concerned, the annual provisions allowed by the Seventh Commission were Rs 100.55 crores while they were only Rs.50.71 crores in the Sixth Commission and a meagre Rs.14.47 crores in the Fifth Commission. The Seventh Commission also recommended a substantial debt relief to the States. It estimated that over the period 1979-84, the non-plan capital gap of all States considered together was expected to amount to Rs.3512.18 crores. Of this, the Commission recommended a relief of Rs.2155.80 crores which was about 61% of the total debt.

The total transfer of resources recommended by the Seventh Finance Commission for the period 1979-84 was Rs.20,907 crores which was approximately double the transfer recommended by the Sixth Finance Commission. Of this amount, Rs.4,791 crores was the share of States in income-tax, Rs.11,347 crores was their share in excise duties, Rs.1,173.12 crores was to be paid to them as general grants, and Rs.436.79 crores was to be paid to them as upgradation grants.

OTHER SOURCES OF TRANSFER

In addition to transfer of resources from the Centre to the States according to the recommendations of the Finance Commission, there are two other sources of transfer—(i) assistance for plan purposes from the Planning Commission, and (ii) discretionary grants from the Centre to the States. The total transfer of resources from the Centre to the States during the planning period and the shares of these sources in the total transfer are given in Table 4. The table shows that non-statutory transfers (which are constituted of 'transfers through the Planning Commission' and 'other transfers' [i.e. (B) + (C) in Table 4] have contributed a sizable proportion of total transfers from the Centre to the States. During the First, Second, and Third Plans they were 69.7%, 68.0% and 71.6% of the total transfers respectively. This shows that the statutory transfers (which are transfers through the Finance Commission) remained less than one-third of total transfers during a considerable period of planning. Thus, transfers through the Planning Commission and discretionary transfers from the Government of India have played an important role. As is clear from the table, discretionary transfers alone constituted about one-third of the total transfers during the Fourth Plan period. As the name itself suggests, their size and distribution depend upon the 'discretion' of the Central government. This gives considerable power to the Central government to influence the decision-making process at the State-level.

As regards transfers from the Planning Commission, they were 40% of the total transfers made during the entire period from the First to the Fifth Plan (calculated from Table 4). If we consider the period up to the Fourth Plan (i.e. till 1968-69) we find that transfers through the Planning Commission accounted for 52% of the total transfers. What is interesting to note is the fact that there were no objective criteria to decide the distribution of such transfers as among different States. Much depended on what the Planning Commission and the Central government thought about their needs. Basically, plan assistance was meant to enable the States to undertake certain schemes according to plan priorities. In actual practice, however, the States were presented with a choice of schemes—each with predetermined proportions of loans and grants assistance. According to Bhatia, "this procedure helped the financially better-off States which could use their own resources for those schemes which carried larger loan assistance and choose those schemes for Central assistance which carried greater proportion of grant component".[16] Though the Planning Commission had no statutory basis (as against the Finance Commission which is an ad hoc quinquennial body statutorily set up to recommend devolution of resources from the Centre to the States), it tended to take up the functions of the Finance Commission

TABLE 4: Transfer of resources from Centre to States

(Rs. crores)

	First Plan (Actuals)	Second Plan (Actuals)	Third Plan (Actuals)	Three Annual Plans (Actuals)	Fourth Plan (Actuals)	Fifth Plan	Sixth Plan
A. Transfer under Finance Commission's Recommendations	429	918	1590	1782	5420	13079	20845
B. Transfer through Planning Commission	880	1344	2738	1917	4900	10595	13245
C. Other Transfers	104	606	1272	1648	4922	4045	—
D. Grand Total (A+B+C)	1413	2868	3600	5347	15312	27728	34090
% of (A) to (D)	30.3	32.0	28.4	33.3	35.4	47.2	61.1
% of (B) to (D)	62.3	46.9	48.9	55.9	32.0	38.2	38.9
% of (C) to (D)	7.4	21.1	22.7	30.8	32.6	14.6	—

Source: D.T. Lakdawala, "Plan Finances in a Federal Economy", *Yojana*, 16 May 1979, Table II, p. 7.

and, for a considerable period of planning, has remained the more important source of transfer. Since it was not guided by any objective criteria, the whole scheme introduced an arbitrariness in the determination of resource transfers.

THE GADGIL FORMULA

It was only from 1969-70 onwards that objective criteria were adopted for the distribution of plan assistance among the States. The formula used for the purpose is known as the Gadgil formula which gives 60% weightage to population, 10% to per capita income if below national average, 10% to tax effort in relation to per capita income, 10% to continuing major and medium irrigation projects, and 10% to special problems of individual States (such as those relating to metropolitan areas, floods, chronically drought affected areas, and tribal areas). Under the new formula, it was stated that 30% of total plan assistance would be given in the form of grants and 70% in the form of loans (the corresponding all States' proportions wen 24 and 76 respectively in the Second Plan, and 21 and 79 in the Third Plan). This provision does not apply to Jammu & Kashmir, Assam, and north-eastern States. In their case the distribution is 10% in the form of loans and 90% in the form of grants.

In its meeting held in August 1980, the National Development Council accepted a modified Gadgil formula raising the resources to be transferred to the States whose per capita income was less than the national average from 10% to 20%. Under the modified Gadgil formula, 60% of the assistance is to be given on the basis of population, 20% to States having per capita income below the national average, 10% on the basis of per capita tax effort, and 10% for special problems.

One form of plan assistance is the adoption of Centrally sponsored schemes. Problems having national and inter-State importance (for example, population planning, inter-State power transmission lines, etc.) have to be tackled through this device. Programmes such as the SFDA, MFAL, DPAP, etc. have also come through Centrally sponsored schemes.

A committee was appointed by the Prime Minister to determine plan assistance over the period of the Sixth Five Year Plan. Its report was submitted to the National Development Council by the then Deputy Chairman of the Planning Commission, D.T. Lakdawala, on 24 February 1979. The committee divided Central assistance into the following two parts:

(a) that available without any transfer of Centrally sponsored schemes (Rs.4200 crores) to be distributed according to the Gadgil formula; and

(b) the amount likely to be available as a result of modifications in the Centrally sponsored schemes (Rs.2000 crores) which could be distributed differently.

The committee proposed that Rs.1800 crores should be provided to the special category States. On account of the importance of the family planning programme, it suggested that 8% of Central assistance (as in the past) should be released for the achievement of family planning targets.

The National Development Council, in its meeting held on 25 February 1979 endorsed the Planning Commission proposal for the distribution of Rs.4200 crores Central plan assistance to the 14 States on the basis of the Gadgil formula. As far as the distribution of Rs.2000 crores was concerned, it was decided to adopt the Income Adjusted Total Population (IATP) formula (population multiplied by the inverse of per capita income).

Under the new Sixth Five Year Plan, it has been decided to transfer Rs.15,350 crores to the States as Central assistance.[17] Of this, Rs.2805 crores is proposed to be distributed as follows:

	Rs. crores
Hill areas	560
Tribal areas	470
North-Eastern Council	325
Externally-aided projects	1450
Total	2805

Of the balance of Central assistance of Rs.12,545 crores, Rs.3245 crores has been allocated to eight special-category States, viz., Assam, Himachal Pradesh, Jammu & Kashmir, Manipur, Meghalaya, Nagaland, Sikkim, and Tripura, and the remaining amount of Rs.9300 crores has been distributed among the fourteen non-special category States as under:

Modified Gadgil Formula	Rs.7,700 crores
IATP Formula	Rs.1,600 crores

RESOURCE TRANSFERS AND BACKWARD STATES : A CRITICAL REVIEW OF THE POLICY OF RESOURCE TRANSFERS FROM THE CENTRE TO THE STATES

Under this heading, let us first of all consider the distribution of Central plan assistance among the States. We have already noted that this assistance is provided 70% in the form of loans and 30% in the form of grants. The grant-loan ratio is a fixed one (30 : 70) for all States (except Jammu & Kashmir, Assam, north-eastern States for whom the ratio is 90 : 10). Since the ratio is a fixed one and does not discriminate between the advanced and the backward States, it amounts to discrimination against the backward States. Since the advanced States have a relatively better economic position they should be granted a greater percentage of resources in the form of loans while in the case of the backward States, a greater percentage of resources should be given in the form of grants. Non-compliance of this requirement and distribution to all States in a *fixed* ratio has led to a paradoxical situation where the comparatively richer States received a higher per capita grant than the poorer States. The situation is depicted in Table 5. The table shows that in 1960-61 the comparatively advanced States of Punjab and Tamil Nadu received a higher per capita grant than the poorer States such as Uttar Pradesh, Bihar, Rajasthan, Madhya Pradesh, Andhra Pradesh, etc. During 1969-70 also, richer States such as Punjab and Haryana received a higher per capita grant than did some of the poorer States such as Uttar Pradesh, Bihar, Andhra Pradesh, Kerala, etc. Bihar with the lowest per

TABLE 5: **Per capita plan grants and loans to States in relation to per capita income**

(Rupees)

States	1960-61			1969-70		
	Per capita income	Per capita grant	Per capita loan	Per capita income	Per capita grant	Per capita loan
Andhra Pradesh	314	2.63	9.88	513	7.50	21.07
Assam	349	5.00	6.77	545	19.94	44.12
Bihar	216	3.42	6.52	402	5.70	10.87
Gujarat	380	2.36	7.84	635	10.34	15.15
Haryana	—	—	—	788	8.59	17.37
Jammu & Kashmir	267	15.93	45.20	513	63.24	40.24
Kerala	278	3.23	10.93	505	6.16	13.52
Madhya Pradesh	274	3.46	7.16	569	7.56	10.48
Maharashtra	419	2.55	7.87	731	5.17	9.79
Mysore	292	3.68	6.77	515	4.67	22.73
Nagaland	—	—	—	NA	519.13	21.56
Orissa	266	4.26	7.44	325	8.20	35.29
Punjab	383	3.45	11.74	945	7.91	19.75
Rajasthan	271	3.27	14.25	480	17.55	58.47
Tamil Nadu	344	4.10	5.39	616	7.04	12.57
Uttar Pradesh	244	2.90	5.73	506	6.31	13.90
West Bengal	286	2.13	7.30	562	5.53	12.90

Source: D.M. Nanjundappa and G.V.K. Rao, "Bases of Resource Transfer from Centre to States" *Economic and Political Weekly*, 15 September 1973, Table 1, p. 1696.

capita income range received the lowest per capita grant. When one comes to study the loan burden on States, one finds that the poorer States had a larger burden in the form of loans compared with the richer States. Thus, in 1969-70, the per capita loan in the case of poorer States such as Assam, Andhra Pradesh, Orissa, Jammu & Kashmir, Nagaland, and Rajasthan was higher than in the case of the relatively more developed States of Maharashtra, Gujarat, Punjab, Haryana, Tamil Nadu, and West Bengal. In fact, the most advanced State (viz., Maharashtra) had the lowest per capita loan in 1969-70.

Per Capita Plan Outlay

It has been pointed out by the poor States that from plan to plan their per capita plan outlay does not only compare badly with that of richer States but has also undergone a relative deterioration. To illustrate this point, let us consider the position of Bihar, Madhya Pradesh, Rajasthan, Orissa, and Uttar Pradesh (all of which are backward States) vis-a-vis Maharashtra, the most advanced industrial State of India. The position is summarized in Table 6.

The long-term trend of per capita plan outlay for the five backward States seems to be declining more or less consistently as a proportion of the per capita plan outlay of Maharashtra.

In this context, it is pertinent to note that the Gadgil formula has not favoured the backward States as much as it was expected to do. Disbursement of 10% assistance according to tax effort (as given under the Gadgil formula) has been to the advantage of the developed States. This criterion can be criticised, at least, on the following three grounds: "Firstly, tax effort was judged as a proportion of revenue to State income and given State tax structure, poor States were not in a position to score on this ground. Secondly, since plan assistance was governed by a formula and plan outlay was determined by plan assistance plus State's own resources, in which tax mobilisation entered as a powerful element, this arrangement penalised poor States doubly. Thirdly, it was not generally noticed that population had no weightage in the tax effort formula with the result that between two States with equal tax effort, the State with lower population gained."[18]

TABLE 6 : Per capita plan outlay of five underdeveloped States vis-a-vis Maharashtra

(in Rs.)

State	First Plan	Second Plan	Third Plan	Fourth Plan	Fifth Plan
Bihar	25	40	67	85	155
	(68)	(70)	(65)	(43)	(42)
Madhya Pradesh	34	48	84	114	254
	(92)	(84)	(81)	(58)	(68)
Orissa	56	54	120	113	207
	(151)	(95)	(117)	(57)	(56)
Rajasthan	39	53	97	120	237
	(105)	(93)	(94)	(60)	(64)
Uttar Pradesh	25	32	72	132	237
	(68)	(56)	(70)	(66)	(64)
Maharashtra	37	57	103	199	372

Note: Figures in parentheses indicate the per capita plan outlay of the State as a percentage of the per capita plan outlay of Maharashtra.

Source: Computed from D.T. Lakdawala, "Plan Finances in a Federal Economy," op. cit., Table V, p. 9.

Transfers by the Finance Commissions

Let us now turn to consider the transfer of resources recommended by the Finance Commissions. We have already noted the attempts made by the different Finance Commissions to incorporate the considerations relating to regional imbalances in deciding the share of States in the tax revenue and grants-in-aid. By giving 80% weightage to population in determining the share of different States in income-tax, the First Finance Commission helped some of the backward States as population has been regarded as a broad measure of need. We also noted that similar considerations continued to prevail in the devolution of income-tax with the Second and the Fifth Finance Commissions increasing the weightage of population to 90% because it was felt that the advanced States were cornering a large share of income-tax revenue on considerations of collection. As already noted, population was given a major weightage in determining the allocation of excise duties also among different States by all the Finance Commissions. In addition, relative financial weakness was incorporated as a factor determining allocation by the Third Finance Commission which was abandoned by the Fourth and the Fifth Commissions in favour of economic and social backwardness. This change explicitly brought into focus the requirements of the backward States. In addition, as already noted, the Fifth Finance Commission also paid specific attention to States having per capita income level less than the average per capita income of all States. However, in actual devolution of resources from the Centre to the States, the more advanced States seem to have cornered the major share of the resources. As we have already noted, the four advanced industrial States of Maharashtra, Gujarat, Tamil Nadu, and West Bengal have consistently received more than one-third of the income-tax transfers despite the fact that the Second and the Fifth Finance Commissions had tried to increase the share of the backward States by increasing the weightage to the population factor from 80% to 90%.

Though the First Finance Commission spoke of reducing inter-State inequalities it only attempted to equalize "standards of basic social services". States having poor basic social services are not necessarily the backward States. Also, the importance given to "budgetary needs" in the allocation of grants-in-aid did not fully recognize the equity principle for the advanced States could also incur large budget deficits (even deliberately at times) and qualify for larger grants-in-aid. Thus, while the relatively advanced States of Punjab and West Bengal qualified for grants-in-aid, the backward States of Bihar and Uttar Pradesh were left out. The subsequent Commissions also basically followed the approach of 'filling up gaps in budget deficits'. The Second Finance Commission discontinued the specific purpose grants-in-aid for primary education and stated that it was the responsibility the Planning Commission to ensure the equalization of the standard of essential social services in the various States. It restricted its task to allocation of tax revenue among States and sanctioning of grants-in-aid to help the States to close their revenue gaps. The Third Finance Commission also accepted the position of the Second Commission that it was no longer the job of the Finance Commission to seek to improve (or equalize) the standards of services provided by the State governments. The Fourth Finance Commission also recommended grants-in-aid to the States on the basis only of its assessment of their non-plan revenue gaps. Though the Fifth Finance Commission expressly stated its desire to help the relatively backward States, as already noted, it did not undertake to help these States in improving their level of social services on the ground that such an attempt "would blur the entire division of functions between this Commission and the Planning Commission".

Though the Finance Commissions had full right to determine the allocation of shared taxes and grants so as to achieve some degree of regional equality, the methods of devolution adopted by them benefited the richer States more in comparison with the poorer States. As can be seen from Table 7, the three richest States of Punjab, Haryana, and Maharashtra have enjoyed sizable surplus in their non-plan revenue accounts under the awards of the Finance Commissions. Such surpluses were comparatively much lower in the case of poorer States such as Bihar and Uttar Pradesh.[19] This tendency is undesirable as far as the objective of reduction in regional inequalities is concerned. Because of their larger surpluses, the richer States have a higher plan outlay while the plan outlay of poorer States remains considerably lower. This state of affairs is caused basically by two factors: (i) instead of considering the financial needs within the revenue accounts of the States in totality different criteria have been adopted for the distribution of shared taxes and grants-in-aid of revenue; and (ii) the criteria adopted for distribution have been themselves inequitable.[20]

The second point is important and needs some further comment. We have already noted that as far as distribution of the income-tax share among States is concerned, population and collection were the bases. Population was regarded to be a broad measure of need and collection was to compensate, at least in part, for the drain of incomes of local origin due to income-tax. But 'population' is a 'neutral criterion' "and can serve as an index of need only when it is assumed that the existing discrepancies in fiscal capacities and needs of the States is in conformity with the social norm".[21] Provision of compensation to take into account the factor of collection has favoured the rich urban States. As already noted, 10% weightage was given to this factor by the Second, the Fifth, and the Sixth

TABLE 7: Estimated surplus in non-plan revenue account of States after devolution

(Rs. crores)

State	Fourth Finance Commission	Fifth Finance Commission	Sixth Finance Commission	Seventh Finance Commission
Bihar	89.25	199.46	—	1092.32
Gujarat	8.00	158.99	355.46	1127.89
Haryana	*	79.88	223.35	678.63
Madhya Pradesh	—	15.09	110.18	1111.25
Maharashtra	215.66	419.29	748.42	3004.75
Karnataka	—	20.57	232.74	1006.15
Punjab	29.83	117.22	341.48	809.50
Tamil Nadu	—	—	184.53	627.39
Uttar Pradesh	17.02	280.87	—	1943.86
West Bengal	13.97	—	—	715.27
Total	373.73	1291.37	2176.16	13582.44**

*Included in the composite State of Punjab,

**Includes surplus for some other States as follows:

Rs.923.18 crores for Andhra Pradesh, Rs.86.82 crores for Assam.

Rs.235.05 crores for Kerala, and Rs.220.28 crores for Rajasthan.

Sources: (a) Reports of the Fourth and the Fifth Finance Commissions, p. 59 and p. 65 respectively.

(b) D.T. Lakdawala, "Plan Finances in a Federal Economy", op. cit., Table III, p. 7.

Commissions and 20% by the First, the Third, and the Fourth Commissions. As far as distribution of proceeds from Union excise duties is concerned, population was again assigned predominant weightage. Some Commissions did indeed try to give weightage to some criteria of social, economic, and financial backwardness but the overall approach was "only a patchwork" and did not consider comprehensively the needs of the States.[22]

The approach adopted for the distribution of statutory grants is basically a 'revenue-gap filling' approach. Grants-in-aid are given to the States to fill their residuary budget gaps. However, the method of determining gap is not satisfactory. No uniform methodology or technique is adopted by the States to determine the gap between the projected revenue and expenditure forecasts. The second weakness arises from the procedure of considering only time as the 'determinant' of the revenue and expenditures of the States. The States generally project their own revenues and expenditures (to be supplied to the Finance Commission) on the basis of the expected growth rates. Assuming relative price stability, the expenditures and revenues of the States are supposed to conform to their past behaviour with respect to time, and thus forecasts for the relevant period are made. According to Govinda Rao, this procedure is objectionable on two grounds: "First, it is not known to what extent the forecasts which are made assuming only time to be the determinant of the States' revenues and expenditures are realistic and reliable. A host of factors, economic, social, political and cultural determine the revenues and expenditures of the States and subsuming all these factors into a single variable 'time' may not explain the changes in revenues and expenditures as much as when these determinants are considered. . . . Second, the devolutions made on the basis of the forecasts made by assuming price stability have been consistently found to have been eroded in real terms due to the continuous rise in the price levels."[23] On account of factors such as these, the Sixth Finance Commission, unlike the previous Commissions, practically re-estimated the States' revenues and expenditures on the basis of the observed, and in some cases expected, growth rates. The Seventh Finance Commission also did similar exercises.

Seventh Finance Commission and Backward States

Against this backdrop of the performance of the first six Finance Commissions vis-a-vis the needs of the backward States, it would be interesting to consider how the Seventh Finance Commission has fared. This is all the more necessary because in recent times a lot of thought has been devoted to the development of backward areas and backward States. In fact, practically every policy measure of the Government of India talks in terms of reducing regional inequalities and promoting the development of backward areas more rapidly.

Let us start by considering the distribution of proceeds from additional excise duties. We have already noted that while the Sixth Finance Commission distributed the receipts from this source on the basis of population, State domestic product and State output of the relevant commodities giving a weightage of 0.7, 0.2, and 0.1 respectively to these factors, the Seventh Finance Commission has set up two principles: for sugar on the basis of the average despatches to the States during the recent past, and for tobacco and textiles on the basis of the product of the population and per capita State domestic product. By assuming that receipts from the duties on tobacco and textiles will continue to be four times the receipts from sugar, Bhabatosh Dutta has computed a weighted average of the percentage share of States in receipts from additional excise in lieu of sales tax and has compared it with the award under the Sixth Finance

Commission. This exercise shows that the percentage share of the poor States such as Bihar and Uttar Pradesh has declined while the percentage share of the rich States such as Punjab and Maharashtra has increased. Thus, the percentage share of Bihar which was 9.36 under the Sixth Commission comes down to 6.96 under the award of the Seventh Commission and that of Uttar Pradesh comes down from 16.10 to 12.67. As against this, the percentage share of Punjab rises from 4.17 to 4.44 and that of Maharashtra rises from 11.65 to 14.20.[24] Thus, concludes Dutta, "if the ultimate objective of the distribution of tax shares is to reduce disparities, the problem is being accentuated by the inequality resulting from the allocation of the receipts from the additional excises."

Basic Excises: Let us now turn to basic excise duties. The distribution of proceeds from this source is crucial because by raising the share of the States from 20% to 40% the Seventh Finance Commission has increased the divisible pool by approximately Rs.6000 crores at one stroke. While the earlier Commission had given 75% or more weightage to the factor of population, the Seventh Finance Commission made an important departure. We have already stated earlier that the new formula adopted by the Seventh Commission gives equal 25% weightage to the factors of population, the inverse of the per capita State domestic product, a specially calculated poverty ratio, and a revenue equalization factor. This formula, the Seventh Finance Commission believes, is more progressive compared with the previous ones. The poverty ratios used by the Commission were worked out by Raj Krishna. "Poverty percentage" were also calculated. The "poverty percentage" for a State is the percentage of persons below the poverty line in that State to the 15-State population of such persons. For example, Bihar has a poverty percentage of 13.03 and has 10.35% of the total population of the 15 States. Thus, its share in the number of poor persons is substantially larger than its share in the total population. The States in which the poverty percentage is higher than the share in the total population are Bihar, Kerala, Orissa, Madhya Pradesh, Tamil Nadu, and West Bengal. This again presents a perplexing situation. States such as West Bengal and Tamil Nadu, which are generally considered to be rich States, show high poverty percentages. Accordingly, by using this criterion, the Seventh Finance Commission has actually helped some of the rich States vis-a-vis States such as Uttar Pradesh which have a lower poverty percentage compared with their share in total population but are nevertheless considerably behind West Bengal and Tamil Nadu in the development race.

Another point that needs emphasis is that, though the Seventh Finance Commission claims to have introduced an element of 'progressiveness' in the distribution of Union excise duties vis-a-vis the previous Finance Commissions by opting for a formula which gives an equal 25% weightage to population, inverse of State domestic product, poverty ratio, and a revenue equalization factor, the actual inter-State distribution shows that, with a few exceptions, the shares of individual States in Union excise duties are almost the same as recommended by the Fifth Finance Commission. The shares of Bihar, Orissa, Kerala, and Uttar Pradesh have actually declined somewhat compared with the recommendations of the Fifth Finance Commission.

Raj Krishna's Note of Dissent

One of the members of the Seventh Finance Commission, Raj Krishna (who was also a member of the Planning Commission at the time), in his 'Note of Dissent' entitled 'A More Equitable Distribution of Resources', has pointed out that the distribution of the total transfers among different States is not sufficiently progressive. He criticises the approach of all the Seven Finance Commissions appointed so far in determining the distribution of income-tax revenue. We have noted that the Finance Commissions have so far attached 10% or 20% weightage to the factor of collection (or contribution). The use of 'collection' as a criterion for distribution of income-tax revenue is criticised by Raj Krishna on the following grounds.

Any weight given to collection is regressive because a larger collection is invariably associated with a higher level of the State domestic product. Raj Krishna has shown that collections are mainly a function of the gross income generated in the factory sector (every increase of Rs.1 lakh in net factory income across States producing about Rs.23,000 as additional income-tax revenue). Because of this relationship between collections and State incomes, weightage to collection implies weightage to per capita income. Thus, more industrialized or more advanced a State, higher the devolution it will get via this mechanism. Weightage to collection reduces the progressivity of transfers due to other criteria.

It has been argued that a larger share should be given to advanced industrial States because they have to incur heavy expenditure on the infrastructure that supports the high revenue-yielding organized sector. Raj Krishna rejects this argument on the basis that "if a higher concentration of high-income units requires larger public expenditure, it also generates correspondingly higher revenues from subjects of taxation in the State list, namely, sales-taxes, property taxes, entertainment taxes, fees, etc." Accordingly, the industrial States are in a better position to raise resources and their need for transferred revenue is less than that of poorer States.

It has been frequently stated that some part of income-tax disbursement should be done on the criterion of collection because this provides an incentive to the fiscal effort of a State (since more collection will imply more transfer of resources in favour of the State). Raj Krishna rejects this argument on the ground that income-tax collections in a State do not depend on the efforts of the government of that State. They depend mainly upon factory income which, in turn, depends upon the geographical distribution of industries. On account of historical and other processes (not within the control of the State governments), industries have tended to gravitate to advanced industrial States.

On account of these reasons, Raj Krishna is against giving any weightage to 'collection' or 'contribution'. Accordingly, he recommends a common formula for the distribution of both revenue from income-tax and revenue from excise duties. He recommends the distribution of the divisible pool of these taxes on the basis of what he calls the "income-adjusted poverty population" of each State. This is calculated by multiplying the population of the State by the poverty ratio (i.e., by taking the total number of persons below the augmented poverty line) and dividing it by the per capita income. Thus,

$$\text{IAPP} = \frac{(\text{Population}) \times (\text{Poverty Ratio})}{(\text{Per Capita Income})}$$

The percentage share of a State in the divisible pool of income-tax and excise revenue is simply the percentage of this adjusted poverty population in the total adjusted poverty population of all States.

Raj Krishna's scheme of devolution of shareable income-tax and excise duties is more progressive compared with the scheme finally adopted by the Seventh Commission and looks after the needs of the poorer States in a better way. This is achieved by Raj Krishna by (i) attaching no weight to collection in the devolution of income-tax revenue; (ii) applying the same formula of inter-States allocation to the devolution of shareable excise as well as income-tax revenues; and (iii) using IAPP by applying the formula given above instead of the formula used by the majority wherein equal weights (of 0.25) were given to the four criteria of population, inverse of per capita income, revenue distance, and poverty percentage. In Raj Krishna's formula, the product of population and poverty ratio is multiplied by the inverse of per capita income only to ensure that rich States are not able to corner the major part of the divisible resources.

As far as the objective of reducing regional disparities is concerned, the superiority of Raj Krishna's scheme over the majority's award can be easily seen by comparing per capita transfers and per capita surpluses under two schemes. In the majority's award, the highest per capita surplus is Rs.675 for Haryana and the lowest is Rs.15 for Orissa. The disparity ratio is as high as 45. In Raj Krishna's scheme, the highest per capita surplus is Rs.577 while the lowest is Rs.100. This gives a disparity ratio less than 6. Raj Krishna has classified the States into the following six categories: (i) *Group A* comprising Punjab, Haryana, and Maharashtra, (ii) *Group B* comprising Gujarat, Karnataka, and West Bengal, (iii) *Group C* comprising Kerala, Tamil Nadu, and Andhra Pradesh, (iv) *Group D* comprising Rajasthan, Orissa, and Assam, (v) *Group E* comprising Madhya Pradesh, Uttar Pradesh, and Bihar, and (vi) *Group F* comprising the hill-States of Himachal Pradesh, Jammu & Kashmir, Manipur, Meghalaya, Nagaland, Sikkim, and Tripura. This classification has been done according to per capita income. Group A contains States with the highest per capita income level and Group E contains States with the lowest per capita income levels. The hill States have been classified into a separate group and do not follow the above rule. A comparison between the majority's award and Raj Krishna's scheme is presented in Table 8. The table shows that per capita transfers and per capita surpluses are both less for richer States under Raj Krishna's scheme (as compared with majority's award) and greater for the poorer States. By reducing per capita transfers by Rs.103 for Group A States and Rs.31 for Group B States, Raj Krishna has been able to increase per capita transfers for States in all other groups. The States in the poorest group (Group E) benefit the most. Simi-

TABLE 8: **Transfers and surpluses per capita of groups of States in majority award and Raj Krishna's scheme**

(in Rupees)

States	Per capita transfers		Difference (3)−(2)	Per capita surplus		Difference (6)−(5)
	Majority Award	RK's scheme		Majority Award	RK's scheme	
(1)	(2)	(3)	(4)	(5)	(6)	(7)
Group A	319	216	−103	623	520	−103
Group B	355	324	− 31	308	280	− 28
Group C	355	371	+ 16	163	175	+ 12
Group D	385	424	+ 39	58	100	+ 42
Group E	384	472	+ 88	240	329	+ 89
Group F	1799	1850	+ 54	49	100	+ 51

Source: Raj Krishna's 'Note of Dissent' to the *Report of the Seventh Finance Commission.*

larly by reducing the per capita surplus of Group A States by Rs.103 and of Group B States by Rs.28, Raj Krishna increased the per capita surpluses of all other groups. Again, Group E benefits the most.

Let us now consider the surplus in non-plan revenue account of the States after devolutions. The surpluses that occur under the Seventh Finance Commission's award are given in the last column of Table 7. Raj Krishna advocated small reductions in the surpluses thus made available to the richer States such as Maharashtra, Gujarat, Punjab, and Haryana so that surpluses of the relatively poor States could be increased. In his scheme he has succeeded in reducing the surplus of Maharashtra from Rs.3004 crores to Rs.2580 crores, of Punjab from Rs.810 crores to Rs.640 crores, of Haryana from Rs.679 crores to Rs.579 crores, and of Gujarat from Rs.1128 crores to Rs.922 crores. This has released considerable resources for the backward States of Uttar Pradesh, Bihar, Madhya Pradesh, and Orissa.[25]

One more observation before we conclude this chapter. This relates to the share of divisible taxes and grants in the total transfers of resources. In the scheme adopted by the Sixth Finance Commission, 70.12% of the total transfer was through tax-sharing and 29.88% was through grants. Under the award of the Seventh Finance Commission, 92.3% transfer is through tax devolution and only 7.7% is through grants. While under the award of the Sixth Finance Commission Rs.2510 crores were given as grants to 14 States and special upgradation grants (for improving administration and social services) amounted to Rs.833 crores, the Seventh Finance Commission gives grants of only Rs.1173 crores to 8 States (7 hill States and Orissa) and the upgradation grants at Rs.437 crores are also considerably lower compared with the Sixth Finance Commission.

This increased dependence on taxes and the reduced share of grants has made the whole approach of the Seventh Finance Commission regressive. Such a scheme is bound to increase inequalities among the States despite all intentions of securing 'progressiveness' according to needs. It is the grants component of the total transfers that can be effectively used to reduce disparities. The reduction in the grants content can only help in accentuating the problems of disparities in non-plan surpluses. Thus, the Seventh Finance Commission appears to have set a wrong precedent. Between the two prominent sources of transfer, Planning Commission and Finance Commission, it is the Finance Commission which, with its statutory powers and 'autonomy', is in a better position to introduce a strong redistributive bias in favour of the poorer States. The failure of the Seventh Finance Commission in this regard is, therefore, a big disappointment.

In conclusion it is pertinent to note the observations of Bhabatosh Dutta that if an equitable transfer of resources from the Centre to the States is the final objective then, as a minimum condition, "the Plan plus non-

Plan expenditure on the developmental services per person below the poverty line should be the same all over the country". Dutta has very rightly appealed for a re-examination of the whole problem "with a view to establishing a continuously operating and fully integrated machinery that has within its purview all finances, that eliminates the need for harmful strategies used both by the Centre and the States in the game of federal finance".[26]

NOTES

1. Thus, revenue from income-tax which was Rs.664.1 crores during the period of the First Plan rose to Rs.1148.3 crores during the period of the Third Plan, to Rs.2833.5 crores during the period of the Fourth Plan, and further to Rs.5463.3 crores during the period 1974-75 to 1978-79. The most remarkable increase has been registered by Union excise duties. The revenue from this source was merely Rs.517.3 crores during the First Plan. This went up to Rs.1554 crores in the Second Plan, to Rs.3517.2 crores in the Third Plan, to Rs.10270.4 crores in the Fourth Plan, and to a staggering figure of Rs.20,576.4 crores during the five-year period 1974-75 to 1978-79.

   On account of factors such as these, the budgetary receipts of the Central government (gross of States' share) registered an increase from Rs.2577.2 crores during the First Plan and Rs.4231.6 crores during the Second Plan to Rs.9906.1 crores during the Third Plan, to Rs.51820 crores during the five-year period 1974-75 to 1978-79. As against this, States' own revenue receipts increased from Rs.1802.9 crores in the First Plan to Rs.2945.8 crores in the Second Plan, to Rs.4925.2 crores in the Third Plan, to Rs.12,458.9 crores in the Fourth Plan, and further to Rs.21,448.9 crores during the five-year period 1974-75 to 1978-79.
2. The States' share in income-tax revenue which was Rs.278.2 crores in the First Plan rose to Rs.555.5 crores in the Third Plan, to Rs.2138.5 crores in the Fourth Plan, and to Rs.3313.3 crores in the five-year period 1974-75 to 1978-79. Thus, in percentage terms, it registered an increase from 42% in the First Plan to 48% in the Third Plan and 75.5% in the Fourth Plan (see note 1 for figures on total revenue from income-tax). In a similar way, the share of the States in the total revenue from the Union excise duties has shown an increase, in both absolute and percentage terms. It rose from Rs.64.1 crores in the First Plan to Rs.281.2 crores in the Second Plan, to Rs.614.8 crores in the Third Plan, to Rs.2383.6 crores in the Fourth Plan, and further to Rs.4880.4 crores during the five-year period 1974-75 to 1978-79. In percentage terms, the increase was from 12% in the First Plan to approximately 18% in the Second and the Third Plans, to 23.2% in the Fourth Plan, and further to 24% during the five-year period 1974-75 to 1978-79.
3. See section on "Other Sources of Transfer".
4. *Report of the First Finance Commission*, 1952, Ch. I, para 22. Emphasis added.
5. From the point of view of reducing regional disparities, it is necessary to provide a built-in mechanism in the distribution of grants-in-aid that ensures a greater proportion to backward States. However, no attempts were made in this direction and the broad approach adopted by all the Finance Commissions was to fill up the budgetary deficits of the States. A State incurring a heavy budgetary deficit gets more grants in compair

son with a State with a low budgetary deficit. Such a scheme has, at least, two basic defects: (i) it gives no incentive to good fiscal management, and (ii) it need not be consistent with the objective of reducing regional disparities. It can happen that comparatively richer States incur heavier deficits than the poorer States on account of their larger expenditure on social and economic overheads. Under this scheme, they will then get more grants-in-aid vis-a-vis poorer States. Such a practice can only increase regional disparities.

6. At a meeting of the NDC in December 1956, the Chief Ministers agreed to refrain from imposing sales tax on mill-made textiles, sugar, and tobacco since these were articles of nation-wide consumption. It was agreed therefore that the Central government would, in lieu thereof, levy and collect additional excises on them and distribute the whole of the net proceeds among the States.

7. Under Article 269 of the Constitution, taxes on railway fares and freights are to be levied and collected by the Union but the net proceeds are to be distributed among the States. A tax on railway passenger fares was imposed for the first time in 1957 and the Second Finance Commission was entrusted with the task of determining the principle on which it should be distributed among States. The Commission recommended that each State should get a share which might be as nearly equal as possible to the net proceeds on account of the actual travel on railway within its limits. The tax remained in force for four years only and during this period it yielded Rs.44.36 crores of which Rs.42.56 crores were assigned to the States. The Railway Passenger Fares Act was repealed in 1961 and the tax was merged in passenger fares. Since then, the railways are giving a fixed grant of Rs.12.50 crores annually (which represents the actual collection of the tax in 1958-59 and 1959-60) to be distributed among States on the principles recommended by the Finance Commission. As far as distribution of this grant among the States is concerned, the Third Finance Commission recommended the principle of 'compensation' so as to place the States on the same footing as they were before the tax was abolished. The amount of grant under this heading was increased to Rs.16.25 crores in 1966-67. The Fifth Finance Commission felt that the system of a fixed annual grant had deprived the States of a potentially elastic source of revenue and accordingly regarded the States' desire for reimposition of the tax as legitimate. However, on grounds of the adverse effects it might have and the unsatisfactory state of finances of the railways, the Commission saw no scope for its reimposition. The principle determining the distribution of this grant was left unchanged by the Commission.

8. This would be clear from the following statement—"We consider that while population should continue to be the major factor of distribution, the relative financial weaknesses of the States, the disparity in the levels of development reached, the percentage of scheduled castes and tribes and backward classes in their population, etc. should also be taken into account in determining the share to be allocated to each State individually." *Report of the Third Finance Commission*, 1961, p. 22.

9. Ibid., p. 32. In his note of dissent, the Member-Secretary of the Commission, G.R. Kamat, objected to specific grants for improving communications. The Central government accepted his plea and rejected the Commission's recommendation in this regard.

10. *Report of the Fourth Finance Commission*, 1965, pp. 28-29.

11. Ibid., p. 34.

12. *Report of the Fifth Finance Commission*, 1969, p. 36.

13. Ibid., p. 36.

14. *Report of the Sixth Finance Commission*, 1973, p. 17.

15. The Commission has not included in this amount the grant of Rs.10.02 crores given to Gujarat under the heading 'General Administration' and the grants of Rs.1.11 crores

and Rs.6.54 crores given to Haryana and Tamil Nadu respectively under the heading 'Police'. If these grants are also included, the total rises to Rs.833.51 crores. See *Report of the Sixth Finance Commission*, p. 51.

16. H.L. Bhatia, *Centre-State Financial Relations in India*, Study sponsored by Birla Institute of Scientific Research (New Delhi: Abhinav Publications, 1979), p. 120.
17. Planning Commission, Government of India, *Sixth Five Year Plan, 1980-85*, p. 68.
18. D.T. Lakdawala, "Plan Finances in a Federal Economy", *Yojana*, 16 May 1979, p. 9.
19. What is important is the fact that whatever surplus arose in the case of poorer States such as Bihar and Uttar Pradesh was on account of their inability to provide services at adequate levels, in comparison with other States. This can be broadly inferred from the fact that their per capita expenditure has normally remained less than the average of per capita expenditure for all States taken together. See M. Govinda Rao, "Federal Fiscal Transfers in India", *Economic and Political Weekly*, 30 July 1977, p. 1229.
20. Ibid., p. 1229.
21. Ibid., p. 1229.
22. Ibid., p. 1230.
23. Ibid., p. 1230.
24. Bhabatosh Datta, "Our Crumbling Federal Finance System: Seventh Finance Commission's Award", *Economic and Political Weekly*, 13 January 1979, Table 2, p. 75.
25. In this context Raj Krishna stated that "since the whole Indian nation is a Commonwealth the better endowed States should not grudge small reduction in their large surpluses for the sake of improving substantially the financial position of their weaker neighbours". Raj Krishna's 'Note of Dissent' to *Report of the Seventh Finance Commission*, p. 144. Unfortunately the rich States do 'grudge' and are generally not willing to look beyond their boundaries. Thus, instead of inter-State cooperation we have inter-State rivalry.
26. Bhabatosh Datta, op. cit., p. 78.

Chapter 10

Experiments in Inter-State Regional Planning

We propose to discuss two experiments in inter-State regional planning in this country—the Damodar Valley Corporation and the Dandakaranya project. Both of these experiments are unique in certain respects. While the Damodar Valley project was the first attempt at multi-purpose planning of a river basin, the Dandakaranya project was the first large inter-State effort to reclaim land for the resettlement of refugees. Both projects were genuine attempts in regional planning where regions cut across State boundaries. The Damodar region lies partly in Bihar and partly in West Bengal, while the Dandakaranya region lies partly in Madhya Pradesh and partly in Orissa.

THE DAMODAR VALLEY CORPORATION

The Damodar river is 541 km (about 336 miles) long and flows through Bihar and West Bengal, across the coal and steel belt of India. The river is also known as Deonadi in its initial reaches. It rises in western Bihar in the hills of Chotanagpur and drains areas in the Ranchi, Hazaribagh, Dhanbad, and Santhal Parganas districts of Bihar and the Bankura and Burdwan districts of West Bengal. After flowing for about 40 km from its initial point, it forms the boundary between the Hazaribagh and Ranchi districts. From here it enters the Hazaribagh district and flows in an easterly direction for approximately 145 km and receives an important tributary—the Bokaro. The river then enters the Dhanbad district and, while flowing through this district, receives the tributary Barakar. After its confluence with Barakar it enters West Bengal. Here it flows through the Bankura district and then the Burdwan district. It suddenly bends southwards below Burdwan town and finally falls in the river Hooghly opposite Falta, approximately 50 km from Calcutta. The river has a total catchment area of 25,820 km^2.

The Damodar Basin can be conveniently divided into two parts—the Chotanagpur districts of Bihar comprise the Upper Valley and the West Bengal districts comprise the Lower Valley. The topography of the basin is sharply defined. "The Upper Valley is a tumbled-down confusion of bare rocks indented by deep forest-clad gorges. The area is sparsely populated, but land-hunger of the people is so acute that agriculture has unwittingly encroached upon forest areas. Extensive jungles have disappeared, and with the disappearance of vegetation, the rich top-soil on hill slopes has been eroded, and what has been ultimately left is a desolate waste of thorny shrubs. This devastating process has gone on through centuries. Most of the Ranchi and Hazaribagh hills have thus been rendered almost bare. There is hardly any soil-lining left to hold crops or to absorb any portion of falling rains. Yawning ravines and gullies have been formed, and the rain water, as it falls, rushes down carrying loads of mud and jungle refuse at a terrific speed."[1] As against this, the lower portion of the Damodar basin lying in West Bengal "is a flat, fertile stretch of land made of layers of alluvial soil. The landscape is uniformly uneven, unbroken by hill or ridge. During spells of bumper crop it is a lush, rolling vista of green."[2] The main crop in the lower valley is *aman* paddy which depends on a copious and well-distributed supply of water.

The Damodar river is notorious and is known for its erratic character. During the last hundred and fifty years or so, serious floods have occurred in it in 1823, 1848, 1856, 1859, 1863, 1882, 1890, 1898, 1901, 1905, 1907, 1913, 1916, 1923, 1935, and 1943. The countryside was inundated, crops and cattle were washed away, and communications seriously disrupted. Between 1862 and 1872 floods in the Damodar river caused a malaria epidemic and almost a third of the population on the left bank of the river died of what came to be known as "Burdwan Fever". What drew widespread attention to the problems of the Damodar region were the devastating floods of 1943 which caused heavy damage in the area. The countryside south of Burdwan was submerged and inundated in some places to a depth of six or seven feet, villages were swept away, rice fields were devastated, rail traffic was seriously disrupted since railway bridges were washed away, the grand trunk road was breached, and at a time even the cities of Burdwan and Calcutta were in danger.

Disturbed by the seriousness of the problem, the Bengal government (in consultation with the Government of India) appointed a ten-man Damodar Flood Enquiry Committee with the Maharaja of Burdwan as chairman and

N.K. Bose as secretary. The committee suggested a comprehensive plan for the development of the Damodar basin on the lines of TVA in the USA.[8] On 3 January 1945, representatives of the Government of India, Bengal, and Bihar met to confer on the possibility of a unified development project for the Damodar basin. This was the first time in India when provincial considerations were overridden and serious attempts made to formulate an inter-State plan for action. The Government of India asked the Central Technical Power Board to study the proposal for the construction/implementation of a multi-purpose Damodar Valley project. The Central Technical Power Board secured the services of W.L. Voorduin, a senior engineer with the TVA. He prepared the Preliminary Memorandum that presented a plan of flood control, irrigation, power production, and navigation in the Damodar Valley. This memorandum was submitted for scrutiny to two eminent engineers of the technical mission of the USA. Two Indian engineers, A.N. Khosla and M. Narasimhaiya, were also associated with the task. The expert body approved Voorduin's proposals. Let us see what these proposals were.

Voorduin's Memorandum

The general plan of development submitted by Voorduin envisaged the building of a system of eight dams and a barrage. Seven of the dams were to be constructed for flood control, irrigation, and hydro-electricity in the upper valley and one dam for power generation alone round the year. These seven dams were—Aiyar and Panchet Hill on the Damodar river; Maithon, Belpahari, and Tilaiya on the Barakar river; Konar on the Konar river; and Bokaro on the Bokaro river. The reservoir capacity that would be thus created was thought to be sufficient to meet all requirements and was expected to provide adequate flood protection. Thus, during the monsoon on average the Damodar and its tributaries received approximately 6000 million m^3 of water from their combined catchment while implementation of Voorduin's proposals would have led to impounding of 6540 million m^3.

As far as the provision of irrigation facilities is concerned, the area commanded by the irrigation system served by the Damodar and Eden canals was expected to register a remarkable increase. Thus, as things stood at the time, only 186,000 acres of land had irrigation facilities and even this land was only partially irrigable for water became a scarce commodity in dry weather. Under Voorduin's scheme, it was expected that perennial irrigation to about 760,000 acres (including the 186,000 acres partially irrigated) would be provided.

In addition to providing irrigation facilities over a large area and sufficient means to control floods, the Voorduin memorandum also aimed at the development of a considerable amount of electric power. The memorandum noted that the existing installations of generating capacity (which were all thermal) in the valley were largely obsolete and had a high average cost of generation. It noted that it should be possible to provide 65,000 continuous kilowatts of primary hydro-electric power and an additional amount of intermittent or seasonal power up to a further 65,000 kilowatts. The memorandum also drew attention to the necessity for combining the electric plants with thermal generating plants. The former would contain about 200,000 kW of generating capacity while the latter would contain some 150,000 kW of generating capacity. "Only in this way could the whole of the hydro-electric energy be satisfactorily utilized and the overall costs would then become quite economical. After allowing for all losses the system would be capable of meeting a maximum demand approaching 300,000 kW making available about 1420 m kW hrs annually."[4] Such combined development of hydro and thermal power system would be cheaper compared with total dependence on thermal power alone. Voorduin showed that "the cost per unit delivered in bulk at load centre at 11 KV works out at about 0.24 anna per kW hr for 60% load factor operation. If the same amount of energy had been generated entirely at a modern thermal station in this locality, the estimated cost per unit delivered, using parallel assumptions, would be approx. 0.31 anna. The average annual savings of the combined hydro and thermal power system as compared with all-thermal system would be about Rs.60 lakhs or somewhat more than the estimated annual flood control expenditures."[5]

In addition to these advantages, the Damodar transmission network was expected to serve as a vital link in "a large network connecting large industrial centres at Jamshedpur, Hirapur and Calcutta with large potential sources of energy generation in the Sone Valley".

According to Voorduin, the adoption of the programme advanced by him also offered "promising potentialities" for navigation and water supply and "large indirect benefits in increased health and prosperity of the population of the area". Though the programme did not present any firm conclusions on the issue, yet it was hoped that it might be possible to provide a navigable channel from the Damodar Valley coalfields to industrial Hooghlyside. The programme also hoped to stimulate regional consciousness and raise the living standards of the people living in 8500 square miles of the Damodar basin.

Commenting on Voorduin's proposals, A.E. Green, the Chief Engineer, P.W.D., Bihar, noted that both, Bihar and Bengal, would derive benefits from them though the gains to the latter were likely to exceed considerably the gains accruing to the former. While Bihar was likely to get more power supply and better irrigation facilities, Bengal was likely to obtain the following benefits—(a) flood control, (b) more power supply, (c) better irrigation, water supply, and sanitation facilities, (d) anti-malaria measures and improved health, and (e) possibly navigation facilities. He also noted that adoption of Voorduin's proposals would, in course of time, promote rapid development of urban areas as well as industry and utilities at various points along the Damodar river.[6] The Damodar Valley is very rich in minerals. It contributes more than 60% of all coal raised in India. All the steel plants, excluding one, use Damodar coal and various industries in different parts of the country (such as textiles, chemicals, fertilizer plants, explosives and pharmaceutical manufacturing concerns, etc.) depend on the coal supplied from Damodar fields. Damodar Valley also possesses large reserves of mica, bauxite, iron ore, chromite, fireclay, china clay, copper and a number of othar minerals. It is responsible for 80% of the mica exported to other countries. It was, accordingly, felt that adequate provision of cheap power and electricity could usher the whole region into a new era of economic progress and prosperity.

Birth of the Damodar Valley Corporation

The Preliminary Memorandum prepared by Voorduin had suggested that "the task of continuing the planning, designing, constructing and operating the dams, reservoirs, waterways, power houses and transmission lines be entrusted to an Authority with powers and duties carefully delineated by the three governments concerned". It recommended a study of the TVA Act and hoped that "Damodar Valley Authority could be an example in the multi-purpose development of a watershed for India as the TVA has been for the U.S.A." The legislatures of Bengal and Bihar agreed to set up an authority with the name Damodar Valley Corporation and an agreed draft of the constitution of this body was placed before the Constituent Assembly of India (Legislative) on 1 December 1947. This was passed by the Parliament of India on 18 February 1948 and placed on the statute book on 27 March 1948. Out of this Act of Parliament was born, on 7 July 1948, the Damodar Valley Corporation. The object of setting up of this Corporation was the development of the Damodar Valley region in Bihar and West Bengal. The statutory functions of the Corporation are:—(i) promotion and operation of schemes for irrigation, water supply, and drainage; (ii) generation, transmission, and distribution of electrical energy and flood control; (iii) promotion and control of navigation in the Damodar river and its tributaries and channels; (iv) promotion of afforestation and control of soil erosion in the Damodar Valley and (v) promotion of public health and agricultural, industrial, economic, and the general well-being of the Damodar Valley and its area of operation.

The DVC constituted under the DVC Act consists of a chairman and two members, appointed by the Central government after consultation with the State governments of West Bengal and Bihar. It is provided under the Act that the three participating governments, i.e., the Central government and the State governments of West Bengal and Bihar, have to make available the entire capital required by the Corporation for the execution of any project undertaken by it. The Act requires that the expenditure on the three main objects of the Corporation, viz., power, irrigation, and flood control, should be allocated in a particular manner. Thus, the expenditure allocated to power is to be shared equally by the three participating governments. As regards irrigation, it is provided that the distribution of expenditure between West Bengal and Bihar is to be done as follows:

(i) The government concerned is responsible for the capital cost of the works constructed exclusively for irrigation in its province.

(ii) The balance of the capital cost under irrigation for both the States of West Bengal and Bihar is shared by the State governments in proportion to their guaranteed annual off-takes of water for agricultural purposes.

As regards expenditure on flood control, Bihar is not required to pay anything since it is essentially the State of Bengal that is the likely beneficiary of such measures. The expenditure is to be equally distributed between the Centre and West Bengal up to a maximum of Rs.14 crores. After that, the entire amount is to be contributed by the West Bengal government.

As regards distribution of profits or losses, the Act provides that "the net profits or deficit attributable to any of the three main objects, viz., Power, Irrigation, and Flood Control, shall be credited or made good by the Participating Governments in proportion to their respective shares in the total capital cost attributed to that object, with the proviso that the net deficit in respect of flood control shall be made good entirely by West Bengal and Central government shall have no share in such deficit."

The Damodar Valley Project

The Damodar Valley project is a multi-purpose plan for the development of the Damodar Valley region and has the objectives of (1) flood control, (2) irrigation, (3) generation and transmission of electricity, and (4) promotion of all-the-year-round navigation. In addition to these, the project is also likely to provide many indirect benefits for the overall development of the region. However, as against the Voorduin proposals for the construction of eight dams, the Damodar Valley project as finally implemented contemplated the construction of four dams only. The main features of the project as existing at present are: (i) four multi-purpose dams at Tilaiya, Konar, Maithon, and Panchet, (ii) a barrage at Durgapur with an irrigation canal system of 1550 miles, including a 85-mile-long irrigation-cum-navigation canal on the left bank of Damodar river, (iii) three hydel stations appended to Tilaiya, Maithon, and Panchet dams, and (iv) three large thermal power stations at Chandrapura, Bokaro, and Durgapur with a network of associated transmission and distribution lines. The dam to be completed first was the Tilaiya dam which stands on the Barakar river, about 130 miles above its confluence with the Damodar. Construction of the Konar dam was also started in 1950 across the Konar river, 23 miles above its confluence with the Damodar. The Maithon dam was built on the Barakar river, just above its confluence with the Damodar. The last of the four dams to be started was the Panchet Hill dam, built across the Damodar above its confluence with the Barakar (see Fig. 1). The salient features of the four dams are given in Table 1.

The Durgapur barrage was completed in 1956. This is the lower-most of the structures across the Damodar within the DVC limits (all the four dams are located in the upper valley). The water discharged from the four dams is diverted into a vast network of canals through this barrage which provides irrigation to a large area in the Burdwan, Hooghly, Howrah, and Bankura districts of West Bengal. During 1977-78, the total area brought under kharif irrigation was 325,037 hectares and under rabi irrigation 66,039 hectares (approximately).

Power Generation and Supply

Easy availability of power is a sine qua non of all programmes of industrial development. The hydro-power potential in the Damodar river is woefully inadequate to meet the demands of industrialization, hence the programme of development of the Damodar region envisaged the setting up of a number of thermal power stations. The total installed capacity of the DVC power system during the year 1977-78 was 131MW out of which 1197MW was thermal and 104MW was hydel derived from the three thermal power stations at Durgapur, Bokaro, and Chandrapura, and the three hydel

TABLE 1: Salient features of four dams constructed in Damodar Valley region

Salient feature	Konar	Maithon	Panchet Hill	Tilaiya
Name of the river	Konar	Barakar	Damodar	Barakar
Type of dam	Earth dam with concrete spillway	Earth dam with concrete spillway	Earth dam with concrete spillway	Concrete
Length (metres)	Earth dam 3549 Spillway 110	994	2545	366
Maximum height	49 m above riverbed	49 m above riverbed	49 m above riverbed	30 m above riverbed
Gross storage capacity (m.cu.m.)	337	1357	1497	395
Live storage capacity (m.cu.m)	276		1307	321
Benefits power	Not finalised	Designed primarliy for flood control power 60MW	Designed primarily for flood control power 40MW	Power 4MW
Cost (Rs. m)	97.5	179.7	191.4	37.1
Date of start	1950	1951	1952	1950
Date of completion	1955	1958	1959	1953

Source: Irrigation Commission Report, 1972, Vol. III, Part I.

stations at Maithon, Panchet, and Tilaiya. Table 2 gives details about power generation during the years 1976-77 and 1977-78. It shows that the DVC power system generated 5245 million kWh and 5161 million kWh of energy in 1976-77 and 1977-78 respectively.

The Damodar Valley Corporation power supply has been made available to a number of industries spread over a wide area and for programmes of urban and rural electrification. The important industries that have received power supply from the DVC, among others, are the locomotive works, chemicals, copper mines, copper smelting, aluminium, engineering works, paper, mica mines, collieries, fireclay and ceramics, iron and steel works, rolling mills, cotton mills, cycle manufacturing, and glass works. The DVC power is also supplied to Bihar and West Bengal governments at their various load-distribution points. A number of towns have received power from these distribution points. Some of the important towns to benefit are: Calcutta, Burdwan, Jamshedpur, Patna, Ranchi, Dhanbad, Jharia, Kulti, Chittaranjan, Hirapur, Asansol, Hazaribagh, Gaya, Dalmianagar, Raniganj, Kharagpur, and Ramgarh.

With the object of meeting the future demands of power, the DVC has taken steps to increase its installed capacity by undertaking the construction of Chandrapura 6th unit (120MW), Durgapur 4th unit (200MW), Bokaro

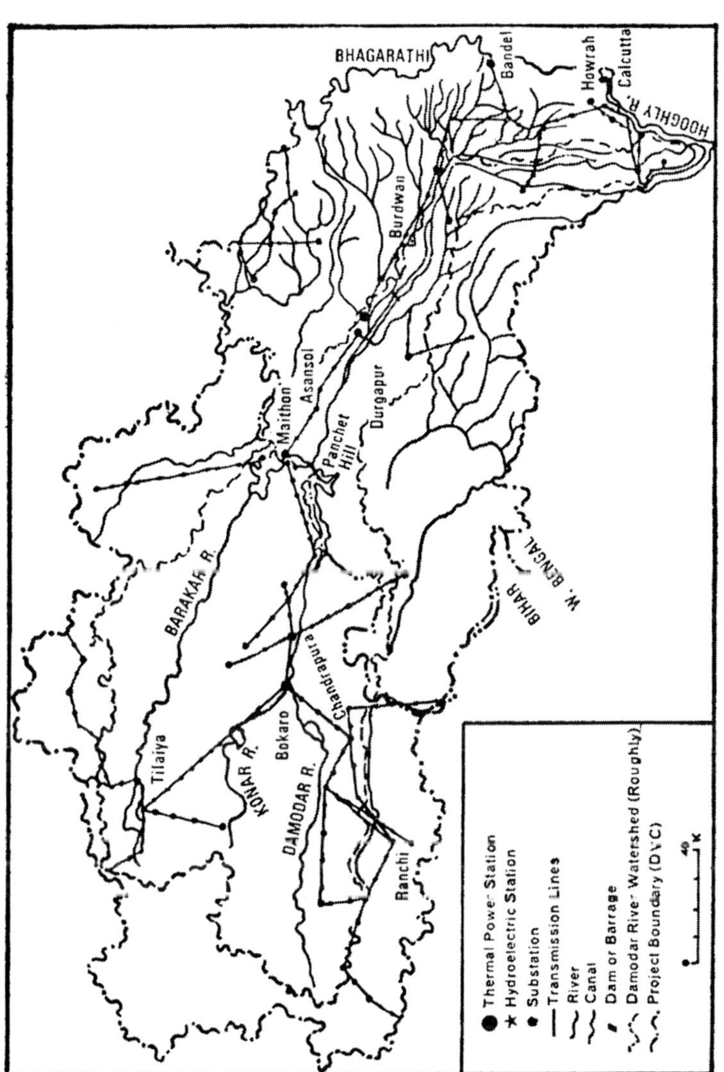

Figure 1: Damodar Valley Corporation Region.

Source: Kanangopal Bagchi, "The Damodar Valley Development and its impact on the Region", Allen G. Noble and Ashok K. Dutt (eds.), *Indian Urbanization and Planning: Vehicles of Modernization* (New Delhi: Tata McGraw Hill Publishing Co. Ltd., 1977), fig. 14.1, p. 237.

'B' Station 1st unit (200MW), and Panchet Hill 2nd unit (40MW).

Soil Conservation and Afforestation

Soil conservation and afforestation are subsidiary activities of the Corporation. Their object is to reduce soil erosion in the catchment and prevent premature sedimentation of the major multi-purpose reservoirs in Damodar Valley. The Corporation has been working since 1949-50 for the treatment of the eroded areas, not only to reduce erosion as such, but also to raise the productivity of land. The problems are being tackled on watershed basis over the major part of the Damodar Valley. During 1977-78 work was carried out in 55 priority watersheds.

The programme of soil conservation is carried out by the soil conservation department in consultation with the leading social scientists of the country. The measures adopted by the department include: (i) survey of soil taking into account "the various physio-chemical properties of the soil, degree of slope, extent of erosion, present land use and suitability for irrigation", (ii) demonstration of better methods of management of land to the farmers and enlisting their cooperation in the task, and (iii) assessing the fertility of the soil at the soils laboratory at Hazaribagh to suggest means of ameliorating the deficient soils.

TABLE 2: **Generation of power in DVC**

Generating station	1976-77		1977-78	
	Max. demand (kW)	Energy generated (million kWh)	Max. demand (kW)	Energy generated (million kWh)
A. *Thermal*				
1. Bokaro	211,000	1158.543	197,000	1136.773
2. Durgapur	222,000	1282.359	218,000	942.996
3. Chandrapura	512,000	2582.263	460,000	2824.069
Total (A)		5023.165		4903.838
B. *Hydel*				
1. Maithon	60,000	98.217	60,000	167.710
2. Panchet	44,000	114.462	44,000	75.853
3. Tilaiya	4,000	9.001	4,000	15.611
Total (B)		221.690		257.174
Grand total		5244.855		5161.012

Source: Damodar Valley Corporation, *Annual Report 1977-78*, Table I, p. 11.

Other land improvement schemes initiated by the DVC include measures such as afforestation, land reclamation, construction of headwater dams, etc. It was expected that the four large reservoirs of the DVC would expose 31,600 acres of their peripheral land annually due to their annual draw-down programme. Because this area is expected to have high agricultural potentialities, a 75-acre research-cum-demonstration farm was started at Sewai on the Tilaiya periphery. A 210-acre agriculture experiment station was started at Panagarh with the intention of carrying out experiments in irrigation farming. The headwater dams perform the dual function of (i) preventing soil erosion and rapid siltration of the main reservoirs and (ii) supplying drinking water to the towns.

The target for the DVC for the year 1977-78 was terracing of 600 hectares, land reclamation of 140 hectares, and construction of 200 silt-detention dams. Against these targets, the achievements were terracing of 233 hectares, land reclamation of 184 hectares, and construction of 273 silt-detention dams. Demonstration of soil conservation farming was done in 1314 hectares; and 10,223 horticultural and other plants were distributed among the farmers free of cost by the DVC. The Corporation also organized four farmers' fairs in different parts of the valley in the same year.[7]

The principal agencies for carrying out afforestation within the Damodar catchment are the forest division of the Corporation and the forest departments of Bihar and West Bengal. During 1977-78, against a target of 2924 hectares, an area of 2268 hectares was afforestated by the DVC in the priority watersheds. In addition, Bihar and West Bengal afforestated 3752 hectares and 147 hectares respectively against the targets of 4000 and 200 hectares respectively, thus bringing the total area afforestated to 6167 hectares during the year.

Capital Structure

According to section 30 of the DVC Act, 1948, the three participating governments, viz., the Union government, West Bengal and Bihar, are to provide the entire capital required by the Corporation for the completion of any project undertaken by it. The capital so provided by the participating governments and the capital outlay up to 31 March 1978 amounted to Rs.214.74 crores and Rs.397.22 crores respectively as shown in Table 3.

An Appraisal

The setting up of the Damodar Valley Corporation was greeted with much fanfare and it was acclaimed as the TVA of Asia that would transform

TABLE 3: Share of participating governments in the capital provided to DVC up to 31 March 1978

(Rs. in crores)

Participating government	Main objects								Excess of outlay over contribution
	Flood control		Irrigation		Power		Total		
	Outlay	Contribution	Outlay	Contribution	Outlay	Contribution	Outlay	Contribution	
1. Union government	7.00	7.00	—	—	109.90	49.09	116.90	56.09	60.81
2. West Bengal government	11.53	7.41	48.71	31.28*	109.90	70.58	170.14	109.27	60.87
3. Bihar government	—	—	0.28	0.12	109.90	49.24	110.18	49.36	60.82
Total	18.53	14.41	48.99	31.40	329.70	168.91	397.22	214.72	182.50

*Does not include capital expenditure amounting to Rs.3.59 crores incurred directly by the Government of West Bengal up to 31 March 1978.

Source: Damodar Valley Corporation, *Annual Report 1977-78*, p. 173.

the face of the Damodar Valley. The emotional zeal of the supporters received perhaps the best description from William Kirk who wrote:

> This is also the first time in the history of the young Indian nation that the resources of a river have been "envisioned in their entirety". Hughes in his survey of the Jharia coalfield referred to the Damodar Basin as the "valles opima" of Bengal; it is rapidly becoming the "valles opima" of India, the valley of the great experiment, the fruits of which will influence the course of Indian geography. For if sectional and local interests are overcome here in the attempt to organize a natural region for the maximum good of its peoples, this will help shape a similar approach to larger regions. And thus a concept reborn into the modern world in the Tennessee Valley returns to a continent where civilized life began with the organization of river basins. The wheel has come full circle.[8]

No one can deny that the Damodar Valley region played an important role in promoting the industrial development of the country. Since this region was endowed with immense mineral resources, it was only natural to expect rapid industrial development in this region, once adequate power supply and the necessary infrastructure was available. Once this happened, there was a rapid spread of industrial activity in the region. A number of public sector plants were set up here. These included the Durgapur steel complex, Bokaro steel complex, heavy machine tools factory at Ranchi, Indian Explosives near Hazaribagh, Sindri Fertilizer Plant, etc. In addition, a number of units in the private sector were also set up. Since the processes of urbanization and industrialization are closely interlinked, the districts having a concentration of industrial units registered a rapid increase in urban population. Both push and pull factors have contributed to the process of rural-urban migration and there is a continuous stream of people migrating from rural areas to the urban and industrial centres. During the decade 1961-71, urban population in the Damodar basin increased by 20% and the overall increase during the two decades of development has been approximately 40%.

Apart from the Howrah-Hooghly riverine industrial belt, the following urban-industrial complexes in the Damodar Valley region have been identified: "(1) Durgapur industrial complex inclusive of thermal power plant, coke oven and by-products of coke oven, iron and steel, alloy steel, mining and allied machinery, cement machinery and boilers, and electrical industries; (2) the Asansol-Kulti Industrial Complex inclusive of steel factory at Burnpur, Chittaranjan locomotives, Kulti foundry works, Kumardhubi engineering works, J.K. Nagar Aluminium, etc.; (3) Dhanbad-Jharia-Sindri industrial area inclusive of Sindri Fertilizers and chemical industries and coal-based industries; (4) the Bokaro industrial area consisting of proposed steel plant at Maraphari near Chas, thermal plant at Chandrapura and Bokaro, Dugdha coal washery, etc; (5) the Ramgarh-Patratu area with thermal power and Indian Explosives industries and lastly (6) the Ranchi Industrial township with H.E.C., H.M.T. and Foundry Forge Plant and others."[9] Thus, a vast urban industrial and commercial belt is emerging in the Damodar Valley region and the processes of modernization are slowly engulfing the valley.

Changes have also occurred in the agricultural scene and the general living conditions in the valley. According to K. Bagchi, "The regulated flow from the Damodar has resulted in perennial water supply, supplemented by subsoil subsidy, for the industrial and service settlements which now bristle with activity the year round. The restriction of flood water spill has released for cultivation more lands bordering the streams resulting in a more intensive agriculture in the Basin. Flood immunity has enabled construction of a denser net of roads with more frequent road services for underdeveloped regions in the Valley. Reduced soil waterlogging and concerted efforts in respect of public health have reduced endemic diseases such as malaria and thereby increased per capita performance."[10]

The most important objective of the Damodar Valley project was to control floods which, as already noted, occurred frequently in the Damodar basin and caused havoc and widespread destruction. How far has been the project successful in fulfilling this objective? A survey of floods occurring in the region shows that the performance of the DVC on this front is far from satisfactory. Since it was decided to construct only four dams against seven suggested by Voorduin (for flood control purposes), floods continue to occur in the Damodar region. Even the four dams constructed are not in a position to retain water up to the design flood levels as the land in the fore-shore of the Maithon and Panchet Hill reservoirs was not acquired up to the design level.[11] In view of this, it is not possible to moderate a peak flow of one million cusecs to 250,000 cusecs. In 1959, a peak flow of 810,000 cusecs could be moderated to 350,000 cusecs at Durgapur. Consequently, a certain amount of flooding in the lower valley was inevitable. The experience was repeated in 1970-71 and more recently in 1978.

In a monsoon affected catchment area (which Damodar basin is), the first regulator of the flow of water downstream is the vegetal cover of the catchment area; the second is the series of flood-control dams which should be designed in such a way that they are able to discharge the waters of each wave of flood at a uniform rate as fast as possible so that the reservoirs impounded by the dams are empty and ready to receive the next wave of flood. The waters so emptied should be discharged into canals upstream and downstream to fill the irrigation tanks. According to K.V. Subrahmanyam, "The fundamental principle of flood-control in areas like that of the Damodar valley should be to treat the virgin forest of the catchment areas as the first line of control, the series of dams as the second line of control, to limit the generation of hydro-power from the dams to the discharge of waters from the first wave of flood to the final emptying of the reservoirs impounded by them before the end of the monsoon, and to concentrate on thermal powers as the main source of power."[12] However, while on the one hand the virgin forest of the catchment area of the Damodar and the Barakar became the special target of attack by the timber contractors and the open-cast minars who did not make any provision for scientific logging, afforestation, reclamation of land, and restoration of the top-soil, on the other the DVC authorities treated the DVC's dams as power dams and not flood-control dams, keeping them filled to the brim (while the appropriate strategy is to keep flood control dams always empty by the time the monsoon comes to an end). When the next wave of flood came in all its fury, the DVC authorities resorted to a panicky discharge of the waters stored behind them. It was the result of this action from Panchet and Maithon that led to the flooding of the site of the Durgapur steel plant in 1959. Since then, the reckless deforestation of the catchment area has resulted in a very high rate of silting in these two dams.[13] As a consequence, the 'shock-absorbing' capacity of the DVC dams and of the denuded catchment area of the rivers has been reduced drastically.[14] It is on account of factors such as these that Bhattacharya is led to conclude in his study that the incidence of floods with bigger peak flows seems to have increased since the inception of the DVC.[15]

THE DANDAKARANYA PROJECT

Another major inter-State planning effort was the Dandakaranya project initiated in 1957. Though the region originally under contemplation extended over 80,000 square miles, it was decided to cover about 30,092 square miles comprising the Koraput and Kalahandi districts of Orissa and the Bastar district of Madhya Pradesh. In actual operation, the Project was restricted to only four administrative zones—Umerkote and Malkangiri in the Koraput district of Orissa and Kondagaon and Paralkote in the Bastar district of Madhya Pradesh.

The Background

As a consequence of partition in 1947, the country was faced with an acute refugee problem on both eastern and western fronts. Approximately a total of 9.8 million people poured in from West Pakistan—4.7 million coming from West Pakistan to Punjab and the remaining 5.1 million coming from East Pakistan (now Bangladesh) to West Bengal. One of the most difficult problems facing the government was to rehabilitate these people and provide them with gainful employment so that they could live in peace and honour. Accordingly, a Ministry of Rehabilitation was set up. Evacuee lands in Punjab were allotted on a quasi-permanent basis to about 477,000 displaced landholders; and about 33,000 families of tenants were settled on land. Land was also allotted on a temporary basis outside Punjab, specially in Rajasthan, to about 58,000 persons. The programme for rural rehabilitation also included grants of loans for building houses and for schemes of agricultural improvement. Problems of displaced persons from urban areas were relatively more complex. To settle these people in business and trade,

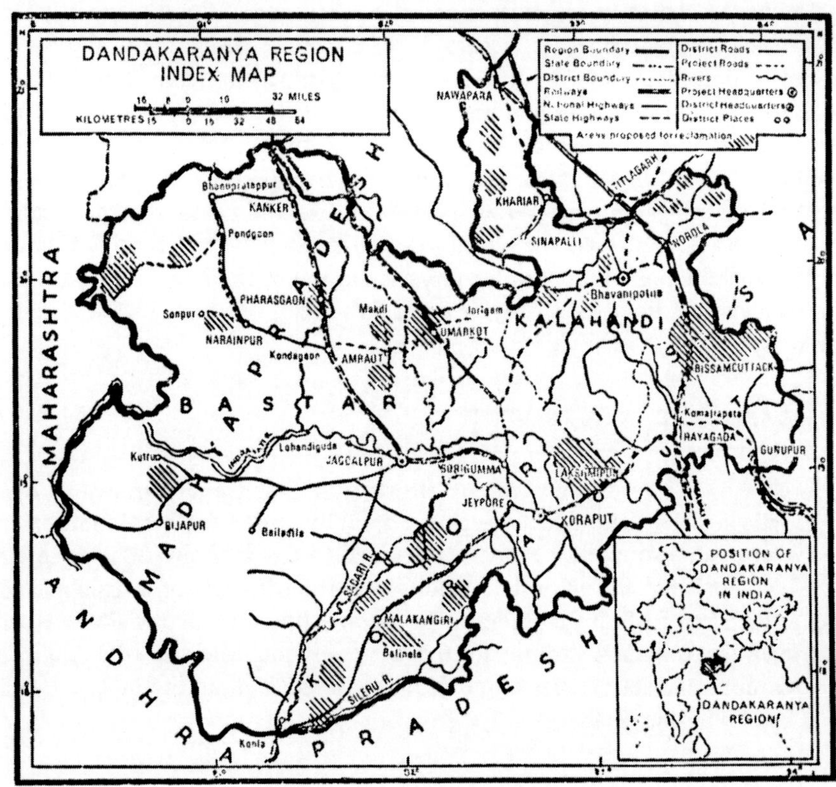

Figure 2: Dandakaranya Region
Source: NCAER, *Development of Dandakaranya*, 1963, Map 1, p. 2.

19 fully developed townships and 136 new colonies were constructed and provided with education, health and other civic amenities, the total number of houses and tenements constructed being about 155,000. Loans were advanced to enable the urban settlers to start business and trade.

The rehabilitation of displaced persons from East Pakistan was rendered difficult in view of the continuing nature of the influx over many years and the heavy pressure on land and economic life in West Bengal. Up to the end of the First Plan, about 500,000 families were rehabilitated in the eastern zone. Of these, about 400,000 were settled on land and in other ancillary occupations in rural areas. The task of rehabilitating displaced persons continued in the Second Plan as well. Housing loans were advanced and a number of colonies developed. Twenty-one schemes for large and medium industries were approved by the Rehabilitation Industries Corporation, which was set up with an authorized capital of Rs.5 crores for putting up industries of its own or in collaboration with private enterprise at centres with large concentrations of displaced persons. Vocational and technical training was given to 28,000 displaced persons during the First Plan and to 22,000 during the Second Plan. Medical facilities were also augmented. A large number of schools and colleges were also established in West Bengal to provide expanded educational facilities to meet the requirements of the displaced persons.[16]

It was being increasingly recognized at the beginning of the Second Plan itself that it would not be possible to rehabilitate all refugees from East Pakistan in West Bengal where the pressure on land was already very heavy and poverty and unemployment were rampant. A large number of refugee families were still living in relief 'camps' and though relief measures were organized on a big scale the living conditions in the camps were bad and deplorable. The burden of providing relief measures was proving very heavy and crushing for the West Bengal economy. Even otherwise, refugees could not continue to live on doles for an unlimited period of time and something had to be done to provide them with permanent homes and permanent employment soon. Land had to be found to resettle them, but where? The first answer to this question was provided by S.V. Ramamurthy, adviser to the Planning Commission, in 1956. He suggested that the Dandakaranya region offered ideal facilities for large-scale settlement, only it called for substantial efforts on the part of the government. A year later, a high-level committee, known as AMPO Committee (consisting of representatives from Andhra Pradesh, Madhya Pradesh, and Orissa) was appointed to investigate the possibilities of his suggestion. The committee made recommendations for integrated development not only to rehabilitate the displaced persons from East Pakistan but also to promote the welfare of the local population particularly the tribals. The recommendations of the committee were approved by the National Development Council and a chief administrator was appointed in November 1957. In September 1958 an autonomous body with the name Dandakaranya Development Authority (DDA) was set up with headquarters at Koraput in Orissa to pursue these objectives. The DDA today has a whole-time chairman and a chief administrator (who is the chief executive officer and secretary) besides six other members—the chief secretaries of the governments of Madhya Pradesh, West Bengal, and Orissa, or their nominees, and a representative each of the ministries of finance, labour and rehabilitation, and home affairs. Expectedly, the first chairman of the DDA was S.V. Ramamurthy himself.

The essential features of the integrated development of the area were spelt out as follows:

1. The eradication of malaria.
2. The improvement of communications by the construction of all-weather roads and a railway.
3. A balanced utilization of land including afforestation, soil conservation, reclamation and the development of colonies with a balanced economy.
4. Evolution of the most beneficial crop pattern appropriate to the quality of the soil, the climate and irrigatian facilities.
5. The development of horticulture.
6. The provision of irrigation facilities.
7. Development of extensive pisciculture, the introduction of new species and improvement of livestock.
8. The establishment of industries, large or small-scale or on cottage basis, having regard to the availability of raw materials, transport, and marketing facilities.
9. The provision of adequate medical, educational, technical, and vocational training facilities.
10. The provision of adequate transport and marketing facilities.
11. The development of power.
12. The exploration and development of mineral resources which are believed to exist in the area.

Initially, the movement of the displaced persons from the relief camps in West Bengal to the Dandakaranya region was kept voluntary. But there was considerable apathy (and also resistance at times) in the refugees to move from Bengal partly because of the fear of an alien land and partly because of their cultural identity with the people of West Bengal. Therefore, their movement to Dandakaranya was halting and slow so much so that it was decided in December 1960 to issue notices to the families still residing in relief camps in West Bengal to vacate the camps and move to Dandakaranya. A decision was made to issue notices at the rate of at least 2000 families per month from 1 May 1961. The notices were to specify that after the expiry of the period of notices (which may be up to 60 days) the families concerned should either move to Dandakaranya or leave the camps. In the latter case, the government will not be responsible for their rehabilitation and resettlement. Notices were given to all families by 15 July 1961. Even then, the movement of people continued to remain halting and slow.

Programmes of Development

Reclamation of Land: The first task that confronted the Dandakaranya

Development Authority was to clear jungles and reclaim land for agricultural purposes and settlement of displaced persons. According to the agreement reached between the DDA on the one hand and the governments of Orissa and Madhya Pradesh on the other, land is to be released by the latter for the resettlement of displaced persons and landless tribal people. This land is to be reclaimed by the DDA and 25% is to be handed back to the State government for settling tribal people. Thus, while the resettlement of the displaced persons is done by the DDA itself, the resettlement of the tribal population is done by the State governments, although the DDA also provides funds for the purpose (to the extent of Rs.2850 per tribal family) These funds are paid by the DDA to the State governments as outright grant. While releasing land to the DDA, both the State governments take appropriate care to keep back sufficient areas of forest lands for the current and future needs of the tribals, to serve as fuel and fodder reserves and for the expansion of the tribals' cultivated land. As is clear from Table 4, the total area released by the governments of Madhya Pradesh and Orissa to DDA was 95,392 acres and 161,613 acres respectively as on 30-11-1977. Of this, an area of 160,335 acres was reclaimed.

The task of reclamation was started by the DDA on a small scale with the help of a small tractor force consisting of five American units taken over from the now defunct Central Tractor Organization. At present, the DDA possesses a large mechanized wing consisting of tractors, bulldozers, heavy crawler tractors, etc.—the size of a small army. The task of reclamation is carried out after proper soil analysis and areas unsuitable for agricultural purposes are eliminated carefully. Also excluded from reclamation is land on steep slopes and land on the banks of rivers, streams, and nullahs. This was thought necessary in the interests of soil conservation and prevention of formation of gullies. Before handing over the reclaimed land to the displaced persons or to the landless tribals, it was not only cleared of trees, stumps, and roots, but was also harrowed and contour-bunded to guard against erosion.

Progress of Resettlement: While planning village settlements, the DDA took into account the fact that most of the refugees and the native people were agriculturists. Accordingly, selection of sites for new villages was made by joint teams of agricultural experts, irrigation engineers, construction officers, and resettlement officers. Each site was selected taking into account the proximity of cultivable lands and the availability of drinking water. Each settler family was given a homestead plot measuring 800 square yards for the erection of a house. In addition, agricultural families were allotted 5 acres in unirrigated areas, or 4 acres in areas where protective irrigation for one crop was available, or 3 acres in areas where perennial irrigation was available.[17] The non-agriculturist families were divided into two categories—those settled in rural areas and those settled in urban and semi-urban areas. Both these categories of settlers were given 800 square yards per family as homestead plot. In addition to this, settlers in rural areas were given an agricultural plot up to 2 acres. Agriculturist family (and non-agriculturist family settled in a rural area) was given a house-building loan of Rs.1700.00. Non-agriculturist family settled in urban and semi-urban areas was given a house-building loan of Rs.2000.00. The construction of the house was left to the initiative of the settler who was asked to construct a house of his own choice for his family. However, some restrictions on standards were imposed and map designs were to be approved by the project engineers. Technical supervision was also provided.

Up to the end of November 1977, a total of 21,323 families (20,120 agriculturist and 1203 non-agriculturist) had been settled in 375 villages (see Table 4). Each village settlement has a primary school, a community centre, and a market place.

The task of rehabilitation does not end with providing shelter to the refugees and housing loans. It should also ensure a proper infrastructure for development (in the form of transport, communications, power, etc.), facilities for education, training, health services, and the like. But what is most important is the provision of gainful employment either directly or through assistance for carrying out some business or trade. As far as direct employment is concerned, the DDA has provided employment to settlers in the following fields—(1) construction of roads, (2) reclamation of land, (3) construction of villages, (4) construction of project buildings, (5) irrigation works, (6) dairy units, (7) small-scale units, (8) manufacture of bricks and tiles, (9) administration of work camps, and other related fields.

As far as assistance for carrying out economic activities is concerned, we have already noted that agriculturist families in rural areas are given land for the cultivation purposes. Non-agriculturist families in rural areas are also given a land of 2 acres. In addition, an agriculturist family is given the following assistance—(1) an agricultural loan of Rs.1725.00 for the purposes of purchasing a pair of bullocks, a milch cow, and a calf, agricultural implements, seeds, manure, and fertilizers, and for carrying out weeding operations; (2) loan of Rs.300.00 for setting up a cottage industry; (3) an irrigation loan of Rs.150.00 for sinking well in the homestead plot; and (4) a short-term loan of Rs.400.00 for purchase of fertilizers. The non-agriculturist family in rural areas is given a loan up to Rs.3000.00 for carrying out some small trade and up to Rs.300.00 as agricultural loan. The family settling in urban and semi-urban areas is given a business loan up to Rs.3000.00 for carrying out some business or trade.

The project authorities are aware of the fact that it takes some time to settle down and start some activity. Accordingly, there is a provision for giving maintenance assistance to the settlers for a fixed period of time. To the agriculturist family, maintenance assistance at full rate is given for the first and second agricultural seasons (of 6 months each) and at half rate for the third agricultural season. To non-agriculturist families the maintenance assistance is provided at cash dole rates for three months following the date of payment of the first instalment of the business/trade loan and at half this rate for three months after the disbursement of the second instalment of the loan.

Agriculture: In addition to direct financial assistance to the displaced persons for carrying out agricultural activities as noted above, a number of other programmes were also undertaken to promote agricultural development. A department of agriculture and soil conservation under a director has been set up which looks after all agricultural activities. The department provides a network of extension services and also maintains a fleet of agricultural tractors to help the settlers in mechanized farming. Two 1000-acre mixed farms have been established—one in Umerkote and the other in Paralkote—to train the settler-farmers. The Government of India undertook in collaboration with the Government of Japan in 1973-74 a scheme for agricultural and community development including land shaping and improvement of irrigation and drainage techniques in the mixed farm and a few selected villages in the Paralkote zone.

In addition to these activities, a pest control branch has been set up to control pest infestation. A directorate of veterinary services and animal husbandry has also been established. By 30-11-1977, 27,820 pairs of bullocks had been distributed among the settlers. Two poultry farms—one at Mana and the other at Kondagaon—are being run by the directorate. Poultry farms are also attached to mixed farms. As for pisciculture, the DDA has taken a number of tanks in the Koraput and Bastar districts on lease from the State governments of Orissa and Madhya Pradesh for rearing fingerlings.

Irrigation: For the success of agricultural programmes, it is necessary to provide irrigation facilities in an ample measure. The average rainfall in the Dandakaranya region is between 62 and 70 inches per annum, but because of the topography and the nature of the soil, water drains away rapidly with the result that there is water shortage (especially in the months of April and May). To remove this difficulty, irrigation facilities are being provided in the Project area in the following ways: (1) Large open surface tanks; (2) Minor bunds across nullahs and streams; and (3) Large earthen dams at or near the reclaimed sites.

Two irrigation projects—Bhaskal, in Umerkote (Orissa), with a culturable command area of 11,000 acres and Pakhanjore, in Paralkote (Madhya Pradesh), with a culturable command area of 1,300 acres—have been completed. The former cost Rs.1.35 crores and the latter Rs.0.08 crores. The Bhaskal project was transferred free of cost to the Government of Orissa on 1-5-1973. Two more projects, viz., Satiguda dam in Koraput and Paralkote dam in Bastar, are under execution. The Satiguda dam has a culturable command area of 28,000 acres and will provide irrigation facilities to 22,400 acres of land in kharif and 11,200 acres in rabi. The project is likely to cost Rs.11.05 crores. The Paralkote dam has a culturable command area of 26,000 acres and will provide irrigation facilities to 26,000 acres in kharif and 13,000 acres in rabi. Irrigation facilities have since become available from the Paralkote dam—14,826 acres up to 31-3-1977 and another 2965 acres up to 30-11-1977 (see Table 4).

In addition to this, 1666 tubewells, 457 masonry wells, 323 headwater tanks, and 37 minor irrigation schemes have also been executed by the project authorities.

Communications: The Dandakaranya region is ill served in respect of rail and road communications. Prior to the project, there were practically no rail links and the road links were also very inadequate serving only a very small area. By 30-11-1977, the project authorities had constructed improved 485.60 km of main roads, 281.20 km of tribal roads, and 750.20 km of link roads. But the most important achievement was the rail link connecting the fabulously rich iron ore deposits at Bailadilla with the port of Visakhapatnam through Jagdalpur, in Bastar, and Jeypore and Koraput in Orissa. Named the Dandakaranya-Bolingir-Kiribur (DBK) railway project, its cost was estimated to be Rs.81 crores. Through its 670 km of railway track, the project links the main town of Dandakaranya with the coast and also with the trunk line between Madras and Calcutta. It has brought the iron ore mines of Bailadilla right into the picture of country's industrial effort. The Bailadilla deposits are estimated at 1135 million tonnes and according to an estimate made by the NCAER in 1963, can fetch foreign exchange to the extent of Rs.20 crores (at 1962-63 prices).[18] The opening up of this railway link has also made the setting up of an integrated iron and steel industry in the Bastar region a viable economic proposition. This is on account of at least two reasons—"Firstly this railway link opens up the possibility of export of steel through Visakhapatnam from the proposed plant. Secondly, it will facilitate the import of metallurgical coal which is not available in the region and which is necessary for this industry. The wagons that will be carrying the ores for export through Visakhapatnam port can be well utilized for carrying the metallurgical coal which can be brought to Visakhapatnam by sea from the coalfields of West Bengal and Bihar."[19] The closeness of the DBK railway to limestone deposits has made their exploitation and transportation easier. Thus, limestone suitable for open hearth furnaces for steel making can be easily made available.

Education and Medical Facilities: Any programme of all-round development of an area must make adequate arrangements for the provision of education and medical facilities in an ample measure. As far as the provision of educational facilities is concerned, there were 295 primary schools, 31 middle schools, and 4 high schools functioning in the four administrative zones of the Dandakaranya project as on 30-11-1977. In the field of health and medical facilities, there were 14 hospitals, primary health centres, and medical mobile units operating in the project area as on 30-11-1977. Besides these, 3 dispensaries, 13 health sub-centres, and 51 primary medical aid points have also been set up. Malaria eradication plan was started as early as in 1958 and covered all the main roads and five-mile belts on either side, every town and village in the operational area and every site earmarked for a colony or a camp. Malaria and its twin black-water fever were totally wiped out from the region.

Industry: To provide an agro-industrial bias to the developing rural economy efforts have been made by the DDA authorities to develop skills (through training of the settlers) and to provide seasonal employment to agriculturists and rural artisans. For this purpose, service units have been set up for carpentry at Boregaon, for agricultural implements and printing at Ambaguda, and for weaving and carpentry at Jagdalpur. Two saw mills and three wood-working centres and an oil extraction unit have been set up at Ambaguda. Industrial centres at these places and at Umerkote, Murthama, Govindapalli, Malkangiri, and Paralkote produce various items including furniture, textiles, carpets, implements, etc. In addition, various cottage industries like bidi making, soap manufacture, paddy husking, and weaving have also been set up. A central workshop has been established at Ambaguda for the project's motor vehicles, earth-moving machinery, etc.

Tribal Welfare: We have already noted that the DDA returns 25% of the reclaimed to the State governments of Madhya Pradesh and Orissa for the rehabilitation of tribals and also provides a grant of Rs.2850 per tribal family (which is paid to the State government concerned). In addition, village tanks are provided for a new tribal settlement with a minimum of 40 families, if it has no suitable water source nearby.

Up to July 1977, 32,877 acres of reclaimed land have been returned by DDA to the governments of Orissa and Madhya Pradesh for tribal settlement. In all, 3304 tribal families have been settled by the two State governments. Besides this, 300 tribal families have been settled by the DDA itself.

As already noted, the DDA has undertaken the construction/financing of 281.20 km of roads in Orissa and Madhya Pradesh primarily for the benefit of tribals; 22 tanks, 61 tubewells, and 9 masonry wells have been constructed in the tribal villages of the Bastar and Koraput districts.

The tribals also share with the new settlers all amenities created by the DDA in fields such as irrigation, animal husbandry, health, and education. The tribals own 60% of the command area (1300 acres) of the Pakhanjore reservoir in the Bastar district and 85% of the command area (11,000 acres) of Bhaskal dam in the Koraput district. A sizable proportion of the ayacut area of the Paralkot dam in the Bastar district and the Satiguda dam in the Koraput district, now under construction, also belongs to the tribals.

The Potteru Irrigation Project: This project was undertaken in 1975 when the Orissa government agreed to release 40,000 acres of cultivable land in the Malkangiri zone of the Dandakaranya project (in the Koraput district) which could be utilized for irrigating agriculture by the construction of a barrage across the Potteru (in which the tail race waters of the Balimela hydel project are being discharged) and two canals. It was estimated that with a holding of 3 acres, 10,000 families could be resettled in agriculture in this area and 1000 families in non-agricultural occupations. This scheme for settlement of 11,000 families of displaced persons (10,000 agricultural and 1000 non-agricultural) has three components—irrigation, resettlement, and afforestation.

(i) *Potteru irrigation scheme:* The barrage except the installation of gates has been constructed at Surlikonda across the river Potteru, a tributary of the Sabari. Besides the barrage, the scheme envisages construction of 2 canals, one on either side of the river. The scheme involves a financial outlay of Rs.14.81 crores, of which an amount of Rs.14.65 crores is to be provided by the Central government. The project is being executed by the State government and is expected to be completed by 1981-82. The Potteru irrigation project will provide irrigation facilities in 150,000 acres of land.

(ii) *Potteru resettlement scheme:* The scheme envisages an outlay of Rs.27.04 crores for the settlement of 1000 families in small trade and 10,000 agriculturist families on 40,000 acres of land, while 2000 tribal families are expected to be settled on 12,000 acres of land. The settlement of displaced persons is to be undertaken by the DDA while the settlement of tribal families will be the responsibility of the State governments, as usual. The whole process is likely to take 8 to 9 years.

(iii) *Afforestation scheme:* For the purpose of keeping an ecological balance against the deforestation of land for the settlement of displaced persons and tribals, an afforestation scheme involving an outlay of Rs.1.80 crores has been taken up for execution by the State governments, covering an area of 36,000 acres, the funds being provided by the Centre.

TABLE 4: Progress of Dandakaranya project (as on 30-11-1977)

1. Area released:			
(a) Madhya Pradesh			95,392 acres
(b) Orissa			1,61,613 acres
2. Area found agriculturally suitable:			1,69,843 acres (up to July 1977)
3. Area reclaimed:			
(a) Mechanically			1,29,697 acres
(b) Manually			30,638 acres
4 Villages:			
(a) Villages set up			375
(b) Village houses constructed			14,020
5. Families resettled:			
	Old	New	Total
(a) Agriculturist	4503	15,617	20,120
(b) Non-agriculturist	322	881	1,203
6. Agriculture:			
(a) Area under cultivation during 1977-78 (up to 30-11-1977)			96,923
7. Animal husbandry:			
bullocks distributed			27,820 pairs
8. Water supply:			
(a) Tubewells			1,666
(b) Masonry wells			457
(c) Village tanks			285
(d) Head water tanks			323
9. Schools established:			
(a) Primary			295
(b) Middle			37
(c) High			4
10. Medical:			
(a) Hospital & primary health centres/medical mobile units			14
(b) Primary emergency aid centres			51
(c) Dispensaries			3
(d) Health sub-centres			13
11. Roads:			
(a) Main roads			486 km
(b) Link roads			750 km
(c) Tribal roads			281 km

(Contd.)

TABLE 4 (*Contd.*)

12. Irrigation:

	Culturable command areas (in acres)	Cost (Rs. in crores)
(a) Bhaskal Dam	11,000	1.35
(b) Pakhanjore Dam	1,300	0.08
(c) Satiguda Dam	28,000	11.05
(d) Paralkote Dam	26,000	5.49

Irrigation facilities have since become available from the Paralkote Dam for 6000 hectares up to 31-3-1977 and another 1200 hectares during 1977-78 (up to 30-11-1977). Irrigation facilities from the Satiguda dam are expected to become available from 1978-79.

Source: Government of India, Ministry of Supply and Rehabilitation, Department of Rehabilitation, *Report 1977-78*, Table X, p. 83-84.

Flight from Dandakaranya

Dandakaranya has been very much in the news recently on account of large-scale desertion of their homes by the displaced persons in Dandakaranya and their flight to West Bengal. The process started in the middle of February 1978 and within months 70% of the refugee families had pulled up their roots and trekked to West Bengal in the fond hope that it would welcome them with open arms. It has often been stated that conditions in Dandakaranya were not conducive enough, that there were tensions between them and the local people, that the land given to them was unfit for cultivation, etc. These factors may or may not have instigated mass-scale desertion but one thing is certain. On account of their cultural identity with the people of West Bengal, the refugees could never accept Dandakaranya as their home. They have continued to nourish dreams of returning to West Bengal one day and though staying in Dandakaranya they are mentally 1000 miles away in West Bengal. The new, strange, and inhospitable environment that they had to encounter in Dandakaranya also contributed in making them dejected, frustrated, and destitute with a longing to go back to their home which for them was West Bengal.

Obviously, the West Bengal government was not in a position to accept these refugees and they had to be virtually pushed back to Dandakaranya. If such mass-scale desertion is to be avoided in the future, it is necessary that the displaced persons are made to realize that their prosperity lies in Dandakaranya alone. There can be no doubt that cultural identity cannot be broken easily, yet its evil effects can be toned down considerably if the displaced persons are convinced that life in Dandakaranya is 'worth living'.

By 'worth living' we imply a standard of life that ensures the satisfaction of all the basic human wants and also provides for some saving and leisure (with attractive outlets to utilize them profitably).

Potentialities of Development

Such a standard of living can be easily provided in the Dandakaranya region because of its richness in mineral resources and potentialities of industrialization which are practically limitless and have not been exploited systematically so far. The study published by the National Council for Applied Economic Research in 1963 (and referred to earlier) has noted that there are extensive mineral resources in the region awaiting exploitation. Bauxite, an immensely important aluminium-bearing mineral of industrial importance, is found here in ample quantities. Iron ore is also found extensively. Maximum concentration is in the Bailadilla iron ore mines of the Bastar district. The reserves in the Bailadilla mines are alone estimated to be 1135 million tonnes. Extensive deposits of limestone (another important resource for development of mineral industries) have been reported in the Bastar and Koraput districts, the estimated reserves being about 1500 million tonnes. Manganese ore and glass sand (quartz and quartzite) are also found in ample quantities. In addition to these five minerals, fourteen other minerals—copper ores, corundum, gold, garnet, graphite, illmenite, andalusite, asbestos, clays, lepidolite, mica, mineral pigments, monazite, and steatite—are also found in the Dandakaranya region.

On account of such considerations, the NCAER report has advocated the setting up of a number of industries in the Dandakaranya region. Because of extensive iron ore reserves in the Bailadilla mines, it has advocated the establishment of an integrated iron and steel industry in the Bastar district. This will provide employment opportunities to the refugees and the tribals inhabiting the region directly and also through the industrial linkage processes (by promoting the development of several metal-processing industries).

Because of extensive limestone resources in the region, the NCAER report has suggested the setting up of cement plants in the area (cement industry is the largest consuming industry of limestone and consumes more than three-fourths of its total production). The NCAER report has advocated the setting of a cement plant in the Umpavalli-Tummiguda area of the region since it is close to the border of the region and can serve as an outlet. This consideration is important because the demand for cement in the Dandakaranya region itself will not be able to exhaust the total supply on its own. The report has also recommended the establishment of a cement plant near Jagdalpur based on the deposits in the Kanger area when the demand for cement grows sufficiently within the region and better transport facilities are available.

Another industry that is based on limestone is calcium carbide. Limestone required to produce calcium carbide should be of high quality and purity. Since about two million tonnes of suitable quality limestone are available in the Umpavalli-Tummiguda area, the NCAER report has recommended the establishment of a calcium carbide plant in this area. For the purpose of producing quicklime and slaked lime (which are used in a number of industries such as the sugar industry, paper industry, building construction, etc.), the report has recommended the establishment of units at the following four locations: (i) Sirivada, (ii) Sunki, (iii) Jagdalpur (in Kanger area), and (iv) Kotpad (near Kondajodi-Dumajodi area). To utilize the china-clay deposits near Sarisa Paddar in the Koraput district, the NCAER report has recommended the location of one plant in this area for washing the clay. The report also notes that with the development of hydro-electric power and transport and communications facilities it will become feasible to develop a number of other large-scale industries.

In addition, there are immense possibilities of developing small-scale industries (both resource-based and non-resource-based). The resource-based industries are mainly based on agricultural products, livestock, and forests. As far as industries based on agricultural products are concerned, the report specifically mentions rice milling and oil milling. Because of the limited livestock resources, there is not much scope for developing industries based on livestock. However, because of the immense forest resources in the area, the report advocates the establishment of a number of small-scale industries based on the forest wealth of the Dandakaranya region. These include the industries engaged in the activity of felling and logging of trees, manufacture of paper in small-scale plants, handmade paper, wood preservation and saw milling, furniture and other wood products, etc. Small-scale non-resource-based industries that are recommended for development in the region include agricultural implements, hand tools, metal work, builders' hardware, bicycle assembling, units for servicing agricultural processing and other machinery, electrical equipment, etc.

We have considered the potentialities of industrialization in detail so as to emphasize the point that there are vast possibilities of developing the Dandakaranya region, only it calls for concerted and sustained efforts on the part of the concerned authorities. Once this is achieved and prosperity rules the land, there is no reason why the displaced persons will not start regarding Dandakaranya as their homeland. Economic progress is frequently a precursor of changes in social and cultural attitudes.

NOTES

1. Damodar Valley Corporation, *Eight Years of D.V.C.* (Calcutta, 1956), p. 3.
2. Ibid., pp. 3-4.
3. The Tennessee Valley Authority (known, in short, as T.V.A.) was established by the U.S. government in 1933 through an Act of Congress to guide the development activities in the Tennessee Valley which was a comparatively underdeveloped area. This experiment was the first multi-purpose development project of a river basin conceived on the basis of inter-State cooperation. Thirty dams have been constructed on the Tennessee River giving opportunities for multipurpose efforts leading to flood control, inland water navigation, soil conservation, development of forestry and fertilizer production, power generation, etc. The experiment has been remarkably successful in bringing about a change in the physical and socio-economic landscape of the region and in improving the standards of living of the people.
4. Voorduin, *Preliminary Memorandum on the Unified Development of the Damodar River,* August 1945.
5. Ibid.
6. Ibid., p. 35.
7. Damodar Valley Corporation, *Annual Report 1977-78*, p. 17.
8. William Kirk, "The Damodar Valley—'Valles Opima'", *Geograpical Review,* Vol. 40, No. 3 (1950).
9. C.R. Pathak, "Damodar Valley Region—A Case Study in Regional Development", in R.P. Misra (ed.), *Regional Planning* (Mysore: The University of Mysore, 1969), p. 473.
10. Kanangopal Bagchi, "The Damodar Valley Development and its Impact on the Region", Allen G. Noble and Ashok K. Dutt (eds.), *Indian Urbanization and Planning: Vehicles of Modernization* (New Delhi: Tata-McGraw Hill Publishing Co. Ltd., 1977), p. 239.
11. Kanwar Sain, *Reminiscences of an Engineer* (New Delhi: Young Asia Publications, 1978), p. 55.
12. K.V. Subrahmanyam, "DVC and Flood Control", *Economic and Political Weekly,* 11 November 1978, p. 1840.
13. According to the Irrigation Commission, "the observed rate of silting in the Maithon Dam is of the order of 7.38 m.cu.m. annually against the designed rate of 0.84 m.cu.m. In the case of the Panchet Hill dam the rate of silting has been observed as 13.74 m.cu.m. annually against a designed rate of 2.44 m.cu.m." See *Irrigation Commission Report*, 1972, Vol. III, Part I, p. 178.
14. Subrahmanyam, op. cit., p. 1840.
15. Thus, "According to data available the peak flow of floods exceeding 1130m^3/sec. at Rhondia occurred only twice between 1933 and 1949. Between 1958 July and 1963 Oct., however, such peak flows occurred 5 times. On 1967 August 19, the peak flow was 10.5m^3/sec. Leaving the two years of drought 1965 and 1966, we find that in the 5 years 1967 to 1971 a peak flow of nearly 11m^3/sec. or more occurred twice. We therefore, conclude that while the lower Damodar Valley is now liable to be flooded at any flow over 18m^3/sec. the possibility of having peak flows of greater volume has increased since the inception of the Damodar Valley Corporation." Asit K. Bhattacharyya, "Flood Control in the Damodar Valley", *Geographical Review of India,* Vol. XXXV, No. 2, p. 141.
16. Planning Commission, Government of India, *The Third Five Year Plan*, pp. 725-727.

17. Earlier, 6.7 acres of cultivable land was given to each agricultural family. But keeping in view the fact that agricultural productivity is bound to be highest in areas, with perennial irrigation and lowest in unirrigated areas, a policy of discrimination has been adopted—families settled on areas of perennial irrigation getting only 3 acres and families settled on unirrigated areas getting 5 acres.
18. National Council of Applied Economic Research, *Development of Dandakaranya*, 1963, p. 50.
19. Ibid., p. 51.

Chapter 11

Planning for Tribal Development

It is not easy to define a tribe, and no definition in India has proved satisfactory and precise. In general, the tribals are expected to possess some, if not all, of the following characteristics: (i) their roots in the soil date back to a very early period; (ii) they live in relative isolation of the hills and forests; (iii) their sense of history is shallow in the sense that after some generations, the remembered history tends to shade off into mythology; (iv) they have a low level of techno-economic development; (v) in terms of their cultural ethos (language, institutions, beliefs, and customs) they stand out from the other sections of the society; and (vi) even if they are not egalitarian, they are at least non-hierarchic and undifferentiated.[1] Taking account of these characteristics, the Government of India has specified 427 communities and has included them in the schedule of tribes. These tribes are known as scheduled tribes and are entitled to special protection and privileges under the Constitution of India. Numerically, the three most important tribes are the Gonds, the Bhils, and the Santhals, each having a population of more than 30 lakhs. Next to them are the Minas, the Mundas, and the Oraons, each having a population of more than 10 lakhs. Then come the Hos, the Khonds, and the Kols, each having a population of more than 5 lakhs. Then there are 42 tribes each having a population between 1 and 5 lakhs. After this come a number of smaller tribes. The smallest tribal community is the Great Andamanese whose numerical strength was only 18 in the 1971 census. In 1976, their population was reported as 23.[2]

In the 1951 census, the tribal population of the country was given as 19.17 million which was 5.29% of the country's total population. After adopting the new definition of scheduled tribes in 1956, their population rose to 22.51 million which was 6.25% of the country's population. In the 1961 census, the tribal population rose to 29.88 million which was 6.87% of the total population. In the 1971 census, their number was originally given as 38.015 million. Later this figure was revised upwards to 41.09 million which comes to 7.5% of the total population.

TABLE 1: Statewise distribution of tribal population, 1971

(in lakhs)

State/Union territory	Total population of the State	Scheduled tribe population		Col. 4 as percentage of col. 2
		Original	Revised	
(1)	(2)	(3)	(4)	(5)
1. Andhra Pradesh	435.02	16.58	22.26	5.12
2. Assam	146.15	16.07	16.07	10.99
3. Bihar	563.53	49.33	49.33	8.75
4. Gujarat	266.97	37.34	37.57	14.07
5. Himachal Pradesh	34.60	1.42	1.42	4.10
6. Karnataka	292.99	2.31	2.62	0.89
7. Kerala	213.47	2.69	1.93	0.90
8. Madhya Pradesh	416.54	83.87	98.15	23.56
9. Maharashtra	504.12	29.54	38.41	7.62
10. Manipur	10.73	3.34	3.34	31.13
11. Meghalaya	10.12	8.14	8.14	80.43
12. Nagaland	5.16	4.57	4.57	88.57
13. Orissa	219.45	50.72	50.75	22.13
14. Rajasthan	257.66	31.26	31.35	12.17
15. Tamil Nadu	411.99	3.12	4.50	1.09
16. Tripura	15.56	4.51	4.51	28.98
17. Uttar Pradesh	883.41	1.99	1.99	0.22
18. West Bengal	443.12	25.33	26.03	5.87
Union territories				
1. Arunachal Pradesh	4.67	3.69	3.69	79.01
2. Aadaman & Nicobar Islands	1.15	0.18	0.18	15.65
3. Dadra & Nagar Haveli	0.74	0.64	0.64	86.49
4. Goa, Daman & Diu	8.58	0.08	0.08	0.93
5. Lakshadweep	0.32	0.29	0.29	90.62
6. Mizoram	3.32	3.13	3.13	94.28
All India	5481.60	380.15	410.95	7.5

Note: The States of Jammu & Kashmir, Haryana, and Punjab and the Union territories of Chandigarh, Delhi, and Pondicherry had no scheduled tribes.

Sources: (i) *Report of the Commissioner for Scheduled Castes and Scheduled Tribes*, 1975-76 and 1976-77, Part I, p. 16.

(ii) L.P. Vidyarthi and B.K. Rai, *The Tribal Culture of India*, p. 67.

(iii) Census of India, 1971, *General Population Tables* Series I, Part II-A(i).

Table 1 gives a State-wise break-up of the tribal population. It shows that the maximum number of tribals are concentrated in Madhya Pradesh followed by Orissa, Bihar, Maharashtra, Gujarat, Rajasthan, and West Bengal in that order (see col. 4). In the States of Meghalaya and Nagaland and the Union territories of Andaman & Nicobar Islands, Lakshadweep and Mizoram more than 80% of the population was constituted by the tribals. For Arunachal Pradesh, the figure was 79.01%.

ECONOMIC LIFE OF THE TRIBALS

The economy of the tribals can be termed a subsistence economy or a primitive economy. It is not infrequent to find the tribals still in the food-gathering and fruit-collecting stages and some of them lead a nomadic or semi-nomadic life. However, as a result of interaction between the tribal and the non-tribal people and as a consequence of the planning efforts of the government during the five year plans, members of some important tribes have assumed the role of industrial labour. Thus, tribals in all different stages of economic development can be found in India. For example, the Andamanese of Andaman & Nicobar Islands are still in the food-gathering stage of civilization and subsist on the bounties of nature available in their immediate environment. Their skills are oriented towards an optimum exploitation of naturally available food. Two of the most isolated tribes, the Jarawa and the Sentinelese, are found in this region. These two tribes continue to live as they have lived for thousands of years, unaffected by civilization. However, most of the tribes living as forest dwellers are neither isolated nor independent. These include the Birhor, the Mallar, and the Kharia of Bihar and Orissa, the Kadar of Kerala, and the Chenchu of Andhra Pradesh, among others. They gather various roots and tubers, fruits, honey, manufacture ropes from wild creepers and keep their collection for personal use or exchange with agricultural produce. They occasionally indulge in fishing and hunting as well. The Todas, inhabiting the Nilgiris in south India, are a pastoral tribe subsisting on the products of their buffaloes. Naturally their maximum time is devoted to dairy operations.

A large number of tribes have entered the 'cultivation stage' while some are still in the transition stage. The shopmen of Great Nicobar are in the latter stage. "They are, like the Andamanese, a semi-nomadic people and go out hunting for wild pig and honey and other plant products in the forests but at the same time they also keep small herds of pigs and cultivate small gardens of coconuts, yams and tobacco-like plants."[8] Similarly, the

Todas have also started the cultivation of some vegetables and cereals. The major tribes of India have entered the cultivation stage and since agricultural activities are more easily carried out by settled inhabitants, the settlements of this vast majority of tribals are generally permanent. Thus, the Gonds, the largest tribe of India, found mostly in Madhya Pradesh (especially in Mandla and Bastar) and scattered in some parts of Maharashtra, Andhra Pradesh, Bihar, Orissa, and West Bengal, are basically dependent on cultivation for their livelihood. They practise both shifting and settled methods of cultivation. The Bhils, spread mostly over the uplands of the States of Madhya Pradesh, Gujarat, Rajasthan, and Maharashtra, also depend on cultivation. The traditional method of cultivation is a type of shifting cultivation. Another important tribe of India, viz. the Santhals, whose main concentration is in Bihar, especially in the districts of Santhal Parganas, Bhagalpur, Hazaribagh, Purnea, Manbhum, Singhbhum, and Mungyr, also has agriculture as its basic occupation. These three tribes supplement their incomes by collecting, hunting, and fishing. In addition, the Bhils also do jobs for contractors such as felling the trees, carrying them to the transportation centres, etc. Another numerically large tribe of India, viz. the Oraons, distributed over the States of Bihar, West Bengal, Madhya Pradesh, and Orissa (Ranchi district in Bihar is the centre of their present habitation), are settled agriculturists and cultivate varieties of paddy, millet, pulses, and oilseeds. Many hill tribes, like the Ao Nagas of Nagaland and the Khasis of Khasia & Jaintia Hills (in Assam) have also adopted cultivation as a basic means of existence. The principal method of cultivation adopted by the Ao Nagas is shifting cultivation while the Khasis practise both dry and wet cultivation and also shifting cultivation.

Thus, agriculture is now the basic occupation of most of the tribes in India. In fact, according to the 1971 census, approximately 90% of the tribal population is dependent on agriculture. The 1971 census figures show that out of every 1000 scheduled tribe workers, as many as 906 are absorbed in agriculture (576 as cultivators and 330 as agricultural labourers). This pattern is followed, more or less, in all the States the only exceptions being Karnataka, Andaman & Nicobar Islands, Goa, Daman & Diu, and Lakshadweep. In Karnataka, e.g., less than 80% of the tribal population is engaged in agriculture. In Andaman & Nicobar Islands, livestock and fisheries is the main occupation followed by manufacturing (household industry). In Goa, Daman & Diu agriculture is the main occupation but engages less than 70% of workers. In Lakshadweep, the main occupation is manufacturing (household industry) followed by livestock and fisheries and other services. In other States, where agriculture engages more than 80% of tribal workers, the only point to be noted is the relative number of cultivators and agricultural labourers. In the States of Kerala, West Bengal, Andhra

Pradesh, Maharashtra, and the Union territories of Goa, Daman & Diu the number of agricultural labourers is considerably more than the number of cultivators. Though one should refrain from passing any judgement on the economic condition of the tribals in the States only on the basis of the relative strength of agricultural labourers vis-a-vis cultivators, one cannot ignore the general impression that agricultural labourers normally possess a lower standard of living compared with cultivators. In Karnataka also, where 71.30% of tribal workers depend upon agriculture, the number of agricultural labourers is considerably greater than the number of cultivators.

PATTERNS OF AGRICULTURE

The three major agricultural patterns adopted by the tribals in the different parts of the country are: (i) shifting cultivation (practised mainly in hilly areas and some plains), (ii) settled cultivation (practised mainly by the plains dwellers), and (iii) cultivation of plantation crops such as coconut, arecanuts, and pineapple.

The method of shifting cultivation practised by the tribals is known as *jhooming*. It was estimated in the Report of the Commissioner for Scheduled Classes and Scheduled Tribes, 1960-61, that approximately 2.6 million tribals were dependent upon shifting cultivation which was practised in an area of 3555 sq. miles. Under this type of cultivation (i.e., *jhooming*), every year thousands of acres of forests are cut, burnt, and planted in successive cycles. In many cases, divine blessings are invoked before a site is finally selected for 'slash and burn' cultivation. After such a selection, vegetation is cut and the jungle is allowed to dry before it is set on fire. While selecting a plot for cultivation, a number of factors such as type of soil, nearness to water source, availability of sunshine, danger of animals and pests, etc. are also taken into account. Cultivation is done without terracing and without the use of modern technology and inputs. The only inputs used are labour and seeds. The ash derived from the fire of the jungle serves as manure. After cultivation for a season or two, the land is allowed to lie fallow for a number of years before it is again brought under cultivation.

The disadvantages of such a method of cultivation are many and multifarious. The shifting cultivation in the long run denudes the hills covered by beautiful forests, runs the generative soil down the hills, and greatly increases the dangers of soil erosion. The soil which was built by nature over the centuries runs down the slopes in a matter of seasons. Leaching, erosion, and loss of fertility take place with rapidity and the yields per unit of land become progressively lesser and lesser.[4]

Majumdar and Madan mention the following nine important traits of the tribal economy in India: (i) there is an absence of *technological aids* in a tribal economy which results in inefficient, inadequate, or even wasteful exploitation of nature. Consequently, the bare minimum of sustenance is raised with great difficulty and the appearance of an economic surplus is a rare phenomenon; (ii) the economic relations among the tribals themselves are based mostly on *barter and exchange*; (iii) the *profit motive* in economic dealings is generally absent. The role of an incentive is fulfilled by a sense of mutual obligation, sharing, and solidarity; (iv) *cooperative and collective endeavour* is a strongly developed feature of their economy; (v) the rate of *innovation*, internal or induced, is very low and consequently they are stabler and make hardly any progress; (vi) *regular market* as an institution is absent (what comes nearest to it is the weekly market or festival and season meets); (vii) the manufacture of consumer rather than capital goods is common and the same are consumed nothing being saved or exchanged in trade; (viii) *specialization* based on specially acquired specific technical abilities is absent; and (ix) the *notion of property* is closely related to display and expenditure of wealth rather than to its accumulation.[5]

All these economic factors have combined with numerous social and cultural factors in keeping the levels of living of the tribal poor depressingly low. In fact, they are at the lowest rung of development with some other non-tribal communities. Incomes are low, social status is very inferior, level of education is low, housing and sanitary conditions are bad, and general standard of health is poor.

SOURCES OF AUTHORITY IN TRIBAL AREAS

As already noted, in tribes having agriculture as the main occupation the settlements are generally permanent and the tribals live in well-defined villages. In most of the tribes, village community is the most important socio-economic and political unit. In the case of the Santhals, it is governed by a *panchayat* consisting of seven officials, viz. (i) *Manjhi* (the headman), (ii) *Paranik* (the assistant headman), (iii) *Naeke* (the village priest), (iv) *Kudam Naeke* (priest), (v) *Jog-manjhi* (arranges communal feasts and entrusted to guard the morals of village youth), (vi) *Jog-paranik* (assistant to *paranik*), and (vii) *Godet* (messenger of the panchayat). Ten or twelve village communities together constitute a large political unit, the headman of which is called *Pargana* or *Parganait*. Each village community has a *panchayat* and all the headmen together with other prominent persons of the village constitute another panchayat under the leadership of *Parganait*. The supreme authority of the Santhal society rests in the body known as *Lo Bir* or Hunt Council. *Lo Bir sits once every year and here all the San-*

thals, with or without any official position, have equal status.[6]

The highest official in a Bhil village is known as *vasawo*. He settles quarrels, restores peace, and also functions as a link between the government and the villages. The next highest position is that of *punjaro* who acts as intermediary between the gods and the Bhils. He also works as the medicine man. The *pradhan* is the second official appointed by the government and officiates for *vasawo* in his absence. Next in importance is the *vartanio* who carries out the commands of the *vasawo*. The Bhils have a village panchayat, *panch*, which is an inevitable part of their social organization. "The panchayat is however not formal. *All the oldmen of the village meet for all important matters and confer among themselves*. These matters include social and magico-religious affairs. *In affairs of inter-village concern the elderly men of both the villages meet to reach a compromising decision*."[7]

The Gonds do not possess any strong tribal organization but within each village there is some authority which includes persons belonging to all castes. "Each caste has its own leaders who are usually the heads of the joint families. *In matters which affect the interest of the village in general, all the constituent members of the council discuss and settle the issue*."[8] Another important tribe, viz. the Oraons, is divided into a number of territorial segments known as the *parhas*. The *parhas* are divided into a number of villages which is the smallest political unit. In each Oraon village, there are three officials—*Baiga* or *Pahan*, *Piyar* (assistant of *Pahan*), and *Mahato*. "The *Mahato* presides over the village panchayat constituted by the village elders. *The authority of this panchayat is supreme in all matters—social or religious*."[9]

Among the smaller tribes, "the Nicobarese have village councils with a headman referred to as Captain. The various village captains constitute the islands' council and one of them officiates as the Chief Captain or Rani if a woman is elected to the post."[10] The basic organization in the Ao Nagas (of Nagaland) is *morung*. It is a miniature form of a village and possesses a council formed by senior boys. It settles all disputes and quarrels arising in the *morung*. The Khasi state (of the Khasi tribe inhabiting the Khasi and Jaintia Hills in Meghalaya) is formed by the voluntary association of villages or groups of villages. The heads of the state is known as *Siem*. His authority is very limted and "*he cannot perform any important act without consulting his durbar which is an executive council having judicial powers*."[11] The institution of *Kebangs* among the Siang also works on a democratic basis. It directs and watches over the welfare and well-being of the village community and provides a forum where all matters are discussed and without its sanction nothing can be done. Even in the case of *Aka Melo* (the council of Akas, a tribal group living in the lower belt of the Kameng district) where the authority vests in a single individual acting as the headman, *the whole community can take away the authority and confer it on itself.*[12] This provision acts as a check on the headman.

This short discussion on the sources of authority in tribal areas illustrates the role of democratic institutions in the tribal set-up. These institutions have been part and parcel of the tribal life and have succeeded in bringing about respect for the socio-cultural order and discipline in the life of the tribals. They can become vehicles for implementing the welfare and development programmes of the government if the tribals are brought into confidence. Along with other factors, these democratic institutions also highlight the cooperative spirit of the tribals and their willingness to solve their problems in mutual consultation with each other. Thus, the cooperative movement should have a fair chance of success in tribal areas provided it is properly planned.

TRIBAL DEVELOPMENT UNDER THE PLANS

The basic problem of the tribal people, as of the vast majority of the non-tribal population is that of poverty. The problems of low standard of living, hunger, starvation, malnutrition, illiteracy, disease, poor sanitary and housing facilities, etc., are all common to the tribal and a vast majority of the non-tribal population. The difference is only of degree. Then, why is it necessary to formulate special plans for tribal development? Because the tribals, in addition to the problems mentioned above, face problems that are specific (and confined) to them alone. Thus, they have been subjected to exploitation for centuries together by the non-tribals such as money-lenders, forest contractors, traders, landlords, officials, and politicians. Compared with the exploitation of the non-tribal rural poor, the exploitation of the tribals is more monopolistic in nature. They continue to be subjected to this exploitation because they do not generally move out of their immediate environment in search of employment opportunities. This is due to a lack of awareness of such opportunities on the part of the tribals, their distrust of an alien situation, and the fear that outsiders will exploit them even more. Also, centuries of isolation from the main civilization has kept the tribals ignorant of modern institutions, scientific and technological developments, and changing environment and has contributed to their ignorance, illiteracy, primitive mode of living, and poor resource base of their economy.

Keeping all these considerations in view, the Government of India initiated special schemes for the development of tribal areas to supplement the benefits accruing from general programmes of development in different fields such as agriculture, cooperation, communications, health, housing, etc. They can be grouped broadly under four headings—(a) communications, (b) education and culture, (c) development of tribal economy, and (d) health, housing, and water supply.[13] To carry out these programmes, tribal development blocks were established on the lines of the community development blocks. Such tribal development blocks were constituted in areas predominantly inhabited by the tribals and each block was intended to cover only about 25,000 persons against the average coverage of 66,000 persons in the community development blocks. This is accounted for by the fact that the population in tribal areas is sparse and terrain difficult. As in the community development programme, success here depended to a considerable degree on the cooperation and the participation of the people for whom the programmes were intended. Such cooperation and participation was unfortunately not forthcoming on account of reasons not dissimilar to those that made the experiment of community development a failure.[14]

The Second Plan advocated the establishment of 40 multi-purpose pilot projects in the plan period (the actual number of projects started was 43) for 'intensive and coordinated development in tribal areas on the general pattern of community development, but modified to suit tribal conditions and supplemented by additional resources'. The task of these pilot projects was defined by the Second Plan thus: "In the pilot projects all aspects of tribal life will be taken up at the same time, such as encouragement of settled forms of agriculture in place of shifting cultivation, improvement of agriculture, provision of medical and public health services, improvement of communications, development of arts and crafts, organisation of cooperatives and the establishment of community welfare centres."[15] Each block involved an outlay of Rs.27 lakhs (Rs.12 lakhs being found under the community development and Rs.15 lakhs by the Ministry of home affairs) The Third Plan set a target of 300 tribal development blocks. In this scheme, a total outlay of Rs.22 lakhs was to be provided in stages II and III. It was proposed that "about 60 percent of the funds should be allotted for economic uplift, 25 percent for communications and 15 percent for social services". It was suggested that to procure additional resources for tackling the problem of drinking water supply, resources from the programmes for economic uplift could be diverted. The actual number of tribal development blocks initiated in the Third Plan was 415. During the Fourth Plan period, 4 new blocks were started and 8 blocks in Manipur were reorganized into 20 sub-blocks functioning in the various tribal regions of the country. Table 2 gives a state-wise distribution of these blocks.

Table 2 shows that Madhya Pradesh (having the largest tribal population) has the maximum number of tribal development blocks. In fact, approximately 25% of blocks are located in this State alone. Madhya Pradesh is followed by Orissa, Bihar, and Gujarat in that order. The expenditure

TABLE 2: **Tribal development blocks: State-wise distribution**

State/Union territory	No. of tribal development blocks
1. Andhra Pradesh	28
2. Assam	26
3. Bihar	63
4. Gujarat	53
5. Himachal Pradesh	7
6. Kerala	1
7. Madhya Pradesh	126
8. Maharashtra	44
9. Manipur	8*
10. Meghalaya	24
11. Nagaland	15
12. Orissa	75
13. Rajasthan	13
14. Tamil Nadu	2
15. Tripura	5
Union territories	
16. Dadra & Nagar Haveli	2
Total	492*

*Since the 8 blocks of Manipur were reorgan zed into 20 sub-blccks in the Fourth Plan, the number of tribal development blocks was reduced to 484 at the end of the Fourth Plan. Thus, the total number of blccks (deveiopment blocks and sub-blocks combined) increased to 484+20=504.

Note: The States and Union territories not possessing any tribal development blocks have not been included in the table. Such States are Haryana, Jammu & Kashmir, Mysore, Punjab, Uttar Pradesh, and West Bengal.

Source: NICD. *Perspectives on Tribal Development and Administration*, August 1975, p. 196.

incurred on tribal development blocks was Rs.15.83 crores in the Third Plan and Rs.20.04 crores in the three Annual Plans. The outlay in the Fourth Plan was kept at Rs.32.50 crores and the anticipated expenditure was Rs.32.94 crores. The tribal development blocks covered a population of 11,934,695 out of 27,533,634 in 15 States which amounts to 43.35% of the tribal population.[16]

The actual expenditure incurred on different schemes of tribal development under the first three plans by the Centre and State governments is given in Table 3.

Table 4 gives a detailed break-up of expenditure under the Third Plan, the three Annual Plans, the Fourth Plan, and the first three years of the

TABLE 3: **Plan expenditure under State and Union schemes for scheduled tribes**

(Rs. crores)

Scheme	First Plan Total	Second Plan			Third Plan		
		State plan schemes	Union plan schemes	Total	State plan schemes	Union plan schemes	Total
Economic uplift	8.46	11.59	11.11	22.70	12.13	18.59	30.72
Education	5.10	6.49	1.56	8.05	11.66	1.57	13.23
Health, housing, communication and others	3.81	4.45	5.31	9.76	6.17	0.93	7.10
All groups	17.37	22.53	17.96	40.51*	29.96	21.09	51.05**

*Excludes grants of Rs.0.68 crores to all-India voluntary organizations.
**Excludes grants of Rs.10.5 crores to all-India voluntary organizations.
Source: L.P. Vidyarthi and B.K. Rai, op. cit., p. 436.

Fifth Plan on various programmes undertaken for the welfare of the backward classes. The figures in the table include expenditure on scheduled castes and scheduled tribes (separate data for scheduled tribes are not available). Column 6 gives the revised Fifth Plan outlay. The original Fifth Plan outlay under the Central and the State Programmes for the welfare of scheduled castes and scheduled tribes was Rs.85.00 crores and Rs.173.14 crores respectively. Under the revised outlay, this amount was raised to Rs.119 crores and Rs.208 crores respectively.

A break-up of expenditure in 1974-75, 1975-76, and 1976-77 for scheduled tribes (State sector) is available in the latest report of the Commissioner for the year 1975-76 and 1976-77. Table 5 is computed from the data given in that report.

The Fifth Plan had kept a total outlay of Rs.80.73 crores for the welfare of the scheduled tribes of which Rs.36.44 crores were to be spent on education, Rs.28.94 crores for programmes of economic uplift, and Rs.15.11 crores on other schemes such as health and housing. The actual expenditure during the first three years of the plan was Rs.31.67 crores of which Rs.17.51 crores were spent on education, Rs.13.05 crores on programmes of economic uplift, and Rs.93.11 crores on schemes such as health and housing.

PROGRAMMES FOR THE DEVELOPMENT OF TRIBALS

Various programmes have been initiated by the Central and State govern-

TABLE 4: Expenditure on welfare of backward classes

(Rs. crores)

Programme	Third Plan expenditure	Three Annual Plans antici-pated ex-penditure	Fourth Plan outlay	Fourth Plan anticipated expenditure	Revised Fifth Plan outlay	Expen-diture incurred during Fifth Plan (1974-78)	Expenditure incurred during 1977-78 and 1978-79
1	2	3	4	5	6	7	8
I. Centre							
1. tribal development blocks	15.83	20.04	32.50	32.94	7.29		
2. post-matric scholarships	9.48	13.01	11.00	23.13	100.00	52.21	35.76
3. girls' hostels	0.14	0.58	2.00	1.96	3.77	2.70	1.81
4. coaching and allied schemes	—	0.11	1.00	1.00	1.58	0.94	0.60
5. research, training and special projects	0.39	0.39	1.50	0.74	1.32	0.82	0.50
6. cooperation (special schemes)	3.06	1.13	2.50	2.95	1.44		
7. improvement in working and living condition of those engaged in unclean occupations	3.44	1.13	3.00	2.96			
8. denotified tribes and nomadic tribes	3.82	1.77	4.50	4.41			
9. aid to voluntary organisations	1.05	0.76	2.00	1.82	2.97		
Total	*36.91*	*38.92*	*60.00*	*71.91*	*118.88**	*58.68***	*41.77****

II. States							
1. education	32.70	19.22		59.65			
2. economic development	14.73	4.06	79.98	17.46			
3. health, housing & other programmes	11.26	4.36		21.63			
Total	*58.69*	*27.64*	*79.98*	*98.74*			
III. Union territories							
1. education	0.49	0.45		0.28			
2. economic development	1.96	1.09	1.36	0.23			
3. health, housing & other programmes	1.09	0.39		1.54			
Total	*3.54*	*1.93*	*1.36*	*2.05*			
Total (States & Union territories)	62.23	29.57	81.34	100.79	208.10		
Grand Total	99.14	68.49	141.34	172.70	326.98		
Special Central Assistance for tribal sub-plans						119.31	125.00

*Includes Rs.51 lakhs for 'Machinery for Enforcement of Untouchability (Offences) Act'.

**Includes Rs.1 lakh for 'Pre-matric Scholarships for children of those engaged in unclean occupations', and Rs.18 lakhs for 'Machinery for implementation of the Protection of Civil Rights Act'.

***Includes Rs.16 lakhs for 'Pre-matric Scholarships for children of those engaged in unclean occupations', Rs.50 lakhs for 'Book Banks for Medical and Engineering students', Rs.65 lakhs for 'Machinery for implementation of Protection of Civil Rights Act', and Rs.50 lakhs for 'Financial Development Corporation for Scheduled Castes'.

Sources: (i) For cols. 2 & 3, *Fourth Five Year Plan*, Ch. 21, Table I, pp. 415-16.
(ii) For cols. 4 & 5, *Draft Fifth Five Year Plan*, Vol. II, Ch. 13, Table I, p. 277.
(iii) For col. 6, *Report of the Commissioner of Scheduled Castes and Scheduled Tribes, 1975-76 & 1976-77*, Part I, Ch. 4, p. 78.
(iv) For cols. 7 & 8, *Report of the Commissioner of Scheduled Castes and Scheduled Tribes, 1978-79*, Part I, Ch. 4, p. 99.

TABLE 5: Expenditure for the development of scheduled tribes in the State sector, 1974-75, 1975-76, 1976-77

(Rs. in lakhs)

Head	Revised Fifth Plan outlay	1974-75	1975-76	1976-77	Total for the three years
Education	3643.58	461.216	578.486	710.395	1750.097
Economic uplift	2894.31	362.654	467.188	475.379	1305.221
Health, housing and others	1510.90	264.647	291.564	374.876	931.087
Total	8048.79 +23.80= 8072.59	1088.517	1337.238	1560.650	3167.395

Source: Report of the Commissioner for Scheduled Castes and Scheduled Tribes 1975-76 & 1976-77, Part II, Statement No. II, pp. 18-20.

ments for the development and welfare of the scheduled tribes. They can be classified as follows:

Centrally Sponsored Programmes:
1. Post-matric scholarships
2. Girls hostels
3. Pre-examination training
4. Tribal Development Blocks
5. Cooperation
6. Research, Training and Special Projects
7. Improvement of working and living conditions of those engaged in unclean occupations
8. Coaching-cum-Guidance Centres
9. Grants to All-India non-official organizations doing welfare work among the scheduled tribes and scheduled castes.

Programmes in the State Sector:
1. Pre-matric scholarships and stipends
2. Exemption from tuition and examination fees
3. Provision of educational equipments
4. Provision of mid-day meals
5. Setting up of Ashram Schools
6. Grants for the construction and maintenance of hostel and school buildings
7. Provision of land and irrigation

8. Supply of bullocks, agricultural implements, seeds, and manures
9. Development of cottage industries
10. Development of communications
11. Cooperation
12. Colonization of shifting cultivators
13. Supply of poultry, sheep, pigs, goats, etc.
14. Medical facilities
15. Drinking water supply schemes
16. Provision of house sites and houses
17. Legal aid
18. Grants-in-aid to non-official organizations working at State level

Education and Employment

Since education can play an important role in bridging the gap between the tribals and non-tribals and in helping the processes of change and modernization, a considerable amount of money is being spent on the provision of education facilities to the tribals. The important. schemes included in the programme for the expansion of education facilities among the scheduled tribes are the opening of various types of schools, award of scholarships, providing hostel facilities, stipends, stationery grants, boarding grants, mid-day meals, etc. The Central and State governments have also provided for the reservation of seats in educational institutions for students belonging to scheduled tribes. Some relaxation in the criteria for admission is also practised. The educational programmes of the Central government include award of post-matric scholarships, provision of girls' hostels, pre-examination training centres, and coaching-cum-guidance facilities to tribal students appearing for IAS and overseas scholarships. In addition to these, there are schemes in the State sector for provision of pre-matric scholarships and stipends, exemptions from tuition fees and examination fees, educational equipment, mid-day meals, etc. Schemes are also being operated to train the tribals to work as teachers in their own areas.

The progress registered during the First Plan in this field was summed up by the draft Second Plan in these words: "To facilitate teaching through tribal dialects, special text books have been prepared in Hyderabad, Assam, NEFA and Bihar. So far eight tribal dialects have been taken up in this manner. Assistance has been given through scholarships, grant for books, hostel fees and other ways to tribal students. Over 4,50,000 tribal students were in receipt of assistance. By the end of the first plan about 4,000 schools will have been established in tribal areas of different kinds. This includes more than one thousand Ashram and Sevashram schools which have been established in tribal areas, specially in Bombay, Bihar, Orissa and Madhya Pradesh."[17] In addition to these, about 8500 scholariships were awarded to the tribal studies for post-matric students. The year-wise details of the award of post-matric scholarships to the students belonging to scheduled tribes from 1948-49, the year of inauguration of the scheme, are shown in Table 6.

Table 6 shows the spectacular increase in the number of scholarships granted and the expenditure incurred. Thus, during the First Plan, 8494 post-matric scholarships involving an expenditure of Rs.41.66 lakhs were granted. The number of scholarships rose to 25,592 (involving an expenditure of Rs.110.36 lakhs) in the Second Plan, and further to 60,058 in the Third Plan (involving an expenditure of Rs.262.63 lakhs). The total number of post-matric scholarships granted in the three Annual Plans was 65,637 (involving an expenditure of Rs.311.04 lakhs) which rose to 199,978 (involving an expenditure of Rs.928.42 lakhs) in the Fourth Plan.

Since 1954-55, the Government of India has been awarding overseas scholarships to the students of scheduled castes and scheduled tribes for post-graduate research. Till 1971-72, every year nine such scholarships were granted. Of these, 4 were awarded to scheduled castes, 4 to scheduled tribes, and 1 to denotified, nomadic castes, and semi-nomadic tribes. The number of scholarships was increased to 21 from 9 in 1972-73 and to

TABLE 6: **Year-wise progress of the post-matric scholarship scheme for students belonging to scheduled tribes**

Year	Number of scholarships awarded	Expenditure incurred (Rs. in lakhs)
(1)	(2)	(3)
1948-49	84	0.46
1949-50	186	0.95
1950-51	348	1.85
Pre-First Plan Total	618	3.26
First Plan		
1951-52	575	2.82
1952-53	1093	5.22
1953-54	1597	8.19
1954-55	2356	12.38
1955-56	2883	13.05
First Plan Total	8494	41.66

(Contd.)

TABLE 6 (*Contd.*)

(1)	(2)	(3)
Second Plan		
1956-57	3482	16.78
1957-58	4300	18.97
1958-59	4821	20.76
1959-60	6112	23.89
1960-61	6877	30.96
Second Plan Total	25592	110.36
Third Plan		
1961-62	8548	36.78
1962-63	10249	44.37
1963-64	11836	50.28
1964-65	13500	60.62
1965-66	15925	70.58
Third Plan Total	60058	262.63
Three Annual Plans		
1966-67	17760	83.84
1967-68	21261	106.34
1968-69	26616	120.86
Total of Three Annual Plans	65637	311.04
Fourth Plan		
1969-70	31324	136.89
1970-71	33776	149.50
1971-72	38842	197.76
1972-73	44668	N.A.
1973-74	51368	N.A.
Fourth Plan Total	19978	928.42
1974-75	55000	
1975-76	57000	
1978-79	70000*	353.00*

*Anticipated.

Sources: (i) *Report of the Commissioner for Scheduled Castes and Scheduled Tribes*, 1971-72 & 1972-73, Appendix IV, p. 274-275.

(ii) *Report of the Commisssioner for Scheduled Castes and Scheduled Tribes* 1975-76 & 1976-77, Part I, p. 93.

(iii) *Report of the Commissioner for Scheduled Castes and Scheduled Tribes, 1978-79, Part I*, p. 170,

49 during the year 1977-78. Of these, 21 were earmarked for scheduled castes, 16 for scheduled tribes, 6 for other economically backward classes, 4 for denotified, nomadic and semi-nomadic tribes, and 2 for neo-Buddhists.[18]

During the Third Plan period, the percentage enrolment of students belonging to scheduled tribes increased in all States. By the end of the Fourth Plan, one million students belonging to scheduled tribes (and three million belonging to scheduled castes) were awarded pre-matric scholarships or stipends. Coaching centres were organized for assisting students to compete in the examinations conducted by the UPSC for recruitment to Class I and Subordinate services. The centres located at Allahabad and Madras imparted training to candidates belonging to scheduled castes and scheduled tribes for appearing in IAS, IPS, and Allied Services examinations. The government decided in 1967-68 to start training courses for entry into State Civil and Subordinate Services of the Central government, etc. Such centres are functioning in Andhra Pradesh, Bihar, Gujarat, Haryana, Karanataka, Kerala, Madhya Pradesh, West Bengal, and the Union territory of Delhi. Four coaching-cum-guidance centres at Madras, Kanpur, Delhi, and Jabalpur were set up in the Fourth Plan. During this plan, a provision of Rs.100 lakhs was made for these centres and it is estimated that Rs.83.09 lakhs were spent by the end of the plan. The Draft Fifth Plan provided for an outlay of Rs.3.00 crores for coaching and allied schemes. Coaching for Engineering Services examination is also being planned for students of scheduled tribes and funds have been sanctioned for the setting up of two centres —one at Allahabad and the other at Tiruchirapalli.

The Union government also recommended that 15% and 5% seats for scheduled caste and scheduled tribe candidates respectively for admission to undergraduate courses in all medical colleges should be reserved. A relaxation of 5% in marks was also recommended for candidates belonging to these communities, in cases where admission was restricted to candidates who obtained a certain minimum percentage of marks. Similar recommendations were made for admission to post-graduate medical courses as well. The State governments of Maharashtra, Kerala, Andhra Pradesh, Punjab, and Tamil Nadu have agreed to make the necessary reservation of seats in post-graduate medical courses but the recommendation regarding 5% relaxation in minimum marks for admission in post-graduate medical courses has not been accepted by many States so far. Since students belonging to scheduled tribes are generally very poor, they cannot afford to purchase all the costly books of medical and engineering courses. Accordingly, a Centrally sponsored scheme for establishing book-banks in various medical and engineering colleges in the country was undertaken in 1978-79.

The Union Ministry of Education issued directions to the three Institutes of Management at Ahmedabad, Bangalore, and Calcutta in 1964 to reserve 20% of seats (15% for scheduled castes and 5% for scheduled tribes) for admission. The Institutes at Ahmedabad and Bangalore have implemented the directive while the Indian Institute of Management, Calcutta, has yet to follow suit. Some relaxation in minimum marks for admission is, however, granted by all the three Institutes. Similar relaxations and reservations were observed in admissions to the Institutes of Technology located at Bombay, Delhi, Kanpur, Kharagpur, and Madras and the Institute of Technology located at Varanasi. Since admission of scheduled tribe candidates through joint entrance examinations was very poor, direct admission was granted for the first time to all scheduled tribe candidates who had secured more than 50% marks in Higher Secondary examination in the academic session 1975-76. However, this privilege was withdrawn from the academic year 1979. As on 1-1-1975, there were 356 Industrial Training Institutes in the country imparting training in engineering and non-engineering trades, under the Craftsman Training Scheme of the Directorate General of Employment and Training, Ministry of Labour. "Seats are reserved in these Institutes for Scheduled Castes and Scheduled Tribe candidates in proportion to the percentage of their population in the State/Union Territory concerned."[19] The Report of the Commissioner for 1974-75 notes with concern the decrease in enrolment of scheduled tribe candidates from 2.7% in the beginning of 1974 to 2.5% at the end of 1974. A fall was registered in Gujarat, Karnataka, Madhya Pradesh, Orissa, Rajasthan, and Tripura.

Till the academic year 1975-76 no reservations were made for admissions to Kendriya Vidyalayas. However, from 1976-77 onwards, it was agreed to reserve 15% of seats for scheduled caste candidates and 7½% for scheduled tribe candidates. Despite this decision, only 0.9% of the total number of students on rolls during 1977-78 belonged to scheduled tribes. During 1977-78, only 1.3% of the total students admitted belonged to scheduled tribes.[20]

Keeping in view the employment needs of the scheduled tribes, increase in educational facilities to them, and their meagre representation in government services, reservations in different services and posts have been allowed for the members of the scheduled tribes. In the case of recruitment made on the basis of an all-India competition, 7½% of the vacancies are reserved for the scheduled tribes. Reservations in direct recruitment to Class III and Class IV posts which normally attract candidates from a locality or region are fixed in proportion to the population of the scheduled tribe in the respective States and Union territories. In certain cases where promotions are to be made from departmental candidates in Class II, III, and IV posts, reservation for scheduled tribes is made at 7.5% of the vacancies. In the cases of promotion by selection from Class II to Class I posts (and within Class II posts), employees belonging to scheduled tribes are given one higher grading in categorization of merit. This concession is confined to 25% of the total vacancies, in a grade in a year.[21]

As a result of these steps, the percentage of scheduled tribes in Central government services has gone up. Their representation in Class I services increased from 0.1% in 1957 to 0.57% in 1968. This increased further to 0.62% in 1975 and to 0.94% in 1979. The representation of scheduled tribes in Class II services rose from 0.3% in 1957 to 0.57% in 1968 and was 0.43% in 1971. This increased further to 0.59% in 1975 and to 1.03% in 1979. The representation in Class III and Class IV services has increased considerably. Thus, the increase was from 0.6% in 1957 to 1.70% in 1971 in the former case, and from 2.4% in 1957 to 3.65% in 1971 in the latter case. The Report of the Commissioner for 1978-79 reveals that the representation of scheduled tribes in Class III and Class IV services stood at 3.11% and 5.19% respectively as on 1-1-1979.

Information regarding representation of scheduled tribes in the services under the State governments and Union territory administrations is highly inadequate. For example, no information is available for the States of Andhra Pradesh, Assam, Bihar, Himachal Pradesh, Jammu & Kashmir, Karnataka, Meghalaya, Manipur, Nagaland, Rajasthan, Tamil Nadu, and Uttar Pradesh and for the Union territories of Chandigarh, Delhi, and Goa, Daman & Diu. Whatever scanty information is available reveals that actual performance of the States in this field is disappointing. In Gujarat, e.g., while the reservation was 10% in Class I and Class II services, the actual representation was only 1.6% in Class I and 1.28% in Class II services as on 1-1 1978. In Class III and Class IV services the reservation was 14% but actual representation was only 8.9% in Class III and 12% in Class IV services as on 1-1-1978. In Madhya Pradesh, while the reservation was 18% in Class I and Class II services, the actual representation was only 0.6% in Class I services and 1.05% in Class II services as on 1-1-1978. As against 20% reservation for Class III and Class IV services, the actual representation was 5.61% in Class III and 7.14% in Class IV services as on 1-1-1978. The situation was disappointing in the case of Maharashtra, Orissa, Rajasthan, Tripura, and the Union territories of Andaman & Nicobar Islands and Delhi as well where the actual representation in Class I and Class II services fell considerably short of the reservations. In a number of States such as Orissa, Rajasthan, Manipur, etc., representation of scheduled tribes in Class III and Class IV services is considerably higher than in Class I and Class II services. Similar situation prevails in the Union territories of

Arunachal Pradesh, Dadra & Nager Haveli, and Lakshadweep.

Agriculture

As has already been noted, a number of tribals practise the method of shifting cultivation which has a number of disadvantages. In all such areas and in all other tribal areas, in general, agricultural production and productivity are very low. The techniques of production are primitive, irrigation facilities are available only in a very small area (according to the Report of the Commissioner for Scheduled Castes and Scheduled Tribes for 1971-72 and 1972-73, only 1% to 2% of total cultivated area had irrigation facilities in tribal areas, as against the national average of 21%) and holdings are extremely small. In those areas where settled cultivation is followed, there is a need to lay stress on the supply of improved seeds, fertilizers and credit, increase in irrigation facilities, soil conservation and land reclamation, adoption of better implements and new technology. In areas practising shifting cultivation, it is necessary to see that such cultivation is carried out on a scientific basis till the final conversion to settled cultivation takes place. Keeping this end in view, an attempt is being made to minimize the evils of jhooming and in bringing up the fertility of the jhoom areas. Colonization schemes have been introduced in tribal middle India, Kerala, and Tripura. For example, in Tripura, about two-thirds of the families practising shifting cultivation have changed over to settled agriculture and have been allotted 2 acres of cultivable land, some cash for seeds, bullocks, and implements. In some tribal areas of the country, mechanized reclamation of hilly and forested tracts is being carried out. In some tribal areas (especially in Rajasthan), high-yielding varieties have been successfully adopted.

The agricultural policy adopted in tribal areas includes the following: (i) promotion of improved methods and techniques in agriculture (through organization of demonstration farms, distribution of improved agricultural implements, better seeds, fertilizers, etc.), (ii) protection of land against soil erosion, (iii) credit facilities to tribal agriculturists for the purchase of implements, bullocks, etc., and (iv) provision of irrigation facilities (this programme includes digging of new wells, renovation of old wells, installation of diesel pumping sets, and construction of irrigation tanks). Programmes of animal husbandry and setting up of cottage and small industries have been initiated to provide subsidiary income to tribal agriculturists.

Cooperation

To achieve a transformation of tribal agriculture and to prevent the exploitation of the tribals from the moneylenders, forest contractors, and other non-tribals, it is necessary to think in terms of 'cooperation and co-operatives'. Because of their extreme poverty, most of the tribals have to borrow money from the moneylenders and traders. However, once they incur a debt, they land into the clutches of the moneylenders from which they find it difficult to extricate themselves. The moneylenders charge ex-orbitant rates of interest ranging from 25% to 100% and since the tribals are mostly illiterate they do not understand the interest calculations of the moneylenders. In many cases the first instalment of interest is deducted at the time of giving the loan itself. Thus, if a loan of Rs.100 is needed by the tribal, the moneylender gives him only Rs.70 or Rs.75 deducting the difference towards interest and obtains the thumb impression of the tribal for the full amount. In case of default, the moneylender charges compound rate of interest and practises various techniques of harassment on the tribal. In many cases, loan is granted against the mortgage of land which passes on to the moneylender in course of time. Various legislative measures have been adopted by different State governments to check these practices. In this regard, mention may be made of the Andhra Pradesh (Scheduled Tribes) Debt Relief Regulation, 1960, Andhra Pradesh (Scheduled Areas) Money-lenders Regulation 1960, Bihar Scheduled Area Regulation 1969, Madhya Pradesh Scheduled Tribe Debt Relief Regulation 1965, the Bengal Money-lenders Act, 1940 (as modified in 1971), etc. However, all such legislative acts are useless for (i) the tribals are generally ignorant about them, and (ii) alternative sources of credit are not properly developed. Unless an alternative source of credit is provided to the tribals—a source that can provide all types of loans (short, medium, and long-term) for all types of purposes, productive as well as unproductive, it is difficult to break the stranglehold of the moneylenders on the tribal people.

Along with exploitation at the hands of the moneylenders, the tribals also face exploitation at the hands of the forest contractors. The latter engage tribal labour for work in forests at miserably low wages. In the absence of alternative sources of employment or in the absence of the knowledge of such sources, the tribals are generally forced to work for these contractors.

Keeping all these considerations in view, the government has, ever since the inauguration of the First Plan, emphasized the role of cooperatives in the tribal economy. In the First Plan, 312 multi-purpose cooperative societies were set up in tribal areas and 350 grain golas (now functioning as grain banks) were set up in Orissa, Bihar, and Madhya Pradesh. During the same plan, 653 forest labour cooperatives were established so that forest contracts could be given to such cooperatives instead of to forest contractors. In the First Plan, the State governments undertook schemes involving financial commitments to the extent of Rs.49.75 lakhs in the field of cooperation. During the Second Plan, an amount Rs.139.71 lakhs was allocated for the development of cooperative institutions. During the Third Plan period, an allocation of Rs.2.98 crores was made under the centrally sponsored scheme while the actual expenditure was of Rs.3.06 crores. The expenditure on cooperatives under the same scheme was Rs.103.02 lakhs in the three Annual Plans. During the Fourth Plan, allocation under the centrally sponsored programme was of Rs.2.51 crores while the anticipated expenditure was Rs.2.78 crores. Apex tribal cooperative organizations were set up in Andhra Pradesh, Bihar, Madhya Pradesh, Maharashtra, and Orissa to co-ordinate the activities of the primary societies and to extend financial and technical assistance to them. A specific provision of Rs.3 crore was made in the Draft Fifth Plan to help cooperatives in tribal areas.

Communications

Since many tribal areas are isolated from the rest of the economy, it is necessary to provide adequate roads, transport, and other means of communication if they are to be absorbed and assimilated in the national economy. There is another aspect of the problem as well. We have already emphasized the subsistence nature of agriculture in tribal areas. If the tribals are to be encouraged to increase agricultural production, it is necessary that ample marketing facilities are provided to them so that agricultural surplus can be unloaded in the markets. In the absence of such an arrangement, the economic compulsion (and incentive) to increase agricultural production does not exist. Since the majority of the tribals depend on agriculture, improvement in their standard of living depends upon increases in agricultural production and the market outlets for such increased production. This brings into prominence the importance of ample communication facilities. Keeping these considerations in view, Rs.6 crores were spent during the First Plan on developing roads in the tribal areas of Assam and other States. Bridle and hill paths to the extent of 2340 miles were constructed in a number of States including Assam, Bihar, Orissa, Madhya Pradesh, Andhra Pradesh, and Vindhya Pradesh. The Second Plan laid down the task of improving 450 miles of motorable roads and 7200 miles of bridle paths in tribal areas; Rs.4 crores were prescribed for the task. During the Third Plan, Rs.5.1 crores were spent for building roads and improving communication facilities.

Land Distribution and Land Alienation

The scarcity of land for purposes of cultivation has led to the creation of many uneconomic holdings on the one hand, and to a large number of landless workers on the other. To solve the problem of uneconomic holdings, the government has promoted and supported the spirit of cooperation among the tribals and to solve the problem of landless tribal workers, it has been decided in many States to give them priority in land distribution programmes.

As already noted, the problem of land alienation is a serious one in tribal areas. Moneylenders, *sahukars*, and other non-tribal people have continued to grab the land belonging to the tribals on one pretext or another. To cope with this problem, safeguards along the following lines have been provided: "(a) provisions restricting the transfer of tribal land to non-tribals by sale, as found in Gujarat, Orissa and Rajasthan, (b) provisions restricting transfer of tribal land to any person—tribal or non-tribal, as found in West Bengal, and (c) provisions restricting the transfer of tribal land by any means."[22] Numerous Acts and Regulations have been adopted by the State governments to safeguard the interests of the tribals. These are: "Assam Land and Revenue Regulation (Amendment) Act, 1964; Bihar Scheduled Areas Regulation, 1969; Land Revenue (Amendment) Rule, 1960 of Karnataka; Kerala Land Assignment Rule 1964; Land Revenue Code 1959; (Section 165) of Madhya Pradesh and 1966 (Section 36) of Maharashtra; Orissa Scheduled Areas Transfer of Immovable Property (by Scheduled Tribes) Regulation, 1956 and amended in 1965; Rajasthan Tenancy Act, 1955 (Sections 42, 43, 46A and 49A); a 10-year binding for land alienation in Tamil Nadu; Tripura Land Revenue and Land Reform Act, 1968 (Section 187); U.P. Zamindari Vinash and Bhumi Vyavastha (Sanshodhan) Adhiniyam, 1969 (Section 157 *ka*); West Bengal Land Reform (Amendment) Act 1965; Andaman and Nicobar Islands (Protection of Aboriginal Tribes) Regulation, 1956; Organisacao Agraria of Dadra and Nagar Haveli and Protection of Scheduled Tribes Regulation Act of 1964 of Lakshadweep."[23]

Despite all these elaborate legal arrangements, it has not been found possible to check land alienation. The tribals are generally ignorant of their rights and wherever they know them, they are afraid to exercise them either because they do not have enough resources to pull through the legal proceedings or they are afraid to challenge the superior wielders of money power who grab their lands.

Industrialization

During the First Plan, several States carried out programmes for developing cottage industries and subsidiary occupations among the tribal people. These included bee-keeping, sheep rearing, weaving, sericulture, and palm gurs. In 1955-56, about 800 tribals received training in weaving, sericulture, and fruit preservation and about 750 persons received assistance in starting trades in which they were trained. During the same plan, 111 cottage industry centres were established. During the Second Plan, the State governments laid down the target of establishment of 825 cottage industries centres and training to 4000 persons in various crafts; 45 training-cum-production centres were included in Orissa's Second Plan, while other States sought to provide for 87 industrial and technical training centres for tribal students. Programmes for promotion of cottage industries were continued in all subsequent plans as well. During the Third Plan, an amount of Rs.2.29 crores was made available for their development. The Draft Fourth Plan stated that "Assistance will also be given for the promotion of cottage industries, including financial assistance for improving trade or business marketing facilities, technical guidance and setting up production and training centres". Further, it was proposed that these programmes would be linked together and integrated with general sector programmes so that 'the intensity of effort is large enough to produce an impact'.

Since industrialization is considered a sine qua non of economic development, some important major industrial projects were located in tribal areas. These included Rourkela, Ranchi, and Bokaro steel plants. These projects have provided considerable employment opportunities to tribal people as unskilled labour. Technical training is also being provided to tribals to enable them to work as skilled labour in these and other projects. Of the 138,729 trainees on rolls as on 31-12-1974 in 356 ITIs, 3719 (i.e., 2.54%) belonged to scheduled tribes. In Nagaland, Arunachal Pradesh, and Mizoram all trainees belonged to scheduled tribes. The position in other States (having a relatively larger proportion of tribals) is as under—in Madhya Pradesh, out of 11,245 persons on rolls in ITIs as on 31-12-1974, 857 (i.e., 7.62%) belonged to scheduled tribes. In Bihar 6.47%, in Manipur 34.06%, in Tripura 6.21%, and in Orissa 11.35% belonged to scheduled tribes.

Tribal Development Agency Projects

On the pattern of SFDA/MFAL[24] projects in rural areas, Tribal Development Agency Projects were established in some tribal areas on an experimental basis. Initially six such pilot projects were started in 1971-72 in the Srikakulam district of Andhra Pradesh, Singhbhum district of Bihar, Dantewada and Konta tehsils of the Bastar district in Madhya Pradesh, and the Ganjam and Koraput districts of Orissa. Two more projects were later added in Orissa State to be located in the Keonjhar and Phulbani districts. The Tribal Development Agency (TDA) is an autonomous body registered under the Societies Registration Act, 1860, and entrusted with the task of developing the selected tribal areas within the district in a comprehensive manner. The salient features of these projects are as under:

(i) each project is being implemented by a tribal development agency with the district collector as the chairman. The agency also has a full-time project officer and other district officer as members;
(ii) in addition to obtaining the help of the development machinery of the government in the actual execution of programmes, help from the financial institutions (such as the land development banks and commercial banks), public sector bodies (such as State Electricity Boards, Tribal Development Corporations, Forest Corporations, etc.), and representatives of the tribal communities can also be obtained;
(iii) the jurisdiction of each project is a few selected blocks where the concentration of tribals is high;
(iv) the TDA adopts a comprehensive approach to the problems of the area under its jurisdiction, its major attempt being to develop the infrastructural base of the area in respect of irrigation, land development, communication, credit and marketing, etc. Such programmes of infrastructure development are to be integrated with programmes as horticulture, land improvement, soil conservation, animal husbandry, etc.;
(v) locating and developing the potential 'growth centres' of the project area; and
(vi) the TDA is expected to provide 50-75% subsidy for the promotion of economic activity and the rest of the funds are to be found by the beneficiaries themselves.

The outlay for each of the agencies was Rs.2 crores and the target was to cover 10,000 deserving tribal families or 50,000 deserving tribals in each agency project. A total amount of Rs.440 lakhs was released during the Fourth Plan for these projects. Half of the amount released went for the Ganjam and Koraput projects in Orissa. The total amount released from the date of inception to 31-8-1975 was Rs.746.51 lakhs of which Rs.641.31 lakhs was actually utilized by the end of June 1975. Approximately half of the amount released was for the TDAs in Orissa alone. Thus, of the total amount utilized approximately 47.04% went to projects in Orissa. Improved agricultural practices were adopted in 243,557 acres of land under the projects, 3653 pairs of bullocks were supplied, 885 km of link roads and arterial roads were constructed and approximately one and a half lakh persons benefited from the TDA projects. The largest number of beneficiaries seems to be in the Singhbhum district of Bihar.[25]

A new approach to tribal development was initiated in the Fifth Plan period with the introduction of the scheme of tribal sub-plans. Against the ad hoc and piecemeal approach adopted in the previous plans, this new scheme emphasized an integrated and comprehensive approach to the problems of tribal areas. It was also recognized that there was no uniform solution to the variety of problems facing tribal areas and communities which were at different levels of socio-economic development. Consequently, while preparing the tribal sub-plans, needs of the areas coming under these sub-plans were given specific importance.[26]

Other Schemes of Development

A number of schemes were also undertaken to improve the housing and sanitary conditions of the tribals and in providing adequate medical facilities to them. The State governments provided Rs.60 lakhs in the Second Plan for the costruction of 18,800 houses. It was also proposed to form 56 housing societies for undertaking construction programmes. The number of houses constructed for the scheduled tribes in the first three plans with the assistance of the Central and State governments was 19,620 in the First Plan, 46,718 in the Second Plan, and 12,172 in the Third Plan. During the first three years of the Fourth Plan, a sum of Rs.69.28 lakhs was granted as subsidy to scheduled tribes for construction of houses. A programme for the provision of house-sites to landless workers in rural areas has also been taken up by the Ministry of Works and Housing. In this programme, priority is to be given to districts having sizable concentration of landless workers belonging to scheduled castes and scheduled tribes. To take care of the health of tribals, 3144 dispensaries and mobile health units were established in tribal areas by the end of the Fifth Plan. Health surveys were conducted to study the general condition of health among the tribals and the methods and practices adopted by them for healing. The Second Plan provided for the setting up of 600 dispensaries and mobile health units.

Some of the schemes undertaken by the States in the Fourth Plan for provision of medical facilities included the following. In Andhra Pradesh a scheme for the construction of a 10-bed hospital was undertaken and Rs.16.20 lakhs were provided for the purpose. The State government sanctioned an amount of Rs.6.25 lakhs for mobile medical units and Rs. 11.75 lakhs for a crash nutrition programme. The Assam government sanctioned (i) grants to patients suffering from T.B. etc., (ii) grants to non-official organizations for anti-leprosy work, (iii) stipends for nursing courses, and (iv) financial assistance to leprosy control units. The governments of Bihar and Gujarat sanctioned Rs.2.50 lakhs and Rs.2.00 lakhs respectively for medical aid. The Karnataka government set apart Rs.0.91 lakhs for mobile health units and Rs..05 lakhs for maternity health assistance. The Kerala government provided for an expenditure of Rs.1.90 lakhs for an Ayurvedic dispensary and Rs.1.50 lakhs for a mid-wifery training centre. The Government of Tamil Nadu provided Rs.3.08 lakhs for medical units and the Orissa government sanctioned Rs.2.04 lakhs for anti-yaws campaign and Rs.0.75 lakhs for the establishment of a Homeopathic dispensary. The Tripura government provided Rs.1.00 lakh for the training of tribal girls as dais, Rs.0.50 lakh as financial assistance for carrying tribal patients to the nearest hospital, and Rs.0.50 lakhs as financial assistance for T.B. and other patients. The total amount made available for medical facilities by all the States taken together was Rs.50.93 lakhs during the Fourth Plan. To provide ample drinking water, the Government of India gives subsidies for the construction of drinking water wells, and pumps and small tanks in localities and areas predominantly inhabited by scheduled tribes.

Voluntary organizations engaged in the task of tribal welfare are given grants-in-aid mostly for schemes of education and for removal of social disabilities. During the Third Plan, an amount of Rs.11.07 crores was spent on health, housing and other schemes for scheduled castes and scheduled tribes and during the Fourth Plan an outlay of Rs.14.05 crores was kept for these purposes while the anticipated expenditure was Rs.23.17 crores. Schemes of legal aid for scheduled tribes are in operation in Bihar, Gujarat, Himachal Pradesh, Karnataka, Madhya Pradesh, Orissa, Rajasthan, and Tripura.

An Appraisal of Development Efforts of the Government

None can ignore the genuine desire of the government to uplift the tribal people and the role played by its efforts in changing the mode of thinking and attitudes of many tribals. Thus, the educational policies of the government, provision of reservation in jobs, policies in the fields of agriculture, cooperation, communications, industrialization, social services, etc., have brought the tribals closer to the main stream of national life. Tribal markets have been linked up with urban markets providing greater economic opportunities to the tribals and creating a commercial aptitude in them, the concept of saving is gaining acceptance, and there is a definite shift in the consumption pattern of the tribals from need base to impersonal needs. Yet, all said and done, the efforts so far have not helped in solving the problems of poverty, malnutrition, and exploitation faced by the tribals. Let us discuss some of the drawbacks of the government programmes systematically, one by one.

Let us first of all take up the field of education and employment. According to the 1971 census, the percentage of literacy among the scheduled tribes was only 11.29 against the general literacy rate of 29.35. The literacy rate among the tribal women was only 4.85. As far as the State-wise position is concerned, literacy rate was particularly low in Madhya Pradesh, Andhra Pradesh, and Rajasthan and in the Union territory of Arunachal Pradesh. The literacy rate was only 5.34% in Andhra Pradesh and 5.20% in Arunachal Pradesh. The highest literacy rate among the States was noted in Manipur (28.71%) and among the Union territories in Mizoram (53.49%).[27] Thus, the impact of the educational programmes of the government has been uneven. It has been seen that a large number of post-matric scholarships have gone to students belonging to a few selected tribes only.

The Commissioner for Scheduled Castes and Scheduled Tribes pointed out in his Report of 1968-69 that nearly three-fourths of the total scholarships had been awarded to scheduled tribe students belonging to Assam and Bihar, though the tribal population of these States constituted only one-fifth of the total tribal population in the country. Even within States, the distribution of scholarships was highly skewed in favour of some tribes. Thus, in Gujarat, the Dhodias and the Chodhras (including the Chaudharis) who accounted for only 10% of the tribal population in 1966-67, received 46.17% and 21.64% of total post-matric scholarships while the Bhils constituting 40.80% of the tribal population received only 16.98% of such scholarships. In Maharashtra, students belonging to the tribes of the Halbas and Gonds, who constituted merely 0.22% and 11.30% of the total scheduled tribe population in the State, received 32.49% of the total post-matric scholarships in 1967-68. The Mahadev Kolis and the Bhils constituting 11.40% and 24.02% of the scheduled tribes, received only 9.60% and 21.37% of such scholarships. In Tamil Nadu, the Konda Kapus, the Kattunayakans and the Kammaras constituting merely 0.001%, 2.5%, and 0.01% of the tribal population received respectively 19%, 17%, and 11% of the post-matric scholarships in 1967-68. As against this, the Malayalis and the Irulas constituting 51.50% and 31.60% of the tribal population received only 19% and 5% of such scholarships. In Rajasthan, the Minas, constituting 50.04% of the total scheduled tribe population, received 72.36% of the post-matric scholarships while the Bhils forming 39.26% of the population received only 16.69%.

Thus, it would seem that some advanced scheduled tribes have gained educational benefits out of all proportion while a number of tribes have failed to benefit. The Commissioner notes that the provisions of keeping reservations for scheduled tribes in admission seats are not adhered to by some institutions. Thus, the Central university of Aligarh does not follow the policy of Central government regarding reservation of seats for scheduled tribes students. The irony of the matter is that Mahatma Gandhi Institute of Medical Sciences at Sevagram—Gandhiji's headquarters for many years—has no reserved seats for the students of scheduled tribes. The Draft Fourth Plan points to the various weaknesses of the programme. According to it, "the incidence of stagnation and wastage has been high, particularly at the primary and secondary stages. There is also considerable variation in extent of literacy between different tribes as well as between different castes. . . . Enrolment in technical and professional courses has been low. Schemes of economic development have tended to rely on standardised patterns They have not been coordinated properly with other programmes of development in the district. The functioning of the tribal research institutes has not been sufficiently development-oriented."[28]

When one comes to reservations for scheduled tribes in services, the position does not seem to be better. As the Commissioner noted in one of his Reports, "while at the policy-making level there does exist, as stated above, an ardent desire and anxiety to provide persons from amongst these communities with adequate employment under the state, in as short a period as possible, the various bottlenecks created at the implementation level, do not allow the progress being achieved at the desired speed". It has also been found that reserve vacancies are mostly filled in for Class III and Class IV posts only. In some public sector undertakings, labour unions are opposed to the policy of reservations. There are also numerous cases of humiliation, harassment, and ill-treatment faced by workers of scheduled castes and scheduled tribes in respect of promotions, transfers, and other related matters.

Criticism of Tribal Development Blocks Project

The tribal development blocks failed in their task on account of reasons similar to the reasons that made the community development blocks a failure. The benefits failed to reach the lower strata of the society and got concentrated in the hands of the upper crust of the tribal community. The Shilu Ao Committee (1969) observed that though the TD blocks had brought about a change in the outlook of the tribals, particularly in the field of education and agriculture, the impact had fallen short of expectations. The Committee pointed out the following limitations of the TD blocks: (i) smallness of the area in each TD block, (ii) fragmented approach to development planning, (iii) application of a large number of standardized schemes in vogue among advanced communities to tribal areas, (iv) neglect of the employment aspects of development, and (v) failure to take up settlement of land disputes in the pre-extension stage.[29]

The Commissioner stated in his Report of 1971-72 and 1972-73 that the TDB programme succeeded in making only a limited impact due to certain inherent problems such as subsistence level of living of tribals, undeveloped infrastructure and high percentage of illiteracy among them. It was also noted that land alienation problem and shifting cultivation as practised by the tribals hampered development of these blocks. Other problems are—dearth of trained personnel to work among these people and frequent transfers of block level officials. The cooperatives have often been started by block officials without much education or preparation of the tribal people. It is also reported that 60 to 70% of the funds are spent on "brick and mortar" schemes.

The most important criticism of the TDBs is that the whole programme has been carried without the participation of the tribal people. The tribals had practically no say in the programmes formulated for their own development nor was their cooperation obtained in the implementation of these programmes. The planners were fully aware of the need to involve the tribal people in the programmes formulated for their development.[30] Yet, as has happened in so many other spheres, the spirit and pious intentions of the planners could not be translated into practice. This is not unexpected in a framework where formulation aspects of planning have no connection (or relation) whatsoever to the implementation of planning. The latter aspect is the wholesole responsibility of an unchanging bureaucracy that has failed to fulfil the role of a developmental agency.

A more basic criticism has been offered by H.S. Verma and B.L. Tripathi. According to them, the power structure in the tribal areas is such that it perpetuates exploitation of the tribal people and independence from foreign rule in 1947 did not bring about any institutional changes in this framework. In fact, the interests of the politicians, administrators, and local power elite connive to perpetuate and strengthen the system. "This ensures status, power and money to the politicians, reward, power and continuity to the administrators, and continuity of economic dominance to the local power elite. Each of these elements gives something to the other in return for what it gets. Together, they confer some peripheral benefits for the tribal poor, the politicians in the form of ameliorative programmes and laws controlling exploitation, the administrators by implementing them, and the local elite by doling out charity. What is important in this web of relationships is the manner in which the dominants behave towards those dominated. In this situation the local power elites act as gatekeepers, take the maximum benefit from the development programmes, and deprive the tribal poor of their share. The dominance of the prevailing power structure continues even though programmes aiming at its removal are operating. In addition the system stabilises itself, and succeeds remarkably in reproducing itself."[31]

Problems Created by Industrialization

Industrialization has created at least two complex problems. Firstly, establishment of large industrial projects in tribal areas has caused a large-scale displacement of the tribals and, secondly, the tribal population is assuming more and more a migratory character and the tribal life is getting disintegrated. Industrialization needs a large area for construction of the project, allied activities, industrial townships, etc., and this results in displacement of the natives from their land. Thus, in Bihar alone, industrialization programmes started in Hatia, Jamshedpur, Patratu, Bokaro, and Rourkela had resulted in the acquisition of 137 villages. In Hatia 25 villages were acquired and 2198 families involving 12,990 persons were displaced; in Jamshedpur 18 villages were acquired and 635 families displaced; in Patratu, 19 villages were acquired and 202 families displaced; in Rourkela 30 villages were acquired and 2500 families involving 15,200 persons were displaced. The Bokaro steel plant had acquired 45 villages and the number of families likely to be displaced was 6066 involving 37,185 persons.[32]

Such deprivation from land pushed the tribals into a state of insecurity. Though compensation was paid, it was too insufficient. Thus, persons displaced from the Rourkela complex were granted a compensation of Rs.200 to Rs.900 per acre depending on the quality of land which 'was too inadequate to afford any prolonged sustenance'. Some land was also given to rehabilitate them. However, almost all such lands "were hilly, without any irrigation facilities, and situated at long distances of 10-15 miles from their housing sites. The tribals who had already exhausted their little cash in hand in the construction and maintenance of their dwellings, could ill afford to have these lands reclaimed so as to continue their traditional occupation."[33] Thus, they were forced to seek employment in the industrial projects where also they faced a raw deal.

Naidu notes that being illiterate the tribals could not seek any technical posts while in low posts, such as peons and chowkidars etc. "they had to face competition from their non-tribal counterparts, besides being subjected to the prejudices and indifference of the non-tribal recruiting officials".[34] Subsequently, the tribals were assured that one member from each displaced family would be provided employment in the steel complex. However, only about 400 displaced persons were given employment. Naidu mentions two other important flaws of the scheme—(i) while in agriculture, the whole tribal family got some task to do, under the new arrangement only one member of the family was given employment leading to under-utilization of tribal labour, and (ii) the tribals could not adjust to the new environment which compelled daily work at regular hours. This was very much against the traditional and care-free previous life of the tribals. Many indulged in unauthorized absence for days together and had to lose their jobs.

On account of industrial urbanization, the tribal population is forced to migrate here and there in search of employment opportunities. The tribals are forced to abandon their villages and try for employment in the industrial town. According to Naidu, "this migration, whether seasonal or otherwise, has a devastating effect on the tribal villages as it shatters the very foundations of the tribal economy which are based on cooperation and group solidarity. Those left in the villages find it difficult to carry on their agricultural operations, let alone their ceremonial hunting and fishing operations which have thus almost disappeared from the scene. . . . As a result the tribal villages have become dry and drab—which further increases the outflow." In the industrial townships, the tribals are condemned to living in slum areas and to a life 'that is segmented and heterogeneous in culture'. This takes away their 'emotional energy' and 'sense of identity'.

Criticism on Some other Aspects of Tribal Development Programmes

As noted by the Commissioner in his Report for 1971-72 and 1972-73, no authentic land records are available 'as a result of which the Scheduled Tribes persons are not able to get many of the benefits which flow due to planned economic development'. In the seven districts of Bihar predominantly inhabited by tribals, complete land surveys have not been undertaken in the three districts of Palamau, Hazaribagh, and Ranchi. In Rajasthan and Madhya Pradesh, adequate data on land records are not available. In the Bastar district of Madhya Pradesh, more than 50% of the area is unsurveyed. Since no priority has been accorded to the programme of preparation of land records and conducting of land surveys, a considerable area remains unsurveyed in Orissa. The Commissioner also reports that no cadastral survey has so far been undertaken in Arunachal Pradesh.

It is generally stated that tribal development plans have brought the tribals nearer to the non-tribals and have helped in the processes of integration of the tribal economy with the national economy. While this is a welcome development, it should not be considered an unmixed blessing. It can create serious problems and the planners should remain prepared to tackle them with advance planning so that they are not caught napping. It is frequently found that the process of integration generally confers a low social status on the tribals. Thus, they are integrated with other people as peons, unskilled labour, or bonded labour. They are despised by the non-tribals who call them beef-eaters, non-bathers, etc. Obviously these things cause distrust and unrest in the minds of the tribals making them hostile. This can prove destructive if curative steps are not taken in time.

As noted in Chapter 3, the planning strategy adopted in our country was an investment-based strategy that regarded investment as the kingpin of all development efforts. Industrialization, introduction of technological practices etc., assumed a central role in such investment-oriented planning. Financial allocations were made to carry out such programmes and there was a competition among States to spend money. Nobody bothered about the actual achievements and everybody forgot the basic input of all development—*the man*. No attempt was made to involve the tribal people themselves in the implementation of programmes that concerned them and no regional studies were carried out in different tribal regions to understand their development requirements in a true perspective.

The Report of the Commissioner (1971-72 and 1972-73) has pointed out a serious flaw in the tribal development programmes. According to it, there are many backward communities which have remained outside the purview of development efforts. Some State governments have not even so far tried to identify such communities.

There are certain structural deficiencies in the tribal development administration as well. Though there is a directorate of tribal welfare/backward classes' welfare/social welfare in all States, the tribal welfare programmes are implemented by various departments such as agriculture, cooperation, etc. The usual practices is to transfer funds to these departments. The director of tribal welfare/social welfare is not vested with enough powers to ensure adequate implementation of the programmes through a judicious expenditure of the funds. Thus, there is no effective mechanism to ensure proper execution of the programmes. Also, since the work of tribal welfare is looked after by the directorate of social welfare it does not receive sufficient attention. In some of the States there is no State-level officer in the directorate to look after the execution of the tribal development programmes. If this problem is to be tackled effectively, it is necessary to create a special and separate unit for tribal welfare in the social welfare departments.

Another problem of tribal administration is staff absenteeism. It is difficult to find willing workers in tribal areas and the staff that is posted in these areas tries to get itself transferred from these places as early as possible. Administrators who are serious about their task, receive opposition from vested interests and are transferred. This has a demoralizing effect on them and forbades the 'in-comers' or new administrators to work faithfully and enthusiastically.

Since tribal development is linked with social services, a cut in the latter when imposed on account of shortage of funds affects tribal development programmes adversely. Thus, a reduction in expenditure on health, education, and housing programmes also entails a cut in the tribal development programmes.

As pointed out by various committees, the funds allocated for tribal development are too insufficient keeping in view the magnitude of the task. The Shilu Ao Study Team (1969) advocated that the State governments should be asked to surrender a part of the budget based on percentage of tribal population and special State level committees should be constituted to ensure free flow of funds for tribal development.

The tribal development efforts have not so far succeeded in making the tribals fully conscious of their rights on the one hand, and have failed in bringing dedicated, articulate, and enlightened tribals in the forefront, on the other.

Bureaucracy's apathy in understanding the problems of tribal people and red-tapism result in wastage of already meagre resources provided for tribal development. An example is provided by Patnaik in his study of the tribal village of Narayanpatna in Orissa.[35] He points out that in this village, Rs.33,997.24 were spent on digging and repairing 22 wells, but they all lie unused because the tribals prefer stream water. It would have been cheaper (and more desirable from the point of view of the tribals) to construct a large reservoir in which water from hill streams could be collected.

It would be desirable to conclude this section with the following comments from the Commissioner on the condition of scheduled tribes in India: "With the enforcement of forest laws without much consideration to the human life in the forest areas; land restrictions and alienation of their lands; the indifference shown towards the human problems of the tribal communities by the planners of the industrial projects in the tribal areas; their dependence on, and exploitation by the moneylenders, landlords, and other unscrupulous elements, like liquour contractors have greatly disturbed their way of life. No doubt since Independence efforts have been made to ameliorate their economic and social conditions and steps have been taken by the concerned State governments for development. It is, however, unfortunate that, in spite of specific safeguards provided in the Constitution for their protection and advancement, most of the tribals have not only remained neglected but an exploited lot also."[36]

INTEGRATED DEVELOPMENT OF TRIBAL AREAS

In Chapter 8 we have mentioned four aspects of integrated development—(a) sectoral-cum-temporal integration, (b) spatial integration, (c) integration between the development of different people and groups of people, and (d) integration of the conflicting goals of economic, social and environmental development.[37] Such integrated planning is necessary to ensure popular interest and participation in the planning process and equitable distribution of the fruits of economic growth. The tribal development agency projects (TDA projects) initiated in the Fourth Plan period had comprehensive and integrated development of the tribal areas as the ultimate objective. However, these projects were generally formulated on a uniform basis for all regions of the country and hence lacked the necessary appreciation of the local needs and flexibility to adjust according to local situations. Also, no effective measures were initiated to link up these projects with the State plans properly. As a result, the projects were reduced to Centrally sponsored schemes lacking the necessary local orientation and participation by State governments.

To take account of these factors, the Fifth Plan introduced the concept of a sub-plan. The distinctive features of the sub-plan are:

(i) It caters to the special needs of the designated areas.
(ii) It employs a total (as against sectoral), approach to problems of the area.
(iii) It accepts the uniqueness of the problem of each viable area and community and formulates programmes with reference to it.
(iv) Its resources will be the sum total of resources of the State Plan for the sub-plan area, the Central sectoral outlays, special central assistance and institutional finance.[38]

As noted elsewhere in this chapter, the approach up to the Fourth Plan was to implement schemes having a limited coverage. The schemes included provision of education facilities, post-matric scholarships, hostels, research and training, etc. The tribal development blocks were also set up on the lines of the CD blocks but they failed to deliver the goods. The pilot projects included in the Fourth Plan faced difficulties on account of the reasons just discussed above. The introduction of the idea of the sub-plan in the Fifth Plan marked an important change of emphasis from ad hoc and disjointed efforts to comprehensive, well-knit, and integrated programmes for special development of specific areas. Strategies for the development of a specific area, financial aspects, physical planning, administrative considerations of the government, semi-government, and voluntary agencies are all sought to be integrated into a single programme of development under the sub-plan concept. The objectives of these sub-plans in tribal regions are the elimination of exploitation of all types, speeding up economic and social development, bridging the gaps between the levels of development of these areas and rest of the country, and improving the quality of life of the inhabitants of the tribal regions. The contents of the tribal sub-plans are as under:

(i) Identification and demarcation of areas of tribal concentration.
(ii) Identification of socio-cultural barriers and promoters of change and development.
(iii) Assessment of potentialities, special problems, and felt-needs of the tribal areas.
(iv) Assessment of the resources available for the tribal sub-plan from the normal plan funds, special Central assistance and institutional sources.
(v) Formulation of sectoral programmes.
(vi) Devising a suitable administrative set-up.

The States were asked to prepare tribal sub-plans for areas having more than 50% tribal population. Such sub-plans were prepared in respect of 16 States and 2 Union territories during the Fifth Plan period. Approximately 63% of the tribal population has been covered under the programme. Along with the formulation of the tribal sub-plans, the Planning Commission envisaged the preparation of Integrated Tribal Development Projects which are the implementing agencies of the sub-plans. The total number of such projects started is 180.

In the tribal sub-plan areas an outlay of the order of Rs.644 crores from States plans (including Rs.120 crores special central assistance) was made in the Fifth Plan (1974-78). Of this amount, 29% was spent on agriculture and allied sectors, 5% on cooperation, 27% on irrigation and power development, 10% on transport and communication, 4% on industries, 22% on social and community services, and 3% on economic and general services. In addition, pockets with 50% or more tribals in a population of 10,000 in a contiguous area, have been included in the tribal sub-plan areas from 1979-80 onwards raising the tribal population covered under the tribal sub-plan to 75% at the beginning of the Sixth Plan.

In terms of physical achievements, 5.72 lakh hectares of additional area was brought under minor irrigation, 1.68 lakh hectares under soil conservation, about 8000 hectares under horticulture, approximately 52,000 hectares of land was restored to tribal families, more than 8000 villages provided with water supply, and 6528 villages were electrified. A total of Rs.140 crores were provided as special central assistance for tribal sub-plans during the years 1978-79 and 1979-80 (combined). The Sixth Plan aims at providing Rs.470 crores to these sub-plans during 1980-85.[39]

Recently Gujarat, which has 10% of the total tribal population of the country, came up with a detail sub-plan for the tribal areas. This is said to be one of the first completed tribal sub-plans and envisages an expenditure of Rs.68 crores in the State sector and a Central commitment of another Rs.55 crores. The Rajasthan government's tribal sub-plan envisages an expenditure of Rs.154.66 crores of which Rs.43.57 crores is expected to be made available through institutional resources, Rs.24.53 crores as sectoral inflow in the State plan, and Rs.86.5 crores by the Centre from its tribal development fund.[40] Since the plains tribals of Assam are now not in the stage of primitive agriculture, they have to be encouraged to take up new scientific techniques of increasing agricultural production and productivity. Accordingly, the government has divided the entire State into 19 projects and 55 tribal blocks in identified areas where 19 programmes under agriculture were to be taken up during the year 1977-78. The programmes include fertilizer distribution, plant protection, development of sugarcane and pulses together with HYV wheat and paddy, land reclamation, demonstration, distribution of agricultural implements and machinery, and a few others. Of these programmes, while equal emphasis is stated to be laid on all items, priority will be given to demonstration, HYV wheat and paddy, fertilizer distribution, and plant protection. This sub-plan envisages an expenditure of Rs.83.80 lakhs under the State sector and Rs.40 lakhs under the Centrally divided sector. This amount is expected to help increase in production in about 24,410 hectares.[41]

The structure of planning proposed in a tribal sub-plan is a three-tier structure involving micro, meso, and macro levels of planning. The micro region will be conterminous with a development block, the meso region will be a contiguous block involving 3 to 5 lakh people having comparable levels of socio-economic development, and the macro region will be formed of bigger tribal belts for planning of tribal development. The functions at the micro, meso, and macro levels have been visualized as follows.

At the micro level, the functions included are: (a) education upto higher secondary level, (b) elementary health services, (c) agricultural extension, (d) supply of agricultural inputs, (e) minor irrigation schemes, (f) elementary veterinary services, (g) multi-purpose cooperatives, (h) local panchayat, (i) household industry, and (j) village approach roads.

At the meso level, the functions included are: (a) higher general education, (b) technical and vocational training, (c) manpower planning and employment services, (d) advanced health services with referral facilities, (e) agricultural research extension, (f) seed multiplication farms, (g) soil conservation and land management, (h) apex integrated credit marketing structure with adequate godowning and buffer stock facilities, (i) development of road and communication infrastructure connecting market with State/district highways, (j) distribution of network of power, rural electrification, etc., (k) local resource based industries with adequate market linkages, (l) forest management, (m) horticulture development, (n) complementary development programme in the hinterland, and of bigger industries, (o) minor and medium irrigation projects, and (p) research statistics and evaluation.

At the macro level, the functions include: (a) coordination of activities in tribal development projects, (b) agricultural research on a regional basis, (c) direction of the various sectoral programmes in the project, (d) major irrigation projects, (e) river valley development, (f) industrial and mineral development of the region to ensure complementarity of the project level development programme, (g) marketing support projects and (h) evaluation.[42]

The sub-plan is to be prepared in two parts, which are complementary to each other. In Part I, an attempt will be made to specify the basic problems of development and development potential of the area and a plan will be prepared to bridge the gap between these areas and the neighbouring non-tribal areas. Part II will deal with sectoral programmes in which time-bound programmes of agriculture and allied sector development, cottage and village industries development, etc., will be given the central role. An attempt is also to be made to involve the tribal people at various stages of plan implementation processes. Each State is being given freedom to devise the administrative set-up for its tribal regions on its own, keeping the specific problems of the regions in view. This is likely to introduce a sufficient element of flexibility in tribal sub-plans. In many States, an attempt is being made to create a separate budget head for the tribal sub-plans. This will ensure that these outlays are 'non-divertible'.

The idea behind such integrated area planning is to ensure a *collective utilization* of the resources of a particular area keeping in view the problems and needs of development of that area and the structure of socio-economic relations prevailing therein. The spectrum of the problems of development that still await solution in tribal areas includes the follows: (i) land alienation, (ii) indebtedness and exploitation, (iii) bonded labour, (iv) low educational standards, (v) low agricultural production and productivity, (vi) inadequate supply of essential consumer goods, (vii) land reclamation, (viii) inadequate irrigation facilities, (ix) shortage of drinking water, (x) inadequate communication facilities, (xi) housing problem, (xii) inadequate marketing facilities, (xiii) inadequate employment opportunities, and (xiv) underdeveloped state of health services. However, merely injecting financial resources to solve these problems will not be sufficient. Such a thing was done in the past (though not on a sufficiently big scale) without much success. What is necessary is to bring about *institutional changes* in the tribal society.

The basic problem of tribal areas is the existence of an agrarian structure that condemns the tribals to a life of exploitation and deprivation. As emphasized by Shreekant Sambrani,[43] the problem of poverty is common to both tribal and non-tribal areas but what distinguishes the problems of the former from the latter is the existence of widespread exploitation and deprivation in tribal areas. This issue can be dealt with effectively only by introducing far-reaching and permanent institutional changes in the existing tribal set-up. Thus, along with developing resources potential, infrastructure and economic activities in tribal areas, any comprehensive plan should also aim at (i) developing the local human capital in tribal areas and (ii) changing the socio-politico-economic framework in which this capital should function. For this purpose it is necessary to evolve an integrated strategy of development, consisting of the following main planks.

1. Development programmes aimed at increasing agricultural production and productivity. Such programmes will include: (i) development of irrigation facilities, (ii) schemes of soil conservation, (iii) provision of modern agricultural inputs at reasonable prices, (iv) making the size of farm holdings economic, (v) improving agricultural marketing facilities, (vi) educating the tribal farmers in new agricultural techniques, etc.

2. Taking necessary steps to tackle the problem of land alienation. Since tribals have lost a considerable extent of land to moneylenders, forest contractors, etc., there is a need to evolve steps such as (i) legal protection to tribals and (ii) making the tribals conscious of their rights and such legal protection available to them. However, before any such steps can be taken, it is necessary to prepare authentic land records. In most of the tribal areas no land records are available. This appreciably reduces the effectiveness of legal protection guaranteed to the tribals.

3. Development of transport and communication facilities so that the process of social interation between tribal and non-tribal areas and the process of integration of the tribal economy into the national economy can be accelerated.[44] Such infrastructural facilities are also required to generate economic progress in tribal regions.

4. Since forests have an important place in the tribal economy it is necessary to carry out a review of the forestry policy with a view to providing maximum benefits to the tribal people. For example, the processing of minor and major forest produce could be augmented in the tribal areas

themselves.

5. Development of activities allied to agriculture such as dairying, poultry keeping, animal husbandry, etc., with a view to providing employment all the year round to small and marginal farmers, and agricultural labourers.

6. Development of a public distribution system to supply essential consumer goods to the tribals at reasonable prices.

7. Setting up of cottage and small scale industries in selected growth centres of tribal areas. Also in those areas where major industrial projects are located, it is necessary to plan a network of such cottage and small industries to provide employment to persons displaced from their lands. The industrial framework should be able to absorb and rehabilitate the uprooted tribals.

8. Provision of social services such as medical and health facilities, drinking water, nutrition, rural housing, etc.

9. Since the tribals have a strong community feeling and long tradition of democratic institutions,[16] the cooperative movement and the panchayati raj institutions have a tremendous scope of success. They failed in the past on account of government's apathy and because they fell into the hands of vested interests (of some tribals and non-tribals). Since the tribals could not provide landed securities, they could not obtain loans from cooperative societies. Sometimes non-tribals obtained loans from these societies and gave them to the tribals at higher rates of interest. Then, the cooperatives did not give loans for unproductive purposes. The commercial banks were apprehensive about giving loans to the tribals. Thus, the dependence of the tribals on moneylenders continued as usual. Keeping these considerations in view, the rebuilding of the cooperative movement has once again to be done from cooperative credit societies and all mistakes of the past have to be remedied. In addition to this, as noted by the Bawa Committee on Cooperative Credit Structure in Tribal Areas (constituted in 1971), the primary cooperative societies should provide a comprehensive range of services to the tribals so that they do not have to approach a multiplicity of institutions for assistance. A start can be made by organizing credit-cum-marketing societies, as is being done in some States.

10. Development of educational facilities in tribal areas and entrepreneurial faculties in tribals. This is necessary to 'sustain' the programmes of economic development. It is also necessary to carry out a massive programme of 'entrepreneurial hunt' in these areas.

11. Adoption of protective measures to prevent exploitation of the tribals. In addition to economic exploitation, various cases of atrocities on scheduled tribes are also reported in different parts of the country. Most of these atrocities are committed by landlords, forest contractors, government

employees (including police), panchayat members, etc. It is necessary to take preventive steps to stop such crimes committed on the tribals.

12. Special programmes should be launched for the benefit of the tribals belonging to small, isolated, and primitive tribes that have remained more or less untouched by the plans so far.

13. Changes in the administrative set-up to make the administration more responsive to the needs of development of the tribal people. It is necessary to appreciate that the issue of tribal administration is not the simple one of creating some department, breaking up some other departments, redistributing financial resources, etc. It is a more basic issue of evolving some administrative arrangements wherein the tribals have an effective say. The institutions of the tribals are not modern enough to effect changes in the traditional structure of the tribal society while the administrative institution of the government is almost alien to tribals' thinking and not acceptable to them. It is necessary to strike a balance somewhere. This can be done by enlisting the cooperation of the tribal people in programmes of tribal administration. Such cooperation should be enlisted at all stages of programme formulation, execution, and evaluation. The local tribal should be trained in the task of administration and posted in tribal areas. It may even be necessary to relax the recruitment standards to make this possible.

14. A periodic evaluation of the programmes adopted in tribal areas should be carried out to ensure 'timely corrective action'.

Shreekant Sambrani points to a basic weakness in such area planning. According to him, if successful, it can only make a few tribals viable farmers/entrepreneurs/service class members, while a large number of the tribals will remain where they were or can be pushed to a worse plight. He feels that unless the elements of exploitation are eliminated by restructuring the existing agrarian set-up, the vast majority of the tribals cannot benefit from such area planning. For this purpose he advocates the setting up of *collective projects* which can create centres of 'countervailing influence'. Initiating and nursing such collective projects based on the collective action of the tribals themselves can usher them into a new era of 'progress without exploitation'. The million dollar question that remains to be answered even now is: 'who will take the lead in such collective projects'? Tribals themselves have failed to do so. Sambrani thinks that the voluntary organizations working in the tribal areas can perhaps take on this role. But where is the guarantee that once they assume such a role, they will not themselves become exploitative? Where is the guarantee that economic power, once given to their hands, will not be wielded against the poor tribals?

This guarantee can be provided by an ever-vigilant, sympathetic, and innovative bureaucracy. It is necessary to create a class of administrators which live in close proximity to tribal culture, can understand the problems of the tribals, is dedicated to the task of their upliftment and zealously guards them against all types of exploitation—economic, social, and moral. It will be necessary to induct the tribal people into such an administrative framework so that it can have a wide acceptability and popularity among the tribal people. A number of voluntary agencies engaged in the task of tribal development and distinguished individuals working in those areas and commanding respect among tribals should also be invited to collaborate with the government in this field. In fact, a regional tribal body should be set up to supervise the programmes of tribal development. Such a body should have representatives from the tribals themselves, district administration departments of State governments engaged in the task of tribal welfare, Central government, and voluntary organizations working in tribal areas. Men of public importance and academicians having interest in tribal problems should also be invited to participate in the task. The regional tribal body should be a permanent one and should work in close collaboration with the Central and State planning departments. It can be vested with legal and administrative powers to ensure that its voice cannot be overruled.

NOTES

1. S.C. Dube *Tribal Heritage of India* (New Delhi: Vikas Publishing House Pvt. Ltd., 1977), p. 2. As noted by Dube, these characteristics are only rough indicators and cannot withstand a critical scrutiny. Thus, neither all tribals are 'original' inhabitants of the soil nor all of them live in isolation. In fact, the three biggest tribes of India, viz., Gonds, Bhils, and Santhals, live in close proximity of non-tribals. The third, fourth, and fifth characteristics are not the legacy of tribals alone. They are to be found among non-tribals as well. The sixth characteristic is also not universally applicable to all tribes. There are many tribes which are divided into a number of endogamous sub-divisions which behave like castes.
2. T.N. Pandit, "The Original Inhabitants of the Andaman & Nicobar Islands", *Yojana*, Vol. XX, Nos. 13 & 14, 15 August 1976, p. 83.
3. Ibid., p. 85.
4. See Barthakur, "Jhooming and its Consequences", *Yojana*, Annual Number, Vol. XXI/1 (26 January 1977), pp. 122-123. A survey conducted under the auspices of the Agro-Economic Centre, Jorhat, on Banshidua (a Garo village in Assam) points out the ill effects of *jhooming*. According to it, continuous jhooming in the hill lands in the village "has brought about complete change in the texture of soil and nature of vegetation" so that availablity of fresh jhum land has become a problem. Also, on account of jhooming, there has been a continuous decline in the productivity of the hill soil resulting in fall in the cultivation of cash crops such as cotton and their replacement by mesta or sesamum. The jhumias, in fact, earn the lowest per capita

income in the village while settled farmers earn the highest. See the review of Niranjan Saha *et.al.*, *Banshidua: A Socio-Economic Survey of a Garo Village in Assam*, Agro-Economic Centre, Jorhat in *Economic and Political Weekly*, 3,33,1968 by B.K. Bhattacharya (reprinted in *ICSSR Journal of Abstracts and Reviews*, Vol. 1, Nos. 1 & 2, January-December 1972, pp. 62-64).

However, from the point of view of tribals, the practice of jhooming has a number of advantages. Thus, "the Jhoom fire quickly renders a dense forest fit for growing crops. Fire is thus a great labour saving device and clears the cut jungle in a very short time. The ashes correct the soil acidity, and the admixture of ashes with the soil makes the soil more fertile. The soils of hill slopes of high rain zones are generally acidic, which are thus partly neutralised by the alkali content of the ashes. Further, fire clears the areas of extensive preponderance of fungi, insects and pests. Not only the insects and pests of the Jhoom plots with their larva and eggs are burnt but the Jhoom fires which are usually lit at night and continued for a few days, attracts insects and pests from the surrounding forests. This rids the area of these pests which later would have destroyed the crops. The clearance of insects and pests from the surrounding area to the Jhoom plot creates a protective belt and keeps the crops safe from the heavy inroads of insects and pests . . . . Burning also retards the growth of weeds in the Jhoom clearing by destroying the roots of the tubers and seeds of the weeds. It renders the tubers and roots dormant for a period of time.

The shifting cultivator thus reaps a number of very tangible technological advantages i.e. lesser input of labour, the pests and insects and fungi destroyed, the soil neutralized and fertilized, and less time and labour spent on weeding etc. If the fire had not helped him in this manner, he would have laboured more and reaped less." Barthakur, op. cit., pp. 121-122.

5. As quoted by L.P. Vidyarthi and B.K. Rai, *Tribal Culture of India* (Delhi: Concept Publishing Company, 1977), p. 98.
6. M. Chakrabarti and D. Mukherjee, *Indian Tribes* (Calcutta: Saraswati Library, 1971), pp. 136-137.
7. Ibid., p. 110. Emphasis added.
8. Ibid., pp. 88-89. Emphasis added.
9. Ibid., Emphasis added.
10. T.N. Pandit, op.cit., p. 87.
11. Chakrabarti and Mukherjee, op.cit., Emphasis added.
12. Prem Khandu Thungon, "Traditional Democratic Institutions in Arunachal Pradesh", *Yojana*, Vol. XX1/1 (26 January 1977), p. 100.
13. Planning Commission, Government of India, *Second Five Year Plan*, p. 590.
14. See Chapter 7 for a discussion on the community development programme and reasons that led to the failure of this experiment.
15. Planning Commission, Government of India, *Second Five Year Plan*, p. 593. These special multipurpose tribal development (SMPT) blocks were renamed as tribal development blocks in the Third Plan. For the TD blocks, 100% assistance was provided by the Central government.
16. *Report of the Commissioner for Scheduled Castes and Scheduled Tribes*, 1971-72 and 1972-73 (New Delhi: Government of India, 1974), p. 382.
17. *Second Five Year Plan*, p. 590.
18. *Report of the Commissioner for Scheduled Castes and Scheduled Tribes*, 1978-79, Part I, p. 176.
19. *Report of the Commissioner for Scheduled Castes and Scheduled Tribes*, 1974-75, p. 77.

20. *Report of the Commissioner for Scheduled Castes and Scheduled Tribes*, 1978-79, part I, p. 180-181.
21. K.V. Narayana Rao, "Education and Employment Policy Towards Scheduled Tribes in India", in National Institute of Community Development, *Perspectives on Tribal Development and Administration*, Hyderabad, August 1975. pp. 209-210.
22. A.K. Mukhopadhyay, "The Structure of Land Relations in Tribal Communities in India", NICD, Ibid., p. 204.
23. Vidyarthi and Rai, op.cit., p. 439.
24. See Chapter 7 for a discussion on SFDA/MFAL projects.
25. K.V. Sundaram and R.P. Misra, "Micro Level Planning and Development Processes", Vol. I (University of Mysore Institute of Development Studies, 1976), Cyclostyled Report, Annexure V, pp. 196-197, and Annexure VI, p. 198.
26. For a detailed discussion of tribal sub-plans, see the later part of the present chapter.
27. Census of India 1971, Part II-C(i), Tables C-VIII, Part A, pp. 146-147.
28. *Fourth Five Year Plan*, p. 417.
29. B.K. Roy Burman, "Perspectives for Administration and Development of the Scheduled Tribes", NICD, August 1975, op. cit., p. 54.
30. This would appear to be in direct contrast to the original intentions of the planners as would be clear from the following statement contained in Second Plan: "Welfare programmes for tribal people have to be based on respect and understanding of their culture and traditions and an appreciation of the social, psychological and economic problems with which they are faced. The welfare and development programmes in tribal areas inevitably involve a measure of disturbance in relation to traditional beliefs and practices. *In their implementation, therefore, the confidence of the people and, in particular, the understanding and goodwill of the elders of tribal communities are of the highest importance. It is, therefore, necessary that welfare extension workers of all kinds should be found as far as possible from amongst the educated youth in tribal communities. In commending the adoption of new techniques tribal leadership should have a major role and any suggestion of imposition from without should be avoided*, and for each step the ground should be carefully prepared in advance. The anthropologist, the administrator, the specialist and the social worker have to work together as a team, approaching the problems of the tribal people with sympathy, understanding and knowledge of the social psychology and needs of tribal communities. *Tribal people have to be assisted largely through their own institutions. Details of development programmes should be formulated in consultation with members of advisory councils, leaders of tribal opinion and institutes engaged in the study of tribal problems. The tribal people should feel that these programmes are, in a real sense, a response to their own urge for better standards of living and the development of their culture.* If the programmes are implemented with popular support, they will give the tribal people in all parts of the country a sense of partnership and integration with the nation as a whole." (Emphasis added) pp. 58 -590.
31. H.S. Verma and B.L. Tripathi, "Integrating Research, Training and Education", in Ranjit Gupta (ed.), *Planning for Tribal Development* (New Delhi: Ankur Publishing House, 1976), pp. 259-260.
32. *Report of the Commissioner for Scheduled Castes and Scheduled Tribes*, 1971-72 and 1972-73, p. 377.
33. N.Y. Naidu, "Tribals Pains of Industrialization", *Economic and Political Weekly*, 5 June 1976, p. 830.
34. Ibid., p. 831.
35. N. Patnaik, *Tribes and Their Development: A Study of Two Tribal Developme*

Blocks in Orissa (Hyderabad: National Institute of Community Development), p. 34.

36. *Report of the Commissioner for Schedule Castes and Schedule Tribes*, 1971-72 and 1972-73, p. 5. In his Report for 1975-76 and 1976-77, the Commissioner laments thus: "The planned efforts of the last four Five Year Plans were supposed to go a long way in raising the levels of the Scheduled Castes and the Scheduled Tribes and to ensure them to occupy their rightful place with other sections of the people. Facts, however, have belied this expectation so far. Indeed it is not a happy commentary on the methodology of our planning that even now some of the communities amongst Scheduled Tribes should be known as primitive tribes and confined to isolated hilly tracts living at the pre-agricultural level of technology . . . . Large scale exploitation of Scheduled Castes and Scheduled Tribes at the hands of money lenders and traders is even now the order of the day." p. 4.
37. See Chapter 8.
38. K.V. Sundaram and R.P. Misra, op. cit., Vol. I, pp. 82-84.
39. Planning Commission, Government of India, *Sixth Five Year Plan, 1980-85*, p. 418 and Annexure 26.2, p. 422.
40. *The Economic Times*, ed., "Tribal Welfare", 8 July 1974, p. 5.
41. *The Economic Times*, 16 April 1977, p. 3.
42. B.K. Roy Burman, "Perspectives for Administration and Development of the Scheduled Tribes", NICD, op. cit., pp. 57-58.
43. Shreekant Sambrani, "Area Planning and Tribal Development: Concepts and Experiments", in Ranjit Gupta (ed.), *Planning for Tribal Development* op. cit., p. 205.
44. As mentioned elsewhere in this chapter such interaction and integration has brought exploitation to the tribal people. In fact, the present links of tribal areas with advanced sectors were forged largely for the exploitation of tribals. Yet, interaction and integration is necessary to accelerate the processes of economic development. Therefore, it is necessary to plan carefully to ensure that advanced sector benefits and not exploits the tribal sector. For example, "in tribal tracts near cities, activities such as dairying, poultry and vegetable production should be organised in such a manner as would permit retention of the bulk of profits within tribal areas". "Plans for Tribes", *The Economic Times*, ed., 7 May 1976, p. 5.
45. See discussion on 'Sources of Authority in Tribal Areas' in this chapter.

Chapter 12

Directions of Regional Policy—Multi-Level Planning in India and Some Other Issues in Regional Planning

MULTI-LEVEL PLANNING IN INDIA

The various levels of planning in India are: (1) Centre, (2) States, (3) districts, (4) blocks, and (5) villages. The task of plan formulation is basically carried out by the Centre and the State governments and the other levels of planning process enter only at the implementation stage of planning. As far as the stage of plan formulation is concerned, the dominant and decisive role has been played by the Centre and it was only during the Fourth Plan that some States tried to formulate plans on their own. However, since the States did not generally possess a planning machinery and since they remained heavily dependent on the Centre for financial and other resources, their own plans remained only 'exercises' in planning. The task of plan formulation has, for all content and purposes, remained the prerogative of the Central government.

The First Level

Therefore, in the context of multi-level planning in India, the first (and foremost level) is constituted by the Central government. The head of government is the President who acts under the advice of the Council of Ministers headed by the Prime Minister. The advice of the Council of Ministers is binding on the President. The business of the government is transacted through a three-tier set-up. The Prime Minister, Cabinet Ministers, Ministers of State, Deputy Ministers, and Parliamentary Secretaries constitute the first or top layer. The second layer is constituted by the secretariat organization of the ministry with the secretary as head. The executive organization of the department, comprising the ministry, forms the third layer. The actual task of plan formulation is done by the Planning Commission at the Centre which has Prime Minister as its chairman, and some members of the Cabinet and three or four full-time professional experts as members.

The Second Level

The second level is constituted by the States. The executive head of a State is the Governor, who is appointed by the President of India. As in the case of the Centre, the Governor does not directly exercise the powers that are vested in him. They are exercised by a Council of Ministers headed by the Chief Minister. The advice of the Council of Ministers is binding on the Governor. The Council of Ministers works through the secretariat that is headed by a secretary. The main functions of the secretariat relate to assisting the ministers in policy-making and in discharging their legislative responsibilities, coordination of policies and programmes, suprevision and control of expenditure, efficient running of administration, etc. The Council of Ministers has a number of departments functioning under it which can be broadly classified into three categories—(a) development departments (having the departments of agriculture and animal husbandry, rural development, public works and industries), (b) social welfare departments (having the departments of education, health and social welfare), and (c) coordinating departments (having home, revenue, finance and planning departments).[1]

Since the Indian Union is a federation of States, the framers of the Constitution have provided for division of powers as between the Centre and the States so that the chances of confrontation between these two levels of government can be minimized. The division of powers between the Centre and the States is according to the seventh schedule and Article 246 of the Constitution. Article 246 gives three lists of subjects: *Union List* (containing 97 items), *State List* (containing 66 items), and *Concurrent List* (containing 49 items). The Central government has the power to legislate on the subjects given in the Union List while the State governments have powers to legislate on the subjects given in the State List. As far as subjects contained in the Concurrent List are concerned, both Central and State governments have powers to legislate on them, but in case of a conflict, the Central law prevails. Organized activities such as industries, minerals, railways and telecommunications come under the Centre's responsiblities while agriculture, collection of land revenue, irrigation, power, public health, education, local self-government and several other important subjects come under the control of the States.

Levels Below the State

There are generally three levels below the State level—district, block, and village. The district administration is under the overall charge of the collector (also known as deputy commissioner in some States). He is responsible for maintaining law and order in the district. He also works as a coordinator among various departments. Important departments located in the district are agriculture, minor, medium and major irrigation, animal husbandry, dairying, forestry, industries, public works, cooperation, education, medical and public health, social welfare and pancahyati raj, etc. Besides, there are autonomous agencies with offices in the district such as the electricity board, state transport and special agencies set up for special programmes such as the SFDA, DPAP, etc. Though the collector generally works as a coordinator, his role is not defined properly and differs in different States. This introduces complexities and difficulties in the task of administration.

The complexities are further enhanced when we consider the relationship between the collector and the panchayati raj bodies. As noted in Chapter 2, the relationship between the collector and the zilla parishad is not uniform in all the States. In some States such as Karnataka and Tamil Nadu, the collector is the chairman of the zilla parishad. In some States such as U.P. and Bihar he can only attend the meetings of the zilla parishad but cannot vote. In some other States he is associated as an advisory member. As noted by Reddy, it is difficult to identify a well-established planning agency at the district level.

> Planning function may be performed by a district planning officer under the overall charge of a collector. Sometimes, a district planning officer is appointed only for the period of the formulation of five-year plans. In some cases, there is no institution for planning at all and the collector may, depending on his initiative, prepare a plan. In some states thedistrict planning officer is placed under the control of the *zilla parishad.* In certain others, special committees are formed which are either headed by the collector, or convened by him with a state-level minister as the head of the committee. However, in all states some sort of district plans, covering some segments but ensuring integration with other schemes, have to be prepared mostly under the overall guidance of the collector, and occasionally under a specified committee set up for

special agencies such as a tribal sub-plan, the SFDA and so on. Barring these, there have been very few systematic attempts at district planning.[3]

At levels below the district, there are blocks and villages. These levels are basically 'levels of implementation' and have not so far been utilized for the purpose of formulation of plans. This would be clear from the staffing pattern in blocks. The set-up basically consists of a block development officer who is assisted by five extension officers, one each in the fields of agriculture, animal husbandry, cooperation, panchayats, aud rural industries. The other staff consists of an overseer, a social education organiser, a progress assistant and village level workers. In the block, there are also veterinary stockmen, a medical officer, a sanitary inspector, and a lady health visitor, some of them with the necessary supporting staff. In some States there is also an extension officer for programmes relating to women and children.

While at the district level, the developmental tasks are looked after by the zilla parishad, at the block level they are looked after by the panchayat samiti. The lowest level is the village and the agency entrusted with the task of its development and welfare is the panchayat. The village panchayat (known as gram panchayat in most States) is normally constituted for a village or a group of villages. A group of such villages (usually accounting for a total of about a hundred thousand people) are constituted into a block—with a panchayat samiti (known as janapada samiti in Madhya Pradesh and kshetra samiti in Uttar Pradesh) to run the affairs. In some States, instead of blocks, we have talukas which in some cases correspond to blocks while in other cases account for more than one block. Corresponding to panchayat samitis at the block level, we have taluka panchayats at the taluka level. At the top tier of hierarchy of panchayati raj institutions, are the zilla parishads constituted at the district level (known as Mokhuma parishad in Assam, district panchayat in Gujarat, and district development council in Karnataka and Tamil Nadu). As shown by Table 1, the panchayati raj institutions at the village, block, and district level are mutually interlinked. In most States, sarpanches of all panchayats are members of the panchayat samitis and presidents of all panchayat samitis are members of zilla parishads.

PLAN FORMULATION AND CONTACTS BETWEEN DIFFERENT LEVELS

As noted in the beginning of this chapter, the most important level, as far as plan formulation is concerned, is the Centre. The first step for formulat-

TABLE 1: **Structure of panchayat samitis and zilla parishad (State Acts)**

State	Composition	
	Panchayat samiti	Zilla parishad
(1)	(2)	(3)
1. Andhra Pradesh	(i) Sarpanches of all panchayats and town committees in the block. (ii) Local MLAs and MLCs with right to vote but not to hold office. (iii) One person each nominated by district collector for the units, where panchayats do not exist.	(i) Presidents of all panchayat samitis. (ii) District collector. (iii) Local MPs, MLAs and MLCs as associate members.
2. Assam (Mohkuma Parishad at sub-division level)		(1) One councillor of the mohkuma parishad to be elected by the voters of gram panchayats from amongst themselves. (2) One representative each (not being the member of State legislature or Parliament) from the municipality, town committee, elementary education and the central cooperative bank. (3) Such other government officers as ex-officio councillors as the State govt. may appoint them from time to time. The govt. also nominates councillors from tea garden areas.
3. Bihar	1. Mukhiyas from gram panchayats in the block. 2. Chairman of municipalities and vice-chairman of notified area committees. 3. Presidents of the union Boards (deleted by amendment). 4. Three representatives of the	1. All pramukhs of panchayat samitis. 2. Local MPs and MLCs as associate members. 3. Three persons elected by electoral college of members of the municipalities and notified area committees.

(Contd.)

TABLE 1 (*Contd.*)

(1)	(2)	(3)
	cooperative societies. 5. One representative of cane growers' society. 6. One representative of cooperative societies other than cane growers' and multi-purpose societies, etc. 7. Local MPs and MLAs & MLCs as associate members.	4. Two persons elected by the electoral college of members of managing committee of central cooperative banks.
4. Gujarat (Taluk Panchayat and District Panchayat)	1. 15-31 members from amongst the qualified voters of taluk panchayat. 2. Members elected by the sarpanches of all gram panchayats (about 1/3rd of total members at 1 above). 3. A representative each from district cooeperative union, district cooperative bank, taluka cooperative purchase & sale union, agricultural marketing produce committee. 4. Local MLAs, president of municipalities, local members of district panchayat and mamlatdar or mahalbari as associate members.	1. President (in his absence vice-president) of taluka panchayat. 2. 31-51 members elected from amongst qualified voters representing taluk panchayat. 3. Local MPs, MLAs, president of municipalities, D.C. as associate members. 4. One representative each of district cooperative union/ district cooperative bank/ district coeperative purchase and sale union.
5. Haryana	1. 16 Members elected by panches/sarpanches in the block. 2. Two members representing cooperative societies. 3. One member representing market committees in the block. 4. Sub-divisional officer, BDO and panchayat officer, ex-officio members. 5. MLAs as associate members.	
6. Himachal Pradesh	1. Up to 20 members from the block by the panches, up-pradhans and pradhans of gram panchayats from	1. One representative of every panchayat samiti. 2. Chairman of every panchayat samiti.

(*Contd.*)

TABLE 1 (*Contd.*)

(1)	(2)	(3)
	amongst themselves. 2. MLAs as associate members. 3. Sub-divisional officer as ex-officio member. 4. 2 members from the co-operative society.	3. MP, MLA, MLCs. 4. Deputy commissioner
7. Kerala	...	...
8. Karnataka	1. 15-19 members directly elected by secret ballot by the electorate of the taluka. 2. Local MLAs and MLCs.	1. Deputy commissioner (as president). 2. Local MPs, MLAs & MLCs (with right to vote). 3. Presidents of taluka boards. 4. Such officers (not more than 15) as nominated by the government.
9. Madhya Pradesh (Janapada panchayat) (Zilla Parishads do not exist)	1. 15-30 members elected by the panches of gram panchayat. 2. One councillor representing municipal corporation, council or notified area committee in the block. 3. Local MLAs as associate members. 4. One representative of cooperative institutions.	...
10. Maharashtra	1. Directly elected councillor of zilla parishad from electoral divisions in the blocks and coopted councillors to the zilla parishad. 2. Members elected by direct election from electoral colleges in the block. 3. Chairman of a cooperative society conducting purchase and sale of agricultural produce. 4. Chairman of cooperative society conducting business relating to agriculture.	1. 40-60 councillors directly elected from electoral divisions in the district. 2. The chairman of panchayat samitis as ex-officio member. 3. Chairman of 5 federal co-operative societies dealing with credit, land development, marketing, industries and cooperative training and education as associate councillors.
11. Orissa (Zilla Pari-	1. Sarpanches of all panchayts.	...

(*Contd.*)

TABLE 1 (*Contd.*)

(1)	(2)	(3)
shad abolished since November 1968)	2. Chairman of municipality and notified area council. 3. BDO and one officer from each of the development and revenue departments.	
12. Punjab	1. 16 members elected by panches. 2. Local MLAs and MLCs as associate members. 3. SDO/BDO as ex-officio member. 4. 2 members representing cooperative societies and one member representing market committees.	1. 3 members from panchayat and coopted members of panchayat samitis at district level. 2. Chairman of all panchayat samitis. 3. Deputy commissioner as associate member. 4. Local MPs, MLAs, and MLCs as associate members.
13. Rajasthan	1. Sarpanches of all panchayats. 2. Local MLAs with right to vote but not to hold office. 3. SDO as associate member. 4. *Elected Members* One or more members from the presidents of all the gram sabhas according to population. 5. One representative each elected by the chairman of the: (i) service cooperative societies, (ii) cooperative societies other than service cooperative societies and (iii) marketing cooperative societies (as associate members).	1. Pradhans of all panchayat samitis. 2. Local MPs and MLAs with right to vote and hold office. 3. District development officer as associate member. 4. President of central cooperative bank as associate member. 5. Chairman of the district cooperative as associate member. 6. Pramukh, who is otherwise not a member of the zilla parishad (as additional member).
14. Tamil Nadu	1. President of every panchayat and non-official member of each township. 2. Local MLAs, MLCs in the area as associate members.	1. District collector (as chairman). 2. Local MPs & MLAs and MLCs with right to vote. 3. Chairman of panchayat unions and municipal councils. 4. Presidents of cooperative

(*Contd.*)

TABLE 1 (*Contd.*)

(1)	(2)	(3)
		central banks. 5. Such officers connected with planning and development as nominated by government.
15. Uttar Pradesh	1. Pradhans of gaon sabhas. 2. Chairman of town area and notified area committee. 3. 2-5 representatives of cooperative societies. 4. Local MPs, MLAs and MLCs with right to vote but note to hold office.	1. Pramukhs of kshetra samitis. 2. Members to be chosen by each khsetra samiti from amongst its members as specified by the government. 3. Presidents of municipal boards. 4. Chairman/administrator of a cooperative bank/ district cooperative banks. 5. A representative from each of the (i) district cooperative federation to be chosen by the board of directors from amongst the members of the board; (ii) cooperative society; (iii) cane unions. 6. Persons up to 3 to be chosen by the State government from those engaged in social, cultural and literary activities. 7. All local MPs, MLAs and MLCs, with right to vote but not to hold office.
16. West Bengal	1. Note more than 3 persons to be elected from each gram with the block on the basis of population. 2. Pradhans of all gram panchayats within the block. 3. MPs, MLAs, with right to vote but not to hold office.	1. Sabhapattis of panchayat samitis within the district. 2. Two persons elected from each block within the district. 3. MPs, MLAs with right to vote but not to hold offiee.

Source: Government of India, *Report of the Committee on Panchayati Raj Institutions*, August 1978, Annexure 3-A, pp. 215-223.

ing a plan is taken by the Planning Commission two or three years in advance of the commencement of the new plan when it lays down the approach to the new plan after taking into account the existing economic situation, objectives, and the desired perspectives of development. Concurrently, a perspective plan is also prepared which analyses the state of the economy with reference to the past and takes a long-term view of the future progress of the economy. The approach submitted by the Planning Commission is discussed in the National Development Council, and after it receives the approval, work starts on the details of the plan.

In the second stage, the Planning Commission works out the details of the plan on the basis of the general approach decided in the first stage. The Planning Commission has, so far, tended to restrict itself to the task of investment planning alone. The task that the Planning Commission sets before itself is best described in the words of Datta-Chaudhuri: "Given the initial levels of productive capacities in the different sectors of the economy, assuming that the productive capacities *can be* fully utilized (subject only to the non-availability of certain other complementary inputs), a picture of the commodity flows in the base year is constructed. The problem, as posed in the Planning Commission, is to find a feasible and 'desirable' structure of commodity production at the target year which is consistent with the 'potentialities' of domestic savings (or the estimates of domestic consumption) and the foreign trade and aid possibilities".[4] The problem is tackled basically with the help of inter-industry investment allocation models. Several working groups are constituted for the purpose where representatives of the Planning Commission, technical experts, and ministers sort out the issues that arise in the wake of such exercises.

While at the Central level the working groups are busy in the task of plan formulation, the Planning Commission gives a rough indication of the size of the plan to the States. The States then set up their own working groups which prepare detailed sectoral plans based on the framework decided upon by the State planning department and the guidelines received from the Centre. The broad issues concerning total outlay, sectoral allocations, major projects to be taken up, and resources to be devoted to them are decided either by the Chief Minister or the cabinet or some sub-committee of the cabinet. Keeping these considerations in view, a draft outline of the plan is prepared.

The draft outline thus prepared is discussed with the Central working groups in Delhi and the Chief Minister confers with the Planning Commission. If necessary, the State plan is revised and finalized in the light of the Draft Outline published by the Planning Commission. After the plan is approved by the NDC, it is put before the State cabinet and State legislature.

The formulation of State plans is a comparatively recent phenomenon. For a considerable period of planning, many States did not have any planning machinery worth the name. Some States do not even now possess a proper machinery that can be entrusted with the task of plan formulation. In all these States, the department of planning is just like any other department of the secretariat and functions in a routine manner.[5] The whole process is mechanical. On the one hand, the department is busy trying to inflate the State plan (so that more assistance could be procured from the Centre) and, on the other, it is busy piecing together the demands and needs submitted by different departments of the government (in fact, it is such demands and needs pieced together that form the State plan).

We have discussed above the process of formulation of five year plans at the Centre and State levels. In addition to the five year plans, perspective plans and annual plans are also prepared. A perspective plan is a long-term plan, say, for a period of 15 to 20 years. It is not a detailed plan and just lays down the objectives and targets for the major sectors of the economy to be achieved within that period. It is necessary to have a perspective plan because it gives the likely path of development and knowledge of the policies and instruments that have to be adopted to follow the determined path. Also, there are many projects (especially multi-purpose river valley projects and heavy, capital goods industries) which are not likely to be completed (and, in any case, are not likely to fructify) within a short span of five years. Hence, they have to be planned for a longer period than a five-year period. This can only be done within the overall context of a perspective plan. As against the perspective plan, the annual plan is limited to a one-year period. The annual plans introduce an element of flexibility into the planning process and are operational in character. As far as planning process in India is concerned, perspective plans have generally been prepared by the Planning Commission at the Centre. Generally in such plans, projections of population, urbanization, balance of payments, income distribution, outputs of principal commodities, etc., are made at the national level. State-wise long-term projections are not made. However, as the importance of regional elements is getting more and more recognized in recent years, the States have been encouraged to formulate their own perspective plans. At least three States (Gujarat, Tamil Nadu, and Andhra Pradesh) have already formulated perspective plans while some other States have completed the computation of basic data and inter-industry input-output tables. Gujarat has prepared a ten-year perspective plan, covering the Fifth and the Sixth Plans. It aims at a growth rate of 7% per year and gives sectoral break-up of outlays under the State public sector, the Central sector, and the private sector. The perspective plan for Tamil Nadu also covers a period of ten years (from 1974-75 to

1983-84) and aims at increasing the growth rate of per capita income from 2.22% in 1974-75 to 8.96% by 1983-84. The perspective plan for Andhra Pradesh is also a ten-year plan covering the periods of the Fifth and the Sixth Plans. A simple projection of investments and income of the State has been made on certain assumed investment-income ratios, and three alternative paths of growth worked out.[6]

As already noted, the annual plans are operationally very important. For the purpose of formulating an annual plan at the Centre, the Planning Commission takes into account the provisions regarding the five year plans, progress of development, and the policy changes introduced by the Union government. The financial resources are estimated a few months in advance, broad magnitudes are discussed, and details of the schemes examined by working groups (as in the case of five year plans). The annual plans are also prepared at the State level within the overall guidelines issued by the Planning Commission. Deliberations between the Planning Commission and the State Chief Minister are held to sort out differences regarding outlays, if any.

At levels below the State, practically no machinery exists for formulating perspective, five-year, and annual plans. However, some efforts have been made in these directions. For example, in Andhra Pradesh an attempt was recently made to prepare a perspective plan for three 'policy regions' —Rayalaseema, Telengana, and Coastal Andhra. Maharashtra and Tamil Nadu have made significant attempts in preparing perspective plans for districts. However, for all practical purposes, levels below the State have not participated in the task of plan formulation. Only in those cases where special programmes such as the SFDA and DPAP were undertaken, the district-level agencies were engaged in the task of formulating plans because in such cases there was a direct contract between the Centre and the district-level agencies. At levels below the district, there is no plan formulation because there is no planning organization worth the name.

MULTI-LEVEL PLANNING AND POPULAR PARTICIPATION

Planning process cannot be considered successful unless it is able to elicit the willing cooperation of the persons whose economic and social welfare it aims to increase. The common man should *feel* a sense of involvement in the process and should be enthusiastic and ready to cooperate. This object can be realized only if popular participation of the people is obtained both at the level of plan formulation and at the level of plan implementation. As far as the stage of plan formulation is concerned, the central question is: "How to ensure that the mass of the population have access to decision-making process; in other words—how to make the plan more democratic and more a reflection of the people's real aspirations and needs?"[7] The issues to be studied in this context are: attitudes prevailing in key groups (such as the local power elite, large industries, business, etc.). prevailing Centre-local relationship (and the extent to which changes have to be brought in the attitude of the Central authorities towards 'local participation'), attitude of 'service institutions' including banks and credit institutions, attitude of medium and small private enterprises, and attitude of the large majority of the population from whom participation in plan formulation is sought. As far as the organizational structure for ensuring wider popular participation in the process of plan formulation at the regional level is concerned, the regional planning agencies can experiment with one or more of the following alternatives: (i) appointment of an ad hoc advisory council with some members appointed and others elected (elected members can be chosen from the general public); (ii) public hearings on draft regional plans prepared by the regional plan office; and (iii) appointment of a 'people's spokesman' assigned and paid by the regional planning authorities to take initiative in exploring the demands of the general public in order to transmit them to the regional planners for their consideration.[8]

At the plan implementation level, popular participation is closely related to the problem of *motivation*. Effective motivation depends upon a number of factors such as appropriate social and physical infrastructure, confidence of the general public in the official policies and in the persons who are entrusted with the task of direct implementation (especially the bureaucracy and political leadership), a fair amount of understanding about the objectives, targets, and purposes of planning, and, most importantly, the existence of a development plan which has a number of projects of a local nature so that people can easily identify themselves with the planning process. Janusz A. Ziolkowski feels that it is not the lack of motivation that is the basic problem—the basic problem is "finding ways of capitalizing on motivation that is already present". For this purpose, it is necessary to find out "what people want and expect from development, or to put it another way, what must be done to make them willing and effective participants in regional development."[9]

No popular participation can be effected unless there is proper *communication* between the people and the regional administration. This is essentially a problem relating to the flow of *information*. Planners should have information about the needs of the people and the people, in general, should have information on the planners' proposals and the reasons for them. In addition, each planner needs to know what other planners are doing. Central, regional, and local authorities and other levels of administration and bureaucracy should have an information flow amongst themselves; and each group among the people should know the needs, interests, and responses of other groups. Establishing such a vast information system is not an easy task and has to be performed with the help of a number of governmental agencies, voluntary organizations, labour unions, and citizen organizations. Care has to be taken to ensure that communication channels do not get *overloaded*. Because of the importance of the information flows at the regional planning level, considerable attention is being devoted to develop *information systems* and models are being prepared.[10]

POPULAR PARTICIPATION AND INDIAN PLANNING

We have already noted above the relatively insignificant role played by the lower levels and democratic institutions (such as panchayati raj) in the tasks of plan formulation and plan implementation in this country.[11] The causes which led to the failure of the community development programmes, panchayati raj and cooperation in eliciting popular participation are also examined in Chapter 7. We have noted that there is a sort of apathy towards panchayati raj institutions among the villagers in general. Though all adult members are expected to participate in the deliberations of the gram sabha and especially in the meetings convened to consider the audit report, administrative report, taxation and other programmes, very few people attend these meetings and still fewer participate effectively in the discussions.

The basic cause responsible for this state of affairs is that the richer sections of the village community have gained control over these institutions and the common villager feels isolated and neglected. Right from the election to the panchayats to the wielding of whatever influences and powers there may be, the rural landlords and the rural rich exercise a decisive control over the whole apparatus. In the process of the election to panchayats itself, pressures from the rural rich are very much in evidence. Terror, bribery, personal influence, and various other ingenious methods galore. Though generally panchayat elections are not fought on party basis (basically on the plea that local problems have nothing to do with ideologies) the State leadership and the political parties show a keen interest in the elections. This is the easiest way to influence the local governments, control the decision-making process at the local level, and make a truck with the rural rich who can ensure them votes of a considerable majority in the general elections. Because the financial dependence of the local authorities on the State government is very heavy and they are themselves not willing to increase taxation and raise additional resources for meeting their ever-increasing expenditures, they have to strike a 'double-edged' (mutual) benefit scheme with the State leadership and the party that be in power.[12]

In many cases the sanction and approval of projects to be undertaken in the area within the jurisdiction of the panchayat is also decided by the State government. Naturally, those areas and villages receive more aid and more projects where the touts of the ruling party control the apparatus. In the election campaign itself, these touts go about telling people to vote for them because they have contacts at the State level and are thus in a better position to extract developmental and other benefits. Since they normally succeed in their endeavours, the panchayati raj institutions only help make the powerful more powerful. The poor are left out and feel isolated and cornered. In fact, they are victims of all kinds of pressure and terror. There are examples where they were beaten up and even tortured to death because they refused to vote for a particular candidate.

As noted by K. Seshadri, "It is idle to pretend that there were always factions and PR has nothing to do with them. Factions get aggravated and politicised involving State level leadership which tries to bale out the culprits and thus reduce the law enforcing authorities to helplessness. PR may not be the only cause but PR is an aggravator. The general election also creates certain problems, but PR problems vitiate the day-to-day life of the villages while the disturbances caused by the general election tend to get ameliorated."[13]

Thus, it seems that in many cases, the institution of panchayati raj was less inspired by the genuine concern for popular participation as expected by the Balwantrai Mehta Committee and more inspired by an attempt on the part of the State leadership to develop and reward its rural-based activists, and to dig its roots deep into the rural soil. Commenting on the institutions in Rajasthan, Mathur elaborates how the ruling party (Indian National Congress) which had a weak rural base initially and was constantly threatened by the offences of the erstwhile princes and jagirdars, found the instrument of panchayati raj handy for consolidating its political base "by providing institutional arrangements for local leaders' control over the distribution of developmental benefits".[14] Since there was no genuine concern for popular participation, no genuine attempts were made to elicit the participation of masses in the planning process. As a consequence, the new enthusiasm generated at the time of the launching of the panchayati raj experiment gradually gave way to disillusionment and dismay and people lost all interest in the programme. The phase of ascendancy was followed by a phase of stagnation and finally by the phase of decline.[15] With the onset of the phase of decline, pressures began to build up for starting Centrally sponsored programmes such as the SFDA, MFAL, DPAP, ITDP, etc. This further reduced the orbit of programmes under the control of the panchayati raj institutions.[16] The bureaucracy also played a negative role. Accustomed to working within its own framework (and assuming that it was responsible only to the State government), it did not adjust itself to working under the supervision of the elected representatives at levels below the State. It was not, in general, in favour of entrusting more functions to the panchayati raj institutions and under the garb of various pretences withdrew the staff from the block level. All this helped to further weaken the panchayati raj institutions and the scope of popular participatian in the planning process.

REORGANIZATION OF LEVELS BELOW THE STATE

In recent years there has been an increasing recognition of the regional planning needs, decentralized planning, and popular participation of the people in the planning process. With its heavy reorientation towards rural planning and rural development, the Sixth Plan document emphasized specifically the need for strengthening the levels below the State (especially district and block levels) and the need to revitalize the panchayati raj institutions. To suggest ways and means to accomplish this task, the Planning Commission appointed two committees towards the end of 1977—the Dantwala Working Group on Block Level Planning and the Asoka Mehta Committee on Panchayati Raj Institutions.

The Working Group on Block Level Planning was asked by the Planning Commission to draw up "detailed guidelines for block level planning". The desire to revitalize the planning process at the block level was a result of the belief of the Planning Commission that 'the block is the primary area for local planning' and immensely useful for adopting 'programmes suitable to local environment and local capacity' and is fulfilling the full employment goal. We have already discussed some of the recommendations of the Working Group in Chapter 3[17] and need not repeat them here. However, it is necessary to list the objectives of block-level planning as given in the report of the Working Group because it throws considerable light on the nature of planning that is being conceived at the block level and the immensity of the task involved. The objectives, as mentioned, are:

1. Optimum utilisation of the growth potential of the area leading to increase in income and employment.
2. Ensuring that a larger than proportionate gains of development accrue to the weaker sections of the population—small and marginal farmers, share-croppers, agricultural labourers, rural artisans, etc.
3. Fulfilment of the minimum needs programme—health and medical facilities, drinking water, housing, education and supply of essential commodities through a public distribution system.
4. Building up of social and economic infrastructure to achieve the

above objectives.

5. Reorienting the existing institutions/organisations in order to protect the interests of the poor.
6. Building up of appropriate organisations of the poor especially to protect them from exploitation.
7. Promotion of a progressively more egalitarian structure of ownership of assets.
8. Augmenting the duration and productivity of employment of the poor and the underemployed in their existing occupations *inter alia* through upgrading of technology, imparting of skills and setting up of non-exploitative institutions of credit, marketing and extension.
9. Alleviating residual unemployment through employment on public works.[18]

Can block-level planning fulfil the complex and multifarious objectives mentioned above? We have already noted the non-existence of any planning machinery at the block level. The administrative machinery at this level has been basically engaged in the task of carrying out directions from above and has failed miserably as a development agency. The panchayati raj institution at this level (known as panchayat samiti) has failed to elicit popular participation in the planning process because it was itself engaged in political bickerings of various sorts. It became the pipeline through which the influence of the parties at the State level percolated down to the village level. There is no guarantee that adoption of the recommendations of the report and instituting the proposed reforms will radically transform the situation. However, our criticism is of a more basic nature—is block (as conceived so far) the appropriate unit of planning? In Chapter 8, while discussing Integrated Area Development we had noted that if economic development is to be achieved and a propulsive mechanism started, it would be necessary to (i) create viable economic units by combining villages into clusters, (ii) select dynamic clusters, and (iii) locate growth centres within such dynamic clusters. It is only by adopting such a regional planning approach to problems of development that sufficient spread effects can be generated in underdeveloped areas and the problem of development solved. The existing approach towards block-level planning and the approach as revealed in the report of the Working Group do not take these considerations into account and therefore cannot hope to accomplish much. Unless spatial and regional planning is interwoven into the planning process by adopting the growth foci approach,[19] planning efforts are not likely to yield any positive results. In any case, development benefits are not likely to be distributed equitably over different areas and groups of people.

THE CONCEPT OF A MANDAL PANCHAYAT

The Asoka Mehta Committee on Panchayati Raj Institutions takes into consideration the above facts. In the view of the committee there should be two levels of decentralization below the State level—the district level and the *mandal* level. The committee feels that on account of the smallness of its size, the village is not a viable unit of planning. Hence, it advocates the adoption of the concept of a cluster of villages or central village service centre. Normally, this service centre with a population of 15 to 20 thousand will cover the central village in this complex and the villages in the hinterland. Mandal panchayats will be located at this level and will therefore cover a population of 15,000 to 20,000 and would also facilitate forging of necessary linkages with schemes of development. The committee feels that in view of the developments that are likely to take place in the rural areas, the block may prove to be too large and the village too small. The mandal panchayat, therefore, appears to be the logical choice as a unit for developmental activities. Since it will be located in the central village, it will serve the needs of a number of hinterland villages by providing marketing outlets, inputs for agricultural development, transport and communication infrastructure, social facilities such as hospitals and schools, warehousing facilities, and a number of other facilities.

Thus, the Asoka Mehta Committee suggests a two-tier panchayati raj structure—a district level zilla parishad and a mandal panchayat. The committee proposes that the block-level panchayat samitis, where they exist now, should be converted into non-statutory executive committees of zilla parishads and when the mandal panchayats become active, most of their functions should be taken up by the mandal panchayats. As a transitional structure, the block can, therefore, continue as per the convenience of the States keeping in view their requirements and the stage of development. At the village level, the people would be involved in mandal panchayats through village committees which would look after the municipal functions and related welfare activities.

The proposal of the committee to set up mandal panchayats on the above lines is, in our view, a very important recommendation that needs full consideration and implementation. The services which are intended to be provided at the central village level (mentioned above) clearly shows that mandal panchayats would facilitate the forging of necessary linkages with schemes of development of focal points and growth centres and would ensure efficient management of the growing rural-urban linkages. Thus conceived, the mandal panchayat (at the central village level) will form an important link in the hierarchy of growth foci. As we have been emphasizing again and again, only such an approach can ensure a balanced development of all regions of the country. Viewed in this context, the decision of the conference of Chief Ministers held on 19 May 1979 rejecting the proposal for mandal panchayats and retaining the existing structure is very unfortunate.[20] We feel that an excellent opportunity for revitalizing panchayat raj institutions in the overall framework of integrated area development has been missed. Invaluable recommendations of the committee have been thrown to the winds without giving them any serious thought.

SOME OTHER ISSUES IN REGIONAL PLANNING

Before we conclude this chapter, it would be imperative to point out at least two directions of regional policy towards which attention is being increasingly diverted. The first concerns itself with the social dimensions of regional planning and the other with the environmental issues.

Social Issues in Regional Planning

Following the economic theories and models originating in the western countries, many developing countries have given a central role to investment programmes in their planning processes. While none can deny the relationship between the rate of investment and the rate of economic growth, undue emphasis on the former has led to a situation where inadequate attention is being paid to wider issues of social development. In the framework of the policies adopted, it is assumed that social development and social transformation will automatically follow the process of economic growth. Thus, the sequence seems to be—increase in rate of investment→increase in rate of economic growth→social development and social transformation. Again, since the rate of investment was the kingpin of all activities, all efforts were concentrated on devising ways and means to maximize it and to direct investment to those sectors and regions where returns were expected to be maximum. In some countries deliberate attempts were made to accomplish this, while in others a policy of 'non-interference' in market forces was adopted. Both the attitudes encouraged *polarization* of economic activities (and consequently economic development) in some selected sectors and regions while other sectors and regions languished. This has created many social problems such as "(1) the clash between economic goals formulated in terms of output only and social development objectives and needs (for instance, when introducing highly specialized, labour-saving industries against the needs of maximum possible employment in the over-populated region), (2) the concentration of industry and infrastructure in a few areas thus creating enclaves of modernization in the midst of growing economic stagnation".[21] Planning devoid of social considerations also led to undue emphasis on heavy industry to the neglect of agriculture (this proved to be highly undesirable in those countries that were basically agrarian societies), emphasis on general education unsuited to the needs of development of particular countries, and unrealistic planning.

The basic justification for adopting a regional planning approach is that it is capable of correcting all these distortions in the planning process. Detailed surveys of different regions of the economy can help us in formulating plans for reducing regional disparities and development of small and medium towns can provide effective counter-magnets to check the growth of unduly large urban centres. Social surveys conducted with the purpose of investigating population characteristics, assessing housing, employment, educational, shopping and communications requirements of the population, and selecting the 'specific points' where the location of these facilities can have maximum spread effects, can go a long way in evolving a correct approach to social problems. It is only within the boundaries of a region that these issues can be properly faced and tackled. A nation is too big an entity to tackle these issues satifactorily.[22]

What should be the objectives of such a social planning approach? The objectives, according to Antoni Kuklinski, are basically three: (1) social equality (2) social transformation, and (3) provision of social infrastructure.[23] Because of the need to educate and involve the local people in the planning process (and thereby generate new social impulses and dynamics in a hitherto stagnant society) in an underdeveloped country, it is necessary that regional policy in such countries also takes into account explicitly the social processes of mobilizing the local and regional community. This is the familiar problem of popular participation in the planning process which we have already discussed earlier in this chapter. We have noted there that because of numerous factors, the common man in rural areas has felt isolated and neglected while the objective is exactly the opposite—that of involving him in the task of planning. We have shown that the leadership of the panchayati raj institutions has gone into the hands of small groups of local politicians and rural landlords who have a stake in perpetuating the conditions of exploitation and social injustice that promote their own vested economic, social, and political interests. In this context, we feel that the most important objective of social regional planning in this country (and perhaps in other underdeveloped countries as well) is to *organize* the local community into a series of functional bodies in such a way that each functional body is a cohesive whole. Care has also be to taken to ensure that there are definite and clear 'meeting-grounds' among these various functional bodies and there is the minimum clash of interests and views. Such functional bodies can form themselves into village committees which can be organically linked up to the mandal panchayats at the mandal level (in terms of Mehta Committee's report) or to whatever organization that exists at the central village level or the block level.

Recognizing the necessity of taking social factors into account while formulating regional plans, planners in the advanced countries are increasingly resorting to the use of social indicators and socio-economic coefficients. Social indicators can play an effective role in analysing past developments and in indicating future directions particularly if they are analysed in correlation with the economic indicators of planning. An idea of what social indicators should be considered can be had from the following fields of social concern specified by OECD in 1971:

1. personal health and safety;
2. personal development and intellectual and cultural enrichment through learning;
3. occupational development and satisfaction;
4. time and leisure;
5. command over goods and services;
6. the physical environment;
7. the social environment (including, e.g., demographic concerns).[24]

Drewe refers to the problems concerning measurement. These centre round two aspects of 'indicators of change in basic well-being': the gauging of 'basic well-being' and of 'change'. Since it is difficult to measure either of them quantitatively and some value-judgements of the researcher cannot be avoided (e.g., in deciding the social indicators to be considered, weightage to be accorded to different indicators, methods of computation to be used, etc.) some observers are not quite optimistic about the value of such indicators. The problems are still more acute in developing countries where data relating to most of the fields mentioned above are either not available at all, or if available are unreliable and totally inadequate. Therefore, social indicators and socio-economic coefficients do not have much utility as far as the underdeveloped countries are concerend. Yet this does not imply that these countries cannot have social planning. Social realities need not be expressed in terms of specific quantifiable indicators and interwoven into complex mathematical models for us to understand their importance. They are there for everyone to see. As regards the methods of tackling them, every region will have to face them in its own way because they may differ from region to region. Yet, if planning process is to be realistic and is to benefit the society at large, it can ill-afford to ignore the social atmosphere in which it operates and the mutual interactions between economic and social development which it will help to generate.

Environmental Issues

Undoubtedly, the process of increased industrial production has been accompanied by more progress, higher income levels, and economic prosperity but it has also brought in its wake serious threats to ecological balance and has resulted in pollution[25] and environmental deterioration. The advanced industrialized countries of the world are entrapped in a sort of vicious circle. They have to go on producing more and more if they have to prevent mass unemployment and economic depression. But rising production is continuously increasing the threats of environmental pollution, mass-produced waste and poisoning of the atmosphere we live and breathe in. As noted by Narindar Singh,[26] the fantastic expansion of the petro-chemical industry since the end of the Second World War has had an intense 'degradative effect' on the environment. Thus, the new chemical industry introduced products which are both extremely toxic and bio-nondegradable. Detergents, introduced in the US market in 1940, "have caused a seven-fold increase in phosphate emissions from the municipal sewage systems during the succeeding thirty years as against an approximate doubling during the preceding thirty".[27] Rapid and unprecedented increase in the production of automobiles has filled the air with smog and carbon monoxide. A relatively new source of massive noxious emission is the super-jet, the pollution-effect of one Boeing 707 take off being the same as that of 6850 accelerating Volkswagens. Fears have been expressed that growing preoccupation with supersonic air travel can pose serious threats to life on this earth "because nitrogen oxides and other trace contaminants emitted by these jets might cause a series of photochemical reactions and bring about a depletion of the ozone that shields the globe".[28] Widespread use of fertilizers and insecticides has disturbed the stability of the ecosphere. Recycling in the ecosphere is automatic for organic substances because nature itself provides an enzyme capable of breaking it down. "But", notes Narindar Singh, "when a new substance is synthetized by man with a molecular structure departing significantly from the types that occur in nature, it is more likely than not that *no* enzyme capable of degrading it exists; so the material has a built-in tendency to *accumulate* and intrude violently into the otherwise self-sustaining eco-cyclical processes. It is in this way that the life-supporting ecosphere is being gradually overwhelmed by the 'technosphere' created by the petrochemical industry which releases into the environment a large and growing variety of noxious product."[29] Narindar Singh gives the example of the D.D.T. in this context which 'threatens to upset the oxygen balance of biosphere'. In ocean waters, it can disable the tiny marine plants (known as the green algae) that produce as much as 70% of the atmospheric oxygen.

The rapid pace of industrialization in the advanced countries has led to a considerable increase in the use of power and energy resources. In this context we may note the fact that "coal mining began eight hundred years ago and that, incredible though it may seem, half of the total quantity ever mined has been extracted in the last thirty years. Also, half of the total production of crude oil has been obtained in the last ten years only!"[30] Such excessive use of the energy resources of the world in such a short period and the immense amount of fuel burnt everyday pollutes the air badly. It has been reported that in big Japanese cities such as Tokyo artificial 'grass' is being 'planted' to simulate green lawns, as natural grass cannot grow any more because of smog![31]

Problem in India

Because of slow industrial progress, these problems have not assumed dangerous magnitudes in the developing countries such as India. Therefore, it is very rare that we find economists and planners in these countries introducing 'environment' as a specific variable in their plan models. Yet, the problem has started appearing in large industrial urban centres. For example, in India the problem has already assumed alarming proportions in areas where industries are concentrated and more specifically in large urban centres such as Calcutta, Bombay, Delhi, and Madras. A study of the air pollution problem shows that Calcutta is the most polluted city. "The dust concentration in this city was found to be about 500Mg/m^3, while the corresponding figure for Bombay was only 283Mg/m^3, Kanpur 200Mg/m^3, Madras 170Mg/m^3. Carbon Monoxide levels in the busy streets during heavy traffic hours were as high as those recorded in western cities."[32] A survey conducted by the Calcutta Metropolitan Development Authority and the National Environmental Engineering Research Institute showed that 50% of the 10 million residents of Calcutta suffered from respiratory disease due to air pollution.

In Bombay, nearly 1000 tonnes of deadly pollutants are released in the atmosphere everyday. Such an alarming rate of air pollution has drastically undermined the health of its citizens. It has been estimated that because of the presence of carbon particles in the air, every individual in south Bombay—though he may be a non-smoker—virtually 'smokes' 20 cigarettes a day.[33]

The pollution of the country's water systems has already reached serious proportions. According to the scientists of NEERI, 70% of India's inland waters are unfit for human consumption due to the indiscriminate and inordinate industrial wastes discharged into them. For example, the Damodar river is highly polluted between Bokaro and Durgapur where metallurgical and chemical units and the coal washeries contaminate it to the hilt with their discharges. It has been estimated that 1800 tonnes out of 82,000 tonnes of coal washed by the Durgapur washery a month are drained into the river. The Kalu river which flows through the industrial areas of Bombay has chemical plants on its banks, discharging all their effluents into it. The river has heavy concentration of mercury, lead and cadmium and poses a serious health hazard.[34] The Hooghly near Calcutta is polluted from the industrial wastes from different industries such as jute textile mills, cotton mills, paper mills, and tanneries. "It is also polluted from the sewage disposal, domestic wastes etc. together amounting to about 4616 tons solid wastes, 1057 tons suspension and about 125 tons in soluble state daily."[35]

In addition to these, we have already noted in Chapter 6 how increasing congestion in urban areas has caused a serious housing problem and has put the civic amenities, drainage system, sewage disposal system, etc., under severe strain.

Environment and Regional Planning

The traditional approach to environmental problems in economics has been that of *negative externalities*. "A negative externality occurs if through his acts of production or consumption an economic agent adversely affects the well-being of other economic agents without compensating them for this cost."[36] This happens under private market organization where an industry disposes of its wastes into common property resources such as air and water. The costs of the resulting pollution and environmental deterioration in such a case are not borne by the industry but are borne by those who must live with the pollutants. Thus, there emerges a difference in social and private costs. The obvious solution to this problem (and the one that has been advocated by most economists) is that of *internalizing externalities* by asking all producers to bear the full cost of treating the wastes they generate. If internalization of all external diseconomies (including social, aesthetic, and other external diseconomies) is ensured for each and every regional development project, the adverse effects of regional development would be considerably reduced. Accordingly, *maximum internalization of external diseconomies can be considered a useful objective in regional development policies.*

The regional development planners should study carefully each and every project to specify the likely environmental impact of the project, cost of that impact, and the socio economic consequences of the costs. They should give top priority to those projects which maximize the differences between regional benefits and regional costs. It is necessary to note here that internalization of externalities does not imply reducing emissions to zero because such a policy is likely to impose extremely heavy costs. What should be aimed at is an optimal level of emissions in which social marginal benefits are equated with social marginal costs.[37] However, this is more easily said than done. In actual practice it is generally not possible to measure social marginal costs and social marginal benefits. Some attempts can be made to measure costs on the basis of empirical studies or engineering analysis. But to measure marginal social benefits is practically impossible. Benefits from improved environmental quality are generally in the nature of 'reduction of damages to health, to welfare and to ecological process'. It is not possible to quantify these gains and, therefore, attractive as it may seem, the actual utility of the model suggesting equalization of marginal social benefits with marginal social costs is not much. The problem is more acute in the underdeveloped countries where even the normal economic data are woefully inadequate and the regional data for many variables are practically absent.

The second, and more important, suggestion as far as regional planning is concerned is to evolve regional development models wherein environment enters as a specific variable. Forecasting economic-environment planning models can go a long way in helping us estimate the potential environmental damage and proper steps can be taken in time to control it. The models available so far for forecasting environmental impacts from economic development "are based upon the use of emission coefficients which have been observed or inferred from engineering studies or observation of existing process".[38] A major advantage of using regional economic-environmental models, according to Cumberland, is that through them it may become "possible to identify optimal combinations of economic activitives such that the wastes of one set of activities could be used as inputs into other activities, minimizing the net residuals discharged into the environment".[39] These models can also help in evaluating the distribution of benefits and costs of development.

Though all these solutions can help us in reducing the dangers of pollution and environmental decay, they are highly inadequate to deal with the threats which the advancing science and technological innovations are increasingly imposing on the environment. The cars, supersonic aircrafts, hazards of the petrochemical industry, nuclear energy have all come to stay with us and their rapidly increasing use is sure tos pell disaster sooner than later.

Accordingly, in very affluent societies and communities, the talks of zero economic growth and stationary state are gaining more and more currency with the passage of time. Admittedly, all such talks sound premature (if not irrelevant) to people living in the underdeveloped countries where the rate of economic growth is meagre and poverty, hunger, and malnutrition are rampant. Yet we can ignore the environment only at our own peril.[40]

NOTES

1. See Y. Venugopal Reddy, *Multilevel Planning in India* (New Delhi: Vikas Publishing House Pvt. Ltd., 1279), pp. 28-29:
2. See Chapter 3.
3. Reddy, op. cit., p. 33. Also see Chapter 3, Section on 'Role of District Planning' of the present book.
4. Mrinal Dutta Chaudhuri, "The Problems of Multi-Level Planning and Decision-making in India", in Antoni Kuklinski (ed.), *Social Issues in Regional Policy and Regional Planning* (The Hague: Mouton & Co., 1977).
5. Also see Chapter 3 in this context.
6. Reddy, op. cit., pp. 52-53.
7. Janusz A. Ziolkowski, "The Integrated Social Science Approach to Regional Planning", in Antoni Kuklinski (ed.), op. cit., p. 447.
8. H.J.A. Morsink, "Sociological Aspects of Regional Development and of Planning for Regional Develepment: Some Issues and Areas of Further Exploration", in Antoni Kuklinski (ed.), Ibid., p. 477.
9. Janusz A. Ziolkowski, op.cit., pp. 448 449.
10. See, e.g., Tormod Hermansen, "Information Systems for Regional Development Control: Framework for a Research Project", in R.P. Misra (ed.), *Regional Planning* (Mysore: The University of Mysore, 1969), pp. 301-342.
11. In this context, see also Chapter 3.
12. The financial dependence of the panchayati raj bodies on the State government would be clear from the following figure.

    Of the six States for which data on the income of zilla parishads are available, the share of 'own receipts' (i.e., resources raised by the zilla parishads themselves) was less than 6% in three States (in Andhra Pradesh it was 4.36% in 1977-78, in Gujarat it was 3.19% in 1973-74, and in Maharashtra it was 5.3% in 1971-72). In all the three States, the zilla parishads were heavily dependent on grants from the State government. Thus, in Andhra Pradesh, Rs.5314.6 lakhs out of a total income of Rs.5682.06 lakhs were in the form of grants from the government in 1977-78. In Gujarat, Rs.9878.67 lakhs out of total income of Rs.10,204.05 lakhs were in the form of government grants in 1973-74, and in Maharashtra Rs.8955.10 lakhs out of Rs.11,039.67 lakhs were in the form of grants in 1971-72. Income data for the Panchayat samitis available for five States of Andhra Pradesh, Haryana, Himachal Pradesh, Orissa, and Tamil Nadu show that in the year 1977-78, the dependence on State government grants was 95% jn the case of Andhra Pradesh and 99.5% in the case of Orissa. The extent of dependence on grants was 67% in the same year in the case of Tamil Nadu. Himachal Pradesh and Haryana showed less dependenceon grants. Thus, in the year 1975-76, 34% of income in Haryana came in the form of grants. In Himachal Pradesh this was still less at 28% in the same year.

The figures given here are computed from the *Report of the Committee on Pancha yati Raj Institutions*, August 1978, Statement 4, pp. 289-290 and Statement 5, pp. 291-292. Data for other States are not available. Yet it is an accepted fact that the financial depenpence of the panchayati raj institutions on the State governments is veryhigh.

13. K. Seshadri, "The Truth and the Myth", *Seminar*, No. 234, February 1979, p. 24.
14. P.C. Mathur, "Report from Rajasthan", *Seminar*, No. 234, p. 18.
15. According to the *Report of the Committee on Panchayati Raj Institutions*, the initial period of 1959-64 marked the period of ascendancy by stagaation. The period after 1969 tells the story of the decline of panchayati raj experiment. See *Report*, op. cit., p. 4.
16. Even during the earlier phase of the programme, no State government (except Maharashtra and Gujarat) gave any opportunity to the panchayati raj institutions to take up planning or implementational work on a sizable scale. Though block was conceived as the most important level in the community development programme and panchayat samiti was conterminus with the block, no attempt was made to regulate the flow of all developmental activities through this organization. The growing vastness and complexity of development programmes was sometimes used as an excuse for bypassing the panchayati raj institutions. Naturally this reduced the scope of popular participation considerably. See *Report of the Committee on Panchayati Raj Institutions*, op. cit., p. 4-5.
17. See Chapter 3.
18. Government of India, *Report of the Working Group on Block Level Planning*, 1978, p. 1.
19. See Chapter 4.
20. For a report on the conference, see *The Economic Times*, 20 May 1979, p. 1.
21. Janusz A. Ziolkowski, op. cit., p. 436.
22. "The entire intricate process of social phenomena in development—which, at the national level, appears as an abstraction—becomes real and valid in a socio-economic space or in a locality, in other words, in the context of a community in a territorial unit of a population associated with a geographical and economic space. Human beings need space to carry out their activities. Most of the resources and process of development, whether of local, national or foreign origin, exist within this context. Social, economic, historical, geographical and other variables converge or contrast within it and combine in complex social processes." Ruben D. Utria, "Some Social Aspects of Regional Development in Latin America", in Kuklinski (ed.) op. cit., p. 212.
23. Antoni Kuklinski, "Social Issues in Regional Policy and Regional Planning", in Kuklinski (ed.), op. cit., p. 167.
24. Paul Drewe, "Regional Policy as Social Planning", in Kuklinski (ed), op.cit., p. 33.
25. "Pollution covers a wide variety of environmental damages: air pollution and smell, noise and vibration, safety, access, privacy, physical space (congestion, crowding and isolation), wind flow, climate (heat, humidity, barometric pressure), radiation (ionizing, ultraviolet, lasers, infrared), microwaves and radio frequencies, aesthetics. These damages are the output of other sectors." Paul Drewe, Ibid., p. 50.
26. Narindar Singh, *Economics and the Crisis of Ecology* (Delhi: Oxford University Press, 1978), p. 20.
27. Ibid., p. 21.
28. Ibid., p. 19.
29. Ibid., p. 21.

30. Georgescu-Roegen quoted by Narindar Singh, Ibid., p. 45.
31. Ibid., p. 46.
32. S. Chatterjee, "Environment Pollution Problem in Urban Planning", in K.G. Bagchi and C.R. Pathak (eds.), *Regional Developm·nt and Planinng* (Regional Science Association, India, 1976), p. 161.
33. "Polluted Industrialization", *The Economic Times*, 28 March 1981, p. 1, (Special Supplement on 'Growth and Environment').
34. Ibid., p. 1.
35. S. Chatterjee, op. cit., p. 162.
36. Martin Pfaff, "Inter-Regional Transfers through Environmental Policy", R.P. Misra, D.V. Urs and V.K. Natraj (eds.) *Regional Planning and National Development* (New Delhi: Vikas Publishing House Pvt. Ltd., 1978), p. 291.
37. John H. Cumberland, "Regional and Environmental Planning in Social Perspective", in Antoni Kuklinski (ed.), op. cit., p. 77.
38. Ibid., p. 80.
39. Ibid., pp. 80-81.
40. The report of the committee for recommending legislative measures and administrative machinery for ensuring environmental protection, submitted in 1980, is an important *milestone* in the history of environmental protection in this country. The report speaks with equal emphasis of the need for creation of bio-sphere reserves, protection of grazing lands, protection of catchment areas of major river basins, protection of wetlands and estuaries, prevention of overfishing in coastal waters, protection of endangered species of wild fauna and flora, scientific land use, mitigating the environmental impact of mining, prevention of noise pollution, the defence of marine ecosystems, the development of national parks, the avoidance of water and air pollution and the achievement of a number of other objectives. It recommends that (i) a department of environment (DOE) should be created at the Centre, (ii) all administrative ministries and agencies whose plans and programmes have an impact on environmental resources should develop the necessary expertise within their own structures to assess the potential environmental impact of their action, (iii) posts of environmental advisers should be created in different ministries and departments, (iv) a Central land commission should be created to serve as a policy planning, coordinating and monitoring agency for issues concerning the health and scientific management of land resources, and (v) a national committee on environmental planning (NCEP) should be set up to serve essentially as a think-tank on environmental policy matters and to provide planning and advisory inputs to the DOE and other Central and State agencies.

Index